SOCIAL SECURITY LEG
SUPPLEMENT 201

General Editor
Nick Wikeley, M.A. (Cantao)

Commentary by
David Bonner, LL.B., LL.M.
Emeritus Professor of Law, University of Leicester
Formerly Member, Social Security Appeal Tribunals

Ian Hooker, LL.B.

John Mesher, B.A., B.C.L., LL.M.

Richard Poynter B.C.L., M.A. (Oxon)
District Tribunal Judge,
Judge of the Upper Tribunal

Mark Rowland, LL.B.
Judge of the Upper Tribunal

Robin White, M.A., LL.M.
Emeritus Professor of Law, University of Leicester,
Judge of the Upper Tribunal

Nick Wikeley, M.A. (Cantab)
Judge of the Upper Tribunal,
Emeritus Professor of Law,
University of Southampton

David W. Williams, LL.M., Ph.D., C.T.A.
Judge of the Upper Tribunal,
Honorary Professor of Tax Law,
Queen Mary College, London

Penny Wood, LL.B., M.Sc.
District Tribunal Judge

Consultant Editor
Child Poverty Action Group

SWEET & MAXWELL      **THOMSON REUTERS**

Published in 2015 by Sweet & Maxwell
part of Thomson Reuters (Professional) UK Limited
(Registered in England and Wales, Company No. 1679046. Registered
Office and address for service:
2nd floor, 1 Mark Square, Leonard Street, London EC2A 4EG)

Typeset by Wright and Round Ltd., Gloucester
Printed and bound in Great Britain by
Ashford Colour Press, Gosport, Hants

For further information on our products and services,
visit www.sweetandmaxwell.co.uk

No natural forests were destroyed to make this product.
Only farmed timber was used and re-planted.

A CIP catalogue record for this book is
available from the British Library

ISBN 978-0-414-04990-1

STOP PRESS

Secretary of State for Work and Pensions v TJ (JSA) [2015] UKUT 56 (AAC) (*CJSA/1266/2013, CJSA/2431/2013* and *CJSA/2542/2013*)

The decision of the three-judge panel of the Upper Tribunal (AAC) on post-*Reilly and Wilson* issues mentioned in the noter-up for p.190 of Vol.II (Jobseekers (Back to Work Schemes) Act 2013) at para.3.010 of this Supplement was signed on February 11, 2015. It imposes a significant restriction on the retrospective effect of the 2013 Act in cases where before the coming into operation of the Act on March 26, 2013 a claimant had appealed to a First-tier Tribunal against an adverse Secretary of State's decision. The Upper Tribunal in its decision gave the Secretary of State permission to appeal to the Court of Appeal on its conclusions on issues (1) and (3), having waived the requirement for an application. It thus seems unlikely that any of such cases stayed to await the outcome of these appeals that depend on the ruling on the non-retrospective effect of the 2013 Act will be determined until the issue has been decided by the Court of Appeal (and potentially the Supreme Court). The rulings related to notices will not enable most cases to be determined unless and until it is authoritatively decided that the Upper Tribunal is wrong. If cases where there had not been an appeal as at March 26, 2013 were stockpiled, they might now be determined.

See the general notes to the 2013 Act and to the Jobseeker's Allowance (Employment, Skills and Enterprise Scheme) Regulations 2011 ("the ESES Regulations") in Vol.II (pp.188 and 1330) for the general legislative and case law background, with references.

The three cases before the Upper Tribunal all stemmed from decisions of the Secretary of State, made before the amendment of the ESES Regulations by the Jobseeker's Allowance (Sanctions) (Amendment) Regulations 2012, to impose a sanction of non-payment of JSA on the claimants under reg.8 for having failed without good cause to participate in a scheme under the ESES Regulations (in two cases the Work Programme and in one the Community Action Programme). Reg.8 as in existence at the time is set out at p.1257 of Vol.II (2012/13 edition). Two tribunals allowed the claimants' appeals on the ground that, following the High Court decision in *Reilly and Wilson*, the notifications requiring participation did not meet the requirements of reg.4. The Secretary of State was given permission to appeal to the Upper Tribunal. The other tribunal disallowed the claimant's appeal without reference to *Reilly and Wilson*.

Subsequently, the Supreme Court in *Reilly and Wilson* confirmed the Court of Appeal's reasoning (but not the result, because of the 2013 Act) in quashing the ESES Regulations as ultra vires because they provided insufficient details of the schemes covered for them to have been "of a prescribed description" under s.17A(1) of the old style Jobseekers Act 1995. The 2013 Act had been passed on the day on which the Secretary of State applied for permission to appeal to the Supreme Court (March

26, 2013), providing that the ESES Regulations were "to be treated for all purposes" as made under s.17A and that notices given were, under certain conditions, to be taken as complying with reg.4(2)(c) and (e).

The Upper Tribunal, by a majority (Judges Rowland and Wright; Charles J. dissenting), dismissed the Secretary of State's appeals and allowed the other claimant's appeal, substituting a decision that JSA remained payable for the weeks in question.

The Issues

The Upper Tribunal identified seven outstanding issues that arose on the cases before it (paras 6–11 of the decision).

(1) Was the 2013 Act properly to be construed on ordinary principles as affecting appeals that had been brought before a First-tier Tribunal before March 26, 2013? The Upper Tribunal had concluded that the Supreme Court in *Reilly and Wilson* had proceeded on the assumption agreed by the parties that the Act had an all-encompassing retrospective effect, so that the Upper Tribunal was not bound to adopt that assumption.

(2) How did the 2013 Act fit with s.12(8)(b) of the Social Security Act 1998 (tribunal prohibited from taking into account circumstances not obtaining at the time of the decision under appeal?

(3) Could the 2013 Act be read under s.3 of the Human Rights Act 1998 so as to avoid the incompatibility with art.6 of the ECHR identified by Lang J. in *Reilly (No 2)*?

(4) If the first three issues were determined against the claimants, should the Upper Tribunal exercise its discretion under s.12(2)(a) of the Tribunals, Courts and Enforcement Act 2007 not to set aside a decision of First-tier Tribunal that involved an error of law, so as to avoid an incompatibility with art.6 of the ECHR?

(5) On the facts of the particular appeals, was a notice complying with the terms of reg.4 of the ESES Regulations served?

(6) Was there a lack of sufficient prior information such that the requirement to participate in the relevant scheme was vitiated (see para.74 of the judgement of the Supreme Court in *Reilly and Wilson*)?

(7) Were the legal requirements for establishing "good cause" under reg.7 of the ESES Regulations met?

The decision

The Upper Tribunal's decision on those issues was as follows (based on its own summary at para.13, with brief further explanation):

(1) By a majority, on ordinary, non-Human Rights Act, canons of statutory construction, the 2013 Act did not apply to cases where an appeal had already been brought before March 26, 2013. That conclusion was based on a close analysis of the terms of the Act and of the Explanatory Notes issued when the Bill was introduced, in the light of the principle that, in cases where an Act was clearly intended to be retrospective, it should be assumed that the

retrospective effect was no greater than was clearly intended. Notwithstanding the literal meaning of the words "for all purposes", the majority concluded that in the absence of discussion of this particular issue in the treatment of Human Rights Act considerations in the Explanatory Notes, a sufficiently clear intent to affect case identified had not been shown. The minority (Charles J.) considered that the force of the words "for all purposes" could not be undermined by the terms of the Explanatory Notes, which were not necessarily inconsistent with an intent to affect the cases identified by the majority.

(2) If the majority were wrong on issue (1), the Upper Tribunal was unanimous (although differing slightly in reasoning) in concluding that s.12(8)(b) of the Social Security Act 1998 could not have prevented a First-tier Tribunal in the present cases from taking account of the retrospective effect of the 2013 Act as a "circumstance obtaining" at the time of the decision under appeal. The current legislative context was different from that of *CAO v McKiernon*, reported as R(I) 2/94, and required not just that the subsequent passing of retrospective legislation be regarded as a relevant change of circumstances but also that the retrospective effect be regarded as altering the circumstances obtaining at the time of the decision. The context requires the same result when the Upper Tribunal or a court gives a decision of law, which inherently declares what the law has always been.

(3) If the majority were wrong on issue (1), by the same majority the 2013 Act had to be read under s.3 of the Human Rights Act 1998 so as to prevent it applying to claimants who had already brought appeals to the First-tier Tribunal, which would have interfered with their rights under art.6 of the ECHR. To read in such an exception would not go against the grain of or disturb a cardinal feature of the Act. The mischief aimed at by the Act was people who had not appealed against adverse decisions and who would otherwise have been able to benefit from the ruling in *Reilly and Wilson* because of the non-applicability of ss.26 and 27 of the Social Security Act 1998 to judicial review decisions. The minority reached a different conclusion.

(4) If the majority conclusions on issues (1) and (3) were wrong, s.12(8)(a) of the 2007 Act could not be used so as not to set aside the decisions of First-tier Tribunals which had decided in favour of claimants based on *Reilly and Wilson*. On the basis assumed, that would be an improper use of the discretion and inconsistent with s.6 of the Human Rights Act 1998.

(5) A requirement to give notice under reg.4(2) of the ESES Regulations, as read with the 2013 Act and its assumed retrospective validating effect, was met by the provision of a WP05 ("start notification") letter from the Secretary of State, but may be constituted by more than one document (such as, in addition or alternatively, an "opportunity letter" or an "appointment letter" from the scheme provider).

(6) In the case of schemes which were mandatory both at the stage of referral onto them and once on them (such as the Work Programme in most JSA cases and the Community Programme) no basis could be identified on which meaningful representations could be made prior to the decision to refer, in the sense of those representations being able to affect the decision to refer. The Upper Tribunal was therefore driven to conclude (unanimously) that the Supreme Court wrongly decided that aspect of Mr Wilson's case in *Reilly and Wilson* based on a false factual premise. Further, even if fairness might require information to be provided is respect of steps taken or decisions to be made once referred onto a scheme, no such case arose on the appeals before the Upper Tribunal.

(7) Regulation 7 of the ESES Regulations required good cause to be shown within five working days of a claimant's being notified of failure to participate in the scheme in question and not within any later period.

The decision contains considerable helpful detail on the operation of the Work Programme and the Community Action Programme and also intriguing paragraphs (214–219) suggesting a qualification to Commissioner's decision R(IS) 11/92 on whether any presumption can be drawn from the destruction of documents by a party to an appeal.

PREFACE

This is the combined Supplement to the 2014/15 edition of the four-volume work, *Social Security Legislation*, which was published in September 2014, and to *Volume V: Universal Credit* from the 2013/14 series, published in March 2014.

Part I of this Supplement contains other new legislation, presented in the same format as the main volumes. This will enable readers to note very quickly relevant new sets of legislation. The most significant additions are the Statutory Shared Parental Pay Regulations 2014 (SI 2014/3051), made under the Children and Families Act 2014, and two new JSA pilot schemes, the Jobseeker's Allowance (Supervised Jobsearch Pilot Scheme) Regulations 2014 (SI 2014/1913) and the Jobseeker's Allowance (18–21 Work Skills Pilot Scheme) Regulations 2014 (SI 2014/3117). Readers should note that new regulations and Commencement Orders governing Universal Credit are collected together in Part VI of this work (see further below).

Parts II, III, IV, V and VI contain the standard updating material—a separate Part for each volume of the main work—which amends the legislative text and key aspects of the commentary, drawing attention to important recent case law, so as to be up to date as at December 31, 2014. Part VII, the final section of the Supplement, gives some notice of changes forthcoming between that date and the date to which the main work (2015/16 edition) will be up to date (mid-April 2015) along with the April 2015 benefit rates.

Among the many changes, particularly noteworthy are those with respect to:

- developments in Upper Tribunal case law relating to both disability living allowance (DLA) and the descriptors for employment and support allowance (ESA), including important decisions of three-judge panels on reg.35(2) (risks from work related activity), mobilising and the meaning of "social engagement";
- further changes impacting on the right to reside;
- new regulations governing the Diffuse Mesothelioma Payment Scheme;
- the introduction of Statutory Shared Parental Pay.

In addition, the new Part VI to the Supplement includes the full text of the new Universal Credit (Transitional Provisions) Regulations 2014 (SI 2014/1230) as well as the text of successive Universal Credit Commencement Orders as amended by subsequent Commencement Orders.

As always we welcome comments from those who use this Supplement. Please address these to the General Editor, Nick Wikeley, c/o

School of Law, The University of Southampton, Highfield, Southampton SO17 1BJ (njw@soton.ac.uk).

David Bonner
Ian Hooker
John Mesher
Richard Poynter
Mark Rowland

Robin White
Nick Wikeley
David Williams
Penny Wood

January 15, 2015

CONTENTS

USING THE UPDATING MATERIAL IN
THIS SUPPLEMENT

The amendments and updating material contained in Parts II–VI of this Supplement are keyed in to the page numbers of the relevant main volume of *Social Security Legislation 2014/15* (or the 2013/14 edition in the case of *Volume V: Universal Credit*). Where there have been a significant number of changes to a provision, the whole section, subsection, paragraph or regulation, as amended will tend to be reproduced. Other changes may be noted by an instruction to insert or substitute new material or to delete part of the existing text. The date the change takes effect is also noted. Where explanation is needed of the change, or there is updating relating to existing annotations but no change to the legislation, you will also find commentary in this Supplement. The updating material explains new statutory material, takes on board Upper Tribunal or court decisions, or gives prominence to points which now seem to warrant more detailed attention.

For the most part any relevant new legislation since the main volumes were published is contained in Part I, while amendments to existing legislative provisions are contained in Parts II–V respectively, together with commentary on new case law. However, statutory material relating to Universal Credit has been treated differently. Section A of Part VI consists of the new Universal Credit (Transitional Provisions) Regulations 2014 (SI 2014/1230) along with the original Commencement Orders as published in Volume V as well as all subsequent new Commencement Orders available up until the time of going to press. This approach has been adopted because the various successive Commencement Orders extensively amend earlier Commencement Orders, and so the material has been presented here in as accessible a format as is possible. Section B of Part VI comprises the usual updating material for Universal Credit along the same lines as Parts II-V for the companion volumes.

This Supplement amends the text of the main volumes of *Social Security Legislation 2014/15* (or the 2013/14 edition in the case of *Volume V: Universal Credit*) to be up to date as at December 31, 2014.

Nick Wikeley
General Editor

PAGES OF MAIN VOLUMES AFFECTED
BY MATERIAL IN THIS SUPPLEMENT

Main volume page affected	Relevant paragraph in supplement
VOLUME I	
xxxv	2.001
42	2.002
44	2.003
46	2.004
48	2.005
50	2.006
54	2.006.1
56	2.007
60	2.008
61	2.009
63	2.010
71	2.011
83	2.012
87	2.013
89	2.014
89	2.015
89	2.016
91	2.017
91	2.018
94	2.019
95	2.020
96	2.021
96	2.022
104	2.023
143	2.024
178	2.025
180	2.026
181	2.027
241	2.028
253	2.029
258	2.030
283	2.031
284	2.033
286	2.035
329	2.037
335	2.038
356	2.039
405	2.040
408	2.041
424	2.042
443	2.043

VOLUME II

VOLUME III

VOLUME IV

VOLUME V

Pages of Main Volumes Affected by Material in this Supplement

TABLE OF ABBREVIATIONS USED IN THIS SERIES

1978 Act	Employment Protection (Consolidation) Act 1978
1979 Act	Pneumoconiosis (Workers' Compensation) Act 1979
1995 Regulations	Social Security (Incapacity for Work) (General) Regulations 1995
1998 Act	Social Security Act 1998
1999 Regulations	Social Security and Child Support (Decisions and Appeals) Regulations 1999
2002 Act	Tax Credits Act 2002
2004 Act	Child Trust Funds Act 2004
AA	Attendance Allowance
AA 1992	Attendance Allowance Act 1992
AA Regulations	Social Security (Attendance Allowance) Regulations 1991
AAC	Administrative Appeal Chamber
AACR	Administrative Appeals Chamber Reports
AAW	Algemene Arbeidsongeschiktheidswet (Dutch General Act on Incapacity for Work)
A.C.	Law Reports Appeal Cases
A.C.D.	Administrative Court Digest
ADHD	Attention Deficit Hyperactivity Disorder
Adjudication Regs	Social Security (Adjudication) Regulations 1986
Admin	Administrative Court
Admin L.R.	Administrative Law Reports
Administration Act	Social Security Administration Act 1992
AIDS	Acquired Immune Deficiency Syndrome
AIIS	Analogous Industrial Injuries Scheme
AIP	assessed income period
All E.R.	All England Reports
All E.R. (E.C.)	All England Reports (European Cases)
AMA	American Medical Association
AO	Adjudication Officer
AO	Authorised Officer
AOG	*Adjudication Officers Guide*
art.	article
Art.	Article
ASD	Autistic Spectrum Disorder

ASPP	Additional Statutory Paternity Pay
A.T.C.	Annotated Tax Cases
Attendance Allowance Regulations	Social Security (Attendance Allowance) Regulations 1991
AWT	All Work Test
BA	Benefits Agency
BAMS	Benefits Agency Medical Service
B.C.L.C.	Butterworths Company Law Cases
B.H.R.C.	Butterworths Human Rights Cases
B.L.G.R.	Butterworths Local Government Reports
Blue Books	*The Law Relating to Social Security*, Vols 1–11
BMI	body mass index
B.M.L.R.	Butterworths Medico Legal Reports
B.P.I.R.	Bankruptcy and Personal Insolvency Reports
B.T.C.	British Tax Cases
BTEC	Business and Technology Education Council
B.V.C.	British Value Added Tax Reporter
B.W.C.C.	Butterworths Workmen's Compensation Cases
C	Commissioner's decision
c.	chapter
C&BA 1992	Social Security Contributions and Benefits Act 1992
CAA 2001	Capital Allowances Act 2001
CAB	Citizens Advice Bureau
CAO	Chief Adjudication Officer
CBA 1975	Child Benefit Act 1975
CBJSA	Contribution-Based Jobseeker's Allowance
C.C.L. Rep.	Community Care Law Reports
CCM	HMRC New Tax Credits Claimant Compliance Manual
CCN	New Tax Credits Claimant Compliance Manual
C.E.C.	European Community Cases
CERA	cortical evoked response audiogram
CESA	Contribution-based Employment and Support Allowance
CFS	chronic fatigue syndrome
Ch.	Chancery Division Law Reports
Child Benefit Regulations	Child Benefit (General) Regulations 2006
CIR	Commissioners of Inland Revenue
Citizenship Directive	Directive 2004/38

Table of Abbreviations used in this Series

CJEC	Court of Justice of the European Communities
CJEU	Court of Justice of the European Union
Claims and Payments Regulations	Social Security (Claims and Payments) Regulations 1987
Claims and Payments Regulations 1979	Social Security (Claims and Payments) Regulations 1979
CMA	Chief Medical Adviser
CMEC	Child Maintenance and Enforcement Commission
C.M.L.R.	Common Market Law Reports
C.O.D.	Crown Office Digest
Com. L.R.	Commercial Law Reports
Commissioners Procedure Regulations	Social Security Commissioners (Procedure) Regulations 1999
Community treaties	EU treaties
Community institution	EU institution
Community instrument	EU instrument
Community law	EU law
Community legislation	EU legislation
Community obligation	EU obligation
Community provision	EU provision
Computation of Earnings Regulations	Social Security Benefit (Computation of Earnings) Regulations 1978
Computation of Earnings Regulations 1996	Social Security Benefit (Computation of Earnings) Regulations 1996
Con. L.R.	Construction Law Reports
Consequential Provisions Act	Social Security (Consequential Provisions) Act 1992
Const. L.J.	Construction Law Journal
Contributions and Benefits Act	Social Security Contributions and Benefits Act 1992
Council Tax Benefit Regulations	Council Tax Benefit (General) Regulations 1992 (SI 1992/1814)
CP	Carer Premium
CP	Chamber President
CPAG	Child Poverty Action Group
C.P.L.R.	Civil Practice Law Reports
CPR	Civil Procedure Rules
C.P. Rep.	Civil Procedure Reports
Cr. App. R.	Criminal Appeal Reports
Cr. App. R. (S.)	Criminal Appeal Reports (Sentencing)
CRCA 2005	Commissioners for Revenue and Customs Act 2005
Credits Regulations 1974	Social Security (Credits) Regulations 1974

Credits Regulations 1975	Social Security (Credits) Regulations 1975
Crim. L.R.	Criminal Law Review
CRU	Compensation Recovery Unit
CSA 1995	Child Support Act 1995
CSIH	Inner House of the Court of Session
CSOH	Outer House of the Court of Session
CS(NI)O	Child Support (Northern Ireland) Order 1995
CSO	Child Support Officer Act 2000
CSPSSA 2000	Child Support, Pensions and Social Security Act 2000
CTA	Common Travel Area
CTB	Council Tax Benefit
CTC	Child Tax Credit
CTC Regulations	Child Tax Credit Regulations 2002
CTF	child trust fund
CTS	Carpal Tunnel Syndrome
CV	curriculum vitae
DAT	Disability Appeal Tribunal
DCA	Department for Constitutional Affairs
DCP	Disabled Child Premium
Decisions and Appeals Regulations 1999	Social Security Contributions (Decisions and Appeals) Regulations 1999
Dependency Regulations	Social Security Benefit (Dependency) Regulations 1977
DfEE	Department for Education and Employment
DHSS	Department of Health and Social Security
DIY	do it yourself
Digital Service Regulations 2014	Universal Credit (Digital Service) Amendment Regulations 2014
Disability Living Allowance Regulations	Social Security (Disability Living Allowance) Regulations
DLA	Disability Living Allowance
DLA Regulations	Social Security (Disability Living Allowance) Regulations 1991
DLAAB	Disability Living Allowance Advisory Board
DLAAB Regs	Disability Living Allowance Advisory Board Regulations 1991
DLADWAA 1991	Disability Living Allowance and Disability Working Allowance Act 1991
DM	Decision Maker
DMA	Decision-making and Appeals
DMG	Decision Makers' Guidance

Table of Abbreviations used in this Series

DMP	Delegated Medical Practitioner
DP	Disability Premium
DPTC	Disabled Person's Tax Credit
D.R.	European Commission of Human Rights Decisions and Reports
DRO	Debt Relief Order
DSD	Department for Social Development (Northern Ireland)
DSDNI	Department for Social Development, Northern Ireland
DSS	Department of Social Security
DTI	Department of Trade and Industry
DWA	Disability Working Allowance
DWP	Department of Work and Pensions
DWPMS	Department for Work and Pensions Medical Service
EAA	Extrinsic Allergic Alveolitis
EAT	Employment Appeal Tribunal
EC	Treaty establishing the European Economic Community
ECHR	European Convention on Human Rights
ECJ	European Court of Justice
ECSMA Agreement	European Convention on Social and Medical Assistance
E.C.R.	European Court Report
ECtHR	European Court of Human Rights
Ed.C.R.	Education Case Reports
EEA	European Economic Area
EEA Regulations	Immigration (European Economic Area) Regulations 2006
EEC	European Economic Community
EESSI	Electronic Exchange of Social Security Information
E.G.	Estates Gazette
E.G.L.R.	Estates Gazette Law Reports
EHIC	European Health Insurance Card
E.H.R.L.R.	European Human Rights Law Review
E.H.R.R.	European Human Rights Reports
E.L.R.	Education Law Reports
EMA	Education Maintenance Allowance
EMO	Examining Medical Officer
EMP	Examining Medical Practitioner
Employment and Support Allowance Regulations	Employment and Support Allowance Regulations 2008
Enforceable Community right	Enforceable EU right

English Regulations (eligible children)	Care Planning, Placement and Case Review (England) Regulations 2010
English Regulations (relevant children)	Care Leavers (England) Regulations 2010
Eq. L.R.	Equality Law Reports
ERA	Employment, Retention and Advancement Scheme
ERA	Evoked Response Audiometry
ERA 1996	Employment Rights Act 1996
ER(NI)O	Employers Rights (Northern Ireland) Order 1996
ES	Employment Service
ESA	Employment and Support Allowance
ESA Regulations	Employment and Support Allowance Regulations 2008
ESA WCAt	Employment and Support Allowance Work Capability Assessment
ETA 1973	Employment and Training Act 1973
ETA(NI) 1950	Employment and Training Act (Northern Ireland) 1950
EU	European Union
Eu.L.R.	European Law Reports
European Coal and Steel Communities	European Union
EWCA Civ	Civil Division of the Court of Appeal in England and Wales
EWHC Admin	Administrative Court division of the High Court (England and Wales)
F(No.2)A 2005	Finance (No.2) Act 2005
FA 1990	Finance Act 1990
FA 1993	Finance Act 1993
FA 1996	Finance Act 1996
FA 2000	Finance Act 2000
FA 2004	Finance Act 2004
Fam. Law	Family Law
FAS	Financial Assistance Scheme
F.C.R.	Family Court Reporter
FIS	Family Income Supplement
FISMA 2000	Financial Services and Markets Act 2000
Fixing and Adjustment of Rates Regulations 1976	Child Benefit and Social Security (Fixing and Adjustment of Rates) Regulations 1976
F.L.R.	Family Law Reports
Former Regulations	Employment and Support Allowance (Transitional Provisions, Housing Benefit and Council Tax Benefit) (Existing Awards) Regulations 2010
FME	further medical evidence

Table of Abbreviations used in this Series

FOTRA	Free of Tax to Residents Abroad
FRAA	flat rate accrual amount
FSCS	Financial Services Compensation Scheme
FSMA 2000	Financial Services and Markets Act 2000
FSVG	Bundesgestez über die Sozialversicherung freiberuflich selbständig Erwerbstätiger (Austrian Federal Act of 30 November 1978 on social insurance for the self-employed in the liberal professions)
FTT	First-tier Tribunal
GA	Guardians Allowance
GA Regulations	Social Security (Guardian's Allowance) Regulations 1975
General Benefit Regulations 1982	Social Security (General Benefit) Regulations 1982
General Regulations	Statutory Maternity Pay (General) Regulations 1986
GMP	Guaranteed Minimum Pension
G.P.	General Practitioner
GRA	Gender Recognition Act
GRB	Graduated Retirement Benefit
GRP	Graduated Retirement Pension
G.W.D.	Greens Weekly Digest
HASSASSA	Health and Social Services and Social Security Adjudication Act 1983
HB	Housing Benefit
HCD	House of Commons Debates
HCP	health care professional
HCWA	House of Commons Written Answer
HESC	Health, Education and Social Care
HIV	Human Immunodeficiency Virus
H.L.R.	Housing Law Reports
HMIT	Her Majesty's Inspector of Taxes
HMRC	Her Majesty's Revenue and Customs
HMSO	Her Majesty's Stationery Office
HNCIP	(Housewives') Non-Contributory Invalidity Pension
Hospital In-Patients Regulations 1975	Social Security (Hospital In-Patients) Regulations 1975
Housing Benefit Regulations	Housing Benefit Regulations 2006
HP	Health Professional
HPP	Higher Pensioner Premium
HRA 1998	Human Rights Act 1998
H.R.L.R.	Human Rights Law Reports–UK Cases
HSE	Health and Safety Executive

IAC	Immigration and Asylum Chamber
IAP	Intensive Activity Period
IB	Invalidity Benefit
IB/IS/SDA	Incapacity Benefits' Regime
IBJSA	Incapacity Benefit Job Seekers Allowance
IBJSA	Income-Based Jobseeker's Allowance
IB PCA	Incapacity Benefit Personal Capability Assessment
IB Regs	Social Security (Incapacity Benefit) Regulations 1994
IB Regulations	Social Security (Incapacity Benefit) Regulations 1994
IBS	Irritable Bowel Syndrome
ICA	Invalid Care Allowance
ICA Regulations	Social Security (Invalid Care Allowance) Regulations 1976
ICA Unit	Invalid Care Allowance Unit
I.C.R.	Industrial Cases Reports
ICTA 1988	Income and Corporation Taxes Act 1988
I(EEA) Regulations	Immigration (European Economic Area) Regulations 2006
IFW Regulations	Incapacity for Work (General) Regulations 1995
I.I.	Industrial Injuries
IIAC	Industrial Injuries Advisory Council
IIDB	Industrial Injuries Disablement Benefit
ILO	International Labour Organization
ILO Convention	International Labour Organization Convention
Imm. A.R.	Immigration Appeal Reports
Immigration and Asylum Regulations	Social Security (Immigration and Asylum) Consequential Amendments Regulations 2000
Incapacity for Work Regulations	Social Security (Incapacity for Work) (General) Regulations 1995
Income Support General Regulations	Income Support (General) Regulations 1987
Income Support Regulations	Income Support (General) Regulations 1987
Increases for Dependants Regulations	Social Security Benefit (Dependency) Regulations 1977
IND	Immigration and Nationality Directorate of the Home Office
I.N.L.R.	Immigration and Nationality Law Reports
IO	Information Officer
I.O.	Insurance Officer

Table of Abbreviations used in this Series

IPPR	Institute of Public Policy Research
IRC	Inland Revenue Commissioners
IRESA	Income-Related Employment and Support Allowance
I.R.L.R.	Industrial Relations Law Reports
IS	Income Support
IS Regs	Income Support Regulations
IS Regulations	Income Support (General) Regulations 1987
IS	Income Support
ISA	Individual Savings Account
ITA 2007	Income Tax Act 2007
ITEPA	Income Tax (Earnings and Pensions) Act 2003
ITEPA 2003	Income Tax, Earnings and Pensions Act 2003
I.T.L. Rep.	International Tax Law Reports
ITS	Independent Tribunal Service
ITTOIA	Income Tax (Trading and Other Income) Act 2005
ITTOIA 2005	Income Tax (Trading and Other Income) Act 2005
IVB	Invalidity Benefit
IWA 1994	Social Security (Incapacity for Work) Act 1994
IW	Incapacity for Work
IW (Dependants) Regs	Social Security (Incapacity for Work) (Dependants) Regulations
IW (General) Regs	Social Security (Incapacity for Work) (General) Regulations 1995
IW (Transitional) Regs	Incapacity for Work (Transitional) Regulations
JD(NI)O 1995	Jobseekers (Northern Ireland) Order 1995
Jobseeker's Allowance Regulations	Jobseekers Allowance Regulations 1996
Jobseeker's Regulations 1996	Jobseekers Allowance Regulations 1996
J.P.	Justice of the Peace Reports
J.P.L.	Journal of Public Law
JSA	Job Seekers Allowance
JSA 1995	Jobseekers Act 1995
JSA (NI) Regulations	Jobseeker's Allowance (Northern Ireland) Regulations 1996
JSA (Transitional) Regulations	Jobseeker's Allowance (Transitional) Regulations 1996
JSA Regs 1996	Jobseekers Allowance Regulations 1996
JSA Regulations 1996	Jobseekers Allowance Regulations 1996
JSA Regulations	Jobseeker's Allowance Regulations 1996

JS(NI)O 1995	Jobseekers (Northern Ireland) Order 1995
J.S.S.L.	Journal of Social Security Law
J.S.W.F.L.	Journal of Social Welfare and Family Law
J.S.W.L.	Journal of Social Welfare Law
K.B.	Law Reports, King's Bench
K.I.R.	Knight's Industrial Law Reports
L.& T.R.	Landlord and Tenant Reports
LCW	limited capability for work
LCWA	Limited Capability for Work Assessment
LCWRA	Limited Capability for Work-Related Activity
LEA	local education authority
LEL	Lower Earnings Limit
LET	low earnings threshold
L.G.R.	Local Government Law Reports
L.G. Rev.	Local Government Review
L.J.R.	Law Journal Reports
Ll.L.Rep	Lloyd's List Law Report
Lloyd's Rep.	Lloyd's Law Reports
LRP	liable relative payment
L.S.G.	Law Society Gazette
LTAHAW	Living Together as Husband and Wife
Luxembourg Court	Court of Justice of the European Union (also referred to as CJEC and ECJ)
MA	Maternity Allowance
MAF	Medical Assessment Framework
MAT	Medical Appeal Tribunal
Maternity Allowance Regulations	Social Security (Maternity Allowance) Regulations 1987
Maternity Benefit Regulations	Social Security (Maternity Benefit) Regulations 1975
ME	myalgic encephalomyelitis
Medical Evidence Regulations	Social Security (Medical Evidence) Regulations 1976
M.H.L.R.	Mental Health Law Reports
MHP	mental health problems
MIG	minimum income guarantee
Migration Regulations	Employment and Support Allowance (Transitional Provisions, Housing Benefit and Council Tax Benefit (Existing Awards) (No.2) Regulations 2010
MIRAS	mortgage interest relief at source
MRI	Magnetic resonance imaging
MRSA	methicillin-resistant Staphylococcus aureus

MS	Medical Services
NACRO	National Association for the Care and Resettlement of Offenders
NCB	National Coal Board
NDPD	Notes on the Diagnosis of Prescribed Diseases
NHS	National Health Service
NI	National Insurance
N.I.	Northern Ireland Law Reports
NI Com	Northern Ireland Commissioner
NI	National Insurance
NICA	Northern Ireland Court of Appeal
NICs	National Insurance Contributions
NICom	Northern Ireland Commissioner
NINO	National Insurance Number
NIQB	Northern Ireland, Queen's Bench Division
NIRS 2	National Insurance Recording System
N.L.J.	New Law Journal
NMC	Nursing and Midwifery Council
Northern Ireland Contributions and Benefits Act	Social Security Contributions and Benefits (Northern Ireland) Act 1992
N.P.C.	New Property Cases
NTC Manual	Clerical procedures manual on tax credits
NUM	National Union of Mineworkers
OA	Osteoarthritis
OCD	Obsessive Compulsive Disorder
OGA	Agricultural Insurance Organisation
Ogus, Barendt and Wikeley	A. Ogus, E. Barendt and N. Wikeley, *The Law of Social Security* (4th edn, Butterworths, 1995)
O.J.	Official Journal
Old Cases Act	Industrial Injuries and Diseases (Old Cases) Act 1975
OPA	Overseas Pensions Act 1973
OPB	One Parent Benefit
O.P.L.R.	Occupational Pensions Law Reports
OPSSAT	Office of the President of Social Security Appeal Tribunals
Overlapping Benefits Regulations	Social Security (Overlapping Benefits) Regulations 1979
Overpayments Regulations	Social Security (Payments on account, Overpayments and Recovery) Regulations
P. & C.R.	Property and Compensation Reports
pa	per annum

para.	paragraph
PAYE	Pay As You Earn
Payments on Account Regulations	Social Security (Payments on account, Overpayments and Recovery) Regulations
PCA	Personal Capability Assessment
PD	prescribed disease
P.D.	Practice Direction
Pens. L.R.	Pensions Law Reports
Persons Abroad Regulations	Social Security Benefit (Persons Abroad) Regulations 1975
Persons Residing Together Regulations	Social Security Benefit (Persons Residing Together) Regulations 1977
PIE	Period of Interruption of Employment
PILON	pay in lieu of notice
P.I.Q.R.	Personal Injuries and Quantum Reports
PIW	Period of Incapacity for Work
P.I.W.R.	Personal Injury and Quantum Reports
P.L.R.	Estates Gazette Planning Law Reports
Polygamous Marriages Regulations	Social Security and Family Allowances (Polygamous Marriages) Regulations 1975
PPF	Pension Protection Fund
Prescribed Diseases Regulations	Social Security (Industrial Injuries) (Prescribed Diseases) Regulations 1985
Present Regulations	Employment and Support Allowance (Transitional Provisions, Housing Benefit and Council Tax Benefit) (Existing Awards) (No.2) Regulations 2010
PSCS	Pension Service Computer System
Pt	Part
PTA	pure tone audiometry
P.T.S.R.	Public and Third Sector Law Reports
PTWR 2000	Part-time Workers (Prevention of Less Favourable Treatment) Regulations 2000
PVS	private or voluntary sectors
pw	per week
Q.B.	Queen's Bench Law Reports
QBD (NI)	Queen's Bench Division (Northern Ireland)
QEF	qualifying earnings factor
QYP	qualifying young person
R	Reported Decision
r.	rule
RC	Rules of the Court of Session
REA	Reduced Earnings Allowance
Recoupment Regulations	Social Security (Recoupment) Regulations 1990

reg.	regulation
RIPA	Regulation of Investigatory Powers Act 2000
RMO	Responsible Medical Officer
rr.	rules
R.T.R.	Road Traffic Reports
S	Scottish Decision
s.	section
SAP	Statutory Adoption Pay
SAYE	Save As You Earn
SB	Supplementary Benefit
SBAT	Supplementary Benefit Appeal Tribunal
SBC	Supplementary Benefits Commission
S.C.	Session Cases
S.C. (H.L.)	Session Cases (House of Lords)
S.C. (P.C.)	Session Cases (Privy Council)
S.C.C.R.	Scottish Criminal Case Reports
S.C.L.R.	Scottish Civil Law Reports
Sch.	Schedule
SDA	Severe Disablement Allowance
SDP	Severe Disability Premium
SEC	Social Entitlement Chamber
SERPS	State Earnings Related Pension Scheme
Severe Disablement Allowance Regulations	Social Security (Severe Disablement Regulations Allowance) Regulations 1984
SI	Statutory Instrument
SIP	Share Incentive Plan
S.J.	Solicitors Journal
S.J.L.B.	Solicitors Journal Law Brief
S.L.T.	Scots Law Times
SMP	Statutory Maternity Pay
SMP (General) Regulations 1986	Statutory Maternity Pay (General) Regulations 1986
SP	Senior President
SPC	State Pension Credit
SPC Regulations	State Pension Credit Regulations 2002
SPCA	State Pension Credit Act 2002
SPCA 2002	State Pension Credit Act 2002
SPCA(NI) 2002	State Pension Credit Act (Northern Ireland) 2002
SPP	Statutory Paternity Pay
SPP and SAP (Administration) Regs 2002	Statutory Paternity Pay and Statutory Adoption Pay (Administration) Regulations 2002

SPP and SAP (General) Regulations 2002	Statutory Paternity Pay and Statutory Adoption Pay (General) Regulations 2002
SPP and SAP (National Health Service)	Statutory Paternity Pay and Statutory Adoption Pay (National Health Service Employees) Regulations 2002
SPP and SAP (Weekly Rates) Regulations	Statutory Paternity Pay and Statutory Adoption Pay (Weekly Rates) Regulations 2002
SS(MP)A 1977	Social Security (Miscellaneous Provisions) Act 1977
ss.	sections
SSA 1975	Social Security Act 1975
SSA 1977	Social Security Act 1977
SSA 1978	Social Security Act 1978
SSA 1979	Social Security Act 1979
SSA 1981	Social Security Act 1981
SSA 1986	Social Security Act 1986
SSA 1988	Social Security Act 1988
SSA 1989	Social Security Act 1989
SSA 1990	Social Security Act 1990
SSA 1998	Social Security Act 1998
SSAA 1992	Social Security Administration Act 1992*
SSAC	Social Security Advisory Committee
SSAT	Social Security Appeal Tribunal
SSCB(NI)A	Social Security Contributions and Benefits (Northern Ireland) Act 1992
SSCBA 1992	Social Security Contributions and Benefits Act 1992*
SSCPA 1992	Social Security (Consequential Provisions) Act 1992
SSHBA 1982	Social Security and Housing Benefits Act 1982
SSHD	Secretary of State for the Home Department
SS(MP) A 1977	Social Security (Miscellaneous Provisions) Act 1977
SS (No.2) A 1980	Social Security (No.2) Act 1980
SSPP	statutory shared parental pay
SSP	Statutory Sick Pay
SSP (General) Regulations	Statutory Sick Pay (General) Regulations 1982
SSPA 1975	Social Security Pensions Act 1975
SSWP	Secretary of State for Work and Pensions
State Pension Credit Regulations	State Pension Credit Regulations 2002
S.T.C.	Simon's Tax Cases
S.T.C. (S.C.D.)	Simon's Tax Cases: Special Commissioners Decisions

S.T.I.	Simon's Tax Intelligence
STIB	Short-Term Incapacity Benefit
Strasbourg Court	European Court of Human Rights
Students Directive	Directive 93/96/EEC
subpara.	subparagraph
subs.	subsection
T	Tribunal of Commissioners' Decision
Taxes Act	Income and Corporation Taxes Act 1988
(TC)	Tax and Chancery
T.C.	Tax Cases
TC (Claims and Notifications) Regs 2002	Tax Credits (Claims and Notifications) Regulations 2002
TCA	Tax Credits Act
TCA 1999	Tax Credits Act 1999
TCA 2002	Tax Credits Act 2002
TCEA 2007	Tribunals, Courts and Enforcement Act 2007
TCGA	Taxation of Chargeable Gains Act 1992
TCGA 1992	Taxation of Chargeable Gains Act 2002
TCTM	Tax Credits Technical Manual
TEC	Treaty Establishing the European Community
TEU	Treaty on European Union
TFEU	Treaty on the Functioning of the European Union
The Board	Commissioners for Revenue and Customs
TIOPA 2010	Taxation (International and Other Provisions) Act 2010
TMA 1970	Taxes Management Act 1970
T.R.	Taxation Reports
Transfer of Functions Act	Social Security Contributions (Transfer of Functions etc.) Act 1999
Transitional Provisions Regulations	Employment and Support Allowance (Transitional Provisions Regulations 2008
Treaty	Rome Treaty
Tribunal Procedure Rules	Tribunal Procedure (First-tier Tribunal)(Social Entitlement Chamber) Rules 2008
UB	Unemployment Benefit
UC	Universal Credit
UCITS	Undertakings for Collective Investments in Transferable Securities
UKAIT	UK Asylum and Immigration Tribunal
UKBA	UK Border Agency of the Home Office
UKCC	United Kingdom Central Council for Nursing, Midwifery and Health Visiting

UKFTT	United Kingdom First-tier Tribunal Tax Chamber
UKHL	United Kingdom House of Lords
U.K.H.R.R.	United Kingdom Human Rights Reports
UKSC	United Kingdom Supreme Court
UKUT	United Kingdom Upper Tribunal
Unemployment, Sickness and Invalidity Benefit Regs	Social Security (Unemployment, Sickness and Invalidity Benefit) Regulations 1983
USI Regs	Social Security (Unemployment, Sickness and Invalidity Benefit) Regulations 1983
UT	Upper Tribunal
VAMS	Veterans Agency Medical Service
VAT	Value Added Tax
VCM	vinyl chloride monomer
VERA 1992	Vehicle Excise and Registration Act 1992
VWF	Vibration White Finger
W	Welsh Decision
WAO	Wet op arbeidsongeschiktheidsverzekering (Dutch Act on Incapacity for Work)
WAZ	Wet arbeidsongeschiktheidsverzekering (Dutch Act on Self-employed Persons' Incapacity for Work)
WCA/WCAt	Work Capability Assessment
Welsh Regulations	Children (Leaving Care) (Wales) Regulations 2001 (SI 2001/2189)
WFHRAt	Work-Focused Health-Related Assessment
WFI	work-focused Interview
WFTC	Working Families Tax Credit
WIA	Wet Werk en inkomen naar arbeidsvermogen (Dutch Act on Work and Income according to Labour Capacity)
Widow's Benefit and Retirement Pensions Regs	Social Security (Widow's Benefit and Retirement Pensions) Regulations 1979
Wikeley, Annotations	N. Wikeley, "Annotations to Jobseekers Act 1995 (c.18)" in *Current Law Statutes Annotated* (1995)
Wikeley, Ogus and Barendt	Wikeley, Ogus and Barendt, *The Law of Social Security* (5th ed., Butterworths, 2002)
W.L.R.	Weekly Law Reports
Workmen's Compensation Acts	Workmen's Compensation Acts 1925 to 1945
WPS	War Pensions Scheme
W-RA Regs	Employment and Support Allowance (Work-Related Activity) Regulations 2011 (SI 2011/1349)

Table of Abbreviations used in this Series

WRA 2007	Welfare Reform Act 2007
WRA 2009	Welfare Reform Act 2009
WRA 2012	Welfare Reform Act 2012
WRAAt	Work-Related Activity Assessment
WRPA 1999	Welfare Reform and Pensions Act 1999
WRP(NI)O 1999	Welfare Reform and Pensions (Northern Ireland) Order
WTC	Working Tax Credit
WTC (Entitlement and Maximum Rate) Regulations 2002	Working Tax Credit (Entitlement and Maximum Rate) Regulations 2002
WTC Regulations	Working Tax Credit (Entitlement and Maximum Rate) Regulations 2002
W.T.L.R.	Wills & Trusts Law Reports

TABLE OF CASES

TABLE OF SOCIAL SECURITY COMMISSIONERS' DECISIONS

TABLE OF EU LEGISLATION

TABLE OF STATUTES

TABLE OF STATUTORY INSTRUMENTS

PART I

NEW LEGISLATION

Important preliminary note

The text of new legislation relating to Universal Credit is to be found in Part VI below, not this Part.

NEW REGULATIONS AND ORDERS

The Welfare Reform Act 2012 (Commencement No. 16 and Transitional and Transitory Provisions) Order 2014

(SI 2014/209) (C. 7)

See Part VI   1.001

The Universal Credit (Transitional Provisions) Regulations 2014

(SI 2014/1230 (as amended))

See Part VI   1.002

The Immigration (European Economic Area) (Amendment) Regulations 2014

(SI 2014/1451)

In force July 1, 2014

The Secretary of State, being a Minister designated for the purposes of   1.003
section 2(2) of the European Communities Act 1972 in relation to
measures relating to rights of entry into, and residence in, the United
Kingdom, in exercise of the powers conferred by that section, makes the
following Regulations.

Citation and commencement

1. These Regulations may be cited as the Immigration (European   1.004
Economic Area) (Amendment) Regulations 2014 and come into force
on 1st July 2014.

Interpretation

2. In these Regulations, "the 2006 Regulations" means the Immigra-   1.005
tion (European Economic Area) Regulations 2006.

3

Amendments to regulation 6 of the 2006 Regulations

1.006   **3.** *[Omitted: see the amendments to reg.6 of the Immigration (European Economic Area) Regulations 2006 in the Noter-up]*

Transitional provision

1.007   **4.** Any period after 31st December 2013 during which a person was a jobseeker for the purposes of regulation 6(1)(a) of the 2006 Regulations is, where relevant, to be taken into consideration when determining—
    (a) the length of the relevant period; and
    (b) whether condition C applies,
for the purposes of regulation 6 of the 2006 Regulations as amended by these Regulations.

(SI 2014/1583) (C. 61)

The Welfare Reform Act 2012 (Commencement No. 17 and Transitional and Transitory Provisions) Order 2014

(SI 2014/1583) (C. 61)

See Part VI

1.008

The Welfare Reform Act 2012 (Commencement No. 9, 11, 13, 14, 16 and 17 and Transitional and Transitory Provisions (Amendment)) Order 2014

(SI 2014/1661) (C.69)

See Part VI

1.009

The Jobseeker's Allowance (Supervised Jobsearch Pilot Scheme) Regulations 2014

(SI 2014/1913)

In force July 17, 2014 to April 29, 2015

ARRANGEMENT OF REGULATIONS

PART 1

GENERAL

1.010

PART 2

SELECTION FOR AND PARTICIPATION IN THE SUPERVISED JOBSEARCH PILOT SCHEME

PART 3

CONSEQUENTIAL AMENDMENTS

PART 4

CONTRACTING OUT

The Secretary of State for Work and Pensions makes the following Regulations in exercise of the powers conferred by sections 123(1)(d), 136(5)(a) and (b), 137(1) and 175(1), (3), (4) and (6) of the Social Security Contributions and Benefits Act 1992, sections 12(4)(a) and (b), 17A(1), (2), (4) and (5)(a), 20E(3)(a), 29, 35(1) and 36(2), (4) and (4A) of the Jobseekers Act 1995 and sections 30 and 146(1) and (2) of the Housing Grants, Construction and Regeneration Act 1996.

These Regulations are made with a view to ascertaining whether their provisions will, or will be likely to, encourage persons to obtain or remain in work or will, or will be likely to, make it more likely that persons will obtain or remain in work or be able to do so.

These Regulations are made with the consent of the Treasury in respect of provisions relating to section 30 of the Housing Grants, Construction and Regeneration Act 1996.

In respect of provisions in these Regulations relating to housing benefit, organisations appearing to the Secretary of State to be representative of the authorities concerned have agreed that consultations need not be undertaken.

The Social Security Advisory Committee has agreed that the proposals in respect of these Regulations should not be referred to it.

A draft of this instrument was laid before Parliament in accordance with section 37(2) of the Jobseekers Act 1995 and approved by a resolution of each House of Parliament.

PART 1

GENERAL

Citation, commencement and duration

1.—(1) These Regulations may be cited as the Jobseeker's Allowance (Supervised Jobsearch Pilot Scheme) Regulations 2014 and come into force on the day after the day on which they are made.

(2) They cease to have effect on 30th April 2015.

1.011

Interpretation

2.—(1) In these Regulations—

"the Jobseeker's Allowance Regulations" means the Jobseeker's Allowance Regulations 1996;

"the Housing Renewal Grants Regulations" means the Housing Renewal Grants Regulations 1996;

"the Housing Benefit Regulations" means the Housing Benefit Regulations 2006;

"claimant" means a person who claims a jobseeker's allowance, except that in relation to a joint-claim couple claiming a joint-claim jobseeker's allowance, it means either or both of the members of the couple;

"the Scheme" has the meaning given to it in regulation 3(2);

"the Scheme provider" means the person or persons delivering the Scheme pursuant to arrangements made by the Secretary of State;

"working day" means any day other than a Saturday, a Sunday, Christmas Day, Good Friday or a bank holiday under the Banking and Financial Dealings Act 1971 in England.

(2) For the purpose of these Regulations, where a written notice is given by sending it by post it is taken to have been received on the second working day after posting.

1.012

PART 2

SELECTION FOR AND PARTICIPATION IN THE SUPERVISED JOBSEARCH PILOT SCHEME

The Supervised Jobsearch Pilot Scheme

3.—(1) The Supervised Jobsearch Pilot Scheme is prescribed for the purposes of section 17A(1) (schemes for assisting persons to obtain employment: "work for your benefit" schemes etc) of the Jobseekers Act 1995.

1.013

7

(2) The Supervised Jobsearch Pilot Scheme ("the Scheme") is a scheme—

(a) that is designed to provide support and assistance to a claimant in their search to find employment, in a supervised environment, for up to 35 hours per week over a period of up to 13 weeks; and

(b) which involves an initial interview with the Scheme provider to discuss what the claimant is required to do by way of participation in the Scheme and may also involve training or other activity to help improve a claimant's job search skills, help preparing for job interviews and assistance with job applications and preparing a curriculum vitae.

DEFINITIONS

"claimant"—see reg.2(1).
"employment"—see Jobseekers Act 1995 s.35(1) and JSA Regulations 1996 reg.3.
"prescribed"—see Jobseekers Act 1995 s.35(1).

Selection for participation in the Scheme

1.014 **4.** The Secretary of State may select a claimant ("C") for participation in the Scheme either—

(a) in accordance with regulation 5, where C has never been selected for participation in the Work Programme within the meaning of regulation 3(8) of the Jobseeker's Allowance (Schemes for Assisting Persons to Obtain Employment) Regulations 2013; or

(b) in accordance with regulation 6, in all other cases.

DEFINITIONS

"claimant"—see reg.2(1).
"the Scheme"—see regs 2(1) and 3(2).

1.015 **5.** Where the Secretary of State is satisfied that the claimant ("C") is not taking sufficiently effective steps to secure employment (for example, because C is failing to secure job interviews), the Secretary of State may select C on a sampling basis, for participation in the Scheme if the conditions in regulation 6(2) to (4) are met.

DEFINITIONS

"claimant"—see reg.2(1).
"employment"—see Jobseekers Act 1995 s.35(1) and JSA Regulations 1996 reg.3.
"the Scheme"—see regs 2(1) and 3(2).

1.016 **6.**—(1) The Secretary of State may select a claimant ("C") on a sampling basis for participation in the Scheme if the following conditions are met.

(2) The first condition is that C has reached the age of 18.

(3) The second condition is that C is registered at a Jobcentre Plus office within a Jobcentre Plus district of the Department for Work and Pensions, by whatever name it is from time to time known, which is

identified by reference to its name at the date these Regulations come into force

(4) The third condition is that C is required to meet the jobseeking conditions.

(5) The fourth condition is that C is not under a current requirement to participate in the Work Programme under regulation 5 of the Jobseeker's Allowance (Schemes for Assisting Persons to Obtain Employment) Regulations 2013.

DEFINITIONS

> "claimant"—see reg.2(1).
> "the jobseeking conditions"—see Jobseekers Act 1995 ss.17A(10) and 1(2)(a)–(c).
> "the Scheme"—see regs 2(1) and 3(2).

Requirement to participate in the Scheme and initial notification

7.—(1) Subject to regulation 9, a claimant ("C") selected in accor- **1.017**
dance with regulation 4 is required to participate in the Scheme where the Secretary of State gives C a notice in writing complying with paragraph (2).

(2) The notice must specify—

(a) that C is required to participate in the Scheme;

(b) that C is required to attend an initial interview with the Scheme provider;

(c) a description of the Scheme in which C is required to participate;

(d) the day on which C is required to start participation in the Scheme;

(e) the day on which the requirement for C to participate in the Scheme will end; and

(f) the consequences of failing to attend the interview with the Scheme provider or failing to participate in the Scheme.

(3) Any changes to the details mentioned in paragraph (2), must be notified by the Secretary of State to C in writing.

DEFINITIONS

> "claimant"—see reg.2(1).
> "the Scheme"—see regs 2(1) and 3(2).
> "the Scheme provider"—see reg.2(1).
> "writing"—see Interpretation Act 1978 Sch.1.

Subsequent notifications

8.—(1) The Scheme provider must hold an initial interview with a **1.018**
claimant ("C") required to participate in the Scheme.

(2) At the initial interview the Scheme provider must discuss with C what C is required to do by way of participation in the Scheme.

(3) The Scheme provider must give C a notice in writing at C's initial interview or within 4 working days of the interview, complying with paragraph (4).

(4) The notice must specify—

(a) what C is required to do by way of participation in the Scheme; and

(b) the consequences of C failing to participate in the Scheme.

(5) Any changes to the details mentioned in paragraph (4), must be notified by the Scheme provider to C in writing.

DEFINITIONS

"claimant"—see reg.2(1).
"the Scheme"—see regs 2(1) and 3(2).
"the Scheme provider"—see reg.2(1).
"writing"—see Interpretation Act 1978 Sch.1.

Circumstances in which requirement to participate in the Scheme is suspended or ceases to apply

1.019   **9.**—(1) The requirement for a claimant ("C") to participate in the Scheme does not apply for any period during which C is not required to meet the jobseeking conditions.

(2) Where the Scheme provider fails to give a notice in writing in accordance with regulation 8, the requirement for C to participate in the Scheme is treated as not applying until such a notice is issued by the Scheme provider.

(3) A requirement to participate in the Scheme ceases to apply to C if—

(a) the Secretary of State gives C notice in writing that C is no longer required to participate in the Scheme; or

(b) C ceases to be entitled to jobseeker's allowance.

(4) If the Secretary of State gives the claimant a notice in writing under paragraph (3)(a), the requirement to participate in the Scheme ceases to apply on the day specified in the notice.

DEFINITIONS

"claimant"—see reg.2(1).
"the jobseeking conditions"—see Jobseekers Act 1995 ss.17A(10) and 1(2)(a)–(c).
"the Scheme"—see regs 2(1) and 3(2).
"the Scheme provider"—see reg.2(1).
"writing"—see Interpretation Act 1978 Sch.1.

Requirement to recommence participation in the Scheme

1.020   **10.**—(1) Where—

(a) the claimant's ("C") requirement to participate in the Scheme ceased to apply in accordance with regulation 9(3); and

(b) the requirement ceased before the date specified in the notice given to C in accordance with regulation 7(2)(e),

the Secretary of State may require C to recommence participation in the Scheme by giving C a new written notice complying with regulation 7(2).

10

(2) Where C is required to recommence participation in the Scheme, the Scheme provider must give a new notice to C in accordance with regulation 8.

DEFINITIONS

"claimant"—see reg.2(1).
"the Scheme"—see regs 2(1) and 3(2).
"the Scheme provider"—see reg.2(1).

PART 3

CONSEQUENTIAL AMENDMENTS

Notional Income

11.—(1) This regulation applies to the following provisions (which   1.021
relate to notional income)—
  (a) regulation 42(7) of the Housing Benefit Regulations;
  (b) regulation 31(9A) of the Housing Renewal Grants Regulations;
  (c) regulation 105(10A) of the Jobseeker's Allowance Regulations.
(2) In each of the provisions to which this regulation applies, after sub-paragraph (cc) insert—

"(cd) in respect of a person's participation in a scheme prescribed in regulation 3 of the Jobseeker's Allowance (Supervised Job-search Pilot Scheme) Regulations 2014;".

DEFINITIONS

"the Jobseeker's Allowance Regulations"—see reg.2(1).
"the Housing Renewal Grant Regulations"—*ibid.*
"the Housing Benefit Regulations"—*ibid.*

Notional Capital

12.—(1) This regulation applies to the following provisions (which   1.022
relate to notional capital)—
  (a) regulation 49(4) of the Housing Benefit Regulations;
  (b) regulation 38(3A) of the Housing Renewal Grants Regulations;
  (c) regulation 113(3A) of the Jobseeker's Allowance Regulations.
(2) In each of the provisions to which this regulation applies, after sub-paragraph (bc) insert—

"(bd) in respect of a person's participation in a scheme prescribed in regulation 3 of the Jobseeker's Allowance (Supervised Job-search Pilot Scheme) Regulations 2014;".

DEFINITIONS

"the Jobseeker's Allowance Regulations"—see reg.2(1).
"the Housing Renewal Grant Regulations"—*ibid.*
"the Housing Benefit Regulations"—*ibid.*

Income to be disregarded

1.023   **13.**—(1) This regulation applies to the following Schedules (which relate to sums to be disregarded in the calculation of income other than earnings)—

(a) Schedule 5 to the Housing Benefit Regulations;
(b) Schedule 3 to the Housing Renewal Grants Regulations;
(c) Schedule 7 to the Jobseeker's Allowance Regulations.

(2) In each of the Schedules to which this regulation applies, after paragraph A3 insert—

> "**A4.** Any payment made to the claimant in respect of any child care, travel or other expenses incurred, or to be incurred, by the claimant in respect of the claimant's participation in a scheme prescribed in regulation 3 of the Jobseeker's Allowance (Supervised Jobsearch Pilot Scheme) Regulations 2014.".

DEFINITIONS

> "the Jobseeker's Allowance Regulations"—see reg.2(1).
> "the Housing Renewal Grant Regulations"—*ibid.*
> "the Housing Benefit Regulations"—*ibid.*

Capital to be disregarded

1.024   **14.**—(1) This regulation applies to the following Schedules (which relate to capital to be disregarded)—

(a) Schedule 6 to the Housing Benefit Regulations;
(b) Schedule 4 to the Housing Renewal Grants Regulations;
(c) Schedule 8 to the Jobseeker's Allowance Regulations.

(2) In each of the Schedules to which this regulation applies, after paragraph A3(**e**) insert—

> "**A4.** Any payment made to the claimant in respect of any child care, travel or other expenses incurred, or to be incurred, by the claimant in respect of the claimant's participation in a scheme prescribed by regulation 3 of the Jobseeker's Allowance (Supervised Jobsearch Pilot Scheme) Regulations 2014, but only for 52 weeks beginning with the date of receipt of the payment.".

DEFINITIONS

> "the Jobseeker's Allowance Regulations"—see reg.2(1).
> "the Housing Renewal Grant Regulations"—*ibid.*
> "the Housing Benefit Regulations"—*ibid.*

Further modifications of the Jobseeker's Allowance Regulations

1.025   **15.** In regulation 25(1A) of the Jobseeker's Allowance Regulations, in the definition of "relevant notification", after "2013" insert the words ", under a scheme prescribed in regulation 3 of the Jobseeker's Allowance (Supervised Jobsearch Pilot Scheme) Regulations 2014".

DEFINITION

> "the Jobseeker's Allowance Regulations"—see reg.2(1).

12

PART 4

CONTRACTING OUT

Contracting out certain functions

16.—(1) Any function of the Secretary of State specified in paragraph   1.026
(2) may be exercised by, or by employees of, such person (if any) as may
be authorised by the Secretary of State.

(2) The functions are any function under—

(a) regulation 7 (requirement to participate in the Scheme and notification);

(b) regulation 9(3)(a) (notice that requirement to participate ceases);

(c) regulation 10 (requirement to recommence participation in the Scheme).

The Welfare Reform Act 2012 (Commencement No. 9, 11, 13, 14, 16 and 17 and Transitional and Transitory Provisions (Amendment) (No. 2)) Order 2014

(SI 2014/1923) (C.88)

1.027   See Part VI

The Immigration (European Economic Area) (Amendment) (No. 2) Regulations 2014

(SI 2014/1976)

In force July 28, 2014

1.028   The Secretary of State, being a Minister designated for the purposes of section 2(2) of the European Communities Act 1972 in relation to measures relating to rights of entry into, and residence in, the United Kingdom, in the exercise of powers conferred by that section, and of the powers conferred by section 109 of the Nationality, Immigration and Asylum Act 2002, makes the following Regulations.

Citation and commencement

1.029   **1.** These Regulations may be cited as the Immigration (European Economic Area) (Amendment) (No. 2) Regulations 2014 and come into force on 28th July 2014.

Interpretation

1.030   **2.** In these Regulations, "the 2006 Regulations" means the Immigration (European Economic Area) Regulations 2006(4).

Amendments to the 2006 Regulations

1.031   **3.** The 2006 Regulations are amended as set out in the Schedule.

Transitional provision

1.032   **4.** The amendments made by these Regulations have no effect in relation to any decision under the 2006 Regulations to remove a person from the United Kingdom taken before these Regulations came into force.

SCHEDULE

Amendments to the 2006 Regulations

1.033   *Omitted: See the amendments to regs 2, 11 and 15B of the Immigration (European Economic Area) Regulations 2006 in the Noter-up.*

The Social Security (Jobseeker's Allowance and Employment and Support Allowance) (Waiting Days) Amendment Regulations 2014

(SI 2014/2309)

In force October 27, 2014

The Secretary of State makes the following Regulations in exercise of the powers conferred by sections 21, 35(1) and 36(2) and (4)(a) of, and paragraphs 4 and 10(1) of Schedule 1 to, the Jobseekers Act 1995 and sections 22, 24(1) and 25(2), (3) and (5)(a) of, and paragraph 2 of Schedule 2 to, the Welfare Reform Act 2007.   **1.034**

In accordance with section 172(1) of the Social Security Administration Act 1992, the Secretary of State has referred the proposals for these Regulations to the Social Security Advisory Committee.

Citation and commencement

1. These Regulations may be cited as the Social Security (Jobseeker's Allowance and Employment and Support Allowance) (Waiting Days) Amendment Regulations 2014 and come into force on 27th October 2014.   **1.035**

Increase in waiting days

2. *[Omitted: see the amendments to reg.46 of the JSA Regulations 2006, reg.144 of the Employment and Support Allowance Regulations 2008, reg.36(2) of the Jobseeker's Allowance Regulations 2013 and reg.85(1) of the Employment and Support Allowance Regulations 2013 in the Noter-up]*   **1.036**

Consequential amendments

3. *[Omitted: see the amendments to regs 141 and 146C of the Jobseeker's Allowance Regulations 2006 in the Noter-up]*   **1.037**

Transitional provision

4.—(1)Regulations 2(1), (3) and 3 do not apply where the jobseeking period for the purposes of paragraph 4 of Schedule 1 (supplementary provisions) to the Jobseekers Act 1995 began before 27th October 2014.   **1.038**

(2) Regulations 2(2) and (4) do not apply where the period of limited capability for work for the purposes of paragraph 2 of Schedule 2 (supplementary provisions) to the Welfare Reform Act 2007 began before 27th October 2014.

(3) The amendment to regulation 144(2)(d) of the Employment and Support Allowance Regulations 2008 made by regulation 2(2) does not apply where the beginning of the period of limited capability for work which relates to the former claimant's entitlement began before 27th October 2014.

The Welfare Reform Act 2012 (Commencement No. 19 and Transitional and Transitory Provisions and Commencement No. 9 and Transitional and Transitory Provisions (Amendment)) Order 2014

(SI 2014/2321) (C.99)

1.039

See Part VI

The Jobseeker's Allowance (Habitual Residence) Amendment Regulations 2014

(SI 2014/2735)

In force November 9, 2014

1.040 The Secretary of State for Work and Pensions makes the following Regulations in exercise of the powers conferred by sections 4(5) and (12), 35(1) and 36(2) of the Jobseekers Act 1995.

In accordance with section 173(1)(b) of the Social Security Administration Act 1992, the Secretary of State has obtained the agreement of the Social Security Advisory Committee that proposals in respect of these Regulations should not be referred to it.

Citation and commencement

1.041 1. These Regulations may be cited as the Jobseeker's Allowance (Habitual Residence) Amendment Regulations 2014 and come into force on 9th November 2014.

Amendment of the Jobseeker's Allowance Regulations 1996

1.042 2. *[Omitted: see the amendments to reg.1(3) of the Jobseeker's Allowance Regulations 1996 in the Noter-up].*

3. *[Omitted: see the amendments to reg.85A(2) and (2A) of the Jobseeker's Allowance Regulations 1996 in the Noter-up].*

Saving

1.043 4. The amendment in regulation 3 does not apply in relation to a claim for a jobseeker's allowance which is made or treated as made before these Regulations come into force.

16

The Immigration (European Economic Area) (Amendment) (No. 3) Regulations 2014

(SI 2014/2761)

In force November 10, 2014

The Secretary of State, being a Minister designated for the purposes **1.044** of section 2(2) of the European Communities Act 1972 in relation to measures relating to rights of entry into, and residence in, the United Kingdom, in the exercise of powers conferred by that section, makes the following Regulations.

Citation and commencement

1. These Regulations may be cited as the Immigration (European **1.045** Economic Area) (Amendment) (No. 3) Regulations 2014 and come into force on 10th November 2014.

Interpretation

2. In these Regulations— **1.046**
"the 2006 Regulations" means the Immigration (European Economic Area) Regulations 2006;
"the relevant period" has the same meaning as in regulation 6(8) of the 2006 Regulations.

Amendments to the 2006 Regulations

3. *[Omitted: see the amendments to regs 6(8)(b) and (9)(b) of the Immi-* **1.047** *gration (European Economic Area) Regulations 2006 in the Noter-up]*

Transitional provisions

4.—(1) Any period after 31st December 2013 during which a person **1.048** enjoyed a right to reside under the 2006 Regulations as a jobseeker is to be taken into account for the purposes of—
(a) determining the relevant period in relation to that person; and
(b) determining whether condition C in regulation 6(9) of the 2006 Regulations applies.
(2) But where calculation of the relevant period pursuant to paragraph (1)(a) would result in a negative balance, the relevant period is to be treated as though it were zero days.

Social Security Contributions and Benefits Act 1992
(Application of Parts 12ZA, 12ZB and 12ZC to Parental Order Cases) Regulations 2014

(SI 2014/2866)

In force November 19, 2014 and later dates

ARRANGEMENT OF REGULATIONS

This instrument contains only regulations made by virtue of, or consequential upon, sections 119(1) and 122(5)(c) and (6)(c) of the Children and Families Act 2014 and is made before the end of the period of 6 months beginning with the coming into force of that enactment.

The Secretary of State, in exercise of the powers conferred by sections 171ZK(2), 171ZT(2) and 171ZZ5(2) of the Social Security Contributions and Benefits Act 1992, makes the following Regulations.

GENERAL NOTE

1.050 These Regulations apply Parts 12ZA, 12ZB and 12ZC of the SSCBA 1992, as modified by these Regulations, to parental order parents. A "parental order parent" is a person who has applied, or intends to apply, with another person, under s.54 of the Human Fertilisation and Embryology Act 2008 for a parental order in respect of a child or someone who has such an order. Part 12ZA provides for entitlement to statutory paternity pay. Part 12ZB provides for entitlement to statutory adoption pay. Part 12ZC (inserted into SSCBA 1992 by Part 7 of the Children and Families Act 2014) provides for entitlement statutory shared parental pay. Official estimates are that the numbers of employees likely to be affected by these Regulations are very small. In 2013, only 185 parental orders were granted. Of those who apply or intend to apply for a parental order (regardless of whether they subsequently obtain one), only a proportion will meet the eligibility requirements to be entitled to adoption leave and pay, paternity leave and pay or to be able to opt into shared parental leave and pay.

Citation, commencement and application

1.051   1. (1) These Regulations may be cited as the Social Security Contributions and Benefits Act 1992 (Application of Parts 12ZA, 12ZB and 12ZC to Parental Order Cases) Regulations 2014.

(2) Subject to paragraphs (3) and (4), these Regulations come into force on 19th November 2014.

18

(3) The modification of section 171ZA of the Social Security Contributions and Benefits Act 1992 by the insertion of subsection (3C) as set out in Schedule 1 to these Regulations comes into force on the date that section 171ZA(2)(ba) comes into force.

(4) The modification of section 171ZL of the Social Security Contributions and Benefits Act 1992 by the insertion of subsection (3B) as set out in Schedule 2 to these Regulations comes into force on the date that section 171ZL(2)(ba) comes into force.

(5) Regulation 4 does not have effect in cases involving children whose expected week of birth ends on or before 4th April 2015.

Interpretation

2. In these Regulations—   1.052

"the Act" means the Social Security Contributions and Benefits Act 1992;

"intended parent", in relation to a child, means a person who, on the day of the child's birth—

    (a) applies, or intends to apply during the period of 6 months beginning with that day, with another person for a parental order in respect of the child, and

    (b) expects the court to make a parental order on that application in respect of the child;

"parental order" means an order under section 54(1) of the Human Fertilisation and Embryology Act 2008; and

"parental order parent" means a person—

    (a) on whose application the court has made a parental order in respect of a child, or

    (b) who is an intended parent of a child.

Application of Part 12ZA of the Act to parental order parents

3. Part 12ZA of the Act (statutory paternity pay) has effect in relation   1.053
to parental order parents with the modifications of sections 171ZA, 171ZB and 171ZE of the Act specified in the second column of Schedule 1 to these Regulations.

Application of Part 12ZB of the Act to parental order parents

4. Part 12ZB of the Act (statutory adoption pay) has effect in relation   1.054
to parental order parents with the modifications of sections 171ZL and 171ZN of the Act specified in the second column of Schedule 2 to these Regulations.

Application of Part 12ZC of the Act to parental order parents

5. Part 12ZC of the Act (statutory shared parental pay) has effect in   1.055
relation to parental order parents with the modifications of section 171ZV of the Act specified in the second column of Schedule 3 to these Regulations.

SCHEDULE 1   Regulation 3

APPLICATION OF PART 12ZA OF THE ACT TO PARENTAL ORDER CASES

1.056

Provision	Modification
Section 171ZA	After subsection (4) insert—
	"(4A) A person who satisfies the conditions in section 171ZB(2)(a) to (d) in relation to a child is not entitled to statutory paternity pay under this section in respect of that child.".
Section 171ZB	For paragraph (a) of subsection (2) substitute—
	"(a) that he satisfies prescribed conditions as to being a person— (i) on whose application the court has made a parental order in respect of a child, or (ii) who is an intended parent of a child; (ab) that he satisfies prescribed conditions as to relationship with the other person on whose application the parental order was made or who is an intended parent of the child;".
	In paragraph (d) of subsection (2), for "placed for adoption" substitute "born".
	In paragraph (e) of subsection (2), omit "where he is a person with whom the child is placed for adoption,".
	For subsection (3) substitute—
	"(3) The references in this section to the relevant week are to the week immediately preceding the 14th week before the expected week of the child's birth.".
	After subsection (3) insert—
	"(3B) In a case where a child is born earlier than the 14th week before the expected week of the child's birth— (a) subsection (2)(b) shall be treated as satisfied in relation to a person if, had the birth occurred after the end of the relevant week, the person would have been in employed earner's employment with an employer for a continuous period of at least 26 weeks ending with the relevant week; (b) subsection (2)(c) shall be treated as satisfied in relation to a person if the person's normal weekly earnings for the period of 8 weeks ending with the week immediately preceding the week in which the child is born are not less than the lower earnings limit in force under section 5(1)(a) immediately before the commencement of the week in which the child is born; and (c) subsection (2)(d) shall not apply. (3C) In a case where a child is born before the end of the relevant week, subsection (2)(ba) shall be treated as satisfied in relation to a person if, had the birth occurred after the end of the relevant week, the person would have been entitled to be in the relevant employment at the end of the relevant week.

Provision	Modification
Section 171ZB—*cont*	In this subsection "the relevant employment" means the employment by reference to which the person satisfies the condition in subsection (2)(b).".
	In subsection (6), for "placement for adoption of more than one child as part of the same arrangement" substitute "birth, or expected birth, of more than one child as a result of the same pregnancy".
	For subsection (7) substitute—
	"(7) In this section— "intended parent", in relation to a child, means a person who, on the day of the child's birth— (a) applies, or intends to apply during the period of 6 months beginning with that day, with another person for a parental order in respect of the child, and (b) expects the court to make a parental order on that application in respect of the child; and "parental order" means an order under section 54(1) of the Human Fertilisation and Embryology Act
	Omit subsection (8).
	Omit subsection (9).
Section 171ZE	In paragraph (b) of subsection (3), for "placement for adoption" substitute "birth".
	In subsection (4)— (a) in paragraph (a), for "sub-paragraph (i) of section 171ZA(2)(a)" substitute "section 171ZA(2)(a)(i)"; (b) in paragraph (b), for "sub-paragraph (ii) of that provision" substitute "section 171ZA(2)(a)(ii) or 171ZB(2)(ab)".
	In subsection (9), for "the reference in subsection (3)(a) to the date of the child's birth shall be read as a reference" substitute "the references in subsection (3)(a) and (b) to the date of the child's birth shall be read as references".
	Omit subsection (10).
	Omit subsection (12).

SCHEDULE 2

Regulation 4

APPLICATION OF PART 12ZB OF THE ACT TO PARENTAL ORDER CASES

Provision	Modification	
Section 171ZL	For paragraph (a) of subsection (2) substitute—	1.057
	"(a) that he is— (i) a person on whose application the court has made a parental order in respect of a child, or (ii) an intended parent of a child;".	
	For subsection (3) substitute—	
	"(3) The references in this section to the relevant week are to the week immediately preceding the 14th week before the expected week of the child's birth.".	

Provision	Modification
Section 171ZL—*cont*	After subsection (3) insert—

"(3A) In a case where a child is born earlier than the 14th week before the expected week of the child's birth—

(a) subsection (2)(b) shall be treated as satisfied in relation to a person if, had the birth occurred after the end of the relevant week, the person would have been in employed earner's employment with an employer for a continuous period of at least 26 weeks ending with the relevant week; and

(b) subsection (2)(d) shall be treated as satisfied in relation to a person if the person's normal weekly earnings for the period of 8 weeks ending with the week immediately preceding the week in which the child is born are not less than the lower earnings limit in force under section 5(1)(a) immediately before the commencement of the week in which the child is born.

(3B) In a case where a child is born before the end of the relevant week, subsection (2)(ba) shall be treated as satisfied in relation to a person if, had the birth occurred after the end of the relevant week, the person would have been entitled to be in the relevant employment at the end of the relevant week.

In this subsection "the relevant employment" means the employment by reference to which the person satisfies the condition in subsection (2)(b).".

For paragraph (b) of subsection (4), substitute—

"(b) the other person on whose application the court has made a parental order in respect of the child or who is an intended parent of the child—

(i) is a person to whom the conditions in subsection (2) above apply, and

(ii) has elected to receive statutory adoption pay.".

Omit subsection (4A).

Omit subsection (4B).

In subsection (5), for "placement, or expected placement, for adoption of more than one child as part of the same arrangement" substitute "birth, or expected birth, of more than one child as a result of the same pregnancy".

After subsection (8) insert—

"(8A) In this section—

"intended parent", in relation to a child, means a person who, on the day of the child's birth—

(a) applies, or intends to apply during the period of 6 months beginning with that day, with another person for a parental order in respect of the child, and

(b) expects the court to make a parental order on that application in respect of the child; and

"parental order" means an order under section 54(1) of the Human Fertilisation and Embryology Act 2008.".

Provision	Modification
Section 171ZL—*cont*	Omit subsection (9).
	Omit subsection (10).
Section 171ZN	In subsection (2F) (5), for "in which the person is notified that the person has been matched with a child for the purposes of adoption" substitute "immediately preceding the 14th week before the expected week of the child's birth".
	Omit subsection (9).

SCHEDULE 3   Regulation 5

APPLICATION OF PART 12ZC OF THE ACT TO PARENTAL ORDER CASES

Provision	Modification	
Section 171ZV	In subsection (1), for "with whom a child is, or is expected to be, placed for adoption under the law of any part of the United Kingdom" substitute "on whose application the court has made a parental order in respect of a child or who is an intended parent of a child".	**1.058**
	In paragraph (a) of subsection (2), for "another person" substitute "the other person on whose application the court has made a parental order in respect of the child or who is an intended parent of the child".	
	In paragraph (g) of subsection (2), for "the placement for adoption of the child" substitute "being a person on whose application the court has made a parental order in respect of the child or being an intended parent of the child".	
	In paragraph (a) of subsection (4), for "with whom a child is, or is expected to be, placed for adoption under the law of any part of the United Kingdom" substitute "on whose application the court has made a parental order in respect of a child or who is an intended parent of a child".	
	In paragraph (h) of subsection (4), for "the placement for adoption of the child" substitute "being a person on whose application the court has made a parental order in respect of the child or being an intended parent of the child".	
	In subsection (16), for "the placement for adoption of more than one child as part of the same arrangement" substitute "the birth of more than one child as a result of the same pregnancy".	
	After subsection (16) insert—	
	"(16A) In this section— "intended parent", in relation to a child, means a person who, on the day of the child's birth— (a) applies, or intends to apply during the period of 6 months beginning with that day, with another person for a parental order in respect of the child, and (b) expects the court to make a parental order on that application in respect of the child; and	

Provision	Modification
Section 171ZV—*cont*	"parental order" means an order under section 54(1) of the Human Fertilisation and Embryology Act 2008.".
	Omit subsection (17).
	Omit subsection (18).

The Universal Credit (Digital Service) Amendment Regulations 2014

(SI 2014/2887)

In force November 26, 2014

The Secretary of State for Work and Pensions, in exercise of the powers conferred by section 1(1) of the Social Security Administration Act 1992 and sections 4(3), 7(3), 8(3), 9(2), 10(3), 11(4), 12(1) and (3), 19(2)(d), 32(1) and (4), 42(2) and (3) of, and paragraph 3(2) of Schedule 1 to, the Welfare Reform Act 2012, makes the following Regulations:
In accordance with section 173(1)(b) of the Social Security Administration Act 1992, the Social Security Advisory Committee has agreed that the proposals for these Regulations need not be referred to it. **1.059**

Citation and commencement

1. These Regulations may be cited as the Universal Credit (Digital Service) Amendment Regulations 2014 and, subject to regulation 5 (saving), come into force on 26th November 2014. **1.060**

Universal credit – childcare costs

2. *[Omitted: see the amendments to regs 33, 34 and 34A of the Universal Credit Regulations 2013, in the Noter-up.]* **1.061**

Universal Credit – assessment periods

3. *[Omitted: see the amendments to regs 15, 21 and 22A of the Universal Credit Regulations 2013; regs 6, 9 and 26 of the Universal Credit, Personal Independence Payment, Jobseeker's Allowance and Employment and Support Allowance (Claims and Payments) Regulations 2013 and reg. 7b of the Universal Credit (Transitional Provisions) Regulations 2013 in the Noter-up.]* **1.062**

Universal Credit—calculation of unearned income

4. *[Omitted: see the amendment to reg. 73 of the Universal Credit Regulations 2013, in the Noter-up.]* **1.063**

Saving

5. (1) These Regulations do not apply to an award of universal credit that has been made by virtue of any of the following orders— **1.064**
  (a) the Welfare Reform Act 2012 (Commencement No. 9 and Transitional and Transitory Provisions and Commencement No. 8 and Savings and Transitional Provisions (Amendment)) Order 2013;
  (b) the Welfare Reform Act 2012 (Commencement No. 11 and Transitional and Transitory Provisions and Commencement No. 9 and

Transitional and Transitory Provisions (Amendment)) Order 2013;

(c) the Welfare Reform Act 2012 (Commencement No. 13 and Transitional and Transitory Provisions) Order 2013;

(d) the Welfare Reform Act 2012 (Commencement No. 14 and Transitional and Transitory Provisions) Order 2013;

(e) the Welfare Reform Act 2012 (Commencement No. 16 and Transitional and Transitory Provisions) Order 2014;

(f) the Welfare Reform Act 2012 (Commencement No. 17 and Transitional and Transitory Provisions) Order 2014;

(g) Welfare Reform Act 2012 (Commencement No. 19 and Transitional and Transitory Provisions and Commencement No. 9 and Transitional and Transitory Provisions (Amendment)) Order 2014,

unless it is an award to which paragraph (2) applies.

(2) This paragraph applies to—

(a) an award made to members of a couple jointly as a consequence of a previous award having ended when the couple formed; or

(b) an award made to a single claimant as a consequence of a previous award having ended when the claimant ceased to be a member of couple,

where either member of the couple in question is a digital service claimant.

(3) A "digital service claimant" is a person who has become entitled to an award of universal credit—

(a) by reference to residence in the postcode part-district SM5 2;

(b) by forming a couple with a person who became entitled to an award of universal credit by reference to residence in that postcode;

(c) by forming a couple with a person who became entitled to an award of universal credit by virtue of sub-paragraph (b); or

(d) by forming a couple with a person who became entitled to an award of universal credit by virtue of sub-paragraph (c).

Diffuse Mesothelioma Payment Scheme (Levy) Regulations 2014

(SI 2014/2904)

In force November 28, 2014

ARRANGEMENT OF REGULATIONS

Citation, commencement and interpretation

1. (1) These Regulations may be cited as the Diffuse Mesothelioma   1.066
Payment Scheme (Levy) Regulations 2014.

(2) These Regulations come into force on 28th November 2014.

(3) In these Regulations—

"a financial year" means the 12 month period ending with the 31st
March in any year;

"individual gross written premium" means the sum, before commission and the cost of reinsurance are taken out, of all employers'
liability insurance premiums written in a calendar year by an
individual active insurer;

"reference period" has the meaning given in regulation 3;

"the payment amount" means the share of the total amount of the levy
that an active insurer is required to pay;

"the scheme" means the Diffuse Mesothelioma Payment Scheme
established by the Diffuse Mesothelioma Payment Scheme Regulations 2014;

"total amount of the levy" means an annual sum decided by the
Secretary of State under section 13 of the Mesothelioma Act 2014
in each financial year with a view to meeting the costs of the
scheme;

"total gross written premium" means the sum, before commission and
the cost of reinsurance are taken out, of all employers' liability
insurance premiums written in a calendar year by all active
insurers.

The requirement to pay a share of the total amount of the levy

2. (1) An active insurer is required to pay a share of the total amount   1.067
of the levy based on that insurer's relative market share in the reference
period as determined in accordance with regulation 4.

(2) The requirement in paragraph (1) is a requirement—

(a) to pay the Secretary of State the payment amount specified in the notice under regulation 5(1) in accordance with the notice under regulation 5(2); and

(b) subject to details given in a notice under regulation 5(2)(a), to pay the payment amount by the end of a financial year in respect of which the Secretary of State decides the total amount of the levy.

The reference period

1.068   **3.** (1) The reference period is a 12 month period ending on 31st December falling in a financial year.

(2) The reference period for the payment amount for the first financial year ends on 31st December 2014.

(3) In this regulation the "first financial year" means the year ending 31st March 2015.

Determination of relative market share and amounts

1.069   **4.** (1) An active insurer's relative market share in the reference period is determined in accordance with paragraph (2) and the payment amount an active insurer must pay is determined in accordance with paragraphs (3) to (5).

(2) For the purpose of these Regulations, relative market share in the reference period is to be treated as if it were the same as the relative market share for the calendar year two years before the reference period.

(3) The payment amount an active insurer must pay in a financial year is to be determined by multiplying the total amount of the levy for that financial year by the figure for their relative market share for the calendar year two years before the reference period.

(4) In this regulation "relative market share for the calendar year two years before the reference period" means A divided by B where—

(a) "A" equals the individual gross written premium for that calendar year;

(b) "B" equals the total gross written premium attributable to the active insurer whose individual gross written premium has been ascertained for the purpose of "A".

(5) In paragraph (4) where "A" cannot be ascertained, an active insurer's relative market share for the calendar year two years before the reference period is nil.

Information and publication

1.070   **5.** (1) The Secretary of State must notify active insurers in writing of the payment amount due from them.

(2) The Secretary of State must also notify active insurers in writing of—

(a) the date or dates in the financial year by which the payment amount is required; and

(b) details of how the payment amount can be made.

(3) The Secretary of State must give active insurers sufficient information to enable them to determine how the payment amount in their case was calculated.

(4) In particular the Secretary of State may give each active insurer information concerning—

(a) the basis on which they are considered to be an active insurer;

(b) the action the Secretary of State may take if the payment amount is not made in accordance with the notice under paragraphs (1) and (2).

(5) The Secretary of State must publish annually the costs of the scheme and must in particular publish information on—

(a) the costs of payments made under the scheme;

(b) the costs of administering the scheme; and

(c) any costs incurred by the Secretary of State in establishing a body to administer the scheme.

Recovery of the payment amount

6. If the payment amount notified to an active insurer is not paid in accordance with the notices under regulation 5(1) and (2), the payment amount, or any part of it, which has not been paid, is recoverable as a debt due to the Secretary of State.   1.071

Statutory Shared Parental Pay (Administration) Regulations 2014

(SI 2014/2929)

In force December 1, 2014

ARRANGEMENT OF REGULATIONS

The Secretary of State makes these Regulations in exercise of powers conferred by sections 7, 8, 10 and 51(1) of the Employment Act 2002 and sections 8(1)(f) and (ga) and 25(3) and (6) of the Social Security Contributions (Transfer of Functions, etc.) Act 1999 with the concurrence of the Commissioners for Her Majesty's Revenue and Customs.

GENERAL NOTE

1.073   Part 7 of the Children and Families Act 2014 inserted a new Part 12ZC into the SSCBA 1992 giving the Secretary of State the power to make regulations to create an entitlement to statutory shared parental pay (ShPP). These Regulations provide for the funding of employers' liabilities to make ShPP payments and also impose obligations on employers in connection with such payments and confer powers on the Commissioners for HMRC. Under reg.3, an employer is entitled to an amount equal to 92 per cent of ShPP payments made by the employer, or the whole of such payments if the employer is a small employer. Regulations 4 to 7 provide for employers to be reimbursed through deductions from income tax, national insurance and other payments that they would otherwise make to HMRC (and for HMRC to fund payments to the extent that employers cannot be fully reimbursed in this way). Regulation 8 enables HMRC to recover overpayments to employers. Regulation 9 requires employers to maintain records relevant to ShPP payments to employees or former employees, while reg.10 empowers HMRC officers to inspect, copy or remove employers' payment records. Regulation 11 requires an employer who decides not to make any (or any further) ShPP payments to an employee (or former employee) to give that person the details of the decision and the reasons for it. Regulations 12 and 13 provide for HMRC officers to determine issues relating to a person's ShPP entitlement. Regulation 14 provides for employers, employment agencies, ShPP claimants and others to furnish information or documents to HMRC officers on request.

Citation and commencement

1. These Regulations may be cited as the Statutory Shared Parental Pay (Administration) Regulations 2014 and come into force on 1st December 2014.

1.074

Interpretation

2. (1) In these Regulations—

1.075

"the 1992 Act" means the Social Security Contributions and Benefits Act 1992;

"the Commissioners" means the Commissioners for Her Majesty's Revenue and Customs;

"contributions payments" has the same meaning as in section 7 of the Employment Act 2002;

"the Contributions Regulations" means the Social Security (Contributions) Regulations 2001;

"income tax month" means the period beginning on the 6th day of any calendar month and ending on the 5th day of the following calendar month;

"income tax quarter" means the period beginning on—

    (a) the 6th day of April and ending on the 5th day of July;

    (b) the 6th day of July and ending on the 5th day of October;

    (c) the 6th day of October and ending on the 5th day of January;

    (d) the 6th day of January and ending on the 5th day of April;

"period of payment of statutory shared parental pay" means each week during which statutory shared parental pay is payable to a person under section 171ZY(2) of the 1992 Act;

"statutory shared parental pay" means statutory shared parental pay payable in accordance with the provisions of Part 12ZC of the 1992 Act;

"tax year" means the 12 months beginning with 6th April in any year;

"writing" includes writing delivered by means of electronic communications to the extent that the electronic communications are approved by directions issued by the Commissioners pursuant to regulations under section 132 of the Finance Act 1999.

(2) Any reference in these Regulations to the employees of an employer includes the employer's former employees.

Funding of employers' liabilities to make payments of statutory shared parental pay

1.076　**3.** (1) An employer who has made any payment of statutory shared parental pay shall be entitled—

(a) to an amount equal to 92% of such payment; or

(b) if the payment qualifies for small employer's relief by virtue of section 7(3) of the Employment Act 2002—

(i) to an amount equal to such payment; and

(ii) to an additional payment equal to the amount to which the employer would have been entitled under section 167(2)(b) of the 1992 Act had the payment been a payment of statutory maternity pay.

(2) The employer shall be entitled in either case (a) or case (b) to apply for advance funding in respect of such payment in accordance with regulation 4, or to deduct it in accordance with regulation 5 from amounts otherwise payable by the employer.

Applications for funding from the Commissioners

1.077　**4.** (1) An employer may apply to the Commissioners for funds to pay the statutory shared parental pay (or so much of it as remains outstanding) to the employee or employees in a form approved for that purpose by the Commissioners where—

(a) the conditions in paragraph (2) are satisfied; or

(b) the condition in paragraph (2)(a) is satisfied and the employer considers that the condition in paragraph (2)(b) will be satisfied on the date of any subsequent payment of emoluments to one or more employees who are entitled to payment of statutory shared parental pay.

(2) The conditions in this paragraph are—

(a) the employer is entitled to a payment determined in accordance with regulation 3 in respect of statutory shared parental pay which the employer is required to pay to an employee or employees for an income tax month or income tax quarter; and

(b) the payment exceeds the aggregate of—

(i) the total amount of tax which the employer is required to pay to the collector of taxes in respect of the deduction from the emoluments of employees in accordance with the Income Tax (Pay as You Earn) Regulations 2003 for the same income tax month or income tax quarter;

(ii) the total amount of the deductions made by the employer from the emoluments of employees for the same income tax month or income tax quarter in accordance with regulations under section 22(5) of the Teaching and Higher Education Act 1998 or under section 73B of the Education (Scotland)

Act 1980 or in accordance with article 3(5) of the Education (Student Support) (Northern Ireland) Order 1998;

(iii) the total amount of contributions payments which the employer is required to pay to the collector of taxes in respect of the emoluments of employees (whether by means of deduction or otherwise) in accordance with the Contributions Regulations for the same income tax month or income tax quarter; and

(iv) the total amount of payments which the employer is required to pay to the collector of taxes in respect of the deductions made on account of tax from payments to sub-contractors in accordance with section 61 of the Finance Act 2004 for the same income tax month or income quarter.

(3) An application by an employer under paragraph (1) shall be for an amount up to, but not exceeding, the amount of the payment to which the employer is entitled in accordance with regulation 3 in respect of statutory shared parental pay which the employer is required to pay to an employee or employees for the income tax month or income tax quarter to which the payment of emoluments relates.

Deductions from payments to the Commissioners

5. An employer who is entitled to a payment determined in accordance with regulation 3 may recover such payment by making one or more deductions from the aggregate of the amounts specified in sub-paragraphs (i) to (iv) of regulation 4(2)(b) except where and in so far as—   1.078

(a) those amounts relate to earnings paid before the beginning of the income tax month or income tax quarter in which the payment of statutory shared parental pay was made;

(b) those amounts are paid by the employer later than six years after the end of the tax year in which the payment of statutory shared parental pay was made;

(c) the employer has received payment from the Commissioners under regulation 4; or

(d) the employer has made a request in writing under regulation 4 that the payment to which the employer is entitled in accordance with regulation 3 be paid and the employer has not received notification by the Commissioners that the request is refused.

Payments to employers by the Commissioners

6. The Commissioners shall pay the employer such amount as the employer was unable to deduct where—   1.079

(a) the Commissioners are satisfied that the total amount which the employer is or would otherwise be entitled to deduct under regulation 5 is less than the payment to which the employer is entitled in accordance with regulation 3 in an income tax month or income tax quarter; and

(b) the employer has in writing requested the Commissioners to do so.

Date when certain contributions are to be treated as paid

1.080   **7.** Where an employee has made a deduction from a contributions payment under regulation 5, the date on which it is to be treated as having been paid for the purposes of subsection (5) of section 7 (funding of employers' liabilities) of the Employment 2002 is—

(a) in a case where the deduction did not extinguish the contributions payment, the date on which the remainder of the contributions payment or, as the case may be, the first date on which any part of the remainder of the contributions payment was paid; and

(b) in a case where deduction extinguished the contributions payment, the 14th day after the end of the income tax month or income tax quarter during which there were paid the earnings in respect of which the contributions payment was payable.

Overpayments

1.081   **8.** (1) This regulation applies where funds have been provided to the employer pursuant to regulation 4 in respect of one or more employees and it appears to an officer of Revenue and Customs that the employer has not used the whole or part of those funds to pay statutory shared parental pay.

(2) An officer of Revenue and Customs shall decide to the best of the officer's judgement the amount of funds provided pursuant to regulation 4 and not used to pay statutory shared parental pay and shall serve notice in writing of this decision on the employer.

(3) A decision under this regulation may cover funds provided pursuant to regulation 4—

(a) for any one income tax month or income tax quarter, or more than one income tax month or income tax quarter, in a tax year; and

(b) in respect of a class or classes of employees specified in the decision notice (without naming the individual employees), or in respect of one or more employees named in the decision notice.

(4) Subject to the following provisions of this regulation, Part 6 of the Taxes Management Act 1970 (collection and recovery) shall apply with any necessary modifications to a decision under this regulation as if it were an assessment and as if the amount of funds determined were income tax charged on the employer.

(5) Where an amount of funds determined under this regulation relates to more than one employee, proceedings may be brought for the recovery of that amount without distinguishing the amounts making up that sum which the employer is liable to repay in respect of each employee and without specifying the employee in question, and the amount determined under this regulation shall be one cause of action or one matter of complaint for the purposes of proceedings under section 65, 66 or 67 of the Taxes Management Act 1970.

(6) Nothing in paragraph (5) prevents the bringing of separate proceedings for the recovery of any amount which the employer is liable to repay in respect of each employee.

Records to be maintained by employers

9. Every employer shall maintain for three years after the end of a tax year in which the employer made payments of statutory shared parental pay to any employee a record of— 1.082
  (a) if the employee's period of payment of statutory shared parental pay began in that year—
    (i) the date of which that period began; and
    (ii) the evidence of entitlement to statutory shared parental pay provided by the employee pursuant to regulations made under section 171ZW(1)(b) of the 1992 Act;
  (b) the weeks in that tax year in which statutory shared parental pay was paid to the employee and the amount paid in each week;
  (c) any week in that tax year which was within the employee's period of payment of statutory shared parental pay but for which no payment of statutory shared parental pay was made to the employee and the reason no payment was made.

Inspection of employers' records

10. (1) Every employer, whenever called upon to do so by any author- 1.083
ised officer of Revenue and Customs, shall produce the documents and records specified in paragraph (2) to that officer for inspection, at such time as that officer may reasonably require, at the prescribed place.
  (2) The documents and records specified in this paragraph are—
  (a) all wage sheets, deductions working sheets, records kept in accordance with regulation 9 and other documents relating to the calculation or payment of statutory shared parental pay to employees in respect of the years specified by such officer; or
  (b) such of those wages sheets, deductions working sheets, or other documents and records as may be specified by the authorised officer.
  (3) The "prescribed place" mentioned in paragraph (1) means—
  (a) such place in Great Britain as the employer and the authorised officer may agree upon; or
  (b) in default of such agreement, the place in Great Britain at which the documents and records referred to in paragraph (2)(a) are normally kept; or
  (c) in default of such agreement and if there is no such place as it referred to in sub-paragraph (b), the employer's principal place of business in Great Britain.
  (4) The authorised officer may—
  (a) take copies of, or make extracts from, any document or record produced to the authorised officer for inspection in accordance with paragraph (1); and
  (b) remove any document or record so produced if it appears to the authorised officer to be necessary to do so, at a reasonable time and for a reasonable period.
  (5) Where any document or record is removed in accordance with paragraph (4)(b), the authorised officer shall provide—
  (a) a receipt for the document or record so removed; and

(b) a copy of the document or record, free of charge, within seven days, to the person by whom it was produced or caused to be produced where the document or record is reasonably required for the proper conduct of business.

(6) Where a lien is claimed on a document produced in accordance with paragraph (1), the removal of the document under paragraph (4)(b) shall not be regarded as breaking the lien.

(7) Where records are maintained by computer, the person required to make them available for inspection shall provide the authorised officer with all facilities necessary for obtaining information from them.

Provision of information relating to entitlement to statutory shared parental pay

1.084   **11.** (1) An employer shall furnish the employee with details of a decision that the employer has no liability to make payments of statutory shared parental pay to the employee and the reason for it where the employer—

(a) has been given evidence of entitlement to statutory shared parental pay pursuant to regulations made under section 171ZW(1)(b) of the 1992 Act; and

(b) decides that they have no liability to make payments of statutory shared parental pay to the employee.

(2) An employer who has been given such evidence of entitlement to statutory shared parental pay shall furnish the employee with the information specified in paragraph (3) where the employer—

(a) has made one or more payments of statutory shared parental pay to the employee but,

(b) decides, before the end of the period of payment of statutory shared parental pay, that they have no liability to make further payments to the employee because the employee has been detained in legal custody or sentenced to a term of imprisonment which was not suspended.

(3) The information specified in this paragraph is—

(a) details of the employer's decision and the reasons for it; and

(b) details of the last week in respect of which a liability to pay statutory shared parental pay arose and the total number of weeks within the period of payment of statutory shared parental pay in which such liability arose.

(4) The employer shall—

(a) return to the employee any evidence provided by the employee as referred to in paragraph (1) or (2);

(b) comply with the requirements imposed by paragraph (1) within 28 days of the day the employee gave evidence of entitlement to statutory shared parental pay pursuant to regulations made under section 171ZW(1)(b) of the 1992 Act; and

(c) comply with the requirements imposed by paragraph (2) within seven days of being notified of the employee's detention or sentence.

Application for the determination of any issue arising as to, or in connection with, entitlement to statutory shared parental pay

12. (1) An application for the determination of any issue arising as to, 1.085
or in connection with, entitlement to statutory shared parental pay may
be submitted to an officer of Revenue and Customs by the employee
concerned.

(2) Such an issue shall be decided by an officer of Revenue and
Customs only on the basis of such an application or on their own initiative.

Applications in connection with statutory shared parental pay

13. (1) An application for the determination of any issue referred to in 1.086
regulation 12 shall be made in a form approved for the purpose by the
Commissioners.

(2) Where such an application is made by an employee, it shall—

(a) be made to an officer of Revenue and Customs within six months
of the earliest day in respect of which entitlement to statutory
shared parental pay is an issue;

(b) state the period in respect of which entitlement to statutory shared
parental pay is in issue; and

(c) state the grounds (if any) on which the applicant's employer had
denied liability for statutory shared parental pay in respect of the
period specified in the application.

Provision of information

14. (1) Where an officer of Revenue and Customs— 1.087

(a) reasonably requires information or documents from a person
specified in paragraph (2) to ascertain whether statutory shared
parental pay is or was payable, and

(b) gives notification to that person requesting such information or
documents, that person shall furnish that information within 30
days of receiving the notification.

(2) The requirement to provide such information or documents
applies to—

(a) any person claiming to be entitled to statutory shared parental
pay;

(b) any person who is, or has been, the spouse, civil partner or partner
of such a person as is specified in sub-paragraph (a);

(c) any person who is, or has been, an employer of such a person as
is specified in sub-paragraph (a);

(d) any person carrying on an agency or other business for the introduction or supply of persons available to do work or to perform
services to persons requiring them; and

(e) any person who is a servant or agent of any such person as is
specified in sub-paragraphs (a) to (d).

Statutory Paternity Pay and Statutory Adoption Pay (Parental Orders and Prospective Adopters) Regulations 2014

(SI 2014/2934)

In force December 1, 2014

1.088   This instrument contains only regulations made by virtue of, or consequential upon, section 119 of the Children and Families Act 2014 and is made before the end of the period of 6 months beginning with the coming into force of that enactment.

The Secretary of State in exercise of the powers conferred by sections 171ZB(2)(a), 171ZC(1A) and (3)(a), (c), (d), (f) and (g), 171ZD(2) and (3), 171ZE(2), (3), (7) and (8), 171ZG(3), 171ZJ(1), (3), (4), (7) and (8), 171ZL(8)(b) to (d), (f) and (g), 171ZM(2) and (3), 171ZN(2), (5) and (6), 171ZP(6), 171ZS(1), (3), (4), (7) and (8) and 175(4) of the Social Security Contributions and Benefits Act 1992, section 5(1)(g), (i) and (p) of the Social Security Administration Act 1992 and sections 8(1) and (2)(c) and 51(1) of the Employment Act 2002 and with the concurrence of the Commissioners for Her Majesty's Revenue and Customs, in so far as such concurrence is required, makes the following Regulations:

GENERAL NOTE

1.089   Part 1 of these Regulations deals with citation, commencement and interpretation issues.

Part 2 of these Regulations amends the Statutory Paternity Pay and Statutory Adoption Pay (General) Regulations (SI 2002/2822) to make provision for a new right to statutory adoption pay for local authority foster parents who are prospective adopters if they have been notified that a child is to be placed with them under s.22C of the Children Act 1989 (following consideration in accordance with s.22C(9B)(c)). The amendments made also make provision for new rights to statutory paternity pay to the spouses, civil partners and partners of these prospective adopters.

Part 3 of these Regulations make provision for an entitlement to statutory adoption pay and statutory paternity pay (adoption) in respect of cases which involve a person who has applied with another person for a parental order under s.54 of the Human Fertilisation and Embryology Act 2008. Under s.54 a court may make an order providing for a child of a surrogate mother to be treated as the child of the applicants if certain conditions are satisfied. Part 3 needs to be read in conjunction with the Social Security Contributions and Benefits Act 1992 (Application of Parts 12ZA, 12ZB and 12ZC to Parental Order Cases) Regulations 2014 (SI 2014/2866). This Part should also be read in conjunction with the Statutory Paternity Pay and Statutory Adoption Pay (General) Regulations (SI 2002/2822) which this Part applies with modifications.

Part 4 amends to Statutory Paternity Pay and Statutory Adoption Pay (Administration) Regulations 2002 (SI 2002/2820) to cover the situation where statutory paternity pay or statutory adoption pay is paid to local authority foster parents who are prospective adopters. Part 5 modifies those 2002 Regulations in a case where statutory paternity pay or statutory adoption pay is paid to a person who has applied with another person for a parental order.

PART 1

GENERAL

Citation and commencement

1. These Regulations may be cited as the Statutory Paternity Pay and   1.090
Statutory Adoption Pay (Parental Orders and Prospective Adopters)
Regulations 2014 and come into force on 1st December 2014.

Interpretation

2. In these Regulations—   1.091
"Administration Regulations" means the Statutory Paternity Pay and
Statutory Adoption Pay (Administration) Regulations 2002;
"parental order parent" means a person on whose application the
court has made a parental order in relation to a child;
"Pay Regulations" means the Statutory Paternity Pay and Statutory
Adoption Pay (General) Regulations 2002.
3. (1) The amendments made in Part 2 and 4 of these Regulations
have effect only in relation to children matched with a person who is
notified of having been matched on or after 5th April 2015.
(2) For the purposes of paragraph (1)—
(a) a person is matched with a child for adoption when an adoption
agency decides that that person would be a suitable adoptive
parent for the child;
(b) in a case where paragraph (a) applies, a person is notified as
having been matched with a child on the date that person receives
notification of the agency's decision, under regulation 33(3)(a) of
the Adoption Agencies Regulations 2005, regulation 28(3) of the
Adoption Agencies (Wales) Regulations 2005 or regulation 8(5) of
the Adoption Agencies (Scotland) Regulations 2009;
(c) a person is also matched with a child for adoption when a decision
has been made in accordance with regulation 22A of the Care
Planning, Placement and Case Review (England) Regulations
2010 and an adoption agency has identified that person with
whom the child is to be placed in accordance with regulation 12B
of the Adoption Agencies Regulations 2005;
(d) in a case where paragraph (c) applies, a person is notified as
having been matched with a child on the date on which that
person receives notification in accordance with regulation
12B(2)(a) of the Adoption Agencies Regulations 2005.
(3) In paragraph (2) "adoption agency" has the meaning given, in
relation to England and Wales, by section 2 of the Adoption and Children Act 2002 and in relation to Scotland, by section 119(1) of the
Adoption and Children (Scotland) Act 2007.

AMENDMENT OF THE PAY REGULATIONS

1.092   **4.** (1) Regulation 2 (interpretation) of the Pay Regulations is amended as follows.

(2) For paragraph (2) substitute—

"(2) For the purposes of these Regulations—
  (a) a person is matched with a child for adoption when an adoption agency decides that that person would be a suitable adoptive parent for the child;
  (b) in a case where paragraph (a) applies, a person is notified as having been matched with a child on the date that person receives notification of the agency's decision, under regulation 33(3)(a) of the Adoption Agencies Regulations 2005, regulation 28(3) of the Adoption Agencies (Wales) Regulations 2005 or regulation 8(5) of the Adoption Agencies (Scotland) Regulations 2009;
  (c) a person is also matched with a child for adoption when a decision is has been made in accordance with regulation 22A of the Care Planning, Placement and Case Review (England) Regulations 2010 and an adoption agency has identified that person with whom the child is to be placed in accordance with regulation 12B of the Adoption Agencies Regulations 2005.
  (d) in a case where paragraph (c) applies, a person is notified as having been matched with a child on the date on which that person receives notification in accordance with regulation 12B(2)(a) of the Adoption Agencies Regulations 2005.".

(3) After paragraph (2), as substituted by this regulation, insert—

"(3) A reference (however expressed) in these Regulations to "placed for adoption" means—
  (a) placed for adoption under the Adoption and Children Act 2002 or the Adoption and Children (Scotland) Act 2007; or
  (b) placed in accordance with section 22C of the Children Act 1989 with a local authority foster parent who is also a prospective adopter.

(4) The reference to "prospective adopter" in paragraph (3) means a person who has been approved as suitable to adopt a child and has been notified of that decision in accordance with regulation 30B(4) of the Adoption Agencies Regulations 2005.

5. (1) Regulation 22 (adoption pay period in cases where adoption is disrupted) of the Pay Regulations is amended as follows.

(2) Paragraph (1)(a)(ii) is substituted by—

"(ii) the child is returned after being placed, or".

(3) After paragraph (4) insert—

"(5) In paragraph (1) "returned after being placed" means—
  (a) returned to the adoption agency under sections 31 to 35 of the Adoption and Children Act 2002;
  (b) in Scotland, returned to the adoption agency, adoption society or nominated person in accordance with section 25(6) of the Adoption and Children (Scotland) Act 2007; or
  (c) where the child is placed in accordance with section 22C of the Children Act 1989, returned to the adoption agency following termination of the placement.".

PART 3

APPLICATION AND MODIFICATION OF THE PAY REGULATIONS IN PARENTAL ORDER CASES

Application of the Pay Regulations to intended parents and parental order parents

6. (1) The provisions of the Pay Regulations in so far as they apply to   1.093
statutory paternity pay (adoption) and statutory adoption pay shall apply to an intended parent or a parental order parent with the modifications set out in this Part of these Regulations.

(2) In this regulation—
"statutory adoption pay" means statutory adoption pay payable in accordance with the provisions of Part 12ZB of the Social Security Contributions and Benefits Act 1992;
"statutory paternity pay (adoption)" means statutory paternity pay payable in accordance with the provisions of Part 12ZA of the Social Security Contributions and Benefits Act 1992 where the conditions specified in section 171ZB of that Act are satisfied.

Application of the Pay Regulations to intended parents and parental order parents

7. In regulation 2 (interpretation) of the Pay Regulations as they apply   1.094
to an intended parent or a parental order parent—
  (a) paragraph (1) shall read as if—
      (i) the definition of "adopter" were omitted;
      (ii) there were the following definitions—

        ""Parent A" in relation to a child means the intended parent or parental order parent who has elected to be Parent A;
        "parental order parent" means a person on whose application the court has made an order in respect of the child under section 54(1) of the Human Fertilization and Embryology Act 2008;
        "statutory shared parental pay" means statutory shared parental pay payable in accordance with Part 12ZC of the Act;";

(b) paragraph (2) shall apply as if that paragraph read—

"(2) An intended parent or a parental order parent elects to be Parent A in relation to a child if that person (A) agrees with the other intended parent or parental order parent of the child (B) that A and not B will be parent A.".

Application of the Pay Regulations to intended parents and parental order parents

1.095   **8.** In regulation 3 (application) of the Pay Regulations as they apply an intended parent or a parental order parent—
(a) paragraph (1)(b) shall read as if sub-paragraphs (i) and (ii) were omitted and replaced by—

"whose expected week of birth begins on or after 5th April 2015".

(b) paragraph (2) shall read as if sub-paragraphs (a) and (b) were omitted and replaced by—

"whose expected week of birth begins on or after 5th April 2015".

Application of the Pay Regulations to intended parents and parental order parents

1.096   **9.** In regulation 11 (conditions of entitlement) of the Pay Regulations as they apply to an intended parent or a parental order parent—
(a) paragraph (1) shall apply as if sub-paragraphs (a) and (b) were omitted and replaced by—

"(a) is an intended parent or parental order parent in relation to the child;
(b) is married to, the civil partner or the partner of Parent A; and
(c) has or expects to have the main responsibility for the upbringing of the child (apart from the responsibility of Parent A)."

(b) paragraph (2) shall read as if the words "the adopter" in both places where those words occur were "Parent A";
(c) paragraph (2A) shall read as if the words "the adopter" in both places where those words occur were "Parent A".

Application of the Pay Regulations to intended parents and parental order parents

1.097   **10.** Regulation 11A (notice of entitlement to statutory paternity pay (adoption)) of the Pay Regulations as they apply to an intended parent or a parental order parent shall apply as if paragraphs (a) and (b) read—

"(a) in or before the 15th week before the expected week of the child's birth; or

42

(b) in a case where it was not reasonably practicable for the employee to give the notice in accordance with paragraph (a), as soon as reasonably practicable.".

Application of the Pay Regulations to intended parents and parental order parents

11. In regulation 12 (period of payment of statutory paternity pay (adoption)) of the Pay Regulations as they apply to an intended parent or a parental order parent—   1.098

(a) paragraph (1) shall apply as if that paragraph read—

> "(1) Subject to regulation 14, a person entitled to statutory paternity pay (adoption) may choose the statutory pay period to begin—
>
> > (a) on the date on which the child is born or, where the person is at work on that day, the following day;
> > (b) the date falling such number of days after the date on which the child is born as the person may specify; or
> > (c) a predetermined date, specified by the person which is later than the expected week of the child's birth.";

(b) paragraph (2) shall not apply;

(c) paragraph (4) shall apply as if sub-paragraphs (a) to (c) read—

> "(a) where the variation is to provide for the employee's statutory paternity pay period to begin on the date on which the child is born, or where the employee is at work on that day, the following day, at least 28 days before the first day of the expected week of the child's birth,
>
> (b) where the variation is to provide for the employee's statutory paternity pay period to begin on a date that is a specified number of days (or a different specified number of days) after the date on which the child is born, at least 28 days before the date falling that number of days after the first day of the expected week of the child's birth,
>
> (c) where the variation is to provide for the employee's statutory paternity pay period to begin on a predetermined date (or a different predetermined date), at least 28 days before that date,".

Application of the Pay Regulations to intended parents and parental order parents

12. In regulation 13 (additional notice requirements for statutory paternity pay (adoption)) of the Pay Regulations as they apply to an intended parent or a parental order parent—   1.099

(a) paragraph (1) shall read as if the words "the date on which the placement occurred" were "the date on which the child was born";

(b) paragraph (2) shall read as if the words "is placed for adoption" were "is born".

Application of the Pay Regulations to intended parents and parental order parents

1.100   **13.** In regulation 14 (qualifying period for statutory paternity pay (adoption)) of the Pay Regulations as they apply to an intended parent or a parental order parent shall read as if the words "of 56 days" to the end were omitted and replaced by—

"which begins on the date of the child's birth and ends—
(a) except in the case referred to in paragraph (b), 56 days after that date;
(b) in a case where the child is born before the first day of the expected week of its birth, 56 days after that day.".

Application of the Pay Regulations to intended parents and parental order parents

1.101   **14.** In regulation 15 (evidence of entitlement for statutory paternity pay (adoption)) of the Pay Regulations as they apply to an intended parent or a parental order parent—
(a) paragraph (2)(b) shall apply as if that paragraph read—

"(b) the expected week of the child's birth;";

(b) paragraph (2)(e) shall apply as if that paragraph read—

"(e) the date on which the child was born";

(c) paragraph (3) shall apply as if sub-paragraphs (a) and (b) read—

"(a) in or before the 15th week before the expected week of the child's birth;
(b) in a case where it was not reasonably practicable for the employee to provide it in accordance with sub-paragraph (a), as soon as reasonably practicable.";

(d) paragraph (4) shall read as if the words "child's placement" were "child's birth".

Application of the Pay Regulations to intended parents and parental order parents

1.102   **15.** In regulation 16 (entitlement to statutory paternity pay (adoption) where there is more than one employer) of the Pay Regulations as they apply to an intended parent or a parental order parent, paragraph (b) shall read as if the words "in which the adopter is notified of being matched with the child" were "immediately preceding the 14th week before the expected week of the child's birth".

Application of the Pay Regulations to intended parents and parental order parents

1.103   **16.** In regulation 20 (avoidance of liability for statutory paternity pay) of the Pay Regulations as they apply to an intended parent or a parental order parent, paragraph (2)(a) shall read as if the words "or, as the case may be, the placement of the child for adoption" were omitted.

Application of the Pay Regulations to intended parents and parental order parents

17. (1) In regulation 21 (adoption pay period) of the Pay Regulations as they apply to an intended parent or a parental order parent, paragraph (1) shall read as if that paragraph read— 1.104

"(1) The adoption pay period in respect of a person entitled to statutory adoption pay shall begin on the day on which the child is born or, where the person is at work on that day, the following day.".

(2) Paragraph (2), (3), (4) and (6) shall not apply.

Application of the Pay Regulations to intended parents and parental order parents

18. In regulation 22 (adoption pay period in cases where adoption is disrupted) of the Pay Regulations as they apply to an intended parent or a parental order parent— 1.105

(a) paragraph (1) shall apply as if that paragraph read—

"(1) The adoption pay period shall terminate in accordance with the provisions of paragraph (2) where—
(a) the child dies;
(b) the person entitled to statutory adoption pay does not apply for a parental order in respect of the child within the time limit set in section 54(3) of the Human Fertilisation and Embryology Act 2008; or
(c) the that person's application for a parental order in respect of the child is refused, withdrawn or otherwise terminated and any time limit for an appeal or a new application has expired;";

(b) in paragraph (3)—
(i) sub-paragraph (a) shall apply as if the reference to paragraph (1)(a)(i) were a reference to paragraph (1)(a);
(ii) sub-paragraph (b) shall apply as if that sub-paragraph read—

"(b) in a case falling within paragraph (1)(b) the week during which the time limit in section 54(3) of the Human Fertilisation and Embryology Act 2008 for an application for a parental order for the child expires;";

(iii) sub-paragraph (c) shall apply as if that sub-paragraph read—

"(c) in a case falling within paragraph (1)(c) the week during which the person's application for a parental order is refused, withdrawn or otherwise terminated without the order being granted.".

Application of the Pay Regulations to intended parents and parental order parents

1.106   **19.** In regulation 23 (additional notice requirements for statutory adoption pay) of the Pay Regulations as they apply to an intended parent or a parental order parent—

(a) paragraph (1) shall read as if the words "the date on which the child is expected to be placed for adoption" were "the expected week of the child's birth";

(b) paragraph (2) shall read as if—

    (i) the words from "Where the choice" to "sub-paragraph (a) of that paragraph," were omitted;

    (ii) the words "the date the child is placed for adoption" were "the date on which the child is born".

Application of the Pay Regulations to intended parents and parental order parents

1.107   **20.** In regulation 24 (evidence of entitlement to statutory adoption pay) of the Pay Regulations as they apply to an intended parent or a parental order parent—

(a) in paragraph (1), sub-paragraph (a) shall apply as if that sub-paragraph read—

    "(a) a statutory declaration specified in paragraph (2) where the person who will be liable to pay the statutory adoption pay requests it in accordance with paragraph (3)";

(b) paragraph (2) shall apply as if that paragraph read—

    "(2) The statutory declaration referred to in paragraph (1)(a) is a statutory declaration stating that the person making the declaration—

        (a) has applied, or intends to apply, under section 54 of the Human Fertilisation and Embryology Act 2008 with another person for a parental order in respect of the child within the time limit for making such an application; and

        (b) expects the court to make a parental order on that application in respect of the child.";

(c) paragraph (3) shall apply as if that paragraph read—

    "(3) The declaration in referred to—

        (a) in paragraph (1)(a) shall be provided to the person liable to pay statutory adoption pay within 14 days of that person requesting that declaration where the person requests it within 14 days of receiving the notice under section 171ZL(6) of the Act;

        (b) in paragraph (1)(b) shall be provided to the person liable to pay statutory adoption pay at least 28 days before the beginning of the adoption pay period, or if that is not reasonably practicable , as soon as reasonably practicable after that date.".

Application of the Pay Regulations to intended parents and parental order parents

21. In regulation 25 (entitlement to statutory adoption pay where 1.108 there is more than one employer) of the Pay Regulations as they apply to an intended parent or a parental order parent, paragraph (b) shall read as if the words "in which he is notified of being matched with the child" were "immediately preceding the 14th week before the expected week of the child's birth".

Application of the Pay Regulations to intended parents and parental order parents

22. In regulation 29 (termination of employment before start of adop- 1.109 tion pay period) of the Pay Regulations as they apply to an intended parent or a parental order parent, paragraph (1) shall apply as if—
  (a) the words "chosen in accordance with regulation 21" were omitted;
  (b) the words "14 days before the expected date of placement" to the end were "on the day on which the child is born".

Application of the Pay Regulations to intended parents and parental order parents

23. In regulation 30 (avoidance of liability for statutory adoption pay) 1.110 of the Pay Regulations as they apply to an intended parent or a parental order parent, in paragraph (2), sub-paragraph (a) shall read as if the words "in which he was notified of having been matched with the child for adoption" read "immediately preceding the 14th week before the expected week of the child's birth".

Application of the Pay Regulations to intended parents and parental order parents

24. In regulation 40 (normal weekly earnings) of the Pay Regulations 1.111 as they apply to an intended parent or a parental order parent, in paragraph (2), the definition of "the appropriate date" shall read—

""the appropriate date" means in relation to statutory paternity pay (adoption) and statutory adoption pay , the first day of the 14th week before the expected week of the child's birth or the first day in the week in which the child is born, whichever is earlier;".

PART 4

AMENDMENT OF THE ADMINISTRATION REGULATIONS

25. In regulation 11 (provision of information relating to entitlement 1.112 to statutory paternity pay or statutory adoption pay) of the Administration Regulations—

(a) for paragraph (4), substitute—

"(4) For the purposes of paragraph (3)(b)(ii), an adopter is notified as having been matched with a child—

    (a) on the date that person receives notification of the adoption agency's decision under regulation 33(3)(a) of the Adoption Agencies Regulations 2005, regulation 28(3) of the Adoption Agencies (Wales) Regulations 2005 or regulation 8(5) of the Adoption Agencies (Scotland) Regulations 2009; or

    (b) on the date on which that person receives notification in accordance with regulation 12B(2)(a) of the Adoption Agencies Regulations 2005.";

(b) after paragraph (4) insert—

"(5) In this regulation "adoption agency" has the meaning given, in relation to England and Wales, by section 2 of the Adoption and Children Act 2002 and, in relation to Scotland, by section 119(1) of the Adoption and Children (Scotland) Act 2007.".

PART 5

MODIFICATION OF THE ADMINISTRATION REGULATIONS IN PARENTAL ORDER CASES

1.113   **26.** In the case of entitlement to statutory paternity pay or statutory adoption pay under section 171ZB or 171ZL of the Social Security Contributions and Benefits Act 1992 as those sections apply to an intended parent or to a parental order parent—

    (a) paragraph (3)(b)(ii) of regulation 11 (provision of information) of the Administration Regulations shall read as if the words from "the end of the seven day period that starts on the date on which the adopter is notified of having been matched with the child" were—

"the day the employee gave notice of the employee's intended absence or the end of the fifteenth week before the expected week of birth, whichever is later;";

    (b) paragraph (4) and (5) of that regulation shall not apply.

Statutory Shared Parental Pay (General) Regulations 2014

(SI 2014/3051)

In force December 1, 2014

ARRANGEMENT OF REGULATIONS

PART 1

PART 2

PART 3

Part 4

Part 5

A draft of these Regulations was laid before Parliament in accordance with section 176(1) of the Social Security Contributions and Benefits Act 1992 and approved by resolution of each House of Parliament.

This instrument contains only regulations made by virtue of, or consequential upon, section 119 of the Children and Families Act 2014 and is made before the end of the period of 6 months beginning with the coming into force of that enactment.

The Secretary of State, in exercise of the powers conferred by sections 171ZU(1), (2), (3), (4), (5), (12), (13), (14) and (15), 171ZV(1), (2), (3), (4), (5), (12), (13), (14), (15) and (17), 171ZW(1)(a) to (f), 171ZX(2) and (3), 171ZY(1), (3), (4) and (5), 171ZZ1(3), 171ZZ4(3), (4), (7) and (8) and 175(3) of the Social Security Contributions and Benefits Act 1992 and by section 5(1)(g), (i), (l) and (p) of the Social Security Administration Act 1992 and with the concurrence of the Commissioners for Her Majesty's Revenue and Customs in so far as such concurrence is required, makes the following Regulations:

GENERAL NOTE

These Regulations introduce a new entitlement for mothers, fathers or the partners of mothers who are employed earners and for adopters and their partners who are employed earners to receive a statutory payment from their employers called statutory shared parental pay (ShPP). Part 7 of the Children and Families Act 2014 inserted a new Chapter 1B into Part 8 of the Employment Rights Act 1996, giving the Secretary of State the power to make regulations to create an entitlement to shared parental leave. Part 7 of the 2014 Act also inserts a new Part 12ZC into the SSCBA 1992 giving the Secretary of State the power to make regulations to create an entitlement to ShPP. Eligible employees will be able to share up to 50 weeks of shared parental leave and up to 37 weeks of ShPP. Shared parental leave and pay can be taken at any time between the birth of a child, or the placement of a child for adoption or with prospective adopters, and must be taken before the child's first birthday or the first anniversary of the placement.

1.115

Part 1 of the Regulations is introductory and in particular specifies for what children the new entitlement arises by reference to the time of their expected week of birth or placement for adoption.

Part 2 (regs 4-16) relates to entitlement to ShPP in connection with the birth of a child. Regulations 4 and 5 set out the conditions which a mother, mother's partner or father must satisfy in order to be entitled to this pay. Regulations 6 and 7 detail what notices and information the claimant mother, mother's partner or father must provide. Regulation 8 provides for the claimants to vary their entitlement once they have claimed it. Regulation 9 provides for the modification of the notice provisions in the case of an early birth. Regulation 10 details how many weeks of ShPP are available to claimants. Regulation 11 sets out when ShPP is not to be paid. Regulations 12 to 15 deal with further circumstances relating to such matters as work or absence from work which mean that pay may, or may not be, payable.

Part 3 (regs.17-28) concerns ShPP in connection with adoption. The provisions correspond to the provisions in Part 2.

Part 4 (regs 29-39) sets out the conditions relating to employment and earnings that a claimant and the claimant's partner (or child's father) must satisfy in order for the claimant to be entitled to ShPP (regs 29-32). This Part also contains further provisions relating to employment (regs 33-39).

Part 5 (regs 40-48) contains provisions as to the rate of ShPP, how it is paid, when it is paid and who pays it.

The Schedule contains provisions modifying the regulations in various cases where a claimant, a claimant's partner or father of the child dies or where the child dies or, in the case of adoption, is returned after being placed.

PART 1

Citation and commencement

1.116   **1.** These Regulations may be cited as the Statutory Shared Parental Pay (General) Regulations 2014 and come into force on 1st December 2014.

Definitions

1.117   **2.** (1) In these Regulations—

"1992 Act" means the Social Security Contributions and Benefits Act 1992;

"A" means a person with whom C is, or is expected to be, placed for adoption under the law of any part of the United Kingdom;

"AP" means a person who at the date C is placed for adoption is married to, or is the civil partner of, or is the partner of A;

"C" means the child in relation to whom entitlement to statutory shared parental pay arises;

"M" means the mother (or expectant mother) of C;

"P" means the father of C or a person who at the date of C's birth is married to, or is the civil partner of, or is the partner of M;

"actual week of birth", in relation to a child, means the week beginning with midnight between Saturday and Sunday, in which the child was born;

"adoption agency" has the meaning given, in relation to England and Wales, by section 2 of the Adoption and Children Act 2002 and in relation to Scotland, by section 119(1) of the Adoption and Children (Scotland) Act 2007;

"child", in relation to A, means a person who is, or when placed with A for adoption was, under the age of 18;

"the Commissioners" means the Commissioners for Her Majesty's Revenue and Customs;

"expected week of birth", in relation to a child, means the week, beginning with midnight between Saturday and Sunday, in which, as appropriate, it is expected that the child will be born, or was expected that the child would be born;

"partner", in relation to M or A, means a person (whether of a different sex or the same sex) who lives with, as the case may be, M or A as well as C in an enduring family relationship but is not a relative of M or A of a kind specified in paragraph (2);

"placed for adoption" means—

    (a) placed for adoption under the Adoption and Children Act 2002 or the Adoption and Children (Scotland) Act 2007; or

    (b) placed in accordance with section 22C of the Children Act 1989 with a local authority foster parent who is also a prospective adopter;

"processing", in relation to information, has the meaning given by section 1(1) of the Data Protection Act 1998;

"shared parental leave" means leave under section 75E or 75G of the Employment Rights Act 1996;

"statutory shared parental pay" means statutory shared parental pay payable in accordance with Part 12ZC of the 1992 Act;

"statutory shared parental pay (adoption)" means statutory shared parental pay payable where entitlement to that pay arises under regulation 17 or 18;

"statutory shared parental pay (birth)" means statutory shared parental pay payable where entitlement to that pay arises under regulation 4 or 5;

"week" in Parts 2, 3 and 5 means a period of seven days.

(2) The relatives of M or A referred to in the definition of "partner" in paragraph (1) are M's, or, A's parent, grandparent, sister, brother, aunt, uncle, child, grandchild, niece or nephew.

(3) References to relationships in paragraph (2)—

(a) are to relationships of the full-blood or half-blood or, in the case of an adopted person, such of those relationships as would exist but for the adoption; and

(b) include the relationship of a child with his adoptive, or former adoptive parents, but do not include any other adoptive relationship.

(4) For the purpose of these Regulations—

(a) a person is matched with a child for adoption when an adoption agency decides that that person would be a suitable adoptive parent for the child;

(b) in a case where paragraph (a) applies, a person is notified as having been matched with a child on the date that person receives notification of the agency's decision, under regulation 33(3)(a) of the Adoption Agencies Regulations 2005, regulation 28(3) of the Adoption Agencies (Wales) Regulations 2005 or regulation 8(5) of the Adoption Agencies (Scotland) Regulations 2009;

(c) a person is also matched with a child for adoption when a decision has been made in accordance with regulation 22A of the Care Planning, Placement and Case Review (England) Regulations 2010 and an adoption agency has identified that person with whom the child is to be placed in accordance with regulation 12B of the Adoption Agencies Regulations 2005;

(d) in a case where paragraph (c) applies, a person is notified as having been matched with a child on the date on which that person receives notification in accordance with regulation 12B(2)(a) of the Adoption Agencies Regulations 2005.

(5) The reference to "local authority foster parent" in the definition of "placed for adoption" in paragraph (1) means a person approved as a local authority foster parent in accordance with regulations made by virtue of paragraph 12F of Schedule 2 to the Children Act 1989.

(6) The reference to "prospective adopter" in the definition of "placed for adoption" in paragraph (1) means a person who has been approved as suitable to adopt a child and has been notified of that decision in

accordance with regulation 30B(4) of the Adoption Agencies Regulations 2005.

Application

1.118   **3.** These Regulations apply in relation to—

(a) statutory shared parental pay (birth) in respect of children whose expected week of birth begins on or after 5th April 2015;

(b) statutory shared parental pay (adoption) in respect of children placed for adoption on or after 5th April 2015.

Part 2

Entitlement of mother to statutory shared parental pay (birth)

1.119   **4.** (1) M is entitled to statutory shared parental pay (birth) if M satisfies the conditions specified in paragraph (2) and if P satisfies the conditions specified in paragraphs (3).

(2) The conditions referred to in paragraph (1) are that—

(a) M satisfies the conditions as to continuity of employment and normal weekly earnings specified in regulation 30;

(b) M has at the date of C's birth the main responsibility for the care of C (apart from the responsibility of P);

(c) M has complied with the requirements specified in regulation 6 (notification and evidential requirements of M);

(d) M became entitled by reference to the birth or expected birth of C to statutory maternity pay in respect of C;

(e) the maternity pay period that applies as a result of M's entitlement to statutory maternity pay is, and continues to be, reduced under section 165(3A) of the 1992 Act;

(f) it is M's intention to care for C during each week in respect of which statutory shared parental pay (birth) is paid to her;

(g) M is absent from work during each week in respect of which statutory shared parental pay (birth) is paid to her (except in the cases referred to in regulation 15 (entitlement to shared parental pay: absence from work)); and

(h) where M is an employee (within the meaning of the Employment Rights Act 1996) M's absence from work as an employee during each week that statutory shared parental pay (birth) is paid to her is absence on shared parental leave in respect of C;

(3) The conditions referred to in paragraph (1) are that—

(a) P has at the date of C's birth the main responsibility for the care of C (apart from the responsibility of M); and

(b) P satisfies the conditions relating to employment and earnings in regulation 29 (conditions as to employment and earnings of claimant's partner).

Entitlement of father or partner to statutory shared parental pay (birth)

5. (1) P is entitled to statutory shared parental pay (birth) if P satisfies the conditions specified in paragraph (2) and M satisfies the conditions specified in paragraph (3).   1.120

(2) The conditions specified in paragraph (1) are that—

(a) P satisfies the conditions as to continuity of employment and normal weekly earnings specified in regulation 30;

(b) P has at the date of C's birth the main responsibility for the care of C (apart from the responsibility of M);

(c) P has complied with the requirements specified in regulation 7 (notification and evidential requirements of P);

(d) it is P's intention to care for C during each week in respect of which statutory shared parental pay (birth) is paid to P;

(e) P is absent from work during each week in respect of which statutory shared parental pay (birth) is paid to P (except in the cases referred to in regulation 15 (entitlement to statutory shared parental pay: absence from work)); and

(f) where P is an employee (within the meaning of the Employment Rights Act 1996 P's absence from work as an employee during each week that statutory shared parental pay (birth) is paid to P is absence on shared parental leave in respect of C.

(3) The conditions specified in paragraph (1) are—

(a) M has at the date of C's birth the main responsibility for the care of C (apart from the responsibility of P);

(b) M meets the conditions as to employment and earnings in regulation 29 (conditions as to employment and earnings of claimant's partner);

(c) M became entitled by reference to the birth, or expected birth, of C to statutory maternity pay or maternity allowance; and

(d) the maternity pay period or the maternity allowance period which applies to M as a result of her entitlement to statutory maternity pay or maternity allowance is, and continues to be, reduced under sections 35(3A) or 165(3A) of the 1992 Act.

Notification and evidential requirements relating to the mother

6. (1) The notice and evidential requirements referred to in regulation 4(2)(c) are that M gives the employer who will be liable to pay statutory shared parental pay (birth) to M the notice and information specified in—   1.121

(a) paragraphs (2) and (3)(a), (b), (d) and (e) at least 8 weeks before the beginning of the first period specified by M pursuant to paragraph (2)(d);

(b) paragraph (3)(c) at least 8 weeks before the beginning of the first period specified by M pursuant to paragraph (2)(d) or, where C is not born by that time, as soon as reasonably practicable after the birth of C but in any event before the beginning of that first period; and

(c) paragraph (4) within 14 days of that employer requesting that information where the employer requests it within 14 days of receiving the notice and information specified in paragraph (2) and (3)(a),(b),(d) and (e).

(2) The notice specified in this paragraph is notice of—

(a) the number of weeks in respect of which M would be entitled to claim statutory shared parental pay (birth) in respect of C if entitlement were fully exercised disregarding any intention of P to claim statutory shared parental pay in respect of C;

(b) the number of weeks out of those specified under sub-paragraph (a) in respect of which M intends to claim statutory shared parental pay (birth) in respect of C;

(c) the number of weeks out of those specified under sub-paragraph (a) in respect of which P intends to claim statutory shared parental pay (birth) in respect of C;

(d) the period or periods during which M intends to claim statutory shared parental pay (birth) in respect of C.

(3) The information specified in this paragraph is—

(a) a written declaration signed by P who in connection with M's claim is required to satisfy the conditions specified in regulation 4(3)—

   (i) that P consents to M's intended claim for statutory shared parental pay;

   (ii) that P meets, or will meet, the conditions in regulation 4(3) (conditions to be satisfied by P);

   (iii) specifying P's name, address and national insurance number or, if P has no national insurance number, stating that P has no such number; and

   (iv) providing P's consent as regards the processing by the employer who will be liable to pay statutory shared parental pay (birth) to M of the information in the written declaration;

(b) C's expected week of birth;

(c) C's date of birth;

(d) M's name;

(e) a written declaration signed by M—

   (i) that the information given by M under paragraphs (2) and (3) is correct;

   (ii) that M meets, or will meet, the conditions in regulation 4(2);

   (iii) that M will immediately inform the person who will be liable to pay statutory shared parental pay (birth) if M ceases to meet the condition in regulation 4(2)(e); and

   (iv) specifying the date on which M's maternity pay period or maternity allowance period in respect of C began and the number of weeks by which it is, or will be, reduced.

(4) The information specified in this paragraph is—

(a) a copy of C's birth certificate or, if one has not been issued, a declaration signed by M which states that it has not been issued; and

(b) the name and address of P's employer or, if P has no employer, a written declaration signed by M that P has no employer.

Notification and evidential requirements relating to the father or partner

7. (1) The notification and evidential requirements referred to in regulation 5(2)(c), are that P gives the employer who will be liable to pay statutory shared parental pay (birth) to P the notice and information specified in—

1.122

(a) paragraphs (2) and (3)(a), (b), (d) and (e) at least 8 weeks before the beginning of the first period specified by P pursuant to paragraph (2)(d);

(b) paragraph 3(c) at least 8 weeks before the beginning of the first period specified by P pursuant to paragraph (2)(d) or, where C is not born by that time, as soon as reasonably practicable after the birth of C but in any event before the beginning of that first period; and

(c) paragraph (4) within 14 days of that employer requesting that information where the employer requests it within 14 days of receiving all the notices and information specified in paragraphs (2) and (3)(a), (b), (d) and (e).

(2) The notice specified in this paragraph is notice of—

(a) the number of weeks in respect of which P would be entitled to claim statutory shared parental pay (birth) in respect of C if entitlement were fully exercised disregarding any intention of M to claim statutory shared parental pay in respect of C;

(b) the number of weeks out of those specified under sub-paragraph (a) in respect of which P intends to claim statutory shared parental pay (birth) in respect of C;

(c) the number of weeks out of those specified under sub-paragraph (a) in respect of which M intends to claim statutory shared parental pay (birth) in respect of C;

(d) the period or periods during which P intends to claim statutory shared parental pay (birth) in respect of C.

(3) The information specified in this paragraph is—

(a) a written declaration signed by M who in connection with P's claim is required to satisfy the conditions specified in regulation 5(3)—

(i) that M consents to P's intended claim for statutory shared parental pay;

(ii) that M meets, or will meet, the conditions in regulation 5(3) (conditions to be satisfied by M);

(iii) that M will immediately inform P if M ceases to meet the condition in regulation 5(3)(d);

(iv) specifying M's name, address and national insurance number or, if M has no national insurance number, stating that M has no such number;

    (v) specifying the date on which M's maternity pay period or maternity allowance period in respect of C began and the number of weeks by which it is, or will be, reduced; and

    (vi) providing M's consent as regards the processing by the person who is, or will be, liable to pay statutory shared parental pay (birth) to P under section 171ZX(1) of the 1992 Act of the information in the written declaration;

(b) C's expected week of birth;

(c) C's date of birth;

(d) P's name;

(e) a written declaration signed by P—

    (i) that the information given by P is correct;

    (ii) that P meets, or will meet, the conditions in regulation 5(2); and

    (iii) that P will immediately inform the person who will be liable to pay statutory shared parental pay (birth) if M ceases to meet the condition in regulation 5(3)(d).

(4) The information specified in this paragraph is—

(a) a copy of C's birth certificate or, if one has not been issued, a declaration signed by P which states that it has not been issued; and

(b) the name and address of M's employer (or, if M has no employer a written declaration signed by P that M has no employer.

Variation of number of weeks of pay to be claimed and of periods when pay is to be claimed

1.123   **8.** (1) M or, as the case may be, P may vary the period or periods during which they intend to claim statutory shared parental pay (birth) by notice in writing given to the employer who will be liable to pay that pay to M or P at least 8 weeks before the beginning of the first period specified in that notice.

(2) M may vary the number of weeks in respect of which M intends to claim statutory shared parental pay (birth) by notice in writing given to the employer who will be liable to pay statutory shared parental pay (birth) to M—

(a) of the number of weeks during which M and P have exercised, or intend to exercise, an entitlement to statutory shared parental pay (birth) in respect of C; and

(b) which is accompanied by a written declaration signed by P who in connection with M's claim is required to satisfy the conditions specified in regulation 4(3) that P consents to that variation.

(3) P may vary the number of weeks in respect of which P intends to claim statutory shared parental pay (birth) by notice in writing given to the employer who will be liable to pay statutory shared parental pay (birth) to P—

(a) of the number of weeks during which P and M have exercised, or intend to exercise, an entitlement to statutory shared parental pay (birth) in respect of C; and

(b) which is accompanied by a written declaration by M who in connection with P's claim is required to satisfy the conditions specified in regulation 5(3) that M consents to that variation.

Modification of notice conditions in case of early birth

9. (1) This paragraph applies where— 1.124
(a) one or more of the periods specified in a notice given under regulation 6, 7, or 8 during which M or, as the case may be, P intends to claim statutory shared parental pay (birth) start in the 8 weeks following the first day of C's expected week of birth;
(b) C's date of birth is before the first day of the expected week of birth; and
(c) M or, as the case may be, P varies by notice under regulation 8(1) the period or periods referred to in sub-paragraph (a) so that that period or those periods start the same length of time following C's date of birth as that period or those periods would have started after the first day of the expected week of birth.

(2) Where paragraph (1) applies the requirement in regulation 8(1) to give notice at least 8 weeks before the first period specified in the notice is satisfied if such notice is given as soon as reasonably practicable after C's date of birth.

(3) This paragraph applies where—
(a) C is born more than 8 weeks before the first day of the expected week of birth; and
(b) M or, as the case may be, P has not given the notice and information under regulations 6 or 7 before the date of C's birth.

(4) Where paragraph (3) applies and M, or as the case may be, P specifies in a notice under regulation 6 or 7 a period or periods of statutory shared parental pay (birth) which start in the 8 weeks following C's date of birth, then the following modifications apply—
(a) in regulation 6—
(i) paragraph (1)(a) shall apply as if it read—

"(a) paragraphs (2) and (3) as soon as reasonably practicable after the date of C's birth but in any event before the first period specified by M pursuant to paragraph (2)(d);";

(ii) paragraph (1)(b) and (c) shall not apply;
(iii) paragraph (4) shall not apply.
(b) in regulation 7—
(i) paragraph (1)(a) shall apply as if it read—

"(a) paragraphs (2) and (3) as soon as reasonably practicable after the date of C's birth but in any event before the first period specified by P pursuant to paragraph (2)(d). ";

(ii) paragraph (1)(b) and (c) shall not apply;
(iii) paragraph (4) shall not apply.

Extent of entitlement to statutory shared parental pay (birth)

1.125   **10.** (1) The number of weeks in respect of which M or P is entitled to payments of statutory shared parental pay (birth) in respect of C is 39 weeks less—

(a) the number of weeks—

   (i) in respect of which maternity allowance or statutory maternity pay is payable to M in respect of C up to the time M has returned to work (where M has returned to work without satisfying the condition in regulations 4(2)(e) or 5(3)(d) (condition as to reduction of the maternity pay period or the maternity allowance period)); or

   (ii) in any other case, to which the maternity allowance period is reduced by virtue of section 35(3A) of the 1992 Act or, as the case may be, the maternity pay period is reduced by virtue of section 165(3A); and

(b) the number of weeks of statutory shared parental pay in respect of C which—

   (i) in the case of M, P has notified P's intention to claim under regulation 7 or 8; or

   (ii) in the case of P, M has notified M's intention to claim under regulation 6 or 8.

(2) In a case where—

(a) P was entitled to payments of statutory shared parental pay (birth) in respect of C; and

(b) P ceases to be so entitled because M ceases to satisfy the condition in regulation 5(3)(d); and

(c) P becomes entitled again to such payments as a result of M satisfying the condition in regulation 5(3)(d);

the number of weeks in which P claimed statutory shared parental pay (birth) up to the time P ceases to be so entitled is also to be deducted from the number of weeks specified in paragraph (1).

(3) Where paragraph (2) applies the number of weeks of statutory shared parental pay (birth) which P notified P's intention to claim under regulation 7(2)(b) (as varied under regulation 8(3)) before P ceases to be entitled to statutory shared parental pay (birth) is to be disregarded for the purposes of this regulation.

(4) In the case where M has more than one entitlement to statutory maternity pay in respect of C and in relation to all those entitlements she returns to work without satisfying the conditions in regulation 4(2)(e) or (5)(3)(d), paragraph (1)(a)(i) shall apply as though it read—

"(i) in respect of which statutory maternity pay is payable to M in respect of C up to the last day M returns to work;".

(5) In the case where M has more than one entitlement to statutory maternity pay in respect of C and the maternity pay periods which apply as a result of those entitlements are all reduced by virtue of section 165(3A) of the 1992 Act before she returns to work, paragraph (1)(a)(ii) shall apply as though it read—

"(ii) falling in the period beginning with the first day of the maternity pay period which is the earliest to begin and ending on the last day of the maternity pay period which is the last to end;".

(6) In the case where M has more than one entitlement to statutory maternity pay in respect of C and—

(a) M returns to work in relation to one or more of those entitlements without satisfying the condition regulation 4(2)(e) or 5(3)(d), and

(b) in relation to one or more of the maternity pay periods which apply as a result of those entitlements that period or those periods are reduced by virtue of section 165(3A) before M returns to work,

paragraph (1)(a) shall apply as though it read—

"(a) the number of weeks falling within the period beginning with the first day of the maternity pay period which is the earliest to begin and ending with the later of—

(i) the last day of the maternity pay period which is reduced by virtue of section 165(3A) before M returns to work (or, where there is more than one such period, the last of those periods); and

(ii) the day on which M returned to work without satisfying the condition in regulation 4(2)(e) or 5(3)(d) in relation to that period (or, where there is more than one such period, the last of those periods);".

(7) In a case where P has more than one entitlement to statutory shared parental pay in respect of C, paragraph (1)(b)(i) shall apply as though it read—

"(i) in the case of M, P has notified P's intention to claim under regulation 7 or 8 falling within the period beginning with the first day of the earliest period so notified and ending with the last day of the latest period so notified;".

(8) In a case where M has more than one entitlement to statutory shared parental pay in respect of C, paragraph (1)(b)(ii) shall apply as though it read—

"(ii) in the case of P, M has notified M's intention to claim under regulations 6 or 8 falling within the period beginning with the first day of the earliest period so notified and ending with the last day of the latest period so notified;".

(9) In a case where P has more than one entitlement to statutory shared parental pay in respect of C, paragraph (2) shall apply as though the number of weeks referred to were the number of weeks which P claimed statutory shared parental pay in respect of C falling within the period beginning with the first day of the earliest period P claimed statutory shared parental pay and ending with the time P ceases to be so entitled.

(10) In this regulation a person is treated as returning to work if one of the following situations apply—

(a) in a case where the person is entitled to maternity allowance, the allowance is not payable to her by virtue of regulations made under section 35(3)(a)(i) of the 1992 Act;

(b) in a case where the person is entitled to statutory maternity pay, that payment is not payable to her in accordance with section 165(4) or (6) of the 1992 Act.

(11) In determining in paragraph (1)(a)(i) the number of weeks in respect of which maternity allowance is payable to M in respect of C up to the time M has returned to work, part of a week in respect of which maternity allowance is payable is to be treated as a whole week.

(12) In paragraph (1)(a)(ii), (6), (7), (8) and (9) part of a week is to be treated as a whole week.

(13) In paragraph (1)(a) "week" has the meaning given by section 122(1) of the 1992 Act, in relation to maternity allowance, or the meaning given by section 165(8) in relation to statutory maternity pay.

When statutory shared parental pay (birth) is not to be paid

1.126   **11.** (1) Statutory shared parental pay (birth) is not payable after the day before C's first birthday (or where more than one child is born as a result of the same pregnancy the first birthday of the first child so born).

(2) Statutory shared parental pay (birth) is not payable to M before the end of M's maternity pay period.

Work during period of payment of statutory shared parental pay (birth)

1.127   **12.** (1) Despite section 171ZY(4) of the 1992 Act (statutory shared parental pay not payable to a person in respect of a week during any part of which the person works for any employer) statutory shared parental pay (birth) is payable to M or, as the case may be, P—

(a) in respect of a statutory pay week during any part of which M or, as the case may be, P works only for an employer—

    (i) who is not liable to pay that person statutory shared parental pay; and

    (ii) for whom that person worked in the week immediately preceding the 14th week before the expected week of birth; or,

(b) where M or, as the case may be, P does any work on any day under a contract of service with an employer during a statutory pay week during which that employer is liable to pay that person statutory shared parental pay (birth) in respect of C and where that day and any previous days so worked do not exceed 20.

(2) Where statutory shared parental pay (birth) is paid to M or P in respect of any week falling within a period specified in a notice under regulation 6, 7, and 8 during which M or P works for an employer falling within paragraph (1)(a)(i) but not paragraph (1)(a)(ii), M or, as the case may be, P shall notify the employer liable to pay statutory shared parental pay (birth) within seven days of the first day during which the former does such work.

(3) The notification mentioned in paragraph (2) shall be in writing, if the employer who has been liable to pay statutory shared parental pay (birth) so requests.

(4) In this regulation "statutory pay week" means a week in respect of which that person has chosen to exercise an entitlement to statutory shared parental pay (birth).

Care of child during period of payment of statutory shared parental pay

13. Despite section 171ZY(3) of the 1992 Act (statutory shared parental pay not payable to a person in respect of a week if it is not the person's intention at the beginning of the week to care for C) statutory shared parental pay (birth) is payable in the cases referred to in paragraph 6 of the Schedule (death of child).

1.128

Other cases where there is no liability to pay statutory shared parental pay

14. (1) There is no liability to pay statutory shared parental pay (birth) to M or, as the case may be, P in respect of any week—

1.129

(a) during any part of which the person who is entitled to that pay is entitled to statutory sick pay under Part 11 of the 1992 Act;

(b) following that in which the person who is claiming that pay has died; or

(c) during any part of which the person who is entitled to that pay is detained in legal custody or sentenced to a term of imprisonment except where the sentence is suspended (but see paragraph (2)).

(2) There is liability to pay statutory shared parental pay (birth) to M or, as the case may be, P in respect of any week during any part of which the person who is entitled to that pay is detained in legal custody where that person—

(a) is released subsequently without charge;

(b) is subsequently found not guilty of any offence and is released; or

(c) is convicted of an offence but does not receive a custodial sentence.

Conditions of entitlement to statutory shared parental pay: absence from work

15. (1) The condition in regulation 4(2)(g) and 5(2)(e) does not apply where M or, as the case may be, P—

1.130

(a) during any part of a statutory pay week works other than for an employer;

(b) during any part of a statutory pay week works only for an employer who falls within paragraph (1)(a) of regulation 12 (work during period payment of statutory shared parental pay);

(c) works in circumstance where paragraph (1)(b) of regulation 12 applies.

(2) In this regulation "statutory pay week" means a week in respect of which that person has chosen to exercise an entitlement to statutory shared parental pay (birth).

Entitlement to statutory shared parental pay (birth) in cases relating to death

1.131   **16.** The Part 1 of the Schedule (statutory shared parental pay in special circumstances) has effect.

PART 3

Entitlement of adopter to statutory shared parental pay (adoption)

1.132   **17.** (1) A is entitled to statutory shared parental pay (adoption) if A satisfies the conditions specified in paragraph (2) and AP satisfies the conditions specified in paragraph (3).

(2) The conditions referred to in paragraph (1) are that—

(a) A satisfies the conditions as to continuity of employment and normal weekly earnings specified in regulation 31 (conditions as to claimant's continuity of employment and normal weekly earnings);

(b) A has at the date of C's placement for adoption the main responsibility for the care of C (apart from the responsibility of AP);

(c) A has complied with the requirements specified in regulation 19 (notification and evidential requirements);

(d) A became entitled to statutory adoption pay by reference to the placement for adoption of C;

(e) the adoption pay period that applies as a result of A's entitlement to statutory adoption pay is, and continues to be, reduced under section 171ZN(2A) of the 1992 Act;

(f) it is A's intention to care for C during each week in respect of which statutory shared parental pay (adoption) is paid to A;

(g) A is absent from work during each week in respect of which statutory shared parental pay is paid to A (except in the cases referred to in regulation 27 (entitlement to statutory shared parental pay (adoption): absence from work); and

(h) where A is an employee (within the meaning of the Employment Rights Act 1996) A's absence from work as an employee during each week that statutory shared parental pay is paid to A is absence on shared parental leave in respect of C.

(3) The conditions referred to in paragraph (1) are that—

(a) AP has at the date of C's placement for adoption the main responsibility for the care of C (apart from the responsibility of A); and

(b) AP satisfies the employment and earnings conditions in regulation 29 (conditions relating to employment and earnings of claimant's partner).

Entitlement of partner to statutory shared parental pay (adoption)

18. (1) AP is entitled to statutory shared parental pay (adoption) if AP satisfies the conditions specified in paragraph (2) and A satisfies the conditions specified in paragraph (3). 1.133

(2) The conditions specified in paragraph (1) are that—

(a) AP satisfies the conditions as to continuity of employment and normal weekly earnings specified in regulation 31 (conditions as to continuity of employment and normal weekly earnings);

(b) AP has at the date of C's placement for adoption the main responsibility for the care of C (apart from the responsibility of A);

(c) AP has complied with the requirements specified in regulation 20 (notification and evidential requirements);

(d) it is AP's intention to care for C during each week in respect of which statutory shared parental pay (adoption) is paid to AP;

(e) AP is absent from work during each week in respect of which statutory shared parental pay (adoption) is paid to AP (except in the cases referred to in regulation 27 (entitlement to statutory shared parental pay: absence from work)); and

(f) where AP is an employee (within the meaning of the Employment Rights Act 1996) AP's absence from work as an employee during each week that statutory shared parental pay is paid to AP is absence on shared parental leave in respect of C.

(3) The conditions specified in paragraph (1) are that—

(a) A has at the date of C's placement for adoption the main responsibility for the care of C (apart from any responsibility of AP);

(b) A satisfies the employment and earnings conditions in regulation 29;

(c) A became entitled to statutory adoption pay by reference to the placement for adoption of C; and

(d) the adoption pay period that applies as a result A's entitlement to statutory adoption pay is, and continues to be, reduced under section 171ZN(2A) of the 1992 Act.

Notification and evidential requirements relating to the adopter

19. (1) The notification and evidential requirements referred to in regulation 17(2)(c) are that A gives the employer who will be liable to pay statutory shared parental pay (adoption) to A the notice and information specified in— 1.134

(a) paragraphs (2) and (3)(a), (b), (d) and (e) at least 8 weeks before the beginning of the first period specified by A pursuant to paragraph (2)(d);

(b) paragraph (3)(c) at least 8 weeks before the beginning of the first period specified by A pursuant to paragraph (2)(d) or, if C is not placed for adoption by that time, as soon as reasonably practicable after the placement of C but in any event before the beginning of that first period; and

(c) paragraph (4) within 14 days of that employer requesting that information where the employer requests it within 14 days of receiving the notice and information specified in paragraph (2) and (3)(a), (b), (d) and (e).

(2) The notice specified in this paragraph is notice of—

(a) the number of weeks in respect of which A would be entitled to claim statutory shared parental pay (adoption) in respect of C if entitlement were fully exercised disregarding any intention of AP to claim statutory shared parental pay (adoption) in respect of C;

(b) the number of weeks (out of those specified under paragraph (2)(a)) in respect of which A intends to claim statutory shared parental pay (adoption) in respect of C;

(c) the number of weeks (out of those specified under paragraph (2)(a)) in respect of which AP intends to claim statutory shared parental pay (adoption) in respect of C; and

(d) the period or periods during which A intends to claim statutory shared parental pay (adoption) in respect of C.

(3) The information specified in this paragraph is—

(a) a written declaration signed by AP who in connection with A's claim is required to satisfy the conditions specified in regulation 17(3)—

  (i) that AP consents to A's intended claim for statutory shared parental pay;

  (ii) that AP meets or will meet the conditions in regulation 17(3) (conditions to be satisfied by AP);

  (iii) specifying AP's name, address and national insurance number or, if AP has no national insurance number, stating that AP has no such number; and

  (iv) providing AP's consent as regards the processing by the employer who will be liable to pay statutory shared parental pay (adoption) to A of the information in the written declaration;

(b) the date on which A was notified that A had been matched with C;

(c) the date of C's placement for adoption;

(d) A's name; and

(e) a written declaration signed by A—

  (i) that the information given by A under paragraph (2) and (3) is correct;

  (ii) that A meets or will meet the conditions in regulation 17(2); and

  (iii) that A will immediately inform the person who will be liable to pay statutory shared parental pay (adoption) if A ceases to meet the condition in regulation 17(2)(e); and

  (iv) specifying the date on which A's adoption pay period in respect of C began and the number of weeks by which it is, or will be, reduced.

(4) The information specified in this paragraph is—

(a) evidence, in the form of one or more documents issued by the adoption agency that matched A with C, of—

  (i) the name and address of the adoption agency;

    (ii) the date on which A was notified that A had been matched with C; and

    (iii) the date on which the adoption agency was expecting to place C with A; and

  (b) the name and address of AP's employer or, if AP has no employer, a written declaration signed by A that AP has no employer.

Notification and evidential requirements relating to the partner

20. (1) The notification and evidential conditions referred to in regulation 18(2)(c) are that AP gives the employer who will be liable to pay statutory shared parental pay (adoption) to AP the notice and information specified in—

  (a) paragraphs (2) and (3)(a), (b), (d) and (e) at least 8 weeks before the beginning of the first period specified by AP pursuant to paragraph (2)(d);

  (b) paragraph (3)(c) at least 8 weeks before the beginning of the first period specified by AP pursuant to paragraph (2)(d) or if C is not placed for adoption by that time, as soon as reasonably practicable after the placement of C but in any event before that first period; and

  (c) paragraph (4) (where applicable) within 14 days of that employer requesting this information where the employer requests it within 14 days of receiving all the notice and information specified in paragraph (2) and (3)(a), (b), (d) and (e).

(2) The notice specified in this paragraph is notice of—

  (a) the number of weeks in respect of which AP would be entitled to claim statutory shared parental pay (adoption) in respect of C if entitlement were fully exercised disregarding any intention of A to claim statutory shared parental pay (adoption) in respect of C;

  (b) the number of weeks (out of those specified under paragraph (2)(a)) in respect of which AP intends to claim statutory shared parental pay (adoption) in respect of C;

  (c) the number of weeks (out of those specified under paragraph (2)(a)) in respect of which A intends to claim statutory shared parental pay (adoption) in respect of C;

  (d) the period or periods during which AP intends to claim statutory shared parental pay (adoption) in respect of C.

(3) The information specified in this paragraph is—

  (a) a written declaration signed by A who in connection with AP's claim is required to satisfy the conditions in regulation 18(3)—

    (i) that A consents to AP's intended claim for statutory shared parental pay (adoption);

    (ii) that A meets, or will meet, the conditions in regulation 18(3) (conditions to be satisfied by A);

    (iii) that A will immediately inform AP if A ceases to meet the conditions in regulation 18(3)(d);

    (iv) specifying A's name, address and national insurance number or, if A has no national insurance number, stating that A has no such number;

1.135

(v) specifying the date on which A's adoption pay period in respect of C began and the number of weeks by which it is, or will be, reduced; and

(vi) providing A's consent as regards the processing by the employer who is, or will be, liable to pay statutory shared parental pay (adoption) to AP of the information in the written declaration;

(b) the date on which A was notified that A had been matched with C;

(c) the date of C's placement for adoption;

(d) AP's name;

(e) a written declaration signed by AP—

(i) that the information given by AP is correct;

(ii) that AP meets, or will meet, the conditions in regulation 18(2); and

(iii) that AP will immediately inform the person who will be liable to pay statutory shared parental pay (adoption) if A ceases to meet the condition 18(3)(d) .

(4) The information specified in this paragraph is—

(a) evidence, in the form of one or more documents issued by the adoption agency that matched A with C, of —

(i) the name and address of the adoption agency;

(ii) the date on which A was notified that A had been matched with C; and

(iii) the date on which the adoption agency was expecting to place C for adoption with A; and

(b) the name and address of A's employer or, if A has no employer, a written declaration signed by AP that A has no employer.

Variation of number of weeks of pay to be claimed and of periods when pay is to be claimed

1.136   **21.** (1) A or, as the case may be, AP may vary the period or periods during which they intend to claim statutory shared parental pay (adoption) by notice in writing given to the employer who will be liable to pay that pay to A or AP at least 8 weeks before the beginning of the first period specified in that notice.

(2) A may vary the number of weeks in respect of which A intends to claim statutory shared parental pay (adoption) by notice in writing given to the employer who will be liable to pay that pay to A—

(a) of the number of weeks during which A and AP have exercised, or intend to exercise, an entitlement to statutory shared parental pay in respect of C; and

(b) which contains a written declaration signed by AP who in connection with A's claim is required to satisfy the conditions in regulation 17(3) that AP consents to that variation.

(3) AP may vary the number of weeks in respect of which AP intends to claim statutory shared parental pay (adoption) by notice in writing given to the employer who will be liable to pay that pay to AP—

(a) of the number of weeks during which AP and A have exercised, or intend to exercise, an entitlement to statutory shared parental pay (adoption) in respect of C; and

(b) which is accompanied by a written declaration by A who in connection with AP's claim is requires to satisfy the conditions in regulation 18(3) that A consents to that variation.

Extent of entitlement to statutory shared parental pay (adoption)

22. (1) The number of weeks in respect of which A or, as the case may be, AP is entitled to payments of statutory shared parental pay (adoption) in respect of C is 39 weeks less—   1.137

(a) the number of weeks—

    (i) in respect of which statutory adoption pay is payable to A in respect of C up to the time that person has returned to work (where that person has returned to work without satisfying the conditions in regulations 17(2)(e) or 18(3)(d)) (condition as to reduction in adoption pay period); or

    (ii) in any other case, to which the adoption pay period is reduced by virtue of section 171ZN(2A) of the 1992 Act; and

(b) the number of weeks of statutory shared parental pay (adoption) in respect of C which—

    (i) in the case of A, AP has notified AP's intention to claim under regulation 20 or 21; or

    (ii) in the case of AP, A has notified A's intention to claim under regulation 19 or 21.

(2) In the case where A has more than one entitlement to statutory adoption pay in respect of C and in relation to all those entitlements A returns to work without satisfying the conditions in regulation 17(2)(e) or 18(3)(d), paragraph (1)(a)(i) shall apply as though it read—

"(i) in respect of which statutory adoption pay is payable to A in respect of C up to the last day A returns to work;".

(3) In the case where A has more than one entitlement to statutory adoption pay in respect of C and the adoption pay periods which apply as a result of those entitlements are all reduced by virtue of section 171ZN(2A) of the 1992 Act before A returns to work, paragraph (1)(a)(ii) shall apply as though it read—

"(ii) falling in the period beginning with the first day of the adoption pay period which is the earliest to begin and ending with the last day of the adoption pay period which is the last to end;".

(4) In a case where A has more than one entitlement to statutory adoption pay in respect of C and—

(a) A returns to work in relation to one or more of those entitlements without satisfying the conditions in regulation 17(2)(e) or 18(3)(d), and

(b) in relation to one or more of the adoption pay periods which apply as a result of those entitlements that period or those periods are reduced by virtue of section 171ZN(2A) of the 1992 Act before A returns to work,

paragraph (1)(a) shall apply as though it read—

"(a) the number of weeks falling within the period beginning with the first day of the adoption pay period which is the earliest to begin and ending with the later of—

(i) the last day of the adoption pay period which is reduced by virtue of section 171ZN(2A) of the 1992 Act before A returns to work (or, where there is more than one such period, the last of those periods); and

(ii) the day on which A returned to work without satisfying the conditions in regulation 17(2)(e) or 18(3)(d) in relation to that period (or, where there is more than one such period, the last of those periods);".

(5) In the case where AP has more than one entitlement to statutory shared parental pay in respect of C, paragraph (1)(b)(i) shall apply as though it read—

"(i) in the case of A, AP has notified AP's intention to claim under regulation 20 or 21 falling within the period beginning with the first day of the earliest period so notified and ending with the last day of the latest period so notified;".

(6) In the case where A has more than one entitlement to statutory shared parental pay in respect of C, paragraph (1)(b)(ii) shall apply as though it read—

"(ii) in the case of AP, A has notified A's intention to claim under regulation 19 or 21 falling within the period beginning with the first day of the earliest period so notified and ending with the last day of the latest period so notified;".

(7) In this regulation a person is treated as returning to work if statutory adoption pay is not payable to A in accordance with section 171ZN(3) or (5) of the 1992 Act.

(8) In paragraph (1)(a)(ii), (4), (5) and (6) part of a week is to be treated as a whole week.

(9) In paragraph (1)(a) "week" has the meaning given by section 171ZN(8) of the 1992 Act.

When statutory shared parental pay (adoption) is not to be paid

1.136   **23.** (1) Statutory shared parental pay (adoption) is not payable after the day before the first anniversary of the date on which C was placed for adoption (or where more than one child is placed for adoption through a single placement, the first anniversary of the date of placement of the first child).

(2) Statutory shared parental pay (adoption) is not payable to A before the end of A's adoption pay period.

Work during period of payment of statutory shared parental pay (adoption)

24. (1) Despite section 171ZY(4) of the 1992 Act (statutory shared parental pay not payable to a person in respect of a week during any part of which person works for any employer) statutory shared parental pay (adoption) is payable to A or, as the case may be, AP— 1.137

- (a) in respect of a statutory pay week during any part of which A or, as the case may be, AP works only for an employer—
  - (i) who is not liable to pay that person statutory shared parental pay; and
  - (ii) for whom that person worked in the week immediately preceding the 14th week before the expected week of the placement for adoption; or
- (b) where A or, as the case may be, AP does any work on any day under a contract of service with an employer during a statutory pay week during which that employer is liable to pay that person statutory shared parental pay (adoption) in respect of C and where that day and any previous days so worked do not exceed 20.

(2) Where statutory shared parental pay (adoption) is paid to A or AP in respect of any week falling within a period specified in a notice under regulation 19, 20 or 21 during which A or AP works for an employer falling within paragraph (1)(a)(i) but not paragraph (1)(a)(ii) A or, as the case may be, AP shall notify the employer liable to pay statutory shared parental pay within seven days of the first day during which the former does such work.

(3) The notification mentioned in paragraph (2) shall be in writing, if the employer who has been liable to pay statutory shared parental pay so requests.

(4) In this regulation "statutory pay week" means a week in respect of which that person has chosen to exercise an entitlement to statutory shared parental pay (adoption).

Care of child during period of payment of statutory shared parental pay

25. Despite section 171ZY(3) of the 1992 Act (statutory shared parental pay not payable to a person in respect of a week if it is not the person's intention at the beginning of the week to care for C) statutory shared parental pay (adoption) is payable in the cases set out in paragraph 12 of the Schedule (disrupted placement or death of child). 1.138

Other cases where there is no liability to pay statutory shared parental pay

26. (1) There is no liability to pay statutory shared parental pay (adoption) to A or, as the case may be, AP in respect of any week— 1.139

- (a) during any part of which the person who is entitled to that pay is entitled to statutory sick pay under Part 11 of the 1992 Act;
- (b) following that in which the person who is claiming that has died; or

71

(c) during any part of which the person who is entitled to it is detained in legal custody or sentenced to a term of imprisonment except where the sentence is suspended (but see paragraph (2)).

(2) There is liability to pay statutory shared parental pay to A or, as the case may be, AP in respect of any week during any part of which the person entitled to that pay is detained in legal custody where that person—

(a) is released subsequently without charge;

(b) is subsequently found not guilty of any offence and is released; or

(c) is convicted of an offence but does not receive a custodial sentence.

Conditions of entitlement to statutory shared parental pay: absence from work

1.140   **27.** (1) The condition in regulations 17(2)(g) and 18(2)(e) does not apply are where A or, as the case may be, AP—

(a) during any part of a statutory pay week works other than for an employer;

(b) during any part of a statutory pay week works only for an employer who falls within paragraph (1)(a) of regulation 24 (work during period payment of statutory shared parental pay);

(c) works in circumstances where paragraph (1)(b) of regulation 24 applies.

(2) In this regulation "statutory pay week" means a week in respect of which that person has chosen to exercise an entitlement to statutory shared parental pay (adoption).

Entitlement to statutory shared parental pay (adoption) in cases relating to death

1.141   **28.** Part 2 of the Schedule (statutory shared parental pay in special circumstances) has effect.

PART 4

Conditions relating to employment and earnings of a claimant's partner

1.142   **29.** (1) In relation to the entitlement of M, P, A or AP to statutory shared parental pay a person satisfies the conditions as to earnings and employment specified in regulations 4(3)(b), 5(3)(b), 17(3)(b) and 18(3)(b) if that person—

(a) has been engaged in employment as an employed or self-employed earner for any part of the week in the case of at least 26 of the 66 weeks immediately preceding the calculation week; and

(b) has average weekly earnings (determined in accordance with paragraph (2)) of not less than the amount set out in section 35A(6A) (state maternity allowance) of the 1992 Act in relation to the tax year before the tax year containing the calculation week.

(2) A person's average weekly earnings are determined by dividing by 13 the specified payments made, or treated as being made, to or for the benefit of that person in the 13 weeks (whether or not consecutive) in the period of 66 weeks immediately preceding the calculation week in which the payments are greatest.

(3) Where a person receives any pay after the end of the period in paragraph (1) in respect of any week falling after that period, the average weekly amount is to be determined as if such sum had been paid in that period.

(4) Where a person is not paid weekly, the payments made or treated as made for that person's benefit for the purposes of paragraph (1), are to be determined by dividing the total sum paid to that individual by the nearest whole number of weeks in respect of which that sum is paid.

(5) In this regulation—

"calculation week" means in relation to—

(a) statutory shared parental pay (birth) the expected week of birth of C; and

(b) statutory shared parental pay (adoption), the week in which A was notified as having been matched for adoption with C;

"employed earner" has the meaning given by section 2 of the 1992 Act, subject for these purposes to the effect of regulations made under section 2(2)(b) of that Act;

"self-employed earner" has the meaning given by section 2 of the 1992 Act, subject for these purposes to the effect of regulations made under section 2(2)(b) of that Act;

"specified payments"—

(a) in relation to a self-employed earner who satisfies the conditions in paragraph (6), are to be treated as made to the self-employed earner at an amount per week equal to the amount set out in section 35(6A) of the 1992 Act that is in force at the end of the week;

(b) in relation to an employed earner, are all payments made to the employed earner or for that employed earner's benefit as an employed earner specified in regulation 2 (specified payments for employed earners) of the Social Security (Maternity Allowance) (Earnings) Regulations 2000;

"tax year" means the 12 months beginning with the 6th April in any year.

(6) The conditions referred to in paragraph (a) of the definition of "specified payments" are that, in respect of any week, the self-employed earner—

(a) does not hold a certificate of exception issued pursuant to regulation 44(1) of the Social Security (Contributions) Regulations

2001 and has paid a Class 2 contribution (within the meaning of section 1 of the 1992 Act), or

(b) holds such a certificate of exception.

Conditions as to continuity of employment and normal weekly earnings relating to a claimant for statutory shared parental pay (birth)

1.143   **30.** (1) The conditions as to continuity of employment and normal weekly earnings referred to in regulation 4(2)(a) and 5(2)(a) are—

(a) the person has been in employed earner's employment with an employer for a continuous period of at least 26 weeks ending with the relevant week;

(b) the person's normal weekly earnings (see regulation 32) with the employer by reference to which the condition in sub-paragraph (a) is satisfied for the period of eight weeks ending with the relevant week are not less than the lower earnings limit in force under subsection (1)(a) of section 5 (earnings limits and thresholds for class 1 contributions) of the 1992 Act at the end of the relevant week;

(c) the person continues in employed earner's employment with the employer by reference to which the condition in sub-paragraph (a) is satisfied for a continuous period beginning with the relevant week and ending with the week before the first week falling within the relevant period relating to that person under section 171ZY(2) of the 1992 Act.

(2) Where C's birth occurs earlier than the 14th week before C's expected week of birth paragraph (1) shall have effect as if, for the conditions set out there, there were substituted conditions that—

(a) the person would have been in employed earner's employment for a continuous period of at least 26 weeks ending with the relevant week had C been born after the relevant week;

(b) the person's normal weekly earnings for the period of eight weeks ending with the week immediately preceding C's actual week of birth are not less than the lower earnings limit in force under section 5(1)(a) of the 1992 Act immediately before the commencement of C's actual week of birth; and

(c) the person continues in employed earner's employment with the employer by reference to whom the condition in sub-paragraph (a) is satisfied for a continuous period beginning with the date of C's birth and ending with the week before the first week falling within the relevant period relating to that person under section 171ZY(2) of the 1992 Act.

(3) The references in this regulation to the relevant week are to the week immediately preceding the 14th week before C's expected week of birth.

(4) Where more than one child is born as a result of the same pregnancy the date the first child is born is to be used to determine C's actual week of birth or the date of C's birth.

Conditions as to continuity of employment and normal weekly earnings in relation to a claimant for statutory shared parental pay (adoption)

31. (1) The conditions as to continuity of employment and normal weekly earnings referred to in regulations 17(2)(a) and 18(2)(a) relating to the entitlement of A and AP to statutory shared parental pay (adoption) are—   **1.144**

(a) the person has been in employed earner's employment with an employer for a continuous period of at least 26 weeks ending with the relevant week;

(b) the person's normal weekly earnings (see regulation 32) with the employer by reference to which the condition in sub-paragraph (a) is satisfied for the period of eight weeks ending with the relevant week are not less than the lower earnings limit in force under subsection (1)(a) of section 5 (earnings limits and thresholds for class 1 contributions) of the 1992 Act at the end of the relevant period;

(c) the person continues in employed earner's employment with the employer by reference to which the condition in sub-paragraph (a) is satisfied for a continuous period beginning with the relevant week and ending with the week before the first week falling within the relevant period relating to that person under section 171ZY(2) of the 1992 Act.

(2) The references in paragraph (1) to the relevant week are to the week in which A was notified of having been matched with C.

Normal weekly earnings of a claimant for statutory shared parental pay

32. (1) For the purpose of section 171ZZ4(6) (which defines normal weekly earnings for the purposes of Part 12ZC of the 1992 Act) "earnings" and "relevant period" have the meanings given in this regulation.   **1.145**

(2) The relevant period is the period—

(a) ending on the last normal pay day to fall before the appropriate date; and

(b) beginning with the day following the last normal pay day to fall at least eight weeks earlier than the normal pay day mentioned in sub-paragraph (a).

(3) In a case where a person has no identifiable normal pay day, paragraph (2) shall have effect as if the words "day of payment" were substituted for the words "normal pay day" in each place where they occur.

(4) In a case where a person has normal pay days at intervals of or approximating to one or more calendar months (including intervals of or approximating to a year) that person's normal weekly earnings shall be calculated by dividing their earnings in the relevant period by the number of calendar months in that period (or, if it is not a whole number, the nearest whole number), multiplying the result by 12 and dividing by 52.

(5) In a case to which paragraph (4) does not apply and the relevant period is not an exact number of weeks, the person's normal weekly earnings shall be calculated by dividing their earnings in the relevant period by the number of days in the relevant period and multiplying the result by seven.

(6) In any case where a person receives a back-dated pay increase which includes a sum in respect of a relevant period, normal weekly earnings shall be calculated as if such a sum was paid in that relevant period even though received after that period.

(7) The expression "earnings" refers to gross earnings and includes any remuneration or profit derived from a person's employment except any amount which is—

(a) excluded from the computation of a person's earnings under regulation 25 (payments to be disregarded) of, and Schedule 3 to, the Social Security (Contributions) Regulations 2001 and regulation 27 (payments to directors to be disregarded) of those Regulations (or would have been so excluded had they not been made under the age of 16);

(b) a chargeable emolument under section 10A (class 1B contributions) of the 1992 Act except where, in consequence of such a chargeable emolument being excluded from earnings, a person would not be entitled to statutory shared parental pay (or where such a payment or amount would have been so excluded and in consequence the person would not have been entitled to statutory shared parental pay had they not been aged under the age of 16).

(8) The expression "earnings" includes—

(a) any amount retrospectively treated as earnings by regulations made by virtue of section 4B(2) of the 1992 Act;

(b) any sum payable in respect of arrears of pay in pursuance of an order for reinstatement or re-engagement under the Employment Rights Act 1996;

(c) any sum payable by way of pay in pursuance of an order made under the Employment Rights Act 1996 for the continuation of a contract of employment;

(d) any sum payable by way of remuneration in pursuance of a protective award under section 189 of the Trade Union and Labour Relations (Consolidation) Act 1992;

(e) any sum payable by way of statutory sick pay, including sums payable in accordance with regulations made under section 151(6) of the 1992 Act;

(f) any sum payable by way of statutory maternity pay;

(g) any sum payable by way of statutory paternity pay;

(h) any sum payable by way of statutory shared parental pay; and

(i) any sum payable by way of statutory adoption pay.

(9) In paragraphs (2) to (4)—

(a) "the appropriate date" means—

(i) in relation to statutory shared parental pay (birth), the first day of the 14th week before the expected week of the child's birth or the first day in the week in which the child is born, whichever is earlier (but see paragraph (10)),

(ii) in relation to statutory shared parental pay (adoption) the first day of the week after the week in which A is notified of being matched with the child for the purposes of adoption;

(b) "day of payment" means a day on which the person was paid; and

(c) "normal pay day" means a day on which the terms of a person's contract of service require the person to be paid, or the practice in that person's employment is for that person to be paid if any payment is due to them.

(10) Where more than one child is born as a result of the same pregnancy, the date the first child is born is to be used to determine the week in which the child is born.

Treatment of persons as employees

33. (1) A person is treated as an employee for the purposes of Part 12ZC of the 1992 Act (even though not falling within the definition of 'employee' in section 171ZZ4(2) of that Act) where, and in so far as, that person is treated as an employed earner by virtue of the Social Security (Categorisation of Earners) Regulations 1978 (but see paragraph (3)).   **1.146**

(2) A person shall not be treated as an employee for the purposes of Part 12ZC of the 1992 Act (even though falling within the definition of 'employee' in section 171ZZ4(2) of that Act) where, and in so far as, that person is not treated as an employed earner by virtue of those Regulations (but see paragraph (3)).

(3) Paragraphs (1) and (2) shall have effect in relation to a person who—

(a) is under the age of 16; and

(b) would, or as the case may be, would not have been treated as an employed earner by virtue of those Regulations had they been over that age;

as they have effect in relation to a person who is, or as the case may be, is not treated as an employed earner by virtue of those Regulations.

(4) A person is treated as an employee for the purpose of Part 12ZC of the 1992 Act (even though not falling within the definition of 'employee' in section 171ZZ4(2) of that Act) where that person is in employed earner's employment under a contract of apprenticeship.

(5) A person is not to be treated as an employee for the purposes of Part 12ZC of the 1992 Act (even though falling within the definition of 'employee' in section 171ZZ4(2) of that Act) where that person is in employed earner's employment but that person's employer—

(a) does not fulfil the conditions prescribed in regulation 145(1) (conditions as to residence or presence) of the Social Security (Contributions) Regulations 2001 in so far as that provision relates to residence or presence in Great Britain; or

(b) is a person who, by reason of any international treaty to which the United Kingdom is a party or of any international convention binding the United Kingdom—

  (i) is exempt from the provisions of the 1992 Act; or

  (ii) is a person against whom the provisions of the 1992 Act are not enforceable.

Continuous employment

1.148 **34.** (1) A week is to be treated for the purposes of sections 171ZU and 171ZV of the 1992 Act (see also regulations 30 and 31) as part of a period of continuous employment with the employer even though no contract of service exists with that employer in respect of that week in the circumstances mentioned in paragraph (2) and subject to paragraphs (3) and (4).

  (2) The circumstances mentioned in paragraphs (1) are that in any week the person is, for the whole or part of the week—

  (a) incapable of work in consequence of sickness or injury;

  (b) absent from work on account of a temporary cessation of work; or

  (c) absent from work in circumstances such that, by arrangement or custom, that person is regarded as continuing in the employment of their employer for all or any purposes;

and returns to work for their employer after the incapacity for or absence from work.

  (3) Incapacity for work which lasts for more than 26 consecutive weeks shall not count for the purposes of paragraph (2)(a).

  (4) Where a person—

  (a) is an employee in employed earner's employment in which the custom is for the employer—

   (i) to offer work for a fixed period of not more than 26 consecutive weeks;

   (ii) to offer work for such period on two or more occasions in a year for periods which do not overlap; and

   (iii) to offer the work available to those persons who had worked for the employer during the last or a recent such period; but

  (b) is absent from work because of incapacity arising from some specific disease or bodily or mental disablement;

then in that case paragraph (2) shall apply as if the words "and returns to work for their employment for their employer after the incapacity for or absence from work" were omitted.

Continuous employment and unfair dismissal

1.149 **35.** (1) Where in consequence of specified action in relation to a person's dismissal, the person is reinstated or re-engaged by their employer or by a successor or associated employer of that employer then—

  (a) the continuity of their employment shall be preserved for the purposes of sections 171ZU and 171ZY of the 1992 Act (see also regulations 30 and 31) for the period beginning with the effective date of termination and ending with the date of reinstatement or re-engagement; and

(b) any week which falls within the interval beginning with the effective date of termination and ending with the date of reinstatement or re-engagement, as the case may be, shall count in the computation of their period of continuous employment.

(2) In this regulation—

(a) "associated employer" shall be construed in accordance with section 231 of the Employment Rights Act 1996;

(b) "dismissal procedures agreement" and "successor" have the same meanings as in section 235 of the Employment Rights Act 1996;

(c) "specified action in relation to a person's dismissal" means action which consists of—

  (i) the presentation by that person of a complaint under section 111(1) (complaints to employment tribunal) of the Employment Rights Act 1996;

  (ii) that person making a claim in accordance with a dismissal procedure agreement designated by an order under section 110 of that Act; or

  (iii) any action taken by a conciliation officer under section 18 (conciliation) of the Employment Tribunals Act 1996.

Continuous employment and stoppages of work

36. (1) Where a person does not work for any week or part of a week   **1.150** because there is a stoppage of work at that person's place of employment due to a trade dispute within the meaning of section 35(1) of the Jobseekers Act 1995 then—

(a) that person's continuity of employment shall be treated as continuing throughout the stoppage (but see paragraph (2) for the purposes of sections 171ZU and 171ZY of the 1992 Act (see also regulations 30 and 31); and

(b) no such week shall count in the computation of their period of continuous employment (but see paragraph(3)).

(2) Where during the stoppage of work a person is dismissed from their employment, that person's continuity of employment shall not be treated under paragraph (1) as continuing beyond the commencement of the day that person stopped work (but see paragraph (3)).

(3) Paragraph (1)(b) and paragraph (2) do not apply to a person who proves that at no time did they have a direct interest in the trade dispute in question.

Change of employer

37. (1) Where a person's employer changes, a person's employment is   **1.151** to be treated for the purposes of sections 171ZU and 171ZV of the 1992 Act (see also regulations 30 and 31) as continuous employment with the second employer in the following circumstances—

(a) the employer's trade or business or an undertaking (whether or not it is an undertaking established by or under an Act of Parliament) is transferred from one person to another;

(b) a contract of employment between any body corporate and the person is modified by or under an Act of Parliament, whether public or local and whenever passed and some other body corporate is substituted as that person's employer;

(c) on the death of the employer, the person is taken into the employment of the personal representatives or trustees of the deceased;

(d) the person is employed by partners, personal representatives or trustees and there is a change in the partners, or as the case may be, personal representatives or trustees;

(e) the person is taken into the employment of an employer who is, at the time the person entered into to the employer's employment, an associated employer of the person's previous employer; or

(f) on the termination of the person's employment with an employer that person is taken into the employment of another employer and those employers are governors of a school maintained by a local education authority.

(2) In paragraph (1)(e) "associated employer" shall be construed in accordance with section 231 of the Employment Rights Act 1996.

Reinstatement after service with the armed forces etc

1.152   **38.** Where a person—

(a) is entitled to apply to their employer under the Reserve Forces (Safeguard of Employment) Act 1985; and

(b) enters the employment of that employer within the six month period mentioned in section 1(4)(b) (obligation to reinstate) of that Act;

that person's previous period of employment with that employer (or if there was more than one such period, the last of those periods) and the period of employment beginning in that six month period shall be treated as continuous for the purposes of sections 171ZU and 171ZV of the 1992 Act (see also regulations 30 and 31).

Treatment of two or more employers or two or more contracts of service as one

1.153   **39.** (1) In a case where the earnings paid to a person in respect of two or more employments are aggregated and treated as a single payment of earnings under regulation 15(1) (aggregation of earnings paid in respect of different employed earner's employments by different persons) of the Social Security (Contributions) Regulations 2001, the employers of that person in respect of those employments shall be treated as one for the purposes of Part 12ZC of the 1992 Act (and these Regulations).

(2) Where two or more employers are treated as one under the provisions of paragraph (1), liability for statutory shared parental pay shall be apportioned between them in such proportions as they may agree, or in default of agreement, in the proportions which the person's normal weekly earnings from each employment bear to the amount of the aggregated normal weekly earnings over the relevant period as defined in regulation 32(2).

(3) Where two or more contracts of service exist concurrently between one employer and one employee, they shall be treated as one for the purposes of Part 12ZC of the 1992 Act (and these Regulations) except where, by virtue of regulation 14 (aggregation of earnings paid in respect of separate employed earner's employments under the same employer) of the Social Security (Contributions) Regulations 2001, the earnings from those contracts of service are not aggregated for the purpose of earnings-related contributions.

PART 5

Weekly rate of payment of statutory shared parental pay

40. (1) The weekly rate of payment of statutory shared parental pay is   1.154
the smaller of the following two amounts—
  (a) £138.18;
  (b) 90% of the normal weekly earnings of the individual claiming statutory shared parental pay determined in accordance with section 171ZZ4(6) of the 1992 Act and regulation 32).
  (2) Where the amount of any payment of statutory shared parental pay is calculated by reference to—
  (a) the weekly rate specified in paragraph (1)(b), or
  (b) the daily rate of one-seventh of the weekly rate specified in paragraph (1)(a) or (b),
and that amount includes a fraction of a penny, the payment shall be rounded up to the nearest whole number of pence.

Statutory shared parental pay and contractual remuneration

41. For the purposes of section 171ZZ1(1) and (2) (payment of   1.155
contractual remuneration to go towards discharging liability to pay statutory shared parental pay and payment of statutory shared parental pay to go towards discharging liability to pay contractual remuneration) the payments which are to be treated as contractual remuneration are sums payable under a contract of service—
  (a) by way of remuneration;
  (b) for incapacity for work due to sickness or injury; and
  (c) by reason of birth, adoption or care of a child.

Avoidance of liability for statutory shared parental pay

42. (1) A former employer is liable to make payments of statutory   1.156
shared parental pay to a former employee in any case where the employee has been employed for a continuous period of at least eight weeks and the employee's contract of service was brought to an end by the former employer solely, or mainly, for the purpose of avoiding liability for statutory shared parental pay.
  (2) In a case falling within paragraph (1)—
  (a) the employee shall be treated as if the employee had been employed for a continuous period ending with the period of seven

days beginning with Sunday before the first week falling within the relevant period relating to that employee under section 171ZY(2) of the 1992 Act; and

(b) regulation 32(2) (relevant period for the purpose of the calculation of normal weekly earnings) shall apply as if it read—

"(2) The relevant period is the period—

(a) ending on the last day of payment under the former contract of employment; and

(b) beginning with the day following the day of payment under that contract to fall at least 8 weeks earlier than the day of payment mentioned in sub-paragraph (a).".

Payment of statutory shared parental pay

1.157   **43.** Payments of statutory shared parental pay may be made in like manner to payments of remuneration but shall not include payment in kind or by way of the provision of board and lodgings.

Time when statutory shared parental pay is to be paid

1.158   **44.** (1) In any case where—

(a) a decision has been made by an officer of Revenue and Customs under section 8(1) (decisions by officers) of the Social Security Contributions (Transfer of Functions, etc) Act 1999 as a result of which a person is entitled to an amount of statutory shared parental pay; and

(b) the time for bringing an appeal against the decision has expired and either—

(i) no such appeal has been brought; or

(ii) such appeal has been brought and has been finally disposed of;

that amount of statutory shared parental pay shall be paid within the time specified in paragraph (2).

(2) The employer or former employer shall pay the amount not later than the first pay day after the following days (but see paragraphs (3) and (4))—

(a) where an appeal has been brought, the day on which the employer or former employer receives notification that it has been finally disposed of;

(b) where leave to appeal has been refused, and there remains no further opportunity to apply for leave, the day on which the employer or former employer receives notification of the refusal; and

(c) in any other case, the day on which the time for bringing an appeal expires.

(3) Where it is impracticable, in view of the employer's or former employer's methods of accounting for and paying remuneration, for the requirement of payment referred to in paragraph (2) to be met by the pay day referred to in that paragraph, it shall be met not later than the next following pay day (but see paragraph (4)).

(4) Where the employer or former employer would not have remunerated the employee for their work in the week in respect of which statutory shared parental pay is payable as early as the pay day specified in paragraph (2) or (if it applies) paragraph (3), the requirement of payment shall be met on the first day on which the employee would have been remunerated for his work in that week.

(5) In this regulation "pay day" means a day on which it has been agreed, or it is the normal practice between an employer or former employer to agree and a person who is or was an employee of theirs, that payments by way of remuneration are to be made, or, where there is no such agreement or normal practice, the last day of a calendar month.

Liability of the Commissioners to pay statutory shared parental pay

45. (1) Despite section 171ZX(1) of the 1992 Act (liability to make payments of statutory shared parental pay is liability of the employer) where the conditions in paragraph (2) are satisfied, liability to make payments of statutory shared parental pay to a person is to be liability of the Commissioners and not the employer for— **1.159**

(a) any week in respect of which the employer was liable to pay statutory shared parental pay to that person but did not do so; and

(b) for any subsequent weeks that person is entitled to payments of statutory shared parental pay.

(2) The conditions in this paragraph are that—

(a) an officer of the Revenue and Customs has decided under section 8(1) of the Social Security Contributions (Transfer of Functions, etc) Act 1999 that an employer is liable to make payments of statutory shared parental pay;

(b) the time for appealing against the decision has expired; and

(c) no appeal against the decision has been lodged or leave to appeal against the decision is required and has been refused.

(3) Despite section 171ZX(1) of the 1992 Act, liability to make payments of statutory shared parental pay to a person is to be a liability of the Commissioners and not the employer as from the week in which the employer first becomes insolvent (see paragraphs 4 and 5) until the last week that person is entitled to payment of statutory shared parental pay.

(4) For the purposes of paragraph (3) an employer shall be taken to be insolvent if, and only if, in England and Wales—

(a) the employer has been adjudged bankrupt or has made a composition or arrangement with its creditors;

(b) the employer has died and the employer's estate falls to be administered in accordance with an order made under section 421 Insolvency Act 1986; or

(c) where an employer is a company or a limited liability partnership—

(i) a winding-up order is made or a resolution for a voluntary winding-up is passed (or, in the case of a limited liability

83

partnership, a determination for voluntary winding-up has been made) with respect to it,

(ii) it enters administration,

(iii) a receiver or manager of its undertaking is duly appointed,

(iv) possession is taken, by or on behalf of the holders of any debentures secured by a floating charge, of any property of the company or limited liability partnership comprised in or subject to the charge, or

(v) a voluntary arrangement proposed for the purposes of Part 1 of the Insolvency Act 1986 is approved under that Part.

(5) For the purposes of paragraph (3) an employer shall be taken to be insolvent if, and only if, in Scotland—

(a) an award of sequestration is made on the employer's estate;

(b) the employer executes a trust deed for its creditors;

(c) the employer enters into a composition contract;

(d) the employer has died and a judicial factor appointed under section 11A of the Judicial Factors (Scotland) Act 1889 is required by that section to divide the employer's insolvent estate among the employer's creditors; or

(e) where the employer is a company or a limited liability partnership—

(i) a winding-up order is made or a resolution for voluntary winding-up is passed (or in the case of a limited liability partnership, a determination for a voluntary winding-up is made) with respect to it,

(ii) it enters administration,

(iii) a receiver of its undertaking is duly appointed, or

(iv) a voluntary arrangement proposed for the purposes of Part I of the Insolvency Act 1986 is approved under that Part.

Liability of the Commissioners to pay statutory shared parental pay in case of legal custody or imprisonment

1.160   **46.** Where there is liability to pay statutory shared parental pay—

(a) in respect of a period which is subsequent to the last week falling within paragraph (1)(c) of regulations 14 and 26 (cases where there is no liability to pay statutory shared parental pay); or

(b) during a period of detention in legal custody by virtue of paragraph (2) of those regulations;

that liability, despite section 171ZX(1) of the 1992 Act, shall be that of the Commissioners and not the employer.

Payments by the Commissioners

1.161   **47.** Where the Commissioners become liable in accordance with regulation 45 (liability of the Commissioners to pay statutory shared parental pay) or regulation 46 (liability of the Commissioners to pay statutory shared parental pay in case of legal custody or imprisonment) then—

(a) the first payment is to be made as soon as reasonably practicable after they become so liable; and

(b) subsequent payments are to be made at weekly intervals;

by means of an instrument of payment or by such other means as appear to the Commissioners to be appropriate in the circumstances of any particular case.

Persons unable to act

48. (1) This regulation applies where— 1.162
- (a) statutory shared parental pay is payable to a person or it is alleged that statutory shared parental pay is payable to a person;
- (b) that person is unable for the time being to act;
- (c) no deputy has been appointed by the Court of Protection with power to receive additional statutory paternity pay on their behalf or, in Scotland, their estate is not being administered by a guardian acting or appointed under the Adults with Incapacity (Scotland) Act 2000; and
- (d) a written application has been made to the Commissioners by a person, who, if a natural person, is over the age of 18 to exercise any right, or deal with any sums payable, under Part 12ZC of the 1992 Act on behalf of the person unable to act.

(2) Where this regulation applies the Commissioners may appoint the person referred to in paragraph (1)(d)—
- (a) to exercise, on behalf of the person unable to act, any right which the person unable to act may be entitled under Part 12ZC of the 1992 Act; and
- (b) to deal, on behalf of the person unable to act, with any sums payable to the person unable to act under Part 12ZC of the 1992 Act.

(3) Where the Commissioners have made an appointment under paragraph (2)—
- (a) they may at any time revoke it;
- (b) the person appointed may resign their office after having given one month's notice in writing to the Commissioners of that person's intention to do so; and
- (c) the appointment shall end when the Commissioners are notified that a deputy or other person to whom paragraph (1)(c) applies has been appointed.

(4) Anything required by Part 12ZC of the 1992 Act to be done by or to the person who is unable to act may be done by or to the person appointed under this regulation to act on behalf of the person unable to act, and the receipt of the person so appointed shall be a good discharge to the employer or former employer of the person unable to act for any sum paid.

Service of notices

49. (1) Where a notice is to be given under these Regulations, it may 1.163
be given—
- (a) where paragraph (2) applies, by electronic communication;
- (b) by post; or
- (c) by personal delivery.

(2) This paragraph applies where the person who is to receive the notice has agreed that the notice may be given to the person by being transmitted to an electronic address and in an electronic form specified by the person for that purpose.

(3) Where a notice is to be given under these Regulations it is to be taken to have been given—

(a) if sent by electronic communication, on the day of transmission;

(b) if sent by post in an envelope which is properly addressed and sent by prepaid post, on the day on which it is posted;

(c) if delivered personally, on the day of delivery.

SCHEDULE **Regulations 16 and 28**

STATUTORY SHARED PARENTAL PAY IN SPECIAL CIRCUMSTANCES

PART 1

STATUTORY SHARED PARENTAL PAY (BIRTH)

Entitlement of father or partner to statutory shared parental pay (birth) in the event of the death of M before curtailment

1.164   1. (1) In a case where M dies—

(a) before the end of her maternity allowance period in respect of C and without reducing that period under section 35(3A) of the 1992 Act, or

(b) before the end of her maternity pay period in respect of C and without reducing that period under section 165(3A) of the 1992 Act,

then these Regulations shall apply, in respect of any period after M dies, subject to the modifications in the following provisions of this paragraph.

(2) In regulation 2(1) a person is to be regarded as falling within the definition of P it that person would have done so but for the fact that M had died.

(3) In regulation 5 (entitlement of father or partner)—

(a) paragraph (3)(d) shall not apply;

(b) in a case where M dies before her maternity allowance period or maternity pay period in respect of C starts then the condition in paragraph (3)(c) shall be taken to be satisfied if it would have been satisfied but for the fact that M had died.

(4) In regulation 7 (notification and evidential requirements relating to father or mother's partner)—

(a) paragraph (1)(a) shall apply as if it read—

"(a) paragraphs (2) and (3) at least 8 weeks before the beginning of the first period specified by P pursuant to paragraph (2)(d) or, where it is not reasonably practicable for P to satisfy this requirement, as soon as reasonably practicable after the death of M, but in any event before that period;";

(b) paragraph (1)(b) and (c) shall not apply;

(c) in paragraph (2)—

(i) sub-paragraph (a) shall apply as if the words "disregarding any intention of M to claim statutory shared parental pay (birth) in respect of C" were omitted; and

(ii) sub-paragraph (c) shall not apply;

(d) in paragraph (3)—

(i) sub-paragraph (a) shall not apply;

(ii) sub-paragraph (d) shall apply as if it read—

"(d) the following information relating to P and M—

(i) P's name, M's name and national insurance number (where this number is known to P), M's address immediately before she died and the date of M's death; and

(ii) the start date of M's maternity pay period or maternity allowance period in respect of C or, where M's death occurred before her maternity allowance period or maternity pay period in respect of C started, the date that period would have started but for the fact that M had died;"; and

      (iii) sub-paragraph (e)(iii) shall not apply;

(e)   paragraph (4) shall not apply.

(5) In regulation 8(3) (variation)—

(a) sub-paragraph (a) shall apply as if the reference to M were omitted; and

(b) sub-paragraph (b) shall not apply.

(6) In regulation 10 (extent of entitlement), paragraph (1)(a) shall apply as if the number of weeks referred to is the number of weeks in which maternity allowance or statutory maternity pay was payable to M in respect of C up to the time of M's death.

Notification and variation: death of mother or partner after curtailment

2. (1) In the case where—   **1.165**

(a) P, who in connection with a claim by M would be required to satisfy the conditions specified in regulation 4(3), dies after M has reduced her maternity allowance period in respect of C under section 35(3A) of the 1992 Act or her maternity pay period in respect of C under section 165(3A) of the 1992 Act; and

(b) before P dies M has not given the notices and information specified in regulation 6 (notice and evidential requirements relation to the mother),

then these Regulations apply in respect of any period after P dies, subject to the modifications in the following provisions of this paragraph.

(2) In regulation 6 (notification and evidential requirements relating to the mother)—

(a) paragraph (1)(a) shall apply as if it read—

> "(a) paragraphs (2) and (3) at least 8 weeks before the beginning of the first period specified by M pursuant to paragraph (2)(d) or where it is not reasonably practicable for M to satisfy this requirement as soon as reasonably practicable after the death of P, but in any event before that period;";

(b) paragraph (1)(b) and (c) shall not apply;

(c) in paragraph (2)—

      (i) sub-paragraph (a) shall apply as if the words "disregarding any intention of P to claim statutory shared parental pay in respect of C" were omitted;

      (ii) sub-paragraph (c) shall not apply;

(d) in paragraph (3)—

      (i) sub-paragraph (a) shall not apply;

      (ii) sub-paragraph (d) shall apply as if it read—

> "(d) M's name, P's name and national insurance number (where this number is known to M), P's address immediately before P died and the date of P's death";

(e) paragraph (4) shall not apply.

(3) In regulation 8 (variation)—

(a) paragraph (2)(a) shall apply as if it read—

> "(a) of the number of weeks during which M and P have exercised, and the number of weeks M intends to exercise, an entitlement to statutory shared parental pay (birth) in respect of C";

(b) paragraph (2)(b) shall not apply.

(4) In regulation 10 (extent of entitlement)—

(a) paragraph (1)(b)(i) shall apply as if the words "P has notified P's intention to claim" to the end read "the number of weeks in which P claimed statutory shared parental pay (birth) in respect of C up to the time of P's death.";

(b) paragraph (7) shall apply as if the words "the last day of the latest period so notified" were "the time of P's death".

3. (1) In the case where—

(a) P, who in connection with M's claim is required to satisfy the conditions specified in regulation 4(3), dies after M has reduced her maternity allowance period in respect of C under section 35(3A) of the 1992 Act or her maternity pay period in respect of C under section 165(3A) of the 1992 Act, and

  (b) before P dies M has given the notices and information specified in regulation 6 (notification and evidential requirements relating to the mother),

then these Regulations apply in respect of any period after P dies, subject to the modifications in the following provisions of this paragraph.

  (2) In regulation 8 (variation)—

  (a) paragraph (1) shall apply in relation to the first notice made under that paragraph following P's death as if at the end of that paragraph there is added—

> "or, where it is not reasonably practicable for M to satisfy this requirement, by notice in writing given to that employer as soon as reasonably practicable after the death of P, but in any event before that period and which states the date of P's death";

  (b) paragraph (2)(a) shall apply as if it read—

> "(a) of the number of weeks during which M and P have exercised, and the number of weeks M intends to exercise, an entitlement to statutory shared parental pay (birth) in respect of C";

  (c) paragraph (2)(b) shall not apply.

  (3) In regulation 10—

  (a) paragraph (1)(b)(i) shall apply as if the words "P has notified P's intention to claim" to the end read—

> "the number of weeks in which P claimed statutory shared parental pay (birth) in respect of C up to the time of P's death;";

  (b) paragraph (7) shall apply as if the words "the last day of the latest period so notified" were "the time of P's death".

  4. (1) In the case where—

  (a) M dies after she has reduced her maternity allowance period in respect of C under section 35(3A) of the 1992 Act or her maternity pay period in respect of C under section 165(3A) of the 1992 Act, and

  (b) before M dies P has not given the notices and information specified in regulation 7 (notification and evidential requirements relating to father or partner),

then these Regulations apply in respect of any period after M dies, subject to the modifications in the following provisions of this paragraph.

  (2) In regulation 2(1) (definitions) a person is to be regarded as falling within the definition of P if that person would have done so but for the fact that M has died.

  (3) In regulation 7 (notification and evidential requirements relating to P)—

  (a) in paragraph (1)—

    (i) sub-paragraph (a) shall apply as if it read—

> "(a) paragraphs (2) and (3) at least 8 weeks before the beginning of the first period specified by P pursuant to paragraph (2)(d) or where it is not reasonably practicable for P to satisfy this requirement as soon as reasonably practicable after the death of M, but in any event before that period;";

    (ii) sub-paragraphs (b) and (c) shall not apply.

  (b) in paragraph (2)—

    (i) sub-paragraph (a) shall apply as if the words "disregarding any intention of M to claim statutory shared parental pay in respect of C" were omitted;

    (ii) sub-paragraph (c) shall not apply;

  (c) in paragraph (3)—

    (i) sub-paragraph (a) shall not apply;

    (ii) sub-paragraph (d) shall apply as if it read—

> "(d) P's name, M's name and national insurance number (where this number is known to P), M's address immediately before she died and the date of M's death";

    (iii) sub-paragraph (e)(iii) shall not apply;

  (d) paragraph (4) shall not apply.

  (4) In regulation 8(variation), in paragraph (3)—

(a) sub-paragraph (a) shall apply as if it read—

    "(a) of the number of weeks during which P and M have exercised, and the number of weeks P intends to exercise, an entitlement to statutory shared parental pay (birth) in respect of C";

(b) sub-paragraph (b) shall not apply.

(5) In regulation 10 (extent of entitlement)—

(a) paragraph (1)(b)(ii) shall apply as if the words "M has notified M's intention to claim" to the end read—

    "the number of weeks in which M claimed statutory shared parental pay (birth) in respect of C up to the time of M's death;";

(b) paragraph (8) shall apply as if the words "the last day of the latest period" were "the time of M's death".

5. (1) In the case where—

(a) M dies after she has reduced her maternity allowance period in respect of C under section 35(3A) of the 1992 Act or her maternity pay period in respect of C under section 165(3A) of the 1992 Act, and

(b) before M dies P has given the notice and information specified in regulation 7 (notification and evidential requirements relating to father or mother's partner),

then these Regulations apply in in respect of any period after M dies subject to the modifications in the following provisions of this paragraph.

(2) In regulation 8 (variation)—

(a) paragraph (1) shall apply in relation to the first notice made under that regulation following M's death as if at the end of that paragraph there is added—

    "or, where it is not reasonably practicable for P to satisfy this requirement, by notice in writing given to that employer as soon as reasonably practicable after the death of M, but in any event before that period and which states the date of M's death";

(b) paragraph (3)(a) shall apply as if it read—

    "(a) of the number of weeks during which P and M have exercised, and the number of weeks P intends to exercise, an entitlement to statutory shared parental pay (birth) in respect of C";

(c) paragraph (3)(b) shall not apply.

(3) In regulation 10 (extent of entitlement)—

(a) paragraph (1)(b)(ii) shall apply as if the words "M has notified M's intention to claim" to the end read—

    "the number of weeks in which M claimed statutory shared parental pay (birth) in respect of C up to the time of M's death";

(b) paragraph (8) shall apply as if the words "the last day of the latest period" were "the time of M's death".

Death of child

6. (1) In the case where M has given the notice and information in accordance with regulation 6(1) and then C dies, then in respect of any period after C dies paragraph (2)(f) of regulation 4 (entitlement of mother to statutory shared parental pay), shall not apply, and regulation 8 shall apply in accordance with sub-paragraph (3).   **1.166**

(2) In the case where P has given the notices and information in accordance with regulation 7(1) and then C dies, then in respect of any period after C dies paragraph (2)(d) of regulation 5 (entitlement of father or partner to statutory shared parental pay) shall not apply and regulation 8 shall apply in accordance with sub-paragraph (3).

(3) Where paragraph (1) or (2) applies, regulation 8 (variation) shall apply as if it read—

    "(1) M, or as the case may be, P may cancel the period or periods during which they intend to claim statutory shared parental pay (birth) by notice in writing which is given at least 8 weeks before the first period to be cancelled, or, if this is not reasonably practicable, as soon as reasonably practicable after the death of C, but in any event before that period to the employer who will be liable to pay statutory shared parental pay (birth) to M or P.

(2) M and P may each only give one notice under paragraph (1).".

(4) Where more than one child is born of the same pregnancy—

(a) sub-paragraphs (2) and (3) only apply where all the children die; and

(b) a reference in this paragraph relating to the death of C (however expressed) is to the death of the last of those children to die.

PART 2

STATUTORY SHARED PARENTAL PAY (ADOPTION)

Entitlement of adopter's partner to statutory shared parental pay (adoption) in the event of the death of adopter before curtailment

1.167   7. (1) In a case where A dies before the end of A's adoption pay period in respect of C and without reducing that period under section 171ZN(2A) of the 1992 Act then these Regulations apply in respect of any period after A dies, subject to the modifications in the following provisions of this paragraph.

(2) In regulation 2 a person is to be regarded as falling within the definition of AP if that person would have done so but for the fact that A had died.

(3) In regulation 18 (entitlement of partner to statutory shared parental pay (adoption))—

(a) paragraph (3)(d) shall not apply;

(b) in the case where A dies before A's adoption pay period in respect of C starts, then the condition in paragraph (3)(c) shall be taken to be satisfied if it would have been satisfied but for the fact that A had died.

(4) In regulation 20 (notification and evidential requirements relating to partner)—

(a) paragraph (1)(a) shall apply as if it read—

"(a) paragraphs (2) and (3) at least 8 weeks before the beginning of the first period specified by AP pursuant to paragraph (2)(d) or, where it is not reasonably practicable for AP to satisfy this requirement, as soon as reasonably practicable after the death of A, but in any event before that week";

(b) paragraph (1)(b) and (c) shall not apply;

(c) in paragraph (2)—

(i) sub-paragraph (a) shall apply as if the words "disregarding any intention of A to claim statutory shared parental pay (adoption) in respect of C" were omitted,

(ii) sub-paragraph (c) shall not apply;

(d) in paragraph (3)—

(i) sub-paragraph (a) shall not apply,

(ii) sub-paragraph (d) shall apply as if it read—

"(d) the following information about AP and A—

(i) AP's name, A's name and national insurance number (where this number is known to AP), A's address immediately before she died and the date of A's death; and

(ii) the start date of A's adoption pay period in respect of C;",

(iii) sub-paragraph (e)(iii) shall not apply;

(e) paragraph (4) shall not apply.

(5) In regulation 21 (variation), in paragraph (3)—

(a) sub-paragraph (a) shall apply as if the reference to A were omitted;

(b) sub-paragraph (b) shall not apply.

(6) In regulation 22 (extent of entitlement), paragraph (1)(a) shall apply as if the number of weeks referred to is the number of weeks in which statutory adoption pay was payable to A in respect of C up to the time of A's death.

Notification or variation: death of adopter or adopter's partner after curtailment

8. (1) In the case where—   1.168

(a) AP who in connection with a claim by A would be required to satisfy the conditions in regulation 17(3), dies after A has reduced A's adoption pay period in respect of C under section 171ZN(2A) of the 1992 Act, and

(b) before AP dies A has not given the notice and information specified in regulation 19 (notification and evidential requirements relating to the adopter),

then these Regulations apply in respect of any period after AP dies, subject to the modifications in the following provisions of this paragraph.

(2) In regulation 19 (notification and evidential requirements relating to the adopter)—

(a) paragraph (1)(a) shall apply as if it read—

> "(a) paragraphs (2) and (3) at least 8 weeks before the beginning of the first period specified by A pursuant to paragraph (2)(d) or, where it is not reasonably practicable for A to satisfy this requirement, as soon as reasonably practicable after the death of AP but in any event before that period;";

(b) paragraph (1)(b) and (c) shall not apply;

(c) paragraph (2)(a) shall apply as if the words "disregarding any intention of AP to claim statutory shared parental pay (adoption) in respect of C" were omitted;

(d) paragraph (2)(c) shall not apply;

(e) paragraph (3)(a) shall not apply;

(f) paragraph (3)(d) shall apply as if it read—

> "(d) A's name, AP's name and national insurance number (where this number is known to A), AP's address immediately before AP died and the date of AP's death";

(g) paragraph (4) shall not apply.

(3) In regulation 21 (variation), in paragraph (3) sub-paragraph (a) shall apply as if it read—

> "(a) of the number of weeks during which A and AP have exercised, and the number of weeks A intends to exercise, an entitlement to statutory shared parental pay (adoption) in respect of C;";

(a) paragraph (b) shall not apply.

(4) In regulation 22 (extent of entitlement to statutory shared parental pay (adoption))—

(a) paragraph (1)(b)(i) shall apply as if the words "AP has notified AP's intention to claim" to the end read—

> "the number of weeks in which AP claimed statutory shared parental pay (adoption) in respect of C up to the time of AP's death;";

(b) paragraph (5) shall apply as if the words "the last day of the latest period so notified" were "the time of AP's death".

9. (1) In the case where—

(a) AP, who in connection with A's claim is required to satisfy the conditions specified in regulation 17(3), dies after A has reduced A's adoption pay period under section 171ZN(2A) of the 1992 Act, and

(b) before AP dies A has given the notices and information specified in regulation 19 (notification and evidential requirements relating to the adopter),

then these Regulations apply in respect of any period after AP dies, subject to the modifications in the following provisions of this paragraph.

(2) In regulation 21 (variation)—

(a) paragraph (1) shall apply in relation to the first notice made under that paragraph following AP's death as if at the end of that paragraph there is added—

> "or, where it is not reasonably practicable for A to satisfy this requirement, by notice in writing given to that employer as soon as reasonably practicable after the death of AP, but in any event before that period and which states the date of AP's death";

(b) paragraph (2)(a) shall apply as if it read—

"(a) of the number of weeks during which A and AP have exercised, and the number of weeks A intends to exercise, an entitlement to statutory shared parental pay (adoption) in respect of C;";

(c) paragraph (2)(b) shall not apply.

(3) In regulation 22 (extent of entitlement)—

(a) paragraph (1)(b)(i) shall apply as if the words "AP has notified AP's intention to claim" to the end read "the number of weeks in which AP claimed statutory shared parental pay (adoption) in respect of C up to the time of AP's death;";

(b) paragraph (5) shall apply as if the words "the last day of the latest period so notified" were "the time of AP's death".

10. (1) In the case where—

(a) A dies after A has reduced A's adoption pay period in respect of C under section 171ZN(2A) of the 1992 Act, and

(b) before A dies AP has not given the notice and information specified in regulation 20 (notification and evidential requirements relating to adopter's partner);

then the Regulations apply in respect of any period after A dies subject to the modifications in the following provisions of this paragraph.

(2) In regulation 2(1) (definitions) a person is to be regarded as falling within the definition of AP if that person would have done so but for the fact that A has died.

(3) In regulation 20 (notification and evidential requirements relating to partner)—

(a) paragraph (1)(a) shall apply as if it read—

"(a) paragraphs (2) and (3) at least 8 weeks before the beginning of the first period specified by AP pursuant to paragraph (2)(d) or if it is not reasonably practicable for AP to satisfy this requirement as soon as reasonably practicable after the death of A, but in any event before that period;";

(b) paragraph (1)(b) and (c) shall not apply;

(c) paragraph (2)(a) shall apply as if the words "disregarding any intention of A to claim statutory shared parental pay (adoption) in respect of C" were omitted;

(d) paragraph (2)(c) shall not apply;

(e) paragraph (3)(a) shall not apply;

(f) paragraph (3)(d) shall apply as if it read—

"(d) AP's name, A's name and national insurance number (where this number is known to AP), A's address immediately before A died and the date of A's death;";

(g) paragraph (4) shall not apply.

(4) In regulation 21 (variation), in paragraph (3)—

(a) sub-paragraph (a) shall apply as if it read—

"(a) of the number of weeks during which AP and A have exercised, and the number of weeks AP intends to exercise, an entitlement to statutory shared parental pay (adoption) in respect of C";

(b) sub-paragraph (b) shall not apply.

(5) In regulation 22 (extent of entitlement)—

(a) paragraph (1)(b)(ii) shall apply as if the words "A has notified A's intention to claim" to the end read—

"the number of weeks in which A claimed statutory shared parental pay (adoption) in respect of C up to the time of A's death;".

(b) paragraph (6) shall apply as if the words "the last day of the latest period so notified" were "the time of A's death".

11. (1) In the case where—

(a) A dies after A has reduced A's adoption pay period in respect of C under section 171ZN(2A) of the 1992 Act; and

(b) before A dies AP has given the notice and information specified in regulation 20 (notification and evidential requirements relating to the partner);

then these Regulations apply in respect of any period after A dies subject to the modifications in the following provisions of this paragraph.

(2) In regulation 21 (variation)—

(a) paragraph (1) shall apply in relation to the first notice made under that regulation following A's death as if at the end of that paragraph there is added—

"or, where is it not reasonably practicable for AP to satisfy this requirement, by notice in writing given to that employer as soon as reasonably practicable after the death of A, but in any event before that period and which states the date of A's death;";

(b) paragraph (3)(a) shall apply as it is read—

"(a) of the number of weeks during which AP and A have exercised, and the number of weeks AP intends to exercise, an entitlement to statutory shared parental pay (adoption) in respect of C";

(c) paragraph (3)(b) shall not apply.

(3) In regulation 22 (extent of entitlement)—

(a) paragraph (1)(b)(ii) shall apply as if the words "A has notified A's intention to claim" to the end read—

"the number of weeks in which A claimed statutory shared parental pay (adoption) in respect of C up to the time of A's death.".

(b) paragraph (6) shall apply as if the words "the last day of the latest period so notified" were "the time of A's death".

Death of child or disrupted placement

12. (1) In the case where A has given the notices and information specified in regulation 19(1) and then C dies or is returned after being placed then in respect of any period after C dies or is returned after being placed paragraph (2)(f) of regulation 17 (entitlement of adopter to statutory shared parental pay) shall not apply and regulation 21 shall apply in accordance with sub-paragraph (3).

1.170

(2) In the case where AP has given the notices and information specified in regulation 20(1) and then C dies or is returned after being placed then in respect of any period after C dies or is returned after being placed paragraph (2)(d) of regulation 18 (entitlement of adopter to statutory shared parental pay) shall not apply and regulation 21 shall apply in accordance with sub-paragraph (3).

(3) Where paragraph (1) or (2) applies, regulation 21 (variation) shall apply as if it read—

"(1) A or, as the case may be, AP may cancel the period or periods during which they intend to claim statutory shared parental pay (adoption) by notice in writing which is given at least 8 weeks before the first period to be cancelled or, if this is not reasonably practicable, as soon as reasonably practicable after the death of C or after C is returned after being placed, but in any event before that period to the employer who will be liable to pay statutory shared parental pay (adoption) to A or AP.

(2) A and AP may each only give one notice under paragraph (1).".

(4) Where more than one child is placed for adoption as a result of the same placement—

(a) sub-paragraphs (1) and (2) only apply where all the children die or, as the case may be, all the children are returned after being placed;

(b) a reference in this paragraph to the death of C or to the return of C after being placed (however expressed) is to the death of the last of those children to die or is to the last of those children to be returned after being placed.

(5) In this paragraph "returned after being placed" means—

(a) returned to the adoption agency under sections 31 to 35 of the Adoption and Children Act 2002;

(b) in Scotland, returned to the adoption agency, adoption society or nominated person in accordance with section 25(6) of the Adoption and Children (Scotland) Act 2007; or

(c) where the child is placed in accordance with section 22C of the Children Act 1989, returned to the adoption agency following termination of the placement.

Maternity Allowance (Curtailment) Regulations 2014

(SI 2014/3053)

In force December 1, 2014

ARRANGEMENT OF REGULATIONS

This instrument contains only regulations made by virtue of, or consequential upon, section 120(1) and (2) of the Children and Families Act 2014 and is made before the end of the period of 6 months beginning with the coming into force of that enactment.

The Secretary of State for Work and Pensions, in exercise of the powers conferred by sections 35(3A), (3B), (3C) and (3D) and 175(1), (3), (4) and (5) of the Social Security Contributions and Benefits Act 1992, makes the following Regulations:

GENERAL NOTE

1.172   The Shared Parental Leave Regulations 2014 (SI 2014/3050) and the Statutory Shared Parental Pay (General) Regulations 2014 (SI 2014/3051) provide an entitlement for a mother/adopter and a child's father/adoptive parent or a mother's or adopter's partner to take shared parental leave and pay. The right to shared parental leave and statutory shared parental pay are new statutory rights for employees with a partner who is working, or has recently been working (whether employed or self-employed). Eligible employees will be able to share up to 50 weeks of shared parental leave and up to 37 weeks of statutory shared parental pay (ShPP).

Shared parental leave and ShPP arises from untaken maternity leave and statutory maternity pay or maternity allowance, or untaken adoption leave and statutory adoption pay. An eligible mother or adopter must curtail her maternity or adoption leave in order for shared parental leave to arise. She or he may do this, as now, by simply returning to work. Or she or he may do it giving notice to curtail their maternity or adoption leave at a specified future date. The Maternity and Adoption Leave (Curtailment of Statutory Rights to Leave) Regulations 2014 (SI 2014/3052) enable an expectant mother or a mother on maternity leave, or an adopter or a prospective adopter to give notice to end her maternity leave or his or her adoption leave on a specific future date. Where maternity or adoption leave has been curtailed under the Curtailment of Statutory Rights to Leave Regulations, the balance of the untaken leave may be taken as shared parental leave if the parents satisfy entitlement and notification criteria.

The present Regulations allow eligible women to curtail their maternity allowance period in accordance with s.35(3A) of the SSCBA 1992 so as to enable their partner to take ShPP in accordance with s.171ZU of the SSCBA 1992. The Regulations also allow eligible women to curtail their maternity allowance period in accordance with s.35(3A) of the SSCBA 1992 in order to allow their partner to take shared parental leave in accordance with s.75E of the Employment Rights Act 1996.

Regulation 3 applies to a woman curtailing her maternity allowance period so that her partner can take statutory shared parental pay. Regulation 4 applies to a woman who is not eligible for statutory maternity leave to curtail her maternity allowance period so that her partner can take shared parental leave. In these circumstances, an eligible partner will be entitled to 52 weeks of shared parental leave less the amount of maternity allowance the child's mother has taken at the point of curtailing the maternity allowance period. Regulation 5 prescribes the requirements with which a maternity allowance period curtailment notification must comply. Regulation 6 allows a woman to revoke a maternity allowance period curtailment notification in specified circumstances and subject to certain conditions being satisfied.

Citation and commencement

1. These Regulations may be cited as the Maternity Allowance (Curtailment) Regulations 2014 and come into force on 1st December 2014.   1.173

Interpretation

2. In these Regulations—   1.174

"the 1992 Act" means the Social Security Contributions and Benefits Act 1992;

"the 1996 Act" means the Employment Rights Act 1996;

"C" means the child in respect of whom an entitlement to—
 (a) shared parental leave arises under section 75E (entitlement to shared parental leave: birth) of the 1996 Act; or
 (b) statutory shared parental pay arises under section 171ZU (entitlement: birth) of the 1992 Act;

"M" means the mother (or expectant mother) of C;

"maternity allowance period curtailment date" means, subject to regulation 5(5), the date specified in a maternity allowance period curtailment notification;

"maternity allowance period curtailment notification" means a notification given in accordance with regulation 5 and regulation 6(4);

"P" means the father of C, or the person who is married to, or the civil partner or the partner of, M;

"partner" in relation to M, means a person (whether of a different sex or the same sex) who lives with M and C in an enduring family relationship but is not M's child, parent, grandchild, grandparent, sibling, aunt, uncle, niece or nephew;

"SPL Regulations" means the Shared Parental Leave Regulations 2014;

"ShPP Regulations" means the Statutory Shared Parental Pay (General) Regulations 2014.

Curtailment of maternity allowance period (statutory shared parental pay: P)

1.175   **3.** M's maternity allowance period shall end on the maternity allowance period curtailment date if—

    (a) M gives a maternity allowance period curtailment notification (unless the notification is revoked under regulation 6);

    (b) P satisfies the condition in sub-paragraph (a) of regulation 5(2) (entitlement of father or partner to statutory shared parental pay (birth)) of the ShPP Regulations; and

    (c) M satisfies the conditions in sub-paragraphs (b) and (c) of regulation 5(3) of the ShPP Regulations.

Curtailment of maternity allowance period (shared parental leave: P)

1.176   **4.** M's maternity allowance period shall end on the maternity allowance period curtailment date if—

    (a) M gives a maternity allowance period curtailment notification (unless the notification is revoked under regulation 6);

    (b) P satisfies the condition in sub-paragraph (a) of regulation 5(2) (father's or partner's entitlement to shared parental leave) of the SPL Regulations; and

    (c) M satisfies the conditions in sub-paragraphs (a) and (c) of regulation 5(3) of the SPL Regulations.

Maternity allowance period curtailment notification

1.177   **5.** (1) A maternity allowance period curtailment notification must—

    (a) be given to the Secretary of State; and

    (b) specify the date on which M wants her maternity allowance period to end.

(2) The date specified in accordance with paragraph (1)(b) must be—

    (a) the last day of a week;

    (b) if M has the right to maternity leave under section 71 (ordinary maternity leave) of the 1996 Act, at least one day after the end of the compulsory maternity leave period or, if M does not have that right, at least two weeks after the end of the pregnancy;

    (c) at least eight weeks after the date on which M gives the maternity allowance period curtailment notification; and

    (d) at least one week before the last day of M's maternity allowance period.

(3) Where the Secretary of State considers it appropriate the eight week period set out in paragraph (2)(c) may be reduced in any particular case.

(4) In paragraph (2)(b) "the end of the compulsory maternity leave period" means whichever is the later of—

    (a) the last day of the compulsory maternity leave period provided for in regulations under section 72(2) (compulsory maternity leave) of the 1996 Act; or

(b) where section 205 of the Public Health Act 1936 (women not to be employed in factories or workshops within four weeks after birth of a child) applies to M's employment, the last day of the period in which an occupier of a factory is prohibited from knowingly allowing M to be employed in that factory.

(5) Where M—

(a) returns to work before giving a notification under paragraph (1); and

(b) subsequently gives such a notification;

the "maternity allowance period curtailment date" shall be the last day of the week in which that notification is submitted (irrespective of the date given in that notification under paragraph (1)).

(6) For the purposes of paragraphs (2)(a) and (5), "week" has the meaning given in section 165(8) of the 1992 Act (the maternity pay period).

(7) For the purposes of paragraph (5)(a), a woman is treated as returning to work where maternity allowance is not payable to her in accordance with regulation 2(1) of the Social Security (Maternity Allowance) Regulations 1987 (disqualification for the receipt of a maternity allowance).

Revocation (maternity allowance period curtailment notification)

6. (1) Subject to paragraph (2), M may revoke a maternity allowance period curtailment notification before the maternity allowance period curtailment date if—   **1.178**

(a) M provided the maternity allowance period curtailment notification before the birth of C; or

(b) P dies.

(2) Revocation is effective under paragraph (1) where M gives a notification ("a revocation notification") to the Secretary of State that—

(a) if given under paragraph (1)(a), is given within six weeks of the date of C's birth;

(b) if given under paragraph (1)(b), is given within a reasonable period from the date of P's death.

(3) A revocation notification must—

(a) state that M revokes the maternity allowance period curtailment notification; and

(b) if given under paragraph (1)(b), state the date of P's death.

(4) M may not give a maternity allowance period curtailment notification in respect of the same maternity allowance period subsequent to giving a revocation notification unless the revocation was made in accordance with paragraph (1)(a).

Statutory Maternity Pay and Statutory Adoption Pay (Curtailment) Regulations 2014

(SI 2014/3054)

In force December 1, 2014

ARRANGEMENT OF REGULATIONS

PART 1

GENERAL

PART 2

CURTAILMENT OF MATERNITY PAY PERIOD

PART 3

CURTAILMENT OF ADOPTION PAY PERIOD

This instrument contains only regulations made by virtue of, or consequential upon, section 120(1), (4) and (6) of the Children and Families Act 2014 and is made before the end of the period of 6 months beginning with the coming into force of that enactment.

The Secretary of State for Work and Pensions, in exercise of the powers conferred by sections 165(3A), (3B), (3C) and (3D),

171ZN(2A), (2B), (2C) and (2D) and 175(1), (3) and (4) of the Social Security Contributions and Benefits Act 1992, makes the following Regulations:

GENERAL NOTE

These Regulations allow eligible women to curtail their statutory maternity pay in accordance with s.165(3A) of the SSCBA 1992 in order to enable them to take statutory shared parental pay (ShPP) in accordance with s.171ZU of the 1992 Act. The Regulations also allow eligible women to curtail their statutory maternity pay in accordance with SSCBA 1992, s.165(3A), in order to allow their partner to take ShPP in accordance with SSCBA 1992, s.171ZU, or shared parental leave in accordance with s.75E of the Employment Rights Act 1996.

Regulation 3 prescribes how notices may be given under these Regulations. Regulation 4 applies to a woman curtailing her statutory maternity pay in order to take ShPP. Regulation 5 applies to a woman curtailing her SMP so that her partner can take ShPP. Regulation 6 allows a woman who is not eligible for statutory maternity leave to curtail her SMP so that her partner can take shared parental leave. In these circumstances, an eligible partner will be entitled to 52 weeks of shared parental leave less the amount of SMP the child's mother has taken at the point of curtailing the maternity pay period. Regulation 7 prescribes the requirements with which a maternity pay period curtailment notice must comply. Regulation 8 allows a woman to revoke a notice to curtail her SMP in specified circumstances and subject to certain conditions being satisfied.

These Regulations also make equivalent provisions for adopters. The Regulations allow eligible adopters to curtail their adoption pay period in accordance with SSCBA 1992, s.171ZN(2A) so as to enable them to take ShPP in accordance with SSCBA 1992, s.171ZV. The Regulations also allow eligible adopters to curtail their adoption pay period in accordance with s.171ZN(2A) to allow their partner to take ShPP in accordance with s.171ZV, or shared parental leave in accordance with s.75G of the Employment Rights Act 1996.

1.180

PART 1

GENERAL

Citation and commencement

1. These Regulations may be cited as the Statutory Maternity Pay and Statutory Adoption Pay (Curtailment) Regulations 2014 and come into force on 1st December 2014.

1.181

Interpretation

2. In these Regulations—

"the 1992 Act" means the Social Security Contributions and Benefits Act 1992;

"the 1996 Act" means the Employment Rights Act 1996;

"A" means a person who is entitled to statutory adoption pay;

"adoption pay curtailment date" means, subject to regulation 12(4), the date specified in an adoption pay period curtailment notice;

1.182

"adoption pay period curtailment notice" means a notice given in accordance with regulation 12;

"AP" means the person who is married to, or the civil partner or the partner of, A;

"C" means the child in respect of whom an entitlement to—

    (a) shared parental leave arises under section 75E (entitlement to shared parental leave: birth) or 75G (entitlement to shared parental leave: adoption) of the 1996 Act;

    (b) statutory shared parental pay arises under section 171ZU (entitlement: birth) or 171ZV (entitlement: adoption) of the 1992 Act;

"calendar week" means a period of seven days beginning with a Sunday;

"M" means the mother (or expectant mother) of C;

"maternity pay period curtailment date" means, subject to regulation 7(5), the date specified in a maternity pay period curtailment notice;

"maternity pay period curtailment notice" means a notice given in accordance with regulation 7 and regulation 8(5);

"P" means the father of C, or the person who is married to, or the civil partner or the partner of, M;

"partner" in relation to M or A, means a person (whether of a different sex or the same sex) who lives with M or A and with C in an enduring family relationship but is not M's or A's child, parent, grandchild, grandparent, sibling, aunt, uncle, niece or nephew;

"SPL Regulations" means the Shared Parental Leave Regulations 2014;

"ShPP Regulations" means the Statutory Shared Parental Pay (General) Regulations 2014;

"statutory adoption pay" has the meaning given in section 171ZL (entitlement) of the 1992 Act;

"statutory maternity pay" has the meaning given in section 164(1) (statutory maternity pay—entitlement and liability to pay) of the 1992 Act.

Notices

1.183   **3.** (1) Where a notice is to be given under these Regulations, it may be given—

    (a) where paragraph (2) applies, by electronic communication;

    (b) by post; or

    (c) by personal delivery.

(2) This paragraph applies where the person who is to receive the notice has agreed that the notice may be given to the person by being transmitted to an electronic address and in an electronic form specified by the person for the purpose.

(3) Where a notice is to be given under these Regulations it is to be taken to have been given—

    (a) if sent by electronic communication, on the day of transmission;

(b) if sent by post in an envelope which is properly addressed and sent by prepaid post, on the day on which it is posted;
(c) if delivered personally, on the day of delivery.

PART 2

CURTAILMENT OF MATERNITY PAY PERIOD

Curtailment of maternity pay period (statutory shared parental pay: M)

4. M's maternity pay period shall end on the maternity pay period curtailment date if— **1.184**
 (a) M gives a maternity pay period curtailment notice (unless the notice is revoked under regulation 8);
 (b) M satisfies the conditions in sub-paragraphs (a) and (d) of regulation 4(2) (entitlement of mother to statutory shared parental pay (birth)) of the ShPP Regulations; and
 (c) P satisfies the conditions in sub-paragraph (b) of regulation 4(3) of the ShPP Regulations.

Curtailment of maternity pay period (statutory shared parental pay: P)

5. M's maternity pay period shall end on the maternity pay period curtailment date if— **1.185**
 (a) M gives a maternity pay period curtailment notice (unless the notice is revoked under regulation 8);
 (b) P satisfies the conditions in sub-paragraph (a) of regulation 5(2) (entitlement of father or partner to statutory shared parental pay (birth)) of the ShPP Regulations; and
 (c) M satisfies the conditions in sub-paragraphs (b) and (c) of regulation 5(3) of the ShPP Regulations.

Curtailment of maternity pay period (shared parental leave: P)

6. M's maternity pay period shall end on the maternity pay period curtailment date if— **1.186**
 (a) M gives a maternity pay period curtailment notice (unless the notice is revoked under regulation 8);
 (b) P satisfies the condition in sub-paragraph (a) of regulation 5(2) (father's or partner's entitlement to shared parental leave) of the SPL Regulations; and
 (c) M satisfies the conditions in sub-paragraphs (a) and (c) of regulation 5(3) of the SPL Regulations.

Maternity pay period curtailment notice

7. (1) A maternity pay period curtailment notice must— **1.187**
 (a) be in writing;

    (b) specify the date on which M's statutory maternity pay period is to end; and

    (c) be given to the person who is liable to pay M's statutory maternity pay.

    (2) The date specified in accordance with paragraph (1)(b) must be—

    (a) the last day of a week;

    (b) if M has the right to maternity leave under section 71 (ordinary maternity leave) of the 1996 Act, at least one day after the end of the compulsory maternity leave period, or, if M does not have that right, at least two weeks after the end of the pregnancy;

    (c) at least eight weeks after the date on which M gave the maternity pay period curtailment notice; and

    (d) at least one week before the last day of the maternity pay period.

    (3) In paragraph (2) "the end of the compulsory maternity leave period" means whichever is the later of—

    (a) the last day of the compulsory maternity leave period provided for in regulations under section 72(2) (compulsory maternity leave) of the 1996 Act; or

    (b) where section 205 of the Public Health Act 1936 (women not to be employed in factories or workshops within four weeks after birth of a child) applies to M's employment, the last day of the period in which an occupier of a factory is prohibited from knowingly allowing M to be employed in that factory.

    (4) If M has more than one entitlement to statutory maternity pay in relation to C, M must curtail the maternity pay period in relation to each (or none) of those entitlements, and in relation to each of those entitlements M must specify a maternity pay period curtailment date which falls in the same calendar week.

    (5) Where M—

    (a) returns to work before giving a notice in accordance with paragraph (1); and

    (b) subsequently gives such a notice;

the "maternity pay period curtailment date" shall be the last day of the week in which that notice is given (irrespective of the date given in that notice under paragraph (1)).

    (6) For the purposes of paragraphs (2)(a) and (5), "week" has the meaning given in section 165(8) (the maternity pay period) of the 1992 Act.

    (7) In this regulation, M is treated as returning to work where statutory maternity pay is not payable to her in accordance with section 165(4) or (6) of the 1992 Act.

Revocation (maternity pay period curtailment notice)

1.188   **8.** (1) Subject to paragraph (2), M may revoke a maternity pay period curtailment notice by giving a notice ("a revocation notice") before the maternity pay period curtailment date if—

(a) she gave the maternity pay period curtailment notice before the birth of C; or

(b) P dies.

(2) Revocation is effective under paragraph (1) where M gives a revocation notice to the person who is liable to pay M's statutory maternity pay that—

(a) if given under paragraph (1)(a), is given within six weeks of the date of C's birth; or

(b) if given under paragraph (1)(b), is given within a reasonable period from the date of P's death.

(3) A revocation notice must—

(a) be in writing;

(b) state that M revokes the maternity pay period curtailment notice; and

(c) if given under paragraph (1)(b), state the date of P's death.

(4) Where in accordance with regulation 7(4) M has given a maternity pay period curtailment notice to more than one person, M must give a revocation notice to each of those persons.

(5) M may not give a maternity pay period curtailment notice in respect of the same maternity pay period subsequent to giving a revocation notice unless the revocation was made in accordance with paragraph (1)(a).

PART 3

CURTAILMENT OF ADOPTION PAY PERIOD

Curtailment of adoption pay period (statutory shared parental pay: A)

9. A's adoption pay period shall end on the adoption pay curtailment   1.189
date if—

(a) A gives an adoption pay period curtailment notice (unless the notice is revoked under regulation 13);

(b) A satisfies the conditions in sub-paragraphs (a) and (d) of regulation 17(2) (entitlement of adopter to statutory shared parental pay (adoption)) of the ShPP Regulations; and

(c) AP satisfies the condition in sub-paragraph (b) of regulation 17(3) of the ShPP Regulations.

Curtailment of adoption pay period (statutory shared parental pay: AP)

10. A's adoption pay period shall end on the adoption pay curtailment   1.190
date if—

(a) A gives an adoption pay period curtailment notice (unless the notice is revoked under regulation 13);

(b) AP satisfies the conditions in sub-paragraph (a) of regulation 18(2) (entitlement of adopter's partner to statutory shared parental pay (adoption)) of the ShPP Regulations; and

(c) A satisfies the conditions in sub-paragraphs (b) and (c) of regulation 18(3) of the ShPP Regulations.

Curtailment of adoption pay period (shared parental leave: AP)

1.191   **11.** A's adoption pay period shall end on the adoption pay curtailment date if—

(a) A gives an adoption pay period curtailment notice (unless the notice is revoked under regulation 13);

(b) AP satisfies the condition in sub-paragraph (a) of regulation 21(2) (adopter's partner's entitlement to shared parental leave) of the SPL Regulations; and

(c) A satisfies the conditions in sub-paragraphs (a) and (c) of regulation 21(3) of the SPL Regulations.

Adoption pay period curtailment notice

1.192   **12.** (1) An adoption pay period curtailment notice must—

(a) be in writing;

(b) specify the date on which A's statutory adoption pay period is to end; and

(c) be given to the person who is liable to pay A's statutory adoption pay.

(2) The date specified in accordance with paragraph (1)(b) must be—

(a) the last day of a week;

(b) at least eight weeks after the date on which A gave the adoption pay period curtailment notice;

(c) at least two weeks after the first day of the adoption pay period; and

(d) at least one week before the last day of the adoption pay period.

(3) If A has more than one entitlement to statutory adoption pay in relation to C, A must curtail the adoption pay period in relation to each (or none) of those entitlements, and in relation to each of those entitlements A must specify an adoption pay curtailment date which falls in the same calendar week.

(4) Where A—

(a) returns to work before giving a notice in accordance with paragraph (1); and

(b) subsequently gives such a notice;

the adoption pay curtailment date shall be the last day of the week in which that notice is submitted (irrespective of the date given in that notice under paragraph (1)).

(5) For the purposes of paragraph (2)(a) and (4), "week" has the meaning given in section 171ZN(8) of the 1992 Act.

(6) In this regulation, A is treated as returning to work where statutory adoption pay is not payable to A in accordance with section 171ZN(3) or (5) of the 1992 Act.

Revocation (adoption pay period curtailment notice)

13. (1) Where AP dies before the adoption pay curtailment date, A   **1.193**
may revoke an adoption pay period curtailment notice by giving a notice
("a revocation notice") in accordance with paragraph (2).

(2) A revocation notice must be given to the person who is liable to pay
A statutory adoption pay within a reasonable period from the date of
AP's death and before the adoption pay curtailment date.

(3) A revocation notice must—

(a) be in writing;

(b) state that A revokes the adoption pay period curtailment notice;
and

(c) state the date of AP's death.

(4) Where in accordance with regulation 12(3) A has given an adoption pay period curtailment notice to more than one person, A must give
a revocation notice to each of those persons.

(5) A may not give an adoption pay period curtailment notice subsequent to giving a revocation notice.

The Welfare Reform Act 2012 (Commencement No. 9, 11, 13 14, 16, 17 and 19 and Transitional and Transitory Provisions (Amendment)) Order 2014

SI 2014/3067 (C.129)

1.194   *See Part VI*

Statutory Shared Parental Pay (Parental Order Cases) Regulations 2014

(SI 2014/3097)

1.195   In force December 1, 2014

ARRANGEMENT OF REGULATIONS

1.196   1. Commencement and Citation
2. Interpretation
3. Application of the Pay Regulations to an intended parent or a parental order parent
4.-16. Modifications of the Pay Regulations as they apply to an intended parent or a parental order parent

A draft of these Regulations was laid before Parliament in accordance with section 176(1) of the Social Security Contributions and Benefits Act 1992 and approved by resolution of each House of Parliament.

This instrument contains only regulations made by virtue of, or consequential upon, section 119(1) of the Children and Families Act 2014 and is made before the end of the period 6 months beginning with the coming into force of that enactment.

The Secretary of State, in exercise of the powers conferred by sections 171ZV(1), (2), (3), (4), (5), (12), (13), (14) and (15), 171ZW(1)(a) to (f), 171ZX(2) and (3), 171ZY(1), (3), (4) and (5), 171ZZ1(3), 171ZZ4(3), (4), (7) and (8) and 175(3) of the Social Security Contributions and Benefits Act 1992 and by section 5(1)(g), (i), (l) and (p) of the Social Security Administration Act 1992 and with the concurrence of the Commissioners for Her Majesty's Revenue and Customs, in so far as such concurrence is required, makes the following Regulations:

GENERAL NOTE

1.197   These Regulations provide an entitlement to statutory shared parental pay in respect of cases which involve a person who has applied, with another person, for a parental order under s.54 of the Human Fertilisation and Embryology Act 2008. Under s.54 a court may make an order providing for a child of a surrogate mother to be treated as the child of the applicants for the order if certain conditions are satisfied. These Regulations need to be read in conjunction with the Social Security Contributions and Benefits Act 1992 (Application of Parts 12ZA, 12ZB and 12ZC to Parental Order Cases) Regulations 2014 (SI 2014/2866). They should also be read in conjunction with the Statutory Shared Parental Pay (General) Regulations 2014 (SI 2014/3051) which they apply with modifications.

PART 1

INTRODUCTION

Citation and commencement

1. These Regulations may be cited as the Statutory Shared Parental Pay (Parental Order Cases) Regulations 2014 and come into force on 1st December 2014.

1.198

Interpretation

2. In these Regulations—

1.199

"A" and "AP" have the same meanings as in the Pay Regulations as modified by these Regulations;

"C", "expected week of birth" and "statutory shared parental pay (adoption)" have the same meanings as under the Pay Regulations;

"parental order parent" means a person on whose application the court has made a parental order in respect of C;

"parental statutory declaration" means a statutory declaration stating that the person making the declaration—

(a) has applied, or intends to apply, under section 54 of the Human Fertilisation and Embryology Act 2008 with another person for a parental order in respect of C within the time limit for making such an application; and

(b) expects the court to make a parental order on that application in respect of C;

"Pay Regulations" means the Statutory Shared Parental Pay (General) Regulations 2014.

Application of the Pay Regulations to an intended parent or a parental order parent

3. The provisions of the Pay Regulations in so far as they apply to statutory shared parental pay (adoption) shall apply to an intended parent or a parental order parent with the modifications set out in Part 2 of these Regulations.

1.200

Modifications of the Pay Regulations as they apply to an intended parent or a parental order parent

1.201   **4.** Regulation 2 (interpretation) of the Pay Regulations as they apply to an intended parent or a parental order parent shall read as if—

(a) in paragraph (1)—

    (i) the definition of "A" read "means the intended parent or parental order parent in relation to C who has elected to receive statutory adoption pay under section 171ZL(2)(e) of the 1992 Act and to whom the conditions in that subsection apply;";

    (ii) the definition of "AP" read "means the intended parent or parental order parent in relation to C who at the date of C's birth is married to, or is the civil partner of, or is the partner of A;";

    (iii) the definition of "child" were omitted;

    (iv) there was the following definition—

       ""parental order parent" means a person on whose application the court has made an order in respect of C under section 54(1) of the Human Fertilization and Embryology Act 2008;";

    (v) the definitions of "placed for adoption" and "adoption agency" were omitted;

(b) paragraphs (4), (5) and (6) were omitted.

1.202   **5.** In regulation 3 (application) of the Pay Regulations as they apply to an intended parent or a parental order parent paragraph (b) shall read as if the words in that paragraph were—

"statutory shared parental pay (adoption) in respect of children whose expected week of birth begins on or after 5th April 2015.".

6. In regulation 17 (entitlement of adopter to statutory shared parental pay (adoption)) of the Pay Regulations as they apply to an intended parent or a parental order parent—

(a) in paragraph (2)—

    (i) sub-paragraph (b) shall read as if the words in that sub-paragraph were—

       "A has, or expects to have, at the date of C's birth the main responsibility for the care of C (apart from the responsibility of AP);";

    (ii) sub-paragraph (d) shall read as if the words "to the placement for adoption of C" read "to being the intended parent or parental order parent of C";

(b) in paragraph (3), sub-paragraph (a) shall read as if the words in that sub-paragraph were—

"AP has, or expects to have, at the date of C's birth the main responsibility for the care of C (apart from the responsibility of A);".

7. In regulation 18 (entitlement of partner to statutory shared parental pay (adoption)) of the Pay Regulations as they apply to an intended parent or a parental order parent—

(a) in paragraph (2), sub-paragraph (b) shall read as if the words in that sub-paragraph were—

"AP has, or expects to have, at the date of C's birth the main responsibility for the care of C (apart from the responsibility of A)";

(b) in paragraph (3)—

(i) sub-paragraph (a) shall read as if the words in that sub-paragraph were—

"A has, or expects to have, at the date of C's birth the main responsibility for the care of C (apart from the responsibility of A);";

(ii) sub-paragraph (c) shall read as if the words "to the placement for adoption of C" read "to being the intended parent or parental order parent of C".

8. (1) In regulation 19 (notification and evidential requirements relating to the adopter) of the Pay Regulations as they apply to an intended parent or a parental order parent—

(a) paragraph (1)(b) shall read as if the words "if C is not placed for adoption by that time as soon as reasonably practicable after the placement of C " were "if C is not born by that time as soon as reasonably practicable after the birth of C";

(b) in paragraph (3)—

(i) sub-paragraph (b) shall read as if the words in that sub-paragraph were "the expected week of birth of C";

(ii) sub-paragraph (c) shall read as if the words in that sub-paragraph were "C's date of birth";

(iii) that paragraph shall apply as if there were also specified a parental statutory declaration by A unless the condition in paragraph (2)(a) or (b) of this regulation is satisfied;

(c) paragraph (4) shall apply as if—

(i) sub-paragraph (a) were omitted;

(ii) there were also specified a copy of C's birth certificate or, if one has not been issued, a written declaration signed by A which states that it has not been issued;

(iii) where A has not provided a parental statutory declaration as a result of the condition in paragraph (2)(a) of this regulation being satisfied, there were specified a parental statutory declaration.

(2) The conditions referred to in paragraph (1)(b)(iii) and (c)(iii) are—

(a) that A has given the employer who will be liable to pay statutory shared parental pay (adoption) to A a statutory declaration as evidence of A's entitlement to statutory adoption pay in respect of C in accordance with regulation 24 of the Statutory Paternity Pay and Statutory Adoption Pay (General) Regulations 2002;

   (b) that A is a parental order parent and has given the employer a copy of the order in respect of C made under section 54(1) of the Human Fertilisation and Embryology Act 2008.

1.203   **9.** In regulation 20 (notification and evidential requirements relating to the partner) of the Pay Regulations as they apply to an intended parent or a parental order parent—

   (a) paragraph (1)(b) shall read as if the words "if C is not placed for adoption by that time as soon as reasonably practicable after the placement of C " were "if C is not born by that time as soon as reasonably practicable after the birth of C";

   (b) in paragraph (3)—

      (i) sub-paragraph (b) shall read as if the words in that sub-paragraph were "the expected week of birth of C";

      (ii) sub-paragraph (c) shall read as if the words in that sub-paragraph were "C's date of birth";

      (iii) sub-paragraph (e) shall read as if the written declaration signed by AP was also required to contain the statement that A and AP are the intended parents or the parental order parents of C;

   (c) paragraph (4) shall apply as if—

      (i) sub-paragraph (a) were omitted; and

      (ii) there were specified a copy of C's birth certificate or, if one has not been issued, a written declaration signed by AP which states that it has not been issued.

    10. (1) The Pay Regulations apply to an intended parent or a parental order parent with the modification provided for in paragraph (2) where—

   (a) one or more of the periods specified in a notice under regulation 19, 20 or 21 of the Pay Regulations during which A or, as the case may be, AP intends to claim statutory shared parental pay (adoption) start in the 8 weeks following the first day of C's expected week of birth;

   (b) C's date of birth is before the first day of the expected week of birth; and

   (c) A or, as the case may be, AP varies by notice under regulation 21(1) the period or periods referred to in sub-paragraph (a) so that that period or those periods start the same length of time following C's date of birth as that period or those periods would have started after the first day of the expected week of birth.

    (2) The modification in this paragraph is that the requirement in regulation 21(1) to give notice at least 8 weeks before the first period specified in the notice is satisfied if such notice is given as soon as reasonably practicable after C's date of birth.

    (3) The Pay Regulations apply to an intended parent or a parental order parent with the modifications provided for in paragraph (4) where—

(a) C is born more than 8 weeks before the first day of the expected week of birth;

(b) A or, as the case may be, AP has not given the notice and information under regulations 19 or 20 of the Pay Regulations before the date of C's birth; and

(c) A or, as the case may be, AP specifies in a notice under regulations 19 or 20 a period or periods of statutory shared parental pay (adoption) which start in the 8 weeks following C's date of birth.

(4) The modifications in this paragraph are—

(a) in regulation 19—

    (i) paragraph (1)(a) shall read as if the words in that sub-paragraph were—

> "paragraphs (2) and (3) as soon as reasonably practicable after the date of C's birth but in any event before the first period specified by A pursuant to paragraph (2)(d)";

    (ii) paragraph (1)(b) and (c) shall not apply;

    (iii) paragraph (4) shall not apply.

(b) in regulation 20—

    (i) paragraph (1)(a) shall read as if the words in that sub-paragraph were—

> "paragraphs (2) and (3) as soon as reasonably practicable after the date of C's birth but in any event before the first period specified by AP pursuant to paragraph (2)(d)";

    (ii) paragraph (1)(b) and (c) shall not apply;

    (iii) paragraph (4) shall not apply.

11. In regulation 23 (when statutory shared parental pay (adoption) is not to be paid) of the Pay Regulations as they apply to an intended parent or a parental order parent, paragraph (1) shall read—

> "Statutory shared parental pay (adoption) is not payable after the day before the date of C's first birthday (or, where more than one child is born of the same pregnancy, the birthday of the first child so born).".

12. In regulation 24 (work during period of payment of statutory shared parental pay) of the Pay Regulations as they apply to an intended parent or a parental order parent, paragraph (1)(a)(ii) shall read as if the words "the expected week of placement for adoption" read "the expected week of birth".

13. In regulation 29 (conditions relating to employment and earnings of a claimant's partner) of the Pay Regulations as they apply to an intended parent or a parental order parent, in paragraph (5), the definition of "calculation week" shall read—

> ""calculation week" means the expected week of birth of C;".

14. Regulation 31 (conditions as to continuity of employment and normal weekly earnings in relation to a claimant) of the Pay Regulations as they apply to an intended parent or a parental order parent, shall read as if—

(a) the words in paragraph (2) were—

"Where C's birth occurs earlier than the 14th week before C's expected week of birth paragraph (1) shall have effect as if, for the conditions set out there, there were substituted conditions that—

(a) the person would have been in employer earner's employment for a continuous period of at least 26 weeks ending with the relevant week had C been born after the relevant week;

(b) the person's normal weekly earnings for the period of eight weeks ending with the week immediately preceding C's actual week of birth are not less than the lower earnings limit in force under section 5(1)(a) of the 1992 Act immediately before the commencement of C's actual week of birth; and

(c) the person continues in employed earner's employment with the employer by reference to whom the condition in sub-paragraph (a) is satisfied for a continuous period beginning with the date of C's birth and ending with the week before the first week falling within the relevant period relating to that person under section 171ZY(2) of the 1992 Act.".

(b) the following paragraphs were added—

"(3) The references in this regulation to the relevant week are to the week immediately preceding the 14th week before C's expected week of birth.

(4) Where more than one child is born as a result of the same pregnancy the date the first child is born is to be used to determine C's actual week of birth or the date of C's birth.".

15. In regulation 32 (normal weekly earnings of a claimant for statutory shared parental pay) of the Pay Regulations as they apply to an intended parent or a parental order parent, in paragraph (9), sub-paragraph (a), the definition of "the appropriate date" shall read—

""the appropriate date" means the first day of the 14th week before the expected week of the child's birth or the first day in the week in which the child is born, whichever is earlier (but see paragraph (10)).".

16. In the Schedule (statutory shared parental pay in special circumstances) to the Pay Regulations as they apply to an intended parent or a parental order parent, in paragraph 12—

(a) sub-paragraphs (1) and (2) shall read as if the words "is returned after being placed" (in each place where they occur) read "the parental order does not proceed";

(b) sub-paragraph (4) shall read as if the words in that sub-paragraph were—

"Where more than one child is born of the same pregnancy—
  (a) sub-paragraphs (1) and (2) only apply where all the children die or the parental order does not proceed in respect of all the children; and
  (b) a reference in this paragraph relating to the death of C (however expressed) is to the death of the last of those children to die.".

(c) sub-paragraph (5) shall read as if the words in that sub-paragraph were—

"For the purpose of this paragraph a parental order does not proceed if—
  (a) A and AP have not made an application for an order in respect of C under section 54(1) of the Human Fertilisation and Embryology Act 2008 within the time limit for such an application under section 54(3) of that Act; or
  (b) an application made for such an order in respect of C is refused, withdrawn or otherwise terminated and any time limit for an appeal or a new application has expired."

The Jobseeker's Allowance (18-21 Work Skills Pilot Scheme) Regulations 2014

(SI 2014/3117)

In force November 25, 2014

ARRANGEMENT OF REGULATIONS

PART 1

GENERAL

PART 2

SELECTION FOR AND PARTICIPATION IN PHASE ONE OF THE 18-21 WORK SKILLS PILOT SCHEME

PART 3

SELECTION FOR AND PARTICIPATION IN PHASE TWO OF THE 18-21 WORK SKILLS PILOT SCHEME

PART 4

EXEMPTIONS FROM REQUIREMENT TO MEET THE JOBSEEKING CONDITIONS

14. Exemptions from requirement to meet the jobseeking conditions

PART 5

CONSEQUENTIAL AMENDMENTS

15. Notional income
16. Notional capital
17. Income to be disregarded
18. Capital to be disregarded
19. Further modifications of the Jobseeker's Allowance Regulations

PART 6

CONTRACTING OUT

20. Contracting out certain functions

The Secretary of State for Work and Pensions makes the following Regulations in exercise of the powers conferred by sections 123(1)(d), 136(5)(a) and (b), 137(1) and 175(1), (3), (4) and (6) of the Social Security Contributions and Benefits Act 1992, sections 12(4)(a) and (b), 17A(1), (2), (5)(a) and (b), 20E(3)(a), 29, 35(1) and 36(2), (4) and (4A) of the Jobseekers Act 1995 and sections 30 and 146(1) and (2) of the Housing Grants, Construction and Regeneration Act 1996.

These Regulations are made with a view to ascertaining whether their provisions will, or will be likely to, encourage persons to obtain or remain in work or will, or will be likely to, make it more likely that persons will obtain or remain in work or be able to do so.

These Regulations are made with the consent of the Treasury in respect of provisions relating to section 30 of the Housing Grants, Construction and Regeneration Act 1996.

In respect of provisions in these Regulations relating to housing benefit, organisations appearing to the Secretary of State to be representative of the authorities concerned have agreed that consultations need not be undertaken.

The Social Security Advisory Committee has agreed that the proposals in respect of these Regulations should not be referred to it.

A draft of this instrument was laid before Parliament in accordance with section 37(2) of the Jobseekers Act 1995 and approved by a resolution of each House of Parliament.

PART 1

GENERAL

Citation, commencement and duration

1.205   **1.**—(1) These Regulations may be cited as the Jobseeker's Allowance (18-21 Work Skills Pilot Scheme) Regulations 2014 and come into force on the day after the day on which they are made.

(2) They cease to have effect at the end of the period of 24 months beginning with the day on which they come into force.

Interpretation

1.206   **2.**—(1) In these Regulations—

"the Act" means the Jobseekers Act 1995;

"the Jobseeker's Allowance Regulations" means the Jobseeker's Allowance Regulations 1996;

"the Housing Renewal Grants Regulations" means the Housing Renewal Grants Regulations 1996;

"the Housing Benefit Regulations" means the Housing Benefit Regulations 2006;

"claimant" means a person who claims a jobseeker's allowance, except that in relation to a joint-claim couple claiming a joint-claim jobseeker's allowance, it means either or both of the members of the couple;

"Level 2 qualification" means—

(a) a qualification defined as a Level 2 qualification within the National Qualification Framework regulated by the Office of Qualifications and Examinations Regulation; or

(b) an equivalent qualification within the European Qualifications Framework; or

(c) any other qualification that the Secretary of State considers is equivalent to a qualification mentioned in paragraphs (a) or (b);

"Phase One" has the meaning given to it in regulation 3(3) to (6);

"Phase Two" has the meaning given to it in regulation 3(7);

"pilot area" means a Jobcentre Plus district of the Department for Work and Pensions, by whatever name it is from time to time known, which is identified by reference to its name at the date these Regulations come into force as listed below—

(a) Black Country;

(b) Devon, Somerset and Cornwall;

(c) Kent;

(d) Mercia;

"the Scheme" has the meaning given to it in regulation 3(2);

"the Scheme provider" means the person or persons delivering the Scheme pursuant to arrangements made by the Secretary of State.

(2) For the purpose of these Regulations, where a written notice is given by sending it by post it is taken to have been received on the second

working day (which means any day except for a Saturday, a Sunday, Christmas Day, Good Friday or a bank holiday under the Banking and Financial Dealings Act 1971 in England) after posting.

The 18-21 Work Skills Pilot Scheme

3.—(1) The 18-21 Work Skills Pilot Scheme is prescribed for the purposes of section 17A(1) (schemes for assisting persons to obtain employment: "work for your benefit" schemes etc) of the Act.   **1.207**

(2) The 18-21 Work Skills Pilot Scheme ("the Scheme") is a scheme that consists of two phases as described in paragraphs (3) to (7).

(3) Phase One is designed to provide claimants selected in accordance with regulation 4 with skills training in English or Maths (or both) for up to 16 hours per week for a cumulative period of up to 6 months to help claimants develop skills in one or both subjects in order to assist them to obtain employment.

(4) Phase One begins with an assessment of a claimant by the Scheme provider.

(5) A claimant participating in Phase One may be required to undertake skills training in English or Maths (or both) where, following that assessment, the Secretary of State is satisfied that the claimant does not possess skills in one or both subjects at a standard equivalent to that required to obtain a Level 2 qualification.

(6) Phase One may also include further assessments of claimants' skills.

(7) Phase Two is designed to provide claimants selected in accordance with regulation 10 with work-related activity or skills training (or both) for up to 30 hours per week for a cumulative period of up to 6 months to help claimants develop skills or gain experience (or both) relevant to the work place in order to assist them to obtain employment.

DEFINITIONS

"the Act"—see reg.2(1).
"claimant"—*ibid.*
"employment"—see Jobseekers Act 1995 s.35(1), and JSA Regulations 1996 reg.3.
"Level 2 qualification"—see reg.2(1).
"the Scheme provider"—*ibid.*
"week"—see Jobseekers Act 1995 s.35(1).

PART 2

SELECTION FOR AND PARTICIPATION IN PHASE ONE OF THE 18-21 WORK SKILLS PILOT SCHEME

Selection for participation in Phase One of the Scheme

4.—(1) The Secretary of State may select on a sampling basis a claimant ("C") for participation in Phase One of the Scheme if the following circumstances are met.   **1.208**

(2) The first circumstance is that C has reached the age of 18 and has not yet reached the age of 22 on the day on which C makes or is treated as making a claim for a jobseeker's allowance.

(3) The second circumstance is that C's claim for a jobseeker's allowance is made or treated as made on or after the date that these Regulations come into force.

(4) The third circumstance is that C is registered at a Jobcentre Plus office that is located within a pilot area.

(5) The fourth circumstance is that C is required to meet the jobseeking conditions.

(6) The fifth circumstance is that C has not provided evidence of a Level 2 qualification in English or Maths or both.

DEFINITIONS

"claimant"—see reg.2(1).
"employment"—see Jobseekers Act 1995 s.35(1), and JSA Regulations 1996 reg.3.
"the jobseeking conditions"—see Jobseekers Act 1995 ss.17A(10) and 1(2)(a)–(c).
"Level 2 qualification"—see reg.2(1).
"Phase One"—see regs 2(1) and 3(3)—(6).
"pilot area"—see reg.2(1).
"the Scheme"—see regs 2(1) and 3(2).

Requirement to participate in Phase One of the Scheme and initial notification

1.209 **5.**—(1) Subject to regulation 7, a claimant ("C") selected in accordance with regulation 4 is required to participate in Phase One of the Scheme, including attending an assessment with the Scheme provider, where the Secretary of State gives C a notice in writing complying with paragraph (2).

(2) The notice must specify—

(a) that C is required to participate in Phase One of the Scheme, including attending an assessment with the Scheme provider;

(b) a description of Phase One of the Scheme in which C is required to participate;

(c) the day on which C is required to start participation in Phase One of the Scheme;

(d) the date, time and location at which the assessment will take place;

(e) the purpose of the assessment;

(f) that the requirement to participate in Phase One of the Scheme will continue until any of the circumstances in sub-paragraphs (a) to (d) of regulation 7(2) apply; and

(g) the consequences of failing to participate in Phase One of the Scheme, including failing to attend an assessment with the Scheme provider.

(3) Any changes to the details mentioned in paragraph (2) must be notified by the Secretary of State to C in writing.

DEFINITIONS

"claimant"—see reg.2(1).
"Phase One"—see regs 2(1) and 3(3)—(6).
"pilot area"—see reg.2(1).
"the Scheme"—see regs 2(1) and 3(2).
"the Scheme provider"—see reg.2(1).
"writing"—see Interpretation Act 1978 Sch.1.

Subsequent notifications

6.—(1) Subject to regulation 7, a claimant ("C") who, following an   1.210
assessment in accordance with regulation 5 or 8, the Secretary of State
is satisfied does not possess skills in English or Maths or both at a
standard equivalent to the skills required to obtain a Level 2 qualification
is required to—
(a) attend skills training in English or Maths or both; and
(b) participate in further assessments if appropriate;
where the Secretary of State gives C a notice in writing complying with
paragraph (2).
(2) The notice must specify—
(a) details of what C is required to do by way of continued participation in Phase One of the Scheme; and
(b) information about the consequences of failing to continue to
participate in Phase One of the Scheme.
(3) Any changes to the details mentioned in paragraph (2) must be
notified by the Secretary of State to C in writing.

DEFINITIONS

"claimant"—see reg.2(1).
"Level 2 qualification"—*ibid.*
"Phase One"—see regs 2(1) and 3(3)–(6).
"the Scheme"—see regs 2(1) and 3(2).
"writing"—see Interpretation Act 1978 Sch.1.

Circumstances in which requirement to participate in Phase One of the Scheme is suspended or ceases to apply

7.—(1) The requirement for C to participate in Phase One of the   1.211
Scheme does not apply for any period during which the Jobseeker's
Allowance Regulations apply so that C is not required to meet the
jobseeking conditions.
(2) A requirement to participate in Phase One of the Scheme ceases to
apply to C if—
(a) the Secretary of State gives C notice in writing that C is no longer
required to participate in Phase One of the Scheme; or
(b) C has ceased to be registered at a Jobcentre Plus office that is
located within a pilot area; or
(c) C has participated in Phase One of the Scheme for a cumulative
period of 6 months; or
(d) C ceases to be entitled to a jobseeker's allowance.

(3) If the Secretary of State gives C a notice in writing under paragraph (2)(a), the requirement to participate in Phase One of the Scheme ceases to apply on the date specified in the notice.

DEFINTIONS

"the Jobseeker's Allowance Regulations"—see reg.2(1).
"the jobseeking conditions"—see Jobseekers Act 1995 ss.17A(10) and 1(2)(a)–(c).
"Phase One"—see regs 2(1) and 3(3)—(6).
"pilot area"—see reg.2(1).
"the Scheme"—see regs 2(1) and 3(2).
"writing"—see Interpretation Act 1978 Sch.1.

Requirement to recommence participation in Phase One of the Scheme

1.212   **8.**—(1) Where—

(a) a claimant's ("C") requirement to participate in Phase One of the Scheme ceases to apply in accordance with regulation 7(2)(a), (b) or (d); and

(b) the circumstances specified in regulation 4(2) to (6) are met;

the Secretary of State may require C to recommence participation in Phase One of the Scheme, including attending an assessment, by giving C a notice in writing complying with paragraph (2).

(2) The notice must comply with regulation 5(2)(b), (f) and (g) and specify—

(a) that C is required to recommence participation in Phase One of the Scheme, including—

(i) where C has not previously had an assessment with a Scheme provider in accordance with regulation 5(1), that C is required to attend an assessment with the Scheme provider; or

(ii) where C has previously had an assessment with a Scheme provider in accordance with regulation 5(1), that C is required to attend an additional assessment;

(b) the day on which C is required to recommence participation in Phase One of the Scheme;

(c) the date, time and location at which the assessment will take place; and

(d) the purpose of the assessment.

(3) Any changes to the details mentioned in paragraph (2) must be notified by the Secretary of State to C in writing.

DEFINTIONS

"claimant"—see reg.2(1).
"Phase One"—see regs 2(1) and 3(3)–(6).
"the Scheme"—see regs 2(1) and 3(2).
"the Scheme provider"—see reg.2(1).
"writing"—see Interpretation Act 1978 Sch.1.

Part 1

SELECTION FOR AND PARTICIPATION IN PHASE TWO OF THE 18-21 WORK SKILLS PILOT SCHEME

Selection for participation in Phase Two of the Scheme

9.—(1) The Secretary of State may select a claimant ("C") for   1.213
participation in Phase Two of the Scheme if the following circumstances
are met.

(2) The first circumstance is that C has reached the age of 18 but has
not yet reached the age of 22 on the day on which C has been in receipt
of a jobseeker's allowance for 6 months or longer.

(3) The second circumstance is that C has been in receipt of a
jobseeker's allowance for 6 months or longer.

(4) The third circumstance is that C is registered at a Jobcentre Plus
office that is located within a pilot area.

(5) The fourth circumstance is that C is required to meet the jobseeking conditions.

(6) The fifth circumstance is that C is not required to participate in
Phase One of the Scheme.

DEFINITIONS

"claimant"—see reg.2(1).
"the jobseeking conditions"—see Jobseekers Act 1995 ss.17A(10) and
   1(2)(a)–(c).
"Phase One"—see regs 2(1) and 3(3)–(6).
"Phase Two"—see regs 2(1) and 3(7).
"pilot area"—see reg.2(1).
"the Scheme"—see regs 2(1) and 3(2).

Requirement to participate in Phase Two of the Scheme and initial notification

10.—(1) Subject to regulation 12, a claimant ("C") selected in accor-   1.214
dance with regulation 9 is required to participate in Phase Two of the
Scheme where the Secretary of State gives C a notice in writing complying with paragraph (2).

(2) The notice must specify—

(a) that C is required to participate in Phase Two of the Scheme;
(b) a description of Phase Two of the Scheme in which C is required
    to participate;
(c) the day on which C is required to start participation in Phase Two
    of the Scheme;
(d) that the requirement to participate in Phase Two of the Scheme
    will continue until any of the circumstances in sub-paragraphs (a)
    to (d) of regulation 12(2) apply; and
(e) information about the consequences of failing to participate in
    Phase Two of the Scheme.

(3) Any changes to the details mentioned in paragraph (2) must be notified by the Secretary of State to C in writing.

"claimant"—see reg.2(1).
"Level 2 qualification"—*ibid.*
"Phase Two"—see regs 2(1) and 3(7).
"the Scheme"—see regs 2(1) and 3(2).
"writing"—see Interpretation Act 1978 Sch.1.

Subsequent notifications

1.215   **11.**—(1) Subject to regulation 12, a claimant ("C") notified in accordance with regulation 10 must be given a further notice in writing by the Secretary of State complying with paragraph (2) before C can be required to undertake any work-related activity or skills training.
(2) The notice must specify—
(a) details of what C is required to do by way of participation in Phase Two of the Scheme; and
(b) information about the consequences of failing to participate in Phase Two of the Scheme.
(3) Any changes to the details mentioned in paragraph (2) must be notified by the Secretary of State to C in writing.

"claimant"—see reg.2(1).
"Phase Two"—see regs 2(1) and 3(7).
"the Scheme"—see regs 2(1) and 3(2).
"writing"—see Interpretation Act 1978 Sch.1.

Circumstances in which requirement to participate in Phase Two of the Scheme is suspended or ceases to apply

1.216   **12.**—(1) The requirement for C to participate in Phase Two of the Scheme does not apply for any period during which the Jobseeker's Allowance Regulations apply so that C is not required to meet the jobseeking conditions.
(2) A requirement to participate in Phase Two of the Scheme ceases to apply to C if—
(a) the Secretary of State gives C notice in writing that C is no longer required to participate in Phase Two of the Scheme; or
(b) C has ceased to be registered at a Jobcentre Plus office that is located within a pilot area; or
(c) C has participated in Phase Two of the Scheme for a cumulative period of 6 months; or
(d) C ceases to be entitled to a jobseeker's allowance.
(3) If the Secretary of State gives C a notice in writing under paragraph (2)(a), the requirement to participate in Phase Two of the Scheme ceases to apply on the day specified in the notice.

"the Jobseeker's Allowance Regulations"—see reg.2(1).
"the jobseeking conditions"—see Jobseekers Act 1995 ss.17A(10) and
1(2)(a)–(c).
"Phase Two"—see regs 2(1) and 3(7).
"pilot area"—see reg.2(1).
"the Scheme"—see regs 2(1) and 3(2).
"writing"—see Interpretation Act 1978 Sch.1.

Requirement to recommence participation in Phase Two of the Scheme

13.—(1) Where   1.217
(a) a claimant's ("C") requirement to participate in Phase Two of the
Scheme ceases to apply in accordance with regulation 12(2)(a),
(b) or (d); and
(b) the circumstances specified in regulation 9(2) to (6) are met,
the Secretary of State may require C to recommence participation in
Phase Two of the Scheme by giving C a new written notice complying
with regulation 10(2).

(2) Any changes to the details mentioned in paragraph (1) must be
notified by the Secretary of State to C in writing.

"claimant"—see reg.2(1).
"Phase Two"—see regs 2(1) and 3(7).
"the Scheme"—see regs 2(1) and 3(2).
"writing"—see Interpretation Act 1978 Sch.1.

PART 4

EXEMPTIONS FROM REQUIREMENT TO MEET THE JOBSEEKING CONDITIONS

Exemptions from requirement to meet the jobseeking conditions

14.—(1) A claimant who is participating in the Scheme is not required   1.218
to meet the conditions set out in section 1(2)(a) and (c) of the Act
(conditions for entitlement to a jobseeker's allowance: available for and
actively seeking employment) if the claimant is a full-time student.

(2) A claimant who is participating in the Scheme is not required to
meet the conditions set out in section 1(2)(a) and (c) of the Act if the
claimant has been discharged from detention in a prison, remand centre
or youth custody institution, for one week commencing with the date of
that discharge.

(3) In this regulation, "full-time student" has the same meaning as in
regulation 1(3) of the Jobseeker's Allowance Regulations.

DEFINITIONS

"the Act"—see reg.2(1).
"claimant"—*ibid.*
"the Jobseeker's Allowance Regulations"—*ibid.*
"Phase Two"—see regs 2(1) and 3(7).
"the Scheme"—see regs 2(1) and 3(2).

PART 5

CONSEQUENTIAL AMENDMENTS

Notional income

1.219 **15.**—(1) This regulation applies to the following provisions (which relate to notional income)—
(a) regulation 42(7) of the Housing Benefit Regulations;
(b) regulation 31(9A) of the Housing Renewal Grants Regulations;
(c) regulation 105(10A) of the Jobseeker's Allowance Regulations.
(2) In each of the provisions to which this regulation applies, after sub-paragraph (cd) insert—

"(ce) in respect of a person's participation in a scheme prescribed in regulation 3 of the Jobseekers Allowance (18 - 21 Work Skills Pilot Scheme) Regulations 2014;"

DEFINITIONS

"the Jobseeker's Allowance Regulations"—see reg.2(1).
"the Housing Renewal Grant Regulations"—*ibid.*
"the Housing Benefit Regulations"—*ibid.*

Notional capital

1.220 **16.**—(1) This regulation applies to the following provisions (which relate to notional capital)—
(a) regulation 49(4) of the Housing Benefit Regulations;
(b) regulation 38(3A) of the Housing Renewal Grants Regulations;
(c) regulation 113(3A)(f) of the Jobseeker's Allowance Regulations.
(2) In each of the provisions to which this regulation applies, after sub-paragraph (bd) insert—

"(be) in respect of a person's participation in a scheme prescribed in regulation 3 of the Jobseekers Allowance (18 - 21 Work Skills Pilot Scheme) Regulations 2014;".

DEFINITIONS

"the Jobseeker's Allowance Regulations"—see reg.2(1).
"the Housing Renewal Grant Regulations"—*ibid.*
"the Housing Benefit Regulations"—*ibid.*

Income to be disregarded

17.—(1) This regulation applies to the following Schedules (which 1.221 relate to sums to be disregarded in the calculation of income other than earnings)—

(a) Schedule 5 to the Housing Benefit Regulations;
(b) Schedule 3 to the Housing Renewal Grants Regulations;
(c) Schedule 7 to the Jobseeker's Allowance Regulations.

(2) In each of the Schedules to which this regulation applies, after paragraph A4 insert—

"A5. Any payment made to the claimant in respect of any child care, travel or other expenses incurred, or to be incurred, by the claimant in respect of their participation in a scheme prescribed in regulation 3 of the Jobseekers Allowance (18 - 21 Work Skills Pilot Scheme) Regulations 2014.".

DEFINTIONS

"the Jobseeker's Allowance Regulations"—see reg.2(1).
"the Housing Renewal Grant Regulations"—*ibid.*
"the Housing Benefit Regulations"—*ibid.*

Capital to be disregarded

18.—(1) This regulation applies to the following Schedules (which 1.222 relate to capital to be disregarded)—

(a) Schedule 6 to the Housing Benefit Regulations;
(b) Schedule 4 to the Housing Renewal Grants Regulations;
(c) Schedule 8 to the Jobseeker's Allowance Regulations.

(2) In each of the Schedules to which this regulation applies, after paragraph A4 insert—

"A5. Any payment made to the claimant in respect of any child care, travel or other expenses incurred, or to be incurred, by the claimant in respect of their participation in a scheme prescribed in regulation 3 of the Jobseekers Allowance (18 - 21 Work Skills Pilot Scheme) Regulations 2014, but only for 52 weeks beginning with the date of receipt of the payment.".

DEFINTIONS

"the Jobseeker's Allowance Regulations"—see reg.2(1).
"the Housing Renewal Grant Regulations"—*ibid.*
"the Housing Benefit Regulations"—*ibid.*

Further modifications of the Jobseeker's Allowance Regulations

19. In regulation 25(1A) of the Jobseeker's Allowance Regulations, in 1.223 the definition of "relevant notification", after "2013" insert the words ", under a scheme prescribed in regulation 3 of the Jobseekers Allowance (18 - 21 Work Skills Pilot Scheme) Regulations 2014".

DEFINTION

"the Jobseeker's Allowance Regulations"—see reg.2(1).

PART 6

CONTRACTING OUT

Contracting out certain functions

1.224   **20.**—(1) Any function of the Secretary of State specified in paragraph (2) may be exercised by, or by employees of, such person (if any) as may be authorised by the Secretary of State.

(2) The functions are any function under—

(a) regulations 5 and 10 (requirement to participate in the Scheme and notification);

(b) regulations 6 and 11 (subsequent notifications);

(c) regulations 7 and 12 (circumstances in which requirement to participate ceases);

(d) regulations 8 and 13 (requirement to recommence participation in the Scheme).

Statutory Shared Parental Pay (Persons Abroad and Mariners) Regulations 2014

(SI 2014/3134)

In force December 1, 2014

ARRANGEMENT OF REGULATIONS

The Secretary of State, in exercise of the powers conferred by sections 171ZZ3(1) and 171ZZ4(3)(b) of the Social Security Contributions and Benefits Act 1992, and with the concurrence of the Treasury, makes the following Regulations.

This instrument contains only regulations made by virtue of, or consequential upon, section 119 of the Children and Families Act 2014 and is made before the end of the period of 6 months beginning with the coming into force of that enactment.

GENERAL NOTE

These Regulations relate to the treatment under Part 12ZC of the SSCBA   1.226
1992 of persons abroad, persons who work as mariners and persons who work on the continental shelf. The effect is that persons who would otherwise not fulfil the qualifying conditions for entitlement to statutory shared parental pay (ShPP) because of the nature of their employment or the fact that they are outside the United Kingdom will have an entitlement to such pay.

PART 1

GENERAL

Citation and commencement

1.227   **1.** These Regulations may be cited as the Statutory Shared Parental Pay (Persons Abroad and Mariners) Regulations 2014 and come into force on 1st December 2014.

PART 2

STATUTORY SHARED PARENTAL PAY

Interpretation

1.228   **2.** (1) In these Regulations—
"the Act" means the Social Security Contributions and Benefits Act 1992;
"adopter", in relation to a child, means the person with whom a child is, or is expected to be, placed for adoption under the law of the United Kingdom;
"adoption from overseas" means the adoption of a child who enters Great Britain from outside the United Kingdom in connection with or for the purposes of adoption which does not involve the placement of the child for adoption under the law of any part of the United Kingdom;
"EEA" means European Economic Area;
"foreign-going ship" means any ship or vessel which is not a home-trade ship;
"General Regulations" means the Statutory Shared Parental Pay (General) Regulations 2014;
"home-trade ship" includes—
    (a) every ship or vessel employed in trading or going within the following limits—
        (i) the United Kingdom (including for this purpose the Republic of Ireland),
        (ii) the Channel Islands,
        (iii) the Isle of Man, and
        (iv) the continent of Europe between the river Elbe and Brest inclusive;
    (b) every fishing vessel not proceeding beyond the following limits—
        (i) on the South, Latitude 48°30{27}N,
        (ii) on the West, Longitude 12°W, and
        (iii) on the North, Latitude 61°N;

"mariner" means a person who is or has been in employment under a contract of service either as a master or member of the crew of any ship or vessel, or in any other capacity on board any ship or vessel where—

    (a) the employment in that other capacity is for the purposes of that ship or vessel or her crew or any passengers or cargo or mails carried by the ship or vessel; and

    (b) the contract is entered into in the United Kingdom with a view to its performance (in whole or in part) while the ship or vessel is on her voyage,

but does not include a person in so far as their employment is as a serving member of the forces;

"placed for adoption" means—

    (a) placed for adoption under the Adoption and Children Act 2002 or the Adoption and Children (Scotland) Act 2007; or

    (b) placed in accordance with section 22C of the Children Act 1989 with a local authority foster parent who is also a prospective adopter;

"serving member of the forces" means a person, other than one mentioned in Part 2 of Schedule 1, who, being over the age of 16, is a member of any establishment or organisation specified in Part 1 of that Schedule (being a member who gives full pay service) but does not include any such person while absent on desertion;

"statutory shared parental pay (adoption)" means statutory shared parental pay payable where entitlement to that pay arises under regulation 17 or 18 of the General Regulations;

"statutory shared parental pay (birth)" means statutory shared parental pay payable where entitlement to that pay arises under regulation 4 or 5 of the General Regulations.

(2) For the purposes of these regulations, the expressions "ship" and "ship or vessel" include hovercraft, except in regulation 9(2).

(3) For the purposes of these Regulations—

(a) a person is matched with a child for adoption when an adoption agency decides that that person would be a suitable adoptive parent for the child;

(b) in a case where paragraph (a) applies, a person is notified as having been matched with a child on the date that person receives notification of the agency's decision, under regulation 33(3)(a) of the Adoption Agencies Regulations 2005, regulation 28(3) of the Adoption Agencies (Wales) Regulations 2005 or regulation 8(5) of the Adoption Agencies (Scotland) Regulations 2009;

(c) a person is also matched with a child for adoption when a decision has been made in accordance with regulation 22A of the Care Planning, Placement and Case Review (England) Regulations 2010 and an adoption agency has identified that person with whom the child is to be placed in accordance with regulation 12B of the Adoption Agencies Regulations 2005;

(d) in a case where paragraph (c) applies, a person is notified as having been matched with a child on the date on which that person receives notification in accordance with regulation 12B(2)(a) of the Adoption Agencies Regulations 2005.

(4) The reference to "prospective adopter" in the definition of "placed for adoption" in paragraph (1) means a person who has been approved as suitable to adopt a child and has been notified of that decision in accordance with regulation 30B(4) of the Adoption Agencies Regulations 2005.

(5) The reference to "adoption agency" in paragraph (3) has the meaning given, in relation to England and Wales, by section 2 of the Adoption and Children Act 2002 and in relation to Scotland, by section 119(1) of the Adoption and Children (Scotland) Act 2007.

Application

1.229   **3.** These Regulations apply in relation to—
(a) statutory shared parental pay (birth) in respect of children whose expected week of birth begins on or after 5th April 2015;
(b) statutory shared parental pay (adoption) in respect of children placed for adoption on or after 5th April 2015.

Restriction on scope

1.230   **4.** A person who would not be treated under regulation 33 (treatment of persons as employees) of the General Regulations as an employee for the purposes of Part 12ZC (statutory shared parental pay) of the Act if that person's employment were in Great Britain shall not be treated as an employee under these Regulations.

Treatment of persons in other EEA states as employees

1.231   **5.** A person who is—
(a) gainfully employed in an EEA state other than the United Kingdom in such circumstances that, if the employment were in Great Britain, the person would be an employee for the purposes of Part 12ZC of the Act, or a person treated as such an employee under regulation 33 of the General Regulations; and
(b) subject to the legislation of the United Kingdom under Council Regulation (EEC) No.1408/71,
notwithstanding that person not being employed in Great Britain, shall be treated as an employee for the purposes of Parts 12ZC of the Act.

Treatment of certain persons absent from Great Britain as employees

1.232   **6.** Subject to regulation 9(2), where a person, while absent from Great Britain for any purpose, is gainfully employed by an employer who is liable to pay secondary Class 1 contributions (within the meaning of section 1(2) of the Act) in respect of that person's employment under section 6 of the Act or regulation 146 of the Social Security Contributions Regulations 2001, that person shall be treated as an employee for the purposes of Part 12ZC of the Act.

Entitlement to statutory shared parental pay where person has worked in an EEA state

7. (1) A person who—
  (a) is an employee or treated as an employee under regulation 5;
  (b) in the week immediately preceding the 14th week before the expected week of the child's birth was in employed earner's employment with an employer in Great Britain; and
  (c) had in any week within the period of 26 weeks immediately preceding that week been employed by the same employer in another EEA state,

shall be treated for the purposes of section 171ZU of the Act (entitlement to shared parental pay: birth) as having been employed in employed earner's employment with an employer in those weeks in which the person was so employed in the other EEA state.

(2) A person who—
  (a) is an employee or treated as an employee under regulation 5;
  (b) in the week in which the adopter is notified of having been matched with the child for the purposes of adoption was in employed earner's employment with an employer in Great Britain; and
  (c) had in any week within the period of 26 weeks immediately preceding that week been employed by the same employer in another EEA State,

shall be treated for the purposes of section 171ZV of the Act (entitlement to shared parental pay: adoption) as having been employed in employed earner's employment in those weeks in which the person was so employed in the other EEA State.

Time for compliance with Part 12ZC of the Act or regulations made under it

8. Where—
  (a) a person is outside the United Kingdom;
  (b) Part 12ZC of the Act or regulations made under it require any act to be done forthwith or on the happening of a certain event or within a specified time; and
  (c) because the person is outside the United Kingdom that person or that person's employer cannot comply with the requirement,

the person or the employer, as the case may be, shall be deemed to have complied with the requirement if the act is performed as soon as reasonably practicable.

Mariners

9. (1) A mariner engaged in employment on board a home-trade ship with an employer who has a place of business within the United Kingdom shall be treated as an employee for the purposes of Part 12ZC of the Act, notwithstanding that he may not be employed in Great Britain.

(2) A mariner who is engaged in employment—
  (a) on a foreign-going ship; or

1.233

1.234

1.235

(b) on a home-trade ship with an employer who does not have a place of business within the United Kingdom,

shall not be treated as an employee for the purposes of Part 12ZC of the Act, notwithstanding that the mariner may have been employed in Great Britain.

Continental shelf

1.236   **10.** (1) In this regulation—

"designated area" means any area which may from time to time be designated by Order in Council under section 1(7) of the Continental Shelf Act 1964 as an area within which the rights of the United Kingdom with respect to the seabed and subsoil and their natural resources may be exercised;

"prescribed employment" means any employment (whether under a contract of service or not) in a designated area in connection with continental shelf operations, as defined in section 120(2) of the Act.

(2) A person in prescribed employment shall be treated as an employee for the purposes of Part 12ZC of the Act notwithstanding that that person may not be employed in Great Britain.

Adoptions from overseas

1.237   **11.** Schedule 2 applies to adoptions from overseas.

PART 3

STATUTORY PATERNITY PAY AND STATUTORY ADOPTION PAY

1.238   **12.** The Statutory Paternity Pay and Statutory Adoption Pay (Persons Abroad and Mariners) Regulations 2002 are amended as follows.

13. (1) Paragraph (2) of regulation 1 is amended as follows

(2) For the definition "adopter" substitute—

""adopter", in relation to a child, means the person with whom a child is, or is expected to be, placed for adoption under the law of the United Kingdom;".

(3) Before the definition of "serving member of the forces" insert—

""placed for adoption" means—

(a) placed for adoption under the Adoption and Children Act 2002 or the Adoption and Children (Scotland) Act 2007; or

(b) placed in accordance with section 22C of the Children Act 1989 with a local authority foster parent who is also a prospective adopter;".

14. For paragraph (3) of regulation 1 substitute—

"(3) For the purposes of these Regulations—

(a) a person is matched with a child for adoption when an adoption agency decides that that person would be a suitable adoptive parent for the child;

(b) in a case where paragraph (a) applies, a person is notified as having been matched with a child on the date that person receives notification of the agency's decision, under regulation 33(3)(a) of the Adoption Agencies Regulations 2005, regulation 28(3) of the Adoption Agencies (Wales) Regulations 2005 or regulation 8(5) of the Adoption Agencies (Scotland) Regulations 2009;

(c) a person is also matched with a child for adoption when a decision has been made in accordance with regulation 22A of the Care Planning, Placement and Case Review (England) Regulations 2010 and an adoption agency has identified that person with whom the child is to be placed in accordance with regulation 12B of the Adoption Agencies Regulations 2005;

(d) in a case where paragraph (c) applies, a person is notified as having been matched with a child on the date on which that person receives notification in accordance with regulation 12B(2)(a) of the Adoption Agencies Regulations 2005.

(3A) The reference to "prospective adopter" in the definition of "placed for adoption" in paragraph (2) means a person who has been approved as suitable to adopt a child and has been notified of that decision in accordance with regulation 30B(4) of the Adoption Agencies Regulations 2005.

(3B) The reference to "adoption agency" in paragraph (3) has the meaning given, in relation to England and Wales, by section 2 of the Adoption and Children Act 2002 and in relation to Scotland, by section 119(1) of the Adoption and Children (Scotland) Act 2007.".

SCHEDULE 1   Regulation 2(1)

PART 1

ESTABLISHMENTS AND ORGANISATIONS

1. Any of the regular, naval, military or air forces of the Crown.   **1.239**

2. Royal Fleet Reserve.

3. Royal Naval Reserve

4. Royal Marines Reserve.

5. Army Reserve.

6. Territorial Army.

7. Royal Air Force Reserve.

8. Royal Auxiliary Air Force.

9. The Royal Irish Regiment, to the extent that its members are not members of any force falling within paragraph 1.

PART 2

ESTABLISHMENTS AND ORGANISATIONS OF WHICH HER MAJESTY'S FORCES SHALL NOT CONSIST

10. Her Majesty's forces shall not be taken to consist of any of the establishments or organisations specified in Part 1 of this Schedule by virtue only of the employment in such establishment or organisation of the following persons—   **1.240**

   (a) any person who is serving as a member of any naval force of Her Majesty's forces and who (not having been an insured person under the National Insurance Act 1965 and not being a contributor under the Social Security Act 1975 or the Social Security Contributions and Benefits Act 1992) locally entered that force at an overseas base;

   (b) any person who is serving as a member of any military force of Her Majesty's forces and who entered that force, or was recruited for that force outside the United Kingdom, and the depot of whose unit is situated outside the United Kingdom;

   (c) any person who is serving as a member of any air force of Her Majesty's forces and who entered that force, or was recruited for that force, outside the United Kingdom, and is liable under the terms of his engagement to serve only in a specified part of the world outside the United Kingdom.

SCHEDULE 2   **Regulation 11**

ADOPTIONS FROM OVERSEAS

Interpretation

1.241   1. In this Schedule "the Application Regulations" means the Social Security Contributions and Benefits Act 1992 (Application of Parts 12ZA, 12ZB and 12ZC to Adoptions from Overseas) Regulations 2003.

Application to adoptions from overseas

1.242   2. (1) The provisions of these Regulations, in so far as they apply to statutory shared parental pay (adoption) apply to adoptions from overseas with the modifications set out in paragraphs 3 to 6 and subject to sub-paragraphs (2) and (3).

(2) Any references in these Regulations to the provisions of Part 12ZC of the Act must be construed as references to the provisions of Part 12ZC as modified by the Application Regulations.

Modifications of the Regulations for the purposes of adoptions from overseas

1.243   3. The Regulations are modified as follows.

4. (1) Regulation 2 (interpretation) is modified as follows.

(2) In paragraph 1—

(a) for the definition of "adopter" substitute—

> ""adopter", in relation to C, means the person by whom C has been or is to be adopted; ";

(b) for the definition of "statutory shared parental pay (adoption)" substitute—

> ""statutory shared parental pay (adoption)" means statutory shared parental pay payable where entitlement to that pay arises under regulation 17 or 18 of the General Regulations as modified by the Statutory Shared Parental Pay (Adoption from Overseas) Regulations 2014;";

(c) insert the following definitions in the appropriate places alphabetically—

> ""enter Great Britain" means enter Great Britain from outside the United Kingdom in connection with or for the purposes of adoption;";
>
> ""official notification" means written notification, issued by or on behalf of the relevant central authority, that it is prepared to issue a certificate to the overseas authority concerned with the adoption of the child, or that it has issued a certificate and sent it to that authority, confirming, in either case, that the adopter is eligible to adopt, and has been assessed and approved as being a suitable adoptive parent;";
>
> ""relevant central authority" means—

(a) in the case of an adopter to whom Part 3 of the Adoptions with a Foreign Element Regulations 2005 apply and who is habitually resident in Wales, the Welsh Ministers;

(b) in the case of an adopter to whom the Adoptions with a Foreign Element (Scotland) Regulations 2009 apply and who is habitually resident in Scotland, the Scottish Ministers; and

(c) in any other case, the Secretary of State;".

5. In Regulation 3 (application), for paragraph (1)(b) substitute—

"(b) statutory shared parental pay (adoption) in respect of children who enter Great Britain on or after 5th April 2015.".

6. (1) In regulation 7 (entitlement to shared parental pay where person has worked in an EEA State), for paragraph (2) substitute—

"(2) A person who—

(a) is an employee or treated as an employee under regulation 5;

(b) in the week in which the adopter received the official notification was in employed earner's employment with an employer in Great Britain; and

(c) had in any week within the period of 26 weeks immediately preceding that week been employed by the same employer in another EEA State,

shall be treated for the purposes of section 171ZV of the Act (entitlement to shared parental pay: adoption) as modified by the Application Regulations as having been employed in employed earner's employment in those weeks in which the person was so employed in the other EEA State.".

Marriage and Civil Partnership (Scotland) Act 2014 and Civil Partnership Act 2004 (Consequential Provisions and Modifications) Order 2014

(SI 2014/3229)

In force December 16, 2014

ARRANGEMENT OF ARTICLES INCLUDED

PART 1

STATE PENSIONS

The Secretary of State makes the following Order in exercise of the powers conferred by sections 104, 112(1) and 113(2) to (5) and (7) of the Scotland Act 1998 and section 259(1) of the Civil Partnership Act 2004.

In accordance with paragraphs 1, 2 and 3 of Schedule 7 to the Scotland Act 1998 and section 259(8) of the Civil Partnership Act 2004, a draft of this Order has been laid before and approved by a resolution of each House of Parliament.

PART 1

STATE PENSIONS

Category B retirement pension for married person

1.245   **8.**—(1) Section 48A of the 1992 Act (Category B retirement pension for married person) does not confer a right to a Category B retirement pension on a person by reason of the person being married to a person of the same sex who was born before 6th April 1950.

(2) But that does not prevent section 48A from conferring a right to such a pension on a woman by reason of her marriage to another woman ("the spouse") if—

    (a) the spouse is a woman by virtue of a full gender recognition certificate having been issued under the 2004 Act; and

(b) the marriage subsisted before the time when that certificate was issued.

Category B retirement pension for widows and widowers

9.—(1) Section 48B of the 1992 Act (Category B retirement pension for widows and widowers) does not confer a right to a Category B retirement pension on a woman who attained pensionable age before 6th April 2010 by reason of her marriage to another woman.   **1.246**

(2) But that does not prevent section 48B from conferring a right to such a pension on a woman by reason of her marriage to another woman ("the spouse") if—

(a) the spouse was, at the time of her death, a woman by virtue of a full gender recognition certificate having been issued under the 2004 Act; and

(b) the marriage subsisted before the time when that certificate was issued.

Category B retirement pension for widowers

10.—(1) Section 51(1ZA) of the 1992 Act (category B retirement pension for widowers) does not confer a right to a Category B retirement pension on a person if the person attains pensionable age on or after 6th April 2010.   **1.247**

(2) Section 51(1ZA) of the 1992 Act does not confer a right to a Category B retirement pension on a woman by reason of her marriage to another woman ("the spouse") if—

(a) the spouse was, at the time of her death, a woman by virtue of a full gender recognition certificate having been issued under the 2004 Act; and

(b) the marriage subsisted before the time when that certificate was issued.

Adult dependency increases

11.—(1) In a case where a full gender recognition certificate is issued to a person under the 2004 Act—   **1.248**

(a) section 83 of the 1992 Act (pension increase (wife)) does not cease to apply by virtue of the change of gender; and

(b) in the continued application of section 83 in such a case, references to a pension payable to a man, or references to his wife, are to be construed accordingly.

(2) In a case where a full gender recognition certificate is issued to a person under the 2004 Act—

(a) section 84 of the 1992 Act (pension increase (husband)) does not cease to apply by virtue of the change of gender; and

(b) in the continued application of section 84 in such a case, references to a pension payable to a woman, or references to her husband, are to be construed accordingly.

Converted or changed civil partnerships

1.249   **12.**—(1) This article applies where a civil partnership is converted into a marriage under section 9 of the 2013 Act, or is changed into a marriage in accordance with provision made under the 1977 Act, section 10 of the 2014 Act or Part 5 of this Order.

(2) For the purposes of section 48A of, and paragraph 5A(1)(b) of Schedule 3 to, the 1992 Act—

(a) the civil partnership is to be treated as having subsisted during the period that begins with the day when it was formed and ends with the day before the conversion day; and

(b) the marriage is to be treated as subsisting only from the conversion day.

(3) In this article "conversion day" means the day when the civil partnership is converted into a marriage or changed into a marriage.

PART II

UPDATING MATERIAL
VOLUME I

NON MEANS TESTED BENEFITS AND EMPLOYMENT AND SUPPORT ALLOWANCE

Commentary by

David Bonner

Ian Hooker

Richard Poynter

Robin White

Nick Wikeley

David Williams

Penny Wood

p.xxxv, *Table of Cases*

The year in the entry for "*NH v Secretary of State for Work and Pensions*   2.001
(ESA) [2010] UKUT 82 (AAC) . . . .9.385" should be corrected to
[2011].

p.42, *amendment to the Social Security Contributions and Benefits Act
1992 s.36 (Bereavement payment)*

With effect from March 13, 2014, art.2 and Sch.1, para.22(2) of the   2.002
Marriage (Same Sex Couples) Act 2013 (Consequential and Contrary
Provisions and Scotland) Order 2014 (SI 2014/560) amended s.36(2) by
substituting the following:

> "(2) A bereavement payment shall not be payable to a person if that
> person and a person whom that person was not married to, or in a civil
> partnership with, were living together as a married couple at the time
> of the spouse's or civil partner's death.".

p.44, *amendment to the Social Security Contributions and Benefits Act
1992 s.37 (Widowed mother's allowance)*

With effect from March 13, 2014, art.2 and Sch.1, para.22(3) of the   2.003
Marriage (Same Sex Couples) Act 2013 (Consequential and Contrary
Provisions and Scotland) Order 2014 (SI 2014/560) amended s.37(4) by
inserting "or" after paragraph (a) and substituting for paras.(b) and (c)
the following:

> "(b) for any period during which she and a person whom she is not
> married to, or in a civil partnership with, are living together as a
> married couple.".

p.46, *amendment to the Social Security Contributions and Benefits Act
1992 s.38 (Widow's pension)*

With effect from March 13, 2014, art.2 and Sch.1, para.22(4) of the   2.004
Marriage (Same Sex Couples) Act 2013 (Consequential and Contrary
Provisions and Scotland) Order 2014 (SI 2014/560) amended s.38(3) by
inserting "or" after paragraph (b) and substituting for paras (c) and (d)
the following:

> "(c) for any period during which she and a person whom she is not
> married to, or in a civil partnership with, are living together as a
> married couple."

p.48, *amendment to the Social Security Contributions and Benefits Act
1992 s.39A (Widowed parent's allowance)*

With effect from March 13, 2014, art.2 and Sch.1, para.22(5) of the   2.005
Marriage (Same Sex Couples) Act 2013 (Consequential and Contrary
Provisions and Scotland) Order 2014 (SI 2014/560) amended s.39A(5)

by inserting "or" after paragraph (a) and substituting for paras (b) and (c) the following:

"(b) for any period during which the surviving spouse or civil partner and a person whom she or he is not married to, or in a civil partnership with, are living together as a married couple."

p.50, *amendment to the Social Security Contributions and Benefits Act 1992 s.39B (Bereavement allowance where no dependent children)*

2.006   With effect from March 13, 2014, art.2 and Sch.1, para.22(6) of the Marriage (Same Sex Couples) Act 2013 (Consequential and Contrary Provisions and Scotland) Order 2014 (SI 2014/560) amended s.39B(5) by inserting "or" after paragraph (a) and substituting for paras.(b) and (c) the following:

"(b) for any period during which the surviving spouse or civil partner and a person whom she or he is not married to, or in a civil partnership with, are living together as a married couple."

p.54, *annotation to the Social Security Contributions and Benefits Act 1992 ss.36–39C (Proof of a valid marriage)*

2.006.1   The rule of law that, in Scotland, provided for marriage by cohabitation with habit and repute was abolished with effect from May 6, 2006 (Family Law (Scotland) Act 2006). That abolition is, however, prospective only; couples whose living arrangements began before that date may still take advantage of the rule—see s.3(2) of the Act. Furthermore, in the special case of a widow or a widower whose marriage was celebrated outside the United Kingdom and has subsequently been discovered to have been invalid, the rule may still be applied even if the cohabitation with habit and repute began after May 2006. But this will only apply where the surviving party became aware of the invalidity of the marriage after the spouse's death—see s.3(3) and s.3(4). Note that these provisions require only that the parties are domiciled in Scotland, which does not necessarily mean they are resident in Scotland; however, the rule of marriage by cohabitation with habit and repute applies only when the parties are cohabiting in Scotland, which means that both domicile and residence will need to relate to Scotland.

p.56, *annotation to the Social Security Contributions and Benefits Act 1992 General note to ss.36–39C (Validity of marriage—foreign marriages)*

2.007   Although the capacity of a person to marry is determined by that person's domicile at the time of the marriage it should be noted that the formalities of a marriage (sometimes referred to as the formal validity of that marriage) are determined by the law of the place that the marriage takes place. Thus, an Englishman can effect a valid marriage in Las Vegas, or on the beach in the Bahamas, provided that the ceremony is in accordance with the law of that place. Further complications arise, however, where the place that the marriage occurs is unclear. That was the problem in *SB v SSWP* [2014] UKUT 496 (AAC). The claimant was the widow of a man originally from Pakistan. She married him in Pakistan and had three children by him. Her claim for bereavement benefits had been refused because there was evidence that the deceased had been married already at the time of the claimant's marriage and there was no evidence that that marriage had been dissolved, or that his first wife had predeceased him. The factual background was confused, but by the time the case came before the Upper Tribunal it had become clear that the earlier marriage had been conducted by telephone at a time that the deceased was in the UK and the putative wife was in Pakistan. The question was, therefore, by what law the ceremony of marriage should be governed when the parties were in different places; or to put it another way—what is the place of a marriage transacted on the telephone? The decision of Judge West in the UT is unequivocal—to be valid the marriage must be valid by the laws of both places. As a telephone marriage is not valid in the UK it followed that the first marriage of the deceased had been void and that the claimant's marriage was, therefore, good and her claim succeeded. This appears to be the first time that the validity of a telephonic marriage has been determined in English law. Judge West applied various opinions from earlier cases and the view expressed by the editors of Dicey and Morris *Conflict of Laws* and he rejects the view expressed in a recent decision by the Scottish courts, but the decision that he has reached was in accordance with the revised opinion expressed on behalf of the Secretary of State and represented the considered views of other departments of state (e.g. the Border Agency) to whom these are matters of great concern.

p.60, *annotation to the Social Security Contributions and Benefits Act 1992 s.36-39C*

The Presumption of Death Act 2013 came into force on October 1, 2014. Henceforth, a spouse or civil partner will be able to apply for a declaration of presumption of death where a person who is missing is thought to have died, or where they have not been known to be alive for at least seven years.   2.008

p.61, *annotation to the Social Security Contributions and Benefits Act 1992 ss.36-39C (Forfeiture rule—relief against forfeiture)*

BC v SSWP [2014] UKUT 237 (AAC) is a further example of the claimant's being relieved entirely of the effect of the forfeiture rule. The claimant had been convicted of the manslaughter of her husband after pleading guilty at trial. The death resulted from a drunken brawl after many years in a violent marriage. The trial judge imposed only a three year period of probation as her sentence. The Upper Tribunal Judge took account of the leniency of the sentence in deciding that the relief against forfeiture should be given in full—thus the claimant was able to rely upon her deceased husband's contribution record in now making a claim for retirement pension. Although the claimant had delayed making her claim for many years (and the rules against back-dating a claim would apply) the relief was granted, with effect from the date of her   2.009

conviction, so that she was able to take advantage of the enhancement by deferment that had occurred.

p.63, *annotation to the Social Security Contributions and Benefits Act 1992 ss.36-39C (Living together as husband and wife or as if in a civil partnership)*

2.010   The concept of "living together" continues to show room for development. Although the extension to civil partnership, and now to same-sex marriage may have the effect of moving the focus away from questions involving the sexual relationship it is clear that the courts and the Upper Tribunal judges will insist upon something that shows, not merely mutual support, but a loving and emotional relationship that is fundamental to all forms of marriage (at least at the outset). Furthermore, these recent cases show a return to the idea that the parties must be prepared to acknowledge publicly that that is the nature of their relationship. In *JP v SSWP* [2014] UKUT 17 (AAC) Judge Levenson had to consider the case of a widow who had been in receipt of Income Support for some years when it was stopped because it was learned that she shared her home with another woman. They owned the house as tenants-in-common and had a joint mortgage. They shared all household expenses but otherwise lived separate and independent lives. When giving leave to appeal the judge observed that if two people of the same sex had not entered into a civil partnership he thought it would require compelling evidence to show that they were living together as if they had done. Indeed, in reaching the decision that these two women were not living as civil partners he says (at para.33):

> "It seems to me that in cases involving a suggestion that a couple are living together as if they were husband and wife or as though they were civil partners the current state of the law is that a committed emotional loving relationship must be established and publicly acknowledged. The traditional signposts might be able to help establish these matters but Mr Justice Lewison's reasoning [in *Bayer v Hedger and others* [2008] EWCH 1587 (Ch)] is key on the question of statutory construction. An unacknowledged relationship cannot be the equivalent of marriage or a registered civil partnership which are, in their very nature, public acknowledgement of an emotional relationship. In the case of same sex relationships, for the reasons that I have discussed above, some of the traditional signposts are of less assistance. It is for those alleging that two people are a couple within the meaning of section 137(1) to prove that there is a publicly acknowledged committed emotional loving relationship."

p.71, *annotation to the Social Security Contributions and Benefits Act 1992 s.43 and following—Pensions Act 2014*

2.011   The Pensions Act 2014 received Royal Assent on May 14, 2014. It provides for major changes both to public pensions and private pensions. Part 1 (State Pensions) resets the regime currently established by SSCBA 1992 ss.43 to 55C and s.62. It is being brought into effect in stages, with the most important changes currently scheduled for April 6, 2016. As it does so the relevant provisions of SSCBA 1992 and amending legislation, including prospective amendments in the Pensions Act 2008, are repealed.

At the "headline" level, however, one of its major changes is already in effect. The publicly funded universal pensions for older UK residents are no longer retirement pensions (as they are termed in SSCBA and other previous legislation). They are state pensions. This in part reflects the shifts in state pensionable age (dealt with by Part 3 of the 2014 Act) and the removal of any link between payment of the pension and actual retirement. Part 2 (option to boost old retirement pensions) is also partially in effect. This enables government to introduce regulations to create a new Class 3A contribution to allow contributors to make voluntary contributions to increase their entitlements to a state pension under the "old" provisions. This is not yet fully in effect and is largely beyond the scope of this volume.

For a full statement of the policy behind these changes, including a useful executive summary, see the Government White Paper *The single-tier pension: a simple foundation for saving*, CM 8528.

For a full list of those sections relevant to this work and currently in force see Part 7 of the Act (fully in force), the Pensions Act 2014 (Commencement No. 2) Order 2014 (SI 2014/2377) made on September 2014 and the Pensions Act (Commencement No. 3) Order 2014 (SI 2014/2727) made on October 11, 2014. All relevant provisions currently in effect are noted in this updater.

p.83, *amendment to the Social Security Contributions and Benefits Act 1992 s.45*

With effect from October 1, 2014, Sch.15, para.7 of the Pensions Act 2014 amended s.45(1) by inserting after "shall be" the following: 2.012

"the sum of the following—
  (a) in relation to any surpluses in the pensioner's earnings factors,";

and inserting at the end "; and (b) if the pensioner has one or more units of additional pension, a specified amount for each of those units."

The same amending provision inserted "; and (e) if the pensioner has one or more units of additional pension, a specified amount for each of those units." at the end of paragraph (2)(d) and inserted after subsection (2) the following new paragraph:

"(2A) For the purposes of subsections (1)(b) and (2)(e) the "specified amount" is an amount to be specified by the Secretary of State in regulations."

p.87, *amendment to the Social Security Contributions and Benefits Act 1992 s.46*

With effect from October 1, 2014, the provisions in the Pensions Act 2008 amending this section were repealed, but not further replaced, by   2.013

Pensions Act 2014 Sch.4, para.96. These are noted under amendment 6 to the section.

p.89, *amendment to the Social Security Contributions and Benefits Act 1992 s.48 (Use of former spouse's contributions)*

2.014   With effect from December 10, 2014, Sch.7 para.30 of the Marriage (Same Sex Couples) Act 2013 amended this section (in England and Wales only) by inserting after subsection (4) the following:

"(5) For the purposes of this section, a civil partnership is not to be treated as having terminated by reason of its having been converted into a marriage under section 9 of the Marriage (Same Sex Couples) Act 2013."

However, with effect from December 12, 2014, Sch.4, para.2(7) of the Marriage and Civil Partnership (Scotland) Act 2014 and Civil Partnership Act 2004 (Consequential Provisions and Modifications) Order 2014 (SI 2014/3229) further amended this section (in England, Wales and Scotland) by inserting the following after subsection (4)—

"(5) For the purposes of this section, a civil partnership is not to be treated as having terminated by reason of its having been—
  (a) converted into a marriage under section 9 of the Marriage (Same Sex Couples) Act 2013;
  (b) changed into a marriage under the Marriage (Scotland) Act 1977;
  (c) changed into a marriage in accordance with provision made under section 10 of the Marriage and Civil Partnership (Scotland) Act 2014; or
  (d) changed into a marriage under Part 5 of the Marriage and Civil Partnership (Scotland) Act 2014 and Civil Partnership Act 2004 (Consequential Provisions and Modifications) Order 2014.".

p.89, *amendments to the Social Security Contributions and Benefits Act 1992 s.48A (Category B retirement pension for married person)*

2.015   Note that the modifications made to this section by the Marriage (Same Sex Couples) Act 2013, inserting subss.(2ZA) and (2ZB), have been extended from England and Wales to Scotland with effect from December 16, 2014 by the Marriage and Civil Partnership (Scotland) Act 2014 and Civil Partnership Act 2004 (Consequential Provisions and Modifications) Order 2014 (SI 2014/3229), art.5(3) and Sch.4, para.2(8).

p.89, *annotation to the Social Security Contributions and Benefits Act 1992 s.48A (Category B retirement pension for married person)*

2.016   With effect from October 1, 2014, the provisions in the Pensions Act 2008 amending this section were repealed, but not further replaced, by

Pensions Act 2014 Sch.4, para.96. These are noted under amendment 9 to the section.

p.91, *amendments to the Social Security Contributions and Benefits Act 1992 s.48B (Category B retirement pension for widows and widowers)*

Note that the modifications made to this section by the Marriage (Same Sex Couples) Act 2013, including the insertion of subss.(1ZA)(c) and (1ZB), have been extended from England and Wales to Scotland with effect from December 16, 2014 by the Marriage and Civil Partnership (Scotland) Act 2014 and Civil Partnership Act 2004 (Consequential Provisions and Modifications) Order 2014 (SI 2014/3229), art.5(3) and Sch.4, para.2(9).   2.017

p.91, *annotation to the Social Security Contributions and Benefits Act 1992 s.48B (Category B retirement pension for widows and widowers)*

With effect from October 1, 2014, the provisions in the Pensions Act 2008 amending this section were repealed, but not further replaced, by Pensions Act 2014 Sch.4, para.96. These are noted under amendment 8 to the section.   2.018

p.94, *annotation to the Social Security Contributions and Benefits Act 1992 s.48BB (Category B retirement pension: entitlement by reference to benefits under section 39A or 39B)*

With effect from October 1, 2014, the provisions in the Pensions Act 2008 amending this section were repealed, but not further replaced, by Pensions Act 2014 Sch.4, para.96. These are noted under amendment 7 to the section.   2.019

p.95, *annotation to the Social Security Contributions and Benefits Act 1992 s.48C (Category B retirement pension: general)*

With effect from October 1, 2014, the provisions in the Pensions Act 2008 amending this section were repealed, but not further replaced, by Pensions Act 2014 Sch.4, para.96. These are noted under amendment 6 to the section.   2.020

p.96, *amendments to the Social Security Contributions and Benefits Act 1992 s.51 (Category B retirement pension for widowers)*

Note that the modifications made to this section by the Marriage (Same Sex Couples) Act 2013, including the insertion of subs.(1ZA), have been extended from England and Wales to Scotland with effect from December 16, 2014 by the Marriage and Civil Partnership (Scotland) Act 2014 and Civil Partnership Act 2004 (Consequential Provisions and Modifications) Order 2014 (SI 2014/3229) art.5(3) and Sch.4, para.2(10).   2.021

p.96, *annotation to the Social Security Contributions and Benefits Act 1992 s.51 (Category B retirement pension for widowers)*

2.022   With effect from October 1, 2014, the provisions in the Pensions Act 2008 amending this section were repealed, but not further replaced, by Pensions Act 2014 Sch.4, para.96. These are noted under amendment 5 to the section.

p.104, *amendments to the Social Security Contributions and Benefits Act 1992 s.62 (Graduated retirement benefit)*

2.023   Note that the modifications made to this section by the Marriage (Same Sex Couples) Act 2013, including the insertion of subs.(1ZA), have been extended from England and Wales to Scotland with effect from December 16, 2014 by the Marriage and Civil Partnership (Scotland) Act 2014 and Civil Partnership Act 2004 (Consequential Provisions and Modifications) Order 2014 (SI 2014/3229) art.5(3) and Sch.4, para.2(11).

p.143, *annotation to the Social Security Contributions and Benefits Act 1992 s.72 (Attention in connection with bodily functions)*

2.024   Assistance given to a person by pushing them in a manual wheelchair when they are unable to walk or to move the wheelchair by themselves, is attention given in connection with the function of walking—see *SJ v SSWP* [2014] UKUT 222(AAC).

p.178, *annotation to the Social Security Contributions and Benefits Act 1992 (SSCBA 1992) s.78 (Category C and Category D retirement pensions and other benefits for the aged)*

2.025   The Court of Appeal has, in *SSWP v Garland* [2014] EWCA Civ 1550, allowed the appeal against the decision of Judge White in *SSWP v JG (RP)* [2013] UKUT 300 (AAC) ruling that the claimant did not have residence in Gibraltar which qualified for consideration as residence in the United Kingdom and so could not show residence in the United Kingdom for the required period to be entitled to a Category D retirement pension.

p.180, *annotation to the Social Security Contributions and Benefits Act 1992 s.83 (Pension increase (wife))*

2.026   With effect from December 16, 2014, art.11(1) of the Marriage and Civil Partnership (Scotland) Act 2014 and Civil Partnership Act 2004 (Consequential Provisions and Modifications Order 2001 (SI 2014/3229) provides:

"In a case where a full gender recognition certificate is issued to a person under the 2004 Act—
  (a) section 83 of the 1992 Act (pension increase (wife)) does not cease to apply by virtue of the change of gender; and

(b) in the continued application of section 83 in such a case, references to a pension payable to a man, or references to his wife, are to be construed accordingly."

p.181, *annotation to the Social Security Contributions and Benefits Act 1992 s.84 (Pension increase (husband))*

With effect from December 16, 2014, art.11(2) of the Marriage and Civil Partnership (Scotland) Act 2014 and Civil Partnership Act 2004 (Consequential Provisions and Modifications Order 2001 (SI 2014/3229) provides: 2.027

"In a case where a full gender recognition certificate is issued to a person under the 2004 Act—
  (a) section 84 of the 1992 Act (pension increase (husband)) does not cease to apply by virtue of the change of gender; and
  (b) in the continued application of section 83 in such a case, references to a pension payable to a woman, or references to her husband, are to be construed accordingly."

p.241, *amendment to the Social Security Contributions and Benefits Act 1992 s.122 (Interpretation of Parts I to VI and supplementary provisions)*

With effect from December 12, 2014, Sch.4, para.2(12) of the Marriage and Civil Partnership (Scotland) Act 2014 and Civil Partnership Act 2004 (Consequential Provisions and Modifications) Order 2014 (SI 2014/3229) amended s.122 by omitting subsection (1A).   2.028

p.253, *amendment to the Social Security Contributions and Benefits Act 1992 s.176 (Parliamentary control)*

With effect from October 13, 2014, s.15 and Sch.15 para.11 to the Pensions Act 2014 (brought into force by SI 2014/2727) inserted the following at the appropriate places in s.176(1)(a):   2.029

"section 14A"
"section 45(2A)"

p.258, *amendment to the Social Security Contributions and Benefits Act 1992 Sch.3 (Contribution conditions for entitlement to benefit)*

With effect from December 12, 2014, Sch.4, para.2(14) of the Marriage and Civil Partnership (Scotland) Act 2014 and Civil Partnership Act 2004 (Consequential Provisions and Modifications) Order 2014 (SI 2014/3229) amended Sch.3, para.5A by inserting "or in a case of the kind mentioned in subsection (2ZA)(d) of that section" at the end of sub-para.(1)(b) and inserting "or in a case of the kind mentioned in subsection(1ZA)(c) of that section" at the end of sub-para.(1)(c).   2.030

p.283, *amendments to the Social Security Contributions and Benefits Act 1992 Sch.5 (Pension increase or lump sum where entitlement to retirement pension is deferred), paragraphs 5 and 5A*

2.031 With effect from March 13, 2014, art.4 and Sch.3, para.4 of the Marriage (Same Sex Couples) Act 2013 (Consequential and Contrary Provisions and Scotland) Order 2014 (SI 2014/560) amended Sch.5 para.5(2) (in England and Wales only) by substituting "woman whose deceased spouse was a man" for "widow" in paragraph (a) and substituting "man whose deceased spouse was a woman" for "widower" in paragraph (b); in addition it substituted for paragraph (c) the following —

"(c) where W is—
   (i) a woman whose deceased spouse was a woman,
   (ii) a man whose deceased spouse was a man, or
   (iii) a surviving civil partner,
an amount equal to the sum of the amounts set out in paragraph 6A(2) below."

With effect from December 10, 2014, art.2 and Sch., para.11(2) of the Marriage (Same Sex Couples) Act 2013 (Consequential and Contrary Provisions and Scotland) and Marriage and Civil Partnership (Scotland) Act 2014 (Consequential Provisions) Order 2014 (SI 2014/3168) further amended para.5(2) (in England and Wales only) by substituting the following for paragraph (a):

"(a) where W is a woman—
   (i) whose deceased spouse was a man, or
   (ii) who falls within paragraph 7(3) below,
an amount equal to the sum of the amounts set out in paragraph 5A(2) or (3) below (as the case may be),"

The same amendments substituted for paragraph (c)(i) the following—

"(i) a woman who does not fall within paragraph 7(3) below and whose deceased spouse was a woman,".

With effect from December 12, 2014, art.5(3) and Sch.4, para.2(15) of the Marriage and Civil Partnership (Scotland) Act 2014 and Civil Partnership Act 2004 (Consequential Provisions and Modifications) Order 2014 (SI 2014/3229) further amended Sch.5, para.5(2) (for Scotland only) by substituting for para.(a) the following—

"(a) where W is a woman—
   (i) whose deceased spouse was a man; or
   (ii) who falls within paragraph 7(3) below,
an amount equal to the sum of the amounts set out in paragraph 5A(2) or (3) below (as the case may be),".

2.032 The same amending provision substituted "man whose deceased spouse was a woman" for "widower" in para.(b) and substituted for para.(c) the following—

"(c) where W is—
  (i) a woman who does not fall within paragraph 7(3) below and whose deceased spouse was a woman;
  (ii) a man whose deceased spouse was a man; or
  (iii) a surviving civil partner,
an amount equal to the sum of the amounts set out in paragraph (6A)(2) below.".

With effect from March 13, 2014, art.4 and Sch.3, para.4(3) of the Marriage (Same Sex Couples) Act 2013 (Consequential and Contrary Provisions and Scotland) Order 2014 (SI 2014/560) amended Sch.5 para. 5A(1) (in England and Wales only) by substituting "woman whose deceased spouse was a man" for "widow".

With effect from December 10, 2014, art.2 and Sch., para.11(3) to the Marriage (Same Sex Couples) Act 2013 (Consequential and Contrary Provisions and Scotland) and Marriage and Civil Partnership (Scotland) Act 2014 (Consequential Provisions) Order 2014 (SI 2014/3168) further amended para. 5A(1) (in England and Wales only) by substituting for sub-paragraph (1) the following—

"(1) This paragraph applies where W (referred to in paragraph 5 above) is a woman—
  (a) whose deceased spouse was a man, or
  (b) who falls within paragraph 7(3) below."

The same amending provision (b) substituted "spouse" for "husband" in each place it appears in sub-paras.(2) and (3).

With effect from December 12, 2014, art.5(3) and Sch.4, para.2(16) of the Marriage and Civil Partnership (Scotland) Act 2014 and Civil Partnership Act 2004 (Consequential Provisions and Modifications) Order 2014 (SI 2014/3229) made the same amendment as regards Scotland.

p.284, *amendments to the Social Security Contributions and Benefits Act 1992 Sch.5 (Pension increase or lump sum where entitlement to retirement pension is deferred), paragraphs 6, 6A and 7*

With effect from March 13, 2014, art.4 and Sch.3, para.4(4) of the   2.033
Marriage (Same Sex Couples) Act 2013 (Consequential and Contrary Provisions and Scotland) Order 2014 (SI 2014/560) amended Sch.5 para.6(1) (in England and Wales only) by substituting "man whose deceased spouse was a woman" for "widower".

With effect from December 12, 2014, Sch.4, para.2(17) of the Marriage and Civil Partnership (Scotland) Act 2014 and Civil Partnership Act 2004 (Consequential Provisions and Modifications) Order 2014 (SI 2014/3229) further amended Sch.5, para.6(1) (for Scotland only) by substituting "man whose deceased spouse was a woman" for "widower".

With effect from March 13, 2014, art.4 and Sch.3, para.4(5) of the Marriage (Same Sex Couples) Act 2013 (Consequential and Contrary Provisions and Scotland) Order 2014 (SI 2014/560) amended Sch.5 para.6A (in England and Wales only) by inserting "spouse or" in sub-paragraph (2)(c) before "civil partner" and by substituting for sub-paragraph (1) the following—

"(1) This paragraph applies where W (referred to in paragraph 5 above) is—
(a) a woman whose deceased spouse was a woman,
(b) a man whose deceased spouse was a man, or
(c) a surviving civil partner."

With effect from December 10, 2014, art.2 and Sch., para.11(4) to the Marriage (Same Sex Couples) Act 2013 (Consequential and Contrary Provisions and Scotland) and Marriage and Civil Partnership (Scotland) Act 2014 (Consequential Provisions) Order 2014 (SI 2014/3168) further amended para.6A(1) (in England and Wales only) by substituting for paragraph (a) the following—

"(a) a woman who does not fall within paragraph 7(3) below and whose deceased spouse was a woman,"

2.034   With effect from December 12, 2014, Sch.4, para.2(18) of the Marriage and Civil Partnership (Scotland) Act 2014 and Civil Partnership Act 2004 (Consequential Provisions and Modifications) Order 2014 (SI 2014/3229) amended Sch.5, para.6A (for Scotland only) by inserting "spouse or" before "civil partner" in sub-para.(2)(c) and also substituting for sub-para.(1) the following—

"(1) This paragraph applies where W (referred to in paragraph 5 above) is—
(a) a woman who does not fall within paragraph 7(3) below and whose deceased spouse was a woman;
(b) a man whose deceased spouse was a man; or
(c) a surviving civil partner."

With effect from December 10, 2014, art.2 and Sch., para.11(5) to the Marriage (Same Sex Couples) Act 2013 (Consequential and Contrary Provisions and Scotland) and Marriage and Civil Partnership (Scotland) Act 2014 (Consequential Provisions) Order 2014 (SI 2014/3168) further amended para.7 (in England and Wales only) by inserting after sub-paragraph (2) the following —

"(3) For the purposes of paragraphs 5, 5A and 6A above, a woman falls within this sub-paragraph if—
(a) she was married to another woman who, at the time of her death, was a woman by virtue of a full gender recognition certificate having been issued under the Gender Recognition Act 2004, and
(b) that marriage subsisted before the time when that certificate was issued."

With effect from December 12, 2014, Sch.4, para.2(19) of the Marriage and Civil Partnership (Scotland) Act 2014 and Civil Partnership

Act 2004 (Consequential Provisions and Modifications) Order 2014 (SI 2014/3229) made the same amendment as regards Scotland.

p.286, *annotation to the Social Security Contributions and Benefits Act 1992, Sch.5 (Pension increase or lump sum where entitlement to retirement pension is deferred)*

In *KH v Secretary of State for Work and Pensions* [2014] UKUT 138   2.035
(AAC) Judge Wikeley refused permission to appeal to a claimant because there was no arguable error of law in the decision by the First-tier Tribunal in refusing a claim about deferral put forward by a claimant. The Upper Tribunal reported the decision because the claimant had argued his case on the specific wording of the Departmental leaflet *Your Guide to State Pension deferral (SPD1)*. The leaflet was wrong and did not accurately reflect the law, which the First-tier Tribunal had rightly applied.

p.324, *annotation to the Pension Schemes Act 1993*

In *Secretary of State for Work and Pensions v MH* [2014] UKUT 113   2.036
(AAC) Judge Jacobs found himself unable to read modifications to the pensionable age of women made by subsequent legislation into section 48 of the Pension Schemes Act 1993. He records that the Department for Work and Pensions accepted that this was an error in drafting the legislation but he was unable to interpret the provision to remove the error. Nor, as a judge of the Upper Tribunal, was he able to consider any incompatibility with human rights legislation.

p.329, *annotation to the Pension Schemes Act 1993 s.47 (Further provisions concerning entitlement to guaranteed minimum pensions for the purposes of section 46 and s.46A)*

With effect from December 12, 2014, Sch.5, para.11 of the Marriage   2.037
and Civil Partnership (Scotland) Act 2014 and Civil Partnership Act 2004 (Consequential Provisions and Modifications) Order 2014 (SI 2014/3229) amended s.47(1) by inserting ", surviving same sex spouse" after "widower".

p.335, *amendments to the Pensions Act 1995 Sch.4 (Equalisation of and increase in pensionable age for men and women)*

With effect from July 14, 2014, s.26 of the Pensions Act 2014   2.038
amended Sch.4, para.1 by substituting "6th April 1960" for "6th April 1968" in sub-para.(6) and substituting for sub-para.(7) and Table 3 the following—

"(7) A person born on any day in a period mentioned in column 1 of table 3 attains pensionable age when the person attains the age shown against that period in column 2.

153

TABLE 3

(1) Period within which birthday falls	(2) Age pensionable age attained
6th April 1960 to 5th May 1960	66 years and 1 month
6th May 1960 to 5th June 1960	66 years and 2 months
6th June 1960 to 5th July 1960	66 years and 3 months
6th July 1960 to 5th August 1960	66 years and 4 months
6th August 1960 to 5th September 1960	66 years and 5 months
6th September 1960 to 5th October 1960	66 years and 6 months
6th October 1960 to 5th November 1960	66 years and 7 months
6th November 1960 to 5th December 1960	66 years and 8 months
6th December 1960 to 5th January 1961	66 years and 9 months
6th January 1961 to 5th February 1961	66 years and 10 months
6th February 1961 to 5th March 1961	66 years and 11 months

(7A) For the purposes of table 3—
(a) a person born on 31st July 1960 is to be taken to attain the age of 66 years and 4 months at the commencement of 30th November 2026;
(b) a person born on 31st December 1960 is to be taken to attain the age of 66 years and 9 months at the commencement of 30th September 2027;
(c) a person born on 31st January 1961 is to be taken to attain the age of 66 years and 10 months at the commencement of 30th November 2027."

The same amending provision substituted "5th March 1961" for "5th April 1969" in sub-para.(8).

p.356, *annotation to the Welfare Reform Act 2007 s.1 (Employment and support allowance): subs.(1)*

2.039   In *LH v SSWP (ESA)* [2014] UKUT 480 (AAC), Judge Rowland held that employment and support allowance is a single benefit with two routes to qualification and that it is not necessary to make separate claims for each of the contributory allowance and the income-related allowance (para.12). On the standard claim form a claimant has the opportunity to indicate which of the types s/he seeks (both types or one or the other), something which has advantages both for the claimant (no need to disclose details of financial position if seeking only CESA) and for the Secretary of State (no need to check contribution records where someone seeks only IRESA). However, as Judge Rowland states

"despite the language usually used, an indication that one or other of the allowances is not "claimed" amounts to a waiver of the need for the Secretary of State to consider entitlement to that element of employment and support allowance, rather than amounting to a true failure to claim it. The legislation does not actually contemplate there being a claim for only one element of the allowance" (para.13).

Given that to be the case, then where someone has initially sought only one form and later wishes to seek the other form as well, the matter can be raised not through a new claim but through an application for super-session under SSA 1998 s.10, or through revision under SSA 1998, s.9 or a subsequent appeal under SSA 1998 s.12 (para.15). In this case, because the claimant on appeal to the tribunal had on August 26, 2011 been placed in the support group and was thus entitled to CESA without time limit and to an enhanced disability premium, the supersession terminating entitlement to CESA on expiry of the time-limit on it effected by a decision-maker in ignorance of that appeal should have been for higher award of ESA rather than termination. That was later revised but only with limited award of arrears, and the tribunal hearing the appeal against a refusal to revise that decision erred in law in not recognising that such was the case (para.25). Judge Rowland held that the claimant was entitled to ESA (including both the support component and the enhanced disability premium) from August 26, 2011 (the date she had been placed by the tribunal in the support group).

p.405, *amendment to the Welfare Reform Act 2007 Sch.1 Part 2 para.6 (Income related allowance)*

With effect from December 16, 2014, art.29 and Sch.5, para.17 of the   2.040
Marriage and Civil Partnership (Scotland) Act 2014 and Civil Partnership Act 2004 (Consequential Provisions and Modifications) Order 2014 (SI 2014/3229) amended para.6 of Sch.1 by omitting sub-para.(6) and substituting a definition of "couple" in sub-para.(5) in exactly the same terms as the definition in the main volume. However, the latter definition applies only to England & Wales and the new definition applies to Scotland (see SI 2014/3229, art.3(4)). The result is that the definition in para.6(5) is now the same throughout Great Britain. (Note that the reason for the definition not applying in Scotland until December 16, 2014 is that under the Marriage (Same Sex Couples) Act 2013 (Consequential and Contrary Provisions and Scotland) Order 2014 (SI 2014/560) art.5, effective from March 13, 2014, a same sex marriage in England and Wales was treated as a civil partnership in Scotland. That provision, however, was revoked by the Marriage (Same Sex Couples) Act 2013 (Consequential and Contrary Provisions and Scotland) and Marriage and Civil Partnership (Scotland) Act 2014 (Consequential Provisions) Order 2014 (SI 2014/3168) art.4, with effect from December 16, 2014).

p.408, *annotation to the Welfare Reform Act 2007 Sch.2 para.2 (Waiting days)*

With effect from October 27, 2014, the number of waiting days was   2.041
increased from three to seven with respect to a new claim in respect of a waiting period starting on or after that date. See further, update to pp.1046-1047, below.

p.424, *correction to the Welfare Reform Act 2009 s.13(2)-(4) (Conditions for contributory employment and support allowance)*

For "the ESA Regulations" substitute "Sch.1 to the Welfare Reform   2.042
Act 2007".

p.443, *General Note to the Mesothelioma Act 2014*

2.043   For details of the levy imposed on EL insurers, see now the Diffuse Mesothelioma Payment Scheme (Levy) Regulations 2014 (SI 2014/2904).

pp.453-455, *amendment to the Social Security (Credits) Regulations 1975 (SI 1975/556) reg.2 (Interpretation)*

2.043.1   With effect from April 29, 2013, reg.70(1), (2) of the Universal Credit (Consequential, Supplementary, Incidental and Miscellaneous Provisions) Regulations 2013 (SI 2013/630) made the following amendments to reg.2:

(i) inserted after the definition of "the Act":

""the 2012 Act" means the Welfare Reform Act 2012;";

(ii) substituted for the definition of "contribution-based jobseeker's allowance":

""contribution-based jobseeker's allowance" means an allowance under the Jobseekers Act 1995 as amended by the provisions of Part 1 of Schedule 14 to the 2012 Act that remove references to an income-based allowance, and a contribution-based allowance under the Jobseekers Act 1995 as that Act has effect apart from those provisions;";

(iii) substituted for the definition of "contributory employment and support allowance":

""contributory employment and support allowance" means an allowance under Part 1 of the Welfare Reform Act as amended by the provisions of Schedule 3, and Part 1 of Schedule 14, to the 2012 Act that remove references to an income-related allowance, and a contributory allowance under Part 1 of the Welfare Reform Act as that Part has effect apart from those provisions;";

(iv) inserted after the definition of "relevant past year":

""universal credit" means universal credit under Part 1 of the 2012 Act;".

pp.460-461, *amendment to the Social Security (Credits) Regulations 1975 (SI 1975/556) reg.7 (Credits for approved training)*

2.043.2   With effect from April 29, 2013, reg.70(1), (3) of the Universal Credit (Consequential, Supplementary, Incidental and Miscellaneous Provisions) Regulations 2013 (SI 2013/630) amended para.(1) by replacing "paragraphs (2) and (3)" with "paragraphs (2) to (4)". The same provisions inserted after para.(3) a new para.(4) to read as follows:

"(4) Paragraph (1) shall not apply to a person in respect of any week in any part of which that person was entitled to universal credit."

pp.467–468, *amendment to the Social Security (Credits) Regulations 1975 (SI 1975/556) reg.8A (Credits for unemployment)*

With effect from April 29, 2013, reg.70(1), (4) of the Universal Credit **2.043.3** (Consequential, Supplementary, Incidental and Miscellaneous Provisions) Regulations 2013 (SI 2013/630) amended reg.8A to read as follows:

"Credits for unemployment

8A.—(1) For the purposes of entitlement to any benefit by virtue of a person's earnings or contributions, he shall be entitled to be credited with earnings equal to the lower earnings limit then in force, in respect of each week to which this regulation applies.

(2) Subject to paragraph (5) this regulation applies to a week which, in relation to the person concerned, is—

(a) a week for the whole of which he was paid a jobseeker's allowance;
   or
[(b) a week for the whole of which the person in relation to old style JSA—
   (i) satisfied or was treated as having satisfied the conditions set out in paragraphs (a), (c) and (e) to (h) of section 1(2) of the Jobseekers Act 1995 (conditions for entitlement to a jobseeker's allowance); and
   (ii) satisfied the further condition specified in paragraph (3) below; or
(ba) a week for the whole of which the person in relation to new style JSA—
   (i) satisfied or was treated as having satisfied the conditions set out in paragraphs (e) to (h) of section 1(2) of the Jobseekers Act 1995 (conditions for entitlement to a jobseeker's allowance);
   (ii) satisfied or was treated as having satisfied the work-related requirements under section 6D and 6E of the Jobseekers Act 1995 (work search and work availability requirements); and
   (iii) satisfied the further condition specified in paragraph (3) below; or]
(c) a week which would have been a week described in subparagraph (b) or (ba)] but for the fact that he was incapable of work or had limited capability for work for part of it, or
(d) a week in respect of which he would have been paid a jobseeker's allowance but for a restriction imposed pursuant

to . . . section 6B, 7, 8 or 9 of the Social Security Fraud Act 2001 (loss of benefit provisions).

(3) The further condition referred to in paragraph (2)(b) [and (ba)] is that the person concerned—

(a) furnished to the Secretary of State notice in writing of the grounds on which he claims to be entitled to be credited with earnings—

    (i) on the first day of the period for which he claims to be so entitled in which the week in question fell; or

    (ii) within such further time as may be reasonable in the circumstances of the case; and

(b) has provided any evidence required by the Secretary of State that the conditions referred to in paragraph (2)(b) [or the conditions and requirements in paragraph (2)(ba)] are satisfied.

(4) *Omitted.*

(5) This regulation shall not apply to—

(a) a week in respect of which the person concerned was not entitled to a jobseeker's allowance (or would not have been if he had claimed it) because of section 14 of the Jobseekers Act 1995 (trade disputes); or

(b) a week in respect of which, in relation to the person concerned, there was in force a direction under section 16 of that Act (which relates to persons who have reached the age of 16 but not the age of 18 and who are in severe hardship); or

[(c) a week in respect of which, in relation to the person concerned—

    (i) an old style JSA was reduced in accordance with section 19 or 19A, or regulations made under section 19B, of the Jobseekers Act 1995; or

    (ii) a new style JSA was reduced in accordance with section 6J or 6K of the Jobseekers Act 1995; or]

(d) a week in respect of which a jobseeker's allowance was payable to the person concerned only by virtue of regulation 141 of the Jobseeker's Allowance Regulations 1996 (circumstances in which an income-based jobseeker's allowance is payable to a person in hardship); or

(dd) a week in respect of which a joint-claim jobseeker's allowance was payable in respect of a joint-claim couple of which the person is a member only by virtue of regulation 146C of the Jobseeker's Allowance Regulations 1996 (circumstances in which a joint-claim jobseeker's allowance is payable where a joint-claim couple is a couple in hardship);

[(de) a week where paragraph (2)(b), (ba) or (c) apply and the person concerned was entitled to universal credit for any part of that week; or]

(e) where the person concerned is a married woman, a week in respect of any part of which an election made by her under regulations made under section 19(4) of the Contributions and Benefits Act had effect.

[(6) In this regulation—

"new style JSA" means a jobseeker's allowance under the Jobseekers Act 1995 as amended by the provisions of Part 1 of Schedule 14 to the 2012 Act that remove references to an income-based allowance;

"old style JSA" means a jobseeker's allowance under the Jobseekers Act 1995 as it has effect apart from the amendments made by Part 1 of Schedule 14 to the 2012 Act that remove references to an income-based allowance.]"

pp.470–471, *amendment to the Social Security (Credits) Regulations 1975 (SI 1975/556) reg.8B (Credits for incapacity for work or limited capability for work)*

With effect from April 29, 2013, reg.70(1), (5) of the Universal Credit 2.043.4 (Consequential, Supplementary, Incidental and Miscellaneous Provisions) Regulations 2013 (SI 2013/630) amended reg.8B(2) to insert "(2A)" between "paragraphs" and "(3)". They also substituted after para.(2) a new para.(2A) to read as follows:

"(2A) This regulation shall not apply to a week where—

(a) under paragraph (2)(a)(i) the person concerned was not entitled to incapacity benefit, severe disablement allowance or maternity allowance;

(b) paragraph (2)(a)(ii), (iva) or (v) apply; or

(c) under paragraph (2)(a)(iv) the person concerned was not entitled to an employment and support allowance by virtue of section 1(2)(a) of the Welfare Reform Act,

and the person concerned was entitled to universal credit for any part of that week.".

p.473, *amendment to the Social Security (Credits) Regulations 1975 (SI 1975/556) reg.8C (Credits on termination of bereavement benefits)*

With effect from December 10, 2014 (England and Wales) and 2.044 December 16, 2014 (Scotland) (see art.1), art.2 and Sch.1, para.4(1), (2) of the Marriage (Same Sex Couples) Act 2013 and Marriage and Civil Partnership (Scotland) Act 2014 (Consequential Provisions) Order 2014 (SI 2014/3061) amended reg.8C(2) to read as follows:

"(2) For every year up to and including that in which the recipient ceased to be entitled to a bereavement benefit otherwise than by reason of remarriage, forming a civil partnership, or living together with [another person as a married couple], the recipient shall be credited with such earnings as may be required to enable the condition referred to above to be satisfied."

p.476, *insertion of a new regulation 8G into the Social Security (Credits) Regulations 1975 (SI 1975/556)*

2.044.1   With effect from April 29, 2013, reg.70(1), (6) of the Universal Credit (Consequential, Supplementary, Incidental and Miscellaneous Provisions) Regulations 2013 (SI 2013/630) inserted between regs 8F and 9 a new reg.8G to read as follows:

"Credits for persons entitled to universal credit

8G.—(1) For the purposes of entitlement to a benefit to which this regulation applies, a person shall be credited with a Class 3 contribution in respect of a week if that person is entitled to universal credit under Part 1 of the Welfare Reform Act 2012 for any part of that week.

(2) This regulation applies to—

(a) a Category A retirement pension;

(b) a Category B retirement pension;

(c) a widowed parent's allowance;

(d) a bereavement allowance."

p.478, *amendment to the Social Security (Credits) Regulations 1975 (SI 1975/556) reg.9C (Credits for adoption pay period, additional paternity pay period and maternity pay period)*

2.045   With effect from December 31, 2014, art.2 of the Shared Parental Leave and Statutory Shared Parental Pay (Consequential Amendments to Subordinate Legislation) Order 2014 (SI 2014/3255) amended reg.9C to read as follows:

Credits for adoption pay period, [shared parental pay period,] additional paternity pay period and maternity pay period

9C.—(1) For the purposes of entitlement to any benefit by virtue of—

(a) in the case of a person referred to in paragraph (2)(a) or (aa), that person's earnings or contributions;

(b) in the case of a woman referred to in paragraph (2)(b), her earnings or contributions,

that person or that woman, as the case may be, shall be entitled to be credited with earnings equal to the lower earnings limit then in force in respect of each week to which this regulation applies.

(2) Subject to paragraphs (3) and (4), this regulation applies to each week during—

(a) the adoption pay period in respect of which statutory adoption pay was paid to a person; or

(aa) the additional paternity pay period in respect of which additional statutory paternity pay was paid to a person; or

(b) the maternity pay period in respect of which statutory maternity pay was paid to a woman [; or

(c) the shared parental pay period in respect of which statutory shared parental pay is paid to a person.]

(3) A person or woman referred to above shall be entitled to be credited with earnings in respect of a week by virtue of this regulation only if he or she—

(a) furnished to the Secretary of State notice in writing of his or her claim to be entitled to be credited with earnings; and

(b) did so—

(i) before the end of the benefit year immediately following the tax year in which that week began, or

(ii) within such further time as may be reasonable in the circumstances of his or her case.

(4) This regulation shall not apply to a woman in respect of any week in any part of which she was a married woman in respect of whom an election made by her under regulations made under section 19(4) of the Contributions and Benefits Act had effect.

(5) In this regulation

[(a)] "adoption pay period", "additional paternity pay period", "maternity pay period", "statutory adoption pay", "additional statutory paternity pay" and "statutory maternity pay" have the same meaning as in the Contributions and Benefits Act [;

(b) "statutory shared parental pay" means statutory shared parental pay payable in accordance with Part 12ZC of that Act and "shared parental pay period" means the weeks in respect of which statutory shared parental pay is payable to a person under section 171ZY(2) of that Act.]

pp.484–485, *amendment to the Social Security (Credits) Regulations 1975 (SI 1975/556) Sch para.3 (Persons who may qualify as carers of child under the age of 12)*

With effect from December 10, 2014 (England and Wales) and December 16, 2014 (Scotland) (see art.1), art.2 and Sch.1, para.4(1), (3) of the Marriage (Same Sex Couples) Act 2013 and Marriage and Civil Partnership (Scotland) Act 2014 (Consequential Provisions) Order 2014 (SI 2014/3061) amended para.3 to read as follows: — 2.046

"**3.** For the purposes of paragraph 1(9) and (11)(c), a partner is the other member of a couple consisting of [two people who are not married to or civil partners of each other but are living together as a married couple].

pp.491–493, *amendment to the Social Security (Crediting and Treatment of Contributions, and National Insurance Numbers) Regulations 2001 (SI 2001/769) reg.1 (Citation, commencement and interpretation)*

With effect from April 29, 2013, reg.71 of the Universal Credit (Consequential, Supplementary, Incidental and Miscellaneous Provisions) Regulations 2013 (SI 2013/630) made the following amendments to reg.1(2): — 2.046.1

(i) substituted for the definition of "contribution-based jobseeker's allowance" and "income-based jobseeker's allowance":

""contribution-based jobseeker's allowance" means an allowance under the Jobseekers Act 1995 as amended by the provisions of Part 1 of Schedule 14 to the Welfare Reform Act 2012 that remove references to an income-based allowance, and a contribution-based allowance under the Jobseekers Act 1995 as that Act has effect apart from those provisions;";

(ii) substituted for the definition of "contributory employment and support allowance":

""contributory employment and support allowance" means an allowance under Part 1 of the Welfare Reform Act as amended by the provisions of Schedule 3, and Part 1 of Schedule 14, to the Welfare Reform Act 2012 that remove references to an income-related allowance, and a contributory allowance under Part 1 of the Welfare Reform Act as that Part has effect apart from those provisions;";

and

(iii) inserted after the definition of "earnings factor":

""income-based jobseeker's allowance" has the same meaning as in the Jobseekers Act 1995;".

p.510, *amendment to the Social Security (Computation of Earnings) Regulations 1996 (SI 1996/2745) reg.2(1) (Interpretation)*

2.047   With effect from December 16, 2014, art.29 and Sch.6 para.14 of the Marriage and Civil Partnership (Scotland) Act 2014 and Civil Partnership Act 2004 (Consequential Provisions and Modifications Order 2001 (SI 2014/3229) amended the definition of "couple" by substituting a definition in the same terms as the existing definition. However, the existing definition applied only to England and Wales; the new definition applies to England, Wales, Scotland and Northern Ireland.

p.562, *amendment to the Social Security Dependency Regulations 1977 (SI 1977/343) Sch.2 (Prescribed circumstances for increase of a carer's allowance)*

2.048   With effect from December 16, 2014, art.29 and Sch.6 para.2 of the Marriage and Civil Partnership (Scotland) Act 2014 and Civil Partnership Act 2004 (Consequential Provisions and Modifications Order 2001 (SI 2014/3229) substitutes the following in definition of "couple" in para.2C:

" "couple" means—
(a) two people who are married to, or civil partners of, each other and are members of the same household; or

(b) two people who are not married to, or civil partners of, each other but are living together as a married couple;"

p.676, *annotation to the Social Security (Disability Living Allowance) Regulation 1991 (SI 1991/2890) reg.12(5) (Arrested development or incomplete physical development of the brain)*

In *NMcM v SSWP* [2014] UKUT 312 (AAC) Judge Wikeley has   2.049
decided two important points about para.(5). First, the so called "age 30 cut off" rule in *R (DLA) 2/96* is disapproved and secondly the novel construction of the paragraph that had been suggested by Judge Levenson in *SC v SSWP* [2010] UKUT 76 referred to at the beginning of this note is also disapproved. As to the first, Judge Wikeley finds that the basis upon which the rule was adopted, namely the state of medical knowledge then held about the development of the brain, was no longer sustainable. In the light of more recent medical research, and especially the benefits of MRI imaging, it was no longer possible to assert that the brain could be regarded as fully developed by that age. Judge Wikeley had before him a report agreed by both the parties, which showed that in one sense the brain continues to develop at least into the third decade of life and possibly in some persons into their forties. In another sense, the brain continues to develop when acquiring new skills that can be reflected in physical changes in the brain, throughout life. The present case, which involved a claimant who had suffered brain damage in a road accident at the age of 32, had been rejected on that ground without further consideration at the FTT. The case has now been referred back for further matters to be considered. First among them will be the question of whether the claimant can be said to be suffering from a state of arrested development or incomplete development of the brain. In doing so they will follow the other part of the Judge's decision which is that each of these phrases is to be read as referring to "the brain". Thus, what must be found is "arrested development of the brain" or, alternatively, "incomplete development of the brain". It might be thought that this would present a difficulty, given that the claimant's problems were palpably caused by what we would popularly refer to as "brain damage", but, as the judge points out, the test here is not one of causation; it is, at this stage, just one of medical fact and given the way in which the terms above are now used to describe the medical situation, he thought it possible that the FTT might find accordingly.

p.677, *annotation to the Social Security (Disability Living Allowance) Regulations 1991 (SI 1991/2890) reg. 12(5) (Severe impairment of intelligence and social functioning)*

The approach that treats intelligence and social functioning as parts of   2.050
a combined test of the claimant's ability to function in "real life situations" has been approved in *MP v SSWP* [2014] UKUT 426 (AAC). Judge Knowles QC directed the FTT to whom the case was returned that they should regard *R (DLA) 1/00* as

"authority for the proposition that evidence about a person's insight and sagacity can satisfy both the test of severe impairment of intelligence **and** severe impairment of social functioning required by regulation 12(5)."

This case was another involving a child (four years old) with autistic spectrum disorder. An appeal was allowed largely because insufficient regard had been given to the communication difficulties that the child was experiencing. As the judge put it,

"The emphasis in *R (DLA) 1/00* [. . .] on *"the ability to function in real life situations"* or *"useful intelligence"* invites active consideration of a person's language difficulties when considering their social functioning for the purposes of regulation 12(5)."

The judge directed also that when rehearing the case regard must be had to the child's ability to function in less structured situations rather than just his abilities within the home and at school. Furthermore, she thought it necessary that account should be taken of the child's ability to function in relation to strangers and not just those who were familiar to him. She rejected the suggestion made on behalf of the Secretary of State that it would be difficult to assess a child's ability to interact with strangers because many young children are shy with strangers. To do so, she thought, would be to introduce a comparison with a child of that age who was not disabled; a test she points out that is applied specifically only in para. 4A. However, it is likely that some reference to the generality of youthful shyness is inevitable because it will still be necessary for there to be a finding that the child's condition has resulted in "impairment".

p.787, *annotation to the Social Security (Graduated Retirement Benefit) (No 2) Regulations 1978 (SI 1978/393) reg.3 (continuation in force of sections 36, 37 and 118(1) of the 1965 Act)*

2.051   With effect from December 12, 2014, Sch.6, art.3 of the Marriage and Civil Partnership (Scotland) Act 2014 and Civil Partnership Act 2004 (Consequential Provisions and Modifications) Order 2014 (SI 2014/3229) amended reg.3(2) in exactly the same terms as the existing provision. This is to ensure that the "new" provision applies in Scotland in addition to England and Wales.

p.796 *Amendment to the Additional Pension and Social Security Pensions (Home Responsibilities) (Amendment) Regulations 2001 reg.5A and* insertion of new regs.5B and 5C

2.052   With effect from April 28, 2014 the Additional Pension and Social Security Pensions (Home Responsibilities) (Amendment) Regulations 2001(SI 2001/13223) is amended by the Social Security (Miscellaneous Amendments) Regulations 2014 (SI 2014/591) reg.2 as follows:

In regulation 5A(3) (earnings factor credits eligibility for pensioners to whom employment and support allowance was payable), after "this regulation" insert "and regulation 5C".

After regulation 5B (earnings factor credits eligibility for certain persons entitled to universal credit) insert—

After reg.5A insert a new regulation reg.5B.

"Earnings factor credits eligibility for certain persons entitled to universal credit

5B.—(1) For the purposes of subsection (3) of section 44C (earnings factor credits) of the Contributions and Benefits Act, a pensioner is eligible for earnings factor enhancement in respect of a week if that pensioner was a person entitled to an award of universal credit under Part 1 of the Welfare Reform Act 2012 in respect of any part of that week which includes—

 (a) if the person satisfies the condition in paragraph (2), an amount under regulation 27(1)(a) of the Universal Credit Regulations 2013 in respect of the fact that the person has limited capability for work;

 (b) an amount under regulation 27(1)(b) of those Regulations in respect of the fact that the person has limited capability for work and work-related activity; or

 (c) an amount under regulation 29(1) of those Regulations where the person has regular and substantial caring responsibilities for a severely disabled person,

or would include any of those amounts but for regulation 27(4) or 29(4) of those Regulations.

 (2) The condition referred to in paragraph (1)(a) is that for each of the 52 weeks immediately prior to that week—

 (a) the person was entitled to universal credit in respect of the fact that the person had limited capability for work or would have included an amount in respect of the fact that the person had limited capability for work but for regulation 27(4) or 29(4) of the Universal Credit Regulations 2013; or

 (b) employment and support allowance under Part 1 (employment and support allowance) of the Welfare Reform Act 2007 ("the 2007 Act")—

  (i) was payable to the person;

  (ii) would have been payable to the person but for the fact that the person did not satisfy the contribution condition in paragraph 1 or paragraph 2 of Schedule 1 to the 2007 Act;

  (iii) would have been payable to the person but for the fact that the person had been entitled to it for the relevant maximum number of days under section 1A of the 2007 Act; or

  (iv) would have been payable to the person but for the fact that under regulations the amount was reduced to nil because of—

   (aa) receipt of other benefits; or

   (bb) receipt of payments from an occupational pension scheme or personal pension scheme.

(3) Paragraph (2)(b) of this regulation is satisfied in respect of a week which falls between periods which are linked by virtue of regulations under paragraph 4 (linking periods) of Schedule 2 to the 2007 Act.".

"Earnings factor credit eligibility for pensioners to whom section 1A of the 2007 Act applied

5C.—(1) For the purposes of section 44C(3) (earnings factor credits) of the Contributions and Benefits Act, a pensioner is eligible for earnings factor enhancement in respect of a week to which paragraph (2) applies.

(2) This paragraph applies to a week in which, in relation to the pensioner concerned, each of the days would have been—

(a) a day of limited capability for work; or

(b) a day on which that pensioner would have been treated as having limited capability for work,

for the purposes of Part 1 of the 2007 Act (limited capability for work) where that pensioner would have been entitled to an employment and support allowance but for the application of section 1A of the 2007 Act.".

p.837, *amendments to the Social Security (Widow's Benefits Retirement Pensions and Other Benefits) (Transitional) Regulations 1979 (SI 1979/643) reg.7, (Modifications for widowed mother's allowance, widow's pension and category A and B retirement pensions)*

2.053 With effect from December 10, 2014 (and in respect of Scotland from December 16, 2014) art.2 and Sch.1 of the Marriage (Same Sex Couples) Act 2013 and Marriage and Civil Partnership (Scotland) Act 2014 (Consequential Provisions) Order 2014 (SI 2014/3061) amended reg.7(10) by inserting "or former civil partner" after "former spouse" in each place it occurs, "or civil partner" after "said spouse", "or former civil partner's" after "former spouse's" and "(or, in the case of a civil partnership, the year 1975/76)" after "whichever is the earlier".

p.853, *correction to Part IX title*

2.054 This should read **"OLD STYLE" EMPLOYMENT AND SUPPORT ALLOWANCE**

p.868, *amendment to the Employment and Support Allowance Regulations 2008 (SI 2008/794) reg.2(1) (Interpretation—definition of "couple")*

2.055 With effect from December 16, 2014, art.29 and Sch.6, para.32 of the Marriage and Civil Partnership (Scotland) Act 2014 and Civil Partnership Act 2004 (Consequential Provisions and Modifications) Order 2014 (SI 2014/3229) amended reg.2(1) by substituting a definition of "couple" in exactly the same terms as the definition in the main volume. However, the latter definition applies only to England & Wales and the new definition applies to Scotland—SI 2014/3229, art.3(4). The result is that the definition is now the same throughout Great Britain.

p.872, *amendment to the Employment and Support Allowance Regulations 2008 (SI 2008/794) reg.2(1) (Interpretation—definition of "maternity allowance period)*

With effect from May 18, 2014, reg.5(1) and (2) of the Social Security   2.056
(Maternity Allowance) (Miscellaneous Amendments) Regulations 2014
(SI 2014/884) amended reg.2(1) by revoking the definition of "maternity allowance period".

p.875, *amendment to the Employment and Support Allowance Regulations 2008 (SI 2008/794), reg.2(1) (Interpretation—definition of "shared parental leave")*

With effect from December 31, 2014, reg.20(3)(c) of the Shared   2.057
Parental Leave and Statutory Shared Parental Pay (Consequential
Amendments to Subordinate Legislation) Order 2014 (SI 2014/3255)
amended reg.1(3) by adding the following definition before the definition of "single claimant":

> ""shared parental leave" means leave under section 75E or 75G of the
> Employment Rights Act 1996;".

pp.916-917, *annotation to the Employment and Support Allowance Regulations 2008 (SI 2008/794) reg.25 (Hospital patients)*

The regulation applies not only to those "undergoing medical or other   2.058
treatment as a patient in a hospital or other institution" but also days of
"recovery from that treatment". In *SI v SSWP (ESA)* [2013] UKUT
453 (AAC), Judge Mark was not satisfied

> "that the tribunal did properly consider the question whether the
> claimant was still recovering from the treatment. It does not follow just
> because the wound had scarred over and he had restricted movement
> back in his joint that he was fully recovered. The remaining limitations
> could in part still be due to the fact that he had not fully recovered.
> There does not appear to have been any investigation of the extent of
> his limitation previously or the nature of the operation or of his
> prognosis or the reasons for his continuing therapies and consultations
> or of the expected period within which recovery from the operation
> was to be expected" (para.10).

This lapse did not assist the claimant because the tribunal on the facts
was entitled to conclude that there was no good ground for treating him
as incapable of work.

pp.922-928, *annotation to the Employment and Support Allowance Regulations 2008 (SI 2008/794) reg.29(2(b) (Exceptional circumstances)*

Interpretation and application of reg.29(2)(b) continues to generate   2.059
significant and sometimes conflicting decisions. For clarity, the applicable recent case law can best be considered under several headings.

*The "substantial risk" must arise "by reasons of" a specific disease or
bodily or mental disablement*

In *DR v SSWP (ESA)* [2014] UKUT 188 (AAC); [2014] AACR 38,
Judge May held erroneous in law a tribunal decision that the claimant
satisfied reg. 29 because it had not made the necessary connection
between the risk and the disease or disablement (see para.3). Alcohol
misuse in itself is not such a disablement. To rank as disablement the
misuse of alcohol must rank as "alcohol dependency" in terms of the
"constellation of markers" found in quotations from *R(DLA) 6/06* in the
Three-Judge Panel's decision in *JG v SSWP (ESA)* [2013] UKUT 37
(AAC); [2013] AACR 23 (see paras 5-7, 10 of *DR*). Para.45 of the panel
decision sets out the constellation of markers as follows:

"A maladaptive pattern of substance use, leading to clinically significant impairment or distress, as manifested by three (or more) of
the following, occurring at any time in the same 12-month period
    (1) tolerance, as defined by either of the following:
      (a) a need for markedly increased amounts of the substance to
achieve intoxication or desire effect
      (b) markedly diminished effect with continued use of the same
amount of the substance
    (2) withdrawal, as manifested by either of the following:
      (a) the characteristic withdrawal syndrome for the substance . . .
      (b) the same (or a closely related) substance is taken to relieve or
avoid withdrawal symptoms
    (3) the substance is often taken in larger amounts or over a longer
period than was intended
    (4) there is a persistent desire or unsuccessful efforts to cut down or
control substance use
    (5) a great deal of time is spent in activities necessary to obtain the
substance (e.g. visiting multiple doctors or driving long distances), use
the substance (e.g. chain-smoking), or recover from its effects
    (6) important social, occupational, or recreational activities are
given up or reduced because of substance use
    (7) the substance use is continued despite knowledge of having a
persistent or recurrent physical or psychological problem that is likely
to have been caused or exacerbated by the substance (e.g. current
cocaine use despite recognition of cocaine-induced depression, or
continued drinking despite recognition that an ulcer was made worse
by alcohol consumption)."

The proper approach to the provision

2.060   In *GS v SSWP (ESA)* [2014] UKUT 16 (AAC), Judge Mark affirmed
his approach in *IJ* (see p.924) as the correct one, also citing in support
another decision of Commissioner Parker (as she then was) in *CSIB/
719/2006*.

In *SP v SSWP (ESA)* [2014] UKUT 522 (AAC), considering the
impact on the claimant of a finding that s/he does not have limited
capability for work, Judge Parker again expressed agreement with
para.10 of Judge Mark's decision in *IJ v SSWP (IB)* [2010] UKUT 408

(AAC) (see p.924). The tribunal had failed to address this question and thus erred in law. While she did not categorically reject the possibility of the claimant being accompanied to some interviews at the Jobcentre or elsewhere, she considered that "this would not address some of the potential stress to which Judge Mark referred" (para.7).

The applicability of the Equality Act 2010

The Equality Act 2010 has been mentioned and subject to varying degrees of consideration in a number of Upper Tribunal decisions in a number of contexts. But its specific applicability in the context of reg.29(2)(b) was most fully argued before Judge Wright in *JS v SSWP (ESA)* [2014] UKUT 428, a case in which an oral hearing was held, and the matter analysed in a judgment running to 78 paragraphs. His conclusion was that

> "the assessment of risk under regulation 29(2)(b) of the ESA Regs does not require or involve the decision maker (be that the Secretary of State's delegate or the First-tier Tribunal) in making an assessment as to whether employers would owe a duty under the Equality Act 2010 to make reasonable adjustments in respect of the individual claimant whose case falls for decision, and in my judgment the tribunal therefore erred in law in relying on the Equality Act 2010 to that effect" (para.5).

It is submitted that, for his reasons elaborated below, his conclusion that the Equality Act 2010 is not applicable is the correct approach to the matter.

In contrast, in a much briefer decision in *JB v SSWP (ESA)* [2013] UKUT 518 (AAC), Judge Mark had stated that the Equality Act 2010 could be relevant; indeed, that a tribunal is bound

> "if relevant to an issue before it, to make a determination as to whether a person would be owed a duty by a potential or actual employer under the 2010 Act. In particular, if the existence of such a duty is a prerequisite for there being no substantial risk to a claimant's mental or physical health for the purposes of regulation 29, then plainly a finding must be made as to that duty" (para.15).

Judge Wright argued correctly that this is an *obiter* statement, that the matter was not as fully argued before Judge Mark in *JB* as before him in *JS*, and he thus refused to follow it, both on those grounds and, more fundamentally, because he considered Judge Mark to be wrong.

Judge Gray also referred to the Equality Act 2010 in *AT v SSWP (ESA)* [2013] UKUT 630 (AAC), para.9, but, as Judge Wright notes, she did so to warn of the dangers, particularly acute in mental health cases, of assuming that because there is a duty under that Act to make reasonable adjustments there cannot be a substantial risk to health because of stress-related matters flowing from mental health problems.

Additionally, in *SI v SSWP (ESA)* [2014] UKUT 428 (AAC); [2015] AACR 5, paras.73-74, a three-judge Panel mentioned the Equality Act

2.061

2010 in generalised terms but in the context of the need to look at activities and descriptors in a workplace context and did not deal with its applicability as regards ESA Regs 2008 regs.29 or 35.

2.062   Judge Wright argued, firstly, that the Equality Act 2010 and employment and support allowance schemes have different statutory aims and materially different statutory contents. That the ESA Regs are not to be divorced from the real world (see *AS* and *SI*, above) points to the 2010 Act having potential relevance to the ESA Regs. But, as regards "statutory intendment", against that must be set the plain fact that the ESA Regs (and their predecessors for IB) have never on their face made any express link to the Equality Act 2010 or its predecessor, the Disability Discrimination Act 1995. Indeed, even where as now, para.(3)(a) requires consideration in applying para.(2)(b)to be given to "reasonable adjustments being made in the claimant's workplace" no link was made, pointing   to para.(2)(b) "being intended to embody a test separate to the tests under the Equality Act 2010" (para.48). In addition, the ESA scheme applies to persons not in employment and unable to work, whereas the duties under the Equality Act 2010 apply only to employees or applicants for employment who have made known to the employer their disability. Moreover key elements for assessing disability are different, and noticeably different, under the two schemes (paras. 53, 54).

Secondly, the Equality Act 2010 test sits uneasily with *Charlton*. That case eschewed an "actual employment" test which is essentially the test embodied in that Act (para.51). *Charlton* embraces the impact in respect of travelling to work; the 2010 Act does not (para.55). In addition, *Charlton* took account of the test under para (2)(b) "having to be applied practically". Requiring a decision-maker to consider whether "the claimant would be likely to be owed a duty by an employer or employers to make reasonable adjustments under the statutory machinery contained within the Equality Act 2010" would be likely to render impracticable "a timeous decision" (para.58).

Thirdly, the First-tier Tribunal is ill-equipped to make proper assessments under the Equality Act 2010, which matters are vested in the specialist employment tribunal. While the First-tier tribunal is also specialist in its sphere of operation, "on its face it is not concerned with assessing whether an employer will in fact owe a duty to make reasonable adjustments in respect of an individual disabled person" (para.57).

Finally, *recourse to the Equality Act 2010 is simply unnecessary*. The matter of applying the para (2)(b) test in the light of reasonable adjustments which might be made in the envisaged range of workplaces is now explicit in para.(3), but has also always been inherent in the risk assessment required by para.(2)(b), as interpreted in *Charlton*; as Judge Wright put it the wording is

> "wide enough and flexible enough to encompass reasonable steps that realistically on the evidence may be taken by, or in respect of, the [specific individual] claimant, including by prospective employers. But that does not require an assessment to be made of employers' duties under the Equality Act 2010" (para.61).

There must first be analysis of the range and types of work which as a matter of training or aptitude the claimant is suited to do "and which his or her disabilities do not render him [or her] incapable of performing". There must then be assessed the risk the individual's disease(s) or disablement(s) would, on the balance of probabilities, give rise to

"if the claimant was travelling to and from, and working in, employments he or she was otherwise suited to do. Part of that risk assessment will involve consideration of the steps that, on the evidence and having regard to the individual claimant's health conditions and other circumstances, could reasonably and realistically be taken to avoid any substantial risk to health" (para.62).

Where travelling to work unaccompanied is the potential risk, can the matter of third party assistance be considered as alleviating it?

In *PD v SSWP (ESA)* [2014] UKUT 148 (AAC), Judge Ward con-   2.063
sidered that the risk with respect to travelling to work arising from physical elements was likely to be rare; the traveller contemplated by the Court of Appeal in *Charlton* was "the person whose mental health problems cause difficulties with the journey to work" (para.15). Judge Ward's starting point was that where there was appropriate evidence third party help could be taken into account, that line of argument was open to the Secretary of State (paras 23, 26):

"There will be cases, for instance where a partner is not working, there is no one else at home who uses the car and where the evidence shows a pattern of the partner driving the claimant to wherever s/he wants or needs to go, that it may be open to a tribunal to infer that such help would similarly be available to get a claimant to the *Charlton*-mandated hypothetical workplace. If a scheme such as Access to Work were available on a sufficiently reliable basis, it is hard to see why it should not be taken into account. Such are ultimately conclusions of fact and not matters on which I need say more, except to observe that this may be, par excellence, a field in which tribunals can look to the principles of *Kerr v Department for Social Development* [2004] UKHL 23; [2004] 1 WLR 1372" (para.26).

Judge Ward also stated that

"What is difficult in relation to transport is yet harder in relating to accompaniment within the workplace. Such a setup would be highly unusual, even if only to help with the first few days. I did not hear argument on whether that, unlike the provision of transport, could constitute a reasonable adjustment for Equality Act purposes" (para.27).

Indeed, one should here cross refer to the update to pp.1110-1112 and to the judgment of the three-judge panel in *JC v SSWP (ESA)* [2014] UKUT 352 (AAC), which did not consider that a person could properly be regarded "as able to engage in social contact if she or he can do so only if accompanied by someone, *at least without further explanation as to how it is envisaged that that might be realistic in the workplace*" (para.45, emphasis supplied by commentator).

It should also be noted that in stark contrast in *MT v SSWP (ESA)* [2013] UKUT 545 (AAC), in the context of reg.35(2), Judge Gray firmly rejected looking at capacity to perform activities with third party assistance, observing:

"I do need to deal however with the observation of the FTT in its statement of reasons that the appellant could take another person with her to any work-related activities. It may be that the Secretary of State would be facilitative in any matter which helped a claimant engage so as to improve their ultimate prospects of retaining work. I do not know. Whether or not that is so, is not relevant. As a matter of law any work-related activity which could only be accomplished because of the presence of another person must be looked upon as not being an activity that the claimant can carry out. *The issue under regulation 35 (2)(b) as to whether there would be a substantial risk to the mental or physical health of any person if the claimant were found not to have limited capability for work-related activity cannot be assessed as if the claimant under consideration had somebody else by their side.* There will be claimants who have a need for the personal reassurance of another person, but who do not have anybody available to perform that role. Even if they did, it would not be reasonable for such an assessment to be made on the basis of reliance on another's goodwill. Legal tests cannot depend upon that. Where an appellant who is found to have limited capability for work-related activities wishes to engage voluntarily, it may be that they choose to do so with the help of another person, and it may (or may not, I do not know) be possible for them to do so, but the capacity to engage only with that assistance cannot be part of the test of capability" (para.34, emphasis added by commentator).

In *PD*, Judge Ward agreed with the italicised passage insofar as it meant "without consideration as to whether the third party's presence would be made out in fact" (para.21), but otherwise distinguished the passage as focussing on the claimant's capability to perform activities (agreeing that there third party assistance should be ignored) rather than the different question of what risks would ensue (where, with respect to travelling, at least, third party assistance available in fact might obviate the risk). See also *SP v SSWP (ESA)* [2014] UKUT 522 (AAC), where Judge Parker did not categorically reject as inadmissible the Secretary of State's submission that the claimant could be accompanied (at least initially) to some interviews, but instead concluded that "this would not address some of the potential stress to which Judge Mark referred [in *IJ v SSWP (IB)* [2010] UKUT408 (AAC)"] (para.7).

The need to apply Charlton *in the light of all the available evidence*

2.064   In *GS v SSWP (ESA)* [2014] UKUT 16 (AAC), Judge Mark held:

"It was the duty of the decision maker in relation to the present appeal, under rule 24(4)(b) of the Tribunal Procedure (First-tier Tribunal) (SEC) Rules 2008, to provide with the response to the appeal copies of all documents relevant to the case in the decision maker's possession. It was also the duty of the Secretary of State, under rule 2(4) of the same Rules, to help the tribunal to deal with the case fairly and justly. Under one head or the other, if not both, the tribunal ought to have been provided with copies of the evidence before the previous tribunal which had heard the appeal only 7 months before the new decision now under appeal. It is a duty which the new tribunal [to which he remitted the case] ought to have enforced" (para. 5).

While a Med 3 issued by the claimant's GP is not conclusive on the issue under reg.29(2), the implications of the certificate must be addressed and facts found to the extent possible (*SP v SSWP (ESA)* [2014] UKUT 278 (AAC), para.16).

Should consideration be given to the possibility of working from home?

As noted, in *SM v SSWP (ESA)* [2014] UKUT 241 (AAC), Judge **2.065** Wikeley took the view that a tribunal erred in law in considering whether a claimant could work from home. He cited in support of his interpretation the tenor of Judge Ward's decision in *PD v SSWP (ESA)* [2014] UKUT 148. Judge Wikeley noted that Judge Ward there

"identified the central issue in that appeal as being the impact of regulation 29 "on persons who by reason of mental ill-health have an impaired ability to get to places, such as a hypothetical workplace" (at paragraph 1). If claimants could not avail themselves of regulation 29 simply because they could get a home-working job, then the whole premise of Judge Ward's analysis was flawed. I do not accept that it was" (para.11).

It should be noted, however, that later in *PD*, Judge Ward seemed to indicate that a tribunal *could* look at the viability and suitability of work from home before looking at ability to travel to a workplace. Judge Ward stated

"The tribunal may wish to explore types of work which the person could do from home. Even if the traditional fields for such activity have declined, information technology must bring with it a number of such opportunities for some people. But if such work is not appropriate to the particular claimant, the tribunal will have to conduct the assessment of risk, which is the primary purpose of regulation 29, as best it can in relation to the sort of range of work mandated by *Charlton*, outside the home. If someone has been found to be unable to do something, I find it hard to see how it might be possible to hold that there would be no substantial risk to their health on an assumption that they were effectively made to do that which had been found to be impossible for them (i.e. go to work unaccompanied), though I do not intend to lay that down as a proposition of law. Far more likely is it that what is required is an evaluation of their circumstances when making the hypothetical journey, in particular in relation to being accompanied, in order to see whether the conditions could be satisfied which would alleviate or avoid the risk to health" (para.16).

It is submitted, however, that, for the reasons he gives (set out in the annotation), Judge Wikeley's view is the better one, given *Charlton* and the purposes of reg.29.

Whether work would be good for the claimant is not the correct test

2.066   *CH v SSWP (ESA)* [2014] UKUT 11 (AAC) has been followed and applied by Judge Hemingway in *CS v SSWP (ESA)* [2014] UKUT 550 (AAC) and by Judge Bano in *C McC v SSWP (ESA)* [2014] UKUT 176 (AAC).

Must reg.29(2)(b) always be considered where the claimant has failed to achieve a sufficient score on the LCWA?

2.067   *NS v SSWP (ESA)* [2014] UKUT 0115 (AAC) is reported as [2014] AACR 33. Judge White's approach there was followed by Judge Gray in *KB v SSWP (ESA)* [2014] UKUT 303 (AAC).

In *RU v SSWP (ESA)* [2014] UKUT 77 (AAC), Judge Ward held that:

> "if the claimant's GP was advising his or her patient to refrain from work for 6 months by a Med 3 issued more or less contemporaneously with the decision under appeal, it was incumbent on the tribunal to consider the implications of that. The work capability assessment is an artificial construct, which looks at certain activities only, and there is no necessary correlation between a doctor's views as to what the patient can manage and the outcome of the WCA applied to that person, or vice versa. Regulation 29 has the function of a safety valve addressing that lack of correlation, protecting claimants (and others) from the effect of determinations which in the circumstances set out in that regulation would otherwise result in substantial risk to health" (para.6).

See further *SP v SSWP (ESA)* [2014] UKUT 278 (AAC) noted under the heading "*the need to apply* Charlton *in the light of all the available evidence*", earlier in this update.

Merely reiterating the statutory test is not enough; the need to address the issues, engage in careful fact-finding and provide adequate reasons for the decision

2.068   In *PH v SSWP (ESA)* [2014] UKUT 502 (AAC), Judge Bano rightly stressed that

> "[t]he difficult issues which may arise under regulation 29 will often require detailed findings of fact to be made by the tribunal, rather than mantra-like recitations of the terms of the legislation and unparticularised references to adjustments in the workplace" (para.5).

In *MF v SSWP (ESA)* [2014] UKUT 523 (AAC), Judge Mark allowed the appeal stating that

> " . . . The tribunal does not indicate what occupation or range of occupations it had in mind. More seriously it totally failed to deal with

the points actually made in the written submissions. It was dealing with a claimant who had not worked for 20 years, whose appearance was described by the disability analyst as unkempt, and whose behaviour was described as restless with reduced facial expression, and whom it had found was prone to episodes of depression when he may lack the motivation to do things.

The tribunal needed to address how he would have coped not just with an interview and with some unspecified job when not having a depressive episode, but with all the matters identified by the claimant's representative in his written submissions and then determine whether there was a substantial risk to his mental or physical health (or that of anybody else) if he were found not to have limited capability for work. There have also been raised, at least before me, issues as to the extent to which the claimant can use public transport or travel at busy times and the tribunal may need to consider this both in connection with any requirements imposed in connection with jobseeker's allowance and in connection with any employment he may obtain. In failing to identify the correct issues and to make appropriate reasoned findings, the tribunal was in error of law. Its decision must be set aside and the matter remitted for rehearing by a new tribunal" (paras 7-8).

pp.938–941, *annotation to the Employment and Support Allowance Regulations 2008 (SI 2008/794) reg.35 (Certain claimants to be treated as having limited capability for work-related activity)*

A burgeoning case law on this regulation covers five issues, dealt with in turn, below. 2.069

Issue 1: what evidence of work-related activity must be provided by the Secretary of State and what can a tribunal do where no such evidence is supplied

In *IM v SSWP (ESA)* [2014] UKUT 412 (AAC) a panel of three Upper Tribunal judges dealt with the question of "the amount of detail the regulation 35(2) decision-makers should have of the possible results of the work-focused interview" to which those found not to be incapable of work-related activity will be subject. As is clear from the annotation, this is a question to which different Upper Tribunal judges have given different answers. To the cases already noted there can be added: *AP v SSWP (ESA)* [2013] UKUT 553 (AAC); *PF v SSWP (ESA)* [2013] UKUT 634 (AAC); and *NA v SSWP (ESA)* [2014] UKUT 305 (AAC). In *NA*, Judge Gray deprecated the Secretary of State's failure to provide sufficient information to the tribunal; had the "action plan" seen by Judge Gray on appeal, and which predated the hearing before the First-tier tribunal, been made available to that tribunal the further appeal to the Upper Tribunal might well have been avoided (presumably because that tribunal would then have applied the regulation in the claimant's favour).

The problem with decision-making on reg.35(2) arises because at the stage the decision maker (Secretary of State or First-tier tribunal) has to decide the matter of "substantial risk" exactly what will be required of this particular claimant at any such work-focused interview is unknown, a matter of conjecture, and the decision-maker must perforce engage in a degree of "crystal ball gazing" (para.75), with "substantial risk" bearing the commonly agreed meaning of a risk "that cannot sensibly be ignored having regard to the nature and gravity of the feared harm in the particular case" (para.65).

Having considered the range of case law on the provision covered in the annotation, the panel rightly held that a purposive approach, reflecting practicalities apparent in *Charlton*, must be taken to the regulation (para.83). In the view of the panel,

> "the absence of any system for ensuring that relevant information obtained, and findings made, in the course of carrying out a work capability assessment and applying regulation 35(2) and the reasoning behind the decision made on regulation 35(2) are made available to a person considering whether a requirement to engage in work-related activity should be imposed on the claimant effectively destroys the Secretary of State's argument that only generalised information about some types of work-related activity need be taken into account by the regulation 35(2) decision-maker when considering the possible consequences of a particular claimant being found not to have limited capability for work-related activity. The purpose underlying regulation 35(2) requires that those applying it make predictions about the consequences to the particular claimant of him being found not to have limited capability for work-related activity. In a few cases, the risks of an inappropriate requirement to engage in work-related activity being imposed will be too great to be ignored" (para.101).

2.070 Given the present system of administering the legislation, the First-tier Tribunal needs to know

> "not only what the least demanding types of work-related activity are but also what the most demanding types are in the area where the claimant lives.
>
> . . . .
>
> [O]n an appeal in which regulation 35(2) is in issue, [the Secretary of State] cannot be expected to anticipate exactly what work-related activity a particular claimant would in fact be required to do. This is axiomatic.
>
> But what the Secretary of State can and should provide is evidence of the types of work-related activity available in each area [Wolverhampton in this claimant's case] and by reference thereto what the particular claimant may be required to undertake and those which he considers it would be reasonable for the provider to require the claimant to undertake. The First-tier Tribunal would then be in a position to assess the relevant risks.
>
> [T]he types of work-related activity available may vary from provider to provider, but it should not be beyond the wit of the Department and providers to produce and maintain a list, perhaps for each of the regions into which the First-tier Tribunal is organised, of what is

available in each area within the region. The relevant information could then be included in submissions in individual cases. The First-tier Tribunal would be able to assess the evidential force of such a submission.

. . .

Being unable to carry out an activity does not necessarily imply that there will be a substantial risk to anyone's health if the claimant is required to engage in the activity. Nor does the risk of being sanctioned. Therefore, it may be fairly obvious in most cases that the claimant does not have any realistic argument under regulation 35 and indeed, if made aware of the issues, the claimant may often accept that that is so. But where there turns out to be a serious argument in relation to regulation 35, the provision of the basic information about the more demanding types of work-related activity would enable the First-tier Tribunal to make the necessary predictions by reference to possible outcomes for the particular claimant" (paras 104-107, 110).

The panel considered that where the Secretary of State has accepted that the claimant has limited capability for work, the Secretary of State will be able to aid the tribunal with a more focused submission on why, given the claimant's disablement, reg.35(2) does not apply. It noted that in some cases (see e.g. *CMcC v SSWP (ESA)* [2014] UKUT 176 (AAC)) the work-focused interview will have taken place before the tribunal hears the appeal and its outcome and basis should be provided to it where possible, thereby reducing the element of prediction required, but always remembering that, because of SSA 1998 s.12(8)(b) any such evidence "should only be taken into account so far as it is relevant to the position at the time of the decision of the Secretary of State" (para.113).

The panel held that merely identifying that there is some work-related activity that a claimant could do is insufficient to ground a finding

"that there would not be risk to someone's health if the claimant were found not to have limited capability for work-related activity. That is because it does not wholly answer the statutory question" (para. 116).

But what if the Secretary of State fails to provide the required evidence? In such a case, the panel considered that the First-tier Tribunal has a number of options as to how to proceed. It can use its own knowledge, if it is confident that it is up-to-date and complete as to the more demanding types of work-related activity. It may instead adjourn to obtain that evidence or decide that it can properly determine the case one way or the other without it. The right approach depends on the circumstances and, in particular, on how vulnerable the claimant is (para.118).

Interestingly, the panel also made clear that there were ways in which the reg.35(2) risk could be greatly reduced or even eliminated by a change of practice in the way in which the scheme is administered (paras 98-100). But, unless and until the scheme of decision-making and the legislation is changed the approach in *IM* must be followed (see *EH v SSWP (ESA)* [2014] UKUT 473 (AAC)).

Issue 2: how does reg.35(2) apply if the claimant could never work again or if there is no work-related activity that could reasonably be required of him?

2.071   Here Judge Mark and Judge Jacobs take diametrically opposed positions, the former arguing that in such circumstances the provision can have no application, the latter arguing that it can and must in order to protect the most vulnerable by affording them an opportunity to be placed in the support group in circumstances in which their condition has not met the tailored specifics of ESA Regs 2008 Sch.3. It is submitted that Judge Jacobs' approach is the better one in that promotes the purpose behind reg.35(2) and thus sits better with the purposive approach taken to the provision by the panel in *IM*, above.

Both judges rightly see the position as involving consideration of the WRA 2007, the ESA Regs 2008 and the Employment and Support Allowance (Work-Related Activity) Regulations 2011 (SI 2011/1349) ("the W-RA Regs"). Both note the definition of "work-related activity" in WRA 2007, s.13(7): "activity which makes it more likely that the person will obtain or remain in work or be able to do so". Although s.13(8) was not in force at the date of the decisions concerned, both judges noted its stipulation that such activity "includes work experience or a work placement". Similarly both took on board, reg.3 of the W-RA Regs (see pp.1234-1235) giving the Secretary of State discretion on whether or not to require a person in the work-related activity group actually to undertake any such activity, and providing that any such requirement imposed "must be reasonable in the view of the Secretary of State, having regard to the person's circumstances", and may not require him/her to undergo medical treatment or to apply for a job or undertake work, whether as an employee or otherwise.

In *JS v SSWP (ESA)* [2013] UKUT 635 (AAC), followed by him in *RV v SSWP (ESA)* [2014] UKUT 56 (AAC), Judge Mark held that the initial work-focused interview cannot constitute work-related activity since work-related activities can only be required once it has taken place (para.16). Moreover, the work-focused health assessment was also separate from such activity being an assessment, dealt with separately, and not meeting the s.13(7) definition, above (para.16). Given that definition, he considered "that if a person is patently not going to be able to obtain work at any stage, it is difficult to see how they could be required to carry out work-related activities" (para.15). Accordingly in his judgment, in this case reg.35(2) could not assist this claimant:

"On the basis of the tribunal's finding as to his health problems, there would seem to be no real possibility of his resuming work and it is difficult to see how any interview could come within the definition of work-focused interview in section 12(7) of the 2007 Act since, due to his ill health, there would seem to be no prospect of his getting into work. For the same reason, there would not seem to be any work-related activity that the claimant could be required to do, in that, because of his health problems, there would be no activity which would make it even arguably more likely that he would be able to obtain work.

It follows that, on the basis of the tribunal's findings of fact, there are no work-focused interviews or work-related activities that the Secretary of State could lawfully require the claimant to attend or undertake and that, in the absence of any other issue, there is no risk to his health as a result of not being found to have limited capability for work-related activity. Accordingly he does not fall within regulation 35(2)" (paras 27-28).

Judge Mark reiterated this in *GS v SSWP (ESA)* [2014] UKUT 16 (AAC), para.26.

In marked contrast, in *NS v SSWP (ESA)* [2014] UKUT 149 (AAC), 2.072 Judge Jacobs rejected this way of looking at reg.35(2). Nor, in that case, did the Secretary of State support Judge Mark's analysis. There, Ms Wilkinson, appearing for the Secretary of State, argued that his analysis could not be right because it would remove from the most vulnerable claimants "who will not work again and for whom any WRA [work-related activity] will pose a substantial risk to their health" their final chance of being placed in the support group, final, of course, because reg.35(2) can only be applied where the claimant was not regarded as having limited capability for work-related activity, applying reg.34(1) and Sch.3 (para.23). Her suggested approach, based on s.13(7) requiring only that the activity make it "more likely" that the claimant will be able to obtain work and the chance that circumstances might change (e.g. "through a new form of treatment or medication"), was not accepted by Judge Jacobs as enough to cover the claimant who would clearly never work again. The approach, he thought, required a tribunal to make contradictory findings and, viewed as a statement that there was *at present* no work the claimant could do, left unresolved the question of whether reg.35(2) applied for the time being (para.24). The provision had to be applied effectively, whether before or after consideration had been given to the sort of work-related activity appropriate for a claimant (para.25). For him, it was critical to see reg.35(2) as being a *hypothesis* requiring the identification of "the possible consequences of a particular postulate (the *if* bit)" (para.26). The flaw in Judge Mark's analysis was to ignore the postulate. Judge Jacobs explained further:

"If a possible consequence would be a substantial risk to health, the provision is satisfied and the claimant qualifies for the support group. As I have already said, the postulate cannot be read literally. The tribunal does not simply have to postulate the claimant being found not to have limited capability for work-related activity. It also has to postulate the claimant actually undertaking such activity.

It does not have to identify that activity with precision. That is a separate stage that will only be reached if the tribunal decides that the claimant does not qualify for the support group. If and when that stage is reached, it is a matter for the Secretary of State, not the tribunal. The tribunal's task is preliminary to and necessarily more speculative and more general than the actual application of regulation 3 of the

2011 Regulations. The tribunal has to apply the hypothesis embodied in regulation 35(2). In doing so, it cannot deny the postulate. That, with respect to Judge Mark, is what he did. He denied that the postulate (the *if* bit) could ever apply in certain circumstances. But that is the very foundation of the provision. It is what the tribunal is required to accept. It cannot reject the basis of the hypothesis that forms the structure of regulation 35(2).

In doing so, the tribunal has to limit itself to applying regulation 35(2) and avoid trespassing into the Secretary of State's decision-making under regulation 3 of the 2011 Regulations. . . . The way to remain properly within the tribunal's jurisdiction lies in the level of generality at which the tribunal has to consider work-related activity. Ms Wilkinson accepted that my decision in *AH* was correct. What the tribunal has to do is to identify in a general way 'the range and type of work-related activity which a claimant is capable of performing and might be expected to undertake' (to quote *AH*); and it must do so regardless of whether the Secretary of State would actually require the claimant to undertake any activity and regardless of whether any such activity would have any effect on the claimant's ability to 'obtain or remain in work' (to quote section 13(7))" (paras 26-28).

Judge Jacobs, in effect, requires the tribunal to ignore what might be done under reg.3 of the W-RA Regs. This chimes well with the answer given by the three-judge panel in *IM* to the question in Issue 3, which must now be examined

Issue 3: given that reg.3 of the Employment and Support Allowance (Work-Related Activity) Regulations 2011 (SI 2011/1349) ("the W-RA Regs") stipulates that the work-related activity required must be "reasonable . . . , having regard to the person's circumstances", does this mean that the condition in reg.35(2) cannot be met?

2.073   In *IM v SSWP (ESA)* [2014] UKUT 412 (AAC), the panel of three Upper Tribunal judges answered this in the negative since an affirmative answer would undermine the purpose of the provision. In so deciding they endorsed the decisions on this point given by Judge Jacobs in *NS v SSWP (ESA)* [2014] UKUT 149 (AAC) (paras 30, 34) and Judge Bano in *CMcC v SSWP (ESA)* [2014] UKUT 176 (AAC). As Judge Bano put it (in a passage endorsed by Judge Jacobs as consonant with his own view in *NS*):

"If regulation 35(2) is to have any real meaning, it is not open to a tribunal to find that work-related activity does not present a risk of harm to a claimant on the basis that the claimant will not actually be required to undertake *any* meaningful activity if it turns out to be harmful. I therefore consider that the action of the employment adviser of effectively bringing the claimant's action plan to an end out of concern for her health was evidence which the tribunal should have taken into account when evaluating the risk of harm to the claimant if she were not found to have limited capability for work-related activity" (para.12).

Issue 4: the "substantial risk" must arise "by reasons of" a specific disease or bodily or mental disablement

In *DR v SSWP (ESA)* [2014] UKUT 188 (AAC); [2014 AACR 38,   **2.074**
Judge May held erroneous in law a tribunal decision that the claimant satisfied reg.29 because it had not made the necessary connection between the risk and the disease or disablement (see para.3). He considered the same principle applied to reg.35 (para.10). Alcohol misuse in itself is not such a disablement. To rank as disablement the misuse of alcohol must rank as "alcohol dependency" in terms of the "constellation of markers" found in quotations from *R(DLA) 6/06* in the Three-Judge Panel's decision in *JG v SSWP (ESA)* [2013] UKUT 37 (AAC); [2013] AACR 23 (see paras 5-7, 10 of *DR*). See further, update to p.923, above.

Issue 5: can the availability of third party assistance be taken into account?

In *MT v SSWP (ESA)* [2013] UKUT 545 (AAC), in the context of   **2.075**
reg.35(2) Judge Gray firmly rejected looking at capacity to perform activities with third party assistance, observing:

> "I do need to deal however with the observation of the FTT in its statement of reasons that the appellant could take another person with her to any work-related activities. It may be that the Secretary of State would be facilitative in any matter which helped a claimant engage so as to improve their ultimate prospects of retaining work. I do not know. Whether or not that is so, is not relevant. As a matter of law any work-related activity which could only be accomplished because of the presence of another person must be looked upon as not being an activity that the claimant can carry out. *The issue under regulation 35 (2)(b) as to whether there would be a substantial risk to the mental or physical health of any person if the claimant were found not to have limited capability for work-related activity cannot be assessed as if the claimant under consideration had somebody else by their side.* There will be claimants who have a need for the personal reassurance of another person, but who do not have anybody available to perform that role. Even if they did, it would not be reasonable for such an assessment to be made on the basis of reliance on another's goodwill. Legal tests cannot depend upon that. Where an appellant who is found to have limited capability for work-related activities wishes to engage voluntarily, it may be that they choose to do so with the help of another person, and it may (or may not, I do not know) be possible for them to do so, but the capacity to engage only with that assistance cannot be part of the test of capability" (para.34, emphasis added by commentator).

In *PD v SSWP (ESA)* [2013] UKUT 148 (AAC), in the context of the similarly worded reg. 29(2)(b), Judge Ward agreed with the italicised passage insofar as it meant "without consideration as to whether the third party's presence would be made out in fact" (para.21), but otherwise distinguished the passage as focussing on the claimant's capability to perform activities (agreeing that there third party assistance should be ignored) rather than the different question of what risks would ensue (where, with respect to travelling, at least, third party assistance available in fact might obviate the risk). See further update to pp.922-925, above, and cross refer to the update to pp.1110-1112 and the judgment of the three-judge panel in *JC v SSWP (ESA)* [2014] UKUT 352 (AAC) which did not consider that a person could properly be regarded "as able to engage in social contact if she or he can do so only if accompanied by someone, *at least without further explanation as to how it is envisaged that that might be realistic in the workplace*" (para.45, emphasis supplied by commentator) here substituting for "in the workplace" the different context of "the places where work-related activities might be performed".

p.940, *annotation to the Employment and Support Allowance Regulations 2008 (SI 2008/794) reg.35 (Certain claimants to be treated as having limited capability for work-related activity)*

2.076 *MN v Secretary of State for Work and Pensions (ESA)* is reported at [2014] AACR 6.

p.951, *amendment to the Employment and Support Allowance Regulations 2008 (SI 2008/794) reg.43(3) (Circumstances when partners of claimants entitled to an income-related allowance are not regarded as engaged in remunerative work)*

2.077 With effect from December 31, 2014, reg.20(4) of the Shared Parental Leave and Statutory Shared Parental Pay (Consequential Amendments to Subordinate Legislation) Order 2014 (SI 2014/3255) amended reg.43(3) by adding ", shared parental leave" after "paternity leave".

p.964, *amendment to the Employment and Support Allowance Regulations 2008 (SI 2008/794) reg.63 (Reduction of employment and support allowance)*

2.077.1 With effect from April 29, 2013, reg.37(1), (4) of the Universal Credit (Consequential, Supplementary, Incidental and Miscellaneous Provisions) Regulations 2013 (SI 2013/630) amended reg.63(5) to read as follows:

"(5) For the purposes of determining the amount of any income-related allowance payable, a claimant is to be treated as receiving the amount of any contributory allowance [including new style ESA] which would have been payable but for any reduction made in accordance with this regulation [or section 11J of the Act respectively].".

p.975, *amendment to the Employment and Support Allowance Regulations 2008 (SI 2008/794) reg.70(4) (Special cases: supplemental—persons from abroad)*

2.078 With effect from May 31, 2014, reg.7 of the Social Security (Habitual Residence) (Amendment) Regulations 2014 (SI 2014/902) amended reg.70(4) by substituting the following sub-paragraphs for sub-paras (a) to (f):

"(za) a qualified person for the purposes of regulation 6 of the Immigration (European Economic Area) Regulations 2006 as a worker or a self-employed person;

(zb) a family member of a person referred to in sub-paragraph (za) within the meaning of regulation 7(1)(a), (b) or (c) of those Regulations;

(zc) a person who has a right to reside permanently in the United Kingdom by virtue of regulation 15(1)(c), (d) or (e) of those Regulations;".

p.984, *amendment to the Employment and Support Allowance Regulations 2008 (SI 2008/794): insertion of a new regulation, numbered 82A*

With effect from December 31, 2014, art.20 (1), (6) of the Shared Parental Leave and Statutory Shared Parental Pay (Consequential Amendments to Subordinate Legislation) Order 2014 (SI 2014/3255) inserted after reg.82 a new regulation, numbered 82A, to read as follows: 2.079

"Effect of statutory shared parental pay on a contributory allowance

82A.—(1) This regulation applies where—
(a) a claimant is entitled to statutory shared parental pay and, on the day immediately preceding the first day in the shared parental pay period—
    (i) is in a period of limited capability for work; and
    (ii) satisfies the conditions for a contributory allowance in accordance with section 1(2)(a) of the Act; and
(b) on any day during the statutory shared parental pay period—
    (i) that claimant is in a period of limited capability for work; and
    (ii) that day is not a day where that claimant is treated as not having limited capability for work.

(2) Where this regulation applies, notwithstanding section 20(6) of the Act, a claimant who is entitled to statutory shared parental pay is to be entitled to a contributory allowance in respect of any day that falls within the shared parental pay period.

(3) Where by virtue of paragraph (2) a person is entitled to a contributory allowance for any week (including part of a week), the total amount of such benefit payable to that claimant for that week is to be reduced by an amount equivalent to any statutory shared parental pay to which that claimant is entitled in accordance with Part 12ZC of the Contributions and Benefits Act for the same week (or equivalent part of a week where entitlement to a contributory allowance is for part of a week) and only the balance, if any, of the contributory allowance is to be payable to that claimant.

(4) In this regulation "statutory shared parental pay period" means the weeks in respect of which statutory shared parental pay is payable to a person under section 171ZY(2) of the Social Security Contributions and Benefits Act 1992."

DEFINITIONS

"the Act"—see reg.2(1).
"claimant"—see WRA 2007 s.24(1).
"contributory allowance"—see WRA 2007 s.1(7).
"Contributions and Benefits Act"—see WRA 2007 s.65.
"statutory shared parental pay period"—see para.(4).
"week"—see reg.2(1).

GENERAL NOTE

2.080   In essence this provides that, where a claimant's ongoing entitlement to CESA and statutory shared parental pay (SSPP) overlap, then during the period they coincide, despite WRA 2007 s.20(6), entitlement to CESA is preserved, but the amount payable in respect of the week or part week, as appropriate, is to be reduced (even to nil) by the amount of SSPP for that week or part week—only the balance (if any) of CESA is payable.

p.996, *amendment to the Employment and Support Allowance Regulations 2008 (SI 2008/794) reg.95 (Earnings of employed earners)*

2.081   With effect from December 31, 2014, art.20(7) of the Shared Parental Leave and Statutory Shared Parental Pay (Consequential Amendments to Subordinate Legislation) Order 2014 (SI 2014/3255) amended reg.95(2)(b) by inserting after the words "paternity leave" the words ", shared parental leave".

pp.1046-1047, *amendment to the Employment and Support Allowance Regulations 2008 (SI 2008/794) reg.144 (Waiting days)*

2.082   With effect from October 27, 2014, reg.2(2) of the Social Security (Jobseeker's Allowance and Employment and Support Allowance) (Waiting Days) Amendment Regulations 2014 (SI 2014/2309) amended paras.(1) and (2)(d) by substituting "7" for "3". This increase in the number of waiting days applies with respect to a new claim in respect of a waiting period starting on or after that date; reg.4 of the amending instrument ensures that the changes made to reg.144 do not apply where a waiting period began before that date. For its text, see p.15, above.

p.1076, *correction to the Employment and Support Allowance Regulations 2008 (SI 2008/794) Sch.2 Activity 2 (Standing and sitting): descriptor 2(b)*

2.083   The points available in respect of this descriptor are nine.

p.1078, *correction to formatting of the Employment and Support Allowance Regulations 2008 (SI 2008/794) Sch.2 Activity 9: Absence or loss of control whilst conscious leading to extensive evacuation of the bowel and/or bladder, other than enuresis (bed- wetting), despite the wearing or use of any aids or adaptations which are normally, or could reasonably be, worn or used: descriptor 9(a)*

The words from "sufficient" to "clothing" qualify *both* limbs of each   2.084
descriptor and not just the second limb as is misleadingly the case with the layout in the book. The correct layout is as follows:

"(a) At least once a month experiences:
  (i) loss of control leading to extensive evacuation of the bowel and/or voiding of the bladder; or
  (ii) substantial leakage of the contents of a collecting device
sufficient to require cleaning and a change in clothing."

p.1079, *correction to formatting of the Employment and Support Allowance Regulations 2008 (SI 2008/794) Sch.2 Activity 12: Awareness of everyday hazards (such as boiling water or sharp objects): descriptors (a), (b) and (c)*

For the avoidance of doubt, in each of these descriptors, the words   2.085
from "such that" to "maintain safety" govern *both* sub-paras (i) and (ii), so as to read as follows:

"12. (a) Reduced awareness of everyday hazards leads to a significant risk of:
  (i) injury to self or others; or
  (ii) damage to property or possessions
such that [⁴ the claimant requires] supervision for the majority of the time to maintain safety.
(b) Reduced awareness of everyday hazards leads to a significant risk of
  (i) injury to self or others; or
  (ii) damage to property or possessions
such that [⁴ the claimant requires] supervision for the majority of the time to maintain safety
(c) Reduced awareness of everyday hazards leads to a significant risk of:
  (i) injury to self or others; or
  (ii) damage to property or possessions
such that [⁴ the claimant occasionally requires] supervision to maintain safety."

pp.1097-1100, *annotation to the Employment and Support Allowance Regulations 2008 (SI 2008/794) Sch.2 Activity 1: mobilising unaided by another person with or without a walking stick, manual wheelchair or other aid if such aid is normally, or could reasonably be, worn or used*

"Pausing" is to be equated with "stopping" for the purposes of descriptors (a), (c) and (d) (*GC v SSWP (ESA)* [2014] UKUT 117 (AAC),   2.086

para.21; *DB v SSWP (ESA)* [2014] UKUT 471 (AAC), para.4). So that if a tribunal found that a claimant paused for a few seconds after 30 metres, it should go on to ask "why?" (*DB*, para.5). In addition a tribunal should not confine consideration merely to mobilising on foot but should also consider possible wheelchair use (*DB*, para.7).

In *CS v SSWP (ESA)* [2014] UKUT 519 (AAC), Judge White considered descriptor 1(a). He held that although the phrase "on level ground" appears only in para.(a)(i) and is absent from para.(a)(ii), "the only possible interpretation of the repeatability test is that it is on the same terms as the primary test. That is on level ground" (para.30). Although in this case, the claimant had his own wheelchair and so questions of access to one were not relevant to the appeal, Judge White noted that the three judge panel had in *SI* referred to the Access to Work Scheme. The Secretary of State's submission to Judge White in *CS* provided information on that scheme, which will be useful to other tribunals considering the reasonableness of possible wheelchair use, since it makes clear that the Scheme cannot help:

"The UT judges [in *SI v Secretary of State for Work and Pensions (ESA)*] referred to the Access to Work Scheme as a possible source of assistance with a manual wheelchair. However, that is not the case. The Access to Work Scheme is intended to support the additional costs of employing a disabled person, and helps over 30,000 disabled people to take up and remain in employment every year, providing support such as specialist aids and equipment, as well as help with travel to work. In order to obtain help under the Scheme, a person would need to satisfy the eligibility criteria. In summary, these are that the person must:
- have a disability (as defined in the Equality Act 2010), or long-term health condition; and
- be in or about to start employment or go to a job interview;
- live and work in Great Britain;
- have no other support available;
- not be entitled to an incapacity benefit.

Where a person satisfies the criteria, the DWP disability employment adviser would work with the claimant and the employer to determine how the person's disability can be supported in the workplace, including any reasonable adjustments the employment might have in place. The Scheme would not normally be used to fund purchase of a manual wheelchair, as it is expected that this would be provided by the appropriate wheelchair services in the area . . . However, it could fund the extra costs of a specialist wheelchair if appropriate. Where assistance with travel to work is required, and no other method of transport is available, the Scheme might assist with the cost of taxis. It is my submission this would go some way towards enabling a claimant with mobilising difficulties to look for and start work" (para.42).

As the annotation makes clear, where a claimant has been awarded

HRMC a tribunal in considering ability to mobilise should take into account the evidence on which that award was based (see in addition to the other cases listed, *MA v SSWP (ESA)* [2014] UKUT 185 (AAC); *JC v SSWP (ESA)* [2014] UKUT 257 (AAC)), unless it would add nothing of significance to the other evidence before the tribunal, for example, because the claimant's condition has fundamentally altered since that award or because that award was made in respect of a temporary condition (e.g. restrictions on walking due to an operation) no longer pertaining (*JC*, paras 4-7).

SI v SSWP (ESA) [2014] UKUT 308 (AAC), noted on p.1099, is reported as [2015] AACR 5.

pp.1100-1101, *annotation to the Employment and Support Allowance Regulations 2008 (SI 2008/794) Sch.2 Activity 2: standing and sitting*

It should be noted that in *MM v Department for Social Development (ESA)* [2014] NI Com 48 a tribunal of three Northern Ireland Commissioners disagreed with Judge Wikeley's approach in *MC* to the interpretation of Activity 2 descriptors prior to the January 2013 amendment.   2.087

p.1101, *annotation to the Employment and Support Allowance Regulations 2008 (SI 2008/794) Sch.2 Activity 4: picking up and moving or transferring by the use of upper body or arms: descriptor 4(c): cannot transfer a light but bulky object such as an empty cardboard box*

This descriptor has been considered in two recent cases, each dealing   2.088 with whether the task can be achieved by someone with only one good arm, given that the descriptor, unlike its predecessors no longer stipulates using both hands together.

In *KH v SSWP (ESA)* [2014] UKUT 455 (AAC), Judge Mark accepted that the change in wording means that the use of both hands together is no longer essential, so that if a person could pick the box up and move it by the use of one arm and the upper body, that is by wedging it under the arm, that would suffice as capability to complete the task. But he rightly cautioned that not everyone can be expected to do that. It would depend on all the circumstances of the claimant's condition so that, in this particular case, he considered that the tribunal was entitled to conclude that this claimant "would reasonably require both arms to perform the task", especially so since the object in question is "bulky" (para.4).

In *MT v SSWP (ESA)* [2014] UKUT 548 (AAC), Judge Hemingway agreed with Judge Mark's approach in *KH*, accepting that in principle the task could sometimes be performed by someone with one arm in the way suggested. But he rightly commented that completion of the task is undoubtedly easier for those with two good arms and that it cannot simply be assumed, given the bulky size of the object in question, that someone with one good arm will be capable of accomplishing it (paras

18, 19). It is dependent on all the circumstances of the case. A tribunal should

> "offer some explanation as to how it concludes (if it does so conclude) that the task can be achieved by a claimant who is incapacitated in the way this appellant says he is. In the passage quoted above, the F-tT has not made it clear whether it thinks the appellant could use his left upper limb at all in attempting the task. On the assumption that it does not think he could, it has not explained how it thinks the task might practically be achieved with the use of the rest of his upper body and his right upper limb. Its finding that he is "resolute" does indicate its view that he has determination but that, of itself, will not always be sufficient for a claimant to overcome physical difficulties and does not, of itself, therefore, represent an adequate explanation for its ultimate conclusion. The task of an F-tT in such a case need not be regarded as an exacting one but the standard required has not, for the above reasons, been reached here" (para.20).

pp.1101–1103, *annotation to the Employment and Support Allowance Regulations 2008 (SI 2008/794) Sch.2 Activity 5: manual dexterity; descriptor 5(d); cannot single-handedly use a suitable keyboard or mouse*

2.089   As Judge Mark notes in *KH v SSWP (ESA)* [2014] UKUT 455 (AAC), the disagreement between himself and Judge Wright remains to be resolved on another occasion. They disagree on whether scoring under this descriptor requires inability to use both these items of computer equipment (Judge Wright) or inability to use one (Judge Mark). But in *KH*, Judge Mark agrees with Judge Wright that it is not computer literacy that is being tested, but that rather

> "what is being tested is the physical ability, so far as manual dexterity is concerned, to use a suitable keyboard or mouse. His description in paragraph 48 of his decision of the test is whether the mouse can be gripped and moved over an icon or box and then clicked and using the keyboard to type out letters, numbers and symbols. Again, I would not dissent from that, subject to questions relating to such matters as reasonable repetition and the effects of, for example, repetitive strain injury, and that the purpose of the so using the mouse or typing out letters etc. is to achieve certain results on the computer they are being used with. It is possible that a person may have sufficient control of the hands to be able to move and click the mouse or type letters but insufficient control to do so with any degree of accuracy or with any regularity or for any reasonable time.
>
> When the descriptor speaks of using a keyboard or mouse, as Judge Wright's examples make clear, the use can only be to achieve results on a computer. It follows that in assessing whether hands are so lacking in dexterity as to score points on this descriptor it must be in relation to the operation of a computer. Why that scores the same number of points as not being able to make a meaningful mark with a pen or pencil is unclear, but what is clear is that even Judge Wright's

description of what is required is far more demanding than a physical ability to make a cross on a piece of paper" (paras 10, 11).

p.1104, *annotation to the Employment and Support Allowance Regulations 2008 (SI 2008/794) Sch.2 Activity 9: Absence or loss of control whilst conscious leading to extensive evacuation of the bowel and/or bladder, other than enuresis (bed-wetting), despite the wearing or use of any aids or adaptations which are normally, or could reasonably be, worn or used: correction of case reference*

Please amend the year in the case reference for *NH v SSWP (ESA)* in each of the three places in which it appears to [2011]. The quotation from the case can be found at para.14 of the decision. **2.090**

pp.1107-1108, *annotation to the Employment and Support Allowance Regulations 2008 (SI 2008/794) Sch.2 Pt.II: [C] approaching and interpreting specific descriptors*

In *(1) ST, (2) GF v SSWP (ESA)* [2014] UKUT 547 (AAC), a panel of three Upper Tribunal judges considered the question of **2.091**

"the weight to be given to the observations on mental health descriptors by a physiotherapist (or an appropriately qualified person) when carrying out a Work Capability Assessment under regulation 19 of the Employment and Support Allowance Regulations 2008 ("the ESA Regulations")" (para.1).

It will be recalled that Judge Mark in *JH v SSWP (ESA)* [2013] UKUT 269 (AAC), on which the appellants relied, had rejected the opinion of a HCP who was a physiotherapist as of *no probative value* in assessing the mental health problems of the claimant in that case.

The panel categorically rejected Judge Mark's comments—which it saw as *obiter*—as

"wrong if and to the extent that they purport to create a rule of law or starting point that observations on mental health descriptors by HCP physiotherapists are of no probative value whatsoever or are highly likely or likely to have little probative value and thus should be accorded no or little weight by the decision maker and the First-tier tribunal" (para.33).

Instead the proper approach is that the probative value of an HCP physiotherapist's report is a matter for the decision maker or tribunal dealing with the case, just as it is with other reports and evidence.

The panel so held, firstly, because the legislation makes no distinction between an HCP's ability to deal with mental health descriptors as opposed to physical ones. It merely requires approval by the Secretary of State and registration with the appropriate regulatory body. So any such rule as Judge Mark's would frustrate the statutory framework (para.34). The panel's second rationale noted the difference between the LCW assessment (how a condition affects the claimant's functional capacity) and "a medical examination carried out as part of a process of diagnosis

189

and treatment" (para.35), a distinction acknowledged in Professor Harrington's *First Review* of the ESA process. The panel thus considered that the medical examination carried out by a HCP for the LCW did not require that HCP to be a medical specialist in all the physical and mental problems that might be exhibited by a particular claimant. To require the HCP to be such a specialist "would create insurmountable problems for the assessment process" since many claimants have a variety of problems which might then require assessment in a particular case by several HCPs rather than one (para.35).

2.092   What is required, however, is that the HCP have an informed understanding of the claimant's medical conditions and the difficulties flowing from them. This requires adequate training and supervision. The panel had received detailed information on the current training process (see paras 11-19)—something not available to Judge Mark in *JH*—and, while not commenting on that programme, did observe that none of the independent reviews of the ESA assessment process had criticised the performance of physiotherapists relative to HCPs from other disciplines and that training for HCPs on mental health problems was being reviewed with the aim of increasing the knowledge of all HCPs (para.36).

There is, therefore, no need for a tribunal to adjourn for further particulars on the qualifications of the HCP in a particular case. The specialist tribunal with its medical member must "make its own findings having regard to all the evidence before it" (para.37). The correct starting point was that identified by Judge Ovey in an incapacity benefit appeal (*JF v SSWP (IB)* [2011] UKUT 385 (AAC) at para.25:

" . . . the report is prepared by an HCP who has been trained (whether as part of the training as an HCP or through other training) at least to the level thought appropriate by the Department of Work and Pensions for carrying out examinations where mental health issues are raised. In other words the selection and training procedures ought to have produced an HCP who can conduct a mental health examination competently. It follows that evidence that the HCP has not undergone separate specialist training should not of itself have any effect on the weight which the tribunal attaches to the report . . . "

The panel held that the weight to be accorded to any report "addressing the functional impact of any medical condition on a claimant" is a matter for the specialist tribunal which should consider

"(a) the level of the author's expertise (for example, an HCP or a consultant psychiatrist) and (b) the knowledge of the claimant possessed by the author (for example, knowledge gained from a one-off assessment or that gained as a treating clinician). Additionally the date of the evidence, its comprehensiveness, and its relevance to the issues the tribunal has to determine are also key matters for the tribunal to consider. Importantly the tribunal should explain its reasoning for attaching weight to one type or piece of evidence rather than to another" (para.38 of *ST/GF*).

pp.1110-1112, *annotation to the Employment and Support Allowance Regulations 2008 (SI 2008/794) Sch.2 Activity 16: Coping with social engagement due to cognitive impairment or mental disorder:*

In *SSWP v LC (ESA)* [2014] UKUT 268 (AAC), Judge Williams   2.093
agreed with Judge Ward's comments on "social contact" in *AR v SSWP (ESA)* [2013] UKUT 446 (AAC) and with Judge Mark's "persuasive analysis" of the meaning of "always" in *LM v SSWP (ESA)* [2013] UKUT 552 (AAC). Judge Williams considered that it "can be read as meaning "every day" but not "every moment", something important where the problems of a claimant are variable. His construction of "always" was, however, made without knowing of the decision of the Court of Session in *SSWP v Brade* [2014] AACR 29 (see annotation to ESA Regs 2008 reg.34(2)), and reads "always" somewhat more narrowly than the Court of Session which saw it as connoting "cannot 'for the majority of the time' engage". In addition, his decision was made before that in *JC v SSWP (ESA)* [2014] UKUT 352 (AAC); [2015] AACR 6 in which a panel of three Upper Tribunal judges considered this activity and the case law on it, in particular the conflicting approaches of Judge Parker in *KB v SSWP (ESA)* [2013] UKUT 152 (AAC) and Judge Ward in *AR*, above. Insofar as other decisions are at variance with that of the Three-Judge Panel, *JC* is the authoritative decision to be followed.

In *JC*, the panel considered it "common ground" that the phrases "coping with social engagement" in the definition of the activity and "engagement in social contact" in the definition of the descriptor have the same meaning (para.6). It accepted the submission that "the Activities and their descriptors are intended to assess whether a person is able to engage with others for the purpose of work" (para.16). It also agreed with Judge Wikeley's comments in para.19 of his decision in *AS v SSWP (ESA)* [2013] UKUT 587 (AAC) (see paras 9.374, 9.379 in the main volume) that the activities and descriptors must be "applied on their own terms, but understood against the backdrop of the modern workplace" (para.16). The panel took the view that the differences between Judges Parker and Ward were less than appeared at first sight (para.22). Like Judge Ward it disagreed with Judge Parker that "social" simply meant "relations with other human beings" and did not "carry connotations of leisure and pleasure", but, unlike Judge Ward, did not accept that Parliament's intention was directed only at the difficulties in communication experienced by those with Autistic Spectrum Disorder (ASD) or similar difficulties, although it agreed that Parliament would have had the difficulties of those with ASD in mind (para.25). Instead, the causes "referred to in the Activities and their Descriptors" when read in the context of other relevant provisions in the legislation "show that the intention was not so confined but was directed to the possible impact of a wider range of impairments or disorders" (para.26). The panel saw the words of the definitions in the Activities and Descriptors at issue as a whole and the underlying statutory purposes as being "the most important factors that determine the nature and quality of the behaviour and communications covered by the Activities and their descriptors" (para.27). Applying these factors requires decision-makers and tribunals to consider the following:

> "(i) the range of meanings in common usage of the individual words that are used and so of "coping", "engagement", "social" and "contact" in the context of their combined effect,
>
> (ii) the causes referred to in the Activities for the problems with coping with and engaging in social contact,
>
> (iii) the causes referred to in the Descriptors and their link with the relevant cognitive impairment or mental disorder, and
>
> (iv) the underlying purposes of the legislation and so of the assessments" (para.27).

2.094 Given the underlying purposes (whether a person is able to engage with others for the purpose of work and the context of the modern workplace), the panel could not endorse limitation of

> "the nature and quality of the contact or engagement . . . to contact for pleasure or leisure or characterised by friendliness, geniality or companionship and so the choices that that involves [since such a limitation] would be surprising because that limitation (a) would exclude aspects of communication in the workplace, and (b) would not take proper account of the distinction in the descriptors between communication with people with whom the claimant is familiar and all communication. Indeed, it seems to us that points (a) and (b) dictate that the tests in the Activities and their Descriptors extend to contact for the purposes of work and so to contact with other characteristics and purposes that involve different degrees of choice or no choice because they relate to a structured situation or professional relationship (e.g. doctor and patient, lawyer and client)" (para.28).

On that basis the panel agreed with Judge Parker and the Secretary of State that, taken in isolation, "social" is a reference to "with other human beings" (para.29). However, since "social" is not isolated but qualifies "engagement" or "contact", this left open

> "the nature and quality of the "engagement" or "contact" that is precluded or not possible for the given reasons and thus the assessment of what "engagement or contact with other people" the claimant can cope with due to his cognitive impairment or mental disorder" (para.30).

Key elements here, viewing "coping" and "engagement" in the context of the statutory purposes underlying assessment, were ones of "reciprocity, give and take, initiation and response" (para.32). These can be demonstrated not only by contact characterised by friendliness, geniality or companionship but also "without those elements (and the choices they involve) being present" such as "is often the case in the workplace and elsewhere", although those other contexts might also sometimes display them (para.32). The panel usefully pointed to examples which could equally demonstrate "the necessary degree of reciprocity, give and take, initiation and response": buying a ticket or groceries; contact with a medical examiner or other professional; conversation with a stranger on a park bench or elsewhere; or contact with the First-tier Tribunal itself (para.33). The panel saw the issues, fact finding and value judgements involved as eminently suitable for the First-tier Tribunal, and in the view of the panel:

"it is open to a decision maker to base his decision on an example or examples chosen from a wide range of situations. Whether the evidence and findings relating to the claimant's communications with others and behaviour in the chosen example or examples have the necessary degree of reciprocity, give and take, initiation and response raises issues of fact and degree and of judgment having regard to all the circumstances relating to them. As with other such issues, the authorities show that it is not practical or appropriate to identify the statutory criterion by reference to abstract examples or by reference to a general classification or description other than the statutory test" (para.34).

The proper approach for a tribunal in each case is to consider and determine how 2.095

"The nature and quality of the examples of communications and behaviour they take into account (and thus the reciprocity, give and take, initiation and response shown thereby) would, for the reasons given in the Activities and their Descriptors, be likely to be an effective barrier to the claimant working" (para.35).

The panel accepted that, because the conceptual test thus set out involves value judgments, this leaves "room for different decision-makers applying the right approach in the right way to reach different answers" (para.36 read with paras 9-12).

Good decision-making here involves carrying out the necessary fact-finding "separately from, although with an eye to, the value judgements that have to be applied to those findings" so as to identify and particularise "by reference to primary facts, the situations and events that will be taken into account and so the bedrock of the decision" (para.38). To reach their decision the tribunal must:

"address and decide whether those findings show that:
  (i) the claimant has cognitive impairment or mental disorder,
  (ii) a causative link between that impairment or disorder and his difficulty relating to others or significant distress, and
  (iii) a causative link between that difficulty and distress and a preclusion for all of the time or an impossibility for a majority of the time of contact with all other people, or those who are unfamiliar to the claimant, that has the necessary degree of reciprocity, give and take, initiation and response.
In addressing whether the contact with other people has the necessary nature and quality the tribunal should consider in each individual case how the nature and quality of the communications and behaviour would impact on the ability of the individual to work and so whether or not it would be an effective barrier to him working" (paras 38-39).

As regards the first case under appeal, the panel considered that the tribunal had erred in law in that it may not have understood or applied the statutory test correctly. It had seemed to be concerned about the claimant being able to be helped by someone. The panel did not consider that a person could properly be regarded "as able to engage in social contact if she or he can do so only if accompanied by someone, at least without further explanation as to how it is envisaged that that might be realistic in the workplace" (para.45). The matter was remitted for decision by another tribunal to be decided in light of the guidance proffered by the panel's decision. The panel found no error of law in the second case under appeal (paras 49-60).

pp.1112-1113, *annotation to the Employment and Support Allowance Regulations 2008 (SI 2008/794) Sch.2 Activity 17: Appropriateness of behaviour with other people, due to cognitive impairment or mental disorder*

2.096   In *WC v SSWP (ESA)* [2014] UKUT 363 (AAC), Judge Rowley commended to tribunals considering descriptors under this Activity the following list of questions constituting a "methodical approach":

"(a) Does the claimant have cognitive impairment or mental disorder?

(b) If so, does that cause the claimant to behave in the way described by the descriptor, namely:
   (i) Does the claimant have episodes of aggressive or disinhibited behaviour?
   (ii) Are any such episodes uncontrollable?
   (iii) How often do they occur (noting the words of the descriptor: "on a daily basis," "frequently," "occasionally,").
   (iv) Would such behaviour be unreasonable in any workplace?" (para.10).

Judge Rowley, adopting Judge Gray's observations in the quotation from *WT*, considered that the relevant behaviour could include "sufficiently serious verbal aggression" since its use

"may well create an unacceptable work environment for co-workers, or indeed others with whom the person exhibiting the behaviour may come into contact in the workplace. It would be wrong to say that such conduct can never be enough to satisfy activity 17. Further, in my view it is not necessary for the claimant to have been involved in a fight or argument for activity 17 to apply. There may be examples where his or her behaviour has been aggressive or disinhibited but has not led to another person responding by fighting or arguing. Indeed, in many cases when faced with such behaviour, some people's natural reaction is to walk away. That does not necessarily make the aggressive or disinhibited behaviour any less serious, nor does it necessarily render it any more acceptable to co-workers or others in the workplace. In each case it will be for the tribunal to consider the evidence, find the facts and decide, in the light of those findings, whether a particular claimant's behaviour, whether physical or verbal, is sufficient to satisfy the relevant criteria" (para.16).

Moreover, since the wording of Activity 17 applies to "any work-   2.097
place", he rejected as an "unnecessary gloss" on that wording the sub-mission of the Secretary of State that "the claimant's behaviour would have to be considered unacceptable in an average workplace such as a call centre" (para.18).

It is vital to note that under ESA Regs 2008, reg.19(2), (5) incapability of performing the activity in respect of any descriptor in Pt 2 of Sch.2 must arise from a specific mental illness or disablement. Alcohol misuse in itself is not such a disablement. To rank as disablement the misuse of alcohol must rank as "alcohol dependency" in terms of the "constella-tion of markers" found in quotations from *R(DLA) 6/06* in the Three-Judge Panel's decision in *JG v SSWP (ESA)* [2013] UKUT 37 (AAC); [2013] AACR 23. See further, update to p.923, above. Accordingly, in *DR v SSWP (ESA)* [2014] UKUT 188 (AAC); [2014] AACR 38, Judge May held the tribunal were right to hold that the descriptors did not apply. Moreover, he was persuaded that

"the volume of alcohol the claimant is said to drink on a daily basis would not in itself amount to the disinhibited behaviour referred to in descriptors 17(a) in Schedule 2 and 14 in Schedule 3. I see the force in Mr Webster's submission that disinhibited behaviour requires the context of an inhibition. I cannot see, and it has not been established, what the inhibition in this case is and how the drinking of a certain volume of alcohol amounts in itself to disinhibited behaviour. Disin-hibited behaviour may result as a consequence of drinking specific quantities of alcohol but that is not the basis upon which the claim-ant's argument is put. Mr Orr seeks to widen "disinhibition" beyond the scope of what the statutory provisions can bear. The activity for both descriptors relates to the appropriateness of behaviour "with" other people, which suggests that the descriptor is intended to be applied in respect of behaviour which is more than the passive drink-ing of alcohol" (para.8).

p.1114, *correction to formatting of the Employment and Support Allowance Regulations 2008 (SI 2008/794) Sch.3 Activity 8: Absence or loss of control whilst conscious leading to extensive evacuation of the bowel and/or bladder, other than enuresis (bed-wetting), despite the wearing or use of any aids or adaptations which are normally, or could reasonably be, worn or used: descriptor*

The words from "sufficient" to "clothing" qualify *both* limbs of the   2.098
descriptor and not just the second limb as is misleadingly the case with the layout in the book. The correct layout is as follows:

"At least once a week experiences:
  (a) loss of control leading to extensive evacuation of the bowel and/or voiding of the bladder; or
  (b) substantial leakage of the contents of a collecting device
sufficient to require the individual to clean themselves and change clothing."

p.1114, *correction to formatting of the Employment and Support Allowance Regulations 2008 (SI 2008/794) Sch.3 Activity 10: Awareness of hazard: descriptor*

2.099   For the avoidance of doubt, the words from "such that" to "maintain safety" govern *both* sub-paras (a) and (b), so as to read as follows:

> "Reduced awareness of everyday hazards, due to cognitive impairment or mental disorder, leads to a significant risk of:
> (a) injury to self or others; or
> (b) damage to property or possessions
> such that [³ the claimant requires] supervision for the majority of the time to maintain safety."

pp.1116-1117, *annotation to the Employment and Support Allowance Regulations 2008 (SI 2008/794) Sch.3: the relationship between the terms of the descriptors in the pre-January 2011 Sch. 2 and the correlative provision in Sch.3*

2.100   In *CN v SSWP (ESA)* [2014] UKUT 286 (AAC), Judge Markus applied *CD v SSWP (ESA)* [2012] UKUT 289 (AAC); [2013] AACR 12 to find erroneous in law a tribunal decision finding the claimant not to have limited capability for work-related activity when it had accepted that he had limited capability for work without reviewing the basis on which the decision-maker had proceeded (he had used the "old" pre January 2011 Sch.2), since that limited capability was not disputed. Judge Markus accepted that there are more substantial differences in wording between the two relevant descriptors in this case than between those in issue in *CD*, but was of the opinion that when considering the reasons for the changes in wording it became

> "apparent that the policy intention was that activity 11 in new Schedule 3 is intended to identify the same disability as was in descriptor 16(a) under the old Schedule 2. In its report on the Work Capability Assessment Internal Review dated October 2009 the working group said that activities 14, 15 and 16 in old Schedule 2 all identified "the same disability, the inability to complete a task" (p.44). It therefore proposed that these three activities be amalgamated into one activity, that which is now (with the addition of the word "reliably", but the addition of which is not material for the purpose of this analysis) activity 13 in Schedule 2, and the most severe form of which is activity 11 in Schedule 3. It seems, therefore, that a claimant who fell within old activity 16(a) would fall within new activity 13(a) in the current version of Schedule 2 and so would also fall within activity 11 in Schedule 3.
>
> Activity 12 in new Schedule 3 is "Coping with change" and the descriptor is "Cannot cope with any change, due to cognitive impairment or mental disorder, to the extent that day to day life cannot be managed". The Internal Review of October 2009 found that, if a person cannot cope with planned change, the planned nature of the change is irrelevant (p.47). It therefore equated activity 17(a) under the old Schedule 2 with what became activity 14(a) under the new

Schedule 2 and activity 12 under Schedule 3 (with the addition of the mental cause of the disability). Therefore a person who satisfies activity 17(a) under the old Schedule 2 must satisfy activity 12 of the current Schedule 3, as long as the inability is due to cognitive impairment or mental disorder.

It follows that the FTT made an error of law in concluding that, despite the appellant falling within activities 16(a) and 17(a) in the old Schedule 2, he did not fall within activities 11 or 12 of new Schedule 3.

Even if I am wrong that the application of activities 11 and 12 of new Schedule 3 must follow from the application of activities 16(a) and 17(a) in old Schedule 2, I would nonetheless hold that there is a fundamental error in the reasoning of the FTT and that its decision is irrational. This is because, in deciding whether activities 11 or 12 of Schedule 3 apply to the appellant, the FTT was bound to take into account the obviously relevant conclusions of the French doctor [the claimant lived in France] in relation to activities 16(a) and 17(a) of the old Schedule 2, and the fact that the decision-maker had awarded the appellant the highest scores in respect of those activities. The scoring on those activities was not challenged before the FTT. There was therefore an apparent inconsistency between those scores and a decision that the appellant did not satisfy activities 11 or 12 of Schedule 3" (paras 22-25).

pp.1120-1121, *annotation to the Employment and Support Allowance Regulations 2008 (SI 2008/794) Sch.3 Activity 13*

See further the update to pp.1110-1112 and in particular the decision of the Three-Judge Panel in *JC v SSWP (ESA)* [2014] UKUT 352 (AAC); [2015] AACR 6, which follows Judge Parker on the meaning of "social", identifies the key elements of "engagement" and "coping" as "reciprocity, give and take, initiation and response", and identifies the conceptual test to be applied and the decision-making process to be followed for its application by tribunals. **2.101**

p.1121, *annotation to the Employment and Support Allowance Regulations 2008 (SI 2008/794) Sch.3 Activity 14 Appropriateness of behaviour with other people, due to cognitive impairment or mental disorder: descriptor: Has, on a daily basis, uncontrollable episodes of aggressive or disinhibited behaviour that would be unreasonable in any workplace.*

It is vital to note that under ESA Regs 2008, reg.34(6)(b) incapability of performing the activity in respect of this descriptor must arise from a specific mental illness or disablement. Alcohol misuse in itself is not such a disablement. To rank as disablement the misuse of alcohol must rank as "alcohol dependency" in terms of the "constellation of markers" found in quotations from *R(DLA) 6/06* in para.44 of the Three-Judge Panel's decision in *JG v SSWP (ESA)* [2013] UKUT 37 (AAC); [2013] AACR 23 (see annotation to ESA Regs 2008 reg.19) Accordingly, in *DR v SSWP (ESA)* [2014] UKUT 188 (AAC); [2014] AACR 38, Judge **2.102**

May held the tribunal were right to hold that the descriptor did not apply. Moreover, he was persuaded that

> "the volume of alcohol the claimant is said to drink on a daily basis would not in itself amount to the disinhibited behaviour referred to in descriptors 17(a) in Schedule 2 and 14 in Schedule 3. I see the force in Mr Webster's submission that disinhibited behaviour requires the context of an inhibition. I cannot see, and it has not been established, what the inhibition in this case is and how the drinking of a certain volume of alcohol amounts in itself to disinhibited behaviour. Disinhibited behaviour may result as a consequence of drinking specific quantities of alcohol but that is not the basis upon which the claimant's argument is put. Mr Orr seeks to widen "disinhibition" beyond the scope of what the statutory provisions can bear. The activity for both descriptors relates to the appropriateness of behaviour "with" other people, which suggests that the descriptor is intended to be applied in respect of behaviour which is more than the passive drinking of alcohol" (para.8).

p.1125, *amendment to Employment and Support Allowance Regulations 2008 (SI 2008/794) Sch.4 (Amounts—severe disability premium)*

2.103   With effect from November 26, 2014, reg.3(7)(a) of the Universal Credit and Miscellaneous Amendments (No.2) Regulations 2014 (SI 2014/2888) amended para.6 (severe disability premium) of Sch.1 by substituting the words following for the definition of "blind or severely sight impaired" in sub-para.(9):

> ""blind or severely sight impaired" means certified as blind or severely sight impaired by a consultant ophthalmologist and a person who has ceased to be certified as blind or severely sight impaired where that person's eyesight has been regained is, nevertheless, to be treated as blind or severely sight impaired for a period of 28 weeks following the date on which the person ceased to be so certified;".

p.1134, *amendment to the Employment and Support Allowance Regulations 2008 (SI 2008/794) Sch.6 (Housing costs)*

2.104   With effect from December 31, 2014, art.20(8) of the Shared Parental Leave and Statutory Shared Parental Pay (Consequential Amendments to Subordinate Legislation) Order 2014 (SI 2014/3255) amended para.2(5) of Sch.6 by inserting after the words "paternity leave" the words ", shared parental leave".

p.1149, *amendment to the Employment and Support Allowance Regulations 2008 (SI 2008/794) Sch.6 (Housing costs) para.19 (Non-dependant deductions)*

2.105   With effect from November 26, 2014, reg.3(7)(b) of the Universal Credit and Miscellaneous Amendments (No.2) Regulations 2014 (SI

2014/2888) amended para.19 of Sch.6 by substituting for the existing sub-paragraph (6)(a) a new sub-paragraph (6)(a) as follows:

"(a) certified as blind or severely sight impaired by a consultant ophthalmologist, or who is within 28 weeks of ceasing to be so certified;".

p.1159, *amendment to the Employment and Support Allowance Regulations 2008 (SI 2008/794) Sch.8 (Sums to be disregarded in the calculation of income other than earnings)*

With effect from December 31, 2014, art.20(9)(a) of the Shared   2.106
Parental Leave and Statutory Shared Parental Pay (Consequential Amendments to Subordinate Legislation) Order 2014 (SI 2014/3255) amended para.4 of Sch.8 by inserting after the words "paternity leave" the words "shared parental leave".

p.1159, *amendment to the Employment and Support Allowance Regulations 2008 (SI 2008/794) Sch.8 (Sums to be disregarded in the calculation of income other than earnings)*

With effect from December 31, 2014, art.20(9)(b) of the Shared   2.107
Parental Leave and Statutory Shared Parental Pay (Consequential Amendments to Subordinate Legislation) Order 2014 (SI 2014/3255) amended para.5 of Sch.8 by inserting after the words "paternity leave" the words "shared parental leave".

pp.1162-1163, *amendment to the Employment and Support Allowance Regulations 2008 (SI 2008/794) Sch.8 (Sums to be disregarded in the calculation of income other than earnings)*

With effect from April 22, 2014, art.16 of the Child Arrangements   2.108
Order (Consequential Amendments to Subordinate Legislation) Order 2014 (SI 2014/852) amended para.26(1)(b) of Sch.8 by substituting the words "child arrangements" for the word "residence" before the word "order".

p.1168, *amendment to the Employment and Support Allowance Regulations 2008 (SI 2008/794) Sch.8 (Sums to be disregarded in the calculation of income other than earnings)*

With effect from September 1, 2014, art.27(1) of the Special Educa-   2.109
tional Needs (Consequential Amendments to Subordinate Legislation) Order 2014 (SI 2014/2103) inserted after para.66 in Sch.8 a new paragraph 67 as follows:

"**67.** Any direct payments within the meaning of section 49 of the Children and Families Act 2014 made to a claimant.".

p.1171, *annotation to the Employment and Support Allowance Regulations 2008 (SI 2008/794) Sch.8 para.67 (Sums to be disregarded in the calculation of income other than earnings)*

2.110   The new para.67 inserted at the end of Sch.8 with effect from September 1, 2014 provides for an income disregard of payments under s.49 of the Children and Families Act 2014 (personal budgets and direct payments). Under s.49, parents of a child/young person with an education, health and care plan ("an EHC plan") will have the option of a personal budget, through which they will have control over how some of the provision in the EHC plan will be delivered. EHC plans will gradually replace special educational needs statements and learning disability assessments in England.

p.1179, *amendment to the Employment and Support Allowance Regulations 2008 (SI 2008/794) Sch.9 (Capital to be disregarded)*

2.111   With effect from September 1, 2014, art.27(2) of the Special Educational Needs (Consequential Amendments to Subordinate Legislation) Order 2014 (SI 2014/2103) inserted after para.58 in Sch.9 a new paragraph 59 as follows:

"**59.** Any direct payments within the meaning of section 49 of the Children and Families Act 2014 made to a claimant.".

p.1181, *annotation to the Employment and Support Allowance Regulations 2008 (SI 2008/794) Sch.9 para.59 (Capital to be disregarded)*

2.112   The new para.59 inserted at the end of Sch.9 with effect from September 1, 2014 provides for a capital disregard of payments under s.49 of the Children and Families Act 2014 (personal budgets and direct payments). See further the annotation to para.67 of Sch.8 to the Employment and Support Allowance Regulations 2008 above.

p.1197, *commentary to the Employment and Support Allowance (Transitional Provisions, Housing Benefit and Council Tax Benefit) (Existing Awards) (No. 2) Regulations 2010 (SI 2010/1907) (General Note—The conversion process)*

2.113   The 2010 Regulations are not incompatible with s.17 of the Social Security Act 1998. The appeals by the Secretary of State referred to immediately before para 9.495 of the main volume were allowed by the Upper Tribunal: see *SSWP v PD (ESA)* [2014] UKUT 549 (AAC).

pp.1308-1319, *formatting of the Social Security (Industrial Injuries) (Prescribed Diseases) Regulations 1985 (SI 1985/967) Sch.1 Pt I (List of Prescribed Diseases and the Occupations for which they are prescribed)*

2.114   The phrase *"Any occupation involving:"* should be placed on each page of Part I at the top of the column headed *"Occupation"*.

p.1402, *amendment to the Mesothelioma Lump Sum Payments (Claims and Reconsiderations) Regulations 2008 (SI 2008/1595) reg.4 (Reconsideration)*

With effect from October 28, 2013, reg.5(2) and (3) of the Social Security, Child Support, Vaccine Damage and Other Payments (Decisions and Appeals) (Amendment) Regulations 2013 (SI 2013/2380) omitted "and" at the end of reg.4(1)(a) and inserted after that sub-paragraph the following new sub-paragraphs: **2.115**

"(aa) where a written statement is requested under regulation 4B(3) (reconsideration before appeal) and is provided within the period specified in sub-paragraph (a) above, be made within 14 days of the expiry of that period,

(ab) where a written statement is requested under regulation 4B(3) (reconsideration before appeal) and is provided after the period specified in sub-paragraph (a) above, be made within 14 days of the date on which the statement is provided, or

(ac) be made within such longer period as may be allowed under regulation 4A (late application for reconsideration), and ".

p.1402, *amendment to the Mesothelioma Lump Sum Payments (Claims and Reconsiderations) Regulations 2008 (SI 2008/1595) insertion of new regs 4A and 4B*

With effect from October 28, 2013, reg.5(4) of the Social Security, Child Support, Vaccine Damage and Other Payments (Decisions and Appeals) (Amendment) Regulations 2013 (SI 2013/2380) inserted the following new regulations after reg.4:   **2.116**

"Late application for reconsideration

4A. Where, in a case to which regulation 4B (reconsideration before appeal) applies, the Secretary of State considers there was good cause for not applying for reconsideration of a determination within the time limit specified in regulation 4(1) (reconsideration), he may extend the time limit for such period as he considers appropriate in the circumstances.

Reconsideration before appeal

4B. (1) This regulation applies in a case where—
  (a) the Secretary of State gives a person written notice of a determination made on a claim; and
  (b) that notice includes a statement to the effect that there is a right of appeal to the First-tier Tribunal in relation to the determination only if the Secretary of State has, on an application, decided whether to reconsider the determination.

(2) In a case to which this regulation applies, a person may appeal against the determination only if the Secretary of State has decided on an application whether to reconsider the determination under section

49 of the Child Maintenance and Other Payments Act 2008 ("the 2008 Act").

(3) The notice referred to in paragraph (1) must inform the person—

    (a) of the time limit specified in regulation 4(1) for making an application for reconsideration of the determination; and

    (b) that, where the notice does not include a statement of the reasons for the determination ("written reasons"), he may, within one month of the date of notification of the determination, request that the Secretary of State provide him with written reasons.

(4) Where written reasons are requested under paragraph (3)(b), the Secretary of State must provide them within 14 days of receipt of the request or as soon as practicable afterwards.

(5) Where, as the result of paragraph (2), there is no right of appeal against a determination made on a claim, the Secretary of State may treat any purported appeal as an application for reconsideration of the determination under section 49 of the 2008 Act."

p.1402, *amendment to the Mesothelioma Lump Sum Payments (Claims and Reconsiderations) Regulations 2008 (SI 2008/1595) repeal of regs 5(2) and (3) (Appeal treated as reconsideration) and reg.6 (Appeals)*

2.117   With effect from October 28, 2013, reg.5(5) of the Social Security, Child Support, Vaccine Damage and Other Payments (Decisions and Appeals) (Amendment) Regulations 2013 (SI 2013/2380) omitted reg.5(2) and (3) (appeal treated as a reconsideration) and reg.6 (appeals). These repeals are subject to the transitional and savings provisions in reg.8(1), such that the amendments made by reg.5(5) does not apply in any case where the notice of the decision to which the appeal relates was posted to the appellant's last known address before October 28, 2013.

pp.1466-1467, *annotation to the Employment and Support Allowance Regulations 2013 (SI 2013/379) reg.1 (Citation, commencement and application)*

2.118   The areas and types of case in which IRESA has been abolished have been extended from various dates on or after April 29, 2013. See further Section A of Part VI of this Supplement containing the annotated amended Commencement Orders dealing with "Pathfinder" areas and cases.

p.1468, *amendment to the Employment and Support Allowance Regulations 2013 (SI 2013/379) reg.2 (Interpretation)*

2.119   England and Wales and Scotland now have legislation permitting same sex marriages. Northern Ireland does not. This has consequences with respect to the definition of couples in social security legislation. The position now appears to be as follows.

With effect from December 16, 2014, art.29 and Sch.6, para.23 of the Marriage and Civil Partnership (Scotland) Act 2014 and Civil Partnership Act 2004 (Consequential Provisions and Modifications) Order 2014 (SI 2014/3229) amended reg.2 by substituting a definition of "couple" in exactly the same terms as the existing definition. However, the existing definition applied only to England and Wales (see Amendment 1 for source and date of its insertion and art.1(4) thereof on its extent); the 'new' definition applies to England, Wales, Scotland and Northern Ireland: SI 2014/3229, art.3(1)). Art.6 of the Order stipulates that a same sex marriage in Scotland is to be treated in Northern Ireland as a civil partnership. Under the Marriage (Same Sex Couples) Act 2013 (Consequential and Contrary Provisions and Scotland) Order 2014 (SI 2014/560) art.5, effective from March 13, 2014, a same sex marriage in England and Wales was treated as a civil partnership in Scotland. That provision was revoked by the Marriage (Same Sex Couples) Act 2013 (Consequential and Contrary Provisions and Scotland) and Marriage and Civil Partnership (Scotland) Act 2014 (Consequential Provisions) Order 2014 (SI 2014/3168) art.4, with effect from December 16, 2014. The Marriage (Same Sex Couples) Act 2013 s.10(3) and Sch.2 para.2 provided that from March 13, 2014 a same sex marriage in England and Wales was to be treated as a civil partnership in Northern Ireland.

p.1507, *Amendment 1 to the Employment and Support Allowance Regulations 2013 (SI 2013/379) reg.48 (Claimants subject to work-focused interview requirement only)*

The omitted SI number is SI 2014/1097.   2.120

p.1524, *amendment to the Employment and Support Allowance Regulations 2013 (SI 2013/379): insertion of a new regulation, numbered 75A*

With effect from December 31, 2014, art.30 (1), (3) of the Shared   2.121
Parental Leave and Statutory Shared Parental Pay (Consequential Amendments to Subordinate Legislation) Order 2014 (SI 2014/3255) inserted after reg.75 a new regulation, numbered 75A, to read as follows:

"Effect of statutory shared parental pay on an employment and support allowance

75A.—(1) This regulation applies where—
   (a) a claimant is entitled to statutory shared parental pay and, on the day immediately preceding the first day in the shared parental pay period the claimant—
      (i) is in a period of limited capability for work; and
      (ii) satisfies the conditions of entitlement to an employment and support allowance in accordance with section 1(2)(a) of the Act; and
   (b) on any day during the statutory shared parental pay period—

(i) that claimant is in a period of limited capability for work; and

(ii) that day is not a day where that claimant is treated as not having limited capability for work.

(2) Where this regulation applies, notwithstanding section 20(6) of the Act, a claimant who is entitled to statutory shared parental pay is to be entitled to an employment and support allowance in respect of any day that falls within the shared parental pay period.

(3) Where by virtue of paragraph (2) a person is entitled to an employment and support allowance for any week (including part of a week), the total amount of such benefit payable to that claimant for that week is to be reduced by an amount equivalent to any statutory shared parental pay to which that claimant is entitled in accordance with Part 12ZC of the Contributions and Benefits Act for the same week (or equivalent part of a week where entitlement to an employment and support allowance is for part of a week), and only the balance, if any, of the employment and support allowance is to be payable to that claimant.

(4) In this regulation "statutory shared parental pay period" means the weeks in respect of which statutory shared parental pay is payable to a person under section 171ZY(2) of the Social Security Contributions and Benefits Act 1992."

DEFINITIONS

"the Act"—see reg.2(1).
"claimant"—see WRA 2007, s.24(1).
"contributory allowance"—see WRA 2007 s.1(7).
"Contributions and Benefits Act"—see WRA 2007 s.65.
"statutory shared parental pay period"—see para.(4).
"week"—see reg.2(1).

GENERAL NOTE

2.122   This is the same as ESA Regs 2008 reg.82A (see update to p.984, above).

p.1529, *amendment to the Employment and Support Allowance Regulations 2013 (SI 2013/379) reg.80(2)(b) (Earnings of employed earners)*

2.123   With effect from December 31, 2014, art.30(1), (4)(a) of the Shared Parental Leave and Statutory Shared Parental Pay (Consequential Amendments to Subordinate Legislation) Order 2014 (SI 2014/3255) amended para.(2)(b) to read as follows:

"(b) any remuneration paid by or on behalf of an employer to the claimant in respect of a period throughout which the claimant is on maternity leave, paternity leave[,] adoption leave (which means a period of absence from work on ordinary or additional adoption leave under section 75A or 75B of the Employment Rights Act 1996)[, shared parental leave under section 75E or

75G of that Act] or is absent from work because the claimant is
ill;".

p.1535, *amendment to the Employment and Support Allowance*
Regulations 2013 (SI 2013/379) reg.85 (Waiting days)

With effect from October 27, 2014, reg.2(4) of the Social Security 2.124
(Jobseeker's Allowance and Employment and Support Allowance)
(Waiting Days) Amendment Regulations 2014 (SI 2014/2309) amended
para.(1) by substituting "seven" for "three". This increase in the number
of waiting days applies with respect to a new claim in respect of a waiting
period starting on or after that date; regulation 4 of the amending
instrument ensures that the changes made to reg.85 do not apply where
a waiting period began before that date. For its text, see p.15, above.

p.1550, *correction to formatting of the Employment and Support Allowance*
Regulations 2013 (SI 2013/379) Sch.2 Activity 9: Absence or loss of
control whilst conscious leading to extensive evacuation of the bowel and/or
bladder, other than enuresis (bed- wetting), despite the wearing or use of
any aids or adaptations which are normally, or could reasonably be, worn
or used: descriptor 9(a)

The words from "sufficient" to "clothing" qualify *both* limbs of each 2.125
descriptor and not just the second limb as is misleadingly the case with
the layout in the book. The correct layout is as follows:

"9. (a) At least once a month experiences:
    (i) loss of control leading to extensive evacuation of the bowel
        and/or voiding of the bladder; or
    (ii) substantial leakage of the contents of a collecting device
sufficient to require cleaning and a change in clothing."

p.1554, *correction to formatting of the Employment and Support Allowance*
Regulations 2013 (SI 2013/379) Sch.3 Activity 8: Absence or loss of
control whilst conscious leading to extensive evacuation of the bowel and/or
bladder, other than enuresis (bed-wetting), despite the wearing or use of any
aids or adaptations which are normally, or could reasonably be, worn or
used: descriptor 8

The words from "sufficient" to "clothing" qualify *both* limbs of the 2.126
descriptor and not just the second limb as is misleadingly the case with
the layout in the book. The correct layout is as follows:

"8. At least once a week experiences
    (a) loss of control leading to extensive evacuation of the bowel and/
        or voiding of the bladder; or
    (b) substantial leakage of the contents of a collecting device
sufficient to require the individual to clean themselves and change
clothing."

p.1554, *correction to formatting of the Employment and Support Allowance Regulations 2013 (SI 2013/794) Sch.3 Activity 10: Awareness of hazard: descriptor 10*

2.127   For the avoidance of doubt, the words from "such that" to "maintain safety" govern both sub-paras (a) and (b), so as to read as follows:

"10. Reduced awareness of everyday hazards, due to cognitive impairment or mental disorder, leads to a significant risk of:
  (a) injury to self or others; or
  (b) damage to property or possessions
such that the claimant requires supervision for the majority of the time to maintain safety."

PART III

UPDATING MATERIAL
VOLUME II

INCOME SUPPORT, JOBSEEKER'S ALLOWANCE, STATE PENSION CREDIT AND THE SOCIAL FUND

Commentary by

Penny Wood

Richard Poynter

Nick Wikeley

John Mesher

p.18, *amendment to the Social Security Contributions and Benefits Act 1992 s.137(1) and (1A) (Interpretation—definition of "couple")*

With effect from December 16, 2014, art.5(3) and Sch.4, para.2(13)   **3.001**
of the Marriage and Civil Partnership (Scotland) Act 2014 and Civil Partnership Act 2004 (Consequential Provisions and Modifications) Order 2014 (SI 2014/3229) amended s.137(1) and (1A) by substituting a definition of "couple" in exactly the same terms as the definition in the main volume. However, the latter definition applies only to England & Wales and the new definition applies to Scotland—SI 2014/3229, art.3(4). The result is that the definition is now the same throughout Great Britain.

pp.91-3, *annotation to the old style Jobseekers Act 1995 s.17A (Schemes for assisting persons to obtain employment)*

Add to the list of regulations made under s.17A the Jobseeker's Allow-   **3.002**
ance (Supervised Jobsearch Pilot Scheme) Regulations 2014 (SI 2014/1913) and the Jobseeker's Allowance (18-21 Work Skills Pilot Scheme) Regulations 2014 (SI 2014/3117), set out in this Supplement. A failure without a good reason to participate in any scheme under s.17A(1) attracts a higher-level sanction under s.19(2)(e), but only if the scheme is prescribed for the purposes of s.19. The only scheme so prescribed in reg.70B of the JSA Regulations 1996 is Mandatory Work Activity (MWA). The relevant sanction for these new schemes, and any s.17A scheme other than MWA, therefore appears to be that under s.19A(2)(b) for failing without a good reason to comply with regulations under s.17A. Further regulations implementing pilot schemes are expected to come into operation during 2015.
See also the entry for p.190, below.

p.116, *annotation to the old style Jobseekers Act 1995 s.19C (Hardship payments)*

Note that, if s.19C has never come into force, there appears to be   **3.003**
power to make regs 140–146 of the JSA Regulations 1996 in s.20(4) and (6) of the old style Jobseekers Act 1995.

p.124, *annotation to the old style Jobseekers Act 1995 s.29 (Pilot schemes)*

See the use of this power, as well as that in s.17A(1), in the making of   **3.004**
the Jobseeker's Allowance (Supervised Jobsearch Pilot Scheme) Regulations 2014 (SI 2014/1913) and the Jobseeker's Allowance (18-21 Work Skills Pilot Scheme) Regulations 2014 (SI 2014/3117), set out in this Supplement. See the entry for pp.91-3 above for the sanction for non-compliance. Further regulations implementing pilot schemes are expected to come into operation during 2015.

p.125, *amendment to the Jobseekers Act 1995 s.35 (1) and (1A) (Interpretation—definition of "couple")*

3.005   With effect from December 16, 2014, art.29 and Sch.5, para.12 of the Marriage and Civil Partnership (Scotland) Act 2014 and Civil Partnership Act 2004 (Consequential Provisions and Modifications) Order 2014 (SI 2014/3229) amended s.35(1) and (1A) by substituting a definition of "couple" in exactly the same terms as the definition in the main volume. However, the latter definition applies only to England & Wales and the new definition applies to Scotland—SI 2014/3229, art.3(4). The result is that the definition is now the same throughout Great Britain.

p.148, *annotation to the State Pension Credit Act 2002 s.1(6) (Qualifying age)*

3.006   On some of the difficult evidential issues associated with proof of age, see *LS v SSWP (SPC)* [2014] UKUT 249 (AAC) (the issue was whether the claimant, the wife of a Gurkha, was born on January 1, 1951 or some other date in 1951; tribunal failed to apply correct standard of proof (balance of probabilities) and to consider all relevant evidence).

p.162, *annotation to the State Pension Credit Act 2002 s.9 (Duration of assessed income period)*

3.007   As the commentary notes at the end of the annotation, s.9(6) ceased to have effect on April 6, 2014 (see Pensions Act 2008 ss.105(6)). However, s.29 of the Pensions Act 2014 now provides as follows:

"Preserving indefinite status of certain existing assessed income periods

29.—(1) If this section comes into force before 6 April 2014—
   (a) section 105(6) of the Pensions Act 2008 (which provides that section 9(6) of the State Pension Credit Act 2002 ceases to have effect on 6 April 2014) is repealed, and
   (b) in section 9(6)(a) of the State Pension Credit Act 2002 (duration of assessed income period for certain transitional cases to be treated as indefinite), after "brought to an end" insert " , on or after 6 April 2009 but before 6 April 2014,".
(2) If this section comes into force on or after 6 April 2014—
   (a) section 105(6) of the Pensions Act 2008 (which provides that section 9(6) of the State Pension Credit Act 2002 ceases to have effect on 6 April 2014) is repealed and is to be treated as never having had effect, and
   (b) in section 9(6)(a) of the State Pension Credit Act 2002 (duration of assessed income period for certain transitional cases to be treated as indefinite) as restored by this section, after "brought to an end" insert " , on or after 6 April 2009 but before 6 April 2014,".

In fact s.29 came into force on Royal Assent, which was on May 14, 2014 (see s.56(2)(a)). As a result s.29(1) is otiose and s.29(2) is operative.

Section 9(6) was a transitional provision and was thought to be necessary only until April 6, 2014. It was therefore repealed from that date by section 105(6) of the Pensions Act 2008. The repeal left some doubt about whether existing assessed income periods under s.9(6) would remain in place after April 6, 2014. Section 29 of the Pensions Act 2014 is therefore intended to remove the doubt by ensuring that existing indefinite assessed income periods governed by s.9(6) remain in place on or after that date.

p.183, *amendment to the Child Support Act 1991 s.43 (Recovery of child support maintenance by deduction from benefit)*

With effect from February 4, 2014, s.139 of the Welfare Reform Act 2012 substituted the following new subsections for subs.(1) and (2) of section 43: 3.008

"(1) The power of the Secretary of State to make regulations under section 5 of the Social Security Administration Act 1992 by virtue of subsection (1)(p) of that section may be exercised with a view to securing the making of payments in respect of child support maintenance by a non-resident parent.

(2) The reference in subsection (1) to the making of payments in respect of child support maintenance includes the recovery of-
(a) arrears of child support maintenance, and
(b) fees payable under section 6 of the Child Maintenance and Other Payments Act 2008."

pp.184–186, *annotation to the Child Support Act 1991 s.43 (Recovery of child support maintenance by deduction from benefit)*

The new form of s.43 also allows for the recovery by deduction from benefit of fees payable under s.6 of the Child Maintenance and Other Payments Act 2008 by the non-resident parent. 3.009

p.190, *annotation to the Jobseekers (Back to Work Schemes) Act 2013*

The hearing by a three-judge panel to consider post-*Reilly* issues took place in November 2014, but the decision had not been issued by the date on which the material for this Supplement was delivered to the publishers. A summary of the decision (*Secretary of State for Work and Pensions v TU (USA)* [2015] UKUT 56 (AAC)) appears in the Stop Press part of this Supplement. The appeal to the Court of Appeal by the Secretary of State against Lang J.'s decision in *Reilly (No.2)* is due to be heard in the first three months of 2015, but a date had not been fixed as at December 31, 2014. 3.010

An update on improvements to communications following the independent review of the operation of sanction validated by the 2013 Act was published by the Department for Work and Pensions on December 18, 2014.

p.203, *amendment to the Income Support (General) Regulations 1987 (SI 1987/1967) reg.2(1) (Interpretation—definition of "couple")*

3.011   With effect from December 16, 2014, art.29 and Sch.6, para.5 of the Marriage and Civil Partnership (Scotland) Act 2014 and Civil Partnership Act 2004 (Consequential Provisions and Modifications) Order 2014 (SI 2014/3229) amended reg.2(1) by substituting a definition of "couple" in exactly the same terms as the definition in the main volume. However, the latter definition applies only to England & Wales and the new definition applies to Scotland—SI 2014/3229 art.3(4). The result is that the definition is now the same throughout Great Britain.

p.208, *amendment to the Income Support (General) Regulations 1987 (SI 1987/1967) reg.2(1) (Interpretation—definition of "shared parental leave")*

3.012   With effect from December 31, 2014, reg.5(2)(b) of the Shared Parental Leave and Statutory Shared Parental Pay (Consequential Amendments to Subordinate Legislation) Order 2014 (SI 2014/3255) amended reg.2(1) by adding the following definition before the definition of "single claimant":

> ""shared parental leave" means leave under section 75E or 75G of the Employment Rights Act 1996;".

p.254, *amendment to Income Support (General) Regulations 1987 (SI 1987/1967) reg.5(3A) (Persons treated as engaged in remunerative work)*

3.013   With effect from December 31, 2014, reg.5(3) of the Shared Parental Leave and Statutory Shared Parental Pay (Consequential Amendments to Subordinate Legislation) Order 2014 (SI 2014/3255) amended reg.5(3A) by substituting ", adoption leave or shared parental leave" for "or adoption leave".

p.305, *amendment to the Income Support (General) Regulations 1987 (SI 1987/1967) reg.21AA(4) (Special cases: supplemental—persons from abroad)*

3.014   With effect from May 31, 2014, reg.2(1) of the Social Security (Habitual Residence) (Amendment) Regulations 2014 (SI 2014/902) amended reg.21AA(4) by substituting the following sub-paragraphs for sub-paras (a) to (f):

> "(za)   a qualified person for the purposes of regulation 6 of the Immigration (European Economic Area) Regulations 2006 as a worker or a self-employed person;
>
> (zb)   a family member of a person referred to in sub-paragraph (za) within the meaning of regulation 7(1)(a), (b) or (c) of those Regulations;

(zc)   a person who has a right to reside permanently in the United
       Kingdom by virtue of regulation 15(1)(c), (d) or (e) of those
       Regulations;".

pp.321-324, *annotation to the Income Support (General) Regulations
1987 (SI 1987/1967) reg.21AA (Special cases: supplemental—persons
from abroad—Extended right of residence—Workers—Effective and genuine
work)*

A person who receives carer's allowance for caring for a severely   3.015
disabled person is not providing services for remuneration and so is not
a worker for the purposes of art.7(1)(a) of Directive 2004/38: see *JR v
SSWP (IS)* and *JR v Leeds CC (HB)* [2014] UKUT 154 (AAC).

p.327, *annotation to the Income Support (General) Regulations 1987 (SI
1987/1967) reg.21AA(4) (Special cases: supplemental—persons from
abroad—Extended right of residence—Persons who retain the status of
worker—Pregnancy)*

The decision of the ECJ in *Saint Prix v Secretary of State for Work and*   3.016
Pensions (Case C- 507/12) has been reported as [2014] AACR 18.

p.329, *annotation to the Income Support (General) Regulations 1987 (SI
1987/1967) reg.21AA (Special cases: supplemental—persons from abroad
—Extended right of residence—Persons who retain the status of
worker—Involuntary unemployment)*

The commentary in the main volume must now be read subject to the   3.017
amendments to reg.6 of the 2006 Regulations with effect from July 1,
2014 and November 10, 2014 (see the Noter-up to p.843 of Vol.II).

p.333, *annotation to the Income Support (General) Regulations 1987 (SI
1987/1967) reg.21AA (Special cases: supplemental—persons from abroad—
Extended right of residence—"Workseekers" and "Jobseekers"—Definition
of "Jobseeker")*

The commentary in the main volume must now be read subject to the   3.018
amendments to reg.6 of the 2006 Regulations with effect from July 1,
2014 and November 10, 2014 (see the Noter-up to p.843 of Vol.II).

"Jobseeker" is now defined for the purposes of the 2006 Regulations
by reg.6(4) as "a person who satisfies conditions A, B and, where
relevant, C". Conditions A and B are described in the commentary on
retention of worker status on p.329 of the main volume and have not
changed. Condition C is that "the person has had a period of absence
from the United Kingdom": see reg.6(10).

From July 1, 2014, to November 9, 2014 Condition C applied where
the person had had a right to reside as a person who has retained worker
status for six months, or as a jobseeker for 182 days in total, unless—in
either case—the person concerned has been continuously absent from

the United Kingdom for at least 12 months, since enjoying that right to reside: see reg.6(9).

From November 10, 2014, the 182-day figure was reduced to 91 days.

Where Condition C applies, Condition B must be read as if it said "compelling evidence" rather than "evidence": see reg.6(11).

The length of the period of absence is not specified. In particular, reg.6(9) does not say that the period of absence must be at least 12 months. It only says that Condition C does not apply at all where there has been a continuous absence for 12 months or more. A period of absence of more than three months may have the effect that the claimant will not be entitled to JSA immediately on return to the UK: see the discussion on p.380 of the main volume.

The amendments also reduce the period before which jobseekers (but not those retaining worker status) must provide "compelling" evidence that they have a genuine chance of being engaged. That period, which was previously six months, was reduced on July 1, 2014 to 182 days and on November 10, 2014 to 91 days: see reg.6(7) and (8). However, note the view expressed in para.2.155 on p.329 of the main volume that in practice "compelling evidence" and "evidence" mean the same thing and that the word "compelling" is therefore otiose.

The extent to which those amendments (particularly the reduction of the 182 day period to 91 days) comply with EU law remains to be determined.

p.335, *annotation to the Income Support (General) Regulations 1987 (SI 1987/1967) reg.21AA (Special cases: supplemental—persons from abroad—Extended right of residence—Self-employed persons—Effective and genuine work)*

3.019   A person who receives carer's allowance for caring for a severely disabled person is not providing services for remuneration and so is not a self-employed person for the purposes of art.7(1)(a) of Directive 2004/38: see *JR v SSWP (IS)* and *JR v Leeds CC (HB)* [2014] UKUT 154 (AAC).

p.341, *annotation to the Income Support (General) Regulations 1987 (SI 1987/1967) reg.21AA (Special cases: supplemental—persons from abroad—Extended right of residence—Family members and extended family members)*

3.020   Under reg.11 of the 2006 Regulations (p.852 of Vol.II) family members of EEA nationals who are not themselves EEA nationals and who do not hold a residence card issued by the UK under art.10 of the Directive must obtain a document called an "EEA family permit" (see reg.12) before travelling to the UK. However, in *McCarthy v Secretary of State for the Home Department* (C-202/13), the Grand Chamber of the ECJ ruled that this additional requirement was contrary to the Directive in cases where the family member holds a residence card issued by another member state.

p.358, *annotation to the Income Support (General) Regulations 1987 (SI 1987/1967) reg.21AA (Special cases: supplemental—persons from abroad— Extended right of residence— Rights to reside of children in education and their principal carers:* Baumbast, Ibrahim and Teixeira—*Children of self-employed parents)*

After the citation of *Czop and Punakova v Secretary of State for Work and Pensions* (C-147/11 and C-148/11) immediately before para.2.239 add "and *RM v SSWP (IS)* [2014] UKUT 0401 (AAC)". *RM v SSWP* also contains guidance on the concept of self-employment in EU law. **3.021**

pp.361-362, *annotation to the Income Support (General) Regulations 1987 (SI 1987/1967) reg.21AA (Special cases: supplemental—persons from abroad—Parents of British children: Zambrano—"Assumed")*

The Court of Appeal gave judgment in *Sanneh v Secretary of State for Work and Pensions, and R(HC) v Secretary of State for Work and Pensions* [2015] EWCA Civ 49 on February 10. 2015. The Court held that the *Zambrano* right arises on the first date on which a non-EU citizen who does not have any other right of residence in the UK becomes responsible for the care of an EU citizen child. That might be "on the birth of the child or a later date, for example, the date on which any leave which the carer had to be within the jurisdiction expires" (see Arden LJ at para.23). The fact that the Zambrano right arises on that date rather than on a later date when the UK seeks to take "prohibited national measures" (*i.e.,* measures that would interfere with the effective exercise of the EU citizen child's right to remain in the EU) means that *Zambrano* carers have a right of residence in the UK. As a result Zambrano carers have the right to work and—until specific measures were taken to exclude them from entitlement to social assistance with effect from November 8, 2012—satisfied the right to reside test for social security benefits. Ms Sanneh won her appeal on that basis. **3.022**

The next question was whether the November 8, 2012 amendments were lawful. The Court held that "if the EU citizenship right of the EU citizen child cared for by the *Zambrano* carer is to be effective, then . . . member states must make social assistance available to *Zambrano* carers when it is essential to do so to enable them to support themselves in order to be the carer for the EU citizen children in their care within the EU." The Court described that principle as the "basic support test". However, "the level of social assistance payable to *Zambrano* carers is exclusively governed by national law: the member state might choose to pay more than the amount that the *Zambrano* carer needs to support herself but is not obliged to do so. Second, it does not have to be shown that the *Zambrano* carer would in fact have to leave the EU . . . Third, the EU principle of proportionality does not apply because . . . EU law has no competence in the level of social assistance to be paid to the *Zambrano* carer". In addition, *Zambrano* carers do not have the right to be paid the same level of social assistance as EU citizens with a right of residence in the UK because only EU citizens can rely upon the principle of non-discrimination and EU law does not prevent "reverse discrimination" (*i.e.,* where an EU member state treats its own nationals—in this case the British EU citizen child—less favourably than the nationals of other member states (see Arden LJ at paras 25-29). The duty imposed on local authorities by s.17 of the Children Act 1989 to provide support to children in need (which can include financial support and/or accommodation for both parent and child) was adequate to meet the basic support test. The claimant in *HC* therefore lost her appeal.

It is understood that the Court of Appeal has refused permission to appeal to the Supreme Court to both the Secretary of State and the claimant in *HC*. At the time of going to press, it is not known whether either party will petition the Supreme Court for permission.

pp.362–365, *annotation to the Income Support (General) Regulations1987 (SI 1987/1967) reg.21AA (Special cases: supplemental—persons from abroad—The special position of A8 and A2 nationals)*

3.022.1 The seven-year transitional "accession period" for A8 nationals referred to in the main volume was originally a period of five years from May 1, 2004 to April 30, 2009. However, it was extended for a further two years by the Accession (Immigration and Worker Registration) (Amendment) Regulations 2009 (SI 2009/892) ("the Extension Regulations"). However, in *TG v SSWP (PC)* [2015] UKUT 50 (AAC), the Upper Tribunal (Judge Ward) has held that the making of the Extension Regulations was not a proportionate exercise of the UK's powers under the Treaty of Accession and was therefore incompatible with EU law. The Extension Regulations therefore fell to be disapplied. The consequence is that the accession period for A8 nationals ended on April 30, 2009 rather than on April 30, 2011. A8 nationals who were in genuine and effective work between May 1, 2009 and April 30, 2011 were therefore workers with a right of residence, even if that work was not registered with the Home Office. Similarly, A8 nationals who worked during that period and then became temporarily incapable of work or involuntarily unemployed retained worker status and A8 nationals who, but for the Accession (Immigration and Worker Registration) Regulations 2004, would have had a right of residence as workseekers, had such a right from May 1, 2009 onwards. Although the period from May 1, 2009 to April 30, 2011 ended nearly four years ago, the status of A8 nationals during that period will still be relevant in some cases to the question of whether they have retained worker status or acquired a permanent right of residence.

The Upper Tribunal's decision does not decide the status of the equivalent two-year extension of the A2 scheme. However, there must now at least be a question as to whether that extension was compatible with EU law.

216

pp.365-368, *annotation to the Income Support (General) Regulations 1987 (SI 1987/1967) reg.21AA (Special cases: supplemental—persons from abroad—Compatibility of the right to reside test with EU law)*

The UK case law which holds that there is no general right for EEA 3.023
nationals who are not economically active to reside in a member state of
which they are not a national is reinforced by the Grand Chamber of the
ECJ in *Dano v Jobcenter Leipzig* (C-333/13). The court ruled that:

"Article 24(1) of Directive 2004/38/EC . . . , read in conjunction with
Article 7(1)(b) thereof, and Article 4 of Regulation No 883/2004, . . .
must be interpreted as not precluding legislation of a Member State
under which nationals of other Member States are excluded from
entitlement to certain 'special non-contributory cash benefits' within
the meaning of Article 70(2) of Regulation No 883/2004, although
those benefits are granted to nationals of the host Member State who
are in the same situation, in so far as those nationals of other Member
States do not have a right of residence under Directive 2004/38 in the
host Member State."

The Court's decision received considerable publicity in the UK but does
not actually change the law as it was previously understood: economically inactive EEA nationals who are without sufficient resources do not
have a right to reside and so are not entitled to social assistance.

In *Vestische Arbeit Jobcenter Kreis Recklinghausen v Garcia-Nieto*
(C-299/14), the Landessozialgericht Nordrhein-Westfalen (Social Court
of North Rhine-Westphalia) has referred the following questions to the
ECJ:

"1. Does the principle of equal treatment under Article 4 of Regula-
     tion (EC) No 883/2004—with the exception of the clause in
     Article 70(4) of Regulation (EC) No 883/2004 excluding the
     provision of benefits outside the Member State of residence
     —also apply to the special non-contributory cash benefits
     referred to in Article 70(1) and (2) of Regulation (EC) No
     883/2004?

2.   If the first question is answered in the affirmative: may the
     principle of equal treatment laid down in Article 4 of Regulation
     No 883/2004 be limited by provisions of national legislation
     implementing Article 24(2) of Directive 2004/38/EC which do
     not under any circumstances allow access to those benefits for
     the first three months of residence where European Union cit-
     izens in the Federal Republic of Germany are neither employed
     or self-employed persons nor entitled to exercise freedom of
     movement under Paragraph 2(3) of the Freizügigkeitsgesetz/EU
     (Law on Freedom of Movement for EU Citizens, 'the FreizügG/
     EU') and, if so, to what extent may that principle be limited?

3.   If the first question is answered in the negative: do other princi-
     ples of equal treatment under primary law—in particular Article
     45(2) TFEU in conjunction with Article 18 TFEU—preclude a
     national provision which does not under any circumstances allow

the grant of a social benefit which is intended to ensure sub-sistence and to facilitate access to the labour market in their first three months of residence to European Union citizens who are neither employed or self-employed persons nor entitled to exer-cise freedom of movement under Paragraph 2(3) of the Frei-zügG/EU, but who can demonstrate a genuine link to the host State and, in particular, to the labour market of that host State?"

The first of those questions has already been answered affirmatively by the Court in *Dano*. The second and third questions raise similar issues to those considered in *Dano*. However, the reference in the third question to the ability of the claimants in *Garcia-Nieto* to "demonstrate a genuine link to the host State and, in particular, to the labour market of that host State" indicates that—unlike Mrs Dano—they have previously been economically active in Germany. At the time of going to press, no date has been appointed for the hearing of the reference.

p.367, *annotation to the Income Support (General) Regulations 1987 (SI 1987/1967) reg.21AA (Special cases: supplemental—persons from abroad—Compatibility of the right to reside test with EU law)*

3.024　Replace the commentary in the first two paragraphs of 2.256 with the following:

"The decision in *Patmalniece* applies to child benefit and child tax credit as it does to other social security benefits. In *AS v HMRC (CB)* [2013] NICom 15, the Chief Commissioner of Northern Ireland distinguished *Patmalniece* and held that the right to reside test in reg.27(3) of the Child Benefit (General) Regulations 2006 (i.e. of the Northern Ireland regulations which is equivalent to reg.23(4) of the GB regulations) is unlawfully discriminatory on the grounds of nation-ality contrary to art.3 of Regulation 1408/71. However, the Court of Appeal in Northern Ireland allowed HMRC's appeal (*HM Revenue & Customs v Spiridonova* [2014] NICA 63) and confirmed the validity of the test."

However, see the Noter-up to pp.368-369 of Vol.II below.

pp.368-369, *annotation to the Income Support (General) Regulations 1987 (SI 1987/1967) reg.21AA (Special cases: supplemental—persons from abroad—Compatibility of the right to reside test with EU law—European Commission's challenges to the right to reside test)*

3.025　Information about the grounds on which the Commission has decided to refer the UK to the ECJ in Case C-308/14 are now available. The Commission claims that the Court should declare that the UK, has failed to comply with its obligations under Regulation (EC) No.883/2004, by requiring that a claimant for child benefit or child tax credit should have a right to reside in the UK. It will be observed that this is very much more narrow that the original reasoned grounds of challenge. No date has yet been appointed for the hearing of the reference.

p.380, *annotation to the Income Support (General) Regulations 1987 (SI 1987/1967) reg.21AA (Special cases: supplemental—persons from abroad— Habitual residence—The additional "three-months" requirement for jobseeker's allowance)*

The "three-months" requirement was applied to child benefit and child tax credit with effect from July 1, 2014 by the Child Benefit (General) and the Tax Credits (Residence) (Amendment) Regulations 2014 (SI 2014/1511), subject to a number of exceptions: see further the Noter-Up to Vol.IV.   3.026

pp.381-382, *annotation to the Income Support (General) Regulations 1987 (SI 1987/1967) reg.21ZB (Treatment of refugees)*

The claimant in *HB v SSWP (IS)* [2013] UKUT 433 (AAC) was granted permission to appeal to the Court of Appeal on July 2, 2010 ([2014] EWCA Civ 1040). The appeal (*Blakesley v Secretary of State for Work and Pensions*) was heard on January 27, 2015. Judgment was reserved and had not been delivered at the time of going to press.   3.027

p.413, *amendment to the Income Support (General) Regulations 1987 (SI 1987/1967) reg.35 (Earnings of employed earners)*

With effect from December 31, 2014, art.5(4) of the Shared Parental Leave and Statutory Shared Parental Pay (Consequential Amendments to Subordinate Legislation) Order 2014 (SI 2014/3255) amended reg.35(2)(b) by substituting the words ", adoption leave or shared parental leave" for the words "or adoption leave".   3.028

p.467, *annotation to the Income Support (General) Regulations 1987 (SI 1987/1967) reg.46 (Calculation of capital)*

The question of whether assets subject to a restraint order under the Proceeds of Crime Act 2002 cease to be the claimant's capital, or whether they remain his capital but have a market value of nil, was further considered in *CS v Chelmsford BC* [2014] UKUT 518 (AAC). Judge Markus was of the view that the assets remain the claimant's capital but have no market value. However, like Judge Turnbull in *SH v SSWP* [2008] UKUT 21 (AAC), she did not find it necessary to reach a final conclusion on the point.   3.029

p.482, *annotation to the Income Support (General) Regulations 1987 (SI 1987/1967) reg.49 (Calculation of capital in the UK)*

See *MN v LB Hillingdon (HB)* [2014] UKUT 427 (AAC) and *PE v SSWP (SPC)* [2014] UKUT 387 (AAC) referred to in the annotation to reg.52 of the Income Support (General) Regulations 1987 below.   3.030

p.510, *annotation to the Income Support (General) Regulations 1987 (SI 1987/1967) reg.52 (Capital jointly held)*

3.031   For a further example of a case where the valuation evidence from the District Valuer was wholly inadequate and the tribunal had erred in law in relying on it to make a finding as to the value of the claimant's interest in the matrimonial home occupied by his mentally ill wife, see *MN v LB Hillingdon (HB)* [2014] UKUT 427 (AAC).

    See also *PE v SSWP (SPC)* [2014] UKUT 387 (AAC) which concerned the value of the claimant's interest in his former home, which remained occupied by his wife, son and step-son (the step-son had mental health problems). The District Valuer's valuation was based on an assumption that there had been a hypothetical application under the Trusts of Land and Appointment of Trustees Act 1996. The Secretary of State argued that in the circumstances of the case the District Valuer's assumption was unrealistic. Although no divorce proceedings were in place at the time, any application under the 1996 Act would be likely to generate such proceedings by the other party who was likely to obtain a more favourable outcome under the Matrimonial Causes Act 1973. Judge Jacobs accepted that the evidence relied on by the tribunal as to valuation was therefore flawed.

p.593, *amendment to the Income Support (General) Regulations 1987 (SI 1987/1967) Sch.2 (Applicable amounts— additional condition for the higher pensioner and disability premiums)*

3.032   With effect from November 26, 2014, reg.3(2)(a)(i) of the Universal Credit and Miscellaneous Amendments (No.2) Regulations 2014 (SI 2014/2888) amended para.12 (additional condition for the higher pensioner and disability premiums) of Sch.2 by substituting the following for sub-para.(1)(a)(iii):

"(iii) is certified as severely sight impaired or blind by a consultant ophthalmologist; or"

and the following for sub-para.(2):

"(2) For the purposes of sub-paragraph (1)(a)(iii), a person who has ceased to be certified as severely sight impaired or blind on regaining his eyesight shall nevertheless be treated as severely sight impaired or blind, as the case may be, and as satisfying the additional condition set out in that sub-paragraph for a period of 28 weeks following the date on which he ceased to be so certified.".

pp.594–595, *amendment to the Income Support (General) Regulations 1987 (SI 1987/1967) Sch.2 (Applicable amounts—severe disability premium)*

3.033   With effect from November 26, 2014 reg.3(2)(a)(ii) of the Universal Credit and Miscellaneous Amendments (No.2) Regulations 2014 (SI 2014/2888) amended para.13 (severe disability premium) of Sch. 2 by substituting the words "severely sight impaired or blind or treated as severely sight impaired or blind" for the words "blind or is treated as blind" in sub-paras. (2A) and (3)(d).

p.610, *annotation to the Income Support (General) Regulations 1987 (SI 1987/1967) Sch.2 para.14 (Applicable amounts—disabled child premium)*

The transitional text of para.14 (disabled child premium), which is reproduced in the commentary, was amended with effect from November 26, 2014 by reg.3(2)(a)(iii) of the Universal Credit and Miscellaneous Amendments (No.2) Regulations 2014 (SI 2014/2888). The amendment substituted the words "severely sight impaired or blind or treated as severely sight impaired or blind" for the words "blind or is treated as blind" in sub-para.(1)(b).   **3.034**

p.629, *amendment to the Income Support (General) Regulations 1987 (SI 1987/1967) Sch.3 (Housing costs), para.18 (Non-dependant deductions)*

With effect from November 26, 2014, reg.3(2)(b) of the Universal Credit and Miscellaneous Amendments (No.2) Regulations 2014 (SI 2014/2888) amended para.18(6)(a) of Sch.3 by substituting the words "severely sight impaired or blind or treated as severely sight impaired or blind" for the words "blind or treated as blind".   **3.035**

p.707, *amendment to the Income Support (General) Regulations 1987 (SI 1987/1967) Sch.9 (Sums to be disregarded in the calculation of income other than earnings)*

With effect from December 31, 2014, art.5(6)(a) of the Shared Parental Leave and Statutory Shared Parental Pay (Consequential Amendments to Subordinate Legislation) Order 2014 (SI 2014/3255) amended para.4 of Sch.9 by substituting the words ", adoption leave or shared parental leave" for the words "or adoption leave".   **3.036**

p.707, *amendment to the Income Support (General) Regulations 1987 (SI 1987/1967) Sch.9 (Sums to be disregarded in the calculation of income other than earnings)*

With effect from December 31, 2014, art.5(6)(b)(ii) of the Shared Parental Leave and Statutory Shared Parental Pay (Consequential Amendments to Subordinate Legislation) Order 2014 (SI 2014/3255) amended para.4A of Sch.9 by substituting the words ", statutory adoption pay or statutory shared parental pay" for the words "or statutory adoption pay".   **3.037**

p.711, *amendment to the Income Support (General) Regulations 1987 (SI 1987/1967) Sch.9 (Sums to be disregarded in the calculation of income other than earnings)*

With effect from April 22, 2014, art.2 of the Child Arrangements Order (Consequential Amendments to Subordinate Legislation) Order   **3.038**

2014 (SI 2014/852) amended para.25(1)(c) of Sch.9 by substituting the words "child arrangements" for the word "residence" before the word "order".

p.716, *amendment to the Income Support (General) Regulations 1987 (SI 1987/1967) Sch.9 (Sums to be disregarded in the calculation of income other than earnings)*

3.039   With effect from September 1, 2014, art.3(2) of the Special Educational Needs (Consequential Amendments to Subordinate Legislation) Order 2014 (SI 2014/2103) inserted after para.78 in Sch.9 a new paragraph 79 as follows:

"**79.** Any payments to a claimant made under section 49 of the Children and Families Act 2014 (personal budgets and direct payments).".

p.740, *annotation to the Income Support (General) Regulations 1987 (SI 1987/1967) Sch.9 para.79 (Sums to be disregarded in the calculation of income other than earnings)*

3.040   The new para.79 inserted at the end of Sch.9 with effect from September 1, 2014 provides for an income disregard of payments under s.49 of the Children and Families Act 2014. Under s.49, parents of a child/young person with an education, health and care plan ("an EHC plan") will have the option of a personal budget, through which they will have control over how some of the provision in the EHC plan will be delivered. EHC plans will gradually replace special educational needs statements and learning disability assessments in England.

p.748, *amendment to the Income Support (General) Regulations 1987 (SI 1987/1967) Sch.10 (Capital to be disregarded)*

3.041   With effect from September 1, 2014, art.3(3) of the Special Educational Needs (Consequential Amendments to Subordinate Legislation) Order 2014 (SI 2014/2103) inserted after para.70 in Sch.10 a new paragraph 71 as follows:

"**71.** Any payments to a claimant made under section 49 of the Children and Families Act 2014 (personal budgets and direct payments).".

p.772, *annotation to the Income Support (General) Regulations 1987 (SI 1987/1967) Sch.10 para.71 (Capital to be disregarded)*

3.042   The new para.71 inserted at the end of Sch.10 with effect from September 1, 2014 provides for a capital disregard of payments under s.49 of the Children and Families Act 2014. See further the annotation to para.79 of Sch.9 to the Income Support (General) Regulations 1987 above.

p.837, *amendment to the Immigration (European Economic Area) Regulations 2006 (SI 2006/1003) reg.2(1) (General interpretation— definition of "EEA decision")*

With effect from July 24, 2014, reg.3 of, and para.1(a) of the Schedule **3.043**
to, the Immigration (European Economic Area) (Amendment) (No. 2) Regulations 2014 (SI 2014/1976) amended the definition of "EEA decision" in reg.2(1) by adding the following after sub-para.(d):

";
but does not include decisions under regulations 24AA (human rights considerations and interim orders to suspend removal) or 29AA (temporary admission in order to submit case in person)".

The amendment is subject to the transitional provision in reg.4 of SI 2014/1796: see Part I of this Supplement.

p.837, *amendment to the Immigration (European Economic Area) Regulations 2006 (SI 2006/1003) reg.2(1) (General interpretation— definition of "a qualifying EEA State residence card")*

With effect from July 24, 2014, reg.3 of, and para.1(b) of the Schedule **3.044**
to, the Immigration (European Economic Area) (Amendment) (No. 2) Regulations 2014 (SI 2014/1976) amended the definition of "qualifying EEA State residence card" in reg.2(1) by revoking the word "a" at the beginning of the defined phrase. The amendment is subject to the transitional provision in reg.4 of SI 2014/1796: see Part I of this Supplement.

p.843, *amendment to the Immigration (European Economic Area) Regulations 2006 (2006/1003) reg.6 ("Qualified person")*

With effect from July 1, 2014, reg.3 of the Immigration (European **3.045**
Economic Area) (Amendment) Regulations 2014 (SI 2014/1451) amended reg.6 by substituting the words "A, B and, where relevant, C" for the words "A and B" in para.(4); substituting the words "the relevant period" for the words "six months" in para.(7); and inserting the following after para.(7):

"(8) In paragraph (7), "the relevant period" means—
(a) in the case of a person retaining worker status pursuant to paragraph (2)(b), a continuous period of six months;
(b) in the case of a jobseeker, 182 days, minus the cumulative total of any days during which the person concerned previously enjoyed a right to reside as a jobseeker, not including any days prior to a continuous absence from the United Kingdom of at least 12 months.
(9) Condition C applies where the person concerned has, previously, enjoyed a right to reside under this regulation as a result of satisfying conditions A and B—
(a) in the case of a person to whom paragraph (2)(b) or (ba) applied, for at least six months; or

(b) in the case of a jobseeker, for at least 182 days in total,

unless the person concerned has, since enjoying the above right to reside, been continuously absent from the United Kingdom for at least 12 months.

(10) Condition C is that the person has had a period of absence from the United Kingdom.

(11) Where condition C applies—

(a) paragraph (7) does not apply; and

(b) condition B has effect as if "compelling" were inserted before "evidence".".

The amendment is subject to the transitional provision in reg.4 of SI 2014/1451: see Part I of this Supplement.

With effect from November 10, 2014, reg.3 of the Immigration (European Economic Area) (Amendment) (No. 3) Regulations 2014 (SI 2014/2761) further amended reg.6(8)(b) and (9)(b) be substituting the figures "91" for the figures "182" in each of those sub-paragraphs.

The further amendment is subject to the transitional provisions in reg.4 of SI 2014/27611: see Part I of this Supplement.

p.852, *amendment to the Immigration (European Economic Area) Regulations 2006 (SI 2006/1003) reg.11 (Right of admission to the United Kingdom)*

3.046   With effect from July 24, 2014, reg.3 of, and para.2 of the Schedule to, the Immigration (European Economic Area) (Amendment) (No. 2) Regulations 2014 (SI 2014/1976) amended reg.8(2) by inserting ", (1A)" after the words "regulations 19(1)".

The amendment is subject to the transitional provision in reg.4 of SI 2014/1796: see Part I of this Supplement.

p.859, *amendment to the Immigration (European Economic Area) Regulations 2006 (SI 2006/1003) reg.15B (Continuation of a right of residence)*

3.047   With effect from July 24, 2014, reg.3 of, and para.2 of the Schedule to, the Immigration (European Economic Area) (Amendment) (No. 2) Regulations 2014 (SI 2014/1976) amended reg.15B to read as follows:

"Continuation of a right of residence

15B.—(1) This regulation applies during any period in which, but for the effect of regulation 13(4), 14(5), 15(3) or 15A(9), a person ("P") who is in the United Kingdom would be entitled to reside here pursuant to these Regulations.

(2) Where this regulation applies, any right of residence will (notwithstanding the effect of regulation 13(4), 14(5), 15(3) or 15A(9)) be deemed to continue during any period in which—

(a) an appeal under regulation 26 could be brought, while P is in the United Kingdom, against a relevant decision (ignoring any possibility of an appeal out of time with permission); or

(b) an appeal under regulation 26 against a relevant decision, brought while P is in the United Kingdom, is pending [. . .].

(3) Periods during which residence pursuant to regulation 14 is deemed to continue as a result of paragraph (2) will not constitute residence for the purpose of regulation 15 unless and until—

(a) a relevant decision is withdrawn by the Secretary of State; or

(b) an appeal against a relevant decision is allowed and that appeal is finally determined [. . .].

(4) Periods during which residence is deemed to continue as a result of paragraph (2) will not constitute residence for the purpose of regulation 21(4)(a) unless and until—

(a) a relevant decision is withdrawn by the Secretary of State; or

(b) an appeal against a relevant decision is allowed and that appeal is finally determined [. . .].

(5) A "relevant decision" for the purpose of this regulation means a decision pursuant to regulation 19(3)(b) or (c), 20(1) or 20A(1) which would, but for the effect of paragraph (2), prevent P from residing in the United Kingdom pursuant to these Regulations.

[(6) This regulation does not affect the ability of the Secretary of State to give directions for P's removal while an appeal is pending or before it is finally determined.

(7) In this regulation, "pending" and "finally determined" have the meanings given in section 104 of the 2002 Act(5).]".

The amendment is subject to the transitional provision in reg.4 of SI 2014/1796: see Part I of this Supplement.

p.940, *amendment to the Child Support (Maintenance Calculations and Special Cases) Regulations 2000 (SI 2000/155) reg.4 (Flat rate)*

With effect from May 18, 2014, reg.3(2) of the Social Security (Maternity Allowance) (Miscellaneous Amendments) Regulations 2014 (SI 2014/884) amended reg.4(1)(a)(vii) by inserting the words "or 35B" after the words "section 35".   3.048

p.955, *amendment to the Jobseeker's Allowance Regulations 1996 (SI 1996/207) reg.1(3) (Interpretation—definition of "couple")*

With effect from December 16, 2014, art.29 and Sch.6, para.11 of the Marriage and Civil Partnership (Scotland) Act 2014 and Civil Partnership Act 2004 (Consequential Provisions and Modifications) Order 2014 (SI 2014/3229) amended reg.1(3) by substituting a definition of "couple" in exactly the same terms as the definition in the main volume. However, the latter definition applies only to England & Wales and the new definition applies to Scotland—SI 2014/3229, art.3(4). The result is that the definition is now the same throughout Great Britain.   3.049

p.956, *amendment to the Jobseeker's Allowance Regulations 1996 (SI 1996/207) reg.1(3) (Citation, commencement, interpretation and application—Definition of "Crown Servant")*

3.050   With effect from November 9, 2014, reg.2 of the Jobseeker's Allowance (Habitual Residence) Amendment Regulations 2014 (SI 2014/2735) amended reg.1(3) by adding the following definition after the definition of "course of study":

> ""Crown servant" means a person holding an office or employment under the Crown;".

p.959, *amendment to the Jobseeker's Allowance Regulations 1996 (SI 1996/207) reg.1(3) (Citation, commencement, interpretation and application—Definition of "Her Majesty's forces")*

3.051   With effect from November 9, 2014, reg.2 of the Jobseeker's Allowance (Habitual Residence) Amendment Regulations 2014 (SI 2014/2735) amended reg.1(3) by adding the following definition after the definition of "Health Service Act":

> ""Her Majesty's forces" has the meaning in the Armed Forces Act 2006;".

p.963, *amendment to the Jobseeker's Allowance Regulations 1996 (SI 1996/207) reg.1(3) (Interpretation—definition of "shared parental leave")*

3.052   With effect from December 31, 2014, reg.7(2)(c) of the Shared Parental Leave and Statutory Shared Parental Pay (Consequential Amendments to Subordinate Legislation) Order 2014 (SI 2014/3255) amended reg.1(3) by adding the following definition before the definition of "single claimant":

> ""shared parental leave" means leave under section 75E or 75G of the Employment Rights Act 1996;".

p.977, *amendment to the Jobseeker's Allowance Regulations 1996 (SI 1996/207) reg.3E (Entitlement of a member of a joint-claim couple to a jobseeker's allowance without a claim being made jointly by the couple)*

3.053   With effect from May 18, 2014, reg.4(2) of the Social Security (Maternity Allowance) (Miscellaneous Amendments) Regulations 2014 (SI 2014/884) amended reg.3E(2)(h) by inserting the words "or 35B" after the words "section 35".

pp.1002-1003 *amendment to the Jobseeker's Allowance Regulations 1996 (SI 1996/207) reg.14 (Circumstances in which a person is to be treated as available)*

3.054   With effect from July 21, 2014, reg.2(2) of the Jobseeker's Allowance (Homeless Claimants) Amendment Regulations 2014 (SI 2014/1623) amended reg.14(2) by substituting "paragraphs (2ZB), (2ZC) and

(2ZD)" for "paragraph (2ZB)" and reg.2(3) inserted, after para.(2ZB):

"(2ZC) A person who has recently become homeless shall be treated as available for employment under paragraph (2)(b) only where he takes such steps as are reasonable for him to take to find living accommodation.

(2ZD) A person to whom paragraph (2ZC) applies may be treated as available for employment under paragraph (2)(b) for periods of longer than one week and on more than 4 occasions in any 12 months."

Regulation 14(2)(b) requires a claimant to be treated as available for employment if affected by a domestic emergency, for the time required to deal with the emergency, subject to a maximum of one week in relation to any one emergency and a limit of four periods in 12 months. The new paras (2ZC) and (2ZD) restrict the application of that provision to a claimant who has recently become homeless to those who are taking reasonable steps to find living accommodation, but lift the time limits. Neither "homeless" nor "living accommodation" appears to be given any special definition.

p.1011, *amendments to the Jobseeker's Allowance Regulations 1996 (SI 1996/207) reg.15(1) (circumstances in which a person is not to be regarded as available)*

With effect from December 31, 2014, art.7(3) of the Shared Parental Leave and Statutory Shared Parental Pay (Consequential Amendments and Subordinate Legislation) Order 2014 (SI 2014/3255) amended reg.15(1)(bc) by inserting ", shared parental leave" after "paternity leave".   3.055

With effect from May 18, 2014, reg.4(3) of the Social Security (Maternity Allowance) (Miscellaneous Amendments) Regulations 2014 (SI 2014/884) amended reg.15(1)(c) by substituting this new form of sub-para.(c):

"(c) if she is in receipt of a maternity allowance under section 35 or 35B of the Benefits Act or maternity pay in accordance with sections 164-171 of that Act."

pp.1039-1049, *amendments to the Jobseeker's Allowance Regulations 1996 (SI 1996/207) reg.25(1A) (Entitlement ceasing on a failure to comply with a requirement to participate in an interview: definition of "relevant notification")*

With effect from July 18, 2014 (and ceasing to have effect on April 30, 2015), reg.15 of the Jobseeker's Allowance (Supervised Jobsearch Pilot Scheme) Regulations 2014 (SI 2014/1913) amended the definition of relevant notification" to add after "2013" the words ", under a scheme   3.056

prescribed in regulation 3 of the Jobseeker's Allowance (Supervised Jobsearch Pilot Scheme) Regulations 2014".

With effect from November 25, 2014 (and ceasing to have effect after 24 months), reg.19 of the Jobseeker's Allowance (18-21 Work Skills Pilot Scheme) Regulations 2014 (SI 2014/3117) amended the definition of relevant notification" to add after "2013" (and accordingly before the amendment noted in the previous paragraph) the words ", under a scheme prescribed in regulation 3 of the Jobseeker's Allowance (18-21 Work Skills Pilot Scheme) Regulations 2014".

p.1051, *amendment to the Jobseeker's Allowance Regulations 1996 (SI 1996/207) reg.46 (Waiting days)*

3.057   With effect from October 27, 2014, reg.2(1) of the Social Security (Jobseeker's Allowance and Employment and Support Allowance) (Waiting Days) Amendment Regulations 2014 (SI 2014/2309) amended reg.46(2) by substituting "7" for "3", thus increasing the number of "waiting days" to be served under para.4 of Sch.1 to the Jobseekers Act 1995 before entitlement to benefit can start. The amendment does not apply where the relevant jobseeking period (see regs 47-49) began before October 27, 2014 (reg.4(1) of the amending regulations). This change may well make the provision in the Social Security (Payments on Account of Benefit) Regulations 2013 (Vol.III) for the making of payments on account of benefit, in certain cases of financial need (restrictively defined), more important.

p.1056, *amendment to the Jobseeker's Allowance Regulations 1996 (SI 1996/207) reg.48(2)(c) (linking periods)*

3.058   With effect from May 18, 2014, reg.4(4) of the Social Security (Maternity Allowance) (Miscellaneous Amendments) Regulations 2014 (SI 2014/884) amended reg.48(2)(c) by inserting "or 35B" after "35".

p.1067, *amendment to the Jobseeker's Allowance Regulations 1996 (SI 1996/207) reg.52(1) (Persons treated as engaged in remunerative work)*

3.059   With effect from December 31, 2014, reg.7(4) of the Shared Parental Leave and Statutory Shared Parental Pay (Consequential Amendments to Subordinate Legislation) Order 2014 (SI 2014/3255) amended reg.52(1) by adding ", shared parental leave" after "adoption leave".

p.1125, *amendment to the Jobseeker's Allowance Regulations 1996 (SI 1996/207) reg.85A(4) (Special cases: supplemental—persons from abroad)*

3.060   With effect from May 31, 2014, reg.3 of the Social Security (Habitual Residence) (Amendment) Regulations 2014 (SI 2014/902) amended reg.85A(4) by substituting the following sub-paragraphs for sub-paras (a) to (f):

"(za) a qualified person for the purposes of regulation 6 of the Immigration (European Economic Area) Regulations 2006 as a worker or a self-employed person;

(zb) a family member of a person referred to in sub-paragraph (za) within the meaning of regulation 7(1)(a), (b) or (c) of those Regulations;

(zc) a person who has a right to reside permanently in the United Kingdom by virtue of regulation 15(1)(c), (d) or (e) of those Regulations;".

p.1125, *amendment to the Jobseeker's Allowance Regulations 1996 (SI 1996/207) reg.85A(4) (Special cases: supplemental—persons from abroad)*

With effect from November 9, 2014, reg.3 of the Jobseeker's Allowance (Habitual Residence) Amendment Regulations 2014 (SI 2014/2735) amended reg.85A by inserting the words "subject to the exceptions in paragraph (2A)," at the beginning of para.(2)(a) and a new para.(2A) immediately after para.(2) as follows: **3.061**

"(2A) The exceptions are where the claimant has at any time during the period referred to in paragraph (2)(a)—
(a) paid either Class 1 or Class 2 contributions by virtue of regulation 114, 118, 146 or 147 of the Social Security (Contributions) Regulations 2001(5)or by virtue of an Order in Council having effect under section 179 of the Social Security Administration Act 1992(6); or
(b) been a Crown servant posted to perform overseas the duties of a Crown servant; or
(c) been a member of Her Majesty's forces posted to perform overseas the duties of a member of Her Majesty's forces."

The amendment is subject to the saving provision in reg.4 of SI 2014/2735: see Part I of this Supplement.

p.1145, *amendment to the Jobseeker's Allowance Regulations 1996 (SI 1996/207) reg.98 (Earnings of employed earners)*

With effect from December 31, 2014, art.7(5) of the Shared Parental Leave and Statutory Shared Parental Pay (Consequential Amendments to Subordinate Legislation) Order 2014 (SI 2014/3255) amended reg.98(2)(c) by inserting after the words "adoption leave" the words ", shared parental leave". **3.062**

p.1163, *amendment to the Jobseeker's Allowance Regulations 1996 (SI 1996/207) reg.105 (Notional income)*

With effect from July 18, 2014, reg.11(1)(c) and (2) of the Jobseeker's Allowance (Supervised Jobsearch Pilot Scheme) Regulations 2014 (SI 2014/1913) amended reg.105(10A) by inserting before sub-para.(d) a new sub-paragraph (cd) as follows: **3.063** "(cd) in respect of a person's participation in a scheme prescribed in regulation 3 of the Jobseeker's Allowance (Supervised Jobsearch Pilot Scheme) Regulations 2014;".

With effect from November 25, 2014, reg. 15(1)(c) and (2) of the Jobseeker's Allowance (18-21 Work Skills Pilot Scheme) Regulations 2014 (SI 2014/3117) further amended reg. 105(10A) by inserting after sub-para.(cd) a new sub-paragraph (ce) as follows:

"(ce) in respect of a person's participation in a scheme prescribed in regulation 3 of the Jobseeker's Allowance (18-21 Work Skills Pilot Scheme) Regulations 2014;".

p.1168, *annotation to the Jobseeker's Allowance Regulations 1996 (SI 1996/207) reg.105 (Notional income)*

3.064　　The new sub-para.(cd), which has been inserted into reg.105(10A) with effect from July 18, 2014, ensures that a person who is participating in the pilot scheme known as the Supervised Jobsearch Pilot Scheme will not be treated as possessing notional income as a result of expenses paid in respect of that participation. The pilot scheme is operating in the Jobcentre Plus districts of East Anglia, Black Country, Mercia, Surrey, Sussex and West Yorkshire between October 6, 2014 and April 30, 2015. These Pilot Scheme Regulations cease to have effect on April 30, 2015.

The new sub-para.(ce), inserted into reg.105(10A) with effect from November 25, 2014, makes similar provision in respect of a person who is participating in the 18-21 Work Skills Pilot Scheme. This pilot scheme will operate in the Black Country, Devon, Somerset, Cornwall, Kent and Mercia from early December 2014. These Pilot Scheme Regulations will cease to have effect two years after they came into force.

p.1174, *amendment to the Jobseeker's Allowance Regulations 1996 (SI 1996/207) reg.113 (Notional capital)*

3.065　　With effect from July 18, 2014, reg.12(1)(c) and (2) of the Jobseeker's Allowance (Supervised Jobsearch Pilot Scheme) Regulations 2014 (SI 2014/1913) amended reg.113(3A) by inserting before sub-para.(c) a new sub-paragraph (bd) as follows:

"(bd) in respect of a person's participation in a scheme prescribed in regulation 3 of the Jobseeker's Allowance (Supervised Jobsearch Pilot Scheme) Regulations 2014;".

With effect from November 25, 2014, reg.16(1)(c) and (2) of the Jobseeker's Allowance (18-21 Work Skills Pilot Scheme) Regulations 2014 (SI 2014/3117) further amended reg. 113(3A) by inserting after sub-para.(bd) a new sub-paragraph (be) as follows:

"(be) in respect of a person's participation in a scheme prescribed in regulation 3 of the Jobseeker's Allowance (18-21 Work Skills Pilot Scheme) Regulations 2014;".

p.1177, *annotation to the Jobseeker's Allowance Regulations 1996 (SI 1996/207) reg.113 (Notional capital)*

See the annotation to reg.105 of the Jobseeker's Allowance Regula-   **3.066**
tions 1996 above. The effect of the new sub-para.(bd) of reg.113(3A) is
that a person who is participating in the Supervised Jobsearch Pilot
Scheme will not be treated as possessing notional capital as a result of
expenses paid in respect of that participation. The new sub-para.(be)
makes similar provision in respect of a person who is participating in the
18-21 Work Skills Pilot Scheme.

pp.1211-1212, *amendment to the Jobseeker's Allowance Regulations 1996
(SI 1996/207) reg.141 (Circumstances in which an income-based
jobseeker's allowance is payable to a person in hardship)*

With effect from October 27, 2014, reg.3(1) and (2) of the Social   **3.067**
Security (Jobseeker's Allowance and Employment and Support Allowance) (Waiting Days) Amendment Regulations 2014 (SI 2014/2309)
amended reg.141(2) by substituting "8th" for "4th". The amendment is
subject to the transitional provision in reg.4 of SI 2014/2309: see Part I
of this Supplement.

pp.1220, *amendment to the Jobseeker's Allowance Regulations 1996 (SI
1996/207) reg.146C (Circumstances in which a joint-claim jobseeker's
allowance is payable where a joint-claim couple is a couple in hardship)*

With effect from October 27, 2014, reg.3(1) and (3) of the Social   **3.068**
Security (Jobseeker's Allowance and Employment and Support Allowance) (Waiting Days) Amendment Regulations 2014 (SI 2014/2309)
amended reg.146C(2)(a) by substituting "eighth" for "fourth". The
amendment is subject to the transitional provision in reg.4 of SI
2014/2309: see Part I of this Supplement.

pp.1240-1241, *amendment to the Jobseeker's Allowance Regulations 1996
(SI 1996/207) Sch.1 (Applicable amounts— additional conditions for
higher pensioner and disability premium)*

With effect from November 26, 2014 reg.3(3)(a)(i) of the Universal   **3.069**
Credit and Miscellaneous Amendments (No.2) Regulations 2014 (SI
2014/2888) amended para.14 (additional conditions for higher pensioner and disability premium) of Sch. 1 by substituting the following for
sub-para.(1)(h):

"(h) the claimant or, as the case may be, his partner, is certified as
    severely sight impaired or blind by a consultant ophthalmolo-
    gist."

and the following for sub-para.(2):

"(2) For the purposes of sub-paragraph (1)(h), a person who has
    ceased to be certified as severely sight impaired or blind on regaining
    his eyesight shall nevertheless be treated as severely sight impaired or

blind, as the case may be, and as satisfying the additional condition set out in that sub-paragraph for a period of 28 weeks following the date on which he ceased to be so certified."

pp.1241-1242, *amendment to the Jobseeker's Allowance Regulations 1996 (SI 1996/207) Sch.1 (Applicable amounts—severe disability premium)*

3.070   With effect from November 26, 2014 reg.3(3)(a)(ii) of the Universal Credit and Miscellaneous Amendments (No.2) Regulations 2014 (SI 2014/2888) amended para.15 (severe disability premium) of Sch.1 by substituting the words "severely sight impaired or blind or treated as severely sight impaired or blind" for the words "blind or is treated as blind" in sub-paras (3) and (4)(c).

p.1247, *amendment to the Jobseeker's Allowance Regulations 1996 (SI 1996/207) Sch.1 (Applicable amounts— additional conditions for higher pensioner and disability premium)*

3.071   With effect from November 26, 2014 reg.3(3)(a)(iv) of the Universal Credit and Miscellaneous Amendments (No.2) Regulations 2014 (SI 2014/2888) amended para.20H (additional conditions for higher pensioner and disability premium) of Sch.1 by substituting the following for sub-para.(1)(i):

"(i) is certified as severely sight impaired or blind by a consultant ophthalmologist."

and the following for sub-para.(3):

"(3) For the purposes of sub-paragraph (1)(i), a person who has ceased to be certified as severely sight impaired or blind on regaining his eyesight shall nevertheless be treated as severely sight impaired or blind, as the case may be, and as satisfying the additional condition set out in that sub-paragraph for a period of 28 weeks following the date on which he ceased to be so certified."

p.1248, *amendment to the Jobseeker's Allowance Regulations 1996 (SI 1996/207) Sch.1 (Applicable amounts—severe disability premium)*

3.072   With effect from November 26, 2014 reg.3(3)(a)(v) of the Universal Credit and Miscellaneous Amendments (No.2) Regulations 2014 (SI 2014/2888) amended para.20I (severe disability premium) of Sch.1 by substituting the words "severely sight impaired or blind or treated as severely sight impaired or blind" for the words "blind or is treated as blind" in sub-paras (2) and (3)(c).

p.1254, *annotation to the Jobseeker's Allowance Regulations 1996 (SI 1996/207) Sch. 1 (Applicable amounts—disabled child premium)*

3.073   The transitional text of para.16 (disabled child premium), which is reproduced in the commentary, was amended with effect from November 26, 2014 by reg.3(3)(a)(iii) of the Universal Credit and Miscellaneous Amendments (No.2) Regulations 2014 (SI 2014/2888). The amendment substituted the words "severely sight impaired or blind or treated as severely sight impaired or blind" for the words "blind or is treated as blind" in sub-para.(1)(b).

p.1270, *amendment to the Jobseeker's Allowance Regulations 1996 (SI 1996/207) Sch.2 (Housing costs), para.17 (Non-dependant deductions)*

With effect from November 26, 2014, reg.3(3)(b) of the Universal Credit and Miscellaneous Amendments (No.2) Regulations 2014 (SI 2014/2888) amended para.17(6)(a) of Sch.2 by substituting the words "severely sight impaired or blind or treated as severely sight impaired or blind" for the words "blind or treated as blind".   **3.074**

p.1294, *amendment to the Jobseeker's Allowance Regulations 1996 (SI 1996/207) Sch.7 (Sums to be disregarded in the calculation of income other than earnings)*

With effect from July 18, 2014, reg.13(1)(c) and (2) of the Jobseeker's Allowance (Supervised Jobsearch Pilot Scheme) Regulations 2014 (SI 2014/1913) amended Sch.7 by inserting before para.1 a new paragraph A4 as follows: **3.075**

"**A4.** Any payment made to the claimant in respect of any child care, travel or other expenses incurred, or to be incurred, by the claimant in respect of the claimant's participation in a scheme prescribed in regulation 3 of the Jobseeker's Allowance (Supervised Jobsearch Pilot Scheme) Regulations 2014.".

With effect from November 25, 2014, reg.17(1)(c) and (2) of the Jobseeker's Allowance (18-21 Work Skills Pilot Scheme) Regulations 2014 (SI 2014/3117) further amended Sch.7 by inserting after paragraph A4 a new para.A5 as follows:

"**A5.** Any payment made to the claimant in respect of any child care, travel or other expenses incurred, or to be incurred, by the claimant in respect of their participation in a scheme prescribed in regulation 3 of the Jobseekers Allowance (18-21 Work Skills Pilot Scheme) Regulations 2014.".

p.1294, *amendment to the Jobseeker's Allowance Regulations 1996 (SI 1996/207) Sch.7 (Sums to be disregarded in the calculation of income other than earnings)*

With effect from December 31, 2014, art.7(6)(a)(ii) of the Shared Parental Leave and Statutory Shared Parental Pay (Consequential Amendments to Subordinate Legislation) Order 2014 (SI 2014/3255) amended para.4 of Sch.7 by inserting after the words "statutory adoption pay by virtue of Part 12ZB of the Benefits Act," the words "statutory shared parental pay by virtue of Part 12ZC of the Benefits Act,".   **3.076**

With effect from the same date, art.7(6)(a)(iii) of the same Order further amended para.4 of Sch.7 by substituting the words ", adoption leave or shared parental leave" for the words "or adoption leave".

p.1294, *amendment to the Jobseeker's Allowance Regulations 1996 (SI 1996/207) Sch.7 (Sums to be disregarded in the calculation of income other than earnings)*

3.077   With effect from December 31, 2014, art.7(6)(b)(ii) of the Shared Parental Leave and Statutory Shared Parental Pay (Consequential Amendments to Subordinate Legislation) Order 2014 (SI 2014/3255) amended para.5 of Sch.7 by substituting the words "statutory shared parental pay or statutory adoption pay" for the words "or statutory adoption pay".

p.1298, *amendment to the Jobseeker's Allowance Regulations 1996 (SI 1996/207) Sch.7 (Sums to be disregarded in the calculation of income other than earnings)*

3.078   With effect from April 22, 2014, art.6 of the Child Arrangements Order (Consequential Amendments to Subordinate Legislation) Order 2014 (SI 2014/852) amended para.26(1)(c) of Sch.7 by substituting the words "child arrangements" for the word "residence" before the word "order".

p.1304, *amendment to the Jobseeker's Allowance Regulations 1996 (SI 1996/207) Sch.7 (Sums to be disregarded in the calculation of income other than earnings)*

3.079   With effect from September 1, 2014, art.4(1) of the Special Educational Needs (Consequential Amendments to Subordinate Legislation) Order 2014 (SI 2014/2103) inserted after para.74 in Sch.7 a new paragraph 75 as follows:

> "**75.** Any payments to a claimant made under section 49 of the Children and Families Act 2014 (personal budgets and direct payments).".

p.1310, *annotation to the Jobseeker's Allowance Regulations 1996 (SI 1996/207) Sch.7 paras A4 and A5 (Sums to be disregarded in the calculation of income other than earnings)*

3.080   See the annotation to reg.105 of the Jobseeker's Allowance Regulations 1996 above. The effect of the new para.A4 of Sch.7 is to provide an income disregard of payments of expenses in respect of a person's participation in the Supervised Jobsearch Pilot Scheme. The new paragraph A5 makes similar provision in respect of expenses paid due to a person's participation in the 18-21 Work Skills Pilot Scheme.

p.1310, *annotation to the Jobseeker's Allowance Regulations 1996 (SI 1996/207) Sch.7 para.75 (Sums to be disregarded in the calculation of income other than earnings)*

3.081   The new para.75 inserted at the end of Sch.7 with effect from September 1, 2014 provides for an income disregard of payments under s.49

of the Children and Families Act 2014. See further the annotation to para.79 of Sch.9 to the Income Support (General) Regulations 1987 above.

p.1310, *amendment to the Jobseeker's Allowance Regulations 1996 (SI 1996/207) Sch.8 (Capital to be disregarded)*

With effect from July 18, 2014, reg.14(1)(c) and (2) of the Jobseeker's   **3.082**
Allowance (Supervised Jobsearch Pilot Scheme) Regulations 2014 (SI 2014/1913) amended Sch.8 by inserting before para.1 a new paragraph A4 as follows:

"**A4.** Any payment made to the claimant in respect of any child care, travel or other expenses incurred, or to be incurred, by the claimant in respect of the claimant's participation in a scheme prescribed by regulation 3 of the Jobseeker's Allowance (Supervised Jobsearch Pilot Scheme) Regulations 2014, but only for 52 weeks beginning with the date of receipt of the payment.".

With effect from November 25, 2014, reg.18(1)(c) and (2) of the Jobseeker's Allowance (18-21 Work Skills Pilot Scheme) Regulations 2014 (SI 2014/3117) further amended Sch.8 by inserting after paragraph A4 a new paragraph A5 as follows:

"**A5.** Any payment made to the claimant in respect of any child care, travel or other expenses incurred, or to be incurred, by the claimant in respect of their participation in a scheme prescribed in regulation 3 of the Jobseekers Allowance (18-21 Work Skills Pilot Scheme) Regulations 2014, but only for 52 weeks beginning with the date of receipt of the payment.".

p.1318, *amendment to the Jobseeker's Allowance Regulations 1996 (SI 1996/207) Sch.8 (Capital to be disregarded)*

With effect from September 1, 2014, art.4(2) of the Special Educa-   **3.083**
tional Needs (Consequential Amendments to Subordinate Legislation) Order 2014 (SI 2014/2103) inserted after para.63 in Sch.8 a new paragraph 64 as follows:

"**64.** Any payments to a claimant made under section 49 of the Children and Families Act 2014 (personal budgets and direct payments).".

p.1322, *annotation to the Jobseeker's Allowance Regulations 1996 (SI 1996/207) Sch.8 paras A4 and A5 (Capital to be disregarded)*

See the annotation to reg.105 of the Jobseeker's Allowance Regula-   **3.084**
tions 1996 above. The effect of the new para.A4 of Sch.8 is to provide a capital disregard of payments of expenses in respect of a person's participation in the Supervised Jobsearch Pilot Scheme for 52 weeks from the

date the payment was received. The new para.A5 makes similar provision in respect of expenses paid due to a person's participation in the 18-21 Work Skills Pilot Scheme.

p.1322, *annotation to the Jobseeker's Allowance Regulations 1996 (SI 1996/207) Sch.8 para.64 (Capital to be disregarded)*

3.085 The new para.64 inserted at the end of Sch.8 with effect from September 1, 2014 provides for a capital disregard of payments under s.49 of the Children and Families Act 2014. See further the annotation to para.79 of Sch.9 to the Income Support (General) Regulations 1987 above.

p.1348, *amendment to the State Pension Credit Regulations 2002 (SI 2002/1792) reg.1(2) (Citation, commencement and interpretation)*

3.086 With effect from December 16, 2014, art.29 and Sch.6, para.23 of the Marriage and Civil Partnership (Scotland) Act 2014 and Civil Partnership Act 2004 (Consequential Provisions and Modifications) Order 2014 (SI 2014/3229) amended reg.1(2) by substituting a definition of "couple" in exactly the same terms as the existing definition. However, the existing definition applied only to England & Wales; the 'new' definition applies to England, Wales, Scotland and Northern Ireland: SI 2014/3229 art.3(1)).

p.1350, *amendment to the State Pension Credit Regulations 2002 (SI 2002/1792) reg.1(2) (Citation, commencement and interpretation)*

3.087 With effect from December 31, 2014, art.10(2)(b) of the Shared Parental Leave and Statutory Shared Parental Pay (Consequential Amendments to Subordinate Legislation) Order 2014 (SI 2014/3255) inserted the following new definition after the definition of "qualifying person":

"'shared parental leave' means leave under section 75E or 75G of the Employment Rights Act 1996;"

p.1355, *amendment to the State Pension Credit Regulations 2002 (SI 2002/1792) reg.2(4) (Persons not in Great Britain)*

3.088 With effect from May 31, 2014, reg.4 of the Social Security (Habitual Residence) (Amendment) Regulations 2014 (SI 2014/902) amended reg.2(4) by substituting for sub-paras (a)–(f) the following:

"(za) a qualified person for the purposes of regulation 6 of the Immigration (European Economic Area) Regulations 2006 as a worker or a self-employed person;

(zb) a family member of a person referred to in sub-paragraph (za) within the meaning of regulation 7(1)(a), (b) or (c) of those Regulations;

(zc)   a person who has a right to reside permanently in the United Kingdom by virtue of regulation 15(1)(c), (d) or (e) of those Regulations;".

p.1373, *annotation to the State Pension Credit Regulations 2002 (SI 2002/1792) reg.15 (Income for the purposes of the Act)*

With effect from December 31, 2014, art.10(3)(b) of the Shared   3.089
Parental Leave and Statutory Shared Parental Pay (Consequential Amendments to Subordinate Legislation) Order 2014 (SI 2014/3255) inserted the following new sub-paragraph after sub-paragraph (q):

"(qb)   statutory shared parental pay payable under Part 12ZC of the 1992 Act;"

p.1382, *annotation to the State Pension Credit Regulations 2002 (SI 2002/1792) reg.17A (Earnings of an employed earner)*

With effect from December 31, 2014, art.10(4)(c) of the Shared   3.090
Parental Leave and Statutory Shared Parental Pay (Consequential Amendments to Subordinate Legislation) Order 2014 (SI 2014/3255) inserted the following new sub-paragraph after sub-paragraph (i):

"(ib)   statutory shared parental pay payable under Part 12ZC of the 1992 Act;"

p.1388, *annotation to the State Pension Credit Regulations 2002 (SI 2002/1792) reg.18(2)-(5) (Notional income)*

The correct cross-reference in the commentary should be to par-   3.091
a.2.408 in the main volume, and see the discussion there of *BRG v SSWP (SPC)* [2014] UKUT 246 (AAC).

p.1396, *amendment to the State Pension Credit Regulations 2002 (SI 2002/1792) Sch.I para.1 (Circumstances in which persons are treated as being or not being severely disabled: severe disablement)*

With effect from November 26, 2014, reg.3(4)(a)(i) of the Universal   3.092
Credit and Miscellaneous Amendments (No.2) Regulations 2014 (SI 2014/2888) substituted for sub-para.(1)(c)(ii) the following:

"(ii)   the other partner is certified as severely sight impaired or blind by a consultant ophthalmologist; and";

and substituted for sub-para.(3) the following:

"(3) For the purposes of sub-paragraph (1)(c)(ii), a person who has ceased to be certified as severely sight impaired or blind on regaining his eyesight shall nevertheless be treated as severely sight impaired or blind, as the case may be, and as satisfying the requirements set out in that sub-paragraph for a period of 28 weeks following the date on which he ceased to be so certified."

p.1397, *amendment to the State Pension Credit Regulations 2002 (SI 2002/1792) Sch.I para.2 (Circumstances in which persons are treated as being or not being severely disabled: severe disablement: persons residing with the claimant whose presence is ignored)*

3.093   With effect from November 26, 2014, reg.3(4)(a)(ii) of the Universal Credit and Miscellaneous Amendments (No.2) Regulations 2014 (SI 2014/2888) substituted for sub-para.2(2)(b) the following:

"(b) is certified as severely sight impaired or blind by a consultant ophthalmologist;";

and substituted for sub-para.2(2)(c) the following:

"(c) is no longer certified as severely sight impaired or blind in accordance with head (b) but was so certified not more than 28 weeks earlier;".

p.1400, *amendment to the State Pension Credit Regulations 2002 (SI 2002/1792) Sch.II para.1 (Housing costs)*

3.094   With effect from November 26, 2014, reg.3(4)(b)(i) of the Universal Credit and Miscellaneous Amendments (No.2) Regulations 2014 (SI 2014/2888) substituted for para.1(2)(a)(iii)(cc) the following:

"(cc) is certified as severely sight impaired or blind by a consultant ophthalmologist or who is within 28 weeks of ceasing to be so certified;"

p.1402, *annotation to the State Pension Credit Regulations 2002 (SI 2002/1792) Sch.11 para.2 (Remunerative work)*

3.095   With effect from December 31, 2014, art.10(5) of the Shared Parental Leave and Statutory Shared Parental Pay (Consequential Amendments to Subordinate Legislation) Order 2014 (SI 2014/3255) inserted ", shared parental leave" after "paternity leave".

p.1413, *amendment to the State Pension Credit Regulations 2002 (SI 2002/1792) Sch.II para.14 (Persons residing with the claimant)*

3.096   With effect from November 26, 2014, reg.3(4)(b)(ii) of the Universal Credit and Miscellaneous Amendments (No.2) Regulations 2014 (SI 2014/2888) substituted for para.14(6)(a) the following:

"(a) certified as severely sight impaired or blind by a consultant ophthalmologist, or who is within 28 weeks of ceasing to be so certified; or".

p.1433, *amendment to the State Pension Credit Regulations 2002 (SI 2002/1792) Sch.VI para.4 (Sums disregarded from claimant's earnings)*

3.097   With effect from November 26, 2014, reg.3(4)(c) of the Universal Credit and Miscellaneous Amendments (No.2) Regulations 2014 (SI 2014/2888) substituted for para.4(1)(b) the following:

"(b) is or are certified as severely sight impaired or blind by a consultant ophthalmologist.".

pp.1448-1451, *amendment to the Social Fund Cold Weather Payments (General) Regulations 1988 (SI 1988/1724) Sch.1 (Identification of stations and postcode districts)*

With effect from November 1, 2014, reg.2(1) of and Sch.1 to the   **3.098**
Social Fund Cold Weather Payments (General) Amendment Regulations 2014 (SI 2014/2687) substituted the following Sch.1:

Regulation 2(1), (1A) and (2)

[Schedule 1

IDENTIFICATION OF STATIONS AND POSTCODE DISTRICTS

3.099

Column (1)	*Column (2)*
Meteorological Office Station	*Postcode districts*
1. Aberporth	SA35-48, SA64-65.
2. Aboyne	AB30-34, AB38, AB51-55, DD8-9.
3. Albemarle	DH1-7, DH9, DL4-5, DL14-17, NE1-13, NE15-18, NE20-21, NE23, NE 25-46, SR1-7, TS21, TS28-29.
4. Andrewsfield	CB1-5, CB10-11, CB21-25, CM1-9, CM11-24, CM77, CO9, RM4, SG8-11.
5. Auchincruive	DG9, KA1-26, KA28-30, PA20.
6. Aultbea	IV21-22, IV26.
7. Aviemore	AB37, IV13, PH19-26.
8. Bainbridge	BD23-24, DL8, DL11-13.
9. Bedford	MK1-19, MK40-46, NN1-16, NN29, PE19, SG5-7, SG15-19.
10. Bingley	BB4, BB8-12, BB18, BD1-22, HD3, HD7-9, HX1-7, LS21, LS29, OL13-14, S36.
11. Bishopton	G1-5, G11-15, G20-23, G31-34, G40-46, G51-53, G60-62, G64, G66, G69, G71-78, G81-84, ML4-5, PA1-19, PA21-27, PA32.
12. Boscombe Down	BA12, RG28, SO20-23, SP1-5, SP7, SP9-11.
13. Braemar	AB35-36, PH10-11, PH18.
14. Brize Norton	OX1-6, OX8, OX10-14, OX18, OX20, OX25-29, OX33, OX44, SN7.
15. Capel Curig	LL24-25, LL41.

Column (1)	Column (2)
Meteorological Office Station	*Postcode districts*
16. Cardinham (Bodmin)	PL13-18, PL22-35, TR9.
17. Carlisle	CA1-8, DG12, DG16.
18. Cassley	IV27-28, KW11, KW13.
19. Charlwood	BN5-6, BN44, GU5-6, ME6, ME14-20, RH1-20, TN1-20, TN22, TN27.
20. Charterhall	NE71, TD1-6, TD8, TD10-15.
21. Chivenor	EX23, EX31-34, EX39.
22. Coleshill	B1-21, B23-38, B40, B42-50, B60-80, B90-98, CV1-12, CV21-23, CV31-35, CV37, CV47, DY1-14, LE10, WS1-15, WV1-16.
23. Crosby	CH41-49, CH60-66, FY1-8, L1-40, PR1-5, PR8-9, PR25-26.
24. Culdrose	TR1-8, TR10-20, TR26-27.
25. Dunkeswell Aerodrome	DT6-8, EX1-5, EX8-15, EX24, TA21.
26. Dunstaffnage	PA30-31, PA34-35, PA37-38, PA62-65, PA67-75, PA80.
27. Dyce	AB10-16, AB21-25, AB39, AB41-43.
28. Edinburgh Gogarbank	EH1-42, EH47-49, EH51-55, FK1-7, FK9-10, KY3, KY11-12.
29. Eskdalemuir	DG3-4, DG10-11, DG13-14, ML12, TD7, TD9.
30. Filton	BS1-11, BS13-16, BS20-24, BS29-32, BS34-37, BS39-41, BS48-49, GL11-13, NP16, NP26.
31. Fylingdales	YO13, YO18, YO21-22, YO62.
32. Gravesend	BR5-8, CM0, DA1-18, ME1-5, ME7-8, RM1-3, RM5-20, SS0-17.
33. Hawarden Airport	CH1-8, LL11-14, SY14.
34. Heathrow	BR1-4, CR0, CR2-9, E1-18, EC1-4, EN1-5, EN7-11, HA0-9, IG1-11, KT1-24, N1-22, NW1-11, SE1-28, SL0, SL3, SM1-7, SW1-20, TW1-20, UB1-11, W1-14, WC1-2, WD1-2.
35. Hereford-Credenhill	GL1-6, GL10, GL14-20, GL50-53, HR1-9, NP7-8, NP15, NP25, SY8, WR1-11, WR13-15.
36. Herstmonceux, West End	BN7-8, BN20-24, BN26-27, TN21, TN31-40.
37. High Wycombe	HP5-23, HP27, OX9, OX39, OX49, RG9, SL7-9.

Column (1)	Column (2)
Meteorological Office Station	*Postcode districts*
38. Hurn (Bournemouth Airport)	BH1-25, BH31, DT1-2, DT11, SP6.
39. Isle of Portland	DT3-5.
40. Keele	CW1-3, CW5, CW12, ST1-8, ST11-12, ST14-21.
41. Kinloss	AB44-45, AB56, IV1-3, IV5, IV7-12, IV15-20, IV30-32, IV36.
42. Kirkwall	KW15-17.
43. Lake Vyrnwy	LL20-21, LL23, SY10, SY15-17, SY19, SY21-22.
44. Langdon Bay	CT1-21, ME9-13, TN23-26, TN28-30.
45. Leconfield	DN14, HU1-20, YO11-12, YO14-17, YO25.
46. Leek	DE4, DE45, S32-33, SK13, SK17, SK22-23, ST9-10, ST13.
47. Lerwick	ZE1-3.
48. Leuchars	DD1-7, DD10-11, KY1-2, KY6-10, KY15-16, PH12, PH14.
49. Linton on Ouse	DL1-3, DL6-7, DL9-10, HG1-5, LS1-20, LS22-28, TS9, TS15-16, YO1, YO7-8, YO10, YO19, YO23-24, YO26, YO30-32, YO41-43, YO51, YO60-61.
50. Liscombe	EX16, EX35-36, TA22, TA24.
51. Little Rissington	CV36, GL54-56, OX7, OX15-17, WR12.
52. Loch Glascarnoch	IV4, IV6, IV14, IV23-24, IV63.
53. Loftus	SR8, TS1-8, TS10-14, TS17-20, TS22-27.
54. Lusa	IV40-49, IV51-56, PH36, PH38-41.
55. Machrihanish	KA27, PA28-29, PA41-49, PA60.
56. Marham	CB6-7, IP24-28, PE12-14, PE30-38.
57. Mona	LL33-34, LL42-49, LL51-78.
58. Morpeth, Cockle Park	NE22, NE24, NE61-70.
59. North Wyke	EX6-7, EX17-22, EX37-38, PL19-21, TQ1-6, TQ9-14.
60. Norwich Airport	NR1-35.

Column (1)	Column (2)
Meteorological Office Station	*Postcode districts*
61. Nottingham Watnall	CV13, DE1-3, DE5-7, DE11-15, DE21-24, DE55-56, DE65, DE72-75, LE1-9, LE11-14, LE16-19, LE65, LE67, NG1-22, NG25, NG31-34.
62. Pembrey Sands	SA1-8, SA14-18, SA31-34, SA61-63, SA66-73.
63. Plymouth	PL1-12, TQ7-8.
64. Redesdale	CA9, DH8, NE19, NE47-49.
65. Rhyl	LL15-19, LL22, LL26-32.
66. Rochdale	BL0-9, M24, M26, OL1-12, OL15-16, SK15.
67. Rostherne	CW4, CW6-11, M1-9, M11-23, M25, M27-35, M38, M40-41, M43-46, M50, M90, PR7, SK1-12, SK14, SK16, WA1-16, WN1-8.
68. Rothamsted	AL1-10, EN6, HP1-4, LU1-7, SG1-4, SG12-14, WD3-7, WD17-19, WD23-25.
69. St. Athan	CF3, CF5, CF10-11, CF14-15, CF23-24, CF31-36, CF61-64, CF71-72, NP10, NP18-20, SA10-13.
70. St. Bees Head	CA13-15, CA18-28.
71. Salsburgh	EH43-46, G65, G67-68, ML1-3, ML6-11.
72. Scilly, St. Mary's	TR21-25.
73. Sennybridge	LD1-8, SA19-20, SY7, SY9, SY18.
74. Shap	CA10-12, CA16-17, LA8-10, LA21-23.
75. Shawbury	SY1-6, SY11-13, TF1-13.
76. Sheffield	DN1-8, DN11-12, HD1-2, HD4-6, S1-14, S17-18, S20-21, S25-26, S35, S40-45, S60-66, S70-75, S80-81, WF1-17.
77. South Farnborough	GU1-4, GU7-35, GU46-47, GU51-52, RG1-2, RG4-8, RG10, RG12, RG14, RG18-27, RG29-31, RG40-42, RG45, SL1-2, SL4-6, SO24.
78. Stonyhurst	BB1-3, BB5-7, LA2, LA6-7, PR6.
79. Stornoway Airport	HS1-9.
80. Strathallan	FK8, FK11-19, G63, KY4-5, KY13-14, PH1-7, PH13.
81. Thorney Island	BN1-3, BN9-18, BN25, BN41-43, BN45, PO1-22, PO30-41, SO14-19, SO30-32, SO40-43, SO45, SO50-53.

Column (1)	Column (2)
Meteorological Office Station	*Postcode districts*
82. Threave	DG1-2, DG5-8.
83. Tiree	PA61, PA66, PA76-78, PH42-44.
84. Trawsgoed	LL35-40, SY20, SY23-25.
85. Tredegar	CF37-48, CF81-83, NP4, NP11-13, NP22-24, NP44, SA9.
86. Tulloch Bridge	FK20-21, PA33, PA36, PA40, PH8-9, PH15-17, PH30-35, PH37, PH49-50.
87. Waddington	DN9-10, DN13, DN15-22, DN31-41, LN1-13, NG23-24, PE10-11, PE20-25.
88. Walney Island	LA1, LA3-5, LA11-20.
89. Wattisham	CB8-9, CO1-8, CO10-16, IP1-23, IP29-33.
90. Westonbirt	BA1-3, BA11, BA13-15, GL7-9, RG17, SN1-6, SN8-16, SN25-26.
91. Wick Airport	IV25, KW1-3, KW5-10, KW12, KW14.
92. Wittering	LE15, NN17-18, PE1-9, PE15-17, PE26-29.
93. Yeovilton	BA4-10, BA16, BA20-22, BS25-28, DT9-10, SP8, TA1-20, TA23.]

pp.1452-1453, *amendment to the Social Fund Cold Weather Payments (General) Regulations 1988 (SI 1988/1724) Sch. 2 (Specified alternative stations)*

With effect from November 1, 2014, reg.2(2) of and Sch.2 to the Social Fund Cold Weather Payments (General) Amendment Regulations 2014 (SI 2014/2687) substituted the following Sch.2:   **3.100**

Regulation 2(1A) and (1B)

[Schedule 2

SPECIFIED ALTERNATIVE STATIONS

3.101

Column (1)	*Column (2)*
Meteorological Office Station	*Specified Alternative Station*
Aberporth	Pembrey Sands
Albemarle	Redesdale
Bingley	Stonyhurst
Boscombe Down	Westonbirt
Braemar	Aboyne
Capel Curig	Lake Vyrnwy
Cardinham (Bodmin)	North Wyke
Carlisle	Keswick
Charlwood	Kenley
Coleshill	Pershore College
Crosby	Rhyl
Culdrose	Scilly, St. Mary
Dunstaffnage	Skye, Lusa
Edinburgh, Gogarbank	Strathallan
Eskdalemuir	Redesdale
Gravesend	Kenley
Hawarden Airport	Crosby
Heathrow	Gravesend
Hereford-Credenhill	Pershore College
High Wycombe	Rothamsted
Hurn (Bournemouth Airport)	Swanage
Keele	Shawbury
Kinloss	Lossiemouth
Langdon Bay	Gravesend

Column (1)	Column (2)
Meteorological Office Station	*Specified Alternative Station*
Leconfield	Linton on Ouse
Linton on Ouse	Bramham
Liscombe	North Wyke
Mona	Rhyl
North Wyke	Okehampton
Redesdale	Albemarle
Rhyl	Crosby
Rochdale	Rostherne
Sennybridge	Tredegar
Shap	Keswick
Sheffield	Nottingham, Watnall
St. Athan	Mumbles Head
St. Bees Head	Threave
Stonyhurst	Bingley
Thorney Island	Hurn (Bournemouth Airport)
Threave	Dundrennan
Tiree	Skye, Lusa
Trawsgoed	Aberporth
Tulloch Bridge	Aviemore]

p.1454, *amendment to the Social Fund Winter Fuel Payment Regulations 2000 (SI 2000/729) reg.1(2) (Interpretation—definition of "couple")*

With effect from December 16, 2014, art.29 and Sch.6, para.19 of the Marriage and Civil Partnership (Scotland) Act 2014 and Civil Partnership Act 2004 (Consequential Provisions and Modifications) Order 2014 (SI 2014/3229) amended reg.1(2) by substituting a definition of "couple" in exactly the same terms as the definition in the main volume. However, the latter definition applies only to England & Wales and the new definition applies to Scotland—SI 2014/3229 art.3(4). The result is that the definition is now the same throughout Great Britain. **3.102**

p.1465, *amendment to the Social Fund Maternity and Funeral Expenses (General) Regulations 2005 (SI 2005/3061) reg.3(1) (Interpretation— definition of "child arrangements order")*

3.103   With effect from April 22, 2014, art.12(1) and (2) of the Child Arrangements Order (Consequential Amendments to Subordinate Legislation) Order 2014 (SI 2014/852) amended reg.3(1) by adding the following definition after the definition of "Child":

> ""child arrangements order" means a child arrangements order as defined in section 8(1) of the Children Act 1989 which consists of, or includes, arrangements relating to either or both of the following—
>> (i) with whom the child is to live, and
>> (ii) when the child is to live with any person;"

p.1465, *amendment to the Social Fund Maternity and Funeral Expenses (General) Regulations 2005 (2005/3061) reg.3(1) (Interpretation— definition of "couple")*

3.104   With effect from December 16, 2014, art.29 and Sch.6, para.26 of the Marriage and Civil Partnership (Scotland) Act 2014 and Civil Partnership Act 2004 (Consequential Provisions and Modifications) Order 2014 (SI 2014/3229) amended reg.3(1) by substituting a definition of "couple" in exactly the same terms as the definition in the main volume. However, the latter definition applies only to England & Wales and the new definition applies to Scotland—SI 2014/3229 art.3(4). The result is that the definition is now the same throughout Great Britain.

p.1466, *amendment to the Social Fund Maternity and Funeral Expenses (General) Regulations 2005 (SI 2005/3061) reg.3(1) (Interpretation— definition of "residence order")*

3.105   With effect from April 22, 2014, art.12(1) and (2) of the Child Arrangements Order (Consequential Amendments to Subordinate Legislation) Order 2014 (SI 2014/852) amended reg.3(1) by revoking the definition of "residence order".

p.1470, *amendment to the Social Fund Maternity and Funeral Expenses (General) Regulations 2005 (SI 2005/3061) reg.3A (Provision against double payment: Sure Start Maternity Grants)*

3.106   With effect from April 22, 2014, art.12(1) and (3) of the Child Arrangements Order (Consequential Amendments to Subordinate Legislation) Order 2014 (SI 2014/852) amended reg.3A(6)(c) by substituting the words "child arrangements" for the word "residence".

pp.1478-1479, *annotation to the Social Fund Maternity and Funeral Expenses (General) Regulations 2005, (SI 2005/3061) reg.5A (Entitlement where another member of the claimant's family is under the age of 16)*

At the end of the General Note add the following: **3.107**

"*Legal challenge*
    In *LS v SSWP (SF)* [2014] UKUT 298 (AAC), it was submitted that reg.5A is *ultra vires* on the ground that the Secretary of State had not complied with the public sector equality duty in section 71 of the Race Relations Act 1976 as amended when making it. The Upper Tribunal (Judge Levenson) rejected that submission. However, the claimant was given permission to appeal to the Court of Appeal on November 19, 2014. No date has yet been appointed for that appeal to be heard."

pp.1543-1545, *amendment to the new style Jobseekers Act 1995 s.35(1) and (1A) (Definition of "couple")*

In error, the amendment to the definition of "couple" in s.35(1) and   **3.108**
the omission of subs.(1A) made by art.2 of and Sch.1, para.26, to the Marriage (Same Sex Couples) Act 2013 (Consequential and Contrary Provisions and Scotland) Order 2014 (SI 2014/516) with effect from March 13, 2014, as properly included in relation to the old style Jobseekers Act at pp.125-7 of the main volume, was omitted in relation to the new style Jobseekers Act 1995. See those pages of the main volume for the text. That amendment applied only in England and Wales. The same amendment has now been made with effect from December 16, 2014 by art.29 of and Sch.5, para.12, to the Marriage and Civil Partnership (Scotland) Act 2014 and Civil Partnership Act 2004 (Consequential Provisions and Modifications) Order 2014 (SI 2014/3229). By virtue of art.3(4), this amendment applies only in Scotland.

p.1556, *annotation to the Jobseeker's Allowance Regulations 2013 (SI 2013/378) reg.1 (Commencement)*

See the entries in this Supplement relating to *Vol.V: Universal Credit*   **3.109**
detailing the areas and claimants to which the commencement of the universal credit scheme, and thus the abolition of income-related JSA and the commencement of the Jobseeker's Allowance Regulations 2013, has been extended (see below at paras 6.002 (for a summary of the effect of the Nos.9, 11, 13 and 14 Commencement Orders), 6.154 (No.16 Order), 6.210 (No.17 Order), 6.244 (No.19 Order) and 6.274 (No.20 Order) for the position as at December 31, 2014).

p.1559, *amendment to the Jobseeker's Allowance Regulations 2013 (SI 2013/378) reg.2(2) (General interpretation)*

With effect from December 31, 2014, art.29(2) of the Shared Parental   **3.110**
Leave and Statutory Shared Parental Pay (Consequential Amendments and Subordinate Legislation) Order 2014 (SI 2014/3255) amended

reg.2(2) by inserting this new definition after the definition of "self-employed earner":

""shared parental leave" means a period of absence from work on leave by virtue of section 75E or 75G of the Employment Rights Act 1996;"

p.1595, *amendment to the Jobseeker's Allowance Regulations 2013 (SI 2013/378) reg.36 (Waiting days)*

3.111 With effect from October 27, 2014, reg.2(3) of the Social Security (Jobseeker's Allowance and Employment and Support Allowance) (Waiting Days) Amendment Regulations 2014 (SI 2014/2309) amended reg.36(2) by substituting "seven" for "three", thus increasing the number of "waiting days" to be served under para.4 of Sched.1 to the Jobseekers Act 1995 before entitlement to benefit can start. The amendment does not apply where the relevant jobseeking period (see regs 37-40) began before October 27, 2014 (reg.4(1) of the amending regulations). This change may well make the provision in the Social Security (Payments on Account of Benefit) Regulations 2013 (Vol.III) for the making of payments on account of benefit, in certain cases of financial need (restrictively defined), more important.

p.1599, *amendment to the Jobseeker's Allowance Regulations 2013 (SI 2013/378) reg.39(2)(d) (Linking periods)*

3.112 With effect from May 18, 2014, reg.6(2) of the Social Security (Maternity Allowance) (Miscellaneous Amendments) Regulations 2014 (SI 2014/884) amended reg.39(2)(d) by inserting "or 35B" after "35".

p.1604, *amendment to the Jobseeker's Allowance Regulations 2013 (SI 2013/378) reg.43(1) (Persons treated as engaged in remunerative work)*

3.113 With effect from December 31, 2014, art.29(3) of the Shared Parental Leave and Statutory Shared Parental Pay (Consequential Amendments and Subordinate Legislation) Order 2014 (SI 2014/3255) amended reg.43(1) by inserting "shared parental leave" after "paternity leave,". A new definition is added to reg.2(2) from the same date.

p.1620, *amendment to the Jobseeker's Allowance Regulations 2013 (SI 2013/378) reg.58(2)(c) (Earnings of employed earners: payments not included in earnings)*

3.114 With effect from December 31, 2014, art.29(4) of the Shared Parental Leave and Statutory Shared Parental Pay (Consequential Amendments and Subordinate Legislation) Order 2014 (SI 2014/3255) amended reg.58(2)(c) by inserting "shared parental leave" after "paternity leave,". A new definition is added to reg.2(2) from the same date.

PART IV

UPDATING MATERIAL
VOLUME III

ADMINISTRATION, ADJUDICATION AND THE EUROPEAN DIMENSION

Commentary by

Mark Rowland

Robin White

p.48, *amendment to the Social Security Administration Act 1992 s.15(A)*
(Payment out of benefit of sums in respect of mortgage interest etc.)

With effect from December 16, 2014, art.29 and Sch.5 para.9 of the 4.001
Marriage and Civil Partnership (Scotland) Act 2014 and Civil Partnership Act 2004 (Consequential Provisions and Modifications Order 2001
(SI 2014/3229) amended the definition of "partner" by substituting a
definition in the same terms as the existing definition. However, the
existing definition applied only to England and Wales; the new definition
applies to England, Wales, Scotland and Northern Ireland.

p.54, *annotation to the Social Security Administration Act 1992 s.71*
(Overpayments—general)

KP v RB of Kensington and Chelsea (HB) [2014] UKUT 393 (AAC) 4.002
determines that a compensation order made by the Crown Court does
not act as a cap on the amount of overpaid housing benefit and excess
council tax benefit which is recoverable.

p.117, *amendment to the Social Security Administration Act 1992 s.124*
(Provisions relating to age. Death and marriage)

With effect from December 10, 2014, art.12 of The Marriage (Same 4.003
Sex Couples) Act 2013 (Consequential and Contrary Provisions and
Scotland) and Marriage and Civil Partnership (Scotland) Act (Consequential Provisions) Order 2014 (SI 2014/3168) amended s.124 for
England and Wales only:
  (a) by inserting after the words "in their custody," in subs.(1) "(or in
       the case of marriages converted from civil partnerships, copies or
       extracts from the register of conversions)".
  (b) by inserting the following after subs.(3):

       "(3A) Where it is required to be ascertained or proved for the
       purposes mentioned in subsection (1) above, that a civil part-
       nership has been converted into a marriage, any person—
         (a) on presenting to the superintendent registrar in whose
              district the conversion took place, a duly completed
              requisition in writing in that behalf; and
         (b) on payment of a fee of £10.00;
       is entitled to obtain a copy, certified under the hand of the
       superintendent registrar, of the entry relating to that marriage
       in the register of conversions.".

  (c) by substituting in subs.(4) "subsections (3) and (3A)" for the
       words "subsection (3)".
  (d) by inserting the following in subs.(5)(a) before the definition of
       "Registrar General":

       " "register of conversions" means the register of conversions of
       civil partnerships into marriages kept by the Registrar General
       in accordance with section 9 of the Marriage (Same Sex

Couples) Act 2013 and regulations made under that section."

p.121, *insertion of heading and s.133A (Universal credit information) into the Social Security Administration Act 1972*

4.004   With effect from November 26, 2014, reg.9(1) of the Universal Credit and Miscellaneous Amendments (No.2) Regulations 2014 (SI 2014/2888) inserted a new heading and section as follows:

"Universal Credit Information

Supply of universal credit information

133A.–(1) This section applies to information that is held by—
   (a) the Secretary of State; or
   (b) a person providing services to the Secretary of State, in connection with the provision of those services,
that relates to an award of universal credit.
   (2) Information to which this section applies may be supplied to—
   (a) a local housing authority;
   (b) a licensing authority; or
   (c) a person authorised to exercise any function of a local housing authority or a licensing authority,
for use in connection with obtaining a rent repayment order in respect of an award of universal credit or recovering an amount payable under such an order.
   (3) For the purposes of this section—
"licensing authority" means a person designated by order under section 3 of the Housing (Wales) Act 2014;
"local housing authority" has the meaning given by section 261 of the Housing Act 2004; and
"rent repayment order" means a rent repayment order as referred to in section 73 or 96 of the Housing Act 2004 or section 32 of the Housing (Wales) Act 2014."

p.164, *amendments to the Social Security (Recovery of Benefits) Act 1997 s.1(2) (Cases in which this Act applies)*

4.005   With effect from March 31, 2014, s.11 of, and paras 1 and 2 of Sch.1 to, the Mesothelioma Act 2014 amended s.1(2) of the 1997 Act by omitting "or" at the end of para.(a) and inserting at the end of para.(b):

", or
   (c) under the Diffuse Mesothelioma Payment Scheme (established under the Mesothelioma Act 2014);".

pp.167-168, *amendments to the Social Security (Recovery of Benefits) Act 1997 s.1A (Lump-sum payments: regulation-making power)*

With effect from March 31, 2014, s.11 of, and para.17 of Sch.1 to, the   **4.006** Mesothelioma Act 2014 amended s.1A(2) of the 1997 Act by omitting "and" at the end of para.(b) and inserting at the end of para.(c):

> ", and
>> (d) a payment under the Diffuse Mesothelioma Payment Scheme (established under the Mesothelioma Act 2014),
>
> (but this subsection does not apply to a payment within paragraph (d) in a case where the compensation payment is itself such a payment)."

Section 1A(4)(a) is also amended, by substituting "as specified in section 1(2)(a) or (c)" for the words from "by or" to "extent".

p.176, *annotation to the Social Security (Recovery of Benefits) Act 1997 s.8 (Reduction of compensation payment)*

Add at the end of the annotation: "Nor does it apply in respect of the   **4.007** recovery of payments under the Diffuse Mesothelioma Payment Scheme established under the Mesothelioma Act 2014. See instead s.8A, below."

p.177, *insertion of the Social Security (Recovery of Benefits) Act 1997 s.8A (Reduction of payment under Diffuse Mesothelioma Payment Scheme)*

With effect from March 31, 2014, s.11 of, and paras 1 and 3 of Sch.1   **4.008** to, the Mesothelioma Act 2014 amended the 1997 Act by inserting after s.8:

"Reduction of payment under Diffuse Mesothelioma Payment Scheme

8A.—(1)This section applies instead of section 8 in a case where the compensation payment is a payment under the Diffuse Mesothelioma Payment Scheme.
(2) The gross amount of the compensation payment—
(a) is to be reduced by the amount of the recoverable benefit, and
(b) accordingly, is to be reduced to nil in any case where the amount of the recoverable benefit is equal to or greater than the gross amount of the compensation payment.
(3) Any claim of a person to receive the compensation payment is to be treated for all purposes as discharged if—
(a) the person is paid the gross amount of the compensation payment less the amount of the recoverable benefit, or
(b) the amount of the recoverable benefit is equal to or greater than the gross amount of the compensation payment and the person

is given a statement by the scheme administrator saying that the compensation payment has been reduced to nil."

The Diffuse Mesothelioma Payment Scheme is established under the Mesothelioma Act 2014 (see Vol.I of the main work).

p.177, *amendments to the Social Security (Recovery of Benefits) Act 1997 s.9 (Section 8: supplementary)*

4.009   With effect from March 31, 2014, s.11 of, and paras 1 and 8 of Sch.1 to, the Mesothelioma Act 2014 amended s.9 of the 1997 Act by inserting "or 8A" after "8" in each of subs.(1), (2), (3)(a) and (4)(a). Presumably it was intended that the heading of the section should similarly be amended.

p.178, *amendment to the Social Security (Recovery of Benefits) Act 1997 s.10 (Review of certificate of recoverable benefits)*

4.010   With effect from March 31, 2014, s.11 of, and paras 1 and 4 of Sch.1 to, the Mesothelioma Act 2014 amended s.10 of the 1997 Act by inserting after subs.(3):

"(4) The scheme administrator of the Diffuse Mesothelioma Payment Scheme may not apply for a review under this section."

The "scheme administrator" is defined in s.29 (see below).

p.179, *amendments to the Social Security (Recovery of Benefits) Act 1997 s.11(2) (Appeals against certificates of recoverable benefits)*

4.011   With effect from March 31, 2014, s.11 of, and paras 1, 5 and 8 of Sch.1 to, the Mesothelioma Act 2014 amended s.11 of the 1997 Act by inserting "or 8A" after "8" in subs.(2)(b) and by inserting after subs.(2)(b):

"but the scheme administrator of the Diffuse Mesothelioma Payment Scheme may not appeal under this section."

The "scheme administrator" is defined in s.29 (see below).

p.185, *amendments to the Social Security (Recovery of Benefits) Act 1997 s.13(2) (Appeal to Upper Tribunal)*

4.012   With effect from March 31, 2014, s.11 of, and paras 1, 6 and 8 of Sch.1 to, the Mesothelioma Act 2014 amended s.13 of the 1997 Act by inserting "or 8A" after "8" in subs.(2)(c) and by inserting after subs.(2)(c):

"but the scheme administrator of the Diffuse Mesothelioma Payment Scheme may not appeal under this section."

The "scheme administrator" is defined in s.29 (see below). It is arguable that, if the scheme administrator had for some reason been added as a respondent to the proceedings before the First-tier Tribunal, he would have a right of appeal under s.11 of the Tribunals, Courts and Enforcement Act 2007 as a party, notwithstanding this amendment.

p.185, *amendment to the Social Security (Recovery of Benefits) Act 1997 s.14(4)(a) (Reviews and appeals: supplementary)*

With effect from March 31, 2014, s.11 of, and paras 1 and 8 of Sch.1 to, the Mesothelioma Act 2014 amended s.14(4)(a) of the 1997 Act by inserting "or 8A" after "8".   4.013

p.190, *amendment to the Social Security (Recovery of Benefits) Act 1997 s.19(3)(b) (Payments by more than one person)*

With effect from March 31, 2014, s.11 of, and paras 1 and 8 of Sch.1 to, the Mesothelioma Act 2014 amended s.19(3)(b) of the 1997 Act by inserting "or 8A" after "8".   4.014

p.191, *amendment to the Social Security (Recovery of Benefits) Act 1997 s.20(4)(a) (Amounts overpaid under section 6)*

With effect from March 31, 2014, s.11 of, and paras 1 and 8 of Sch.1 to, the Mesothelioma Act 2014 amended s.20(4)(a) of the 1997 Act by inserting "or 8A" after "8".   4.015

p.192, *amendments to the Social Security (Recovery of Benefits) Act 1997 s.21 (Compensation payments to be disregarded)*

With effect from March 31, 2014, s.11 of, and paras 1 and 8 of Sch.1 to, the Mesothelioma Act 2014 amended s.21 of the 1997 Act by inserting "or 8A" after "8" in each of subs.(1) and (5)(a).   4.016

p.193, *amendment to the Social Security (Recovery of Benefits) Act 1997 s.23 (Provision of information)*

With effect from March 31, 2014, s.11 of, and para.19 of Sch.1 to, the Mesothelioma Act 2014 amended s.23 of the 1997 Act by inserting after subs.(6):   4.017

"(6A) The following persons must give the Secretary of State the prescribed information for the purposes of this Act—
(a) the scheme administrator of the Diffuse Mesothelioma Payment Scheme, and
(b) any person providing services to the scheme administrator."

The "scheme administrator" is defined in s.29 (see below).

p.195, *amendment to the Social Security (Recovery of Benefits) Act 1997 s.29 (General interpretation)*

4.018   With effect from March 31, 2014, s.11 of, and paras 1 and 7 of Sch.1 to, the Mesothelioma Act 2014 amended s.29 of the 1997 Act by inserting at the end:

> ""scheme administrator", in relation to the Diffuse Mesothelioma Payment Scheme, has the meaning given by section 18 of the Mesothelioma Act 2014."

p.204, *amendment to the Social Security Act 1998 s.3(1A) (Use of information)*

4.019   With effect from March 31, 2014, s.11 of, and para.21 of Sch.1 to, the Mesothelioma Act 2014 amended s.3(1A) of the 1998 Act by inserting at the end:

> "(f) the Diffuse Mesothelioma Payment Scheme."

p.205, *annotation to the Social Security Act 1998 s.3 (Use of information)*

4.020   Provision is made for functions under this section to be exercised on behalf of the Secretary of State by the Scottish Ministers (see s.93(1) of the Scotland Act 1998 and art.2(1)(b) of the Scotland Act 1998 (Agency Arrangements) (Specification) Order 2014 (SI 2014/1892)), because the Scottish Ministers exercise relevant functions relating to employment and training.

pp.208–210, *annotation to the Social Security Act 1998 s.8(2) (Decisions by Secretary of State)*

4.021   In *SSWP v HR (AA)* [2014] UKUT 571 (AAC), attention was drawn to Regulation (EC) 987/2009 under which a person may be entitled to sickness benefit (e.g., attendance allowance) from the Member State in which the person lives while any dispute between states as to which is the competent state is determined. However, it was noted that, if a claim was made to the state of residence and it decided it was not the competent state, the proper procedure was for it to refuse the claim and then refer it to the state it regarded as competent. Only if that state then also considered that it was not the competent state would there be a dispute requiring the state of residence to pay the benefit from the date of the first claim. The Upper Tribunal suggested that, in the absence of any relevant power to revise the initial refusal, s.8(2)(b) would preclude the award being made from the date of the original claim after the dispute had arisen and it might be necessary to rely on s.2 of the European Communities Act 1972 in order to give effect to the European Union law.

p.217, *annotation to the Social Security Act 1998 s.10(2) (Decisions superseding earlier decisions)*

MC v SSWP (ESA) [2014] UKUT 125 (AAC) has been reported as [2014] AACR 35.   4.022

pp.223–232, *annotation to the Social Security Act 1998 s.12(1) and (2) (Appeal to First-tier Tribunal)*

AE v SSWP (ESA) [2013] UKUT 5 (AAC) has been reported as [2014] AACR 23 and *MC v SSWP (ESA)* [2014] UKUT 125 (AAC) has been reported as [2014] AACR 35.   4.023

In *John v Information Commissioner* [2014] UKUT 444 (AAC), the Upper Tribunal rejected an argument that a respondent was required to cross-appeal or submit a respondent's notice if disagreeing with a decision being challenged on appeal to the First-tier Tribunal. It was held that new issues could be raised in a response but that the Upper Tribunal could exercise its case-management powers to prevent unfairness to an appellant.

p.237–240, *annotation to the Social Security Act 1998 s.12(8)(b) (Appeal to first-tier Tribunal)*

Although the passing of an Act of Parliament is a change of circumstance (*Chief Adjudication Officer v McKiernon* (reported as *R(I)2/94*)), an Act passed after Secretary v State has made a decision can alter the legal circumstances obtaining at the time of his decision. Thus, in principle, where the Secretary of State has made his decision on the basis of regulations that have been subsequently held to be *ultra vires* and the regulations are then retrospectively validated by Act of Parliament, the Secretary of State is entitled to rely on the effect of that Act in responding to an appeal against his decision, notwithstanding s.12(8)(b) of the 1998 Act (*SSWP v TJ (JSA)* [2015] UKUT 56 (AAC)) in which the majority found that the relevant Act did not in fact have retrospective effect in relation to those who had already appealed before it was passed).   4.023.1

p.251, *annotation to the Social Security Act 1998 s.19(1) and (2) (Medical examination required by Secretary of State)*

JM v SSWP (ESA) [2013] UKUT 234 (AAC) has been reported as [2014] AACR 5. The weight to be given to a physiotherapist's opinion in relation to mental health issues is a matter for the decision-maker or tribunal—see *ST v SSWP (ESA)* [2014] UKUT 547 (AAC) in which the three-judge panel recorded evidence given to it about the recruitment, training and assessment of healthcare professionals.   4.024

p.265, *annotation to the Social Security Act 1998 s.27(1) (Restrictions on entitlement to benefit in certain cases of error)*
There is an incomplete reference in the last line on the page. It should be to *JK v SSWP (DLA)* [2013] UKUT 218 (AAC).   4.025

p.273 *annotation to the Social Security Act 1998 s.39ZA (Certificates)*

4.026   *JM v SSWP (ESA)* [2013] UKUT 234 (AAC) has been reported as [2014] AACR 5.

p.274, *annotation to the Social Security Act 1998 s.39 (Interpretation etc. of Chapter II)*

4.027   The weight to be given to a physiotherapist's opinion in relation to mental health issues is a matter for the decision-maker or tribunal—see *ST v SSWP (ESA)* [2014] UKUT 547 (AAC) in which the three-judge panel recorded evidence given to it about the recruitment, training and assessment of healthcare professionals.

p.281, *annotation to the Social Security Act 1998 Sch.2 paras 3 and 4 (Decision against which no appeal lies)*

4.028   *TD v SSWP (CSM)* [2013] UKUT 282 (AAC) has been reported as [2014] AACR 7. That decision was followed in *SSWP v AK (CA)* [2014] UKUT 415 (AAC) insofar as the judge held that para.3 was also not inconsistent with the European Convention on Human Rights, but the judge also held that, while it precluded an appeal against a decision as to which of two people caring for the relevant disabled person and otherwise entitled to carer's allowance should receive the allowance, para.3 did not preclude an appeal brought on the ground that the other potential claimant was not in fact caring for the disabled person.

p.331, *amendment to the Welfare Benefits Up-rating Act 2013 s.1 (Up-rating of certain social security benefits for the tax years 2014-15 and 2015-16)*

4.029   With effect from November 26, 2014, reg.7(2) of the Universal Credit and Miscellaneous Amendments (No.2) Regulations 2014 (SI 2014/2888) amended s.1 as follows:
   (a) by inserting at the beginning of subsection (2) the words ""Subject to subsection (2A),";
   (b) by inserting the following after subs.(2):

   "(2A) An order under this section shall be framed so that—
      (a) any variation of the relevant sums referred to in paragraphs 1(j) to (1) of the Schedule (sums specified under Part 1 of the Welfare Reform Act 2012) comes into force in relation to a person on the relevant day; and
      (b) any other variation to which the order relates comes into force, for the purposes of determining the amount of universal credit to which a person is entitled, on the relevant day.

   (2B) In subsection (2A) "relevant day", in relation to a person, means the first day of the first universal credit assessment period in respect of the person which begins on or after—

(a) the Monday of the week specified in subsection (2)(a), or

(b) any earlier date specified under subsection (2)(b).

(2C) In subsection (2B) "universal credit assessment period" means an assessment period for the purposes of Part 1 of the Welfare Reform Act 2012.".

p.354, *amendment to the Social Security (Claims and Payments) Regulations 1987 (SI 1987/1868) reg.2(1) (Interpretation)*

With effect from December 16, 2014, art.29 and Sch.6 para.6 of the 4.030 Marriage and Civil Partnership (Scotland) Act 2014 and Civil Partnership Act 2004 (Consequential Provisions and Modifications Order 2001 (SI 2014/3229) amended the definition of "couple" by substituting a definition in the same terms as the existing definition. However, the existing definition applied only to England and Wales; the new definition applies to England, Wales, Scotland and Northern Ireland.

p.422, *annotation to the Social Security (Claims and Payments) Regulations 1987 (SI 1987/1868) reg.19 (Time for claiming benefit)*

S K-G v SSWP (JSA) [2014] UKUT 430 (AAC) decides that 4.031 reg.19(5)(d) does not apply to information in a standard DWP letter and the direct.gov website references to claims being made online or by telephone. Judge Wikeley decides that reg.19(5)(d) is directed to "the situation where a claimant is given information by a DWP officer as part of some specific interchange or transaction relevant to their personal circumstances" (para.17). Furthermore, reg.19(5)(d) is not directed to official information about the process or method of claiming (para. 21).

p.437, *amendment to the Social Security (Claims and Payments) Regulations 1987 (SI 1987/1868) reg.21 (Direct credit transfer)*

With effect from November 26, 2014, reg.5(2) of the Universal Credit 4.032 and Miscellaneous Amendments (No.2) Regulations 2014 (SI 2014/2888) substituted the following for reg.21(1):

"(1) The Secretary of State may arrange for benefit to be paid by way of direct credit transfer into a bank or other account nominated by the person entitled to benefit or a person acting on their behalf."

p.545, *amendment to the Universal Credit, Personal Independence Payment, Jobseeker's Allowance and Employment and Support Allowance (Claims and Payments) Regulations 2013 (SI 2013/380) reg.46 (Direct credit transfer)*

With effect from November 26, 2014, reg.5(3) of the Universal Credit 4.033 and Miscellaneous Amendments (No.2) Regulations 2014 (SI 2014/2888) substituted the following for reg.46(1):

"(1) The Secretary of State may arrange for benefit to be paid by way of direct credit transfer into a bank or other account nominated by the person entitled to benefit, a person acting on their behalf under regulation 57(1) or a person referred to in regulation 57(2)."

p.572, *amendment to the Social Security and Child Support (Decisions and Appeals) Regulations 1999 (SI 1999/991) reg.1(3) (Interpretation)*

4.034   The version of the definition of "couple" that appears in the main work applied only in England and Wales until December 16, 2014, when it was effectively extended to Scotland by para.18 of Sch.6 to the Marriage and Civil Partnership (Scotland) Act 2014 and Civil Partnership Act 2004 (Consequential Provisions and Modifications) Order 2014 (SI 2014/3229). Until that date, the previous version dating from 2005, which assumed that a marriage was between a man and a woman, had continued to apply in Scotland, although this made no practical difference because, until December 16, 2014, a marriage of a same sex couple in England and Wales was treated in Scotland as a civil partnership formed under the law of England and Wales, so that the spouses were treated as civil partners (see art.5 of the Marriage (Same Sex Couples) Act 2013 (Consequential and Contrary Provisions and Scotland) Order 2014 (SI 2014/560), revoked by art.4 of the Marriage (Same Sex Couples) Act 2013 (Consequential and Contrary Provisions and Scotland) and Marriage and Civil Partnership (Scotland) Act 2014 (Consequential Provisions) Order 2014 (SI 2014/3168)).

p.578, *annotation to the Social Security and Child Support (Decisions and Appeals) Regulations 1999 (SI 1999/991) reg.1(3) (Interpretation–"official error")*

4.035   *MB v Christchurch BC (HB)* [2014] UKUT 201 (AAC) has been reported as [2014] AACR 39.

p.596, *annotation to the Social Security and Child Support (Decisions and Appeals) Regulations 1999 (SI 1999/991) reg.3(5E) (Revision of decisions)*

4.036   When a claimant appeals against a decision of the Secretary of State that he or she does not have limited capability for work, the claimant is usually entitled to an award of employment and support allowance at the basic rate while the appeal is pending, without a new claim being made (see reg.3(j) of the Social Security (Claims and Payments) Regulations 1987) and for as long as medical certificates are provided (see reg.30 of the Employment and Support Allowance Regulations 2008—in Vol.I of the main work). If the appeal is unsuccessful, withdrawn, struck out or discontinued, the award is terminated under reg.147A(5) of the 2008 Regulations. If the appeal is successful, reg 3(5E) of the 1999 Regulations permits the award to be revised, for which purpose any finding of fact embodied in or necessary to the decision of the First-tier Tribunal is to be treated as binding up to the date of any relevant change of circumstances (see reg.147A(6) and (7) of the 2008 Regulations). Revision is necessary because the effect of the First-tier Tribunal's decision will be that the claimant is entitled to include the work-related activity component or support component in addition to the basic rate. Thus, implementation of the decision of the First-tier Tribunal is in practice generally effected through this form of revision rather than more directly.

pp.615–616, *annotation to the Social Security and Child Support (Decisions and Appeals) Regulations 1999 (SI 1999/991) reg.6(2)(a)(i) (Supersession for change of circumstances)*

The effect of a binding decision of the Upper Tribunal or a court on the law is to state law as it has always been (*In Re Spectrum Plus Ltd* [2005] UKHL 41; [2005] 2 AC 680). This does not create any difficulty where such a decision shows that an earlier decision of the Secretary of State was wrong in law, because the Secretary of State's decision may be superseded under reg.6(2)(b). However reg.6(2)(b) permits supersession only of decisions of the Secretary of State and it was suggested by the majority of *SSWP v TJ (JSA)* [2015] UKUT 56 (AAC) that, for the purposes of social security adjudication, the making of the binding decision may need to be treated as a change of circumstances affecting the understanding of the law so that a decision of the First-tier Tribunal given before the binding decision was given can be superseded under reg.6(2)(a)(i). Otherwise, where an award of benefit has been made for an indefinite period by the First-tier Tribunal rather than the Secretary of State, it would not be possible to supersede the decision even prospectively so as to give effect to the binding decision. **4.036.1**

p.619, *annotation to the Social Security and Child Support (Decisions and Appeals) Regulations 1999 (SI 1999/991) reg.6(2)(g) (Supersession of incapacity benefit decisions)*

JC v DSD (IB) [2011] NICom 177 has been reported as [2014] AACR 30. **4.037**

p.620, *annotation to the Social Security and Child Support (Decisions and Appeals) Regulations 1999 (SI 1999/991) reg.6(2)(r) (Supersession of employment and support allowance decisions)*

MC v SSWP (ESA) [2014] UKUT 125 (AAC) has been reported as [2014] AACR 35. **4.038**

pp.678-680, *annotation to the Social Security and Child Support (Decisions and Appeals) Regulations 1999 (SI 1999/991) Sch.2 (Decisions against which no appeal lies)*

TD v SSWP (CSM) [2013] UKUT 282 (AAC) has been reported as [2014] AACR 7. **4.039**

There is an important distinction between *ZM and AB v HMRC (TC)* [2013] UKUT 547 (AAC) (now reported as [2014] AACR 17) and *CI v HMRC (TC)* [2014] UKUT 158 (AAC) (both mentioned in the main work). In the former, the Upper Tribunal drew a distinction between issues of fact, in respect of which it was held that an appeal did lie under the Tax Credits Act 2002 because judicial review would not in practice be an adequate remedy, and issues of discretion, in which it was held that judicial review was as effective a remedy and an appeal did not lie. In the latter case, *CI*, the Upper Tribunal declined to draw such a distinction on the ground that it was "over-technical". On this approach, much of Sch.2 to the 1999 Regulations would be inconsistent with art.6 of the European Convention on Human Rights.

p.719, *annotation to the Universal Credit, Personal Independence Payment, Jobseeker's Allowance and Employment and Support Allowance (Decisions and Appeals) Regulations 2013 (SI 2013/381) reg.41(3) (Effect of alterations affecting universal credit)*

4.040   Where the Secretary of State makes a decision under reg.41(3), reg.61(5) of the Universal Credit Regulations 2013 (see below in the amendments to Vol.V) applies so as to enable him either to treat a payment of employed earnings received in one assessment period as paid in a later period or to disregard information received about a payment of employed earnings.

p.762, *amendment to the Social Security (Jobcentre Plus Interviews) Regulations 2002 (SI 2002/1703) reg.4A (Requirement for certain lone parents to take part in an interview)*

4.041   With effect from April 28, 2014, reg.14(2) of the Income Support (Work-Related Activity) and Miscellaneous Amendments Regulations 2014 (SI 2014/1097) amended reg.4A as follows:
(a) by inserting "and" after sub-paragraph (a);
(b) by omitting sub-paragraph (c) and the "and" which preceded it;
(c) by substituting the following for para. (2):

"(2) Subject to regulations 7 to 9, a lone parent to whom this regulation applies is required to take part in one or more interviews as a condition of continuing to be entitled to the full amount of benefit which is payable to him part from these Regulations.";

(d) by omitting the words "waived or" in para, (3)(b).

p.763, *amendment to the Social Security (Jobcentre Plus Interviews) Regulations 2002 (SI 2002/1703) reg.5 (Time when interview is to take place)*

4.042   With effect from April 28, 2014, reg.14(3) of the Income Support (Work-Related Activity) and Miscellaneous Amendments Regulations 2014 (SI 2014/1097) amended reg.5 as follows:

(a) by omitting in para. (2) the words "as soon as reasonably practicable after";
(b) by inserting in para. (2)(a) the words "as soon as reasonably practicable after" before the words "the requirement to take part";
(c) by inserting the following after para. (2)(a):

"(aa) in a case where regulation 4A(2) applies, on such a date as may be determined by the officer; or";

(d) by inserting in para. (2)(b) the words ", as soon as reasonably practicable after" after the words "in any other case";
(e) by omitting sub-para. (i) in para. (2)(b);
(f) by omitting in para. (2)(b)(ii) the words "but regulation 4A(1) does not apply";
(g) by omitting in para. (2)(b)(iii) the words "either" and "or regulation 4A(2)".

p.764, *amendment to the Social Security (Jobcentre Plus Interviews) Regulations 2002 (SI 2002/1703) reg.6 (Waiver of requirement to take part in an interview)*

With effect from April 28, 2014, reg.14(4) of the Income Support (Work-Related Activity) and Miscellaneous Amendments Regulations 2014 (SI 2014/1097) amended reg.6 as follows: **4.043**
(a) by inserting at the beginning of para. (1) "Except in a case where a requirement is imposed by virtue of regulation 4A(2),";
(b) by substituting in para.(2)(a) "4ZA" for "4A)".

p.765, *amendment to the Social Security (Jobcentre Plus Interviews) Regulations 2002 (SI 2002/1703) reg.8 (Exemptions)*

With effect from April 28, 2014, reg.14(5) of the Income Support (Work-Related Activity) and Miscellaneous Amendments Regulations 2014 (SI 2014/1097) amended reg.8(4) by inserting ", 4A" after "4ZA". **4.044**

p.766, *amendment to the Social Security (Jobcentre Plus Interviews) Regulations 2002 (SI 2002/1703) reg.11 (Taking part in an interview)*

With effect from April 28, 2014, reg.14(6) of the Income Support (Work-Related Activity) and Miscellaneous Amendments Regulations 2014 (SI 2014/1097) amended reg.11 as follows: **4.045**
(a) by substituting in para.(4) the words "date on which the person was notified of his failure to take part in the interview" for the words "day on which the interview was to take place";
(b) by inserting the following after para.(4)—

"(5) Where a notice under paragraph (4) is sent by post it is take to have been received on the second working day after it is sent."

p.768, *amendment to the Social Security (Jobcentre Plus Interviews) Regulations 2002 (SI 2002/1703) reg.12 (Failure to take part in an interview)*

4.046   With effect from April 28, 2014, reg.14(7) of the Income Support (Work-Related Activity) and Miscellaneous Amendments Regulations 2014 (SI 2014/1097) amended reg.12 as follows:

    (a) by substituting in para.(9) the words "satisfies a compliance con-dition" for the words "takes part in an interview";

    (b) by substituting in para.(9) the words "compliance condition was satisfied" for the words "requirement to take part in an interview was met";

    (c) by inserting the following after para.(9):

        "(9A) In paragraph (9) "compliance condition" means a require-ment to—

            (a) take part in an interview; or

            (b) undertake work-related activity."

    (d) by substituting in para.(12)(a) the words "date on which the person was notified of his failure to take part in an interview" for the words "day on which the interview was to take place".

p.769, *insertion of reg.12A after reg.12 of the Social Security (Jobcentre Plus Interviews) Regulations 2002 (SI 2002/1703)*

4.047   With effect from April 28, 2014, reg.14(8) of the Income Support (Work-Related Activity) and Miscellaneous Amendments Regulations 2014 (SI 2014/1097) inserted new reg.12A after reg.12 as follows:

"Circumstances where the amount of benefit payable to a claimant is not to be reduced in accordance with regulation 12(2)(c)

12A. (1) The amount of benefit payable to a claimant is not to be reduced in accordance with regulation 12(2)(c) if that amount—

    (a) is at the time the relevant decision falls to be made in respect of the current failure, being paid at a reduced rate in accordance with regulation 12(2)(c), regulations 7(3) and 8 of the Social Security (Work-focused Interviews for Lone Parents) and Mis-cellaneous Amendments Regulations 2000 or regulation 8(1) and (2) of the Income Support (Work-Related Activity) and Miscellaneous Amendments Regulations 2014; and

    (b) was last reduced not more than two weeks before the date of the current failure.

(2) In paragraph (1) "current failure" means a failure which may, in the case of a claimant who has an award of benefit, lead to a reduction in benefit under regulation 12(2)(c) in relation to which the Secretary of State has not yet determined whether the amount of benefit payable to the claimant is to be reduced in accordance with that regula-tion."

p.869, *amendment to the Social Security (Payments on Account of Benefit) Regulations 2013 (SI 2013/383) reg.5 (Payment on account of benefit where there is no award of benefit)*

With effect from November 26, 2014, reg.5(1)(a) of the Universal   4.048
Credit and Miscellaneous Amendments (No. 2) Regulations 2014 (SI 2014/2888) amended reg.5(1)(b) by inserting the words "(or will be satisfied during the period in respect of which the payment is to be made)" after the word "satisfied".

p.870, *amendment to The Social Security (Payments on Account of Benefit) Regulations 2013 (SI 2013/383) reg.9 (Payment by direct credit transfer)*

With effect from November 26, 2014, reg.5(1)(b) of the Universal   4.049
Credit and Miscellaneous Amendments (No. 2) Regulations 2014 (SI 2014/2888) replaced reg.9 with the following:

"Payment by direct credit transfer

9. A payment on account of benefit may be paid by way of direct credit transfer into a bank account or other account nominated by A or a person acting on A's behalf."

p.899, *amendments to the Social Security (Recovery of Benefits) (Lump Sum Payments) Regulations 2008 (SI 2008/1596) reg.1(2) (Interpretation)*

With effect from July 1, 2014, the Social Security (Recovery of Bene-   4.050
fits) (Lump Sum Payments) (Amendment) Regulations 2014 (SI 2014/1456) reg.2, Sch. paras 1 and 2 amended reg.1(2) of the 2008 Regulations by inserting the following definitions in the appropriate places:
""the 2014 Act" means the Mesothelioma Act 2014;";
""Diffuse Mesothelioma Payment Scheme" means the scheme established by the Diffuse Mesothelioma Payment Scheme Regulations 2014;";
""specified lump sum payment" means a lump sum payment within paragraph (a), (b) or (c) of section 1A(2) of the Act;"
It also substituted the following definition for the existing one:
""recoverable lump sum payment"—
    (a) in relation to a compensation payment which is a payment under the Diffuse Mesothelioma Payment Scheme, means any specified lump sum payment which is recoverable by virtue of regulation 4A;
    (b) in relation to any other description of compensation payment, means any lump sum payment which is recoverable by virtue of regulation 4;"

It also amended the definition of "compensator" by inserting after "payment" the words "and includes the scheme administrator who makes a payment in accordance with the Diffuse Mesothelioma Payment Scheme;"

Finally, it replaced the definition of "lump sum payments" with a definition of "lump sum payment" by substituting for the words from ""lump sum payments" are" to "applies" with the words ""lump sum payment" means a payment to which any of paragraphs (a) to (d) of section 1A(2) of the Act applies,".

These and the other amendments made to the 2008 Regulations are in part related to amendments made to the Social Security (Recovery of Benefits) Act 1997 (see above) so as to enable payments made under the Diffuse Mesothelioma Payment Scheme established by the Mesothelioma Act 2014 to be recovered if a compensator later comes to light. They also enable payments under the Pneumoconiosis etc. (Workers' Compensation) Act 1979, the Child Maintenance and Other Payments Act 2008 and certain related extra-statutory payments to be recovered from payments made under the Diffuse Mesothelioma Payment Scheme. For the 1979 Act, the 2008 Act and the 2014 Act, see Vol.1 of the main work.

p.900, *amendments to the Social Security (Recovery of Benefits) (Lump Sum Payments) Regulations 2008 (SI 2008/1596) reg.4 (Recovery of lump sum payments)*

4.051   With effect from July 1, 2014, the Social Security (Recovery of Benefits) (Lump Sum Payments) (Amendment) Regulations 2014 (SI 2014/1456) reg.2, Sch. paras 1 and 3 amended reg.4 of the 2008 Regulations by (a) substituting for the heading "Recovery of lump sum payments from compensation payment made otherwise than under Diffuse Mesothelioma Payment Scheme"; (b) substituting in para.(1) for "a payment to which section 1A(2) of the Act applies ("a lump sum payment")" the words "a lump sum payment"; and (c) inserting after para.(1)(a):

"(ab) the compensation payment is not a payment under the Diffuse Mesothelioma Payment Scheme; and".

It further inserted after para.(1):

"(1A) The Secretary of State may also recover the amount of lump sum payments to which section 1A(2)(d) of the Act applies where—
(a) any such payment has been, or is likely to be, made to one or more dependants of P;
(b) by virtue of a notice given under section 3(3) of the 2014 Act, any other dependant of P has ceased to be eligible for a lump sum payment to which section 1A(2)(d) of the Act applies; and
(c) a compensation payment in consequence of P's diffuse mesothelioma is made to that other dependant.".

266

p.900, *insertion of the Social Security (Recovery of Benefits) (Lump Sum Payments) Regulations 2008 (SI 2008/1596) reg.4A (Recovery of specified lump sum payments from compensation payment under Diffuse Mesothelioma Payment Scheme)*

With effect from July 1, 2014, the Social Security (Recovery of Bene-   4.052
fits) (Lump Sum Payments) (Amendment) Regulations 2014 (SI 2014/1456) reg.2, Sch. paras 1 and 4 inserted into the 2008 Regulations:

"Recovery of specified lump sum payments from compensation payment under Diffuse Mesothelioma Payment Scheme

4A. The Secretary of State may recover the amount of a specified lump sum payment where—

(a) a compensation payment in consequence of diffuse mesothelioma is made to or in respect of P, or to a dependant of P, and a lump sum payment has been, or is likely to be, made to P or in respect of P;

(b) that compensation payment is a payment under the Diffuse Mesothelioma Payment Scheme; and

(c) the disease in consequence of which the specified lump sum payment was made is also diffuse mesothelioma.".

p.900, *amendments to the Social Security (Recovery of Benefits) (Lump Sum Payments) Regulations 2008 (SI 2008/1596) reg.6 (Compensation payments to which these Regulations apply)*

With effect from July 1, 2014, the Social Security (Recovery of Bene-   4.053
fits) (Lump Sum Payments) (Amendment) Regulations 2014 (SI 2014/1456) reg.2, Sch. paras 1 and 5 amended reg.6 of the 2008 Regulations by renumbering the existing provision as paragraph (1), inserting at the beginning of that paragraph the words "Except as stated in paragraph (2)"; and then inserting a new para.(2):

"(2) In any case where—

(a) the lump sum payment falls within section 1A(2)(d) of the Act; or

(b) paragraphs (a) to (c) of regulation 4A apply;

these Regulations apply only in relation to compensation payments which are made on or after 31st March 2014.".

p.900, *amendment to the Social Security (Recovery of Benefits) (Lump Sum Payments) Regulations 2008 (SI 2008/1596) reg.7(1)(g) (Exemption of UK Asbestos Trust)*

With effect from July 1, 2014, the Social Security (Recovery of Bene-   4.054
fits) (Lump Sum Payments) (Amendment) Regulations 2014 (SI 2014/1456) reg.2, Sch. paras 1 and 6 amended reg.7(1)(g) of the 2008

Regulations by inserting after "diseases" the words "provided that any payment made in respect of diffuse mesothelioma out of this Trust is not made to or in respect of a person who has received a payment under the Diffuse Mesothelioma Payment Scheme".

p.902, *insertion of the Social Security (Recovery of Benefits) (Lump Sum Payments) Regulations 2008 (SI 2008/1596) reg.9(2A) (Information contained in certificates)*

4.055   With effect from July 1, 2014, the Social Security (Recovery of Benefits) (Lump Sum Payments) (Amendment) Regulations 2014 (SI 2014/1456) reg.2, Sch. paras 1 and 7 inserted into reg.9 of the 2008 Regulations:

> "(2A) Where a certificate has been applied for by the scheme administrator, the certificate may contain information which would assist the scheme administrator in making a determination in accordance with the Diffuse Mesothelioma Payment Scheme.".

pp.903–904, *amendments to the Social Security (Recovery of Benefits) (Lump Sum Payments) Regulations 2008 (SI 2008/1596) reg.10 (Liability to pay Secretary of State amount of lump sum payments)*

4.056   With effect from July 1, 2014, the Social Security (Recovery of Benefits) (Lump Sum Payments) (Amendment) Regulations 2014 (SI 2014/1456) reg.2, Sch. paras 1 and 8 amended reg.10(3) of the 2008 Regulations by substituting for "is less than the lump sum payments" the words "is less than the recoverable lump sum payments".

It then inserted:

> "(4A) In any case where recoverable lump sum payments include one or more lump sum payments to which section 1A(2)(d) of the Act applies, the liability referred to in paragraph (1) in respect of those lump sum payments arises prior to any such liability in respect of any other recoverable lump sum payment.".

Finally, it inserted at the beginning of para.(7) "Subject to paragraph (8)," and inserted after that paragraph:

> "(8) In the case of a lump sum payment to which section 1A(2)(d) of the Act applies which has been made to one or more dependants of P, this regulation also applies to the extent that the compensator is making any of the payments listed in—
>
> (a) paragraph (7)(a), where such a payment is made to another dependant of P who has ceased to be eligible for a lump sum payment to which section 1A(2)(d) of the Act applies by virtue of having given notice under section 3(3) of the 2014 Act;
>
> (b) paragraph (7)(b), where such a dependant is an intended beneficiary of that payment.".

pp.904-905, *amendments to the Social Security (Recovery of Benefits)*
(Lump Sum Payments) Regulations 2008 (SI 2008/1596) reg.12
(Reduction of compensation payment)

With effect from July 1, 2014, the Social Security (Recovery of Bene-   4.057
fits) (Lump Sum Payments) (Amendment) Regulations 2014 (SI
2014/1456) reg.2, Sch. paras 1 and 9 amended reg.12(1) of the 2008
Regulations by inserting at the beginning "Except where regulation 12A
applies,".

It then inserted at the beginning of reg.12(7) "Subject to paragraph
(8)," and inserted after that paragraph:

"(8) In the case of a lump sum payment to which section 1A(2)(d)
of the Act applies which has been made to one or more dependants of
P, this regulation also applies to the extent that the compensator is
making any of the payments listed in—

(a) paragraph (7)(a), where such a payment is made to another
dependant of P who has ceased to be eligible for a lump sum
payment to which section 1A(2)(d) of the Act applies by virtue
of having given notice under section 3(3) of the 2014 Act;

(b) paragraph (7)(b), where such a dependant is an intended beneficiary of that payment.".

p.905, *insertion of the Social Security (Recovery of Benefits) (Lump Sum*
Payments) Regulations 2008 (SI 2008/1596) reg.12A (Reduction of
compensation payment under Diffuse Mesothelioma Payment Scheme)

With effect from July 1, 2014, the Social Security (Recovery of Bene-   4.058
fits) (Lump Sum Payments) (Amendment) Regulations 2014 (SI
2014/1456) reg.2, Sch. paras 1 and 10 inserted into the 2008 Regulations:

"Reduction of compensation payment under Diffuse
Mesothelioma Payment Scheme

12A. (1) This regulation applies in a case where the compensation
payment is a payment under the Diffuse Mesothelioma Payment
Scheme.

(2) The gross amount of the compensation payment—

(a) is to be reduced by the amount of the recoverable lump sum
payments; and

(b) accordingly, is to be reduced to nil in any case where the
amount of the recoverable lump sum payments is equal to or
greater than the gross amount of the compensation payment.

(3) The reduction in paragraph (2) is to be made before any reduction in respect of recoverable benefits under section 8A of the Act.

(4) Any claim by a person to receive the compensation payment is
to be treated for all purposes as discharged if—

(a) the person is paid the gross amount of the compensation payment less the amount of the recoverable lump sum payments; or

(b) the amount of the recoverable lump sum payments is equal to or greater than the gross amount of the compensation payment and the person is given a statement by the scheme administrator saying that the compensation payment has been reduced to nil.

(5) In the application of paragraph (4) to any case where the compensation payment is to be made to two or more dependants of P, the deduction of the amount of the recoverable lump sum payments is to be made before calculating the amount to be paid to each dependant in accordance with regulation 16(2)(iii) of the Diffuse Mesothelioma Payment Scheme Regulations 2014.".

pp.905-906, *amendments to the Social Security (Recovery of Benefits) (Lump Sum Payments) Regulations 2008 (SI 2008/1596) reg.13 (Regulation 12: supplementary)*

4.059 With effect from July 1, 2014, the Social Security (Recovery of Benefits) (Lump Sum Payments) (Amendment) Regulations 2014 (SI 2014/1456) reg.2, Sch. paras 1 and 11 amended reg.13 of the 2008 Regulations by substituting for "Regulation 12" in the heading the words "Regulations 12 and 12A", by inserting "or 12A" after "regulation 12" in each of paragraphs (1), (2), (3)(a) and (4) and by inserting after "regulation 4(1)(a)" in paragraph (2) the words "or 4A(a) (as the case may be)".

p.906, *amendments to the Social Security (Recovery of Benefits) (Lump Sum Payments) Regulations 2008 (SI 2008/1596) reg.14(4) (Reduction of compensation: complex cases)*

4.060 With effect from July 1, 2014, the Social Security (Recovery of Benefits) (Lump Sum Payments) (Amendment) Regulations 2014 (SI 2014/1456) reg.2, Sch. paras 1 and 12 amended reg.14(4) of the 2008 Regulations by inserting "or 12A" after "regulation 12" (in both places).

p.907, *amendments to the Social Security (Recovery of Benefits) (Lump Sum Payments) Regulations 2008 (SI 2008/1596) reg.16 (Information to be provided by P)*

4.061 With effect from July 1, 2014, the Social Security (Recovery of Benefits) (Lump Sum Payments) (Amendment) Regulations 2014 (SI 2014/1456) reg.2, Sch. paras 1 and 13 amended reg.16 of the 2008 Regulations by inserting "and the scheme administrator" in the heading after "provided by P", by renumbering the existing provision as paragraph (1), by substituting "section 23(2)(a) of the Act" for "section 23(2) of the Act" and by inserting a new para.(2):

"(2) For the purposes of section 23(2)(b) of the Act, the prescribed information is the amount of the lump sum payment falling within section 1A(2)(d) and the date on which it was paid.".

p.908, *amendment to the Social Security (Recovery of Benefits) (Lump Sum Payments) Regulations 2008 (SI 2008/1596) reg.17(b) (Provision of information)*

With effect from July 1, 2014, the Social Security (Recovery of Bene-   4.062
fits) (Lump Sum Payments) (Amendment) Regulations 2014 (SI 2014/1456) reg.2, Sch. paras 1 and 14 amended reg.17(b) of the 2008 Regulations by inserting "or the scheme administrator, as the case may be" after "from P".

p.909, *amendments to the Social Security (Recovery of Benefits) (Lump Sum Payments) Regulations 2008 (SI 2008/1596) reg.19 (Adjustments)*

With effect from July 1, 2014, the Social Security (Recovery of Bene-   4.063
fits) (Lump Sum Payments) (Amendment) Regulations 2014 (SI 2014/1456) reg.2, Sch. paras 1 and 15 amended reg.19 of the 2008 Regulations by inserting the following paragraphs:

"(5A) This paragraph applies where—
(a) the amount of the payment made by the compensator was calculated under regulation 12A; and
(b) the Secretary of State has made a payment under paragraph (1).
(5B) Where paragraph (5A) applies, the amount of the compensation payment is to be recalculated under regulation 12A to take account of the fresh certificate and the compensator must pay the amount of the increase (if any) to the applicant as defined by regulation 3 of the Diffuse Mesothelioma Payment Scheme Regulations 2014.",

and also:

"(8) This paragraph applies where—
(a) the amount of the payment made by the compensator was calculated under regulation 12A; and
(b) the fresh certificate issued after the review or appeal was required as a result of any applicant for payment under the Diffuse Mesothelioma Payment Scheme supplying to the compensator information knowing it to be incorrect or insufficient, and the compensator supplying that information to the Secretary of State without knowing it to be incorrect or insufficient.
(9) Where paragraph (8) applies, the compensator may recalculate the compensation payment under regulation 12A to take account of the fresh certificate and may require the repayment by the applicant responsible for supplying the incorrect or insufficient information of

the difference (if any) between the payment made and the payment so recalculated.".

pp.909–912, *amendments to the Social Security (Recovery of Benefits) (Lump Sum Payments) Regulations 2008 (SI 2008/1596) Sch.1 (Modification of certain provisions of the Social Security (Recovery of Benefits) Act 1997)*

4.064   With effect from July 1, 2014, the Social Security (Recovery of Benefits) (Lump Sum Payments) (Amendment) Regulations 2014 (SI 2014/1456) reg.2, Sch. paras 1 and 16 amended Sch.1 to the 2008 Regulations. Paragraph 16 of the Schedule to the 2014 Regulations is in the following terms:

"**16.** (1) Schedule 1 (which modifies certain provisions of the Social Security (Recovery of Benefits) Act 1997 ("the 1997 Act") in their application to recovery of lump sum payments) is amended as follows.

(2) In paragraph 1 after "regulation 4" insert "or 4A".

(3) In paragraph 4 (which modifies section 11 of the 1997 Act)—

(a) in sub-paragraphs (c)(i) and (d)(i), for "lump sum payments" substitute "recoverable lump sum payments";

(b) in sub-paragraph (g), after "section 8" insert "or 8A" and after "regulation 12" insert "or 12A".

(4) In paragraph 6 (which modifies section 13 of the 1997 Act), for the words from "as if in" to the end, substitute—

"as if in subsection (2)—

(a) in paragraph (b), there were omitted "of recoverable benefits";

(b) in paragraph (bb), for "section 7(2)(a)" there were substituted "regulation 11(2)(a) of the Lump Sum Payments Regulations";

(c) in paragraph (c), for "section 8 or 8A) the injured person" there were substituted "regulation 12 or 12A of the Lump Sum Payments Regulations) P.".

(5) In paragraph 7 (which modifies section 14 of the 1997 Act), in sub-paragraph (c), after "section 8" insert "or 8A" and after "regulation 12" insert "or 12A".

(6) In paragraph 11 (which modifies section 19 of the 1997 Act), in sub-paragraph (c)(ii), after "section 8" insert "or 8A" and after "regulation 12" insert "or 12A".

(7) In paragraph 12 (which modifies section 20 of the 1997 Act), in sub-paragraph (b), after "section 8" insert "or 8A" and after "regulation 12" insert "or 12A".

(8) In paragraph 13 (which modifies section 21 of the 1997 Act), in sub-paragraph (a), after "sections 6 and 8" insert "or 8A" and after "regulations 10 and 12" insert "or 12A".

(9) In paragraph 15 (which modifies section 23 of the 1997 Act)—

(a) after sub-paragraph (b) insert—

"(ba) after subsection (1)(b) there were inserted—

",and
- (c) where the compensation which is sought is a payment under the Diffuse Mesothelioma Payment Scheme, subsection (6A) applies.";";
- (b) in sub-paragraph (c), in the text substituted for subsection (2)—
  - (i) the words from "the prescribed information" to the end become paragraph (a) of subsection (2); and
  - (ii) after paragraph (a) insert—
    "(b)the prescribed information about any lump sum payment which falls within section 1A(2)(d) must be given to the Secretary of State by the scheme administrator.".

(10) In paragraph 18 (which modifies section 29 of the 1997 Act), in sub-paragraph (b)(iii), after "regulation 4" insert "or 4A"."

There was a Schedule 2 to the 2008 Regulations, which is omitted from the main work because it merely made consequential amendments.

p.916, *amendment to the Social Security (Work-focused Interviews) Regulations 2000 (SI 2000/1926) reg.2ZA (Requirement for certain lone parents to take part in an interview)*

With effect from April 28, 2014, reg.13(2) of the Income Support (Work-Related Activity) and Miscellaneous Amendments Regulations 2014 (SI 2014/1097) reg.13(2) amended reg.2ZA as follows: 4.065
- (a) by inserting "and" after sub-paragraph (a);
- (b) by omitting sub-paragraph (c) and the "and" which preceded it;
- (c) by substituting the following for para. (2):

"(2) Subject to regulations 4 and 5, a lone parent to whom this regulation applies is required to take part in one or more interviews as a condition of continuing to be entitled to the full amount of benefit which is payable to him apart from these Regulations.";

- (d) by omitting the words "waived or" in para, (3)(b).

p.918, *amendment to the Social Security (Work-focused Interviews) Regulations 2000 (SI 2000/1926) reg.2C (The interview)*

With effect from April 28, 2014, reg.13(3) of the Income Support (Work-Related Activity) and Miscellaneous Amendments Regulations 2014 (SI 2014/1097) substituted the following for reg.2C(1):   4.066

"(1) An interview under these Regulations shall take place—
- (a) where regulation 2ZA applies, on such date as may be determined by an officer;
- (b) in any other case, as soon as is reasonably practicable after the date on which the requirement to take part in the interview arises."

p.920, *amendment to the Social Security (Work-focused Interviews) Regulations 2000 (SI 2000/1926) reg.4 (Circumstances where requirement to take part in an interview does not apply)*

4.067   With effect from April 28, 2014, reg.13(4) of the Income Support (Work-Related Activity) and Miscellaneous Amendments Regulations 2014 (SI 2014/1097) amended reg.4 as follows:

(a) by inserting in para. (1) ", 2ZA" after the words "Regulation 2";

(b) by substituting in para. (1A) the words "Regulations 2 and 2ZA" for "Regulation 2";

(c) by omitting para. (3).

p.921, *amendment to the Social Security (Work-focused Interviews) Regulations 2000 (SI 2000/1926) reg.6 (Waiver)*

4.068   With effect from April 28, 2014, reg.13(5) of the Income Support (Work-Related Activity) and Miscellaneous Amendments Regulations 2014 (SI 2014/1097) amended reg.6 as follows:

(a) by substituting in para.(1) the words "regulations 2(1) and 2ZB(2)" for "these Regulations";

(b) by omitting in para.(2)(a) ", 2ZA".

p.921, *amendment to the Social Security (Work-focused Interviews) Regulations 2000 (SI 2000/1926) reg.7 (Consequence of failure to take part in an interview)*

4.069   With effect from April 28, 2014, reg.13(6) of the Income Support (Work-Related Activity) and Miscellaneous Amendments Regulations 2014 (SI 2014/1097) amended reg.7 as follows:

(a) by substituting in para.(1) "(2), (5) and (5A)" for "(2) and (5)";

(b) by substituting in para.(1)(b) the words "date on which the person was notified of his failure to take part in the interview" for the words "day on which the interview was to take place";

(c) by inserting the following after para.(1):

"(1A) Where a notice under paragraph (1)(b) is sent by post it is taken to have been received on the second working day after it was sent."

(d) by substituting in para.(2)(a) the words "date on which the person was notified of his failure to take part in the interview" for the words "day on which the interview was to take place";

(e) by inserting the following after para.(5):

"(5A) The amount of income support payable to a person is not to be reduced in accordance with paragraph (3) if that amount—

(a) is, at the time a decision falls to be made in respect of the current failure, being paid at a reduced rate in accordance with paragraph (3) and regulation 8, regulation

12(2)(c) of the Social Security (Jobcentre Plus Interviews) Regulations 2002(2) or regulation 8(1) and (2) of
the Income Support (Work-Related Activity) and Miscellaneous Amendments Regulations 2014; and
(b) was last reduced not more than two weeks before the date
of the current failure.

(5B) In paragraph (5A), "current failure" means a failure
which may, in the case of a claimant who has an award of
income support, lead to a reduction in income support under
paragraph (3) and regulation 8 in relation to which the Secretary of State has not yet determined whether the amount of
income support payable to the person is to be reduced in
accordance with that paragraph and regulation."

p.923, *amendment to the Social Security (Work-focused Interviews)
Regulations 2000 (SI 2000/1926) reg.8 (Reduction of income support)*

With effect from April 28, 2014, reg.13(7) of the Income Support   4.070
(Work-Related Activity) and Miscellaneous Amendments Regulations
2014 (SI 2014/1097) amended reg.8 as follows:
(a) by substituting in para.(3)(c) the words "satisfies a compliance
condition" for the words "meets the requirement to take part in an
interview";
(b) by inserting the following after para.(3)(d):

"(4) In paragraph (3)(c), "compliance condition" means a
requirement to—
(a) take part in an interview; or
(b) undertake work-related activity."

p.1013, *annotation to art.20*

The Court of Appeal has overruled the decision in *SSWP v JS (IS)*   4.070.1
[2013] UKUT 490 (AAC) in a combined decision in *Sanneh v SSWP,
Scott v London Borough of Croydon, Birmingham City Council v Merali, R
(on the application of HC) v SSWP and others* [2015] EWCA Civ 49. In
a complex decision which concerns the situation both before and after
the amendments made by a whole series of amendment regulations (SI
2012/2587; SI 2012/2588; and SI 2012/2612) the effect of which was,
from November 8, 2012, to disqualify from a range of income-related
benefits those with a right to reside arising under art.20 following the
Zambrano case ("the 2012 amendments"). This group is described as
Zambrano carers. They are, by definition, not citizens of the Union, but
are third country nationals.

In a significant development of the case-law, the Court of Appeal ruled
that *Zambrano* carers have a right to reside from the date on which the
carer ceased to be liable to be removed from the United Kingdom (that
is, on the birth of a child who is a citizen of the Union for whom care is
provided, or upon becoming the primary carer of a citizen of the Union,
in both cases where the citizen of the Union might have to leave the

European Union if the carer might be obliged to leave) and not just from the later date on when measures are taken, or are imminent, to seek the removal of the carer from the United Kingdom.

In relation to the circumstances of the *Sanneh* case (the appeal against the decision in *SSWP v JS*), since Sanneh was a *Zambrano* carer in June 2011 when she claimed income support, she was entitled to that benefit since her circumstances predated the 2012 amendments.

The Court of Appeal decides that the rights of *Zambrano* carers are not the same as the rights of citizens of the Union, although the requirement that the EU national's citizenship is effective under EU law requires Member States to provide basic support. Such support was wholly a matter for national law, and assistance provided under s.17 of the Children Act 1989 might well suffice.

The Court of Appeal concluded that the exclusion of *Zambrano* carers by the 2012 amendments was not directly discriminatory. It was accepted that the amendments were indirectly discriminatory, but the Court ruled that the difference in treatment was justifiable both under EU law and under the European Convention on Human Rights. Finally, the Court concluded that in making the amending regulations, the Secretary of State had not failed to comply with the general public sector equality duty under s.149 of the Equality Act 2010.

p.1029, *annotation to the Treaty on the Functioning of the European Union art.45*

4.071   The DWP guidance on whether an EEA national is a worker or self-employed person is set out in Memo DMG 21/14 of September 2014.

In *VW v SSWP (SPC)* [2014] UKUT 573 (AAC) Judge Ward ruled that a person who had undertaken work for three periods of two or four weeks many years before the date of the claim under appeal, and who received board and lodging, reimbursement and certain other expenses in exchange for his work, was not a worker within art.45 TFEU (see paras 21-50).

p.1067, *annotation to Regulation (EU) No.492/2011 art.10*

4.072   *RM v SSWP (IS)* [2014] UKUT 401 (AAC) decides that the logic of the structure of the reasoning of the Court of Justice in responding to references in the *Czop* and *Punakova* cases means that the children of self-employed persons are not entitled to a right of residence as primary carers under art.12 of Regulation 1612/68; and it would follow the successor provision in art.10.

p.1086, *annotation to Directive 2004/38/EC art.7 (Right of residence for more than three months)*

4.073   The DWP guidance in response to the judgment in *Jessy Saint-Prix v SSWP* (C-507/120 is set out in Memo DMG 25/14 of October 2014. Paragraph 9 provides:

"Where a claimant indicates that they have an intention to return to their previous job or that they will find another job, the [decision maker] can award IS for a fixed period until the end of the 15 week period after the expected date of confinement. If the claimant subsequently does not return to work, a recovery of the IS paid will not be required."

p.1107, *annotation to art.17 (Exemptions for persons no longer working in the host Member State and their family members)*

In *TG v SSWP (PC)* [2015] UKUT 50 (AAC), Judge Ward has ruled   4.073.1
that the right of permanent residence contained in art.17, unlike the corresponding right of permanent residence under art.16, is satisfied by actual residence rather than residence strictly in accordance with the provisions of the Citizenship Directive. This is essentially because it corresponds to a right which had originally been contained in Commission Regulation 1251/70, which contained no limitation on the concept of residence comparable to that found in the Citizenship Directive. The Citizenship Directive was designed to preserve existing rights and so could not limit the nature of the residence upon which the right in art.17 depended. In contrast, the right of permanent residence in art.16 was a new right introduced by the Citizenship Directive, and so could contain more restrictive conditions on the nature of the residence. Judge Ward's detailed reasoning can be found at paras 14-68 of the decision.

p.1111, *annotation to Directive 2004/38/EC art.24 (Equal treatment)*

Dano and Dano v Jobcenter Leipzig (C-333/13), judgement of Novem-   4.074
ber 11, 2014, confirms that there is no obligation under art.24 (or art.4 of Regulation 883/2004) to pay means-tested benefits to an EU migrant of more than three months standing who has not been a worker, and is not seeking work. The Court notes that art.7(1)(b) requires those who are economically inactive "to meet the condition that they have sufficient resources of their own" in order to have a right of residence (para.75).

p.1137, *annotation to Regulation (EC) No.883/2004 art.3 (Matters covered)*

The Court of Appeal has, in *SSWP v Garland* [2014] EWCA Civ   4.075
1550, allowed the appeal against the decision in *SSWP v JG (RP)* [2013] UKUT 300 (AAC) ruling that the claimant did not have residence in Gibraltar which qualified for consideration as residence in the United Kingdom and so could not show residence in the United Kingdom for the required period to be entitled to a Category D retirement pension.

p.1143, *annotation to Regulation (EC) No.883/2004 art.4 (Equality of treatment)*

The Northern Ireland Court of Appeal has over-ruled the decision in   4.076
AS v HMRC (CB) [2013] NI Com 15 (CI/10/11 (CB)) and ruled that

the right to reside requirement in relation to entitlement to child benefit is not directly discriminatory under art.3 of Regulation 1408/71 (and, it would follow, art.4 of Regulation 883/2004).

p.1151, *annotation to Regulation (EC) No.883/2004 art.11 (General rules)*

4.077   In *Ministertvo práce a sociálních věcí v B* (C-394/13) the Court of Justice ruled:

> " . . . Regulation No 883/2004, in particular Article 11 thereof, must be interpreted as precluding a Member State from being regarded as the competent State for the purpose of granting a family benefit to a person on the sole ground that the person concerned is registered as being permanently resident in its territory, where neither that person nor the members of his family work or habitually reside in that Member State."

p.1163, *annotation to Regulation (EC) No.883/2004 art.19 (Stay outside the competent Member State)*

GENERAL NOTE

4.078   In *I v Health Service Executive* (C-255/13) Judgment of June 5 2014, the Court ruled as follows:

> "Article 1(j) and (k) of Regulation (EC) No 883/2004 . . . must be interpreted as meaning that, for the purpose of Article 19(1) or Article 20(1) and (2) of that regulation, where a European Union national who was resident in one Member State suffers a sudden serious illness while on holiday in a second Member State and is compelled to remain in the latter State for 11 years as a result of that illness and the fact that specialist medical care is available close to the place where he lives, such a person must be regarded as 'staying' in the second Member State if the habitual centre of his interests is in the first Member State. It is for the national court to determine the habitual centre of such a person's interests by carrying out an assessment of all the relevant facts and taking into account that person's intention, as may be discerned from those facts, the mere fact that that person has remained in the second Member State for a long time not being sufficient in itself alone for him to be regarded as residing in that Member State." (para.59).

p.1166, *annotation to Regulation (EC) No.883/2004 art.24 (No right to benefit in kind under the legislation of the Member State of residence)*

4.079   *Helder and Farrington v College voor zorgverzekeringen* (C-321/12) Judgment of October 10, 2013, concerns the interpretation of art.28(2)(b) of Regulation 1408/71 which corresponds to the provisions of art.24(2)(b) of Regulation 883/2004. The Court ruled that art.28(2)(b) should be interpreted as meaning that the "legislation" to which the pensioner has been subject for the longest period of time, for the purposes of that provision, refers to the legislation concerning pensions.

p.1207, *annotation to Regulation (EC) No.883/2004 art.67 (Members of the family residing in another Member State)*

Würker v Familienkasse Nürnberg (C-32/13) Judgment of February 27, 2014, ruled that a benefit in Germany in the form of a pension for bringing up children which is granted, in the event of death, to the former spouse of the deceased for the purposes of bringing up the children of that former spouse is covered by the concept of a "pension" for the purposes of art.67.   4.080

p.1278, *annotation to art.2 (Scope and rules for exchanges between institutions)*

GENERAL NOTE

In *SSWP v HR (AA)* [2014] UKUT 571 (AAC), Judge Jacobs has drawn attention to the objectives contained in this article in dealing with a case concerning a difference of view between Member State institutions about which State was the competent State for the purposes of a claim for a sickness benefit. See also annotation to art.6 of Regulation 987/2009.   4.080.1

p.1280, *annotation to art.6 (Provisional application of legislation and provisional granting of benefits)*

In *SSWP v HR (AA)* [2014] UKUT 571 (AAC), Judge Jacobs has given detailed guidance on the operation of this article in a case in which there was a difference of view between the United Kingdom and Swedish authorities on which was the competent institution for the award of sickness benefits. The Secretary of State accepted that in a claim for an attendance allowance by a Swedish national resident in the United Kingdom, the legislation of the State of residence should be provisionally applied under the terms of the article. The decision under appeal had been a refusal of the claim on the grounds that the United Kingdom was not the competent State. A difference of view does not require formal decisions from different authorities (see paras 16-19).   4.080.2

Judge Jacobs goes on to provide guidance in three typical situations which can arise. The first situation arises where the United Kingdom concludes that it is the competent State under Regulation 883/2004. Here the only remaining issues will be the application of national law to the claim which has been made (para.26).

The second situation arises where the Secretary of State decides that the United Kingdom is not the competent State and another Member State has expressed a different view. Here there is a difference of view and art.6 must be applied. If the claimant meets the conditions of entitlement under national law to the United Kingdom benefit, the United Kingdom is required to apply its legislation on a provisional basis to award the benefit. No appeal should arise since the claimant will be receiving the benefit (para.27).

The third situation arises where the Secretary of State decides that the United Kingdom is not the competent State, and there is no indication of a difference of view with any other Member State. Here the Secretary of State will be likely to refuse the claim, but is also under a duty under art.81 of Regulation 883/2004 to forward the claim without delay to the State which it considers to be the competent State. This could generate a difference of view which would trigger the operation of the procedures in art.6. Judge Jacobs concludes that any difficulties about the date of claim and the date from which payment could be made will be governed by European Union law which will override any limitations contained in national law (paras 28-31).

p.1354, *annotation to Council Directive 79/7/EEC art.4*

4.081   The Court of Appeal has, in *MB v SSWP* [2014] EWCA Civ 1112, dismissed the appeal against the decision in *MB v SSWP (RP)* [2013] UKUT 290 (AAC).

p.1419, *annotation to art.6 (Right to a fair trial)*

4.082   At para.4.98 it is stated that the detailed treatment of *Gillies v Secretary of State for Work and Pensions* [2006] UKHL 2 can be found in the commentary to the Social Security Act 1998 s.14, whereas it can, in fact, be found in the commentary to the Tribunals, Courts and Enforcement Act 2007 s.3(3) at paras 5.24-5-25.

pp.1449-1453, *annotation to the Tribunals, Courts and Enforcement Act 2007 s.3(1) (The First-tier Tribunal–the inquisitorial role of the tribunal and the burden of proof)*

4.083   In *PM v SSWP (IS)* [2014] UKUT 474 (AAC), the claimant was a 19-year old foreign national who had been in care following estrangement from her father and who, the First-tier Tribunal had been told, was too distressed to attend the hearing. Her entitlement to income support depended on whether her father was a "worker" under European Union law at the material time and the Upper Tribunal held that her circumstances required the First-tier Tribunal to obtain the relevant information through the Secretary of State, who could have obtained the information himself with a bit more effort.

p.1456, *annotation to the Tribunals, Courts and Enforcement Act 2007 s.3(1) (The First-tier Tribunal–evidence)*

4.084   *SA v SSWP (BB)* [2013] UKUT 234 (AAC) has been reported as [2014] AACR 20.

p.1461, *annotation to the Tribunals, Courts and Enforcement Act 2007 s.3(2) (Precedent in the Upper Tribunal)*

4.085   In *Gilchrist v Revenue and Customs Commissioners* [2014] UKUT 162 (TCC); [2015] 2 W.L.R. 1, *Secretary of State for Justice v RB* [2010]

UKUT 454 (AAC); [2012] AACR 31 (mentioned in the main work) was cited when it was held that the Upper Tribunal, as a "superior court of record", was not bound by High Court decisions in tax cases, notwithstanding that many High Court decisions were given on appeal from decisions of the special commissioners for income tax whose functions have been transferred to the Upper Tribunal. It was pointed out that many High Court judges now sit regularly in the Tax and Chancery Chamber of the Upper Tribunal and it was said that: "Although of course conceptually possible, it would be surprising if a decision of a High Court judge sitting in the High Court would be binding on a High Court judge sitting in the Upper Tribunal but not if sitting in the High Court".

In *TG v SSWP (SPC)* [2015] UKUT (AAC), it was noted that, while the criteria for directing that a case can be heard by a three-judge panel are the same in the Immigration and Asylum Chamber of the Upper Tribunal as they are in the Administrative Appeals Chamber, it is not considered that a single judge of the immigration and Asylum Chamber is bound to follow a decision of a three-judge panel, except in a "starred" or "country guidance" case. Nonetheless, the judge considered that a single judge of the Administrative Appeals chamber shoud follow any decision of a three-judge panel in the Asylum and Immigration Chamber "unless there are compelling reasons not to".

pp.1471-1472, *annotation to the Tribunals, Courts and Enforcement Act 2007 s.19(4) (Review of decision of First-tier Tribunal)*

It was said in *Essex CC v TB (SEN)* [2014] UKUT 559 (AAC) that there appeared to be no reason why a discrete part of a decision should not be set aside under s.9(4)(c), but that it was the decision rather than the reasoning that was set aside and it could be unwise formally to limit the scope of the decision to be made by the panel who would re-decide the case and who might look at the case differently. 4.086

pp.1479-1483, *annotation to the Tribunals, Courts and Enforcement Act 2007 s.11(1) (Right of appeal to Upper Tribunal–procedural and other irregularities)*

JM v SSWP (ESA) [2013] UKUT 436 (AAC) has been reported as [2014] AACR 5 and *JM v SSD (WP)* [2014] UKUT 358 (AAC) is to be reported as [2015] AACR 7. 4.087

pp.1487-1490, *annotation to the Tribunals, Courts and Enforcement Act 2007 s.12 (Proceedings on appeal to the Upper Tribunal)*

Nesbitt's Application [2013] NIQB 111 has been reported as [2014] AACR 31. 4.088

The express power to "make such findings of fact as it considers appropriate" and the former long-established practice of the Social Security Commissioners are among reasons for distinguishing the position of the Upper Tribunal in social security cases from that of the

Employment Appeal Tribunal which, it has been held in *Jafri v Lincoln College* [2014] EWCA Civ 449; [2014] 3 W.L.R. 933, is bound to remit a matter when allowing an appeal if the matter is in dispute and more than one outcome is possible, however well placed it might otherwise be to take a decision itself. The context of social security cases, where many hearings are extremely short and the amount at stake is often not huge (at least from the perspective of the public purse) would make it disproportionate for there to be remittal in all disputed cases. However, where the First-tier Tribunal would be constituted so as to include specialist members, their expertise would be a powerful argument for remitting the case. A relevant factor in many cases is simply that the Upper Tribunal determines the overwhelming majority of its cases on paper, particularly in the social security field, and an oral hearing is likely to be necessary if findings of fact are to be made. it will generally be easier for the First-tier Tribunal to arrange a hearing near the claimant's home than it would be for the Upper Tribunal to do so.

pp.1495-1496, *annotation to the Tribunals, Courts and Enforcement Act 2007 s.13(8)–(10) (Right of appeal to Court of Appeal etc.–excluded decisions)*

4.089   The finding made by the High Court in *R. (Kuteh) v Upper Tribunal (Administrative Appeals Chamber)* [2012] EWHC 2196 (Admin), mentioned in the main work, when quashing a refusal of permission to appeal that there had been a serious procedural error by the First-tier Tribunal not only obliged the Upper Tribunal to grant permission to appeal but also obliged it to allow the appeal. This was because it was bound by law to proceed on the footing that the First-tier Tribunal had perpetrated a serious procedural irregularity which was not merely academic of hypothetical, even though the appellant might have been fortunate in the result he had obtained from the High Court (*Kuteh v Secretary of State for Education* [2014] EWCA Civ 1586).

p.1497, *annotation to the Tribunals, Courts and Enforcement Act 2007 s.13(15) (Right of appeal to Court of Appeal etc.–rules of court)*

4.090   The amendments to Practice Direction 52D anticipated in the main work were duly made with effect from October 1, 2014. The time limit for filing an appellant's notice is now "within 28 days of the date on which notice of the Upper Tribunal's decision on permission to appeal to the Court of Appeal is sent to the appellant" (para.3.3, as amended).

p.1511, *annotation to the Tribunals, Courts and Enforcement Act 2007 s.25 (Supplementary powers of Upper Tribunal)*

4.091   For the meaning of "the production . . . of documents" in subs.(2)(b), see the annotation to r.7(3) of the Tribunal Procedure (First-tier Tribunal) (Social Entitlement Chamber) Rules 2008 at p.1553 of the main work, where the meaning of "to produce a document" in r.7(3)(e) is considered.

p.1533, *annotation to the First-tier Tribunal and Upper Tribunal (Composition of Tribunals) Order 2008 (SI 2008/2835) art.2 (Number of members of the First-tier Tribunal)*

MB v SSWP (ESA & DLA) [2013] UKUT 111 (AAC) has been reported as [2014] AACR 1.   **4.092**

p.1543, *annotation to the Tribunal Procedure (First-tier Tribunal) (Social Entitlement Chamber) Rules 2008 (SI 2008/2685) r.4 (Delegation to staff)*

The Senior President of Tribunals has amended his practice statement   **4.093**
so as to give clerks the same powers in relation to late responses to appeals as they have in relation to whether appeals satisfy the requirements set out in r.23(3) and are accompanied by the documents required by r.22(4), i.e., they may waive the requirement to provide a response within the specified time, require the failure to be remedied or strike out the respondent's case (having given any necessary direction) and, if they strike out a case, they may reinstate it. Note, however, that whereas in relation to appeals the clerk is concerned with the adequacy of the content and not with whether they are in time, the reverse is true in relation to responses. These additional powers are conferred with effect from October 1, 2014, which is when r.24 was amended so as for the first time to impose a time limit for responses to appeals in most social security and child support cases (see below).

p.1546, *annotation to the Tribunal Procedure (First-tier Tribunal) (Social Entitlement Chamber) Rules 2008 (SI 2008/2685) r.5(3)(b) (Case management powers)*

In *John v Information Commissioner* [2014] UKUT 444 (AAC), the   **4.094**
Upper Tribunal suggested that, where two parties appealed against the same decision, it would be appropriate to direct that the cases be heard together rather than consolidated. It was noted that consolidation had been described in *Zuckerman on Civil Procedure* (3rd ed) at para.13.12 as an "arcane process". It has a technical meaning that is arguably inappropriate in appeals to tribunals.
The Upper Tribunal also held that it was unnecessary for a respondent to cross-appeal if wishing to challenge the decision being challenged on the appeal and that the Rules made no provision for a respondent's notice. Accordingly, a respondent may raise new issues in a response to an appeal, although the First-tier Tribunal can use its case management powers to prevent unfairness to an appellant.

p.1553, *annotation to the Tribunal Procedure (First-tier Tribunal) (Social Entitlement Chamber) Rules 2008 (SI 2008/2685) r.7(3) (Failure to comply with rules etc.)*

AP v HMRC (Enforcement Reference) [2014] UKUT 182 (AAC) has   **4.095**
been reported as [2014] AACR 37.

pp.1561-1563, *annotation to the Tribunal Procedure (First-tier Tribunal) (Social Entitlement Chamber) Rules 2008 (SI 2008/2685) r.11 (Representatives)*

4.096   In *PM v SSWP (IS)* [2014] UKUT 474 (AAC), the judge expressed surprise that the First-tier Tribunal had not been prepared to accept evidence from the claimant's representative in a case where the claimant was a 19-year old foreign national who had been in care following estrangement from her father and who, the First-tier Tribunal had been told, was too distressed to attend the hearing. The First-tier Tribunal had said that only statements of fact made by representatives as to matters within their own personal knowledge were evidence. The Upper Tribunal referred to *PL v Walsall MBC* [2009] UKUT 27 (AAC), a case where an assertion of a local authority's submission-writer, supported by computer printouts, was held to be sufficient evidence to prove that certain decisions had been made, because the fact that the evidence was not of matters within the submission-writer's personal knowledge merely made it hearsay which might affect its probative worth but did not make it inadmissible. The evidence in *PM* had been as to the claimant's father's last known address and place of work, which the Upper Tribunal commented "was likely to prove an uncontroversial issue capable of objective verification and not one where there was any risk of the evidence being compromised if it was mediated through a representative".

In *CO v LB Havering (HB)* [2015] UKUT 28 (AAC), a notice of appeal was held valid even though it was signed by the claimant's solicitor rather than by the claimant personally as required under r.23(6) and the solicitor had not provided the claimant's written authority to act as her representative for the purposes of r.11 so the r.11(5) did not apply. (A copy of the notice countersigned by the claimant was received only after the absolute time limit for appealing had expired.) The judge left open the question whether a notice of appeal signed by a representative without written authority who was not under a professional obligation to act only on instructions should be treated as having been signed by the appellant. However, even if the signature of such a representative who does not have written authority does not amount to the appellant's signature, it is arguable that the requirement that the notice be signed personally can be waived under r.7 where the appellant has subsequently adopted the notice, see *R(DLA) 2/98* and *CIB/460/2003*, both mentioned in the annotation to r.22(3) and (4) in the main work, and also *Salisvury Independent Living v Wirral MBC* [2011] UKUT 44 (AAC), which was cited in *CO*.

p.1572, *annotation to the Tribunal Procedure (First-tier Tribunal) (Social Entitlement Chamber) Rules 2008 (SI 2008/2685) r.17 (Withdrawal)*

4.097   *AE v SSWP (ESA)* [2014] UKUT 5 (AAC) has been reported as [2014] AACR 23.

pp.1573-1574, *substitution for the Tribunal Procedure (First-tier Tribunal) (Social Entitlement Chamber) Rules 2008 (SI 2008/2685) r.19 (Confidentiality in child support or child trust fund cases)*

With effect from October 20, 2014, the Tribunal Procedure (Amend- **4.098** ment No.3) Rules 2014 (SI 2014/2128) rr.33 to 35 substituted the following rule and heading for the existing rule and heading:

"Confidentiality in social security and child support cases

19. (1) Paragraph (4) applies to—

  (a) proceedings under the Child Support Act 1991 in the circumstances described in paragraph (2), other than an appeal against a reduced benefit decision (as defined in section 46(10)(b) of the Child Support Act 1991, as that section had effect prior to the commencement of section 15(b) of the Child Maintenance and Other Payments Act 2008);

  (b) proceedings where the parties to the appeal include former joint claimants who are no longer living together in the circumstances described in paragraph (3).

(2) The circumstances referred to in paragraph (1)(a) are that the absent parent, non-resident parent or person with care would like their address or the address of the child to be kept confidential and has given notice to that effect—

  (a) in the notice of appeal or when notifying the Secretary of State or the Tribunal of any subsequent change of address; or

  (b) within 14 days after an enquiry is made by the recipient of the notice of appeal or the notification referred to in sub-paragraph (a).

(3) The circumstances referred to in paragraph (1)(b) are that one of the former joint claimants would like their address to be kept confidential and has given notice to that effect—

  (a) in the notice of appeal or when notifying the decision maker or the tribunal of any subsequent change of address; or

  (b) within 14 days after an enquiry is made by the recipient of the notice of appeal or the notification referred to in sub-paragraph (a).

(4) Where this paragraph applies, the Secretary of State or other decision maker and the Tribunal must take appropriate steps to secure the confidentiality of the address and of any information which could reasonably be expected to enable a person to identify the address, to the extent that the address or that information is not already known to each other party.

(5) In this rule—

"absent parent", "non-resident parent" and "person with care" have the meanings set out in section 3 of the Child Support Act 1991;

"joint claimants" means the persons who made a joint claim for a jobseeker's allowance under the Jobseekers Act 1995, a tax credit under the Tax Credits Act 2002 or in relation to whom an award of universal credit is made under Part 1 of the Welfare Reform Act 2012."

Specific provision for confidentiality is no longer made for child trust fund cases, because it is now unlikely there will be further such appeals. Instead, provision is made for confidentiality in a number of social security cases where former partners might both be parties. It is open to the First-tier Tribunal to exercise its case-management powers under r.5 so as to make provision for confidentiality in other types of case should that be appropriate.

pp.1577–1578, *annotation to Tribuanl Procedure (First-tier Tribunal) (Social Entitlement Chamber) Rules 2008 (SI 2008/2685) r.22(3) and (4) (Cases in which the notice of appeal is to be sent to the Tribunal)*

4.098.1   In *CO v LB Havering (HB)* [2015] UKUT 28 (AAC), a notice of appeal was held valid even though it was signed by the claimant's solicitor rather than by the claimant personally as required under r.23(6) (and now r.22(3)) and the solicitor had not provided the claimant's written authority to act as her representative for the purposes of r.11 so that r.11(5) did not apply. (A Copy of the notice countersgned by the claimant was received only after the absolute time limit for appealing had expired). The judge left open the question whether a notice of appeal signed by a representative without written authority who was not under a professional obligation to act only on instructions should be treated as having been signed by the appellant. However, even if the signature of such a representative who does not have written authority does not amount to the appellant's signature, it is arguable that the requirement that the notice be signed personally can be waived under r.7 where the appellant has subsequently adopted the notice, see *R(DLA) 2/98* and *CIB/460/2003*, both mentioned in the annotation to r.22(3) and (4) in the main work, and also *Salisvury Independent Living v Wirral MBC* [2011] UKUT 44 (AAC), which was cited in *CO*.

pp.1580-1581, *substitution for the Tribunal Procedure (First-tier Tribunal) (Social Entitlement Chamber) Rules 2008 (SI 2008/2685) r.24(1) (Responses and replies)*

4.099   With effect from October 1, 2014, the Tribunal Procedure (Amendment) Rules 2013 rr.22 and 27(a), as amended by the Tribunal Procedure (Amendment No.3) Rules 2014 (SI 2014/2128) rr.36-37, substituted for r.24(1) of the 2008 Rules:

"(1) When a decision maker receives a copy of a notice of appeal from the Tribunal under rule 22(7), the decision maker must send or deliver a response to the Tribunal—
   (a)   in asylum support cases, so that it is received within 3 days after the date on which the Tribunal received the notice of appeal;
   [(b)   in—

     (i) criminal injuries compensation cases, or
     (ii) appeals under the Child Support Act 1991,
    within 42 days after the date on which the decision maker received the copy of the notice of appeal; and]

(c) in other cases, within 28 days after the date on which the decision maker received the copy of the notice of appeal.

(1A) Where a decision maker receives a notice of appeal from an appellant under rule 23(2), the decision maker must send or deliver a response to the Tribunal so that it is received as soon as reasonably practicable after the decision maker received the notice of appeal.";

The amendment made by the 2014 Regulations is in square brackets above and removes a specific reference to child trust fund appeals which are now unlikely to be brought.

The overall effect of the new para.(1) is to impose time limits within which responses to appeals must be provided by the Secretary of State in social security and child support cases where there has been direct lodgement or mandatory reconsideration. These are six weeks from the date that the Secretary of State received a copy of the notice of appeal from the First-tier Tribunal in child support cases and four weeks in other cases. (There were already time limits in asylum support and criminal injuries compensation cases.) Clerks have been given the power to waive the time limit or to strike out the respondent's case for failing to comply with it (see the annotation to r.4 above).

Paragraph (1A) applies to housing benefit cases and the few remaining other cases where the appeal was sent directly to the decision-maker and there has not been mandatory reconsideration before the appeal was bought. It does not impose a time limit, maintaining the status quo and giving the decision-maker a substantial opportunity to consider whether to review the decision being challenged before submitting a response.

pp.1582–1584, *annotation to the Tribunal Procedure (First-tier Tribunal) (Social Entitlement Chamber) Rules 2008 (SI 2008/2685) r.24 (Responses and replies)*

MN v SSWP (ESA) [2013] UKUT 262 (AAC) has been reported as   **4.100**
[2014] AACR 6 and further guidance as to the information about work-related activity to be included in responses has been given by a three-judge panel in *IM v SSWP (ESA)* 2014 UKUT 412 (AAC). In particular, it was suggested that, even in relation to an appeal against a decision that the claimant did not have limited capability for work, a response should normally include information that would enable the First-tier Tribunal, should it allow the appeal, fairly to go on and consider whether the claimant had limited capability for work-related activity.

JC v DSD (IB) [2011] NICom 177 has been reported as [2014] AACR 30

In *John v Information Commissioner* [2014] UKUT 444 (AAC), the Upper Tribunal rejected an argument that a respondent was required to cross-appeal or submit a respondent's notice if disagreeing with a decision being challenged on appeal to the First-tier Tribunal. It was held that new issues could be raised in a response but that the Upper Tribunal could exercise its case-management powers to prevent unfairness to an appellant.

The standard of a response by HMRC to a tax credit appeal was severely criticised in *SB v HMRC (TC)* [2014] UKUT 543 (AAC). The response failed adequately to explain the decision-making history, reversed the burden of proof, argued that evidence provided by the appellant had been insufficient to support her case without a copy of her evidence being attached to the submission, revealed an inadequate investigation of the facts and failed to answer the appellant's grounds of appeal. The First-tier Tribunal was in turn criticised for having upheld HMRC's decision on the papers before it, notwithstanding their manifest deficits.

pp.1590–1591, *annotation to the Tribunal Procedure (First-tier Tribunal) (Social Entitlement Chamber) Rules 2008 (SI 2008/2685) r.27(1) and (2) (Decision with or without a hearing–evidence at a hearing)*

4.101   *JP v SSWP (DLA)* [2014] UKUT 275 (AAC) is to be reported as [2015] AACR 2.

Representatives in social security cases are often in a position to give evidence from their own knowledge and it has on several occasions been said that they should not be stopped from doing so (see the note to r.11(1) at pp.1561–1562 of the main work).

pp.1604–1607, *annotation to the Tribunal Procedure (First-tier Tribunal) (Social Entitlement Chamber) Rules 2008 (SI 2008/2685) r.34(2)–(5) (Reasons for decision)*

4.102   In criminal injuries compensation cases, the First-tier Tribunal has had a practice of giving fairly detailed hand-written summary reasons on the decision notice but recording that they are not the full reasons and informing the claimant of the right to ask for full reasons. In *R.(MC) v First-tier Tribunal (CIC)* [2014] UKUT 544 (AAC), the summary reasons were sufficient to enable the Upper Tribunal to reject a challenge to the adequacy of the reasons as though they were full reasons but the judge was critical of the failure of the First-tier Tribunal to provide a full statement of reasons when asked to provide a legible copy of the reasons.

p.1610, *annotation to the Tribunal Procedure (First-tier Tribunal) (Social Entitlement Chamber) Rules 2008 (SI 2008/2685) r.34(2)–(5) (Reasons for decision–detailed guidance)*

4.103   *NS v SSWP (ESA)* [2014] UKUT 115 (AAC) has been reported as [2014] AACR 33 and *JK v SSWP (ESA)* [2014] UKUT 140 (AAC) has been reported as [2014] AACR 34.

pp.1632-1635, *amendments to the Tribunal Procedure (Upper Tribunal) Rules 2008 (SI 2008/2698) r.1(3) (Interpretation)*

With effect from September 1, 2014, the Tribunal Procedure   4.104
(Amendment No.3) Rules 2014 (SI 2014/2128) rr.2 and 4 inserted definitions of "disability discrimination in schools case", "special educational needs case" and "young person" and, with effect from October 20, 2014, they amended the definition of "fast-track case". None of these definitions is relevant to social security cases and so they are not set out here.

p.1639, *amendments to the Tribunal Procedure (Upper Tribunal) Rules 2008 (SI 2008/2698) r.5(4) (Case management powers)*

With effect from October 20, 2014, the Tribunal Procedure (Amend-   4.105
ment No.3) Rules 2014 (SI 2014/2128) rr.2 and 5 amended r.5(4) of the 2008 Rules which relates to "fast-track cases" in the Immigration and Asylum Chamber of the Upper Tribunal. As the amendments are not relevant to social security cases, they are not set out here.

p.1652, *amendments to the Tribunal Procedure (Upper Tribunal) Rules 2008 (SI 2008/2698) r.12 (Calculating time)*

With effect from September 1, 2014, the Tribunal Procedure   4.106
(Amendment No.3) Rules 2014 (SI 2014/2128) rr.2 and 6 omitted r.12(5) of the 2008 Rules and, with effect from October 20, 2014, they omitted r.12(3A)(b) and the preceding "and". Neither of these amendments is relevant to social security cases.

pp.1660-1661, *substitution for the Tribunal Procedure (Upper Tribunal) Rules 2008 (SI 2008/2698) r.19 (Confidentiality in child support or child trust fund cases)*

With effect from October 20, 2014, the Tribunal Procedure (Amend-   4.107
ment No.3) Rules 2014 (SI 2014/2128) rr.2 and 7 substituted the following rule and heading for the existing rule:

"Confidentiality in social security and child support cases

19. (1) Paragraph (4) applies to an appeal against a decision of the First-tier Tribunal—
   (a) in proceedings under the Child Support Act 1991 in the circumstances described in paragraph (2), other than an appeal against a reduced benefit decision (as defined in section 46(10)(b) of the Child Support Act 1991, as that section had effect prior to the commencement of section 15(b) of the Child Maintenance and Other Payments Act 2008); or
   (b) in proceedings where the parties to the appeal include former joint claimants who are no longer living together in the circumstances described in paragraph (3).
(2) The circumstances referred to in paragraph (1)(a) are that—

(a) in the proceedings in the First-tier Tribunal in respect of which the appeal has been brought, there was an obligation to keep a person's address confidential; or

(b) an absent parent, non-resident parent or person with care would like their address or the address of the child to be kept confidential and has given notice to that effect to the Upper Tribunal—

    (i) in an application for permission to appeal or notice of appeal;

    (ii) within 1 month after an enquiry by the Upper Tribunal; or

    (iii) when notifying any subsequent change of address after proceedings have been started.

(3) The circumstances referred to in paragraph (1)(b) are that—

(a) in the proceedings in the First-tier Tribunal in respect of which the appeal has been brought, there was an obligation to keep a person's address confidential; or

(b) one of the former joint claimants would like their address to be kept confidential and has given notice to that effect to the Upper Tribunal—

    (i) in an application for permission to appeal or notice of appeal;

    (ii) within 1 month after an enquiry by the Upper Tribunal; or

    (iii) when notifying any subsequent change of address after proceedings have been started.

(4) Where this paragraph applies, the Secretary of State or other decision maker and the Upper Tribunal must take appropriate steps to secure the confidentiality of the address and of any information which could reasonably be expected to enable a person to identify the address, to the extent that the address or that information is not already known to each other party.

(5) In this rule—

"absent parent", "non-resident parent" and "person with care" have the meanings set out in section 3 of the Child Support Act 1991;

"joint claimants" means the persons who made a joint claim for a jobseeker's allowance under the Jobseekers Act 1995, a tax credit under the Tax Credits Act 2002 or in relation to whom an award of universal credit is made under Part 1 of the Welfare Reform Act 2012."

Specific provision for confidentiality is no longer made for child trust fund cases, because it is now unlikely there will be further such appeals. Instead, provision is made for confidentiality in a number of social security cases where former partners might both be parties. It is open to the Upper Tribunal to exercise its case-management powers under r.5 so as to make provision for confidentiality in other types of case should that be appropriate.

pp.1662-1663, *amendments to the Tribunal Procedure (Upper Tribunal) Rules 2008 (SI 2008/2698) r.21 (Application to the Upper Tribunal for permission to appeal)*

With effect from October 20, 2014, the Tribunal Procedure (Amend- **4.108** ment No.3) Rules 2014 (SI 2014/2128) rr.2 and 8 amended r.21(3)(aa) of the 2008 Rules and omitted r.21(3)(ab) and (3A). None of these amendments is relevant to social security cases.

p.1665, *amendments to the Tribunal Procedure (Upper Tribunal) Rules 2008 (SI 2008/2698) r.22(1) (Decision in relation to permission to appeal)*

With effect from June 30, 2014, the Tribunal Procedure (Amendment **4.109** No.2) Rules 2014 (SI 2014/1505) rr.2 and 3 amended r.22(1) of the 2008 Rules by inserting at the beginning "Subject to rule 40A,". How- ever, with effect from October 20, 2014, the Tribunal Procedure (Amendment No.3) Rules 2014 (SI 2014/2128) rr.2 and 9 replaced those words (except for the comma) with "Except where rule 22A (special procedure for providing notice of a refusal of permission to appeal in an asylum case) applies".

Rules 2 and 10 of SI 2014/2128 inserted the new r.22A into the 2008 Rules but, as that new rule is not relevant to social security cases, it is not set out here.

p.1668, *amendment to the Tribunal Procedure (Upper Tribunal) Rules 2008 (SI 2008/2698) r.24(2)(aa) (Response to the notice of appeal)*

With effect from October 20, 2014, the Tribunal Procedure (Amend- **4.110** ment No.3) Rules 2014 (SI 2014/2128) rr.2 and 11 amended r.24(2)(aa) of the 2008 Rules by substituting "two days" for "one day". This amendment is not relevant to social security cases.

pp.1676-1677, *annotation to the Tribunal Procedure (Upper Tribunal) Rules 2008 (SI 2008/2698) r.30(4A) (Decision on permission to bring immigration judicial review proceedings)*

A claim for judicial review may be "totally without merit" if it is bound **4.111** to fail, even if it is not abusive or vexatious (*R. (Grace) v Secretary of State for the Home Department* [2014] EWCA Civ 1091; [2014] 1 W.L.R. 3432).

p.1682, *amendments to the Tribunal Procedure (Upper Tribunal) Rules 2008 (SI 2008/2698) r.37(4)(e) (Public and private hearings)*

With effect from September 1, 2014, the Tribunal Procedure **4.112** (Amendment No.3) Rules 2014 (SI 2014/2128) rr.2 and 13 amended r.37(4)(e) of the 2008 Rules by substituting for "the age of eighteen years" the words "18, other than a young person who is a party in a special educational needs case or a disability discrimination in schools case".

p.1684, *amendment to the Tribunal Procedure (Upper Tribunal) Rules 2008 (SI 2008/2698) r.40(2) (Decisions)*

4.113   With effect from October 20, 2014, the Tribunal Procedure (Amendment No.3) Rules 2014 (SI 2014/2128) rr.2 and 14 amended r.40(2) of the 2008 Rules by substituting for "rule 40A (special procedure for providing notice of a decision relating to an asylum case)" the words "rule 22 (decision in relation to permission to appeal) or rule 22A (special procedure for providing notice of a refusal of permission to appeal in an asylum case)". Rules 2 and 10 of SI 2014/2128 inserted the new r.22A into the 2008 Rules but, as that new rule is not relevant to social security cases, it is not set out here.

p.1685, *revocation of the Tribunal Procedure (Upper Tribunal) Rules 2008 (SI 2008/2698) r.40A (Special procedure for providing notice of a decision relating to an asylum case)*

4.114   With effect from October 20, 2014, the Tribunal Procedure (Amendment No.3) Rules 2014 (SI 2014/2128) rr.2 and 15 revoked r.40A of the 2008 Rules, which was in any event not relevant to social security cases.

p.1694, *annotation to Practice Direction (First-tier And Upper Tribunals: Child, Vulnerable Adult and Sensitive Witnesses)*

4.115   *JP v SSWP (DLA)* [2014] UKUT 275 (AAC) is to be reported as [2015] AACR 2.

PART V

UPDATING MATERIAL:
VOLUME IV

TAX CREDITS AND HMRC-ADMINISTERED SOCIAL SECURITY BENEFITS

Commentary by

Nick Wikeley

David Williams

Ian Hooker

p.16-18, *amendments to the Taxes Management Act 1970 s.54 (Settling of appeals by agreement)*

With effect from August 12, 2014, s.54 is modified, with the consent 5.001
of the Lord Chancellor, the Scottish Ministers and the Department of
Justice of Northern Ireland, by reg.3 of the Tax Credits (Settlement of
Appeals) Regulations 2014 (SI 2014/1933) as follows:

"(1) Section 54 of the Taxes Management Act 1970 (settling of
appeals by agreement) shall apply to a tax credits appeal, with the
modifications prescribed by paragraphs (2) to (7).
(2) In subsection (1) for "tribunal" (in both places) substitute
"First-tier Tribunal".
(3) In subsections (1) and (4) for "assessment" (in each place)
substitute "determination".
(4) In subsections (1), (2) and (4)(a) for "the inspector or other
proper officer of the Crown" substitute "an officer of Revenue and
Customs".
(5) For subsection (3) substitute—
"(3) Where an agreement is not in writing—
(a) the preceding provisions of this section shall not apply unless
the Board give notice, in such form and manner as they
consider appropriate, to the appellant of the terms agreed
between the officer of Revenue and Customs and the
appellant;
and
(b) the references in those preceding provisions to the time when
the agreement was come to shall be construed as references
to the date of that notice.".
(6) In subsection (4)(b) for "the inspector or other proper officer"
substitute "an officer of Revenue and Customs".
(7) In subsection (4), in the words after paragraph (b), for "the
inspector or other proper officer" substitute "an officer of Revenue
and Customs"."

GENERAL NOTE

These modifications clarify and tidy up the previously messy and 5.002
incomplete provisions seeking to apply the general settlement powers
used by HMRC to deal with income tax and similar disputes to the
settlement of tax credits appeals.

p.53, *amendments to the Social Security Contributions and Benefits Act
1992 s.165 (The maternity pay period)*

With effect from June 30, 2014, s.120(4) of the Children and Families 5.003
Act 2014 inserted after subsection (3) the following new subsections
(Children and Families Act 2014 (Commencement No. 3, Transitional
Provisions and Savings) Order 2014 (SI 2014/1640), art.3(1)(d)):

"(3A) Regulations may provide for the duration of the maternity pay
period as it applies to a woman to be reduced, subject to prescribed
restrictions and conditions.

(3B) Regulations under subsection (3A) are to secure that the reduced period ends at a time—

(a) after a prescribed period beginning with the day on which the woman is confined, and

(b) when at least a prescribed part of the maternity pay period remains unexpired.

(3C) Regulations under subsection (3A) may, in particular, prescribe restrictions and conditions relating to—

(a) the end of the woman's entitlement to maternity leave;

(b) the doing of work by the woman;

(c) the taking of prescribed steps by the woman or another person as regards leave under section 75E of the Employment Rights Act 1996 in respect of the child;

(d) the taking of prescribed steps by the woman or another person as regards statutory shared parental pay in respect of the child.

(3D) Regulations may provide for a reduction in the duration of the maternity pay period as it applies to a woman to be revoked, or to be treated as revoked, subject to prescribed restrictions and conditions."

p.64, *amendments to the Social Security Contributions and Benefits Act 1992 s.171ZB (Entitlement to ordinary statutory paternity pay: adoption)*

5.004   With effect from June 30, 2014, s.121(3) of the Children and Families Act 2014 inserted after subsection (7) the following new subsection (Children and Families Act 2014 (Commencement No. 3, Transitional Provisions and Savings) Order 2014 (SI 2014/1640), art.3(1)(e)):

"(8) This section has effect in a case involving a child placed under section 22C of the Children Act 1989 by a local authority in England with a local authority foster parent who has been approved as a prospective adopter with the following modifications—

(a) the references in subsection (2) to a child being placed for adoption under the law of any part of the United Kingdom are to be treated as references to a child being placed under section 22C in that manner;

(b) the reference in subsection (3) to the week in which the adopter is notified of being matched with the child for the purposes of adoption is to be treated as a reference to the week in which the prospective adopter is notified that the child is to be, or is expected to be, placed with the prospective adopter under section 22C;

(c) the reference in subsection (6) to placement for adoption is to be treated as a reference to placement under section 22C;

(d) the definition in subsection (7) is to be treated as if it were a definition of "prospective adopter".

(9) Where, by virtue of subsection (8), a person becomes entitled to statutory paternity pay in connection with the placement of a child under section 22C of the Children Act 1989, the person may not

become entitled to payments of statutory paternity pay in connection with the placement of the child for adoption."

p.65, *amendments to the Social Security Contributions and Benefits Act 1992 s.171ZB(1) (Entitlement: general)*

With effect from June 30, 2014, s.123(2) of the Children and Families Act 2014 substituted " only if he gives the person who will be liable to pay it notice of the week or weeks in respect of which he expects there to be liability to pay him statutory paternity pay. " for the words from "only if" to the end of subsection (1) (Children and Families Act 2014 (Commencement No. 3, Transitional Provisions and Savings) Order 2014 (SI 2014/1640) art.3(1)(g)). In addition, after subsection (1) there is inserted the following new subsection: 5.005

"(1A) Regulations may provide for the time by which notice under subsection (1) is to be given."

p.67, *amendments to the Social Security Contributions and Benefits Act 1992 s.171ZE (Rate and period of pay)*

With effect from June 30, 2014, s.120(5) of the Children and Families Act 2014 inserted after subsection (3) the following new subsection (Children and Families Act 2014 (Commencement No. 3, Transitional Provisions and Savings) Order 2014 (SI 2014/1640) art.3(1)(d)):   5.006

"(3A) Statutory paternity pay is not payable to a person in respect of a statutory pay week if—
  (a) statutory shared parental pay is payable to that person in respect of any part of that week or that person takes shared parental leave in any part of that week, or
  (b) statutory shared parental pay was payable to that person or that person has taken shared parental leave in respect of the child before that week."

With effect from June 30, 2014, s.121(4) of the Children and Families Act 2014 inserted after subsection (11) the following new subsection (Children and Families Act 2014 (Commencement No. 3, Transitional Provisions and Savings) Order 2014 (SI 2014/1640), art.3(1)(e)):

"(12) Where statutory paternity pay is payable to a person by virtue of section 171ZB(8), this section has effect as if—
  (a) the references in subsections (3)(b) and (10) to placement for adoption were references to placement under section 22C of the Children Act 1989;
  (b) the references in subsection (10) to being placed for adoption were references to being placed under section 22C."

p.75, *amendments to the Social Security Contributions and Benefits Act 1992 s.171ZJ(1) (Part XIIZA: supplementary)*

With effect from June 30, 2014, s.121(7)(a) of the Children and Families Act 2014 inserted the following new definitions in subsection   5.007

(1) before the definition of "modifications" (Children and Families Act 2014 (Commencement No. 3, Transitional Provisions and Savings) Order 2014 (SI 2014/1640) art.3(1)(e)):

""local authority" has the same meaning as in the Children Act 1989 (see section 105(1) of that Act);";

""local authority foster parent" has the same meaning as in the Children Act 1989 (see section 22C(12) of that Act);".

p.79, *amendments to the Social Security Contributions and Benefits Act 1992 s.171ZL (Entitlement to statutory adoption pay)*

5.008   With effect from June 30, 2014, s.121(5) of the Children and Families Act 2014 inserted after subsection (8) the following new subsections (Children and Families Act 2014 (Commencement No. 3, Transitional Provisions and Savings) Order 2014 (SI 2014/1640), art.3(1)(e)):

"(9) This section has effect in a case involving a child who is, or is expected to be, placed under section 22C of the Children Act 1989 by a local authority in England with a local authority foster parent who has been approved as a prospective adopter with the following modifications—

(a) the references in subsections (2)(a) and (4A)(a) to a child being placed for adoption under the law of any part of the United Kingdom are to be treated as references to a child being placed under section 22C in that manner;

(b) the reference in subsection (3) to the week in which the person is notified that he has been matched with the child for the purposes of adoption is to be treated as a reference to the week in which the person is notified that the child is to be, or is expected to be, placed with him under section 22C;

(c) the references in subsection (4B)(a) to adoption are to be treated as references to placement under section 22C;

(d) the reference in subsection (5) to placement, or expected placement, for adoption is to be treated as a reference to placement, or expected placement, under section 22C.

(10) Where, by virtue of subsection (9), a person becomes entitled to statutory adoption pay in respect of a child who is, or is expected to be, placed under section 22C of the Children Act 1989, the person may not become entitled to payments of statutory adoption pay as a result of the child being, or being expected to be, placed for adoption."

p.80, *amendments to the Social Security Contributions and Benefits Act 1992 s.171ZN (Rate and period of statutory adoption pay)*

5.009   With effect from June 30, 2014, s.120(6) of the Children and Families Act 2014 inserted after subsection (2) the following new subsections (Children and Families Act 2014 (Commencement No. 3, Transitional Provisions and Savings) Order 2014 (SI 2014/1640) art.3(1)(d)):

"(2A) Regulations may provide for the duration of the adoption pay period as it applies to a person ("A") to be reduced, subject to prescribed restrictions and conditions.

(2B) Regulations under subsection (2A) are to secure that the reduced period ends at a time—

(a) after a prescribed part of the adoption pay period has expired, and

(b) when at least a prescribed part of the adoption pay period remains unexpired.

(2C) Regulations under subsection (2A) may, in particular, prescribe restrictions and conditions relating to—

(a) the end of A's entitlement to adoption leave;

(b) the doing of work by A;

(c) the taking of prescribed steps by A or another person as regards leave under section 75G of the Employment Rights Act 1996 in respect of the child;

(d) the taking of prescribed steps by A or another person as regards statutory shared parental pay in respect of the child.

(2D) Regulations may provide for a reduction in the duration of the adoption pay period as it applies to a person to be revoked, or to be treated as revoked, subject to prescribed restrictions and conditions."

p.81, *amendment to the Social Security Contributions and Benefits Act 1992 s.171ZN (Rate and period of statutory adoption pay)*

With effect from June 30, 2014, s.121(6) of the Children and Families Act 2014 inserted after subsection (8) the following new subsections (Children and Families Act 2014 (Commencement No. 3, Transitional Provisions and Savings) Order 2014 (SI 2014/1640) art.3(1)(e)): 5.010

"(9) Where statutory adoption pay is payable to a person by virtue of section 171ZL(9), this section has effect as if the reference in subsection (2F) to the week in which the person is notified that he has been matched with a child for the purposes of adoption were a reference to the week in which the person is notified that a child is to be, or is expected to be, placed with him under section 22C of the Children Act 1989."

p.84, *amendments to the Social Security Contributions and Benefits Act 1992 s.171ZS(1) (Part XIIZB: supplementary)*

With effect from June 30, 2014, s.121(7)(b) of the Children and Families Act 2014 inserted the following new definitions in subsection (1) before the definition of "modifications" (Children and Families Act 2014 (Commencement No. 3, Transitional Provisions and Savings) Order 2014 (SI 2014/1640) art.3(1)(e)): 5.011

""local authority" has the same meaning as in the Children Act 1989 (see section 105(1) of that Act);";

""local authority foster parent" has the same meaning as in the Children Act 1989 (see section 22C(12) of that Act);".

p.85, *amendments to the Social Security Contributions and Benefits Act 1992 Part 12ZC (Insertion of new Part 12ZC (Statutory shared parental pay))*

5.012   With effect from June 30, 2014, s.119 of the Children and Families Act 2014 inserted after s.171ZT a new Past 12ZC (ss.171ZE-171ZZ5) as follows (Children and Families Act 2014 (Commencement No. 3, Transitional Provisions and Savings) Order 2014 (SI 2014/1640), art.3(1)(c)):

"PART 12ZC

STATUTORY SHARED PARENTAL PAY

Entitlement: birth

171ZU.—(1) Regulations may provide that, where all the conditions in subsection (2) are satisfied in relation to a person who is the mother of a child ("the claimant mother"), the claimant mother is to be entitled in accordance with the following provisions of this Part to payments to be known as "statutory shared parental pay".

(2) The conditions are—

(a) that the claimant mother and another person ("P") satisfy prescribed conditions as to caring or intending to care for the child;

(b) that P satisfies prescribed conditions—

　(i) as to employment or self-employment,

　(ii) as to having earnings of a prescribed amount for a prescribed period, and

　(iii) as to relationship either with the child or with the claimant mother;

(c) that the claimant mother has been in employed earner's employment with an employer for a continuous period of at least the prescribed length ending with a prescribed week;

(d) that at the end of that prescribed week the claimant mother was entitled to be in that employment;

(e) that the claimant mother's normal weekly earnings for a prescribed period ending with a prescribed week are not less than the lower earnings limit in force under section 5(1)(a) at the end of that week;

(f) if regulations so provide, that the claimant mother continues in employed earner's employment (whether or not with the employer by reference to whom the condition in paragraph (c) is satisfied) until a prescribed time;

(g) that the claimant mother became entitled to statutory maternity pay by reference to the birth of the child;

(h) that the claimant mother satisfies prescribed conditions as to the reduction of the duration of the maternity pay period;

(i) that the claimant mother has given the person who will be liable to pay statutory shared parental pay to her notice of—
  (i) the number of weeks in respect of which she would be entitled to claim statutory shared parental pay in respect of the child if the entitlement were fully exercised (disregarding for these purposes any intention of P to claim statutory shared parental pay in respect of the child),
  (ii) the number of weeks in respect of which she intends to claim statutory shared parental pay, and
  (iii) the number of weeks in respect of which P intends to claim statutory shared parental pay;

(j) that the claimant mother has given the person who will be liable to pay statutory shared parental pay to her notice of the period or periods during which she intends to claim statutory shared parental pay in respect of the child;

(k) that a notice under paragraph (i) or (j)—
  (i) is given by such time as may be prescribed, and
  (ii) satisfies prescribed conditions as to form and content;

(l) that P consents to the extent of the claimant mother's intended claim for statutory shared parental pay;

(m) that it is the claimant mother's intention to care for the child during each week in respect of which statutory shared parental pay is paid to her;

(n) that the claimant mother is absent from work during each week in respect of which statutory shared parental pay is paid to her;

(o) that, where she is an employee within the meaning of the Employment Rights Act 1996, the claimant mother's absence from work during each such week is absence on shared parental leave.

(3) Regulations may provide that, where all the conditions in subsection (4) are satisfied in relation to a person ("the claimant"), the claimant is to be entitled in accordance with the following provisions of this Part to payments to be known as "statutory shared parental pay".

(4) The conditions are—

(a) that the claimant and another person ("M") who is the mother of a child satisfy prescribed conditions as to caring or intending to care for the child;

(b) that the claimant satisfies—
  (i) prescribed conditions as to relationship with the child, or
  (ii) prescribed conditions as to relationship with M;

(c) that M satisfies prescribed conditions—
  (i) as to employment or self-employment, and
  (ii) as to having earnings of a prescribed amount for a prescribed period;

(d) that the claimant has been in employed earner's employment with an employer for a continuous period of at least the prescribed length ending with a prescribed week;

(e) that at the end of that prescribed week the claimant was entitled to be in that employment;

(f) that the claimant's normal weekly earnings for a prescribed period ending with a prescribed week are not less than the lower earnings limit in force under section 5(1)(a) at the end of that week;

(g) if regulations so provide, that the claimant continues in employed earner's employment (whether or not with the employer by reference to whom the condition in paragraph (d) is satisfied) until a prescribed time;

(h) that M became entitled, by reference to the birth of the child, to—
   (i) a maternity allowance, or
   (ii) statutory maternity pay;

(i) that M satisfies prescribed conditions as to—
   (i) the reduction of the duration of the maternity allowance period, or
   (ii) the reduction of the duration of the maternity pay period, as the case may be;

(j) that the claimant has given the person who will be liable to pay statutory shared parental pay to the claimant notice of—
   (i) the number of weeks in respect of which the claimant would be entitled to claim statutory shared parental pay in respect of the child if the entitlement were fully exercised (disregarding for these purposes any intention of M to claim statutory shared parental pay in respect of the child),
   (ii) the number of weeks in respect of which the claimant intends to claim statutory shared parental pay, and
   (iii) the number of weeks in respect of which M intends to claim statutory shared parental pay;

(k) that the claimant has given the person who will be liable to pay statutory shared parental pay to the claimant notice of the period or periods during which the claimant intends to claim statutory shared parental pay in respect of the child;

(l) that a notice under paragraph (j) or (k)—
   (i) is given by such time as may be prescribed, and
   (ii) satisfies prescribed conditions as to form and content;

(m) that M consents to the extent of the claimant's intended claim for statutory shared parental pay;

(n) that it is the claimant's intention to care for the child during each week in respect of which statutory shared parental pay is paid to the claimant;

(o) that the claimant is absent from work during each week in respect of which statutory shared parental pay is paid to the claimant;

(p) that, where the claimant is an employee within the meaning of the Employment Rights Act 1996, the claimant's absence from work during each such week is absence on shared parental leave.

(5) Regulations may provide for—

(a) the determination of the extent of a person's entitlement to statutory shared parental pay in respect of a child;

(b) when statutory shared parental pay is to be payable.

(6) Provision under subsection (5)(a) is to secure that the number of weeks in respect of which a person is entitled to payments of statutory shared parental pay in respect of a child does not exceed the number of weeks of the maternity pay period reduced by—

(a) where the mother of the child takes action that is treated by regulations as constituting for the purposes of this section her return to work without satisfying conditions prescribed under subsection (2)(h) or, as the case may be, subsection (4)(i)—

   (i) the number of relevant weeks in respect of which maternity allowance or statutory maternity pay is payable to the mother, or

   (ii) if that number of relevant weeks is less than a number prescribed by regulations, that prescribed number of weeks, or

(b) except where paragraph (a) applies, the number of weeks to which the maternity allowance period is reduced by virtue of section 35(3A) or, as the case may be, the maternity pay period is reduced by virtue of section 165(3A).

(7) In subsection (6)(a) "relevant week" means—

(a) where maternity allowance is payable to a mother, a week or part of a week falling before the time at which the mother takes action that is treated by regulations as constituting for the purposes of this section her return to work;

(b) where statutory maternity pay is payable to a mother, a week falling before the week in which the mother takes action that is so treated.

For these purposes "week" has the meaning given by section 122(1), in relation to maternity allowance, or the meaning given by section 165(8), in relation to statutory maternity pay.

(8) In determining the number of weeks for the purposes of subsection (6)(b)—

(a) "week" has the same meaning as in subsection (7), and

(b) a part of a week is to be treated as a week.

(9) Provision under subsection (5)(a) is to secure that, where two persons are entitled to payments of statutory shared parental pay in respect of a child, the extent of one's entitlement and the extent of the other's entitlement do not, taken together, exceed what would be available to one person (see subsection (6)).

(10) Provision under subsection (5)(b) is to secure that no payment of statutory shared parental pay may be made to a person in respect of a child after the end of such period as may be prescribed.

(11) Provision under subsection (5)(b) is to secure that no payment of statutory shared parental pay in respect of a child may be made to a person who is the mother of the child before the end of the mother's maternity pay period.

(12) Regulations may provide that, where the conditions in subsection (13) are satisfied in relation to a person who is entitled to statutory shared parental pay under subsection (1) or (3) ("V"), V may vary the period or periods during which V intends to claim statutory shared parental pay in respect of the child in question, subject to complying with provision under subsection (14) where that is relevant.

(13) The conditions are—

(a) that V has given the person who will be liable to pay statutory shared parental pay to V notice of an intention to vary the period or periods during which V intends to claim statutory shared parental pay;

(b) that a notice under paragraph (a)—

(i) is given by such time as may be prescribed, and

(ii) satisfies prescribed conditions as to form and content.

(14) Regulations may provide that, where the conditions in subsection (15) are satisfied in relation to a person who is entitled to statutory shared parental pay under subsection (1) or (3) ("V"), V may vary the number of weeks in respect of which V intends to claim statutory shared parental pay.

(15) The conditions are—

(a) that V has given the person who will be liable to pay statutory shared parental pay to V notice of—

(i) the extent to which V has exercised an entitlement to statutory shared parental pay in respect of the child,

(ii) the extent to which V intends to claim statutory shared parental pay in respect of the child,

(iii) the extent to which another person has exercised an entitlement to statutory shared parental pay in respect of the child, and

(iv) the extent to which another person intends to claim statutory shared parental pay in respect of the child;

(b) that a notice under paragraph (a)—

(i) is given by such time as may be prescribed, and

(ii) satisfies prescribed conditions as to form and content;

(c) that the person who is P or, as the case may be, M in relation to V consents to that variation.

(16) A person's entitlement to statutory shared parental pay under this section is not affected by the birth of more than one child as a result of the same pregnancy.

Entitlement: adoption

171ZV.—(1) Regulations may provide that, where all the conditions in subsection (2) are satisfied in relation to a person with whom a child is, or is expected to be, placed for adoption under the law of any part of the United Kingdom ("claimant A"), claimant A is to be entitled in accordance with the following provisions of this Part to payments to be known as "statutory shared parental pay".

(2) The conditions are—

(a) that claimant A and another person ("X") satisfy prescribed conditions as to caring or intending to care for the child;

(b) that X satisfies prescribed conditions—
   (i) as to employment or self-employment,
   (ii) as to having earnings of a prescribed amount for a prescribed period, and
   (iii) as to relationship either with the child or with claimant A;

(c) that claimant A has been in employed earner's employment with an employer for a continuous period of at least the prescribed length ending with a prescribed week;

(d) that at the end of that prescribed week claimant A was entitled to be in that employment;

(e) that claimant A's normal weekly earnings for a prescribed period ending with a prescribed week are not less than the lower earnings limit in force under section 5(1)(a) at the end of that week;

(f) if regulations so provide, that claimant A continues in employed earner's employment (whether or not with the employer by reference to whom the condition in paragraph (c) is satisfied) until a prescribed time;

(g) that claimant A became entitled to statutory adoption pay by reference to the placement for adoption of the child;

(h) that claimant A satisfies prescribed conditions as to the reduction of the duration of the adoption pay period;

(i) that claimant A has given the person who will be liable to pay statutory shared parental pay to claimant A notice of—
   (i) the number of weeks in respect of which claimant A would be entitled to claim statutory shared parental pay in respect of the child if the entitlement were fully exercised (disregarding for these purposes any intention of X to claim statutory shared parental pay in respect of the child),
   (ii) the number of weeks in respect of which claimant A intends to claim statutory shared parental pay, and
   (iii) the number of weeks in respect of which X intends to claim statutory shared parental pay;

(j) that claimant A has given the person who will be liable to pay statutory shared parental pay to claimant A notice of the period or periods during which claimant A intends to claim statutory shared parental pay in respect of the child;

(k) that a notice under paragraph (i) or (j)—
   (i) is given by such time as may be prescribed, and
   (ii) satisfies prescribed conditions as to form and content;

(l) that X consents to the extent of claimant A's intended claim for statutory shared parental pay;

(m) that it is claimant A's intention to care for the child during each week in respect of which statutory shared parental pay is paid to claimant A;

(n) that claimant A is absent from work during each week in respect of which statutory shared parental pay is paid to claimant A;

(o) that, where claimant A is an employee within the meaning of the Employment Rights Act 1996, claimant A's absence from work during each such week is absence on shared parental leave.

(3) Regulations may provide that, where all the conditions in subsection (4) are satisfied in relation to a person ("claimant B"), claimant B is to be entitled in accordance with the following provisions of this Part to payments to be known as "statutory shared parental pay".

(4) The conditions are—

(a) that claimant B and another person ("Y") who is a person with whom a child is, or is expected to be, placed for adoption under the law of any part of the United Kingdom satisfy prescribed conditions as to caring or intending to care for the child;

(b) that claimant B satisfies—
   (i) prescribed conditions as to relationship with the child, or
   (ii) prescribed conditions as to relationship with Y;

(c) that Y satisfies prescribed conditions—
   (i) as to employment or self-employment, and
   (ii) as to having earnings of a prescribed amount for a prescribed period;

(d) that claimant B has been in employed earner's employment with an employer for a continuous period of at least the prescribed length ending with a prescribed week;

(e) that at the end of that prescribed week claimant B was entitled to be in that employment;

(f) that claimant B's normal weekly earnings for a prescribed period ending with a prescribed week are not less than the lower earnings limit in force under section 5(1)(a) at the end of that week;

(g) if regulations so provide, that claimant B continues in employed earner's employment (whether or not with the employer by reference to whom the condition in paragraph (d) is satisfied) until a prescribed time;

(h) that Y became entitled to statutory adoption pay by reference to the placement for adoption of the child;

(i) that Y satisfies prescribed conditions as to the reduction of the duration of the adoption pay period;

(j) that claimant B has given the person who will be liable to pay statutory shared parental pay to claimant B notice of—
   (i) the number of weeks in respect of which claimant B would be entitled to claim statutory shared parental pay in respect of the child if the entitlement were fully exercised (disregarding for these purposes any intention of Y to claim statutory shared parental pay in respect of the child),
   (ii) the number of weeks in respect of which claimant B intends to claim statutory shared parental pay, and
   (iii) the number of weeks in respect of which Y intends to claim statutory shared parental pay;

(k) that claimant B has given the person who will be liable to pay statutory shared parental pay to claimant B notice of the period or periods during which claimant B intends to claim statutory shared parental pay in respect of the child;

(l) that a notice under paragraph (j) or (k)—

    (i) is given by such time as may be prescribed, and

    (ii) satisfies prescribed conditions as to form and content;

(m) that Y consents to the extent of claimant B's intended claim for statutory shared parental pay;

(n) that it is claimant B's intention to care for the child during each week in respect of which statutory shared parental pay is paid to claimant B;

(o) that claimant B is absent from work during each week in respect of which statutory shared parental pay is paid to claimant B;

(p) that, where claimant B is an employee within the meaning of the Employment Rights Act 1996, claimant B's absence from work during each such week is absence on shared parental leave.

(5) Regulations may provide for—

(a) the determination of the extent of a person's entitlement to statutory shared parental pay in respect of a child;

(b) when statutory shared parental pay is to be payable.

(6) Provision under subsection (5)(a) is to secure that the number of weeks in respect of which a person is entitled to payments of statutory shared parental pay in respect of a child does not exceed the number of weeks of the adoption pay period reduced by—

(a) where the person who became entitled to receive statutory adoption pay takes action that is treated by regulations as constituting for the purposes of this section the person's return to work without satisfying conditions prescribed under subsection (2)(h) or, as the case may be, subsection (4)(i)—

    (i) the number of relevant weeks in respect of which statutory adoption pay is payable to the person, or

    (ii) if that number of relevant weeks is less than a number prescribed by regulations, that prescribed number of weeks, or

(b) except where paragraph (a) applies, the number of weeks to which the adoption pay period has been reduced by virtue of section 171ZN(2A).

(7) In subsection (6)(a) "relevant week" means a week falling before the week in which a person takes action that is treated by regulations as constituting for the purposes of this section the person's return to work, and for these purposes "week" has the meaning given by section 171ZN(8).

(8) In determining the number of weeks for the purposes of subsection (6)(b)—

(a) "week" has the same meaning as in subsection (7), and

(b) a part of a week is to be treated as a week.

(9) Provision under subsection (5)(a) is to secure that, where two persons are entitled to payments of statutory shared parental pay in respect of a child, the extent of one's entitlement and the extent of the other's entitlement do not, taken together, exceed what would be available to one person (see subsection (6)).

(10) Provision under subsection (5)(b) is to secure that no payment of statutory shared parental pay may be made to a person in respect of a child after the end of such period as may be prescribed.

(11) Provision under subsection (5)(b) is to secure that no payment of statutory shared parental pay in respect of a child may be made to a person who became entitled to receive statutory adoption pay in respect of the child before the end of the person's adoption pay period.

(12) Regulations may provide that, where the conditions in subsection (13) are satisfied in relation to a person who is entitled to statutory shared parental pay under subsection (1) or (3) ("V"), V may vary the period or periods during which V intends to claim statutory shared parental pay in respect of the child in question, subject to complying with provision under subsection (14) where that is relevant.

(13) The conditions are—

(a) that V has given the person who will be liable to pay statutory shared parental pay to V notice of an intention to vary the period or periods during which V intends to claim statutory shared parental pay;

(b) that a notice under paragraph (a)—
    (i) is given by such time as may be prescribed, and
    (ii) satisfies prescribed conditions as to form and content.

(14) Regulations may provide that, where the conditions in subsection (15) are satisfied in relation to a person who is entitled to statutory shared parental pay under subsection (1) or (3) ("V"), V may vary the number of weeks in respect of which V intends to claim statutory shared parental pay.

(15) The conditions are—

(a) that V has given the person who will be liable to pay statutory shared parental pay to V notice of—
    (i) the extent to which V has exercised an entitlement to statutory shared parental pay in respect of the child,
    (ii) the extent to which V intends to claim statutory shared parental pay in respect of the child,
    (iii) the extent to which another person has exercised an entitlement to statutory shared parental pay in respect of the child, and
    (iv) the extent to which another person intends to claim statutory shared parental pay in respect of the child;

(b) that a notice under paragraph (a)—
    (i) is given by such time as may be prescribed, and
    (ii) satisfies prescribed conditions as to form and content;

(c) that the person who is X or, as the case may be, Y in relation to V consents to that variation.

(16) A person's entitlement to statutory shared parental pay under this section is not affected by the placement for adoption of more than one child as part of the same arrangement.

(17) Regulations are to provide for entitlement to statutory shared parental pay in respect of a child placed, or expected to be placed,

under section 22C of the Children Act 1989 by a local authority in England with a local authority foster parent who has been approved as a prospective adopter.

(18) This section has effect in relation to regulations made by virtue of subsection (17) as if—

(a) references to a child being placed for adoption under the law of any part of the United Kingdom were references to being placed under section 22C of the Children Act 1989 with a local authority foster parent who has been approved as a prospective adopter;

(b) references to placement for adoption were references to placement under section 22C with such a person.

Entitlement: general

171ZW.—(1) Regulations may—

(a) provide that the following do not have effect, or have effect subject to prescribed modifications, in such cases as may be prescribed—
  (i) section 171ZU(2)(a) to (o),
  (ii) section 171ZU(4)(a) to (p),
  (iii) section 171ZU(13)(a) and (b),
  (iv) section 171ZU(15)(a) to (c),
  (v) section 171ZV(2)(a) to (o),
  (vi) section 171ZV(4)(a) to (p),
  (vii) section 171ZV(13)(a) and (b), and
  (viii) section 171ZV(15)(a) to (c);

(b) impose requirements about evidence of entitlement and procedures to be followed;

(c) specify in what circumstances employment is to be treated as continuous for the purposes of section 171ZU or 171ZV;

(d) provide that a person is to be treated for the purposes of section 171ZU or 171ZV as being employed for a continuous period of at least the prescribed period where—
  (i) the person has been employed by the same employer for at least the prescribed period under two or more separate contracts of service, and
  (ii) those contracts were not continuous;

(e) provide for amounts earned by a person under separate contracts of service with the same employer to be aggregated for the purposes of section 171ZU or 171ZV;

(f) provide that—
  (i) the amount of a person's earnings for any period, or
  (ii) the amount of the person's earnings to be treated as comprised in any payment made to the person or for the person's benefit,
  are to be calculated or estimated for the purposes of section 171ZU or 171ZV in such manner and on such basis as may be prescribed and that for that purpose payments of a particular class or description made or falling to be made

to or by a person are, to such extent as may be prescribed, to be disregarded or, as the case may be, to be deducted from the amount of the person's earnings.

(2) The persons upon whom requirements may be imposed by virtue of subsection (1)(b) include—

(a) a person who, in connection with another person's claim to be paid statutory shared parental pay, is required to satisfy conditions prescribed under section 171ZU(2)(b) or (4)(c) or 171ZV(2)(b) or (4)(c);

(b) an employer or former employer of such a person.

(3) In subsection (1)(d) "the prescribed period" means the period of the length prescribed by regulations under section 171ZU(2)(c) or (4)(d) or 171ZV(2)(c) or (4)(d), as the case may be.

Liability to make payments

171ZX.—(1) The liability to make payments of statutory shared parental pay under section 171ZU or 171ZV is a liability of any person of whom the person entitled to the payments has been an employee as mentioned in section 171ZU(2)(c) or (4)(d) or 171ZV(2)(c) or (4)(d), as the case may be.

(2) Regulations must make provision as to a former employer's liability to pay statutory shared parental pay to a person in any case where the former employee's contract of service with the person has been brought to an end by the former employer solely, or mainly, for the purpose of avoiding liability for statutory shared parental pay.

(3) The Secretary of State may, with the concurrence of the Commissioners for Her Majesty's Revenue and Customs, by regulations specify circumstances in which, notwithstanding this section, liability to make payments of statutory shared parental pay is to be a liability of the Commissioners.

Rate and period of pay

171ZY.—(1) Statutory shared parental pay is payable at such fixed or earnings-related weekly rate as may be prescribed by regulations, which may prescribe different kinds of rate for different cases.

(2) Subject to the following provisions of this section, statutory shared parental pay is payable to a person in respect of each week falling within a relevant period, up to the number of weeks determined in the case of that person in accordance with regulations under section 171ZU(5) or 171ZV(5).

(3) Except in such cases as may be prescribed, statutory shared parental pay is not payable to a person in respect of a week falling within a relevant period if it is not the person's intention at the beginning of the week to care for the child by reference to whom the person satisfies—

(a) the condition in section 171ZU(2)(a) or (4)(a), or

(b) the condition in section 171ZV(2)(a) or (4)(a).

(4) Except in such cases as may be prescribed, statutory shared parental pay is not payable to a person in respect of a week falling

within a relevant period during any part of which week the person works for any employer.

(5) The Secretary of State may by regulations specify circumstances in which there is to be no liability to pay statutory shared parental pay in respect of a week falling within a relevant period.

(6) Where for any purpose of this Part or of regulations it is necessary to calculate the daily rate of statutory shared parental pay, the amount payable by way of statutory shared parental pay for any day shall be taken as one seventh of the weekly rate.

(7) For the purposes of this section a week falls within a relevant period if it falls within a period specified in a notice under—

(a) section 171ZU(2)(j), (4)(k) or (13)(a), or

(b) section 171ZV(2)(j), (4)(k) or (13)(a),

and is not afterwards excluded from such a period by a variation of the period or periods during which the person in question intends to claim statutory shared parental pay.

(8) In this section "week", in relation to a relevant period, means a period of seven days beginning with the day of the week on which the relevant period starts.

Restrictions on contracting out

171ZZ.—(1) An agreement is void to the extent that it purports—

(a) to exclude, limit or otherwise modify any provision of this Part, or

(b) to require a person to contribute (whether directly or indirectly) towards any costs incurred by that person's employer or former employer under this Part.

(2) For the avoidance of doubt, an agreement between an employer and an employee, authorising deductions from statutory shared parental pay which the employer is liable to pay to the employee in respect of any period, is not void by virtue of subsection (1)(a) if the employer—

(a) is authorised by that or another agreement to make the same deductions from any contractual remuneration which the employer is liable to pay in respect of the same period, or

(b) would be so authorised if the employer were liable to pay contractual remuneration in respect of that period.

Relationship with contractual remuneration

171ZZ1.—(1) Subject to subsections (2) and (3), any entitlement to statutory shared parental pay is not to affect any right of a person in relation to remuneration under any contract of service ("contractual remuneration").

(2) Subject to subsection (3)—

(a) any contractual remuneration paid to a person by an employer of that person in respect of any period is to go towards discharging any liability of that employer to pay statutory shared parental pay to that person in respect of that period; and

311

(b) any statutory shared parental pay paid by an employer to a person who is an employee of that employer in respect of any period is to go towards discharging any liability of that employer to pay contractual remuneration to that person in respect of that period.

(3) Regulations may make provision as to payments which are, and those which are not, to be treated as contractual remuneration for the purposes of subsections (1) and (2).

Crown employment

171ZZ2.—The provisions of this Part apply in relation to persons employed by or under the Crown as they apply in relation to persons employed otherwise than by or under the Crown.

Special classes of person

171ZZ3.—(1) The Secretary of State may with the concurrence of the Treasury make regulations modifying any provision of this Part in such manner as the Secretary of State thinks proper in its application to any person who is, has been or is to be—

(a) employed on board any ship, vessel, hovercraft or aircraft;

(b) outside Great Britain at any prescribed time or in any prescribed circumstances; or

(c) in prescribed employment in connection with continental shelf operations, as defined in section 120(2).

(2) Regulations under subsection (1) may, in particular, provide—

(a) for any provision of this Part to apply to any such person, notwithstanding that it would not otherwise apply;

(b) for any such provision not to apply to any such person, notwithstanding that it would otherwise apply;

(c) for excepting any such person from the application of any such provision where the person neither is domiciled nor has a place of residence in any part of Great Britain;

(d) for the taking of evidence, for the purposes of the determination of any question arising under any such provision, in a country or territory outside Great Britain, by a British consular official or such other person as may be determined in accordance with the regulations.

Part 12ZC: supplementary

171ZZ4.—(1) In this Part—

"adoption pay period" has the meaning given in section 171ZN(2);

"employer", in relation to a person who is an employee, means a person who—

(a) under section 6 is liable to pay secondary Class 1 contributions in relation to any of the earnings of the person who is an employee, or

(b) would be liable to pay such contributions but for—

(i) the condition in section 6(1)(b), or

    (ii) the employee being under the age of 16;

"local authority" has the same meaning as in the Children Act 1989 (see section 105(1) of that Act);

"local authority foster parent" has the same meaning as in the Children Act 1989 (see section 22C(12) of that Act);

"maternity allowance period" has the meaning given in section 35(2);

"maternity pay period" has the meaning given in section 165(1);

"modifications" includes additions, omissions and amendments, and related expressions are to be read accordingly;

"prescribed" means prescribed by regulations.

(2) In this Part "employee" means a person who is gainfully employed in Great Britain either under a contract of service or in an office (including elective office) with general earnings (as defined by section 7 of the Income Tax (Earnings and Pensions) Act 2003).

(3) Regulations may provide—

(a) for cases where a person who falls within the definition in subsection (2) is not to be treated as an employee for the purposes of this Part, and

(b) for cases where a person who would not otherwise be an employee for the purposes of this Part is to be treated as an employee for those purposes.

(4) Without prejudice to any other power to make regulations under this Part, regulations may specify cases in which, for the purposes of this Part or of such provisions of this Part as may be prescribed—

(a) two or more employers are to be treated as one;

(b) two or more contracts of service in respect of which the same person is an employee are to be treated as one.

(5) In this Part, except where otherwise provided, "week" means a period of seven days beginning with Sunday or such other period as may be prescribed in relation to any particular case or class of cases.

(6) For the purposes of this Part, a person's normal weekly earnings are, subject to subsection (8), to be taken to be the average weekly earnings which in the relevant period have been paid to the person or paid for the person's benefit under the contract of service with the employer in question.

(7) For the purposes of subsection (6) "earnings" and "relevant period" have the meanings given to them by regulations.

(8) In such cases as may be prescribed, a person's normal weekly earnings are to be calculated in accordance with regulations.

(9) Where—

(a) in consequence of the establishment of one or more National Health Service trusts under the National Health Service Act 2006, the National Health Service (Wales) Act 2006 or the National Health Service (Scotland) Act 1978, a person's contract of employment is treated by a scheme under any of those Acts as divided so as to constitute two or more contracts, or

(b) an order under paragraph 26(1) of Schedule 3 to the National Health Service Act 2006 provides that a person's contract of employment is so divided,

regulations may make provision enabling the person to elect for all of those contracts to be treated as one contract for the purposes of this Part or such provisions of this Part as may be prescribed.

(10) Regulations under subsection (9) may prescribe—

(a) the conditions that must be satisfied if a person is to be entitled to make such an election;

(b) the manner in which, and the time within which, such an election is to be made;

(c) the persons to whom, and the manner in which, notice of such an election is to be given;

(d) the information which a person who makes such an election is to provide, and the persons to whom, and the time within which, the person is to provide it;

(e) the time for which such an election is to have effect;

(f) which one of the person's employers under two or more contracts is to be regarded for the purposes of statutory shared parental pay as the person's employer under the contract.

(11) The powers under subsections (9) and (10) are without prejudice to any other power to make regulations under this Part.

(12) Regulations under any of subsections (4) to (10) must be made with the concurrence of the Commissioners for Her Majesty's Revenue and Customs.

Power to apply Part 12ZC

171ZZ5.—(1) The Secretary of State may by regulations provide for this Part to have effect in relation to cases which involve adoption, but not the placement of a child for adoption under the law of any part of the United Kingdom, with such modifications as the regulations may prescribe.

(2) The Secretary of State may by regulations provide for this Part to have effect in relation to cases which involve a person who has applied, or intends to apply, with another person for a parental order under section 54 of the Human Fertilisation and Embryology Act 2008 and a child who is, or will be, the subject of the order, with such modifications as the regulations may prescribe.

(3) Where section 171ZW(1)(b) has effect in relation to such cases as are described in subsection (2), regulations under section 171ZW(1)(b) may impose requirements to make statutory declarations as to—

(a) eligibility to apply for a parental order;

(b) intention to apply for such an order."

(2) In section 176 of the Social Security Contributions and Benefits Act 1992 (Parliamentary control of subordinate legislation), in subsection (1) (affirmative procedure), in paragraph (a), at the appropriate place there is inserted— " any of sections 171ZU to 171ZY;"

pp.122-123, *annotation to the Tax Credits Act 2002 s.2 (Function of Commissioners)*

The Tax Credits (Exercise of Functions) Order 2014 (SI 2014/3280), 5.013
made on December 10, 2014, empowers the Secretary of State to
exercise some tax credit functions concurrently with HMRC. From
April 1, 2015, those functions are the recovery of overpayments and of
any penalty imposed.

pp.123-128, *annotation to the Tax Credits Act 2002 s.3(5A) (Claims)*

In *SS v HMRC (TC)* [2014] UKUT 383 (AAC) Judge Rowley gives 5.014
a close and critical analysis of the conduct of decision-making by HMRC
officers and a First-tier Tribunal about whether two adults were a couple. The decision is critical of both HMRC and the tribunal but in
discussion the judge examines the evidence that both parties put and
should have put before the tribunal and the approach the tribunal should
have taken.

pp.166-168, *annotation to the Tax Credits Act 2002 s.29 (Recovery of overpayments)*

The Income Tax (Pay as You Earn) (Amendment No 4) Regulations 5.015
2014 (SI 2014/2689) empower Her Majesty's Revenue and Customs to
start recovering tax credit debts by using the PAYE coding and tax
deduction machinery to collect such debts. Separate legislation increases
the HMRC power to use tax coding in this way to a total debt of
£17,000. These regulations allow that maximum to be used for tax
credit debts. This will start with codings for the tax year 2015-16.

p.187, *annotation to the Tax Credits Act 2002 s.39 (Exercise of right of appeal)*

See now, with regard to the second health warning annotated to that 5.016
section, the Tax Credits, Child Benefit and Guardian's Allowance
Appeals (Appointed Day) (Northern Ireland) Order 2014 (SI
2014/2881) applying the provisions in SI 2014/886 to Northern Ireland.

p.189, *annotation to the Tax Credits Act 2002 s.39A (Late appeals)*

There has clearly been both confusion and inconsistency in dealing 5.017
with late appeals, notwithstanding the introduction of the new provisions
of s.39A from April 1, 2014. This is in part because the general view
appears now to be that s.39A only achieved part of its purpose, despite
the views expressed to Parliament in the explanatory note to the statutory instrument introducing it. Historically, it is clear that both HMRC
(and its predecessor) and tribunals had power to deal with late appeals
before November 4, 2008. A minor result— presumably unintended—of
the major reforms in 2008 is now accepted to be that from that date

while HMRC continued to have power to deal with late appeals, the relevant tribunal (the First-tier Tribunal) did not have that power. Then on April 1, 2009—again presumably without any specific intention so to do—other legislative changes took away the power of HMRC to deal with late appeals. While it has been argued that the decision of Judge Rowland is open to criticism for failure to deal with human rights issues and is limited in its binding effect to the position before the introduction of s.39A and supporting provisions, those are arguably weak arguments that must be set against the plainly binding authority of the central elements of the decision and the close reasoning of the whole decision. The position for any period before April 1, 2014 must therefore be that set out in that decision.

Unfortunately, and notwithstanding the careful rehearsal of the legislative history of this topic in Judge Rowland's decision, a third set of errors appear to have been made—yet again, it is assumed, unintentionally—when the new provisions incorporated in s.39A took effect on April 1, 2014. Here the result appears to be that HMRC again has power to deal with late appeals both before and after the new provisions take effect. But there is nothing to give the power back to tribunals retrospectively. And the effect of the one year absolute time limit in s.39A(1) is to bar consideration of any late appeal made before April 1, 2013. So it appears that old late appeals may still be caught by the unintended bar against late appeals and more recent appeals made before the new rules came in may enter a limbo where a tribunal has no jurisdiction to consider the matter. In such a case if HMRC does not agree to admitting a late appeal then tribunals cannot deal with it.

There is often an additional kind of confusion in these cases. Bearing in mind that there are at least two separate operative decisions for each tax year, and often more, it is always necessary to check against which decision or decisions a claimant is seeking to appeal. It may be that the result is that some decisions can be admitted late and considered while others remain late and outside the jurisdiction of a tribunal. A final point is that the time limit only starts when the provisions in s.23(2) of the Act are met. See paras 1.307-308 above. If there has been no proper notice of decision, then time cannot start running.

p.382, *Tax Credits Act 2002 (Commencement No. 4, Transitional Provisions and Savings) Order 2003 (SI 2003/938) art.2 (Commencement of provisions of the Act)*

5.018   The entry for art.2 should read as follows:
"**2.**—(1) Subject to the provisions of articles 3 and 4 (savings and transitional provisions), the provisions of the Act specified in this article shall come into force in accordance with the following paragraphs of this article.

(2) Section 47 (consequential amendments), so far as it relates to paragraphs 4 to 7 of Schedule 3, shall come into force on 1st April 2003.

(3) The following provisions of the Act shall come into force on 6th April 2003—

(a) section 1(3)(a) and (f) (abolition of children's tax credit under section 257AA of the Income and Corporation Taxes Act 1988 and employment credit);

(b) section 47, so far as it relates to the provisions of Schedule 3 specified in sub-paragraph (d);

(c) section 60 (repeals), so far as it relates to the provisions of Schedule 6 specified in sub-paragraph (e);

(d) in Schedule 3 (consequential amendments)—
    (i) paragraphs 1 to 3,
    (ii) paragraphs 8 and 9, and
    (iii) paragraphs 13 to 59; and

(e) in Schedule 6, the entries relating to the enactments specified in column 1 of Schedule 1 to this Order to the extent shown in column 2 of that Schedule.

(4) The following provisions of the Act shall come into force on 8th April 2003—

(a) section 1(3)(b) and (c) (abolition of working families' tax credit and disabled person's tax credit);

(b) section 47 so far as concerns the provisions of Schedule 3 mentioned in this paragraph;

(c) section 60 so far as concerns the entries in Schedule 6 referred to in sub-paragraph (e);
t1i27(d)
paragraphs 10 to 12 of Schedule 3 to the Act; and

(e) in Schedule 6 to the Act, the entries relating to the enactments specified in column 1 of Schedule 2 to this Order to the extent shown in column 2 of that Schedule.

(5) [¹ . . .]

AMENDMENT

1. Tax Credits Act 2002 (Commencement and Transitional Provisions)(Partial Revocation) Order 2014 (SI 2014/1848) art.2 (July 14, 2014).

p.382, *annotation to the Tax Credits Act 2002 (Commencement No. 4, Transitional Provisions and Savings) Order 2003 (SI 2003/938) art.2 (Commencement of provisions of the Act)*

The effect of the revocation of art.2(5) by SI 2014/1848 is to remove   5.019
the time limit for the revocation of the child premia paid on some cases to beneficiaries of income support and jobseeker's allowance.

p.383, *amendment to the Tax Credits Act 2002 (Transitional Provisions) Order 2008 (SI 2008/3151) art.3 (Amendments to the Tax Credits Act 2002 (Commencement No. 4, Transitional Provisions and Savings) Order 2003)*

With effect from July 14, 2014, art.4 of the Tax Credits Act 2002   5.020
(Commencement and Transitional Provisions) (Partial Revocation) Order 2014 (SI 2014/1848) revoked art.3(2).

p.384, *Tax Credits Act 2002 (Transitional Provisions) Order 2010 (SI 2010/644) art.3 (Transitional provisions)*

5.021   The entry for art.3(3) should read as follows:

"(3) Notwithstanding regulation 7 of the Tax Credits (Claims and Notifications) Regulations 2002, a person shall not be entitled to child tax credit in respect of any day prior to the day on which that person makes a claim for it ("the earlier day") if—
   (a) [¹ . . .]
   (b) the claimant is entitled, or in the case of a joint claim, either of the claimants is entitled, to the child premia on the earlier day."

In addition, the correct reference for the amending regulation is SI 2014/1848.

pp.394-397, *annotation to the Working Tax Credit (Entitlement and Maximum Rate) Regulations 2002 (SI 2002/2005) reg.4 (Entitlement to basic element of working tax credit: qualifying remunerative work)*

5.022   As to whether the work concerned has to be in the United Kingdom, see the comments of Judge Rowland in *GC v HMRC (TC)* [2014] UKUT 251 (AAC) noted at pp 579-80 below. In Route 1 of the second condition for the tax credit, the commentary notes that the test is in practical terms the same as for child benefit. This applies in most cases, but a person who is claiming child benefit because he or she is contributing to the child's maintenance costs at the specified rate cannot on that basis also claim child tax credit.

p.397, *amendments to the Working Tax Credit (Entitlement and Maximum Rate) Regulations 2002 (SI 2002/2005) reg.5 (Time off in connection with childbirth and adoption)*

5.023   With effect from December 31, 2014, art.11(2)(e) of the Shared Parental Leave and Statutory Shared Parental Pay (Consequential Amendments to Subordinate Legislation) Order 2014 (SI 2014/3255) inserted after sub-paragraph (ga) the following new sub-paragraphs:

"(h) is paid statutory shared parental pay,
   (i) is absent from work during a period of shared parental leave under section 75E or 75G of the Employment Rights Act 1996.".

Art.11(4) of the same amending regulations inserted after sub-paragraph (3A) the following new sub-paragraph:

"(3B) A person shall only be treated as being engaged in qualifying remunerative work by virtue of paragraph (1)(i) for such period as that person would have been paid statutory shared parental pay had the conditions of entitlement in Parts 2 or 3 of the Statutory Shared Parental Pay (General) Regulations 2014 been satisfied."

p.414, *amendments to the Working Tax Credit (Entitlement and Maximum Rate) Regulations 2002 (SI 2002/2005) reg.14 (Entitlement to childcare element of working tax credit)*

With effect from July 18, 2009, reg.5(2)(a) of the Tax Credits (Miscellaneous Amendments) Regulations 2009 (SI 2009/697) omitted sub-paragraph (1A)(b). 5.024

p.417, *amendments to the Working Tax Credit (Entitlement and Maximum Rate) Regulations 2002 (SI 2002/2005) reg.14 (Entitlement to childcare element of working tax credit)*

With effect from November 28, 2014, reg.4(2) of the Child Benefit (General) and Tax Credits (Miscellaneous Amendments) Regulations 2014 (SI 2014/2924) substituted for sub-paragraph (b) the following: 5.025

"(b) the child is certified as severely sight impaired or blind by a consultant ophthalmologist;"
and in sub-paragraph (c), for "registered as blind in such a register", substituted "certified as severely sight impaired or blind by a consultant ophthalmologist".

p.426, *amendment to the Working Tax Credit (Entitlement and Maximum Rate) Regulations 2002 (SI 2002/2005) Sch.1 (Disability which puts a person at a disadvantage in getting a job), paragraph 9*

With effect from November 28, 2014, reg.4(3) of the Child Benefit (General) and Tax Credits (Miscellaneous Amendments) Regulations 2014 (SI 2014/2924) substituted for paragraph (9) of Part 1 the following: 5.026

"**9.** He is certified as severely sight impaired or blind by a consultant ophthalmologist."

p.427, *annotation to the Working Tax Credit (Entitlement and Maximum Rate) Regulations 2002 (SI 2002/2005) Sch.1 (Disability which puts a person at a disadvantage in getting a job), paragraph 9*

The new paragraph 9 replaces the previous tests that relied on entries in registers maintained by local or health authorities, a process being made more difficult to operate in parallel with the approach adopted centrally for social security benefits as devolved governments adopt different approaches. 5.027

p.441, *amendment to the Tax Credits (Definition and Calculation of Income) Regulations 2002 (SI 2002/2006), reg.4 (Employment income)*

With effect from December 31, 2014, art.12(2)(a)(iii) of the Shared Parental Leave and Statutory Shared Parental Pay (Consequential Amendments to Subordinate Legislation) Order 2014 (SI 2014/3255) 5.028

substituted ", statutory shared parental pay or adoption pay" for "or adoption pay" in paragraph (1)(h).

p.441, *amendment to the Tax Credits (Definition and Calculation of Income) Regulations 2002 (SI 2002/2006), reg.4 (Employment income)*

5.029   With effect from November 28, 2014, reg.5 of the Child Benefit (General) and Tax Credits (Miscellaneous Amendments) Regulations 2014 (SI 2014/2924) inserted after entry 21 the following new entry:

"**22.** The payment of a qualifying bonus within section 312A of ITEPA (limited exemption for qualifying bonus payments)."

p.457, *amendment to the Tax Credits (Definition and Calculation of Income) Regulations 2002 (SI 2002/2006) reg.7 (Social security income)*

5.030   With effect from December 31, 2014, art.12(3)(b) of the Shared Parental Leave and Statutory Shared Parental Pay (Consequential Amendments to Subordinate Legislation) Order 2014 (SI 2014/3255) inserted after entry 21A in Table 3 the following new entry:
"**21B.** Statutory shared parental pay under Part 12ZC of the Contributions and Benefits Act."

pp.484-485, *amendments to the Child Tax Credit Regulations 2002 (SI 2002/2006) reg.2 (Interpretation)*

5.031   With effect from June 4, 2014, reg.2 is amended by reg.3 of the Child Benefit (General) and Child Tax Credit (Amendment) Regulations 2014 (SI 2014/1231) so as to omit the words "full-time education for the purposes of" in the definition of "advanced education" and to omit the definition of "full-time education".

p.495, *amendments to the Child Tax Credit Regulations 2002 (SI 2002/2007) reg.5 (Maximum age and prescribed conditions for a qualifying young person)*

5.032   With effect from November 28, 2014, reg.3(2) of the Child Benefit (General) and Tax Credits (Miscellaneous Amendments) Regulations 2014 (SI 2014/2924) inserted "and shall include gaps between the ending of one course and the commencement of another, where the person enrols on and commences the latter course" at the end of reg.5(5).

With effect from June 4, 2014, reg.3 of the Child Benefit (General) and Child Tax Credit (Amendment) Regulations 2014 (SI 2014/1231), inserted a new para.(5A) after reg.5(5) as follows:

"(5A) If paragraph (5) does not apply, then for the purposes of paragraphs (3) and (4) a person shall be treated as being in full-time education if that person is being provided with "appropriate full-time education" in England within section 4 (appropriate full-time education or training) of the Education and Skills Act 2008."

p.498, *amendments to the Child Tax Credit Regulations 2002 (SI 2002/2007) reg.8 (Prescribed conditions for a disabled or severely disabled child or qualifying young person)*

With effect from November 28, 2014, reg.3(3) of the Child Benefit **5.033** (General) and Tax Credits (Miscellaneous Amendments) Regulations 2014 (SI 2014/2924) substituted for sub-paragraph (2)(b) the following:

"(b) he is certified as severely sight impaired or blind by a consultant ophthalmologist;"
and in sub-paragraph (2)(c), omitted the words "registered or", and inserted "severely sight impaired or" before "blind".

p.499, *annotation to the Child Tax Credit Regulations 2002 (SI 2002/2007) reg.8 (Prescribed conditions for a disabled or severely disabled child or qualifying young person)*

The new sub-paragraph (2)(b) replaces the previous tests that relied **5.034** on entries in registers maintained by local or health authorities, a process being made more difficult to operate in parallel with the approach adopted centrally for social security benefits as devolved governments adopt different approaches.

p.536, *amendments to the Tax Credits (Claims and Notifications) Regulations 2002 (SI 2002/2014), reg.27 (Advance notification)*

With effect from November 1, 2006, reg.7 of the Tax Credits (Claims **5.035** and Notifications) (Amendment) Regulations 2006 (SI 2006/2689) substituted "to" for ", (2A) and" in para.(1) and inserted after paragraph (2A) the following—

"(2B) The circumstances prescribed by this paragraph are those where a child is expected to become a qualifying young person for the purposes of Part 1 of the Act."

p.575, *amendments to the Tax Credits (Residence) Regulations 2003 (SI 2003/654) reg.3 (Circumstances in which a person is treated as not being in the United Kingdom)*

With effect from July 1, 2014, regs 2 and 6 of the Child Benefit **5.036** (General) and the Tax Credits (Residence) (Amendment) Regulations 2014 (SI 2014/1511) substituted "Paragraphs (1) and (6) do" for "Paragraph (1) does" in para.(2), added "and paragraph (6) shall not apply" at the end of para.(3) and inserted after para.(5) the following new paragraphs:

"(6) Subject to paragraph (7), a person is to be treated as being in the United Kingdom for the purposes of Part 1 of the Act where he makes a claim for child tax credit only if that person has been living in the United Kingdom for 3 months before that claim plus any time taken into account by regulation 7 of the Tax Credits (Claims and Notifications) Regulations 2002 for determining for the purpose of that regulation when the claim is treated as having been made.

(7) Paragraph (6) shall not apply where the person—

(a) most recently entered the United Kingdom before 1st July 2014;

(b) is a worker or a self-employed person in the United Kingdom for the purposes of Council Directive 2004/38/EC (rights of citizens of the European Union and their family members to move and reside freely within the territory of the Member States);

(c) retains the status of a worker or self-employed person in the United Kingdom pursuant to Article 7(3) of Council Directive 2004/38/EC;

(d) is treated as a worker in the United Kingdom pursuant to regulation 5 of the Accession of Croatia (Immigration and Worker Authorisation) Regulations 2013 (right of residence of a Croatian who is an "accession State national subject to worker authorisation");

(e) is a family member of a person referred to in sub-paragraphs (b), (c), (d) or (i);

(f) is a person to whom regulation 4 applies (persons temporarily absent from the United Kingdom) and who returns to the United Kingdom within 52 weeks starting from the first day of the temporary absence;

(g) returns to the United Kingdom after a period abroad of less than 52 weeks where immediately before departing from the United Kingdom that person had been ordinarily resident in the United Kingdom for a continuous period of 3 months;

(h) returns to the United Kingdom otherwise as a worker or self-employed person after a period abroad and where, otherwise than for a period of up to 3 months ending on the day of returning, that person has paid either Class 1 or Class 2 contributions pursuant to regulation 114, 118, 146 or 147 of the Social Security (Contributions) Regulations 2001 or pursuant to an Order in Council having effect under section 179 of the Social Security Administration Act 1992;

(i) is not a national of an EEA State and would be a worker or self-employed person in the United Kingdom for the purposes of Council Directive 2004/38/EC if that person were a national of an EEA State;

(j) is a refugee as defined in Article 1 of the Convention relating to the Status of Refugees done at Geneva on 28th July 1951, as extended by Article 1(2) of the Protocol relating to the Status of Refugees done at New York on 31st January 1967;

(k) has been granted leave, or is deemed to have been granted leave, outside the rules made under section 3(2) of the Immigration Act 1971 where that leave is—

    (i) granted by the Secretary of State with recourse to public funds, or

    (ii) deemed to have been granted by virtue of regulation 3 of the Displaced Persons (Temporary Protection) Regulations 2005;

(l) has been granted leave to remain in the United Kingdom by the Secretary of State pending an application for indefinite leave to remain as a victim of domestic violence;

(m) has been granted humanitarian protection by the Secretary of State under Rule 339C of Part 11 of the rules made under section 3(2) of the Immigration Act 1971.

(8) In this regulation, a "family member" means a person who is defined as a family member of another person in Article 2 of Council Directive 2004/38/EC.

(9) In this regulation, "EEA State", in relation to any time, means a state which at that time is a member State, or any other state which at that time is a party to the agreement on the European Economic Area signed at Oporto on 2nd May, together with the Protocol adjusting that Agreement signed at Brussels on 17th March 1993, as modified or supplemented from time to time."

p.575, *annotation to the Tax Credits (Residence) Regulations 2003 (SI 2003/654) reg.3 (Circumstances in which a person is treated as not being in the United Kingdom)*

The amendments to reg.3 are parallel to amendments for child bene-   5.037
fit. Both impose, with a lengthy list of exceptions, a general rule that anyone entering the United Kingdom from July 1, 2014 must be living here for three months before claiming.

pp.579-580, *annotation to the Tax Credits (Residence) Regulations 2003 (SI 2003/654) reg.4 (Persons temporarily absent from the United Kingdom)*

In *GC v HMRC (TC)* [2014] UKUT 251 (AAC) Judge Rowland   5.038
allowed an appeal by an appellant who was refused working tax credit while working in Spain. The appellant had returned to the United Kingdom for periods during the year. In that context, no attention had been paid to the provisions of reg.4 of these Regulations allowing a person to continue to be regarded as being in the UK during the first 8 weeks of a temporary absence. These should be considered to see if the appellant continued to be ordinarily resident in the United Kingdom. Further, there was nothing in the Working Tax Credit (Entitlement and

Maximum Rate) Regulations 2002 (SI 2002/2005) requiring that the work had to be in the United Kingdom.

p.609, *amendment to the Child Benefit (General) Regulations 2006 (SI2006/223) reg. 1 (Citation, commencement and interpretation)*

5.039   With effect from June 4, 2014, reg. 2(2)(a) of the Child Benefit (General) and Child Tax Credit (Amendment) Regulations 2014 (SI 2014/1231) amended reg.1(3) by substituting in the definition of "approved training" for sub-paras (c) and (d) the following:

> "(c) in relation to Scotland, known as "Employability Fund activity"; or,
> (d) in relation to Northern Ireland, known as "Training for Success" including "Programme Led Apprenticeships", the "Pathways for Young People" element of "Pathways for Success" or the "Collaboration and Innovation Programme";".

p.610, *amendment to the Chid Benefit (General) Regulations 2006 (SI 2006/223) reg.1 (citation, commencement and interpretation)*

5.040   With effect from June 4, 2014, reg.2(2)(b) of the Child Benefit (General) and Child Tax Credit (Amendment) Regulations 2014 (SI 2014/1231) amended reg.1(3) by inserting "except in regulation 3(2)(ab)" after "full-time education" in the definition of "full-time education".

p.612, *amendment to the Child Benefit (General) Regulations 2006 (SI 2006/223) reg.3(2) (Education and training condition)*

5.041   With effect from June 4, 2014, reg. 2(3) of the Child Benefit (General) and Child Tax Credit (Amendment) Regulations 2014 (SI 2014/1231) amended reg.3 by inserting in reg.3(2) after sub-para.(a) the following —

> "(ab) is being provided with "appropriate full-time education" in England within section 4 (appropriate full-time education or training) of the Education and Skills Act 2008, which is not—
> > (i) a course in preparation for a degree, a diploma of higher education, a higher national certificate, a higher national diploma, a teaching qualification, any other course which is of a standard of Edexcel, a general certificate of education (advanced level), or Scottish national qualifications at higher or advanced higher level;
> > (ii) provided by virtue of his employment or any office held by him;"

and substituting "paragraph (a) or (ab)" for "paragraph (a)" in sub-para.(b), as well as substituting "paragraph (2)(a), (2)(ab)" for "paragraph (2)(a)" in reg.3(4).

With effect from November 28, 2014, reg.2 of the Child Benefit (General) and Tax Credits (Miscellaneous Amendments) Regulations 2014 (SI 2014/2924) inserted "above ordinary national diploma, a national diploma or national certificate" after "standard" in reg.3(2)(ab)(i).

p.625, *amendment to the Child Benefit (General) Regulations 2006 (SI 2006/223) reg.23 (Circumstances in which person treated as not being in Great Britain)*

With effect from July 1, 2014, regs 2 and 3 of the Child Benefit (General) and the Tax Credits (Residence) (Amendment) Regulations 2014 (SI 2014/1511) substituted "Paragraphs (1) and (5) do" for "Paragraph (1) does" in para.(2), inserted "and paragraph (5) shall not apply" at the end of para.(3) and inserted after para.(4) the following new paragraphs:

5.042

"(5) Subject to paragraph (6), a person is to be treated as being in Great Britain for the purposes of section 146(2) of SSCBA only if that person has been living in the United Kingdom for 3 months ending on the first day of the week referred to in that section.

(6) Paragraph (5) does not apply where the person—

(a) most recently entered the United Kingdom before 1st July 2014;

(b) is a worker or a self-employed person in the United Kingdom for the purposes of Council Directive 2004/38/EC (rights of citizens of the European Union and their family members to move and reside freely within the territory of the Member States);

(c) retains the status of a worker or self-employed person in the United Kingdom pursuant to Article 7(3) of Council Directive 2004/38/EC;

(d) is treated as a worker in the United Kingdom pursuant to regulation 5 of the Accession of Croatia (Immigration and Worker Authorisation) Regulations 2013 (right of residence of a Croatian who is an "accession State national subject to worker authorisation");

(e) is a family member of a person referred to in sub-paragraphs (b), (c), (d) or (i);

(f) is a person to whom regulation 24 applies (persons temporarily absent from Great Britain) and who returns to Great Britain within 52 weeks starting from the first day of the temporary absence;

(g) returns to the United Kingdom after a period abroad of less than 52 weeks where immediately before departing from the United Kingdom that person had been ordinarily resident in the United Kingdom for a continuous period of 3 months;

(h) returns to Great Britain otherwise than as a worker or self-employed person after a period abroad and where, otherwise than for a period of up to 3 months ending on the day of returning, that person has paid either Class 1 or Class 2 contributions by virtue of regulation 114, 118, 146 or 147 of the Social Security (Contributions) Regulations 2001 or pursuant to an Order in Council having effect under section 179 of the Social Security Administration Act 1992;

(i) is not a national of an EEA State and would be a worker or self-employed person in the United Kingdom for the purposes of Council Directive 2004/38/EC if that person were a national of an EEA State;

(j) is a refugee as defined in Article 1 of the Convention relating to the Status of Refugees done at Geneva on 28th July 1951, as extended by Article 1(2) of the Protocol relating to the Status of Refugees done at New York on 31st January 1967;

(k) has been granted leave, or is deemed to have been granted leave, outside the rules made under section 3(2) of the Immigration Act 1971 where the leave is —

(i) granted by the Secretary of State with recourse to public funds, or

(ii) deemed to have been granted by virtue of regulation 3 of the Displaced Persons (Temporary Protection) Regulations 2005;

(l) has been granted leave to remain in the United Kingdom by the Secretary of State pending an application for indefinite leave to remain as a victim of domestic violence;

(m) has been granted humanitarian protection by the Secretary of State under rule 339C of Part 11 of the rules made under section 3(2) of the Immigration Act 1971.

(7) In this regulation, a "family member" means a person who is defined as a family member of another person in Article 2 of Council Directive 2004/38/EC.".

p.628, *amendments to the Child Benefit (General) Regulations 2006 (SI 2006/223) reg.27 (Circumstances in which person treated as not being in Northern Ireland)*

5.043 With effect from July 1, 2014, regs 2 and 4 of the Child Benefit (General) and the Tax Credits (Residence) (Amendment) Regulations 2014 (SI 2014/1511) inserted "and paragraph (4) shall not apply" at the end of para.(2) and inserted after para.(3) the following new paragraphs:

"(4) Subject to paragraph (5), a person is to be treated as being in Northern Ireland for the purposes of section 142(2) of SSCB(NI)A only if that person has been living in the United Kingdom for 3 months ending on the first day of the week referred to in that section.

(5) Paragraph (4) does not apply where the person—

(a) most recently entered the United Kingdom before 1st July 2014;

(b) is a worker or a self-employed person in the United Kingdom for the purposes of Council Directive 2004/38/EC;

(c) retains the status of a worker or self-employed person in the United Kingdom pursuant to Article 7(3) of Council Directive 2004/38/EC;

(d) is treated as a worker in the United Kingdom pursuant to regulation 5 of the Accession of Croatia (Immigration and Worker Authorisation) Regulations 2013 (right of residence of a Croatian who is an "accession State national subject to worker authorisation");

(e) is a family member of a person referred to in sub-paragraphs (b), (c), (d) or (i);

(f) is a person to whom regulation 28 applies (persons temporarily absent from Northern Ireland) and who returns to Northern Ireland within 52 weeks starting from the first day of the temporary absence;

(g) returns to the United Kingdom after a period abroad of less than 52 weeks where immediately before departing from the United Kingdom that person had been ordinarily resident in the United Kingdom for a continuous period of 3 months;

(h) returns to Northern Ireland otherwise than as a worker or self-employed person after a period abroad and where, otherwise than for a period of up to 3 months ending on the day of returning, that person has paid either Class 1 or Class 2 contributions by virtue of regulation 114, 118, 146 or 147 of the Social Security (Contributions) Regulations 2001 or pursuant to an Order in Council having effect under section 179 of the Social Security Administration Act 1992;

(i) is not a national of an EEA State and would be a worker or self-employed person in the United Kingdom for the purposes of Council Directive 2004/38/EC if that person were a national of an EEA State;

(j) is a refugee as defined in Article 1 of the Convention relating to the Status of Refugees done at Geneva on 28th July 1951, as extended by Article 1(2) of the Protocol relating to the Status of Refugees done at New York on 31st January 1967;

(k) has been granted leave, or is deemed to have been granted leave, outside the rules made under section 3(2) of the Immigration Act 1971 where that leave is—

   (i) granted by the Secretary of State with recourse to public funds, or

   (ii) deemed to have been granted by virtue of regulation 3 of the Displaced Persons (Temporary Protection) Regulations 2005;

(l) has been granted leave to remain in the United Kingdom by the Secretary of State pending an application for indefinite leave to remain as a victim of domestic violence;

(m) has been granted humanitarian protection by the Secretary of State under Rule 339C of Part 11 of the rules made under section 3(2) of the Immigration Act 1971.

(6) In this regulation, a "family member" means a person who is defined as a family member of another person in Article 2 of Council Directive 2004/38/EC.".

p.667, *amendment to the Statutory Sick Pay (General) Regulations 1982 (SI 1982/894) reg.17 (Meaning of "earnings")*

5.044   With effect from December 31, 2014, art.3 of the Shared Parental Leave and Statutory Shared Parental Pay (Consequential Amendments to Subordinate Legislation) Order 2014 (SI 2014/3255) replaced the full stop at the end of sub-paragraph (j) with a semi-colon and inserted the following new sub-paragraph:

> "(k) any sum payable by way of statutory shared parental pay, including any sums payable in accordance with regulations made under section 171ZX(3) of the Contributions and Benefits Act.".

p.698, *amendment to the Statutory Maternity Pay (General) Regulations 1986 (SI 1986/1960) reg.11 (Continuous employment)*

5.045   With effect from December 31, 2014, art.4(2) of the Shared Parental Leave and Statutory Shared Parental Pay (Consequential Amendments to Subordinate Legislation) Order 2014 (SI 2014/3255) inserted ", shared parental leave" in para.(1)(e) after "adoption leave".

p.704, *amendment to the Statutory Maternity Pay (General) Regulations 1986 (SI 1986/1960) reg.20 (Meaning of "earnings")*

5.046   With effect from December 31, 2014, art.4(2) of the Shared Parental Leave and Statutory Shared Parental Pay (Consequential Amendments to Subordinate Legislation) Order 2014 (SI 2014/3255) replaced the full stop at the end of sub-paragraph (g) with a semi-colon and inserted the following new sub-paragraph:

> "(h) any sum payable by way of statutory shared parental pay, including any sums payable in accordance with regulations made under section 171ZX(3) of the Contributions and Benefits Act.".

p.766, *amendment to the Statutory Paternity Pay and Statutory Adoption Pay (General) Regulations 2002 (SI 2002/2822) (Insertion of new reg.5A)*

5.047   With effect from December 1, 2014, but as regards entitlement only in respect of children whose expected week of birth begins on or after April 5, 2015 (SPP (birth)) or who are placed for adoption on or after April 5, 2015 ((SPP) adoption), regs.3 and 4 of the Statutory Paternity Pay and Statutory Adoption Pay (General) (Amendment) Regulations 2014 (SI 2014/2862) inserted after reg.5 the following new regulation:

"Notice of entitlement to statutory paternity pay (birth)

5A. The notice provided for in section 171ZC(1) of the Act must be given to the employer—

(a) in or before the 15th week before the expected week of the child's birth, or
(b) in a case where it was not reasonably practicable for the employee to give the notice in accordance with sub-paragraph (a), as soon as is reasonably practicable."

p.766, *amendment to the Statutory Paternity Pay and Statutory Adoption Pay (General) Regulations 2002 (SI 2002/2822) reg.6 (Period of payment of statutory paternity pay (birth))*

With effect from December 1, 2014, but as regards entitlement only in respect of children whose expected week of birth begins on or after April 5, 2015 (SPP (birth)) or who are placed for adoption on or after April 5, 2015 ((SPP) adoption), regs 3 and 5 of the Statutory Paternity Pay and Statutory Adoption Pay (General) (Amendment) Regulations 2014 (SI 2014/2862) substituted a new sub-paragraph (4) as follows: **5.048**

"(4) An employee who has made a choice in accordance with paragraph (1) may vary the date chosen provided that the employee gives the employer notice of the variation—
(a) where the variation is to provide for the employee's statutory paternity pay period to begin on the date on which the child is born, or where he is at work on that day, the following day, at least 28 days before the first day of the expected week of the child's birth;
(b) where the variation is to provide for the employee's statutory paternity pay period to begin on a date that is a specified number of days (or a different specified number of days) after the date on which the child is born, at least 28 days before the date falling that number of days after the first day of the expected week of the child's birth;
(c) where the variation is to provide for the employee's statutory paternity pay period to begin on a predetermined date (or a different predetermined date), at least 28 days before that date,
or, if it is not reasonably practicable to give the notice at least 28 days before whichever day or date is relevant, as soon as is reasonably practicable."

p.768, *amendment to the Statutory Paternity Pay and Statutory Adoption Pay (General) Regulations 2002 (SI 2002/2822) reg.9 (Evidence of entitlement to statutory paternity pay (birth))*

With effect from December 1, 2014, but as regards entitlement only in respect of children whose expected week of birth begins on or after April 5, 2015 (SPP (birth)) or who are placed for adoption on or after April 5, 2015 ((SPP) adoption), regs 3 and 6 of the Statutory Paternity Pay and Statutory Adoption Pay (General) (Amendment) Regulations 2014 (SI 2014/2862) substituted a new sub-paragraph (3) as follows: **5.049**

"(3) The information and declaration referred to in paragraph (1) shall be provided—

    (a) in or before the 15th week before the expected week of the child's birth, or

    (b) in a case where it was not reasonably practicable for the employee to provide it in accordance with sub-paragraph (a), as soon as is reasonably practicable."

p.769, *amendment to the Statutory Paternity Pay and Statutory Adoption Pay (General) Regulations 2002 (SI 2002/2822) (Insertion of new reg.11A)*

5.050   With effect from December 1, 2014, but as regards entitlement only in respect of children whose expected week of birth begins on or after April 5, 2015 (SPP (birth)) or who are placed for adoption on or after April 5, 2015 ((SPP) adoption), regs 3 and 7 of the Statutory Paternity Pay and Statutory Adoption Pay (General) (Amendment) Regulations 2014 (SI 2014/2862) inserted after reg.11 the following new regulation:

"Notice of entitlement to statutory paternity pay (adoption)

11A.- The notice provided for in section 171ZC(1) of the Act must be given to the employer—

    (a) no more than seven days after the date on which the adopter is notified of having been matched with the child, or

    (b) in a case where it was not reasonably practicable for the employee to give notice in accordance with sub-paragraph (a), as soon as is reasonably practicable."

p.770, *amendment to the Statutory Paternity Pay and Statutory Adoption Pay (General) Regulations 2002 (SI 2002/2822) reg.12 (Period of payment of statutory paternity pay (adoption))*

5.051   With effect from December 1, 2014, but as regards entitlement only in respect of children whose expected week of birth begins on or after April 5, 2015 (SPP (birth)) or who are placed for adoption on or after April 5, 2015 ((SPP) adoption), regs 3 and 8 of the Statutory Paternity Pay and Statutory Adoption Pay (General) (Amendment) Regulations 2014 (SI 2014/2862) substituted a new sub-paragraph (4) as follows:

"(4) An employee who has made a choice in accordance with paragraph (1) may vary the date chosen provided that the employee gives the employer notice of the variation—

    (a) where the variation is to provide for the employee's statutory paternity pay period to begin on the date on which the child is placed with the adopter or, where the person is at work on that day, the following day, at least 28 days before the date provided under regulation 15(2)(b) as the date on which the child is expected to be placed for adoption;

    (b) where the variation is to provide for the employee's statutory paternity pay period to begin on a date that is a specified number of days (or a different specified number of days) after the date on which the child is placed with the adopter, at least 28 days before the date falling that number of days after the date provided under regulation 15(2)(b) as the date on which the child is expected to be placed for adoption;

(c) where the variation is to provide for the employee's statutory paternity pay period to begin on a predetermined date, at least 28 days before that date,

or, if it is not reasonably practicable to give the notice at least 28 days before whichever date is relevant, as soon as is reasonably practicable."

p.771, *amendment to the Statutory Paternity Pay and Statutory Adoption Pay (General) Regulations 2002 (SI 2002/2822) reg.15 (Evidence of entitlement to statutory paternity pay (adoption))*

With effect from December 1, 2014, but as regards entitlement only in respect of children whose expected week of birth begins on or after April 5, 2015 (SPP (birth)) or who are placed for adoption on or after April 5, 2015 ((SPP) adoption), regs 3 and 9 of the Statutory Paternity Pay and Statutory Adoption Pay (General) (Amendment) Regulations 2014 (SI 2014/2862) substituted a new sub-paragraph (3) as follows: 5.052

"(3) The information and declaration referred to in paragraph (1) shall be provided—

(a) no more than seven days after the date on which the adopter is notified of having been matched with the child, or

(b) in a case where it was not reasonably practicable for the employee to provide it in accordance with sub-paragraph (a), as soon as is reasonably practicable."

p.787, *amendment to the Social Security Contributions and Benefits Act 1992 (Application of Parts 12ZA and 12ZB to Adoptions from Overseas) Regulations 2003 (SI 2013/499) (Title)*

With effect from November 19, 2014, regs 2 and 3 of the Social Security Contributions and Benefits Act 1992 (Application of Parts 12ZA and 12ZB to Adoptions from Overseas) (Amendment) Regulations 2014 (SI 2014/2857) substituted ", 12ZB and 12ZC" for "and 12ZB" in the title to the Regulations. In addition, regs 2 and 4 accordingly substituted ", 12ZB and 12ZC" for "and 12ZB" in reg.1(1). 5.053

p.788, *amendment to the Social Security Contributions and Benefits Act 1992 (Application of Parts 12ZA and 12ZB to Adoptions from Overseas) Regulations 2003 (SI 2013/499) (Insertion of new reg.4)*

With effect from November 19, 2014, regs 2 and 5 of the Social Security Contributions and Benefits Act 1992 (Application of Parts 5.054

12ZA and 12ZB to Adoptions from Overseas) (Amendment) Regulations 2014 (SI 2014/2857) inserted after reg.3 the following new regulation:

"Application of Part 12ZC of the Act to adoptions from overseas

4. Part 12ZC of the Act shall apply in relation to adoptions from overseas, with the modifications of section 171ZV of the Act specified in the second column of Schedule 3.".

p.788, *amendment to the Social Security Contributions and Benefits Act 1992 (Application of Parts 12ZA and 12ZB to Adoptions from Overseas) Regulations 2003 (SI 2013/499) (Insertion of new Sch.3)*

5.055 With effect from November 19, 2014, regs 2 and 6 of the Social Security Contributions and Benefits Act 1992 (Application of Parts 12ZA and 12ZB to Adoptions from Overseas) (Amendment) Regulations 2014 (SI 2014/2857) inserted after Sch.2 the following new Sch.3:

"SCHEDULE 3   Regulation 4

APPLICATION OF PART 12ZC OF THE ACT TO ADOPTIONS FROM OVERSEAS

Provision	Modification
Section 171ZV	In subsection (1), for "with whom a child is, or is expected to be, placed for adoption under the law of any part of the United Kingdom" substitute "by whom a child is, or is expected to be, adopted from overseas".
	In paragraph (g) of subsection (2), for "placement for adoption of the child" substitute "adoption of the child from overseas".
	In paragraph (a) of subsection (4), for "with whom a child is, or is expected to be, placed for adoption under the law of any part of the United Kingdom" substitute "by whom a child is, or is expected to be, adopted from overseas".
	In paragraph (h) of subsection (4), for "placement for adoption of the child" substitute "adoption of the child from overseas".
	In subsection (16), for "placement for adoption" substitute "adoption from overseas".
	After subsection (16) insert—
	"(16A) For the purposes of this section, a person adopts a child from overseas if the person adopts a child who enters Great Britain from outside the United Kingdom in connection with or for the purposes of adoption which does not involve the placement of the child for adoption under the law of any part of the United Kingdom.".
	Omit subsection (17).
	Omit subsection (18)."

p.852, *amendment to the Child Trust Funds Regulations 2004 (SI 2004/1450) reg.2(1)(b) (Interpretation)*

With effect from August 1, 2014, reg. 2 and para.13 of the Sch. to the 5.056
Co-operative and Community Benefit Societies and Credit Unions Act
2010 (Consequential Amendments) Regulations 2014 (SI 2014/1815)
substituted "a registered society" for "an industrial and provident society" in paragraph (iii) and substituted "registered society"; for "industrial and provident society" in paragraph (iv) of the definition of
"company" in reg.2(1)(b). The same amending provisions omitted the
definition "industrial and provident society" in reg.2(1)(b) and after the
definition of "registered friendly society" inserted the following new
definition:
""registered society" means—
    (a) a registered society within the meaning given by section
        1(1) of the Co-operative and Community Benefit Societies
        Act 2014; or
    (b) a society registered or deemed to be registered under the
        Industrial and Provident Societies Act (Northern Ireland)
        1969;"

p.867, *amendment to the Child Trust Funds Regulations 2004 (SI 2004/1450) reg.9 (Annual limit on subscriptions)*

With effect from July 1, 2014, regs 2 and 3 of the Child Trust Funds 5.057
(Amendment No.2) Regulations 2014 (SI 2014/1453) amended
reg.9(2) and (3) by substituting "£4,000" for "£3,840".

p.867, *amendment to the Child Trust Funds Regulations 2004 (SI 2004/1450) reg.12 (Qualifying investments for an account)*

With effect from July 1, 2014, regs 2 and 4 of the Child Trust Funds 5.058
(Amendment No.2) Regulations 2014 (SI 2014/1453) amended
reg.12(2) by substituting ";" for "." at the end of sub-paragraph (q) and
after sub-paragraph (q) inserting:

"(r) core capital deferred shares within the meaning of regulation 2 of
    the Building Societies (Core Capital Deferred Shares) Regula-
    tions 2013, provided that such shares are listed on the official list
    of a recognised stock exchange."

PART VI

UPDATING MATERIAL
VOLUME V

UNIVERSAL CREDIT

Commentary by

John Mesher

Richard Poynter

Nick Wikeley

Penny Wood

Important preliminary note
This Part is divided into two sections. Section A comprises the full text of the Commencement Orders (as amended) and the new Transitional Provisions Regulations currently in force for Universal Credit. Section B includes the rest of the usual updating material for Volume V.

SECTION A

UNIVERSAL CREDIT: COMMENCEMENT ORDERS AND TRANSITIONAL PROVISIONS REGULATIONS

The Welfare Reform Act 2012 (Commencement No. 9 and Transitional and Transitory Provisions and Commencement No. 8 and Savings and Transitional Provisions (Amendment)) Order 2013

(SI 2013/983) (C. 41) (as amended)

ARRANGEMENT OF ARTICLES   6.001

9. Transitional provision: conversion of incapacity benefits
10. Transition from old style ESA
11. Transition from new style ESA
12. Transition from old style JSA
13. Transition from new style JSA
14. Sanctions: transition from old style ESA in case of a new award
15. Sanctions: transition from old style ESA in case of a continuing award
16. Escalation of sanctions: transition from old style ESA
17. Sanctions: transition from old style JSA in case of a new award
18. Sanctions: transition from old style JSA in case of a continuing award
19. Escalation of sanctions: transition from old style JSA
20. Termination of sanctions under a new style ESA or JSA award
21. Transitory provisions: appeals
22. Transitional provision: references to contributory employment and support allowance and contribution-based jobseeker's allowance
23. Amendment of the Welfare Reform Act 2012 (Commencement No 8 and Savings and Transitional Provisions) Order 2013
24. Appeals relating to ESA and JSA

Schedule 1 Postcode districts
Schedule 2 Universal credit provisions coming into force in relation to certain claims and
awards
Schedule 3 Commencement of repeals in Part 1 of Schedule 14 to the Act
Schedule 4 Modifications of the Transitional Provisions Regulations 2010
Schedule 5 The Gateway conditions

The Secretary of State, in exercise of the powers conferred by section 150(3) and (4)(a), (b)(i) and (c) of the Welfare Reform Act 2012, makes the following Order:

GENERAL NOTE

6.002   This Commencement Order ("the Commencement No. 9 Order") was the first to "roll out" the new universal credit scheme. It has to be read together with the Transitional Provisions Regulations 2013 (now replaced by the Transitional Provisions Regulations 2014). This Order accordingly brought into force, albeit for limited purposes only, provisions of the WRA 2012 that relate to both the introduction of universal credit and the abolition of income-related ESA and income-based JSA. This was achieved by reference to the specific categories of cases set out in arts 3 and 4. However, these provisions applied only to four postcode districts in Manchester, Oldham and Stockport (or "the relevant districts"; see Sch.1) as from April 29, 2013 (also the date on which the Transitional Provisions Regulations 2013 came into force).

This Order was followed by the Commencement No. 11 Order (certain postcodes in Wigan ("the No. 2 relevant districts") and Manchester, Oldham and Warrington ("the No. 3 relevant districts") as from July 1, 2013), the Commencement No. 13 Order (certain postcodes in West London, Manchester and Wigan ("the No. 4 relevant districts") as from October 28, 2013) and the

Commencement No. 14 Order (certain postcodes in Rugby, Inverness and Perth ("the No. 5 relevant districts") as from November 25, 2013). See now, in addition, the Commencement Orders No. 15, No. 16, No. 17, No. 19 and No. 20, covering the No. 6 to No. 28 relevant districts. See also the further amendments made by the Welfare Reform Act 2012 (Commencement No. 9, 11, 13, 14, 16 and 17 and Transitional and Transitory Provisions (Amendment)) Order 2014 (SI 2014/1661) Welfare Reform Act 2012 (Commencement No. 9, 11, 13, 14, 16 and 17 and Transitional and Transitory Provisions (Amendment) (No. 2)) Order 2014 (SI 2014/1923).

In addition, of course, a claimant who lived in one of the four originally **6.003** specified postcode districts had also to be a member of the Pathfinder Group, i.e. be a person who met the requirements of regulations 5 to 12 of the Transitional Provisions Regulations 2013. However, as noted above the No. 9 Commencement Order (along with the No. 11, 13, 14 and 16 Commencement Orders) was amended by the Welfare Reform Act 2012 (Commencement No. 9, 11, 13, 14, 16 and 17 and Transitional and Transitory Provisions (Amendment)) Order 2014 (SI 2014/1661). In conjunction with these changes, the Transitional Provisions Regulations 2013 were revoked and replaced by the Universal Credit (Transitional Provisions) Regulations 2014 (SI 2014/1230). At the same time, the "Pathfinder Group" conditions, previously contained in regs 5 to 12 of the Transitional Provisions Regulations 2013 were omitted from the Transitional Regulations 2014. Instead, similar conditions (now known as the "gateway conditions") appear in Sch.5 to the Commencement No. 9 Order as inserted by art.16 of SI 2014/1661.

The justification for the limited "roll out" was that it would "facilitate an evaluation of the Universal Credit business processes and information technology functionality in a live environment before it is rolled out nationally from October 2013" (*Explanatory Memorandum to the Transitional Provisions Regulations 2013*, para.7.64).

In this Order and its following companions, an award of ESA under Part 1 of the Welfare Reform Act 2007, in a case where income-related ESA has been abolished (i.e. in a Pathfinder area), is referred to as a "new style ESA award". Likewise an award of JSA under the Jobseekers Act 1995, in a case where income-based JSA has been abolished, is referred to as a "new style JSA award". Conversely an award of ESA under Part 1 of the Welfare Reform Act 2007, in a case where income-related ESA has not been abolished, is referred to as an "old style ESA award". Similarly an award of JSA under the Jobseekers Act 1995, in a case where income-based JSA has not been abolished, is referred to as an "old style JSA award".

Citation

1. This Order may be cited as the Welfare Reform Act 2012 (Com- **6.004** mencement No. 9 and Transitional and Transitory Provisions and Commencement No. 8 and Savings and Transitional Provisions (Amendment)) Order 2013.

Interpretation

2.-(1) In this Order- **6.005**
"the Act" means the Welfare Reform Act 2012 (apart from in Schedule 4);
"the 1995 Act" means the Jobseekers Act 1995;
"the 2007 Act" means the Welfare Reform Act 2007;

"the amending provisions" means the provisions referred to in article 4(1)(a) to (c);

[¹] [⁴ "claimant"—

    (a) in relation to an employment and support allowance, has the same meaning as in Part 1 of the Welfare Reform Act 2007, save as mentioned in article 5(1A);

    (b) in relation to a jobseeker's allowance, has the same meaning as in the Jobseekers Act 1995 (as it applies apart from the amendments made by Part 1 of Schedule 14 to the Act that remove references to an income-based jobseeker's allowance), save as mentioned in article 5(1A);

    (c) in relation to universal credit, has the same meaning as in Part 1 of the Act

    "appointed day" means the day appointed for the coming into force of the amending provisions in accordance with article 4(3);]

"the Claims and Payments Regulations 1987" means the Social Security (Claims and Payments) Regulations 1987;

"the Claims and Payments Regulations 2013" means the Universal Credit, Personal Independence Payment, Jobseeker's Allowance and Employment and Support Allowance (Claims and Payments) Regulations 2013;

"contribution-based jobseeker's allowance" means a contribution-based allowance under the 1995 Act as it has effect apart from the amendments made by Part 1 of Schedule 14 to the Act that remove references to an income-based allowance;

"contributory employment and support allowance" means a contributory allowance under Part 1 of the 2007 Act as it has effect apart from the amendments made by Schedule 3, and Part 1 of Schedule 14, to the Act that remove references to an income-related allowance;

[¹ "conversion decision" has the meaning given by the 2010 Transitional Regulations;]

"the Decisions and Appeals Regulations 2013" means the Universal Credit, Personal Independence Payment, Jobseeker's Allowance and Employment and Support Allowance (Decisions and Appeals) Regulations 2013;

[⁵ "the Digital Service Regulations 2014" means the Universal Credit (Digital Service) Amendment Regulations 2014;]

"employment and support allowance" means an employment and support allowance under Part 1 of the 2007 Act;

"the ESA Regulations 2008" means the Employment and Support Allowance Regulations 2008;

"the ESA Regulations 2013" means the Employment and Support Allowance Regulations 2013;

[¹ [³ . . .]

"First-tier Tribunal" has the same meaning as in the Social Security Act 1998;

"gateway conditions" means the conditions specified in Schedule 5;

"housing benefit" means housing benefit under section 130 of the Social Security Contributions and Benefits Act 1992;]

"income-based jobseeker's allowance" means an income-based jobseeker's allowance under the 1995 Act;

"income-related employment and support allowance" means an income-related allowance under Part 1 of the 2007 Act;

[¹ "income support" means income support under section 124 of the Social Security Contributions and Benefits Act 1992;]

"jobseeker's allowance" means an allowance under the 1995 Act;

[¹ [² "joint claimants"], in relation to universal credit, has the same meaning as in Part 1 of the Act;]

"the JSA Regulations 1996" means the Jobseeker's Allowance Regulations 1996;

"the JSA Regulations 2013" means the Jobseeker's Allowance Regulations 2013;

[¹ "new style ESA" means an employment and support allowance under Part 1 of the 2007 Act as amended by the provisions of Schedule 3, and Part 1 of Schedule 14, to the Act that remove references to an income-related allowance and "new style ESA award" shall be construed accordingly;

"new style JSA" means a jobseeker's allowance under the 1995 Act as amended by the provisions of Part 1 of Schedule 14 to the Act that remove references to an income-based allowance and "new style JSA award" shall be construed accordingly;

"old style ESA" means an employment and support allowance under Part 1 of the 2007 Act as it has effect apart from the amendments made by Schedule 3, and Part 1 of Schedule 14, to the Act that remove references to an income-related allowance and "old style ESA award" shall be construed accordingly;

"old style JSA" means a jobseeker's allowance under the 1995 Act as it has effect apart from the amendments made by Part 1 of Schedule 14 to the Act that remove references to an income-based jobseeker's allowance and "old style JSA award" shall be construed accordingly;]

"relevant districts" means the postcode districts specified in Schedule 1;

[¹ "single claimant", in relation to universal credit, has the same meaning as in Part 1 of the Act;

"state pension credit" means state pension credit under the State Pension Credit Act 2002;

"tax credit" (including "child tax credit" and "working tax credit") has the same meaning as in the Tax Credits Act 2002;]

[¹ . . .];

(Transitional Provisions, Housing Benefit and Council Tax Benefit)(Existing Awards)(No.2) Regulations 2010.

[¹ "the 2014 Transitional Regulations" means the Universal Credit (Transitional Provisions) Regulations 2014;

"the Universal Credit Regulations" means the Universal Credit Regulations 2013;

"Upper Tribunal" has the same meaning as in the Social Security Act 1998.]

[¹ (2) For the purposes of this Order—
   (a) the Claims and Payments Regulations 2013 apply for the purpose of deciding—
      (i) whether a claim for universal credit is made or is to be treated as made; and
      (ii) the date on which such a claim is made; and
   (b) where a couple is treated, in accordance with regulation 9(8) of the Claims and Payments Regulations 2013, as making a claim for universal credit, references to the date on which the claim is treated as made are to the date of formation of the couple.]

AMENDMENTS

1. Welfare Reform Act 2012 (Commencement No. 9, 11, 13, 14 and 16 and Transitional and Transitory Provisions (Amendment)) Order 2014 (SI 2014/1452) art.4 (June 16, 2014).
2. Welfare Reform Act 2012 (Commencement No. 9, 11, 13 14, 16 and 17 and Transitional and Transitory Provisions (Amendment)) Order 2014 (SI 2014/1661) art.4(1) (June 30, 2014).
3. Welfare Reform Act 2012 (Commencement No. 9, 11, 13, 14, 16 and 17 and Transitional and Transitory Provisions (Amendment) (No. 2)) Order 2014 (SI 2014/1923) art.4(2) (July 28, 2014).
4. Welfare Reform Act 2012 (Commencement No. 9, 11, 13 14, 16, 17 and 19 and Transitional and Transitory Provisions (Amendment)) Order 2014 (SI 2014/3067) art.6(2)(a) (November 24, 2014).
5. Welfare Reform Act 2012 (Commencement No. 20 and Transitional and Transitory Provisions and Commencement No. 9 and Transitional and Transitory Provisions (Amendment)) Order 2014 (SI 2014/3094) art.7(2)(a) (November 26, 2014).

Day appointed for commencement of the universal credit provisions in Part 1 of the Act

6.006   **3.**-(1) 29th April 2013 is the day appointed for the coming into force of-
   (a) sections 29 (delegation and contracting out), 37(1), (2), (8) and (9) (capability for work or work-related activity), 38 (information) and 39(1), (2), (3)(b) and (c) (couples) of the Act;
   (b) the following paragraphs of Schedule 2 to the Act (universal credit: amendments) and section 31 of the Act (supplementary and consequential amendments) in so far as it relates to those paragraphs, in so far as they are not already in force-
      (i) paragraphs 1, 2, 32 to 35, 37 to 42, 52 to 55 and 65;
      (ii) paragraphs 4, 8, 10 to 23, 25 and 27 to 31 and paragraph 3 in so far as it relates to those paragraphs; and
      (iii) paragraphs 44, 45, 47, 49, 50(2) and 50(1) in so far as it relates to 50(2), and paragraph 43 in so far as it relates to those paragraphs and sub-paragraphs; and
   (c) paragraph 1 of Schedule 5 to the Act (universal credit and other working-age benefits) and section 35 of the Act in so far as it relates to that paragraph.

(2) The day appointed for the coming into force of the provisions of the Act listed in Schedule 2, in so far as they are not already in force, in relation to the case of a claim referred to in paragraph (3)(a) to (d) and any award that is made in respect of such a claim, and in relation to the case of an award referred to in paragraph (3)(e) or (f), is the day appointed in accordance with paragraph (4).

[¹ (3) The claims and awards referred to are—

(a) a claim for universal credit where, on the date on which the claim is made, the claimant resides in one of the relevant districts and meets the gateway conditions;

[² (b) a claim for universal credit where—

   (i) in the case of a single claimant, the claimant gives incorrect information regarding the claimant residing in a relevant district or meeting the gateway conditions and the claimant does not reside in such a district or does not meet the gateway conditions on the date on which the claim is made;

  (ii) in the case of joint claimants, either or both of the joint claimants gives or give incorrect information regarding his or her (or their) residing in such a district or meeting the gateway conditions and one or both of them does not or do not reside in such a district or does not or do not meet those conditions on the date on which the claim is made; and

 (iii) after a decision is made that the single claimant is, or the joint claimants are, entitled to universal credit and one or more payments have been made in respect of the single claimant or the joint claimants, the Secretary of State discovers that incorrect information has been given regarding residence or meeting the gateway conditions.]

(c) a claim for universal credit that is treated as made by a couple in the circumstances referred to in regulation 9(8) of the Claims and Payments Regulations 2013 (claims for universal credit by members of a couple) where the claim complies with paragraph (7);

[² (d) a claim for universal credit by a former member of a couple who were joint claimants of universal credit, whether or not the claim is made jointly with another person, where the former member is not exempt from the requirement to make a claim by virtue of regulation 9(6) of the Claims and Payments Regulations 2013 (claims for universal credit by members of a couple), where the claim is made during the period of one month starting with the date on which notification is given to the Secretary of State that the former joint claimants have ceased to be a couple, and where the claim complies with paragraph (8);]

(e) an award of universal credit that is made without a claim in the circumstances referred to in regulation 6(1) or (2) of the Claims and Payments Regulations 2013 (claims not required for entitlement to universal credit in some cases) where the circumstances referred to in paragraph (9) apply; and

(f) an award of universal credit that is made without a claim in the circumstances referred to in regulation 9(6), (7) or (10) of the

Claims and Payments Regulations 2013 (claims for universal credit by members of a couple) where the circumstances referred to in paragraph (9) apply.]

(4) The day appointed in relation to the cases of the claims and awards referred to in paragraph (2) is-

    (a) in the case of a claim referred to in paragraph (3)(a) to (d), the first day of the period in respect of which the claim is made or treated as made;

    (b) in the case of an award referred to in paragraph (3)(e) or (f), the first day on which a person is entitled to universal credit under that award.

(5) [¹ . . .];

(6) For the purposes of paragraph (4)(a), where the time for making a claim for universal credit is extended under regulation 26(2) of the Claims and Payments Regulations 2013, the reference to the first day of the period in respect of which the claim is made or treated as made is a reference to the first day of the period in respect of which the claim is, by reason of the operation of that provision, timeously made or treated as made.

[¹ (7) A claim that is treated as made by a couple in the circumstances referred to in regulation 9(8) of the Claims and Payments Regulations 2013 complies with this paragraph where, on the date on which the claim is treated as made, the member of the couple who did not previously have an award of universal credit [³ . . .] is not entitled to state pension credit.

(8) A claim by a former member of a couple that is made in the circumstances referred to in paragraph (3)(d) complies with this paragraph where, on the date on which the claim is made, [³ neither the former member nor his or her partner (if any) is entitled to state pension credit].

(9) The circumstances referred to are where the relevant person is not entitled to state pension credit and, save where an award of universal credit is made in the circumstances referred to in regulation 9(7) of the Claims and Payments Regulations 2013, his or her partner (if any) is not entitled to [³ state pension credit].

(10) For the purposes of paragraph (9), "relevant person" means—

    (a) where an award of universal credit is made in the circumstances referred to in regulation 6(1) or (2) of the Claims and Payments Regulations 2013, the former claimant referred to in that regulation 6(1);

    (b) where an award of universal credit is made in the circumstances referred to in paragraph (6) of regulation 9 of the Claims and Payments Regulations 2013, [³ as that paragraph has effect apart from the amendments made by the Digital Service Regulations 2014,] the member of the former couple referred to in that paragraph;

    [³ (ba) where an award of universal credit is made in the circumstances referred to in paragraph (6) of regulation 9 of the Claims and Payments Regulations 2013, as that paragraph has effect as amended by the Digital Service Regulations 2014, the former joint claimant of universal credit to whom a new award of universal credit is made as referred to in sub-paragraph (a) or (b) of that paragraph;]

(c) where an award of universal credit is made in the circumstances referred to in paragraph (7) of regulation 9 of the Claims and Payments Regulations 2013, each of the joint claimants referred to in that paragraph;

(d) where an award of universal credit is made in the circumstances referred to in paragraph (10) of regulation 9 of the Claims and Payments Regulations 2013, the surviving partner referred to in that paragraph.

[³ (10A) In paragraph (3)—

(a) in sub-paragraph (c), the reference to regulation 9(8) of the Claims and Payments Regulations 2013 is a reference to that provision both as it has effect as amended by the Digital Service Regulations 2014 and as it has effect apart from that amendment;

(b) in sub-paragraph (d), the reference to regulation 9(6) of the Claims and Payments Regulations 2013 is a reference to that provision as it has effect apart from the amendment made by the Digital Service Regulations 2014;

(c) in sub-paragraph (f), the reference to regulation 9(6) of the Claims and Payments Regulations 2013 is a reference to that provision both as it has effect as amended by the Digital Service Regulations 2014 and as it has effect apart from that amendment.]

(11) For the purposes of paragraphs (8) and (9), "partner" means a person who forms part of a couple with the person in question, where "couple" has the same meaning as it has in section 39 of the Act.]

AMENDMENTS

1. Welfare Reform Act 2012 (Commencement No. 9, 11, 13, 14 and 16 and Transitional and Transitory Provisions (Amendment)) Order 2014 (SI 2014/1452) art.5 (June 16, 2014).
2. Welfare Reform Act 2012 (Commencement No. 9, 11, 13, 14, 16 and 17 and Transitional and Transitory Provisions (Amendment) (No. 2)) Order 2014 (SI 2014/1923) art.4(3) (July 28, 2014).
3. Welfare Reform Act 2012 (Commencement No. 20 and Transitional and Transitory Provisions and Commencement No. 9 and Transitional and Transitory Provisions (Amendment)) Order 2014 (SI 2014/3094) art.7(2)(b) (November 26, 2014).

DEFINITIONS

"the Act"–art.2(1).
"the Claims and Payments Regulations 2013"–*ibid.*
"relevant districts"–*ibid.*
"the Transitional Regulations"–*ibid.*

GENERAL NOTE

Para. (1)

6.007   This brings into force various provisions relating to universal credit (including some supplementary and consequential provisions set out in Sch.2 to the 2012 Act) on April 29, 2013.

Para. (2)

6.008   This tortuously worded provision has the effect of bringing into force those provisions relating to universal credit in Part 1 of the WRA 2012, as set out in Sch.2, where one of the different categories of case referred to in art.3(3) applies. These relate to claims for universal credit and any resulting award as well as to awards of universal credit without a claim.

Para. (3)

6.009   This specifies the various situations in which para.(2) has the effect of applying the new universal credit rules.

Sub-Para. (3) (a)

6.010   This covers the situation where a person makes a claim for universal credit in respect of a period that begins on or after April 29, 2013 where that individual both resides in a "relevant district" at the time that the claim is made and meets the gateway conditions.

Sub-Para. (3) (b)

6.011   Where a person claims universal credit and incorrectly states that they live in a relevant district, that person remains subject to the new regime.

Sub-Para. (3) (c)

6.012   This covers the case of a single person who becomes a member of a couple where the other member was already entitled to universal credit.

Sub-Para. (3) (d)

6.013   Where a couple separate, and the member of the couple who is not exempt from making a claim for universal credit makes a claim within a period of one month, the new rules apply.

Sub-Para. (3) (e)

6.014   A person may be awarded universal credit without making a claim as a result of changes in their income within six months of their income being such that they were not previously entitled to universal credit.

Sub-Para. (3) (f)

6.015   Again, a person may be awarded universal credit without making a claim where a couple cease to be a couple and an award is made to the member of the couple who is exempt from making a claim. Similarly, an award of universal credit may be made without a claim to a couple where the members of the couple were previously entitled to the new benefit as single claimants. In addition, the new regime applies where an award of universal credit is made without a claim to a member of a couple where the other member of the couple has died.

Paras (4)–(11)

These make supplementary provision dealing with the effective date of univer-   **6.016**
sal credit claims and awards under the preceding rules.

[¹ [² [³ Incorrect information regarding residence in a relevant district or meeting the gateway conditions

3A. (1) This article applies where a claim for universal credit is made and it is subsequently discovered that the single claimant or either or both of two joint claimants gave incorrect information regarding his or her (or their) residing in one of the relevant districts or meeting the gateway conditions and the conditions referred to in paragraph (2) are met.

(2) The conditions referred to are that, on the date on which the claim was made, the claimant—

(a) did not reside in one of the relevant districts (unless paragraph (3) applies); or

(b) did reside in one of the relevant districts but did not meet the gateway conditions.

(3) This paragraph applies where the claimant resided in an area apart from the relevant districts with respect to which the provisions of the Act referred to in Schedule 2 were in force in relation to a claim for universal credit and the conditions (if any) that applied to such a claim, for those provisions to come into force, were met.

(4) Where the discovery is made before the claim for universal credit has been decided—

(a) the claimant is to be informed that the claimant is not entitled to claim universal credit;

(b) if the claimant (or, in the case of joint claimants, either of them) makes a claim for old style ESA, old style JSA or income support ("the specified benefit") and the date on which that claim is made (as determined in accordance with the Claims and Payments Regulations 1987) is after the date on which the claim for universal credit was made, but no later than one month after the date on which the information required by sub-paragraph (a) was given—

(i) the claim for the specified benefit is to be treated as made on the date on which the claim for universal credit was made or the first date on which the claimant would have been entitled to the specified benefit if a claim had been made for it on that date, if later; and

(ii) any provision of the Claims and Payments Regulations 1987 under which the claim for the specified benefit is treated as made on a later date does not apply;

(c) if the claimant (or, in the case of joint claimants, either of them) makes a claim for housing benefit and the date of that claim (as

347

determined in accordance with the Housing Benefit Regulations 2006 or, as the case may be, the Housing Benefit (Persons who have attained the qualifying age for state pension credit) Regulations 2006 (together referred to as "the Housing Benefit Regulations")) is after the date on which the claim for universal credit was made, but no later than one month after the date on which the information required by sub-paragraph (a) was given—

    (i) the claim for housing benefit is to be treated as made on the date on which the claim for universal credit was made or the first date on which the claimant would have been entitled to housing benefit if a claim had been made for it on that date, if later; and

    (ii) any provision of the Housing Benefit Regulations under which the claim for housing benefit is treated as made on a later date does not apply;

(d) if the claimant (or, in the case of joint claimants, either of them) makes a claim for a tax credit and that claim is received by a relevant authority at an appropriate office (within the meaning of the Tax Credits (Claims and Notifications) Regulations 2002 ("the 2002 Regulations")) during the period of one month beginning with the date on which the information required by sub-paragraph (a) was given—

    (i) the claim for a tax credit is to be treated as having been received by a relevant authority at an appropriate office on the date on which the claim for universal credit was made or the first date on which the claimant would have been entitled to a tax credit if a claim had been so received on that date, if later; and

    (ii) any provision of the 2002 Regulations under which the claim is treated as having been made on a later date does not apply.

(5) Where the discovery is made after a decision has been made that the claimant is entitled to universal credit, but before any payment has been made—

    (a) that decision is to cease to have effect immediately, by virtue of this article;

    (b) the claimant is to be informed that they are not entitled to claim universal credit; and

    (c) sub-paragraphs (b) to (d) of paragraph (4) apply.

(6) Where the discovery is made after a decision has been made that the claimant is entitled to universal credit and one or more payments have been made in respect of the claimant, the decision is to be treated as a decision under section 8 of the Social Security Act 1998.

(7) For the purposes of paragraph (4), a person makes a claim for old style ESA or old style JSA where he or she makes a claim for an employment and support allowance or a jobseeker's allowance and the claim is subject to Part 1 of the 2007 Act or the 1995 Act respectively as those provisions have effect apart from the amendments made by the amending provisions.]]]

AMENDMENTS

1. Welfare Reform Act 2012 (Commencement No. 9, 11, 13, 14 and 16 and Transitional and Transitory Provisions (Amendment)) Order 2014 (SI 2014/1452) art.5 (June 16, 2014).
2. Welfare Reform Act 2012 (Commencement No. 9, 11, 13 14, 16 and 17 and Transitional and Transitory Provisions (Amendment)) Order 2014 (SI 2014/1661) art.4(3) (June 30, 2014).
3. Welfare Reform Act 2012 (Commencement No. 9, 11, 13, 14, 16 and 17 and Transitional and Transitory Provisions (Amendment) (No. 2)) Order 2014 (SI 2014/1923) art.4(4) (July 28, 2014).

Day appointed for the abolition of income-related employment and support allowance and income-based jobseeker's allowance

[¹ 4. (1) The day appointed for the coming into force of—   6.017

(a) section 33(1)(a) and (b) and (2) of the Act (abolition of benefits);
(b) paragraphs 22 to 26 of Schedule 3 to the Act (abolition of benefits: consequential provisions) and section 33(3) of the Act in so far as it relates to those paragraphs; and
(c) the repeals in Part 1 of Schedule 14 to the Act (abolition of benefits superseded by universal credit) that are referred to in Schedule 3,

in relation to the case of a claim referred to in paragraph (2)(a) to (d) and (g) and any award that is made in respect of such a claim, and in relation to the case of an award referred to in paragraph (2)(e) and (f), is the day appointed in accordance with paragraph (3).

(2) The claims and awards referred to are—

(a) a claim for universal credit, an employment and support allowance or a jobseeker's allowance where, on the date on which the claim is made [2 or treated as made], the claimant—
  (i) resides in one of the relevant districts; and
  (ii) meets the gateway conditions;
[² (b) a claim for universal credit where—
  (i) in the case of a single claimant, the claimant gives incorrect information regarding the claimant residing in a relevant district or meeting the gateway conditions and does not reside in such a district or does not meet the gateway conditions on the date on which the claim is made;
  (ii) in the case of joint claimants, either or both of the joint claimants gives or give incorrect information regarding his or her (or their) residing in such a district or meeting those conditions and one or both of them does not or do not reside in such a district or does not or do not meet those conditions on the date on which the claim is made; and
  (iii) after a decision is made that the single claimant is, or the joint claimants are, entitled to universal credit and one or more payments have been made in respect of the single claimant or

349

the joint claimants, the Secretary of State discovers that incorrect information has been given regarding residence or meeting the gateway conditions;]

(c) a claim for universal credit that is treated as made by a couple in the circumstances referred to in regulation 9(8) of the Claims and Payments Regulations 2013 (claims for universal credit by members of a couple) where the claim complies with article 3(7) and [³ . . .] ;

[² (d) a claim for universal credit by a former member of a couple who were joint claimants of universal credit, whether or not the claim is made jointly with another person, where the former member is not exempt from the requirement to make a claim by virtue of regulation 9(6) of the Claims and Payments Regulations 2013 (claims for universal credit by members of a couple), where the claim is made during the period of one month starting with the date on which notification is given to the Secretary of State that the former joint claimants have ceased to be a couple, and where the claim complies with article 3(8);]

(e) an award of universal credit that is made without a claim in the circumstances referred to in regulation 6(1) or (2) of the Claims and Payments Regulations 2013 (claims not required for entitlement to universal credit in some cases) where the circumstances referred to in article 3(9) apply;

(f) an award of universal credit that is made without a claim in the circumstances referred to in regulation 9(6), (7) or (10) the Claims and Payments Regulations 2013 (claims for universal credit by members of a couple) where the circumstances referred to in article 3(9) apply; and

(g) a claim for an employment and support allowance or a jobseeker's allowance [² other than one referred to in sub-paragraph (a) that is made or treated as made] —

(i) during the relevant period by a single claimant of universal credit or, in the case of joint claimants of universal credit, by either of the joint claimants, where the single claimant has made or the joint claimants have made, or been treated as having made, a claim for universal credit within sub-paragraphs (a) to (d);

(ii) during the relevant period by a single claimant of universal credit or, in the case of joint claimants of universal credit, by either of the joint claimants, where the single claimant has been awarded, or the joint claimants have been awarded, universal credit without a claim within sub-paragraph (e) or (f);

(iii) by a person who is entitled to make a claim for universal credit in the circumstances referred to in sub-paragraph (d) but has not yet done so; or

(iv) by a person who may be entitled to an award of universal credit in the circumstances referred to in sub-paragraph (e) or (f) but where no decision has yet been made as to the person's entitlement.

(3) Subject to paragraph (4), the day appointed in relation to the cases referred to in paragraph (2) is—

(a) in the case of a claim referred to in paragraph (2)(a) to (d) and (g), the first day of the period in respect of which the claim is made or (in the case of a claim for universal credit) treated as made;

(b) in the case of an award referred to in paragraph (2)(e) or (f), the first day on which a claimant is entitled to universal credit under that award.

(4) In relation to the case of a claim referred to in paragraph (2)(c) (claim for universal credit treated as made by a couple), where the member of the couple referred to in regulation 9(8)(b) of the Claims and Payments Regulations 2013 ("new claimant partner") was entitled during the prior period to an old style ESA award or an old style JSA award, the new claimant partner was at that time a member of a couple and the award included an amount in respect of the new claimant partner and his or her partner ("P"), the day appointed in relation to that case is the day after the day on which the new claimant partner and P ceased to be a couple for the purposes of the ESA Regulations 2008 or the JSA Regulations 1996 as the case may be.

(5) For the purposes of paragraph (4), the "prior period" means the period beginning with the first day of the period for which the claim for universal credit is treated as made and ending with the day before the day on which the claim for universal credit is treated as made.

(6) In paragraph (1), the reference to the case of a claim for universal credit referred to in paragraph (2)(a) to (d) (and any award made in respect of the claim), or of an award of universal credit referred to in paragraph (2)(e) and (f), includes a reference to—

(a) a case where a notice under regulation 4 of the 2010 Transitional Regulations (the notice commencing the conversion phase in relation to an award of incapacity benefit or severe disablement allowance) is issued to a single claimant or in the case of joint claimants, either of those claimants, during the designated period;

(b) where sub-paragraph (a) does not apply, a case where a conversion decision is made during that period in relation to an award of incapacity benefit or severe disablement allowance to which a single claimant or in the case of joint claimants, either of those claimants, is entitled; and

(c) where sub-paragraphs (a) and (b) do not apply, a case where the effective date of a conversion decision in relation to such an award occurs during that period (where "effective date" has the same meaning as in the 2010 Transitional Regulations),

and any award of an employment and support allowance that is made consequent on a conversion decision that relates to the notice referred to in sub-paragraph (a), the conversion decision referred to in sub-paragraph (b) or the conversion decision referred to in sub-paragraph (c), as the case may be.

(7) For the purposes of paragraph (6), the designated period means—

(a) in relation to a claim for universal credit referred to in paragraph (2)(a), (b)(i) [², (ii)] or (d), any period when a decision has not yet been made on the claim;

(b) in relation to a claim for universal credit that is treated as made as referred to in paragraph (2)(c), any period when no decision has yet been made as to the joint claimants' entitlement;

(c) any period, subsequent to the period referred to in sub-paragraph (a) or (b), when the single claimant or joint claimants is or are entitled to an award of universal credit in respect of the claim; and

(d) in relation to an award of universal credit referred to in paragraph (2)(e) or (f), any period when the single claimant or joint claimants to whom the award was made is or are entitled to that award.]

[³ (8) In paragraph (2)—

(a) in sub-paragraph (c), the reference to regulation 9(8) of the Claims and Payments Regulations 2013 is a reference to that provision both as it has effect as amended by the Digital Service Regulations 2014 and as it has effect apart from that amendment;

(b) in sub-paragraph (d), the reference to regulation 9(6) of the Claims and Payments Regulations 2013 is a reference to that provision as it has effect apart from the amendments made by the Digital Service Regulations 2014;

(c) in sub-paragraph (f), the reference to regulation 9(6) of the Claims and Payments Regulations 2013 is a reference to that provision both as it has effect as amended by the Digital Service Regulations 2014 and as it has effect apart from that amendment.]

AMENDMENTS

1. Welfare Reform Act 2012 (Commencement No. 9, 11, 13, 14 and 16 and Transitional and Transitory Provisions (Amendment)) Order 2014 (SI 2014/1452) art.6 (June 16, 2014).
2. Welfare Reform Act 2012 (Commencement No. 9, 11, 13, 14, 16 and 17 and Transitional and Transitory Provisions (Amendment) (No. 2)) Order 2014 (SI 2014/1923) art.4(5) (July 28, 2014).
3. Welfare Reform Act 2012 (Commencement No. 20 and Transitional and Transitory Provisions and Commencement No. 9 and Transitional and Transitory Provisions (Amendment)) Order 2014 (SI 2014/3094) art.7(2)(c) (November 26, 2014).

DEFINITIONS

"the Act"–art.2(1).
"the Claims and Payments Regulations 2013"–*ibid.*
"employment and support allowance"–*ibid.*
"income-based jobseeker's allowance"–*ibid.*
"income-related employment and support allowance"–*ibid.*
"jobseeker's allowance"–*ibid.*
"relevant districts"–*ibid.*

"the Transitional Regulations"–*ibid.*
"the 2010 Transitional Regulations"–*ibid.*

GENERAL NOTE

Para. (1)

This brings into force provisions relating to the abolition of both income-related employment and support allowance and income-based jobseeker's allowance. This includes the repeal of various provisions relating to the abolished allowances as set out in Sch.3. However, these provisions are only brought into force where one of the various different categories of case set out in para.(2) applies.

6.018

Para. (2)

This sets out the various categories of case affected by the amendments made by para.(1).

6.019

Para. (2) (a)

Where a person (i) resides in a relevant district (see Sch.1); (ii) meets the gateway conditions; and (iii) makes a claim for universal credit, employment and support allowance or jobseeker's allowance, then the amendments made by para.(1) above govern both the claim and any award made in respect of that claim.

6.020

Para. (2) (b)

This covers the situation here a person claims universal credit and incorrectly states that they live in a relevant district, or provides incorrect information as to their meeting the Pathfinder Group conditions. Such a claim remains within the universal credit regime despite the error.

6.021

Para. (2) (c)

This is analogous to art.3(3)(c).

6.022

Para. (2) (d)

This is analogous to art.3(3)(d).

6.023

Para. (2) (e)

This is analogous to art.3(3)(e).

6.024

Para. (2) (f)

is analogous to art.3(3)(f).

6.025

Provisions that apply in connection with the abolition of income-related employment and support allowance and income-based jobseeker's allowance under article 4

[¹ **5.** (1) [². ..] [³ In determining, for the purposes of article 4(2)(a), whether a claim for an employment and support allowance or a jobseeker's allowance meets the gateway conditions, Schedule 5 is to be read as though—

6.026

(a) any reference in that Schedule to making a claim for universal credit included a reference to making a claim for an employment and support allowance or a jobseeker's allowance as the case may be; and

(b) the reference in paragraph 4 to a single claimant, or to joint claimants, of universal credit was a reference to a person who would be a single claimant of universal credit or to persons who would be joint claimants of universal credit, if the claimant of an employment and support allowance or a jobseeker's allowance had made a claim for universal credit.

(1A) For the purposes of article 4(2)(a), where a claim for an employment and support allowance or a jobseeker's allowance is made by a couple or a member of a couple, any reference in article 4(2)(a) or Schedule 5 (save in paragraph 4 of that Schedule) to "the claimant" is a reference to each member of the couple.

(1B) For the purposes of paragraph (1A), "couple" has the same meaning as it has in section 39 of the Act.]

(2) [⁴. ..]

(3) For the purposes of article 4(2)(g), "relevant period" means—

(a) in relation to a claim for universal credit within article 4(2)(a) to (d), any UC claim period, and any period subsequent to any UC claim period in respect of which the single claimant or the joint claimants is or are entitled to an award of universal credit in respect of the claim;

(b) in relation to an award of universal credit within article 4(2)(e) or (f), any period when the single claimant or the joint claimants to whom the award was made is or are entitled to the award.

(4) For the purposes of paragraph (3)(a), a "UC claim period" is a period when—

(a) a claim for universal credit within article 4(2)(a), (b)(i) [2, (ii)] or (d) has been made but a decision has not yet been made on the claim;

(b) a claim for universal credit within article 4(2)(c) has been treated as made and no decision has yet been made as to the joint claimants' entitlement; or

(c) a decision has been made that a single claimant or joint claimants is or are not entitled to universal credit and—

  (i) the Secretary of State is considering whether to revise that decision under section 9 of the Social Security Act 1998, whether on an application made for that purpose, or on the Secretary of State's own initiative; or

  (ii) the single claimant or the joint claimants has or have appealed against that decision to the First-tier Tribunal and that appeal or any subsequent appeal to the Upper Tribunal or to a court has not been finally determined.

(5) Subject to paragraph (6), for the purposes of article 4(2)(a) and (g), the Claims and Payments Regulations 1987 apply for the purpose of deciding—

(a) whether a claim for an employment and support allowance or a jobseeker's allowance is made; and

(b) the date on which the claim is made or is to be treated as made.

(6) For the purposes of article 4(2)(g)—

(a) a person makes a claim for an employment and support allowance or a jobseeker's allowance if they take any action which results in a decision on a claim being required under the Claims and Payments Regulations 1987; and

(b) except as provided in paragraph (7), it is irrelevant that the effect of any provision of the Claims and Payments Regulations 1987 is that, for the purposes of those Regulations, the claim is not made or treated as made during the relevant period or at a time referred to in article 4(2)(g)(iii) or (iv).

(7) The following provisions of the Claims and Payments Regulations 1987 apply for the purpose of deciding whether or not a claim for an employment and support allowance or a jobseeker's allowance is made or is to be treated as made during the relevant period or at a time referred to in article 4(2)(g)(iii) or (iv)—

(a) [² in the case of a claim for an employment and support allowance,] regulation 6(1F)(b) or (c); and

(b) [² in the case of a claim for a jobseeker's allowance,] regulation 6(4ZA) to (4ZD) and (4A)(a)(i) and (b).

(8) For the purposes of article 4(3)(a)—

(a) in the case of a claim for universal credit, where the time for making a claim is extended under regulation 26(2) of the Claims and Payments Regulations 2013 (time within which a claim for universal credit is to be made), the reference to the first day of the period in respect of which the claim is made is a reference to the first day of the period in respect of which the claim is, by reason of the operation of that provision, timeously made;

(b) in the case of a claim for an employment and support allowance or a jobseeker's allowance, where the time for making a claim is extended under regulation 19 of, and Schedule 4 to, the Claims and Payments Regulations 1987, the reference to the first day of the period in respect of which the claim is made is a reference to the first day of the period in respect of which the claim is, by reason of the operation of those provisions, timeously made.]

AMENDMENTS

1. Welfare Reform Act 2012 (Commencement No. 9, 11, 13, 14 and 16 and Transitional and Transitory Provisions (Amendment)) Order 2014 (SI 2014/1452) art.7 (June 16, 2014).

2. Welfare Reform Act 2012 (Commencement No. 9, 11, 13, 14, 16 and 17 and Transitional and Transitory Provisions (Amendment) (No. 2)) Order 2014 (SI 2014/1923) art.4(6) (July 28, 2014).

3. Welfare Reform Act 2012 (Commencement No. 9, 11, 13 14, 16, 17 and 19 and Transitional and Transitory Provisions (Amendment)) Order 2014 (SI 2014/3067) art.6(2)(b) (November 24, 2014).

4. Welfare Reform Act 2012 (Commencement No. 20 and Transitional and Transitory Provisions and Commencement No. 9 and Transitional and Transitory Provisions (Amendment)) Order 2014 (SI 2014/3094) art.7(2)(d) (November 26, 2014).

DEFINITIONS

"the Claims and Payments Regulations 1987"–art.2(1).
"the Claims and Payments Regulations 2013"–*ibid.*
"income-based jobseeker's allowance"–*ibid.*
"income-related employment and support allowance"–*ibid.*
"jobseeker's allowance"–*ibid.*
"the Transitional Regulations"–*ibid.*

GENERAL NOTE

6.027   These provisions supplement and further define the provisions of art.4.

[¹ **Transitional provision where Secretary of State determines that claims for universal credit may not be made: effect on claims for employment and support allowance and jobseeker's allowance**

6.028   **5A.** (1) Where a person makes a claim for an employment and support allowance or a jobseeker's allowance at a time when they would not be able to make a claim for universal credit by virtue of a determination under regulation 4(1) of the 2014 Transitional Regulations (claims for universal credit may not be made in an area or category of case) [2 and where the amending provisions would otherwise have come into force in relation to the claim by virtue of article 4(2)(a) or any corresponding provision in any order made under section 150(3) of the Act other than this Order], then—

(a) in relation to a claim for an employment and support allowance, Part 1 of the 2007 Act and the Welfare Reform Act 2009 are to apply as though the amending provisions and the provisions referred to in article 7(1)(c), (d) and (f) had not come into force in relation to the claim;

(b) in relation to a claim for a jobseeker's allowance, the 1995 Act, the Social Security Administration Act 1992(2) and the Social Security Act 1998(3) are to apply as though the amending provisions and the provisions referred to in article 7(1)(a), (b) and (e) had not come into force in relation to the claim.

(2) Paragraph (1) does not apply in relation to a claim for an employment and support allowance or a jobseeker's allowance that falls within article 4(2)(g) (claims for an employment and support allowance or a jobseeker's allowance during specified periods with respect to a claim for universal credit, or an award of universal credit without a claim), or an analogous provision in any other order that brings into force the amending provisions.

(3) For the purposes of this article, paragraphs (5) to (7) of article 5 apply for the purpose of deciding—

(a) whether a claim for an employment and support allowance or a jobseeker's allowance is made; and

(b) the date on which the claim is made or is to be treated as made.]

[² (2) Paragraph (1) does not apply in relation to a claim for an employment and support allowance ("ESA") or a jobseeker's allowance ("JSA") where the claim is made or treated as made—

(a) where the claimant of ESA or JSA has made or been treated as having made a claim for universal credit ("UC") within article 4(2)(a) to (d) (whether or not the claim for UC is made jointly with another person), or has been awarded UC without a claim within article 4(2)(e) or (f) (whether or not the award is made to the claimant of ESA or JSA and another person as joint claimants), during the "relevant period" in relation to that claim or award as referred to in article 5(3)(a) or (b);

(b) where the claimant of ESA or JSA has made a claim for UC within any provision of an order made under section 150(3) of the Act, apart from this Order, that corresponds to article 4(2)(a) or (b) (whether or not the claim for UC is made by the claimant of ESA or JSA and another person as joint claimants), during the "relevant period" in relation to that claim as referred to in the provision of that order that corresponds to article 5(3)(a); or

(c) at a time when the claimant of ESA or JSA may be entitled to an award of UC without a claim in the circumstances referred to in article 4(2)(e) or (f) (whether or not the award may be made to the claimant of ESA or JSA and another person as joint claimants) but where no decision has yet been made as to the claimant's entitlement.]

(3) For the purposes of this article, the Claims and Payments Regulations 1987 apply for the purpose of deciding—

(a) whether a claim for ESA or JSA is made; and

(b) the date on which the claim is made or treated as made.]

AMENDMENTS

1. Welfare Reform Act 2012 (Commencement No. 9, 11, 13, 14 and 16 and Transitional and Transitory Provisions (Amendment)) Order 2014 (SI 2014/1452) art.8 (June 16, 2014).
2. Welfare Reform Act 2012 (Commencement No. 19 and Transitional and Transitory Provisions and Commencement No. 9 and Transitional and Transitory Provisions (Amendment)) Order 2014 (SI 2014/2321) art.7 (September 15, 2014).

Transitional provision: where the abolition of income-related employment and support allowance and income-based jobseeker's allowance is treated as not applying

6.-(1) Paragraph (2) applies where- **6.029**

(a) a person has or had a new style ESA award or a new style JSA award ("the award") [¹ by virtue of the coming into force of the amending provisions under any secondary legislation];

(b) in respect of all or part of the period to which the award relates, the person-

    (i) makes a claim, or is treated as making a claim, for universal credit; or

    (ii) makes an application to the Secretary of State for supersession of the decision to make the award, on the basis of a relevant change of circumstances that would relate to the grounds for entitlement to an income-related employment

and support allowance or an income-based jobseeker's allowance if the amending provisions had not come into force
[¹ . . .];

(c) if the amending provisions had not come into force under [¹ . . .]
and, in the case of a claim for universal credit, an application for
supersession of the decision to make the award had been made,
the person would be entitled to an income-related employment
and support allowance or an income-based jobseeker's allowance,
as the case may be, with respect to the period for which the claim
for universal credit or application for supersession is made;

(d) where the person makes an application for supersession of the
decision to make the award, the period in respect of which the
application is made does not include any period in respect of
which the person has been awarded universal credit; [¹ and]

[¹ (e) (i) on the date on which the claim for universal credit is made,
or the application for supersession is received, as the case
may be, the claim does not, or, in the case of an application
for supersession, a claim for universal credit by the person
would not, fall within any case (including a case with
respect to which an award of universal credit may be made
without a claim) in relation to which the provisions of the
Act referred to in Schedule 2 are in force ("the UC commencement case"); or

(ii) on that date, the claim for universal credit does, or, in the
case of an application for supersession, a claim for universal credit by the person would, fall within the UC commencement case, but the claim does or would fall within a
case (including a case that relates in whole or in part to
residence in an area) that is the subject of a determination
made by the Secretary of State under regulation 4(1) of the
2014 Transitional Regulations (determination that claims
for universal credit may not be made).]

(2) Where this paragraph applies, then, in relation to the award and
with effect from the first day of the period in respect of which the claim
is made or treated as made, or the application for supersession is made,
the 1995 Act or Part 1 of the 2007 Act, as the case may be, is to apply
as though the amending provisions had not come into force [¹ . . .].

(3) For the purposes of paragraph (1) [¹ . . .] -

(a) the Claims and Payments Regulations 2013 apply for the purpose
of deciding-

(i) whether a claim for universal credit is made or is to be treated
as made; and

(ii) the day on which the claim is made or is to be treated as
made; [¹ . . .]

(b) [¹ . . .].

(4) For the purposes of paragraph (2), the reference to the period in
respect of which the application for supersession is made is a reference to
the period beginning with the day from which the superseding decision
takes effect in accordance with section 10(5) of the Social Security Act

1998 and regulation 35 of, and Schedule 1 to, the Decisions and Appeals Regulations 2013 (effectives dates: Secretary of State decisions).

(5) For the purposes of paragraph (2), the reference to the first day of the period in respect of which the claim for universal credit is made or treated as made, in a case where the time for making a claim for universal credit is extended under regulation 26(2) of the Claims and Payments Regulations 2013, is a reference to the first day of the period in respect of which the claim is, by reason of the operation of that provision, timeously made or treated as made.

[¹ (6) For the purposes of this article, "secondary legislation" means an instrument made under an Act.]

AMENDMENTS

1. Welfare Reform Act 2012 (Commencement No. 9, 11, 13, 14 and 16 and Transitional and Transitory Provisions (Amendment)) Order 2014 (SI 2014/1452) art.9 (June 16, 2014).

DEFINITIONS

"the 1995 Act"–art.2(1).
"the 2007 Act"–*ibid.*
"the amending provisions"–*ibid.*
"the award"–para.1(a)
"the Claims and Payments Regulations 2013"–art.2(1).
"employment and support allowance"–*ibid.*
"the Decisions and Appeals Regulations 2013"–*ibid.*
"income-based jobseeker's allowance"–*ibid.*
"income-related employment and support allowance"–*ibid.*
"jobseeker's allowance"–*ibid.*
"new style ESA award"–*ibid.*
"new style JSA award"–*ibid.*
"relevant districts"–*ibid.*
"the Transitional Regulations"–*ibid.*

GENERAL NOTE

This makes transitional provision for cases where the conditions in para.(1) are 6.030 met. These all concern cases where the claimant either moves out of a relevant district or is not in the Pathfinder Group. In these cases, the award is treated as though the provisions in art.4(1)(a)-(c) above had not come into force (para.(2); see further art.9(2)). In consequence the person concerned will be able to claim an existing benefit, i.e. income-related ESA or income-based JSA, once again. The six conditions set out in Para.(1) are (in summary) that (a) the claimant has a new style ESA award or new style JSA award; (b) s/he makes a claim for universal credit or applies for supersession of the decision to make the award; (c) s/he would otherwise be entitled to income-related employment and support allowance or income-based jobseeker's allowance; (d) any award of universal credit has come to an end; (e), any claim for universal credit does not fall within the category of a "UC commencement case" or, if so, is the subject of a determination made by the Secretary of State under reg.4(1) of the 2014 Transitional Regulations. Paras.(3)-(5) make supplementary provision for paras (1) and (2).

Day appointed for commencement of provisions relating to claimant responsibilities with respect to employment and support allowance and jobseeker's allowance, and transitional provisions

6.031   7.-(1) The day appointed for the coming into force of-

(a) section 44(2) of the Act and section 44(1) of the Act in so far as it relates to section 44(2) (claimant commitment for jobseeker's allowance);

(b) section 49(2) and (3) to (5) of the Act (and section 49(1) of the Act in so far as it relates to those provisions) (claimant responsibilities for jobseeker's allowance);

(c) section 54(2) of the Act (and section 54(1) of the Act in so far as it relates to that provision) (claimant commitment for employment and support allowance);

(d) section 57(2), (4), (5) and (9) of the Act (and section 57(1) of the Act in so far as it relates to those provisions) (claimant responsibilities for employment and support allowance);

(e) the repeals in Part 4 of Schedule 14 to the Act (jobseeker's allowance: responsibilities after introduction of universal credit); and

(f) the repeals in Part 5 of Schedule 14 to the Act (employment and support allowance: responsibilities after introduction of universal credit),

in so far as they are not already in force, is, in relation to a particular case, the day on which the amending provisions come into force, under any secondary legislation, in relation to that case.

[1 (2) Where, under any secondary legislation, in relation to a new style JSA award, the 1995 Act applies as though the amending provisions had not come into force, then, with effect from the day on which the 1995 Act so applies, the 1995 Act, the Social Security Administration Act 1992 and the Social Security Act 1998 are to apply in relation to the award as though the provisions referred to in paragraph (1)(a), (b) and (e) had not come into force.

(3) Where, under any secondary legislation, in relation to a new style ESA award, Part 1 of the 2007 Act applies as though the amending provisions had not come into force, then, with effect from the day on which Part 1 of the 2007 Act so applies, Part 1 of the 2007 Act and the Welfare Reform Act 2009 are to apply in relation to the award as though the provisions referred to in paragraph (1)(c), (d) and (f) had not come into force.]

(4) For the purposes of paragraphs (1) to (3), "secondary legislation" means an instrument made under an Act.

AMENDMENTS

1. Welfare Reform Act 2012 (Commencement No. 11 and Transitional and Transitory Provisions and Commencement No. 9 and Transitional and Transitory Provisions (Amendment)) Order 2013 (SI 2013/1511) art.6 (July 1, 2013).

DEFINITIONS

"the Act"–art.2(1).
"the 1995 Act"–*ibid.*
"the 2007 Act"–*ibid.*
"the amending provisions"–*ibid.*
"employment and support allowance"–*ibid.*
"jobseeker's allowance"–*ibid.*
"new style ESA award"–*ibid.*
"new style JSA award"–*ibid.*
"secondary legislation"–para.(4).

GENERAL NOTE

This provides for the appointed day and transitional provisions for the meas-   6.032
ures in the WRA 2012 that relate to claimant responsibilities in relation to a new
style ESA award or a new style JSA award.

Day appointed for commencement of provisions concerning consideration of revision before appeal

8. 29th April 2013 is the day appointed for the coming into force of   6.033
paragraphs 1 to 11 and 15 to 18 of Schedule 11 to the Act (power to
require consideration of revision before appeal) and section 102(6) of
the Act in so far as it relates to those paragraphs, to the extent that those
provisions are not already in force.

DEFINITIONS

"the Act"–art.2(1).

GENERAL NOTE

This simply brings into force those provisions of Sch.11 to the Act concerning   6.034
consideration of revision before appeal.

Transitional provision: conversion of incapacity benefits

9.-(1) Subject to paragraph (2), where the amending provisions come   6.035
into force under article 4(1) in relation to the case of a claim referred to
in article 4(2)(a) to (d) [¹ or (g)] and any award made in respect of the
claim, or the case of an award referred to in article 4(2)(e) or (f), the
2010 Transitional Regulations are to apply in relation to that case as if
the modifications set out in Schedule 4 were made.

(2) Where article 6(2) applies in relation to a new style ESA award
(such that the award continues as an old style ESA award), the 2010
Transitional Regulations are to apply in relation to the award, in its
continuation as an old style ESA award, as if those modifications had not
been made.

AMENDMENTS

1. Welfare Reform Act 2012 (Commencement No. 9, 11, 13, 14 and 16 and
    Transitional and Transitory Provisions (Amendment)) Order 2014 (SI
    2014/1452) art.10 (June 16, 2014).

DEFINITIONS

"the amending provisions"–art.2(1).
"new style ESA award"–*ibid.*
"old style ESA award"–*ibid.*
"the 2010 Transitional Regulations"–*ibid.*

GENERAL NOTE

6.036 The introduction of universal credit was always going to be complicated. That complexity has been made worse by the fact that many existing awards of employment and support allowance have not been assessed for conversion, sometimes described as "reassessment", to ESA, even though that process began on October 11, 2010. This regulation allows for transitional provisions whereby, in relation to cases with respect to which art.4 has come into force, the Transitional Provisions Regulations 2010 are to be read as if the amendments set out in Sch.4 were made. Those amendments substitute references to provisions that apply to new style ESA awards, including the ESA Regulations 2013.

[¹ Transition from old style ESA]

6.037 **10.** [¹ (1) This article applies where a person—
(a) makes, or is treated as making, a claim for an employment and support allowance and, under article 4, Part 1 of the 2007 Act, as amended by the provisions of Schedule 3, and Part 1 of Schedule 14, to the Act that remove references to an income-related allowance, applies in relation to the claim; or
(b)   (i) has an old style ESA award immediately before the appointed day in relation to a case of a claim for universal credit referred to in article 4(2)(a) to (d) (and any award made in respect of the claim), or an award of universal credit referred to in article 4(2)(e) or (f); and
(ii) the old style ESA award consists of or includes a contributory employment and support allowance (which allowance therefore continues as a new style ESA award),
and, in the case of sub-paragraph (a), the condition referred to in paragraph (1A) is satisfied.
(1A) The condition is that—
(a) the person previously made, or was treated as having made, a claim for an employment and support allowance and Part 1 of the 2007 Act, as it has effect apart from the provisions of Schedule 3, and Part 1 of Schedule 14, to the Act that remove references to an income-related allowance, applied in relation to the claim;
(b) a notice was issued to the person under regulation 4 of the 2010 Transitional Regulations and Part 1 of the 2007 Act, as that Part has effect apart from the provisions of Schedule 3, and Part 1 of Schedule 14, to the Act that remove references to an income-related allowance, applied in relation to the notice; or
(c) the person previously had a new style ESA award and article 6(2) applied in relation to the award (which award therefore continued as an old style ESA award).]
(2)Where this article applies, the ESA Regulations 2013 are to be read as if-

362

(a) (i) in the definitions of "period of limited capability for work" in regulations 2 (interpretation) and 3 (further interpretation), the reference to a period throughout which a person has, or is treated as having, limited capability for work included a reference to a period throughout which the person in question had, or was treated as having, limited capability for work under the ESA Regulations 2008; and

(ii) the reference, in the definition in regulation 2, to regulation 28 of the Claims and Payments Regulations 2013 (time within which a claim for employment and support allowance is to be made) included a reference to regulation 19 of, and Schedule 4 to, the Claims and Payments Regulations 1987 (prescribed times for claiming benefit);

(b) in regulation 6 (the assessment phase–previous claimants)-

(i) any reference to an employment and support allowance included a reference to an old style ESA award; and

(ii) in paragraph (2)(b)(v) and (c)(iii), the reference to regulation 26 (conditions for treating a claimant as having limited capability for work until a determination about limited capability for work has been made) included a reference to regulation 30 of the ESA Regulations 2008 (conditions for treating a claimant as having limited capability for work until a determination about limited capability for work has been made);

(c) in regulation 7 (circumstances where the condition that the assessment phase has ended before entitlement to the support component or the work-related activity component arises does not apply)-

(i) any reference to an employment and support allowance included a reference to an old style ESA award; and

(ii) in paragraph (3)(b)(iv), (c)(iii), (c)(iv) and (d)(iii), the reference to regulation 26 included a reference to regulation 30 of the ESA Regulations 2008;

(d) in regulation 11 (condition relating to youth–previous claimants), any reference to an employment and support allowance included a reference to an old style ESA award;

(e) in regulation 15 (determination of limited capability for work)-

(i) the reference in paragraph (7)(a) to a claimant having been determined to have limited capability for work included a reference to such a determination made under Part 5 of the ESA Regulations 2008; and

(ii) the reference in paragraph (7)(b) to a person being treated as having limited capability for work included a reference to a person being so treated under regulation 20 (certain claimants to be treated as having limited capability for work), 25 (hospital patients), 26 (claimants receiving certain regular treatment) or 29 (exceptional circumstances) of the ESA Regulations 2008;

(f) in regulation 26 (conditions for treating a claimant as having limited capability for work until a determination about limited capability for work has been made)-

   (i) in paragraph (2)(b), the reference to regulation 18 (failure to provide information in relation to limited capability for work) and 19 (claimant may be called for a medical examination to determine whether the claimant has limited capability for work) included a reference to regulation 22 (failure to provide information in relation to limited capability for work) and 23 (claimant may be called for a medical examination to determine whether the claimant has limited capability for work) of the ESA Regulations 2008; and

   (ii) in paragraph (4)(c), the reference to regulation 18 included a reference to regulation 22 of the ESA Regulations 2008;

  (g) in regulation 30(4) (determination of limited capability for work-related activity), the reference to a determination about whether a claimant has, or is to be treated as having or not having, limited capability for work-related activity included such a determination that was made under Part 6 of the ESA Regulations 2008; [¹ . . .]

[¹ (ga) in regulation 39(6) (exempt work), the reference to an employment and support allowance included a reference to an old style ESA award;

  (gb) in regulation 85(2)(a) (waiting days), where a claimant was entitled to an old style ESA award with effect from the first day of a period of limited capability for work by virtue of regulation 144(2)(a) of the ESA Regulations 2008 and, with effect from [² a day between the second and the seventh day of that period (including the second and the seventh day)], that award continued as a new style ESA award in the circumstances referred to in paragraph (1)(b) of this article, the reference to an employment and support allowance included a reference to the old style ESA award;]

  (h) in regulation 87(1) (claimants appealing a decision), the reference to a determination that the claimant does not have limited capability for work under the ESA Regulations 2013 included a reference to such a determination under the ESA Regulations 2008.

  (i) in regulation 89 (short absence), where—

   (i) a claimant had an old style ESA award in the circumstances referred to in paragraph (1)(b) of this article;

   (ii) a temporary absence from Great Britain commenced when regulation 152 of the ESA Regulations 2008 applied to the claimant; and

   (iii) the first 4 weeks of the temporary absence had not ended immediately before the first day of entitlement to the new style ESA award,

  the initial words of regulation 89 included a reference to the claimant being entitled to the new style ESA award during the remainder of the first 4 weeks of the temporary absence that commenced when regulation 152 of the ESA Regulations 2008 applied to the claimant;

  (j) in regulation 90 (absence to receive medical treatment), where—

(i) a claimant had an old style ESA award in the circumstances referred to in paragraph (1)(b) of this article;

(ii) a temporary absence from Great Britain commenced when regulation 153 of the ESA Regulations 2008 applied to the claimant; and

(iii) the first 26 weeks of the temporary absence had not ended immediately before the first day of entitlement to the new style ESA award,

the initial words of paragraph (1) of regulation 90 included a reference to the claimant being entitled to the new style ESA award during the remainder of the first 26 weeks of the temporary absence that commenced when regulation 153 of the ESA Regulations 2008 applied to the claimant;

(k) in regulation 93 (disqualification for misconduct etc)—

(i) in paragraph (3), for "Paragraph (2) does" there were substituted "Paragraphs (2) and (5) do"; and

(ii) after paragraph (4) there were inserted—

"(5) Subject to paragraph (3), a claimant is to be disqualified for receiving an employment and support allowance for any period determined by the Secretary of State under regulation 157(2) of the Employment and Support Allowance Regulations 2008(3) less any days during that period on which those Regulations applied to the claimant.

(6) Where paragraph (5) applies to a claimant, paragraph (2) is not to apply to that claimant with respect to any matter referred to in paragraph (1) that formed the basis for the claimant's disqualification under regulation 157(2) of the Employment and Support Allowance Regulations 2008.";

(l) in regulation 95 (treating a claimant as not having limited capability for work), the existing words became paragraph (1) and—

(i) at the beginning of paragraph (1), there were inserted "Subject to paragraph (2),"; and

(ii) after paragraph (1), there were inserted—

"(2) A claimant is to be treated as not having limited capability for work if—

(a) under Part 1 of the Act as it has effect apart from the amendments made by Schedule 3, and Part 1 of Schedule 14, to the Welfare Reform Act 2012 that remove references to an income-related allowance ("the former law"), the claimant was disqualified for receiving a contributory employment and support allowance during a period of imprisonment or detention in legal custody;

(b) Part 1 of the Act as amended by the provisions of Schedule 3, and Part 1 of Schedule 14, to the Welfare Reform Act 2012 that remove references to an income-related allowance ("the current law") applied to the claimant

with effect from a day that occurred during the period of
imprisonment or detention in legal custody referred to in
sub-paragraph (a) and during the period of six weeks
with effect from the day on which the claimant was first
disqualified as referred to in sub-paragraph (a); and

(c) the total of—

    (i) the period for which the claimant was disqualified
for receiving a contributory employment and support allowance during the period of imprisonment
or detention in legal custody when the former law
applied to the claimant; and

    (ii) the period for which the claimant was disqualified
for receiving an employment and support allowance
during the period of imprisonment or detention in
legal custody when the current law applied to the
claimant,

amounts to more than six weeks."]

[¹ (3) Subject to paragraph (4), where this article applies, the 2007 Act
is to be read as though—

(a) the reference to an employment and support allowance in section
1A(1) and (4) to (6);

(b) the first reference to an employment and support allowance in
section 1A(3); and

(c) the first reference to an employment and support allowance in
section 1B(4),

included a reference to a contributory employment and support
allowance.

(4) Where this article applies and the 2010 Transitional Regulations
apply to a person, paragraph (3)(c) becomes paragraph (3)(b) and, for
paragraph (3)(a) and (b), there is substituted—

"(a) in section 1A as substituted by the 2010 Transitional Regulations—

    (i) the reference to an employment and support allowance in
section 1A(1), (4) and (5); and

    (ii) the first reference to an employment and support allowance
in section 1A(3); and".

(5) Where this article applies and a claimant—

(a) had an old style ESA award in the circumstances referred to in
paragraph (1)(b); and

(b) the old style ESA award had not been preceded by a new style
ESA award in the circumstances referred to in paragraph
(1A)(c),

the 2007 Act is to be read as if, in section 24(2), the beginning of the
assessment phase (subject to section 24(3)) was the first day of the
period for which the claimant was entitled to the old style ESA
award.]

AMENDMENTS

1. Welfare Reform Act 2012 (Commencement No. 11 and Transitional and Transitory Provisions and Commencement No. 9 and Transitional and Transitory Provisions (Amendment)) Order 2013 (SI 2013/1511) art.8 (July 1, 2013).
2. Welfare Reform Act 2012 (Commencement No. 9, 11, 13 14, 16, 17 and 19 and Transitional and Transitory Provisions (Amendment)) Order 2014 (SI 2014/3067) art.7(a) (November 24, 2014).

DEFINITIONS

"the amending provisions"–art.2(1)
"appointed day"–*ibid.*
"the Claims and Payments Regulations 1987"–*ibid.*
"the Claims and Payments Regulations 2013"–*ibid.*
"contributory employment and support allowance"–*ibid.*
"employment and support allowance"–*ibid.*
"the ESA Regulations 2008"–*ibid.*
"the ESA Regulations 2013"–*ibid.*
"new style ESA award"–*ibid.*
"old style ESA award"–*ibid.*

GENERAL NOTE

This makes transitional provisions for assessments of limited capability for work or for work and work-related activity where a person has a new style ESA award and previously had an old style ESA award. Article 11 deals with the converse position.   **6.038**

So, for example, under the new style ESA award the definition of a period of limited capability for work includes a period throughout which the claimant had, or was treated as having, limited capability for work for the purposes of old style ESA (para.(2)(a)). Similarly, where the old style and new style awards link, then days of entitlement to old styled ESA in the linked award are included in calculating the end of the assessment phase (para.(2)(b)). To the same end, any earlier period of limited capability for work under the old style ESA award is counted in working out whether the work related activity component or support component is payable from the first day of entitlement (para.(2)(c)). Likewise, the six months rule for the purposes of treating a claimant as having limited capability for work until a further determination is made includes having limited capability for work (or being treated as such) under an old style ESA award (subs.(2)(f)).

[¹ Transition from new style ESA]

11.- [¹ (1) This article applies where a person—   **6.039**
(a) makes, or is treated as making, a claim for an employment and support allowance and Part 1 of the 2007 Act, as it has effect apart from the provisions of Schedule 3, and Part 1 of Schedule 14, to the Act that remove references to an income-related allowance, applies in relation to the claim; or
(b) has a new style ESA award and article 6(2) applies in relation to the award (which award therefore continues as an old style ESA award),
and, in the case of sub-paragraph (a), the condition referred to in paragraph (1A) is satisfied.

(1A) The condition is that—

(a) the person previously made, or was treated as having made, a claim for an employment and support allowance and, under article 4, Part 1 of the 2007 Act, as amended by the provisions of Schedule 3, and Part 1 of Schedule 14, to the Act that remove references to an income-related allowance, applied in relation to the claim;

(b) a notice was issued to the person under regulation 4 of the 2010 Transitional Regulations and, under article 4, Part 1 of the 2007 Act, as amended by the provisions of Schedule 3, and Part 1 of Schedule 14, to the Act that remove references to an income-related allowance, applied in relation to the notice; or

(c) the person previously—

    (i) had an old style ESA award immediately before the appointed day in relation to a case of a claim for universal credit referred to in article 4(2)(a) to (d) (and any award made in respect of the claim), or an award of universal credit referred to in article 4(2)(e) or (f); and

    (ii) the old style ESA award consisted of or included a contributory employment and support allowance (which allowance therefore continued as a new style ESA award).]

(2) Where this article applies, the ESA Regulations 2008 are to be read as if-

(a)   (i) in the definitions of "period of limited capability for work" in regulation 2(1) and (5) (interpretation), the reference to a period throughout which a person has, or is treated as having, limited capability for work included a reference to a period throughout which the person in question had, or was treated as having, limited capability for work under the ESA Regulations 2013; and

    (ii) the reference, in the definition in regulation 2(1), to regulation 19 of the Claims and Payments Regulations 1987 (time for claiming benefit) included a reference to regulation 28 of the Claims and Payments Regulations 2013 (time within which a claim for an employment and support allowance is to be made);

(b) in regulation 5 (the assessment phase–previous claimants)-

    (i) any reference to an employment and support allowance included a reference to a new style ESA award; and

    (ii) in paragraph (2)(b)(v) and (c)(iii), the reference to regulation 30 (conditions for treating a claimant as having limited capability for work until a determination about limited capability for work has been made) included a reference to regulation 26 of the ESA Regulations 2013 (conditions for treating a claimant as having limited capability for work until a determination about limited capability for work has been made);

(c) in regulation 7 (circumstances where the condition that the assessment phase has ended before entitlement to the support component or the work-related activity component arises does not apply)-

(i) any reference to an employment and support allowance included a reference to a new style ESA award; and

(ii) in paragraph (1B)(b)(iv), (c)(iii), (c)(iv) and (d)(iii), the reference to regulation 30 included a reference to regulation 26 of the ESA Regulations 2013;

(d) in regulation 10 (condition relating to youth—previous claimants), any reference to an employment and support allowance included a reference to a new style ESA award;

(e) in regulation 19 (determination of limited capability for work)-

(i) the reference in paragraph (7)(a) to a claimant having been determined to have limited capability for work included a reference to such a determination made under Part 4 of the ESA Regulations 2013; and

(ii) the reference in paragraph (7)(b) to a person being treated as having limited capability for work included a reference to a person being so treated under regulation 16 (certain claimants to be treated as having limited capability for work), 21 (hospital patients), 22 (claimants receiving certain treatment) or 25 (exceptional circumstances) of the ESA Regulations 2013;

(f) in regulation 30 (conditions for treating a claimant as having limited capability for work until a determination about limited capability for work has been made)-

(i) in the initial words of paragraph (2)(b), the reference to regulation 22 (failure to provide information in relation to limited capability for work) and 23 (claimant may be called for a medical examination to determine whether the claimant has limited capability for work) included a reference to regulation 18 (failure to provide information in relation to limited capability for work) and 19 (claimant may be called for a medical examination to determine whether the claimant has limited capability for work) of the ESA Regulations 2013; and

(ii) in [² paragraph (4)(c)], the reference to regulation 22 included a reference to regulation 18 of the ESA Regulations 2013;

(g) in regulation 34(4) (determination of limited capability for work-related activity), the reference to a determination about whether a claimant has, or is to be treated as having or not having, limited capability for work-related activity included such a determination that was made under Part 5 of the ESA Regulations 2013; [¹ . . .]

[¹ (ga) in regulation 45(10) (exempt work), the reference to an employment and support allowance included a reference to a new style ESA award;

(gb) in regulation 144(2)(a) (waiting days), where the claimant was entitled to a new style ESA award with effect from the first day of a period of limited capability for work by virtue of regulation 85(2)(a) of the ESA Regulations 2013 and, with effect from [4 a day between the second and the seventh day of that period (including the second and the seventh day)], that award continued as an old style ESA award in the circumstances referred to in paragraph (1)(c) of this article, the reference to an employment and support allowance included a reference to the new style ESA award;]

(h) in regulation 147A(1) (claimants appealing a decision), the reference to a determination that the claimant does not have limited capability for work included a reference to such a determination under the ESA Regulations 2013.

(i) in regulation 152 (short absence), where—

    (i) a claimant had a new style ESA award in the circumstances referred to in paragraph (1)(b) of this article;

    (ii) a temporary absence from Great Britain commenced when regulation 89 of the ESA Regulations 2013 applied to the claimant; and

    (iii) the first 4 weeks of the temporary absence had not ended immediately before the first day of entitlement to the old style ESA award,

the initial words of regulation 152 included a reference to the claimant being entitled to the old style ESA award during the remainder of the first 4 weeks of the temporary absence that commenced when regulation 89 of the ESA Regulations 2013 applied to the claimant;

(j) in regulation 153 (absence to receive medical treatment)—

    (i) a claimant had a new style ESA award in the circumstances referred to in paragraph (1)(b) of this article;

    (ii) a temporary absence from Great Britain commenced when regulation 90 of the ESA Regulations 2013 applied to the claimant; and

    (iii) the first 26 weeks of the temporary absence had not ended immediately before the first day of entitlement to the old style ESA award,

the initial words of paragraph (1) of regulation 153 included a reference to the claimant being entitled to the old style ESA award during the remainder of the first 26 weeks of the temporary absence that commenced when regulation 90 of the ESA Regulations 2013 applied to the claimant;

(k) in regulation 157 (disqualification for misconduct etc)—

    (i) in paragraph (3), for "Paragraph (2) does" there were substituted "Paragraphs (2) and (4) do"; and

    (ii) after paragraph (3) there were inserted—

        "(4) Subject to paragraph (3), a claimant is to be disqualified for receiving an employment and support allowance for any period determined by the Secretary of State under regulation 93(2) of the Employment and Support Allowance Regulations 2013 less any days during that period on which those Regulations applied to the claimant.

(5) Where paragraph (4) applies to a claimant, paragraph (2) is not to apply to that claimant with respect to any matter referred to in paragraph (1) that formed the basis for the claimant's disqualification under regulation 93(2) of the Employment and Support Allowance Regulations 2013."; [² . . .]

(l) in regulation 159 (treating a claimant as not having limited capability for work), the existing words became paragraph (1) and—

  (i) at the beginning of paragraph (1), there were inserted "Subject to paragraph (2),"; and
  (ii) after paragraph (1), there were inserted—

  "(2) A claimant is to be treated as not having limited capability for work if—

  (a) under Part 1 of the Act as amended by the provisions of Schedule 3, and Part 1 of Schedule 14, to the Welfare Reform Act 2012 that remove references to an income-related allowance ("the former law"), the claimant was disqualified for receiving an employment and support allowance during a period of imprisonment or detention in legal custody;

  (b) Part 1 of the Act as it has effect apart from the amendments made by Schedule 3, and Part 1 of Schedule 14, to the Welfare Reform Act 2012 that remove references to an income-related allowance ("the current law") applied to the claimant with effect from a day that occurred during the period of imprisonment or detention in legal custody referred to in sub-paragraph (a) and during the period of six weeks with effect from the day on which the claimant was first disqualified as referred to in sub-paragraph (a); and

  (c) the total of—

    (i) the period for which the claimant was disqualified for receiving an employment and support allowance during the period of imprisonment or detention in legal custody when the former law applied to the claimant; and

    (ii) the period for which the claimant was disqualified for receiving a contributory employment and support allowance during the period of imprisonment or detention in legal custody when the current law applied to the claimant,

  amounts to more than six weeks."] [³ and

(m) in Schedule 6 (housing costs), in paragraphs 8(1) and 9(1), each reference to an employment and support allowance included a reference to new style ESA.]

[¹ (3) Subject to paragraph (4), where this article applies, the 2007 Act is to be read as though—

(a) the reference to a contributory allowance in section (1A)(1) and (4) to (6);

(b) the first reference to a contributory allowance in section (1A)(3); and

(c) the first reference to a contributory allowance in section 1B,

included a reference to a new style ESA award.

(4) Where this article applies and the 2010 Transitional Regulations apply to a person, paragraph (3)(c) becomes paragraph (3)(b) and, for paragraph (3)(a) and (b), there is substituted—

"(a) in section 1A as substituted by the 2010 Transitional Regulations—

(i) the reference to a contributory allowance in section 1A(1), (4) and (5); and

(ii) the first reference to a contributory allowance in section 1A(3); and".

(5) Where this article applies and a claimant—

(a) had a new style ESA award in the circumstances referred to in paragraph (1)(b); and

(b) the new style ESA award had not been preceded by an old style ESA award in the circumstances referred to in paragraph (1A)(c),

section 24(2) of the 2007 Act is to be read as if the beginning of the assessment phase (subject to section 24(3)) was the first day of the period for which the claimant was entitled to the new style ESA award.]

AMENDMENTS

1. Welfare Reform Act 2012 (Commencement No. 11 and Transitional and Transitory Provisions and Commencement No. 9 and Transitional and Transitory Provisions (Amendment)) Order 2013 (SI 2013/1511) art.9 (July 1, 2013).

2. Welfare Reform Act 2012 (Commencement No. 13 and Transitional and Transitory Provisions) Order 2013 (SI 2013/2657) art.5(a) (October 29, 2013).

3. Welfare Reform Act 2012 (Commencement No. 9, 11, 13, 14 and 16 and Transitional and Transitory Provisions (Amendment)) Order 2014 (SI 2014/1452) art.11 (June 16, 2014).

4. Welfare Reform Act 2012 (Commencement No. 9, 11, 13 14, 16, 17 and 19 and Transitional and Transitory Provisions (Amendment)) Order 2014 (SI 2014/3067) art.7(a) (November 24, 2014).

DEFINITIONS

"the Claims and Payments Regulations 1987"–art.2(1)
"the Claims and Payments Regulations 2013"–*ibid.*
"employment and support allowance"–*ibid.*
"the ESA Regulations 2008"–*ibid.*
"the ESA Regulations 2013"–*ibid.*
"new style ESA award"–*ibid.*
"old style ESA award"–*ibid.*

GENERAL NOTE

This makes transitional provisions for assessments of limited capability for   6.040
work or for work and work-related activity where a person has an old style ESA
award and previously had a new style ESA award. Article 10 deals with the
converse position. The modifications are to similar effect as in art.10.

[¹ Transition from old style JSA

12.—(1) This article applies where a person—   6.041

(a) makes, or is treated as making, a claim for a jobseeker's allowance
     and, under article 4, the 1995 Act, as amended by the provisions
     of Part 1 of Schedule 14 to the Act that remove references to an
     income-based jobseeker's allowance, applies in relation to the
     claim; or

(b) (i) has an old style JSA award (whether or not the award was
          made to the person as a member of a joint-claim couple)
          immediately before the appointed day in relation to a case of
          a claim for universal credit referred to in article 4(2)(a) to (d)
          (and any award made in respect of the claim), or an award of
          universal credit referred to in article 4(2)(e) or (f); and
     (ii) the old style JSA award consists of or includes a contribution-
          based jobseeker's allowance (which allowance therefore con-
          tinues as a new style JSA award),
          and, in the case of sub-paragraph (a), the condition referred
          to in paragraph (2) is satisfied.

(2) The condition is that the person previously—

(a) made, or was treated as having made, a claim for a jobseeker's
     allowance (whether or not as a member of a joint-claim couple)
     and the 1995 Act, as it has effect apart from the provisions of Part
     1 of Schedule 14 to the Act that remove references to an income-
     based jobseeker's allowance, applied in relation to the claim; or

(b) had a new style JSA award and article 6(2) applied in relation to
     the award (which award therefore continued as an old style JSA
     award).

(3) Where this article applies, the JSA Regulations 2013 are to be read
as if—

(a) in regulation 15(3)(b) (victims of domestic violence), the refer-
     ence to regulation 15 applying to the claimant included a refer-
     ence to the claimant having been treated as being available for
     employment under regulation 14A(2) or (6) of the JSA Regula-
     tions 1996;

(b) in regulation 36(1) (waiting days), where a person was entitled to
     an old style JSA award with effect from the first day of a jobseeking
     period by virtue of regulation 46(1)(a) of the JSA Regulations
     1996 and, with effect from [2 a day between the second and the
     seventh day of that period (including the second and the seventh
     day)], that award continued as a new style JSA award in the
     circumstances referred to in paragraph (1)(b) of this article, the
     reference to a jobseeker's allowance included a reference to the
     old style JSA award;

373

(c) in regulation 37 (jobseeking period)—

    (i) the jobseeking period in relation to a claimant included any period that, under regulation 47 of the JSA Regulations 1996 (jobseeking period), forms part of the jobseeking period for the purposes of the 1995 Act; and

    (ii) in paragraph (3), the reference to a day that is to be treated as a day in respect of which the claimant was entitled to a jobseeker's allowance included a reference to any day that, under regulation 47(4) of the JSA Regulations 1996, is to be treated as a day in respect of which the claimant was entitled to a contribution-based jobseeker's allowance;

(d) in regulation 41 (persons temporarily absent from Great Britain), where a person had an old style JSA award in the circumstances referred to in paragraph (1)(b) of this article, the reference in paragraph (2)(b), (3)(a) and (c), (5)(a) and (6)(b) to entitlement to a jobseeker's allowance included a reference to the old style JSA award; and

(e) in regulation 46 (short periods of sickness), after paragraph (5) there were inserted—

"(6) Where—

    (a) a person has been treated under regulation 55(1) of the Jobseeker's Allowance Regulations 1996 as capable of work or as not having limited capability for work for a certain period; and

    (b) these Regulations apply to that person with effect from a day ("the relevant day") within that period,

the person is to be treated for the part of that period that begins with the relevant day as capable of work or as not having limited capability for work.

(7) Where paragraph (6) applies to a person and the conditions in paragraph (1)(a) to (c) are fulfilled in relation to that person on any day within the part of a period referred to in paragraph (6), the requirement of paragraph (1) to treat the person as capable of work or as not having limited capability for work is to be regarded as satisfied with respect to the fulfilment of those conditions on that day.

(8) For the purposes of paragraph (3), where paragraph (6) applies to a person, paragraph (3) is to apply to the person as though the preceding provisions of this regulation had applied to the person with respect to the person having been treated for a period, under regulation 55(1) of the Jobseeker's Allowance Regulations 1996 and paragraph (6), as capable of work or as not having limited capability for work.".

(4) Where this article applies, the 1995 Act is to be read as though, in section 5 of the 1995 Act, the reference to a jobseeker's allowance in subsection (1) and the first reference to a jobseeker's allowance in subsection (2) included a reference to a contribution-based jobseeker's allowance.

(5) For the purposes of this article, "joint-claim couple" has the meaning given in section 1(4) of the 1995 Act.]

AMENDMENTS

1. Welfare Reform Act 2012 (Commencement No. 11 and Transitional and Transitory Provisions and Commencement No. 9 and Transitional and Transitory Provisions (Amendment)) Order 2013 (SI 2013/1511) art.10 (July 1, 2013).
2. Welfare Reform Act 2012 (Commencement No. 9, 11, 13 14, 16, 17 and 19 and Transitional and Transitory Provisions (Amendment)) Order 2014 (SI 2014/3067) art.7(a) (November 24, 2014).

DEFINITIONS

"the amending provisions"–art.2(1).
"the appointed day"–*ibid.*
"contribution-based jobseeker's allowance"–*ibid.*
"jobseeker's allowance"–*ibid.*
"the JSA Regulations 1996"–*ibid.*
"the JSA Regulations 2013"–*ibid.*
"new style JSA award"–*ibid.*
"old style JSA award"–*ibid.*

GENERAL NOTE

This makes transitional provisions for the continuity of jobseeking periods where a person has a new style JSA award and previously had an old style JSA award. Article 13 deals with the converse position.   6.042

[¹ Transition from new style JSA

13. (1) This article applies where a person—   6.043
(a) makes, or is treated as making, a claim for a jobseeker's allowance (whether or not as a member of a joint-claim couple) and the 1995 Act, as it has effect apart from the provisions of Part 1 of Schedule 14 to the Act that remove references to an income-based jobseeker's allowance, applies in relation to the claim; or
(b) has a new style JSA award and article 6(2) applies in relation to the award such that it continues as an old style JSA award,
and, in the case of sub-paragraph (a), the condition referred to in paragraph (2) is satisfied.
(2) The condition is that the person previously—
(a) made, or was treated as having made, a claim for a jobseeker's allowance and, under article 4, the 1995 Act, as amended by the provisions of Part 1 of Schedule 14 to the Act that remove references to an income-based jobseeker's allowance, applied in relation to the claim; or
(b) (i) had an old style JSA award immediately before the appointed day in relation to a case of a claim for universal credit referred to in article 4(2)(a) to (d) (and any award made in respect of the claim), or an award of universal credit referred to in article 4(2)(e) or (f); and

375

(ii) the old style JSA award consisted of or included a contributory employment and support allowance (which allowance therefore continued as a new style JSA award).

(3) Where this article applies, the JSA Regulations 1996 are to be read as if—

[² (za) in regulation 11, the references in paragraph (2)(a) and (b) to a jobseeker's allowance included a reference to new style JSA;]

(a) in regulation 14A (victims of domestic violence), for the purposes of paragraph (3)(b) of that regulation, a person had been treated as available for employment on a day (under paragraph (2) of that regulation) where regulation 15 of the JSA Regulations 2013 applied to that person on that day;

[² (aa) in regulation 17A(7), in paragraph (a) of the definition of "benefit", the reference to a jobseeker's allowance included a reference to new style JSA;

(ab) in regulation 19(1)(r), the reference to a jobseeker's allowance included a reference to new style JSA;]

(b) in regulation 46 (waiting days)—
  (i) where a person was entitled to a new style JSA award with effect from the first day of a jobseeking period by virtue of regulation 36(1) of the JSA Regulations 2013 and, with effect from [³ a day between the second and the seventh day of that period (including the second and the seventh day)], that award continued as an old style JSA award in the circumstances referred to in paragraph (1)(b) of this article, the reference to a jobseeker's allowance in paragraph (1)(a) included a reference to the new style JSA award; and
  (ii) the second reference to a jobseeker's allowance in paragraph (1)(d) included a reference to a new style JSA award;

(c) in regulation 47 (jobseeking period)—
  (i) the jobseeking period in relation to a claimant included any period that, under regulation 37 of the JSA Regulations 2013 (jobseeking period) forms part of the jobseeking period for the purposes of the 1995 Act; and
  (ii) in paragraph (4), the reference to any day that is to be treated as a day in respect of which the claimant was entitled to a contribution-based jobseeker's allowance included a reference to a day that, under regulation 37(3) of the JSA Regulations 2013 (jobseeking period), is to be treated as a day in respect of which the claimant was entitled to a jobseeker's allowance;

(d) in regulation 50 (persons temporarily absent from Great Britain), where a person had a new style JSA award in the circumstances referred to in paragraph (1)(b) of this article, the reference in paragraph (2)(b), (3)(a) and (c), (5)(a) and (c), (6AA)(a) and (6D)(b) to entitlement to a jobseeker's allowance included a reference to the new style JSA award; [² . . .]

(e) in regulation 55 (short periods of sickness), after paragraph (5) there were inserted—

"(6) Where—

    (a) a person has been treated under regulation 46(1) of the Jobseeker's Allowance Regulations 2013 as capable of work or as not having limited capability for work for a certain period; and

    (b) these Regulations apply to that person with effect from a day ("the relevant day") within that period,

the person is to be treated for the part of that period that begins with the relevant day as capable of work or as not having limited capability for work.

  (7) Where paragraph (6) applies to a person and the conditions in paragraph (1)(a) to (c) are fulfilled in relation to that person on any day within the part of a period referred to in paragraph (6), the requirement of paragraph (1) to treat the person as capable of work or as not having limited capability for work is to be regarded as satisfied with respect to the fulfilment of those conditions on that day.

  (8) For the purposes of paragraph (3), where paragraph (6) applies to a person, paragraph (3) is to apply to the person as though the preceding provisions of this regulation had applied to the person with respect to the person having been treated for a period, under regulation 46(1) of the Jobseeker's Allowance Regulations 2013 and paragraph (6), as capable of work or as not having limited capability for work.".

[² (f) in paragraphs 6(1) and 7(1) of Schedule 2 (housing costs), each reference to a jobseeker's allowance included a reference to new style JSA; and

(g) in paragraph 13 of Schedule 2 (housing costs)—

    (i) in paragraph (a) of sub-paragraph (1) (apart from sub-paragraph (ii)(bb) of that paragraph), each of the references to a jobseeker's allowance included a reference to new style JSA;

    (ii) in sub-paragraph (1)(b), the reference to a jobseeker's allowance included a reference to new style JSA; and

    (iii) in sub-paragraph (1)(c)(iv) and (f)(iii), the reference to the making of a claim for a jobseeker's allowance included a reference to the making of a claim for a jobseeker's allowance where the 1995 Act, as it has effect as amended by the amending provisions, applied to the claim and the new style JSA award that resulted from the claim continued as an old style JSA award by virtue of article 6 of this Order.]

(4) Where this article applies, the 1995 Act is to be read as though, in section 5 of the 1995 Act, the reference to a contribution-based jobseeker's allowance in subsection (1) and the first reference to a contribution-based jobseeker's allowance in subsection (2) included a reference to a new style JSA award.

(5) For the purposes of this article, "joint-claim couple" has the meaning given in section 1(4) of the 1995 Act.]

AMENDMENTS

1. Welfare Reform Act 2012 (Commencement No. 11 and Transitional and Transitory Provisions and Commencement No. 9 and Transitional and Transitory Provisions (Amendment)) Order 2013 (SI 2013/1511) art.11 (July 1, 2013).
2. Welfare Reform Act 2012 (Commencement No. 9, 11, 13, 14 and 16 and Transitional and Transitory Provisions (Amendment)) Order 2014 (SI 2014/1452) art.12 (June 16, 2014).
3. Welfare Reform Act 2012 (Commencement No. 9, 11, 13 14, 16, 17 and 19 and Transitional and Transitory Provisions (Amendment)) Order 2014 (SI 2014/3067) art.7(a) (November 24, 2014).

DEFINITIONS

"contribution-based jobseeker's allowance"–art.2(1).
"jobseeker's allowance"–*ibid.*
"the JSA Regulations 1996"–*ibid.*
"the JSA Regulations 2013"–*ibid.*
"new style JSA award"–*ibid.*
"old style JSA award"–*ibid.*

GENERAL NOTE

6.044
This makes transitional provisions for the continuity of jobseeking periods where a person has an old style JSA award and previously had a new style JSA award. Article 12 deals with the converse position.

Sanctions: transition from old style ESA in case of a new award

6.045
14.-(1) This article applies where-
(a) a person is entitled to a new style ESA award and they were previously entitled to an old style ESA award that was not in existence immediately before the first day on which the person in question is entitled to the new style ESA award; and
(b) immediately before the old style ESA award terminated, payments were reduced under regulation 63 of the ESA Regulations 2008 (reduction of employment and support allowance).
(2) Where this article applies-
(a) the failure which led to reduction of the old style ESA award ("the relevant failure") is to be treated for the purposes of Part 8 of the ESA Regulations 2013, as a failure which is sanctionable under section 11J of the 2007 Act (sanctions);
(b) the new style ESA award is to be reduced in relation to the relevant failure, in accordance with the provisions of this article and Part 8 of the ESA Regulations 2013 as modified by this article; and
(c) the reduction referred to in sub-paragraph (b) is to be treated, for the purposes of the ESA Regulations 2013, as a reduction under section 11J of the 2007 Act.
(3) The reduction period for the purposes of the ESA Regulations 2013 is to be the number of days which is equivalent to the length of the fixed period applicable to the person under regulation 63 of the ESA Regulations 2008 in relation to the relevant failure, minus-

(a) the number of days (if any) in that fixed period in respect of which the amount of the old style ESA award was reduced; and

(b) the number of days (if any) in the period starting with the day after the day on which the old style ESA award terminated and ending with the day before the first day on which the person is entitled to the new style ESA award.

(4) Accordingly, regulation 51 of the ESA Regulations 2013 (general principles for calculating reduction periods) applies in relation to the relevant failure as if-

(a) in paragraph (1), for the words "in accordance with regulations 52 and 53" there were substituted the words "in accordance with article 14 of the Welfare Reform Act 2012 (Commencement No. 9 and Transitional and Transitory Provisions and Commencement No. 8 and Savings and Transitional Provisions (Amendment)) Order 2013"; and

(b) in paragraph (3), for the words "in accordance with regulation 52 or 53" there were substituted the words "in accordance with article 14 of the Welfare Reform Act 2012 (Commencement No. 9 and Transitional and Transitory Provisions and Commencement No. 8 and Savings and Transitional Provisions (Amendment)) Order 2013".

DEFINTIONS

"the 2007 Act"–art.2(1).
"employment and support allowance"–*ibid.*
"the ESA Regulations 2008"–*ibid.*
"the ESA Regulations 2013"–*ibid.*
"new style ESA award"–*ibid.*
"old style ESA award"–*ibid.*

GENERAL NOTE

This makes transitional provision in relation to sanctions where a person has   6.046
a new style ESA award and previously had an old style ESA award and was
subject to sanctions.

Sanctions: transition from old style ESA in case of a continuing award

15.-(1) This article applies where-   6.047

(a) the amending provisions have come into force under article 4(1) in relation to the case of a claim for universal credit referred to in [¹ article 4(2)(a)] to (d) (and any award that is made in respect of the claim) or an award of universal credit referred to in article 4(2)(e) or (f);

(b) the person in question had an old style ESA award immediately before the appointed day which consisted of or included a contributory allowance (which allowance therefore continues as a new style ESA award); and

(c) immediately before the appointed day, payments under that award were reduced in accordance with regulation 63 of the ESA Regulations 2008 (reduction of employment and support allowance).

(2) Where this article applies-

(a) the failure which led to reduction of the old style ESA award ("the relevant failure") is to be treated for the purposes of Part 8 of the ESA Regulations 2013, as a failure which is sanctionable under section 11J of the 2007 Act (sanctions);

(b) on and after the appointed day, the award (in its continuation as a new style ESA award) is to be reduced in relation to the relevant failure, in accordance with the provisions of this article and Part 8 of the ESA Regulations 2013 as modified by this article; and

(c) the reduction referred to in sub-paragraph (b) is to be treated, for the purposes of the ESA Regulations 2013, as a reduction under section 11J of the 2007 Act.

(3) The reduction period for the purposes of the ESA Regulations 2013 is to be the number of days which is equivalent to the length of the fixed period applicable to the person under regulation 63 of the ESA Regulations 2008 in relation to the relevant failure, minus the number of days (if any) in that period in respect of which the amount of the old style ESA award was reduced.

(4) Accordingly, regulation 51 of the ESA Regulations 2013 (general principles for calculating reduction periods) applies in relation to the relevant failure as if-

(a) in paragraph (1), for the words "in accordance with regulations 52 and 53" there were substituted the words "in accordance with article 15 of the Welfare Reform Act 2012 (Commencement No. 9 and Transitional and Transitory Provisions and Commencement No. 8 and Savings and Transitional Provisions (Amendment)) Order 2013"; and

(b) in paragraph (3), for the words "in accordance with regulation 52 or 53" there were substituted the words "in accordance with article 15 of the Welfare Reform Act 2012 (Commencement No. 9 and Transitional and Transitory Provisions and Commencement No. 8 and Savings and Transitional Provisions (Amendment)) Order 2013".

AMENDMENT

1. Welfare Reform Act 2012 (Commencement No. 9, 11, 13, 14 and 16 and Transitional and Transitory Provisions (Amendment)) Order 2014 (SI 2014/1452) art.13 (June 16, 2014).

DEFINITIONS

"the 2007 Act"–art.2(1)
"the amending provisions"–*ibid.*
"the appointed day"–*ibid.*
"employment and support allowance"–*ibid.*

"the ESA Regulations 2008"–*ibid.*
"the ESA Regulations 2013"–*ibid.*
"new style ESA award"–*ibid.*

GENERAL NOTE

This makes transitional provision in relation to sanctions where a   **6.048**
person has an award of universal credit and previously had an old style
ESA award which was subject to sanctions.

Escalation of sanctions: transition from old style ESA

16.-(1) This article applies where a person is entitled to a new style   **6.049**
ESA award and, at any time previously, the person was entitled to an old
style ESA award.

(2) Where this article applies, for the purposes of determining the
reduction period under regulation 52 of the ESA Regulations 2013 (low-
level sanction) in relation to a sanctionable failure by the person to
whom the new style award referred to in paragraph (1) was made, other
than a failure which is treated as sanctionable under article 14 or 15-

(a) a reduction of a new style ESA award in accordance with article
14 or 15 as the case may be; and

(b) a reduction of an old style ESA award under the ESA Regulations
2008 which did not result in a reduction under article 14 or 15,

is, subject to paragraph (3), to be treated as arising from a sanctionable
failure for which the reduction period which applies is the number of
days which is equivalent to the length of the fixed period which applied
under regulation 63 of the ESA Regulations 2008 (reduction of employment and support allowance).

(3) In determining a reduction period under regulation 52 of the ESA
Regulations 2013 in accordance with paragraph (2), no account is to be
taken of-

(a) a reduction of a new style ESA award in accordance with article
14 or 15, as the case may be, if, at any time after that reduction,
the person was entitled to an old style ESA award, an old style JSA
award or income support;

(b) a reduction of an old style ESA award under the ESA Regulations
2008 if, at any time after that reduction, the person was entitled to
universal credit, a new style ESA award or a new style JSA award,
and was subsequently entitled to an old style ESA award, an old
style JSA award or income support.

DEFINITIONS

"employment and support allowance"–art.2(1).
"the ESA Regulations 2008"–*ibid.*
"the ESA Regulations 2013"–*ibid.*
"new style JSA award"–*ibid.*
"old style ESA award"–*ibid.*
"old style JSA award"–*ibid.*

GENERAL NOTE

6.050   This ensures that any previous old style ESA fixed period reductions are taken into account when deciding the appropriate reduction period for the purposes of new style ESA award.

Sanctions: transition from old style JSA in case of a new award

6.051   17.-(1) This article applies where-
(a) a person is entitled to a new style JSA award and they were previously entitled to an old style JSA award that was not in existence immediately before the first day on which the person in question is entitled to the new style JSA award;
(b) immediately before that old style award terminated, payments were reduced under section 19 (as it applied both before and after substitution by the Act) (before substitution: circumstances in which a jobseeker's allowance is not payable; after substitution: higher-level sanctions) or 19A (other sanctions) of the 1995 Act, or under regulation 69B of the JSA Regulations 1996 (the period of a reduction under section 19B : Claimants ceasing to be available for employment etc.); and
(c) if the old style JSA award was made to a joint-claim couple within the meaning of the 1995 Act and the reduction related to-
   (i) in the case of a reduction under section 19 as it applied before substitution by the Act, circumstances relating to only one member of the couple; or
   (ii) in the case of a reduction under section 19 as it applied after substitution by the Act, a sanctionable failure by only one member of the couple,
the new style JSA award was made to that member of the couple.
(2) Where this article applies-
(a) the circumstances or failure which led to reduction of the old style JSA award (in either case "the relevant failure") is to be treated, for the purposes of the JSA Regulations 2013, as-
   (i) a failure which is sanctionable under section 6J of the 1995 Act (higher-level sanctions), where the reduction was under section 19 of the 1995 Act; or
   (ii) a failure which is sanctionable under section 6K of the 1995 Act (other sanctions), where the reduction was under section 19A of the 1995 Act or regulation 69B of the JSA Regulations 1996;
(b) the award of new style JSA is to be reduced in relation to the relevant failure, in accordance with the provisions of this article and Part 3 of the JSA Regulations 2013 (sanctions), as modified by this article; and
(c) the reduction is to be treated, for the purposes of the JSA Regulations 2013, as a reduction under section 6J or, as the case may be, section 6K of the 1995 Act.
(3) The reduction period for the purposes of the JSA Regulations 2013 is to be the number of days which is equivalent to the length of the

382

period of reduction of a jobseeker's allowance which is applicable to the person under regulation 69, 69A or 69B of the JSA Regulations 1996, minus-

(a) the number of days (if any) in that period in respect of which the amount of a jobseeker's allowance was reduced; and

(b) the number of days (if any) in the period starting with the day after the day on which the old style JSA award terminated and ending with the day before the first day on which the person is entitled to a new style JSA award.

(4) Accordingly, regulation 18 of the JSA Regulations 2013 (general principles for calculating reduction periods) applies in relation to the relevant failure as if-

(a) in paragraph (1), for the words "in accordance with regulations 19, 20 and 21", there were substituted the words "in accordance with article 17 of the Welfare Reform Act 2012 (Commencement No. 9 and Transitional and Transitory Provisions and Commencement No. 8 and Savings and Transitional Provisions (Amendment)) Order 2013"; and

(b) in paragraph (3), for the words "in accordance with regulation 19, 20 or 21", there were substituted the words "in accordance with article 17 of the Welfare Reform Act 2012 (Commencement No. 9 and Transitional and Transitory Provisions and Commencement No. 8 and Savings and Transitional Provisions (Amendment)) Order 2013".

DEFINITIONS

"the Act"–art.2(1).
"the 1995 Act"–*ibid.*
"jobseeker's allowance"–*ibid.*
"the JSA Regulations 1996"–*ibid.*
"the JSA Regulations 2013"–*ibid.*
"new style JSA award"–*ibid.*
"old style JSA award"–*ibid.*

GENERAL NOTE

This makes transitional provision in relation to sanctions where a 6.052 person has a new style JSA award and previously had an old style JSA award and was subject to sanctions.

Sanctions: transition from old style JSA in case of a continuing award

18.-(1) This article applies where- 6.053

(a) the amending provisions have come into force under article 4(1) in relation to the case of a claim for universal credit referred to in [¹ article 4(2)(a)] to (d) (and any award that is made in respect of the claim) or an award of universal credit referred to in article 4(2)(e) or (f);

(b) the person in question had an old style JSA award immediately before the appointed day which consisted of or included a contribution-based allowance (which allowance therefore continues as a new style JSA award);

(c) immediately before the appointed day, payments under that award were reduced under section 19 (as it applied both before and after substitution by the Act) (before substitution: circumstances in which a jobseeker's allowance is not payable; after substitution: higher-level sanctions) or 19A (other sanctions) of the 1995 Act, or under regulation 69B of the JSA Regulations 1996) (the period of a reduction under section 19B : Claimants ceasing to be available for employment etc.); and

(d) if the old style JSA award was made to a joint-claim couple within the meaning of the 1995 Act and the reduction related to-
    (i) in the case of a reduction under section 19 as it applied before substitution by the Act, circumstances relating to only one member of the couple; or
    (ii) in the case of a reduction under section 19 as it applied after substitution by the Act, a sanctionable failure by only one member of the couple,
    the new style JSA award was made to that member of the couple.

(2) Where this article applies-

(a) the circumstances or failure which led to reduction of the old style JSA award (in either case "the relevant failure") is to be treated, for the purposes of the JSA Regulations 2013, as-
    (i) a failure which is sanctionable under section 6J of the 1995 Act (higher-level sanctions), where the reduction was under section 19 of the 1995 Act; or
    (ii) a failure which is sanctionable under section 6K of the 1995 Act (other sanctions), where the reduction was under section 19A of the 1995 Act or regulation 69B of the JSA Regulations 1996;

(b) the award (in its continuation as a new style JSA award) is to be reduced in relation to the relevant failure, in accordance with the provisions of this article and Part 3 of the JSA Regulations (sanctions), as modified by this article; and

(c) the reduction is to be treated, for the purposes of the JSA Regulations 2013, as a reduction under section 6J or, as the case may be, section 6K of the 1995 Act.

(3) The reduction period for the purposes of the JSA Regulations 2013 is to be the number of days which is equivalent to the length of the period of reduction of a jobseeker's allowance which is applicable to the person under regulation 69, 69A or 69B of the JSA Regulations 1996, minus the number of days (if any) in that period in respect of which the amount of a jobseeker's allowance was reduced.

(4) Accordingly, regulation 18 of the JSA Regulations 2013 (general principles for calculating reduction periods) applies in relation to the relevant failure as if-

(a) in paragraph (1), for the words "in accordance with regulations 19, 20 and 21", there were substituted the words "in accordance with article 18 of the Welfare Reform Act 2012 (Commencement No. 9 and Transitional and Transitory Provisions and Commencement No. 8 and Savings and Transitional Provisions (Amendment)) Order 2013"; and

(b) in paragraph (3), for the words "in accordance with regulation 19, 20 or 21", there were substituted the words "in accordance with article 18 of the Welfare Reform Act 2012 (Commencement No. 9 and Transitional and Transitory Provisions and Commencement No. 8 and Savings and Transitional Provisions (Amendment)) Order 2013".

AMENDMENT

1. Welfare Reform Act 2012 (Commencement No. 9, 11, 13, 14 and 16 and Transitional and Transitory Provisions (Amendment)) Order 2014 (SI 2014/1452) art.13 (June 16, 2014).

DEFINITIONS

"the Act"–art.2(1).
"the 1995 Act"–*ibid.*
"the amending provisions"–*ibid.*
"the appointed day"–*ibid.*
"jobseeker's allowance"–*ibid.*
"the JSA Regulations 1996"–*ibid.*
"the JSA Regulations 2013"–*ibid.*
"new style JSA award"–*ibid.*
"old style JSA award"–*ibid.*

GENERAL NOTE

This is the JSA equivalent to reg.15.   6.054

Escalation of sanctions: transition from old style JSA

19.-(1) This article applies where a person is entitled to a new style   6.055
JSA award and, at any time previously, the person was entitled to an old
style JSA award.

(2) Where this article applies, for the purposes of determining the
applicable reduction period under regulation 19 (higher-level sanction),
20 (medium-level sanction) or 21 (low-level sanction) of the JSA Regulations 2013 in relation to a sanctionable failure by the person other than
a failure which is treated as sanctionable by virtue of article 17 or 18-

(a) a reduction of a new style JSA award in accordance with article 17
or 18; and

(b) a reduction of an old style JSA award under section 19 (as it
applied both before and after substitution by the Act) or 19A of
the 1995 Act, or under regulation 69B of the JSA Regulations
1996, which did not result in a reduction under article 17 or
18,

is, subject to paragraph (3), to be treated as arising from a sanctionable
failure for which the reduction period is the number of days which is

equivalent to the length of the period which applied under regulation 69, 69A or 69B of the JSA Regulations 1996.

(3) In determining a reduction period under regulation 19 (higher-level sanction), 20 (medium-level sanction) or 21 (low-level sanction) of the JSA Regulations 2013 in accordance with paragraph (2), no account is to be taken of-

(a) a reduction of a new style JSA award in accordance with article 17 or 18 if, at any time after that reduction, the person was entitled to an old style JSA award, an old style ESA award or income support;

(b) a reduction of an old style JSA award under section 19 (as it applied both before and after substitution by the Act) or 19A of the 1995 Act, or under regulation 69B of the JSA Regulations 1996, if, at any time after that reduction, the person was entitled to universal credit, a new style JSA award or a new style ESA award, and was subsequently entitled to an old style JSA award, an old style ESA award or income support.

DEFINITIONS

"the Act"–art.2(1).
"the 1995 Act"–*ibid.*
"the JSA Regulations 1996"–*ibid.*
"the JSA Regulations 2013"–*ibid.*
"new style JSA award"–*ibid.*
"old style ESA award"–*ibid.*
"old style JSA award"–*ibid.*

GENERAL NOTE

6.056   This is the JSA equivalent to reg.16.

Termination of sanctions under a new style ESA or JSA award

6.057   **20.**-(1) Paragraph (2) applies where-

(a) a new style ESA award or new style JSA award terminates while there is an outstanding reduction period (within the meaning of regulation 55 of the ESA Regulations 2013 (reduction period to continue where award of employment and support allowance terminates) or regulation 23 of the JSA Regulations 2013 (reduction period to continue where award of jobseeker's allowance terminates)) and the claimant becomes entitled to an old style ESA award, an old style JSA award or income support during that period; or

(b) article 6(2) applies to a new style ESA award or new style JSA award (such that it continues as an old style ESA award or an old style JSA award) and there is such an outstanding reduction period on the last day of the period of the new style ESA award or new style JSA award.

(2) Where this paragraph applies-

(a) regulation 55 of the ESA Regulations 2013 or regulation 23 of the JSA Regulations 2013, as the case may be, are to cease to apply; and

(b) the reduction period is to terminate on the first day of entitlement to an old style ESA award, old style JSA award or income support as the case may be.

DEFINITIONS

"employment and support allowance"–art.2(1).
"the ESA Regulations 2013"–*ibid.*
"jobseeker's allowance"–*ibid.*
"the JSA Regulations 2013"–*ibid.*
"new style ESA award"–*ibid.*
"new style JSA award"–*ibid.*
"old style JSA award"–*ibid.*

GENERAL NOTE

This provides that where a claimant has a new style ESA (or new style JSA) award, is subject to sanctions and subsequently becomes entitled to an old style ESA (or old style JSA) award or income support, then the sanctions cease to have effect.   6.058

Transitory provisions: appeals

21.-(1) Paragraph (2) applies where-   6.059
(a) the amending provisions have come into force under article 4(1) in relation to the case of a claim referred to in article 4(2)(a) to (d) (and any award that is made in respect of the claim) or the case of an award referred to in article 4(2)(e) or (f);
(b) the person is sent notice of a decision relating to a new style ESA award or a new style JSA award; and
(c) the date of notification with respect to that decision is before 28th October 2013.

(2) Where this paragraph applies, the provisions mentioned in paragraph (3) apply for the purposes of any appeal in relation to that decision as if regulation 55 of the Decisions and Appeals Regulations 2013 (consequential amendments) did not apply in that person's case.

(3) The provisions referred to are the following provisions of the Social Security and Child Support (Decisions and Appeals) Regulations 1999-
(a) regulation 32 (late appeals);
(b) regulation 33 (notice of appeal); and
(c) regulation 34 (death of a party to an appeal).

(4) For the purposes of paragraph (1), "the date of notification" means the date on which the decision notice was posted to the person's last known address by the Secretary of State.

DEFINITIONS

"the amending provisions"–art.2(1).
"the Decisions and Appeals Regulations 2013"–*ibid.*
"new style JSA award"–*ibid.*

GENERAL NOTE

6.060   This makes limited transitory provision with respect to appeals where a person is sent a notice relating to a new style ESA award or a new style JSA award before October 29, 2013.

Transitional provision: references to contributory employment and support allowance and contribution-based jobseeker's allowance

6.061   **22.** Where the amending provisions have come into force under article 4(1) in relation to the case of a claim referred to in article 4(2)(a) to (d) [¹ or (g)] (and any award that is made in respect of the claim) or the case of an award referred to in article 4(2)(e) or (f), then, in relation to such a case, any reference in the Social Security Administration Act 1992 or the Social Security Contributions and Benefits Act 1992 to-
   (a)   a contributory employment and support allowance is to be read as if it included a reference to a new style ESA award; and
   (b)   a contribution-based jobseeker's allowance is to be read as if it included a reference to a new style JSA award.

AMENDMENT

1.   Welfare Reform Act 2012 (Commencement No. 9, 11, 13, 14 and 16 and Transitional and Transitory Provisions (Amendment)) Order 2014 (SI 2014/1452) art.14 (June 16, 2014).

DEFINITIONS

"the amending provisions"–*ibid.*
"contribution-based jobseeker's allowance"–*ibid.*
"contributory employment and support allowance"–*ibid.*
"new style JSA award"–*ibid.*

GENERAL NOTE

6.062   This provision seeks to ensure that new style ESA and JSA awards are to be treated to all intents and purposes as awards of a contributory employment or support allowance or to a contribution-based jobseeker's allowance respectively. It does so by providing that, in relation to a case with respect to which art.4 has come into force, references in the SSAA 1992 and the SSCBA 1992 are to be construed as if they included a reference to a new style ESA award or to a new style JSA award respectively.

Amendment of the Welfare Reform Act 2012 (Commencement No 8 and Savings and Transitional Provisions) Order 2013

6.063   **23.**-(1) Article 5 of the Welfare Reform Act 2012 (Commencement No 8 and Savings and Transitional Provisions) Order 2013 (appointed day and saving for provisions relating to overpayments) is amended as follows.

(2) In paragraph (3)(a), at the beginning insert "subject to paragraph (3A),".

(3) After paragraph (3) insert-

"(3A) In so far as section 105(1) of the 2012 Act inserts section 71ZB(1)(b) and (c) of the 1992 Act, those paragraphs come into force on 29th April 2013 only in so far as they relate respectively to a new style JSA award and a new style ESA award.".

(4) In paragraph (6), for "those benefits have been claimed before 29th April 2013" substitute "they relate respectively to an old style JSA award and an old style ESA award".

(5) After paragraph (6) add-

"(7) In this article, "old style JSA award", "new style JSA award", "old style ESA award" and "new style ESA award" have the same meaning as in article 2(1) of the Welfare Reform Act 2012 (Commencement No. 9 and Transitional and Transitory Provisions and Commencement No. 8 and Savings and Transitional Provisions (Amendment)) Order 2013.".

DEFINITIONS

"the appointed day"–art.2(1).
"new style JSA award"–*ibid*.
"old style ESA award"–*ibid*.
"old style JSA award"–*ibid*.

GENERAL NOTE

This amends art.5 of the Commencement No. 8 Order as regards over-payments. It is intended to make it clear that the new rules applying to overpayments of employment and support allowance and of jobseeker's allowance under the WRA 2012 apply only to overpayments of a new style ESA award and a new style JSA award respectively (para.(3)). The amendments also clarify that the old rules relating to overpayments of those benefits will continue to apply to overpayments of an old style ESA award and an old style JSA award respectively (para.(4)). **6.064**

[¹ Appeals relating to ESA and JSA

24. (1) This article applies where, after an award of universal credit **6.065** has been made to a claimant (where that award is made by virtue of the coming into force of the provisions of the Act referred to in Schedule 2, under any secondary legislation) —

    (a) an appeal against a decision relating to the entitlement of the claimant to an old style ESA award or an old style JSA award is finally determined; or

    (b) a decision relating to the claimant's entitlement to such an award is revised under section 9 of the Social Security Act 1998 ("the 1998 Act") or superseded under section 10 of that Act.

(2) Where this article applies, the Secretary of State is to consider whether it is appropriate to revise under section 9 of the 1998 Act the decision in relation to entitlement to universal credit or, if that decision has been superseded under section 10 of that Act, the decision as so superseded (in either case, "the UC decision").

(3) Where it appears to the Secretary of State to be appropriate to revise the UC decision, it is to be revised in such manner as appears to the Secretary of State to be necessary to take account of—

(a) the decision of the First-tier Tribunal, Upper Tribunal or court, or, as the case may be, the decision relating to entitlement to an old style ESA award or an old style JSA award, as revised or superseded; and

(b) any finding of fact by the First-tier Tribunal, Upper Tribunal or court.

(4) For the purposes of this article, "secondary legislation" means an instrument made under an Act.]

AMENDMENT

1. Welfare Reform Act 2012 (Commencement No. 9, 11, 13, 14 and 16 and Transitional and Transitory Provisions (Amendment)) Order 2014 (SI 2014/1452) art.15 (June 16, 2014).

SCHEDULE 1

6.066   POSTCODE DISTRICTS

1. M43
2. OL6
3. OL7
4. SK16

Article 3(2)

6.067   SCHEDULE 2

UNIVERSAL CREDIT PROVISIONS COMING INTO FORCE IN RELATION TO CERTAIN CLAIMS AND AWARDS

1. Section 1 (universal credit).
2. Section 2(1) (claims).
3. Section 3 (entitlement).
4. Section 4(1) and (4) (basic conditions).
5. Section 5 (financial conditions).
6. Section 6 (restrictions on entitlement).
7. Section 7(1) and (4) (basis of awards).
8. Section 8 (calculation of awards).
9. Section 9(1) (standard allowance).
10. Section 10(1) (responsibility for children and young persons).
11. Section 11(1) and (2) (housing costs).
12. Section 12(1) and (2) (other particular needs or circumstances).
13. Section 13 (work-related requirements: introductory).
14. Section 14 (claimant commitment).
15. Section 15(1) and (4) (work-focused interview requirement).
16. Section 16 (work preparation requirement).
17. Section 17(1), (2), (3)(a) to (e), (4) and (5) (work search requirement).
18. Section 18 (work availability requirement).
19. Section 19(1), (2)(a) to (c), (5) and (6) (claimants subject to no work-related requirements).
20. Section 20 (claimants subject to work-focused interview requirement only).
21. Section 21 (claimants subject to work preparation requirement).
22. Section 22 (claimants subject to all work-related requirements).
23. Section 23 (connected requirements).
24. Section 24(2), (3) and (4) (imposition of requirements).
25. Section 26(1) to (5) (higher-level sanctions).
26. Section 27(1) to (3) and (6) to (8) (other sanctions).

Article 4(1)

6.068   SCHEDULE 3

COMMENCEMENT OF REPEALS IN PART 1 OF SCHEDULE 14 TO THE ACT

Short title and chapter	Extent of repeal
Jobseekers Act 1995 (c.18)	Section 1(2A) to (2D) and (4). In section 2, in subsection (3C)(d), "contribution-based". Sections 3 to 3B. In section 4— (a) in subsection (1), "contribution-based"; (b) subsections (3), (3A) and (6) to (11A). Section 4A. In section 5— (a) in the heading and in subsection (1) "contribution-based"; (b) in subsection (2), "contribution-based" in the first two places; (c) in subsection (3), "contribution-based". Section 13. Sections 15 to 17. In section 17A(10), the definition of "claimant". Section 23. Section 26. In section 35(1)— (a) in the definition of "claimant", the words from "except" to the end; (b) the definitions of "contribution-based jobseeker's allowance", "income-based jobseeker's allowance", "income-related employment and support allowance", "joint-claim couple", "joint-claim jobseeker's allowance" and "the nominated member". In section 38— (a) in subsections (3) and (4), "contribution-based"; (b) subsection (6). In Schedule 1— (a) in paragraph 6(1), "contribution-based"; (b) paragraphs 8 and 8A; (c) paragraphs 9 to 10; (d) in paragraph 11(1), "contribution-based"; (e) in paragraph 16(1) and (2)(d), "contribution-based"; (f) paragraph 18(b) and (c).
Welfare Reform and Pensions Act 1999 (c.30)	In Schedule 7, paragraphs 2(3) and (4), 4, 5(3) and (4), 6, 9 to 11, 15 and 16. In Schedule 8, paragraph 29(2).
State Pension Credit Act 2002 (c.16)	In Schedule 2, paragraphs 36 to 38.
Income Tax (Earnings and Payments) Act 2003 (c.1)	In Schedule 6, paragraphs 228 to 230.

Short title and chapter	Extent of repeal
Civil Partnership Act 2004 (c.33)	In Schedule 24, paragraphs 118 to 122.
Welfare Reform Act 2007 (c.5)	In section 1— (a) in subsection (2), in the opening words, "either"; (b) in subsection (2)(a), "Part 1 of" and "that Part of"; (c) subsection (2)(b) and the preceding "or"; (d) in subsection (3)(f), the words from "(and" to "allowance)"; (e) in subsection (3A), "Part 1 of"; (f) in subsection (6), the definition of "joint-claim jobseeker's allowance"; (g) subsections (6A) and (7). In subsection 1A— (a) in the heading "contributory"; (b) in subsections (1) (in both places), (3) and (4), "Part 1 of". Section 1B(2). In section 2, in the heading, "contributory". In section 3, in the heading, "contributory". Sections 4 to 6.
	Section 23. In section 24(1), the definitions of "contributory allowance" and "income-related allowance". In section 26(1)(a), "or 4(4)(c) or (5)(c)". Section 27(2)(a) and (4). In Schedule 1— (a) the heading to Part 1; (b) Part 2. In Schedule 2— (a) in the headings to paragraphs 6 and 7, "Contributory allowance:"; (b) paragraph 8; (c) paragraph 11(b) and (c); (d) paragraph 12, so far as not otherwise repealed.
Welfare Reform Act 2009 (c.24)	In Part 3 of Schedule 7, the entry relating to the Civil Partnership Act 2004.

Article 9

6.069

SCHEDULE 4

MODIFICATIONS OF THE 2010 TRANSITIONAL REGULATIONS

1. The 2010 Transitional Regulations are to be read as if the amendments set out in this Schedule were made.

2. (1) Regulation 2 (interpretation) is amended as follows.

(2) In paragraph (1)—

(a) insert at the appropriate places in the alphabetical order of the definitions—

""the Claims and Payments Regulations" means the Universal Credit, Personal Independence Payment, Jobseeker's Allowance and Employment and Support Allowance (Claims and Payments) Regulations 2013;";

""the Decisions and Appeals Regulations" means the Universal Credit, Personal Independence Payment, Jobseeker's Allowance and Employment and Support Allowance (Decisions and Appeals) Regulations 2013;";

""the ESA Regulations" means the Employment and Support Allowance Regulations 2013;";

(b) omit—
  (i) the definition of "income-related allowance";
  (ii) paragraphs (a) to (d) of the definition of "relevant deduction";
(c) in the definition of "benefit week", for "the 2008 Regulations" substitute "the ESA Regulations".
(3) In paragraph (3), omit "or awards".
3. In regulation 4 (the notice commencing the conversion phase), omit paragraph (6).
4. In regulation 5 (deciding whether an existing award qualifies for conversion)—
(a) in paragraph (1), omit "or awards";
(b) in paragraph (2)(a), for "or awards qualify" substitute "qualifies";
(c) in paragraph (2)(b), for "or awards do" substitute "does";
(d) in paragraph (6)(b), omit "or awards".
5. In regulation 6(2) (application of certain enactments for purpose of making conversion decisions)—
(a) for sub-paragraphs (b) and (c), substitute—

"(b) the ESA Regulations;
(c) regulation 38(2) and (3) of the Claims and Payments Regulations (evidence and information in connection with an award);";

(b) for sub-paragraph (e), substitute—

"(e) the Decisions and Appeals Regulations."

6. In regulation 7 (qualifying for conversion)—
(a) in paragraph (1)—
  (i) omit "or awards";
  (ii) for "qualify" substitute "qualifies";
(b) in paragraphs (2)(b) and (3)(b), for "regulation 30 of the 2008 Regulations" substitute "regulation 26 of the ESA Regulations".
7. In regulation 8(1) (amount of an employment and support allowance on conversion), for "the 2008 Regulations" substitute "the ESA Regulations".
8. In regulation 9(1) (determining entitlement to a transitional addition)—
(a) for "or awards qualify" substitute "qualifies";
(b) omit "or 11(2) (transitional addition: income support)".
9. In regulation 10 (transitional addition: incapacity benefit or severe disablement allowance)—
(a) in paragraph (1), omit "(and for these purposes it is irrelevant whether the person is also entitled to any existing award of income support)";
(b) in paragraph (4)(a), for "paragraph (2) of regulation 67 of the 2008 Regulations (prescribed amounts for purpose of calculating a contributory allowance)" substitute "paragraph (1) of regulation 62 of the ESA Regulations (prescribed amounts)".
10. Omit regulation 11 (transitional addition: income support).
11. In regulation 12 (regulations 10 and 11: supplementary)—
(a) in the title, for "Regulations 10 and 11" substitute "Regulation 10";
(b) in paragraph (1), for "regulations 10 and 11" substitute "regulation 10";
(c) in paragraph (2), for "Amounts A and C are" substitute "Amount A is" and for "Amounts B and D are" substitute "Amount B is";
(d) for paragraph (3)(a), substitute—

"(a) by virtue of an order made under section 150 of the Administration Act (annual up-rating of benefits), there is an increase in the weekly rate which, in accordance with regulation 10(3) (transitional addition: incapacity benefit or severe disablement allowance), is to be used to calculate Amount A; and";

(e) in paragraph (4)(a), for "paragraph (3)(a)(i) or (ii)" substitute "paragraph (3)(a)";

(f) in paragraphs (3) and (4), omit "or C" and "or applicable amount (as the case may be)".

12. In regulation 13(3) (the effective date of a conversion decision), omit "or awards".

13. In regulation 14 (conversion decision that existing award qualifies for conversion)—

    (a) in paragraph (1)—

        (i) for "Subject to paragraph (2A), paragraphs (2) to (6)" substitute "Paragraphs (2) to (5)";

        (ii) for "or awards qualify" substitute "qualifies";

    (b) for paragraph (2), substitute—

        "(2) On the effective date of the conversion decision P's existing award is by virtue of this paragraph converted into, and shall have effect on and after that date as, a single award of an employment and support allowance of such amount as is specified in the conversion decision.";

    (c) omit paragraphs (2A), (2B) and (6);

    (d) in paragraph (4), omit "or awards";

    (e) for paragraph (7), substitute—

        "(7) In this regulation paragraphs (2) to (5) are subject to regulation 17 (changes of circumstances before the effective date).".

14. In regulation 15 (conversion decision that existing award does not qualify for conversion)—

    (a) in paragraph (1)—

        (i) for "Subject to paragraphs (2A) and (4), paragraphs (2), (3) and (6)" substitute "Subject to paragraph (4), paragraphs (2) and (3)";

        (ii) for "or awards do" substitute "does";

    (b) for paragraph (2), substitute—

        "(2) P's entitlement to an existing award of incapacity benefit or severe disablement allowance shall terminate by virtue of this paragraph immediately before the effective date of P's conversion decision.";

    (c) omit paragraphs (2A), (2B) and (6);

    (d) in paragraph (4)(a)—

        (i) for "the 2008 Regulations" substitute "the ESA Regulations";

        (ii) in paragraph (i), for "regulation 22(1) (failure to provide information or evidence requested in relation to limited capability for work)" substitute "regulation 18(1) (failure to provide information in relation to limited capability for work)";

        (iii) in paragraph (ii), for "regulation 23(2) (failure to attend for a medical examination to determine whether the claimant has limited capability for work)" substitute "regulation 19(2) (claimant may be called for a medical examination to determine whether the claimant has limited capability for work)";

    (e) in paragraph (5)—

        (i) in sub-paragraph (c), omit "or awards";

        (ii) in sub-paragraph (d), omit "or those existing awards";

    (f) for paragraph (7), substitute—

        "(7) In this regulation paragraphs (2) and (3) are subject to regulation 17 (changes of circumstances before the effective date).".

15. In regulation 16 (application of other enactments applying to employment and support allowance)—

    (a) in paragraph (1A)(b), for "regulation 145(1) of the 2008 Regulations" substitute "regulation 86 of the ESA Regulations";

    (b) in paragraph (2)(e)(ii), for "the 2008 Regulations" substitute "the ESA Regulations";

    (c) in paragraph (2)(e)(iii), omit "(being regulations consequentially amended by regulations made under Part 1 of the 2007 Act)".

16. In regulation 17 (changes of circumstances before the effective date)—

    (a) omit "or awards" in both places where it occurs;

(b) in paragraph (a)(ii)—
  (i) omit "regulation 14(2B)(a) (termination of an existing award of incapacity benefit or severe disablement allowance where entitlement to award of income support continues),";
  (ii) for "(termination of existing awards which do not qualify for conversion)" substitute "(termination of an existing award which does not qualify for conversion)";
(c) omit paragraph (c).

17. In regulation 18 (reducing the transitional addition: general rule), for paragraph (2) substitute—

"(2) For the purposes of paragraph (1), a relevant increase is an increase in any amount applicable to the person under regulation 62(1) or (2) of the ESA Regulations, which is not excluded by paragraph (3).".

18. In regulation 21 (termination of transitional addition)—
(a) in paragraph (1)(b)—
  (i) for ", (3), (3A) and (4)" substitute ", (3) and (3A)"and (4)";
  (ii) omit "an employment and support allowance (entitlement to which arises from sections 1(2)(a) or 1(2)(b) of the 2007 Act), or to" and "or to an income-related allowance";
(b) omit paragraph (4);
(c) in paragraph (5)(a), for "regulation 145(1) of the 2008 Regulations (linking rules)" substitute "regulation 86 of the ESA Regulations (linking period)";
(d) in paragraph (5)(c)(ii), for "regulation 30 of the 2008 Regulations" substitute "regulation 26 of the ESA Regulations";
(e) in paragraph (5A)(c), for "regulation 145(1) of the 2008 Regulations (linking rules)" substitute "regulation 86 of the ESA Regulations (linking period)";
(f) omit paragraph (6);
(g) in paragraph (7)—
  (i) for ", 1A and 2" substitute "and 1A";
  (ii) omit "or additions, as the case may be," in both places where it occurs;
  (iii) for "an allowance which is referred to in paragraph (1)(b)" substitute "a contributory allowance".

19. In regulation 22 (disapplication of certain enactments following conversion decision), omit paragraphs (c) and (d).

20. In Schedule 1 (modification of enactments: making conversion decisions)—
(a) in paragraph 2(a), for the modified section 1(2) substitute—
    "(2) Subject to the provisions of this Part, a notified person is entitled to an employment and support allowance if the person satisfies the basic conditions and is entitled to an existing award of incapacity benefit or severe disablement allowance.";

(b) for paragraph 6, substitute—

    "6. Schedule 1 to the 2007 Act is to be read as if paragraphs 1 to 6 were omitted.";

(c) in the heading to Part 2, for "the 2008 Regulations" substitute "the ESA Regulations";
(d) in paragraph 10, for "Regulation 30" substitute "Regulation 26";
(e) omit paragraph 10A;
(f) in paragraph 11, for "Regulation 75" substitute "Regulation 68";
(g) in paragraph 12, for "Regulation 144" substitute "Regulation 85";
(h) in the sub-heading to Part 3, for "Social Security (Claims and Payments) Regulations 1987" substitute "The Claims and Payments Regulations";
(i) in paragraph 13—
  (i) for "Regulation 32 of the Social Security (Claims and Payments) Regulations 1987" substitute "Regulation 38 of the Claims and Payments Regulations";
  (ii) in sub-paragraph (a), for "paragraph (1)" substitute "paragraph (2)";
  (iii) in sub-paragraph (b), for "paragraph (1A)" substitute "paragraph (3)".

21. (1) Schedule 2 (modification of enactments: after the conversion phase) is amended as follows.

(2) In paragraph 2—

(a) in sub-paragraph (a), in the modified section 1(2)–

    (i) in paragraph (a), for "or awards into a single award of an employment and support allowance;" substitute "into an award of an employment and support allowance; and";

    (ii) omit paragraph (c) and for "; and" at the end of paragraph (b) substitute "; ";

(b) in sub-paragraph (b) in the modified section 1(7)—

    [¹ (i) for the definition of "contributory allowance" substitute-

    "employment and support allowance" means an employment and support allowance to which a person is entitled by virtue of the Employment and Support Allowance (Transitional Provisions, Housing Benefit and Council Tax Benefit)(Existing Awards)(No.2) Regulations 2010 which was based on an award of incapacity benefit or severe disablement allowance to which the person was entitled.]

    and for "; and" following that definition substitute "."];

    (ii) omit the definition of "income-related allowance".

[¹ (2A) In paragraph 2A-

(a) in paragraph (1), omit "contributory"; and

(b) in paragraph (2), in the substituted section 1A

    (i) in paragraphs (1) and (3) to (5), for " a contributory allowance" substitute "an employment and support allowance"; and

    (ii) in paragraph (3), omit "Part 1 of".]

(3) In paragraph 3(b), for "regulation 147A of the 2008 Regulations" substitute "regulation 87 of the ESA Regulations".

(4) Omit paragraphs 4 and 4A.

(5) In paragraph 6A—

(a) in sub-paragraph (a), after paragraph (iv) insert "and";

(b) in sub-paragraph (b), for "; and" substitute ".";

(c) omit sub-paragraph (c).

(6) In the heading to Part 3, for "the 2008 Regulations" substitute "the ESA Regulations".

(7) In paragraph 8, for "regulation 147A of the 2008 Regulations" substitute "regulation 87 of the ESA Regulations".

(8) In paragraph 10, for "regulation 30" substitute "regulation 26".

"(9) For paragraph 11, substitute—

    11. Regulation 39 (exempt work) is to be read as if, in the definition of "work period" in paragraph (6), after "referred to in paragraph (1)(c)", in both places where it occurs, there were inserted ", or any work done in accordance with regulation 17(4)(a) of the Social Security (Incapacity for Work)(General) Regulations 1995.

(10) For paragraph 12, substitute—"

    "**12.** Regulation 62 (prescribed amounts) is to be read as if, in paragraph (1), for sub-paragraphs (a) and (b) there were substituted—

        (a) (i) where the claimant satisfies the conditions set out in section 2(2) or (3) of the Act, £71.70; or

            (ii) where the claimant does not satisfy the conditions set out in section 2(2) or (3) of the Act—

            (aa) where the claimant is aged not less than 25, £71.70; or

            (bb) where the claimant is aged less than 25, £56.80; and

    (b) the amount of any transitional addition to which the person is entitled under regulation 10 of the Employment and Support Allowance (Transitional Provisions, Housing Benefit and Council Tax Benefit) (Existing Awards) (No.2) Regulations 2010."

(9) Omit paragraph 13.

(10) In paragraph 14—

(a) for "Regulation 75" substitute "Regulation 68";

(b) for "paragraph 38" substitute "paragraph 11".

(11) In paragraph 15—

(a) in the introductory words, for "Regulation 147A" substitute "regulation 87";

(b) in the inserted regulation—

(i) in the description of the number of the regulation, for "147A.—" substitute "87.—";

(ii) in paragraph (2), for "regulation 19" substitute "regulation 15";

(iii) in paragraph (4)(a), for "regulation 22 or 23" substitute "regulation 18 or 19";

(iv) for "regulation 30", in all places where it occurs, substitute "regulation 26";

(v) in paragraph (5)(c), for the words from ", struck out" to "(notice of appeal)", substitute "or struck out";

(vi) in paragraph (5A), for "either—" and sub-paragraphs (a) and (b), substitute "receives the First-tier Tribunal's notification that the appeal is dismissed, withdrawn or struck out.".

(12) Omit paragraph 16.

(13) In the sub-heading before paragraph 17, for "Social Security (Claims and Payments) Regulations 1987" substitute "The Claims and Payments Regulations".

(14) In paragraph 17, for "The Social Security (Claims and Payments) Regulations 1987" substitute "The Claims and Payments Regulations".

(15) For paragraph 18 substitute—

"18. Regulation 7 (claims not required for entitlement to an employment and support allowance in certain cases) is to read as if—

(a) the existing provisions were renumbered as paragraph (1);

(b) after paragraph (1) there were inserted—

(2) It is also not to be a condition of entitlement to an employment and support allowance that a claim be made for it where any of the following conditions are met—

(a) the claimant—

(i) has made and is pursuing an appeal against a conversion decision made by virtue of the Employment and Support Allowance (Transitional Provisions, Housing Benefit and Council Tax Benefit) (Existing Awards) (No. 2) Regulations 2010 which embodies a determination that the beneficiary does not have limited capability for work; or

(ii) was entitled to an employment and support allowance by virtue of the Employment and Support Allowance (Transitional Provisions, Housing Benefit and Council Tax Benefit) (Existing Awards) (No. 2) Regulations 2010 and has made and is pursuing an appeal against a later decision which embodies a determination that the claimant does not have limited capability for work; or

(b) the claimant is entitled to an existing award which is subject to conversion under the Employment and Support Allowance (Transitional Provisions, Housing Benefit and Council Tax Benefit) (Existing Awards) (No. 2) Regulations 2010." "

(16) In paragraph 19, for "regulation 26C" substitute "regulation 51".

(17) In paragraph 20—

(a) for "regulation 32(1B)" substitute "regulation 38(4)";

(b) in sub-paragraph (a), for the words "sub-paragraph (a)" substitute "sub-paragraph (b)";

(c) in sub-paragraph (b), for "(ab)" substitute "(bb)".

(18) Omit paragraph 21.

(19) In paragraph 22, for "Schedule 9B" substitute "Schedule 7".

(20) In paragraph 22A, in the inserted text omit paragraph (2B).

(21) In paragraph 23, in the inserted text omit paragraph (2B).

(22) In paragraph 24, in the inserted text omit paragraph (2B).

(23) In paragraph 25, in the inserted text omit paragraph (2B).

(24) In the sub-heading before paragraph 25A, for "Social Security and Child Support (Decisions and Appeals) Regulations 1999" substitute "Universal Credit, Personal Independence Payment, Jobseeker's Allowance and Employment and Support Allowance (Decisions and Appeals) Regulations 2013".

(25) In paragraph 25A—

(a) in sub-paragraph (1), for "Regulation 3 of the Social Security and Child Support (Decisions and Appeals) Regulations 1999 (revision of decisions)" substitute "Regulation 5 of the Universal Credit, Personal Independence Payment, Jobseeker's Allowance and Employment and Support Allowance (Decisions and Appeals) Regulations 2013 (revision on any grounds)";

(b) in sub-paragraph (1)(b), for "paragraph (9)(a)" substitute "paragraphs (2)(a) and (b)";

(c) for sub-paragraph (1)(c), substitute—

"(c) in paragraph (2)(a), for "in the case of an advance award under regulation 32, 33 or 34 of the Claims and Payment Regulations 2013" there were substituted, "in the case of an advance award under regulation 32, 33 or 34 of the Claims and Payment Regulations 2013 or a conversion decision within the meaning of regulation 5(2)(a) of the Employment and Support Allowance (Transitional Provisions, Housing Benefit and Council Tax Benefit) (Existing Awards) (No. 2) Regulations 2010".";

(d) for sub-paragraph (2), substitute—

"(2) Regulation 23(1)(a) of those Regulations (change of circumstances) is to be read as if for "in the case of an advance award under regulation 32, 33 or 34 of the Claims and Payments Regulations 2013" there were substituted "in the case of an advance award under regulation 32, 33 or 34 of the Claims and Payments Regulations 2013 or a conversion decision within the meaning of regulation 5(2)(a) of the Employment and Support Allowance (Transitional Provisions, Housing Benefit and Council Tax Benefit) (Existing Awards) (No. 2) Regulations 2010." "

(26) Omit paragraph 27.

22. In Schedule 3—

(a) for "The Social Security (Claims and Payments) Regulations 1987" substitute "the Claims and Payments Regulations";

(b) for " The Social Security and Child Support (Decisions and Appeals) Regulations 1999" substitute "the Decisions and Appeals Regulations".

AMENDMENTS

1. Welfare Reform Act 2012 (Commencement No. 11 and Transitional and Transitory Provisions and Commencement No. 9 and Transitional and Transitory Provisions (Amendment)) Order 2013 (SI 2013/1511) art.7 (July 1, 2013).

6.070

[¹ SCHEDULE 5

Article 2(1)

THE GATEWAY CONDITIONS

Personal characteristics

6.071   1. The claimant must be—

(a) aged at least 18 years, but under 60 years and six months;

(b) [³ . . .];

(c) a British citizen who—

(i) has resided in the United Kingdom throughout the period of two years ending with the date on which the claim for universal credit is made; and

(ii) has not, during that period, left the United Kingdom for a continuous period of four weeks or more.

Fitness to work

6.072   2. (1) The claimant must not—

(a) be pregnant; or

(b) have been pregnant, if the date of her confinement occurred during the period of 15 weeks ending with the date on which the claim for universal credit is made.

(2) In this paragraph, "confinement" has the same meaning as in regulation 8(4) of the Universal Credit Regulations.

(3) The claimant—

(a) must not have obtained from a doctor a statement given in accordance with the rules set out in Part 1 of Schedule 1 to the Social Security (Medical Evidence) Regulations 1976(1) ("a statement of fitness for work") in respect of the date on which the claim for universal credit is made, unless it has been determined, since the statement was given, that the claimant does not have limited capability for work within the meaning of the 2007 Act;

(b) must not have applied for a statement of fitness for work;

(c) must declare that the claimant does not consider himself or herself to be unfit for work; and

(d) must not have been the subject of a determination that the claimant has limited capability for work within the meaning of the 2007 Act, unless it has subsequently been determined that the claimant does not have limited capability for work within the meaning of that Act.

Existing benefits

3. (1) The claimant must not be entitled to—   6.073

[² (a) old style ESA;

(b) old style JSA;

(c) income support;]

(d) incapacity benefit or severe disablement allowance, as defined in Schedule 4 to the 2007 Act;

(e) disability living allowance under section 71 of the Social Security Contributions and Benefits Act 1992; or

(f) personal independence payment under Part 4 of the Act.

(2) [² . . .]

(3) The claimant must not be awaiting—

[² (a) a decision on a claim for—

(i) any benefit mentioned in sub-paragraph (1)(a) to (c);

(ii) a tax credit; or

(iii) housing benefit;]; or

(b) the outcome of an application—

(i) to the Secretary of State to consider whether to revise, under section 9 of the Social Security Act 1998, a decision that the claimant is not entitled to old style JSA, old style ESA or income support; or

(ii) to the relevant authority (within the meaning of the Child Support, Pensions and Social Security Act 2000) to consider whether to revise, under Schedule 7 to that Act, a decision that the claimant is not entitled to housing benefit.

(4) If the claimant has appealed against a decision that he or she is not entitled to a benefit mentioned in sub-paragraph (1)(a) to (c), the Secretary of State must be satisfied—

(a) that the appeal to the First-tier Tribunal, and any subsequent appeal to the Upper Tribunal or to a court, is not ongoing; and

(b) where an appeal has been finally determined, that there is no possibility of a further appeal by any party.

(5) [² . . .]

(6) [² . . .]

Income and capital

[³ **4.** (1) If the claimant is a single claimant, the claimant must declare that, during the   6.074
period of one month starting with the date on which the claim for universal credit is made, the claimant's earned income is expected not to exceed £330.

(2) If the claim for universal credit is made by a couple as joint claimants, they must declare that, during the period of one month starting with the date on which the claim is made—

(a) in relation to each member of the couple, the earned income of that member is expected not to exceed £330; and

(b) the couple's total earned income is expected not to exceed £525.

(3) If the claimant is a single claimant and is not a member of a couple, the claimant's capital must not exceed £6,000.

(4) If the claimant is a single claimant and is a member of a couple, the couple's total capital must not exceed £6,000.

(5) If the claim for universal credit is made by a couple as joint claimants, the couple's total capital must not exceed £6,000.

(6) For the purposes of this paragraph, "couple" has the same meaning as it has in section 39 of the Act and "earned income" and "capital" have the same meanings as they have in Part 6 of the Universal Credit Regulations.]

Housing

6.075   5. The claimant must not—

(a) be homeless (within the meaning of section 175 of the Housing Act 1996) and must currently reside at his or her usual address;

(b) reside in accommodation in which care, supervision, counselling, advice or other support services (other than services connected solely with the provision of adequate accommodation) are made available to the claimant by or on behalf of the person by whom the accommodation is provided, with a view to enabling the claimant to live there;

(c) reside in the same household as a person who is a member of the regular forces or the reserve forces (within the meaning of section 374 of the Armed Forces Act 2006) and who is absent from the household in connection with that role; or

(d) own, or partly own, the property in which he or she resides.

Caring responsibilities

6.076   6. (1) There must not be—

(a) a child living with the claimant some or all of the time;

(b) a person ("the young person") living with the claimant some or all of the time if—

    (i) the young person is not a child, but is under the age of 20; and

    (ii) the claimant would be responsible for the young person for the purposes of regulation 4 of the Universal Credit Regulations, if the young person were a qualifying young person within the meaning of regulation 5 of those Regulations.

(2) The claimant must not—

(a) be an adopter (within the meaning of the Universal Credit Regulations) with whom a child is expected to be placed during the period of [2 two months] beginning with the date on which the claim for universal credit is made;

(b) be a foster parent;

(c) be liable to pay child support maintenance under the Child Support Act 1991; or

(d) have any responsibility for providing care to a person who has a physical or mental impairment, other than in the course of paid or voluntary employment.

(3) For the purposes of this paragraph—

(a) "child" has the same meaning as in Part 1 of the Act;

(b) "foster parent" means—

    (i) in relation to England, a person who is approved as a foster parent under the Fostering Services (England) Regulations 2011;

    (ii) in relation to Wales, a person who is approved as a foster parent under the Fostering Services (Wales) Regulations 2003;

    (iii) in relation to Scotland, a person who is approved as a kinship carer or a foster carer under the Looked After Children (Scotland) Regulations 2009.

Other requirements

6.077   7. The claimant—

[2 (a) must not be carrying on a trade, profession or vocation in respect of which he or she receives self-employed earnings (within the meaning of regulation 57 of the Universal Credit Regulations) and must declare that he or she does not expect to carry on such a trade, profession or vocation during the period of one month starting with the date on which the claim for universal credit is made;]

(b) must not be receiving education or undertaking a course of training of any kind and must declare that he or she does not intend to engage in education or training of any kind (other than where required to do so by the Secretary of State, or by agreement with the Secretary of State, in connection with an award of universal credit) during the period of one month starting with the date on which the claim for universal credit is made;

(c) must not have—

   (i) a deputy appointed by the Court of Protection under Part 1 of the Mental Capacity Act 2005 ("the 2005 Act");

   (ii) a receiver appointed under Part 7 of the Mental Health Act 1983 and treated as a deputy by virtue of the 2005 Act; or

   (iii) any other person acting on the claimant's behalf in relation to the claim for universal credit;

(d) must have a national insurance number;

(e) must have an account with a bank, a building society or the Post Office, or a current account with a Credit Union (within the meaning of the Credit Unions Act 1979) [2;

(f) must not be—

   (i) a company director, within the meaning of the Companies Act 2006; or

   (ii) a member of a limited liability partnership, within the meaning of the Limited Liability Partnerships Act 2000.]

Declarations

8. [³ (1)] [² A] declaration which is required by paragraph 2(3)(c), 4(1) , [³ 4(2)] or 7(a) or (b) is to be made by such method as may be required by the Secretary of State in relation to the person by whom it is to be made.]   **6.078**

[³ (2) A declaration which is required by paragraph 4(2) in relation to a couple may be made on behalf of the couple by both members of the couple or by either of them.]

AMENDMENTS

1. Welfare Reform Act 2012 (Commencement No. 9, 11, 13, 14 and 16 and Transitional and Transitory Provisions (Amendment)) Order 2014 (SI 2014/1452) art.16 (June 16, 2014).
2. Welfare Reform Act 2012 (Commencement No. 9, 11, 13 14, 16 and 17 and Transitional and Transitory Provisions (Amendment)) Order 2014 (SI 2014/1661) art.4(4) (June 30, 2014).
3. Welfare Reform Act 2012 (Commencement No. 9, 11, 13, 14, 16 and 17 and Transitional and Transitory Provisions (Amendment) (No. 2)) Order 2014 (SI 2014/1923) art.4(7) (July 28, 2014).

The Welfare Reform Act 2012 (Commencement No. 11 and Transitional and Transitory Provisions and Commencement No. 9 and Transitional and Transitory Provisions (Amendment)) Order 2013

(SI 2013/1511) (C. 60) (as amended)

ARRANGEMENT OF ARTICLES   6.079

The Secretary of State, in exercise of the powers conferred by section 150(3) and (4)(a), (b)(i) and (c) of the Welfare Reform Act 2012, makes the following Order:

GENERAL NOTE

6.080 This Commencement Order ("the Commencement No. 11 Order") extended the universal credit scheme to certain postcode districts in Wigan ("the No. 2 relevant districts") and Manchester, Oldham and Warrington ("the No. 3 relevant districts") as from July 1, 2013. The Order accordingly brought into force in those areas the provisions of the WRA 2012 that relate to both the introduction of universal credit and the abolition of income-related employment and support allowance and income-based jobseeker's allowance. This was achieved by reference to the specific categories of cases set out in arts 3 and 4. In addition, of course, the claimant had to fall within the Pathfinder Group, i.e. be a person who meets the requirements of regs 5 to 12 of the Transitional Provisions Regulations 2013 (or now meet the "gateway conditions" as set out in Sch.5 to the Commencement No. 9 Order (as amended)).

An award of employment and support allowance under Part 1 of the Welfare Reform Act 2007, in a case where income-related ESA has been abolished, is referred to as a "new style ESA award". Likewise an award of a jobseeker's allowance under the Jobseekers Act 1995, in a case where income-based JSA has been abolished, is referred to as a "new style JSA award". Conversely an award of employment and support allowance under Part 1 of the Welfare Reform Act 2007, in a case where income-related ESA has not been abolished, is referred to as an "old style ESA award". Similarly an award of JSA under the Jobseekers Act 1995, in a case where income-based JSA has not been abolished, is referred to as an "old style JSA award".

This Order also amends certain transitional provisions in the Commencement No. 9 Order.

Citation

6.081 1. This Order may be cited as the Welfare Reform Act 2012 (Commencement No. 11 and Transitional and Transitory Provisions and Commencement No. 9 and Transitional and Transitory Provisions (Amendment)) Order 2013.

Interpretation

6.082 2.-(1) In this Order-

"the Act" means the Welfare Reform Act 2012;
"the 1995 Act" means the Jobseekers Act 1995;
"the 2007 Act" means the Welfare Reform Act 2007;
"the amending provisions" means the provisions referred to in article
  4(1)(a) to (c) of the No. 9 Order (day appointed for the abolition

of income-related employment and support allowance and income-based jobseeker's allowance);

"appointed day" means the day appointed for the coming into force of the amending provisions in accordance with article 4(3) of the No. 9 Order;

[¹ . . .] [⁴ "claimant"—

(a) in relation to an employment and support allowance, has the same meaning as in Part 1 of the Welfare Reform Act 2007, save as mentioned in article 5(1A) of the No. 9 Order as applied by article 4(7);

(b) in relation to a jobseeker's allowance, has the same meaning as in the Jobseekers Act 1995 (as it applies apart from the amendments made by Part 1 of Schedule 14 to the Act that remove references to an income-based jobseeker's allowance), save as mentioned in article 5(1A) of the No. 9 Order as applied by article 4(7);

(c) in relation to universal credit, has the same meaning as in Part 1 of the Act;]

"contribution-based jobseeker's allowance" means a contribution-based allowance under the 1995 Act as it has effect apart from the amendments made by Part 1 of Schedule 14 to the Act that remove references to an income-based allowance;

"contributory employment and support allowance" means a contributory allowance under Part 1 of the 2007 Act as it has effect apart from the amendments made by Schedule 3, and Part 1 of Schedule 14, to the Act that remove references to an income-related allowance;

"employment and support allowance" means an employment and support allowance under Part 1 of the 2007 Act;

[¹ "First-tier Tribunal" has the same meaning as in the Social Security Act 1998;

[¹ ²] [⁴ "gateway conditions" means the conditions specified in Schedule 5 to the No. 9 Order save that where, for the purposes of article 3(2) or 4(2)(a) or (b), the claimant resides in one of the specified districts on the date on which the claim is made, it means those conditions as if the No. 9 Order were amended as referred to in paragraph (3);]

"jobseeker's allowance" means an allowance under the 1995 Act;

[³ "joint claimants", in relation to universal credit, has the same meaning as in Part 1 of the Act;]

"joint-claim couple" has the meaning given in section 1(4) of the 1995 Act;

"new style ESA award" means an award of an employment and support allowance under Part 1 of the 2007 Act as amended by the provisions of Schedule 3, and Part 1 of Schedule 14, to the Act that remove references to an income-related allowance;

"new style JSA award" means an award of a jobseeker's allowance under the 1995 Act as amended by the provisions of Part 1 of Schedule 14 to the Act that remove references to an income-based jobseeker's allowance;

"No. 2 relevant districts" means the postcode districts and part-districts specified in Part 1 of the Schedule;

"No. 3 relevant districts" means the postcode districts and part-districts specified in Part 2 of the Schedule;

"the No. 9 Order" means the Welfare Reform Act 2012 (Commencement No. 9 and Transitional and Transitory Provisions and Commencement No. 8 and Savings and Transitional Provisions (Amendment)) Order 2013;

"old style ESA award" means an award of an employment and support allowance under Part 1 of the 2007 Act as it has effect apart from the amendments made by Schedule 3, and Part 1 of Schedule 14, to the Act that remove references to an income-related allowance;

"old style JSA award" means an award of a jobseeker's allowance under the 1995 Act as it has effect apart from the amendments made by Part 1 of Schedule 14 to the Act that remove references to an income-based jobseeker's allowance;

[³ "single claimant", in relation to universal credit, has the same meaning as in Part 1 of the Act;]

[⁴ "specified districts" means the following postcode districts and part-districts—

WA1 and WA2;

WA3 4 to WA3 7;

WA4 and WA5;

WA13 0;

WA13 9;]

[¹ . . .]

[¹ "Upper Tribunal" has the same meaning as in the Social Security Act 1998.]

[¹ (2) For the purposes of this Order, the Universal Credit, Personal Independence Payment, Jobseeker's Allowance and Employment and Support Allowance (Claims and Payments) Regulations 2013 apply for the purpose of deciding—

(a) whether a claim for universal credit is made; and

(b) the date on which such a claim is made.]

[⁴ (3) The amendments of the No. 9 Order referred to are—

(a) in article 2(1)—

    (i) after the definition of "the Decisions and Appeals Regulations 2013" insert—

    ""disability living allowance" means an allowance under section 71 of the Social Security Contributions and Benefits Act 1992;"; and

    (ii) after the definition of "old style JSA award" insert—

    ""personal independence payment" means an allowance under Part 4 of the Act;"; and

(b) in paragraph 6 of Schedule 5 (caring responsibilities)—

    (i) for sub-paragraph (1) substitute—

"(1) There must not be a child or young person living with the claimant some or all of the time if the child or young person—

(a) has been certified as severely sight impaired or blind by a consultant ophthalmologist;

(b) is looked after by a local authority, within the meaning of section 22 of the Children Act 1989 or section 17(6) of the Children (Scotland) Act 1995, save where the child or young person is so looked after during any period referred to in regulation 4A(1)(a) of the Universal Credit Regulations; or

(c) is entitled to a disability living allowance or personal independence payment.";

(ii) for sub-paragraph (2)(a) substitute—

"(a) be an adopter (within the meaning of the Universal Credit Regulations) with whom a child has been placed within the period of 12 months ending immediately before the date on which the claim for universal credit is made or with whom a child is expected to be placed during the period of two months beginning with that date; or";

(iii) omit sub-paragraph (2)(c) and (d); and

(iv) in sub-paragraph (3), at the end insert—

";

(c) "young person" means a person—

(i) who is not a child but who is under the age of 20; and

(ii) for whom the claimant would be responsible for the purposes of regulation 4 of the Universal Credit Regulations, if the person were a qualifying young person within the meaning of regulation 5 of those Regulations."]

AMENDMENTS

1. Welfare Reform Act 2012 (Commencement No. 9, 11, 13, 14 and 16 and Transitional and Transitory Provisions (Amendment)) Order 2014 (SI 2014/1452) art.18(2) (June 16, 2014).

2. Welfare Reform Act 2012 (Commencement No. 9, 11, 13 14, 16 and 17 and Transitional and Transitory Provisions (Amendment)) Order 2014 (SI 2014/1661) art.5(a) (June 30, 2014).

3. Welfare Reform Act 2012 (Commencement No. 9, 11, 13, 14, 16 and 17 and Transitional and Transitory Provisions (Amendment) (No. 2)) Order 2014 (SI 2014/1923) art.6(2) (July 28, 2014).

4. Welfare Reform Act 2012 (Commencement No. 9, 11, 13 14, 16, 17 and 19 and Transitional and Transitory Provisions (Amendment)) Order 2014 (SI 2014/3067) art.4(a), (b) and art.6(3) (November 24, 2014).

Day appointed for commencement of the universal credit provisions in Part 1 of the Act

3.-(1) The day appointed for the coming into force of the provisions of the Act listed in Schedule 2 to the No. 9 Order, in so far as they are not   6.083

already in force, in relation to the case of a claim referred to in paragraph (2), and any award that is made in respect of the claim, is the day appointed in accordance with paragraph (3).

[¹ (2) The claims referred to are—

(a) a claim for universal credit where, on the date on which the claim is made, the claimant resides in one of the No. 2 or No. 3 relevant districts and meets the gateway conditions; and

[³ (b) a claim for universal credit where—

    (i) in the case of a single claimant, the claimant gives incorrect information regarding the claimant residing in a No. 2 or a No. 3 relevant district or meeting the gateway conditions and the claimant does not reside in such a district or does not meet the gateway conditions on the date on which the claim is made;

    (ii) in the case of joint claimants, either or both of the joint claimants gives or give incorrect information regarding his or her (or their) residing in such a district or meeting the gateway conditions and one or both of them does not or do not reside in such a district or does not or do not meet those conditions on the date on which the claim is made; and

    (iii) after a decision is made that the single claimant is, or the joint claimants are, entitled to universal credit and one or more payments have been made in respect of the single claimant or the joint claimants, the Secretary of State discovers that incorrect information has been given regarding residence or meeting the gateway conditions.]

(3) The day appointed in relation to the case of a claim referred to in paragraph (2), and any award that is made in respect of the claim, is the first day of the period in respect of which the claim is made [² . . .].

(4) [¹ . . .]

(5) Article 3(6) of the No. 9 Order applies for the purposes of paragraph (3) as it applies for the purposes of article 3(4)(a) of the No. 9 Order.

[¹ [³ (6) Article 3A of the No. 9 Order applies in connection with a claim for universal credit where a single claimant, or, as the case may be, either or both of joint claimants, gives incorrect information regarding his or her (or their) residing in a No. 2 or a No. 3 relevant district or meeting the gateway conditions, as it applies in connection with the giving of incorrect information regarding a claimant residing in a relevant district (as defined in the No. 9 Order) or meeting the gateway conditions.]]

AMENDMENTS

1. Welfare Reform Act 2012 (Commencement No. 9, 11, 13, 14 and 16 and Transitional and Transitory Provisions (Amendment)) Order 2014 (SI 2014/1452) art.18(3) (June 16, 2014).

2. Welfare Reform Act 2012 (Commencement No. 9, 11, 13 14, 16 and 17 and Transitional and Transitory Provisions (Amendment)) Order 2014 (SI 2014/1661) art.5(b) (June 30, 2014).

3. Welfare Reform Act 2012 (Commencement No. 9, 11, 13, 14, 16 and 17 and Transitional and Transitory Provisions (Amendment) (No. 2)) Order 2014 (SI 2014/1923) art.6(3) (July 28, 2014).

DEFINITIONS

"the Act"–art.2(1).
"No. 2 relevant districts"–*ibid.*
"No. 3 relevant districts"–*ibid.*
"the No. 9 Order"–*ibid.*

GENERAL NOTE

Para. (1)

This brings into force provisions relating to universal credit in Part 1 of the   **6.084**
WRA 2012, as set out in Sch.2 to the Commencement No. 9 Order in relation
to the different categories of case set out in para.(2).

Para. (2) (a)

This covers the making of a claim for universal credit on or after July 1, 2013   **6.085**
in respect of a period that begins on or after that date where a person lives in a
"No. 2 or No. 3 relevant districts" at the time that the claim is made. The "No.
2 relevant districts" are those Wigan postcodes described in Part 1 of the
Schedule. The "No. 3 relevant districts", described in Part 2 of the Schedule,
cover certain postcodes in Manchester, Oldham and Warrington. The other
conditions for making a claim for universal credit, originally known as the
"Pathfinder Group conditions", were set out in the Transitional Provisions
Regulations 2013. These have now been superseded by the "gateway conditions"
in Sch.5 to the Commencement No. 9 Order (as amended).

Para. (2) (b)

This relates to the making of a claim for universal credit on or after July 1,   **6.086**
2013 in respect of a period that begins on or after that date but the claimant
provides incorrect information as to either their residence in a relevant district or
their meeting the gateway conditions, and this is only discovered once payments
of universal credit have been made. Such a claim remains within the universal
credit regime despite the error.

Para. (3)

The day appointed for the commencement of the universal credit provisions in   **6.087**
the above cases is the first day of the period in respect of which the claim is
made.

Para. (5)

Article 3(6) of the Commencement No. 9 Order deals with the situation where   **6.088**
there is an extension of time for making a claim.

Para. (6)

Article 3A of the Commencement No. 9 Order makes consequential provision   **6.089**
for cases where a claimant gives incorrect information about either their area of
residence or meeting the gateway conditions. In particular, it provides for certain
consequences to follow (i) where the discovery of the error is made before the
claim for universal credit has been decided, (ii) where the discovery is made after

407

an entitlement decision has been made, but before any payment of universal credit has been made, and (iii) where it is made after an entitlement decision and after one or more such payments have been made.

Day appointed for the abolition of income-related employment and support allowance and income-based jobseeker's allowance

6.090   [¹ **4.** (1) The day appointed for the coming into force of the amending provisions, in relation to the case of a claim referred to in paragraph (2) and any award that is made in respect of the claim, is the day appointed in accordance with paragraph (3).

(2) The claims referred to are—

(a) a claim for universal credit, an employment and support allowance or a jobseeker's allowance where, on the date on which the claim is made [³ or treated as made], the claimant—

    (i) resides in one of the No. 2 or No. 3 relevant districts; and

    (ii) meets the gateway conditions;

[³ (b)   a claim for universal credit where—

    (i) in the case of a single claimant, the claimant gives incorrect information regarding the claimant residing in a No. 2 or a No. 3 relevant district or meeting the gateway conditions and the claimant does not reside in such a district or does not meet the gateway conditions on the date on which the claim is made;

    (ii) in the case of joint claimants, either or both of the joint claimants gives or give incorrect information regarding his or her (or their) residing in such a district or meeting the gateway conditions and one or both of them does not or do not reside in such a district or does not or do not meet those conditions on the date on which the claim is made; and

    (iii) after a decision is made that the single claimant is, or the joint claimants are, entitled to universal credit and one or more payments have been made in respect of the single claimant or the joint claimants, the Secretary of State discovers that incorrect information has been given regarding residence or meeting the gateway conditions;

(c) a claim for an employment and support allowance or a jobseeker's allowance other than one referred to in sub-paragraph (a) that is made or treated as made during the relevant period by a single claimant of universal credit or by either of two joint claimants of universal credit who has or have made a claim for universal credit within sub-paragraph (a) or (b).]

(3) The day appointed in relation to the case of a claim referred to in paragraph (2), and any award that is made in respect of the claim, is the first day of the period in respect of which the claim is made.

(4) For the purposes of paragraph (2)(c), "relevant period" means, in relation to a claim for universal credit referred to in paragraph (2)(a) or (b), any UC claim period, and any period subsequent to any UC claim

period in respect of which the claimant is entitled to an award of universal credit in respect of the claim.

(5) For the purposes of paragraph (4), a "UC claim period" is a period when—

(a) a claim for universal credit as referred to in paragraph (2)(a) or [² [3 (b)(i) (or (ii))]] has been made but a decision has not yet been made on the claim; or

(b) a decision has been made that the claimant is not entitled to universal credit and—

    (i) the Secretary of State is considering whether to revise that decision under section 9 of the Social Security Act 1998, whether on an application made for that purpose, or on the Secretary of State's own initiative; or

    (ii) the claimant has appealed against that decision to the First-tier Tribunal and that appeal or any subsequent appeal to the Upper Tribunal or to a court has not been finally determined.

(6) Paragraphs (6) and (7) of article 4 of the No. 9 Order apply in relation to the case of a claim for universal credit referred to in paragraph (2) (and any award that is made in respect of the claim) as they apply in relation to the case of a claim for universal credit referred to in sub-paragraphs (a) and (b) of article 4(2) of the No. 9 Order (and any award that is made in respect of the claim).

[⁴ (7) Paragraphs (1) to (1B) of article 5 of the No. 9 Order apply for the purposes of paragraph (2)(a) as they apply for the purposes of article 4(2)(a) of the No. 9 Order.]

(8) Paragraphs (5) to (7) of article 5 of the No. 9 Order apply for the purposes of sub-paragraphs (a) and (c) of paragraph (2) as they apply for the purposes of sub-paragraphs (a) and (g) of article 4(2) of the No. 9 Order.

(9) Article 5(8) of the No. 9 Order applies for the purposes of paragraph (3) as it applies for the purposes of article 4(3)(a) of the No. 9 Order.]

AMENDMENTS

1. Welfare Reform Act 2012 (Commencement No. 9, 11, 13, 14 and 16 and Transitional and Transitory Provisions (Amendment)) Order 2014 (SI 2014/1452) art.18(4) (June 16, 2014).

2. Welfare Reform Act 2012 (Commencement No. 9, 11, 13 14, 16 and 17 and Transitional and Transitory Provisions (Amendment)) Order 2014 (SI 2014/1661) art.5(c) (June 30, 2014).

3. Welfare Reform Act 2012 (Commencement No. 9, 11, 13, 14, 16 and 17 and Transitional and Transitory Provisions (Amendment) (No. 2)) Order 2014 (SI 2014/1923) art.6(4) (July 28, 2014).

4. Welfare Reform Act 2012 (Commencement No. 9, 11, 13 14, 16, 17 and 19 and Transitional and Transitory Provisions (Amendment)) Order 2014 (SI 2014/3067) art.6(4) (November 24, 2014).

DEFINITIONS

"the amending provisions"–art.2(1).
"contributory employment and support allowance"–*ibid.*

"employment and support allowance"–*ibid.*
"jobseeker's allowance"–*ibid.*
"No. 2 relevant districts"–*ibid.*
"No. 3 relevant districts"–*ibid.*
"the No. 9 Order"–*ibid.*

GENERAL NOTE

Para. (1)

6.091   This brings into force provisions relating to the abolition of income-related employment and support allowance and of income-based jobseeker's allowance where one of the different categories of case set out in para.(2) applies.

Para. (2) (a)

6.092   This provides that the new provisions come into force in relation to a claim for (and any subsequent award of) universal credit, employment and support allowance or jobseeker's allowance, where a person makes such a claim on or after July 1, 2013 for a period that begins on or after that date and, at the time that the claim is made, the claimant both lives in a No. 2 or No. 3 relevant district (see Part 1 of Schedule) and meets the Pathfinder Group (now gateway) conditions.

Para. (2) (b)

6.093   This is modelled on art.3(2)(b). As with art.3(2)(b), awards made on the basis of incorrect information as to residence or meeting the gateway conditions remain within the universal credit regime despite the error.

Para. (2) (c)

6.094   This covers universal credit claimants who make an ESA or JSA claim and are not otherwise covered by art.4(2)(a). See further art.4(4) and (5).

Para. (3)

6.095   The day appointed for the coming into force of the amending provisions in the above cases is the first day of the period in respect of which the claim is made.

Para. (7)

6.096   Article 5(1) of the Commencement No. 9 Order provides that the Claims and Payments Regulations 1987 determine whether and when a claim for employment and support allowance or jobseeker's allowance is made or is treated as made.

Application of the No. 9 Order

6.097   **5.** [¹ Articles] 9 to 22 of the No. 9 Order apply in connection with the coming into force of the amending provisions in relation to the case of a claim referred to in article 4(2), and any award made in respect of the claim, as they apply in connection with the coming into force of the amending provisions in relation to the case of a claim referred to in [² sub-paragraphs (a), (b) and (g) of article 4(2)] of the No. 9 Order and any award made in respect of the claim.

410

AMENDMENTS

1. Welfare Reform Act 2012 (Commencement No. 9, 11, 13, 14 and 16 and Transitional and Transitory Provisions (Amendment)) Order 2014 (SI 2014/1452) art.18(5) (June 16, 2014).
2. Welfare Reform Act 2012 (Commencement No. 9, 11, 13, 14, 16 and 17 and Transitional and Transitory Provisions (Amendment) (No. 2)) Order 2014 (SI 2014/1923) art.6(5) (July 28, 2014).

DEFINITIONS

"the amending provisions"–art.2(1).
"the No. 9 Order"–*ibid.*

Amendment of article 7 of the No. 9 Order—transitional provisions in relation to claimant responsibilities with respect to employment and support allowance and jobseeker's allowance

6.-(1) Paragraph (3) applies in relation to a case where, under any **6.098** secondary legislation, in relation to a new style JSA award, the 1995 Act applies as though the amending provisions had not come into force (which award therefore continues as an old style JSA award) and where the day with effect from which the 1995 Act so applies occurs on or after 1st July 2013.

(2) Paragraph (4) applies in relation to a case where, under any secondary legislation, in relation to a new style ESA award, Part 1 of the 2007 Act applies as though the amending provisions had not come into force (which award therefore continues as an old style ESA award) and where the day with effect from which Part 1 of the 2007 Act so applies occurs on or after 1st July 2013.

(3) In relation to a case to which this paragraph applies, for article 7(2) of the No. 9 Order substitute-

"(2) Where, under any secondary legislation, in relation to a new style JSA award, the 1995 Act applies as though the amending provisions had not come into force, then, with effect from the day on which the 1995 Act so applies, the 1995 Act, the Social Security Administration Act 1992 and the Social Security Act 1998 are to apply in relation to the award as though the provisions referred to in paragraph (1)(a), (b) and (e) had not come into force.".

(4) In relation to a case to which this paragraph applies, for article 7(3) of the No. 9 Order substitute-

"(3) Where, under any secondary legislation, in relation to a new style ESA award, Part 1 of the 2007 Act applies as though the amending provisions had not come into force, then, with effect from the day on which Part 1 of the 2007 Act so applies, Part 1 of the 2007 Act and the Welfare Reform Act 2009 are to apply in relation to the award as though the provisions referred to in paragraph (1)(c), (d) and (f) had not come into force.".

(5) For the purposes of this article, "secondary legislation" means an instrument made under an Act.

411

DEFINITIONS

"the 1995 Act"–art.2(1).
"the 2007 Act"–*ibid.*
"the amending provisions"–*ibid.*
"employment and support allowance"–*ibid.*
"new style ESA award"–*ibid.*
"new style JSA award"–*ibid.*
"the No. 9 Order"–*ibid.*
"old style ESA award"–*ibid.*
"old style JSA award"–*ibid.*
"secondary legislation"–para.(5)

GENERAL NOTE

6.099   Article 7 of the Commencement No. 9 Order (claimant responsibilities with respect to ESA and JSA) provides for the appointed day and transitional provisions for the measures in the 2012 Act that relate to claimant responsibilities in relation to a new style ESA or new style JSA awards. By virtue of art.7 of the Commencement No. 9 Order, those new provisions come into force in relation to any case with respect to which the provisions of art.4(1)(a)-(c) of that Order come into force.

This provision amends Article 7 of the Commencement No. 9 Order with respect to certain cases that are to occur after the Order is made. In relation to the case where, under any secondary legislation, Part 1 of the WRA 2007 or the Jobseekers Act 1995 applies in relation to a new style ESA award or a new style JSA award respectively as though the amending provisions had not come into force, then the amendments clarify that such awards remain governed by the previous primary legislation.

Amendment of Schedule 4 to the No. 9 Order

6.100   7. With effect from 1st July 2013, Schedule 4 to the No. 9 Order (modifications of the 2010 Transitional Regulations) is amended as follows-
     (a) for paragraph 21(2)(b)(i) substitute-
     "(i) for the definition of "contributory allowance" substitute-

          "employment and support allowance" means an employment and support allowance to which a person is entitled by virtue of the Employment and Support Allowance (Transitional Provisions, Housing Benefit and Council Tax Benefit)(Existing Awards)(No.2) Regulations 2010 which was based on an award of incapacity benefit or severe disablement allowance to which the person was entitled.",

     and for "; and" following that definition substitute "."; "; and
     (b) after paragraph 21(2) insert-

     "(2A) In paragraph 2A-
     (a) in paragraph (1), omit "contributory"; and
     (b) in paragraph (2), in the substituted section 1A
          (i) in paragraphs (1) and (3) to (5), for " a contributory allowance" substitute "an employment and support allowance"; and

(ii) in paragraph (3), omit "Part 1 of".".

DEFINITIONS

"employment and support allowance"–art.2(1).
"the No. 9 Order"–*ibid*.

GENERAL NOTE

This simply amends Sch.4 to the Commencement No. 9 Order to ensure   6.101
consistency between the wording of ss.1 and 1A of the WRA 2007 as
modified by the Transitional Provisions Regulations 2010, and the wording of that Act as amended by the provisions of Sch.3, and Part 1 of
Sch.14, to the WRA 2012 (that remove references to an income-related
allowance).

Amendment of the No. 9 Order—transition from old style ESA to new style ESA

8.-(1) Paragraph (2) applies in relation to a case where-   6.102
  (a)   (i)   a person makes, or is treated as making, a claim for an
              employment and support allowance;
       (ii)   under article 4 of the No. 9 Order, Part 1 of the 2007 Act, as
              amended by the provisions of Schedule 3, and Part 1 of
              Schedule 14, to the Act that remove references to an income-
              related allowance, applies in relation to the claim; and
      (iii)   the claim is made or treated as made on or after 1st July
              2013; or
  (b)   (i)   a person has an old style ESA award immediately before the
              appointed day in relation to a case of a claim for universal
              credit referred to in article 4(2)(a) to (d) of the No. 9 Order
              (and any award made in respect of the claim), or an award of
              universal credit referred to in article 4(2)(e) or (f) of the No.
              9 Order;
       (ii)   the old style ESA award consists of or includes a contributory
              employment and support allowance (which allowance there-
              fore continues as a new style ESA award); and
      (iii)   the first day on which the person is entitled to an employ-
              ment and support allowance under the new style ESA award
              occurs on or after 1st July 2013.
(2) Where this paragraph applies, article 10 of the No. 9 Order is
amended as follows-
  (a) for the title substitute "Transition from old style ESA";
  (b) for paragraph (1) substitute-

  "(1) This article applies where a person-
    (a) makes, or is treated as making, a claim for an employ-
        ment and support allowance and, under article 4, Part 1
        of the 2007 Act, as amended by the provisions of Sched-
        ule 3, and Part 1 of Schedule 14, to the Act that remove
        references to an income-related allowance, applies in
        relation to the claim; or

413

    (b) (i) has an old style ESA award immediately before the appointed day in relation to a case of a claim for universal credit referred to in article 4(2)(a) to (d) (and any award made in respect of the claim), or an award of universal credit referred to in article 4(2)(e) or (f); and

        (ii) the old style ESA award consists of or includes a contributory employment and support allowance (which allowance therefore continues as a new style ESA award),

and, in the case of sub-paragraph (a), the condition referred to in paragraph (1A) is satisfied.

(1A) The condition is that-

    (a) the person previously made, or was treated as having made, a claim for an employment and support allowance and Part 1 of the 2007 Act, as it has effect apart from the provisions of Schedule 3, and Part 1 of Schedule 14, to the Act that remove references to an income-related allowance, applied in relation to the claim;

    (b) a notice was issued to the person under regulation 4 of the 2010 Transitional Regulations and Part 1 of the 2007 Act, as that Part has effect apart from the provisions of Schedule 3, and Part 1 of Schedule 14, to the Act that remove references to an income-related allowance, applied in relation to the notice; or

    (c) the person previously had a new style ESA award and article 6(2) applied in relation to the award (which award therefore continued as an old style ESA award).";

(c) after paragraph (2)(g) omit "and" and insert-

"(ga) in regulation 39(6) (exempt work), the reference to an employment and support allowance included a reference to an old style ESA award;

(gb) in regulation 85(2)(a) (waiting days), where a claimant was entitled to an old style ESA award with effect from the first day of a period of limited capability for work by virtue of regulation 144(2)(a) of the ESA Regulations 2008 and, with effect from the second or third day of that period, that award continued as a new style ESA award in the circumstances referred to in paragraph (1)(b) of this article, the reference to an employment and support allowance included a reference to the old style ESA award;";

(d) after paragraph (2)(h) insert-

"(i) in regulation 89 (short absence), where-

    (i) a claimant had an old style ESA award in the circumstances referred to in paragraph (1)(b) of this article;

    (ii) a temporary absence from Great Britain commenced when regulation 152 of the ESA Regulations 2008 applied to the claimant; and

(iii) the first 4 weeks of the temporary absence had not ended immediately before the first day of entitlement to the new style ESA award,

the initial words of regulation 89 included a reference to the claimant being entitled to the new style ESA award during the remainder of the first 4 weeks of the temporary absence that commenced when regulation 152 of the ESA Regulations 2008 applied to the claimant;

(j) in regulation 90 (absence to receive medical treatment), where-

    (i) a claimant had an old style ESA award in the circumstances referred to in paragraph (1)(b) of this article;

    (ii) a temporary absence from Great Britain commenced when regulation 153 of the ESA Regulations 2008 applied to the claimant; and

    (iii) the first 26 weeks of the temporary absence had not ended immediately before the first day of entitlement to the new style ESA award,

the initial words of paragraph (1) of regulation 90 included a reference to the claimant being entitled to the new style ESA award during the remainder of the first 26 weeks of the temporary absence that commenced when regulation 153 of the ESA Regulations 2008 applied to the claimant;

(k) in regulation 93 (disqualification for misconduct etc)-

    (i) in paragraph (3), for "Paragraph (2) does" there were substituted "Paragraphs (2) and (5) do"; and

    (ii) after paragraph (4) there were inserted-

"(5) Subject to paragraph (3), a claimant is to be disqualified for receiving an employment and support allowance for any period determined by the Secretary of State under regulation 157(2) of the Employment and Support Allowance Regulations 2008 less any days during that period on which those Regulations applied to the claimant.

(6) Where paragraph (5) applies to a claimant, paragraph (2) is not to apply to that claimant with respect to any matter referred to in paragraph (1) that formed the basis for the claimant's disqualification under regulation 157(2) of the Employment and Support Allowance Regulations 2008.";

(l) in regulation 95 (treating a claimant as not having limited capability for work), the existing words became paragraph (1) and-

    (i) at the beginning of paragraph (1), there were inserted "Subject to paragraph (2),"; and

    (ii) after paragraph (1), there were inserted-

"(2) A claimant is to be treated as not having limited capability for work if-

(a) under Part 1 of the Act as it has effect apart from the amendments made by Schedule 3, and Part 1 of Schedule 14, to the Welfare Reform Act 2012 that remove references to an income-related allowance ("the former law"), the claimant was disqualified for receiving a contributory employment and support allowance during a period of imprisonment or detention in legal custody;

(b) Part 1 of the Act as amended by the provisions of Schedule 3, and Part 1 of Schedule 14, to the Welfare Reform Act 2012 that remove references to an income-related allowance ("the current law") applied to the claimant with effect from a day that occurred during the period of imprisonment or detention in legal custody referred to in sub-paragraph (a) and during the period of six weeks with effect from the day on which the claimant was first disqualified as referred to in sub-paragraph (a); and

(c) the total of-

(i) the period for which the claimant was disqualified for receiving a contributory employment and support allowance during the period of imprisonment or detention in legal custody when the former law applied to the claimant; and

(ii) the period for which the claimant was disqualified for receiving an employment and support allowance during the period of imprisonment or detention in legal custody when the current law applied to the claimant,

amounts to more than six weeks.".."; and

(e) after paragraph (2) insert-

"(3) Subject to paragraph (4), where this article applies, the 2007 Act is to be read as though-

(a) the reference to an employment and support allowance in section 1A(1) and (4) to (6);

(b) the first reference to an employment and support allowance in section 1A(3); and

(c) the first reference to an employment and support allowance in section 1B,

included a reference to a contributory employment and support allowance.

(4) Where this article applies and the 2010 Transitional Regulations apply to a person, paragraph (3)(c) becomes paragraph (3)(b) and, for paragraph (3)(a) and (b), there is substituted-

416

"(a) in section 1A as substituted by the 2010 Transitional Regulations-
- (i) the reference to an employment and support allowance in section 1A(1), (4) and (5); and
- (ii) the first reference to an employment and support allowance in section 1A(3); and".
(5) Where this article applies and a claimant-
(a) had an old style ESA award in the circumstances referred to in paragraph (1)(b); and
(b) the old style ESA award had not been preceded by a new style ESA award in the circumstances referred to in paragraph (1A)(c),
the 2007 Act is to be read as if, in section 24(2), the beginning of the assessment phase (subject to section 24(3)) was the first day of the period for which the claimant was entitled to the old style ESA award.".

DEFINITIONS

"the Act"–art.2(1).
"the 2007 Act"–*ibid.*
"appointed day"–*ibid.*
"contributory employment and support allowance"–*ibid.*
"employment and support allowance"–*ibid.*
"new style ESA award"–*ibid.*
"the No. 9 Order"–*ibid.*
"old style ESA award"–*ibid.*

GENERAL NOTE

This Article, together with arts 9-11, amends arts 10 and 11 of the Commencement No. 9 Order, and substitute new articles 12 and 13 of the Commencement No. 9 Order (transition from old style ESA to new style ESA and vice versa, and old style JSA to new style JSA and vice versa) with respect to claims that are made on or after July 1, 2013 and awards of old style ESA or JSA that continue as awards of new style ESA or JSA (or vice versa) on or after that date. The amendments are intended to clarify the cases to which the modifications made by those articles apply and provide for additional modifications of legislation governing ESA and JSA.   6.103

Transition from new style ESA to old style ESA

9.-(1) Paragraph (2) applies in relation to a case where-   6.104
(a) (i) a person makes, or is treated as making, a claim for an employment and support allowance;
   (ii) Part 1 of the 2007 Act as it has effect apart from the provisions of Schedule 3, and Part 1 of Schedule 14, to the Act that remove references to an income-related allowance, applies in relation to the claim; and
   (iii) the claim is made or treated as made on or after 1st July 2013; or
(b) (i) a person has a new style ESA award and article 6(2) of the No. 9 Order applies in relation to the award (which award therefore continues as an old style ESA award); and

(ii) the first day on which the person in question is entitled to an employment and support allowance under the old style ESA award occurs on or after 1st July 2013.

(2) Where this paragraph applies, article 11 of the No. 9 Order is amended as follows-

(a) for the title substitute "Transition from new style ESA";

(b) for paragraph (1) substitute-

"(1) This article applies where a person-

(a) makes, or is treated as making, a claim for an employment and support allowance and Part 1 of the 2007 Act, as it has effect apart from the provisions of Schedule 3, and Part 1 of Schedule 14, to the Act that remove references to an income-related allowance, applies in relation to the claim; or

(b) has a new style ESA award and article 6(2) applies in relation to the award (which award therefore continues as an old style ESA award),

and, in the case of sub-paragraph (a), the condition referred to in paragraph (1A) is satisfied.

(1A) The condition is that-

(a) the person previously made, or was treated as having made, a claim for an employment and support allowance and, under article 4, Part 1 of the 2007 Act, as amended by the provisions of Schedule 3, and Part 1 of Schedule 14, to the Act that remove references to an income-related allowance, applied in relation to the claim;

(b) a notice was issued to the person under regulation 4 of the 2010 Transitional Regulations and, under article 4, Part 1 of the 2007 Act, as amended by the provisions of Schedule 3, and Part 1 of Schedule 14, to the Act that remove references to an income-related allowance, applied in relation to the notice; or

(c) the person previously-

(i) had an old style ESA award immediately before the appointed day in relation to a case of a claim for universal credit referred to in article 4(2)(a) to (d) (and any award made in respect of the claim), or an award of universal credit referred to in article 4(2)(e) or (f); and

(ii) the old style ESA award consisted of or included a contributory employment and support allowance (which allowance therefore continued as a new style ESA award).";

(c) after paragraph (2)(g), omit "and" and insert-

"(ga) in regulation 45(10) (exempt work), the reference to an employment and support allowance included a reference to a new style ESA award;

(gb) in regulation 144(2)(a) (waiting days), where the claimant was entitled to a new style ESA award with effect from the first day of a period of limited capability for work by virtue of regulation 85(2)(a) of the ESA Regulations 2013 and, with effect from the second or third day of that period, that award continued as an old style ESA award in the circumstances referred to in paragraph (1)(c) of this article, the reference to an employment and support allowance included a reference to the new style ESA award;";

(d) after paragraph (2)(h), insert-

"(i) in regulation 152 (short absence), where-
  (i) a claimant had a new style ESA award in the circumstances referred to in paragraph (1)(b) of this article;
  (ii) a temporary absence from Great Britain commenced when regulation 89 of the ESA Regulations 2013 applied to the claimant; and
  (iii) the first 4 weeks of the temporary absence had not ended immediately before the first day of entitlement to the old style ESA award,
the initial words of regulation 152 included a reference to the claimant being entitled to the old style ESA award during the remainder of the first 4 weeks of the temporary absence that commenced when regulation 89 of the ESA Regulations 2013 applied to the claimant;

(j) in regulation 153 (absence to receive medical treatment)-
  (i) a claimant had a new style ESA award in the circumstances referred to in paragraph (1)(b) of this article;
  (ii) a temporary absence from Great Britain commenced when regulation 90 of the ESA Regulations 2013 applied to the claimant; and
  (iii) the first 26 weeks of the temporary absence had not ended immediately before the first day of entitlement to the old style ESA award,
the initial words of paragraph (1) of regulation 153 included a reference to the claimant being entitled to the old style ESA award during the remainder of the first 26 weeks of the temporary absence that commenced when regulation 90 of the ESA Regulations 2013 applied to the claimant;

(k) in regulation 157 (disqualification for misconduct etc)-
  (i) in paragraph (3), for "Paragraph (2) does" there were substituted "Paragraphs (2) and (4) do"; and
  (ii) after paragraph (3) there were inserted-

"(4) Subject to paragraph (3), a claimant is to be disqualified for receiving an employment and support allowance for any period determined by the Secretary of State under regulation 93(2) of the Employment and Support Allowance Regulations 2013 less any days during that period on which those Regulations applied to the claimant.

(5) Where paragraph (4) applies to a claimant, paragraph (2) is not to apply to that claimant with respect to any matter referred to in paragraph (1) that formed the basis for the claimant's disqualification under regulation 93(2) of the

Employment and Support Allowance Regulations 2013."; and

(l) in regulation 159 (treating a claimant as not having limited capability for work), the existing words became paragraph (1) and-

(i) at the beginning of paragraph (1), there were inserted "Subject to paragraph (2),"; and

(ii) after paragraph (1), there were inserted-

"(2) A claimant is to be treated as not having limited capability for work if-

(a) under Part 1 of the Act as amended by the provisions of Schedule 3, and Part 1 of Schedule 14, to the Welfare Reform Act 2012 that remove references to an income-related allowance ("the former law"), the claimant was disqualified for receiving an employment and support allowance during a period of imprisonment or detention in legal custody;

(b) Part 1 of the Act as it has effect apart from the amendments made by Schedule 3, and Part 1 of Schedule 14, to the Welfare Reform Act 2012 that remove references to an income-related allowance ("the current law") applied to the claimant with effect from a day that occurred during the period of imprisonment or detention in legal custody referred to in sub-paragraph (a) and during the period of six weeks with effect from the day on which the claimant was first disqualified as referred to in sub-paragraph (a); and

(c) the total of-

(i) the period for which the claimant was disqualified for receiving an employment and support allowance during the period of imprisonment or detention in legal custody when the former law applied to the claimant; and

(ii) the period for which the claimant was disqualified for receiving a contributory employment and support allowance during the period of imprisonment or detention in legal custody when the current law applied to the claimant,

amounts to more than six weeks."."; and

(e) after paragraph (2) insert-

"(3) Subject to paragraph (4), where this article applies, the 2007 Act is to be read as though-

(a) the reference to a contributory allowance in section (1A)(1) and (4) to (6);

(b) the first reference to a contributory allowance in section (1A)(3); and

(c) the first reference to a contributory allowance in section 1B,

included a reference to a new style ESA award.

420

(4) Where this article applies and the 2010 Transitional Regulations apply to a person, paragraph (3)(c) becomes paragraph (3)(b) and, for paragraph (3)(a) and (b), there is substituted-

"(a)in section 1A as substituted by the 2010 Transitional Regulations-

    (i) the reference to a contributory allowance in section 1A(1), (4) and (5); and

    (ii) the first reference to a contributory allowance in section 1A(3); and".

(5) Where this article applies and a claimant-

(a) had a new style ESA award in the circumstances referred to in paragraph (1)(b); and

(b) the new style ESA award had not been preceded by an old style ESA award in the circumstances referred to in paragraph (1A)(c),

section 24(2) of the 2007 Act is to be read as if the beginning of the assessment phase (subject to section 24(3)) was the first day of the period for which the claimant was entitled to the new style ESA award.".

DEFINITIONS

    "the Act"–art.2(1).
    "the 2007 Act"–*ibid.*
    "appointed day"–*ibid.*
    "contributory employment and support allowance"–*ibid.*
    "employment and support allowance"–*ibid.*
    "new style ESA award"–*ibid.*
    "the No. 9 Order"–*ibid.*
    "old style ESA award"–*ibid.*

Transition from old style JSA to new style JSA

10.-(1) Paragraph (2) applies in relation to the case where-   6.105

(a) (i) a person makes, or is treated as making, a claim for a job-seeker's allowance;

    (ii) under article 4 of the No. 9 Order, the 1995 Act as amended by the provisions of Part 1 of Schedule 14 to the Act that remove references to an income-based jobseeker's allowance, applies in relation to the claim; and

    (iii) the claim is made or treated as made on or after 1st July 2013; or

(b) (i) a person has an old style JSA award (whether or not the award was made to the person as a member of a joint-claim couple) immediately before the appointed day in relation to a case of a claim for universal credit referred to in article 4(2)(a) to (d) of the No. 9 Order (and any award made in respect of the claim) or an award of universal credit referred to in article 4(2)(e) or (f) of the No. 9 Order;

    (ii) the old style JSA award consists of or includes a contributory employment and support allowance (which allowance therefore continues as a new style JSA award); and

(iii) the first day on which the person in question is entitled to a jobseeker's allowance under the new style JSA award occurs on or after 1st July 2013.

(2) Where this paragraph applies, for article 12 of the No. 9 Order substitute-

"Transition from old style JSA

12.-(1) This article applies where a person-

(a) makes, or is treated as making, a claim for a jobseeker's allowance and, under article 4, the 1995 Act, as amended by the provisions of Part 1 of Schedule 14 to the Act that remove references to an income-based jobseeker's allowance, applies in relation to the claim; or

(b) (i) has an old style JSA award (whether or not the award was made to the person as a member of a joint-claim couple) immediately before the appointed day in relation to a case of a claim for universal credit referred to in article 4(2)(a) to (d) (and any award made in respect of the claim), or an award of universal credit referred to in article 4(2)(e) or (f); and

(ii) the old style JSA award consists of or includes a contribution-based jobseeker's allowance (which allowance therefore continues as a new style JSA award),

and, in the case of sub-paragraph (a), the condition referred to in paragraph (2) is satisfied.

(2) The condition is that the person previously-

(a) made, or was treated as having made, a claim for a jobseeker's allowance (whether or not as a member of a joint-claim couple) and the 1995 Act, as it has effect apart from the provisions of Part 1 of Schedule 14 to the Act that remove references to an income-based jobseeker's allowance, applied in relation to the claim; or

(b) had a new style JSA award and article 6(2) applied in relation to the award (which award therefore continued as an old style JSA award).

(3) Where this article applies, the JSA Regulations 2013 are to be read as if-

(a) in regulation 15(3)(b) (victims of domestic violence), the reference to regulation 15 applying to the claimant included a reference to the claimant having been treated as being available for employment under regulation 14A(2) or (6) of the JSA Regulations 1996;

(b) in regulation 36(1) (waiting days), where a person was entitled to an old style JSA award with effect from the first day of a jobseeking period by virtue of regulation 46(1)(a) of the JSA Regulations 1996 and, with effect from the second or third day of that period, that award continued as a new style JSA award in the circumstances referred to in paragraph (1)(b) of this article, the reference to a jobseeker's allowance included a reference to the old style JSA award;

(c) in regulation 37 (jobseeking period)-
  (i) the jobseeking period in relation to a claimant included any period that, under regulation 47 of the JSA Regulations 1996 (jobseeking period), forms part of the jobseeking period for the purposes of the 1995 Act; and
  (ii) in paragraph (3), the reference to a day that is to be treated as a day in respect of which the claimant was entitled to a jobseeker's allowance included a reference to any day that, under regulation 47(4) of the JSA Regulations 1996, is to be treated as a day in respect of which the claimant was entitled to a contribution-based jobseeker's allowance;
(d) in regulation 41 (persons temporarily absent from Great Britain), where a person had an old style JSA award in the circumstances referred to in paragraph (1)(b) of this article, the reference in paragraph (2)(b), (3)(a) and (c), (5)(a) and (6)(b) to entitlement to a jobseeker's allowance included a reference to the old style JSA award; and
(e) in regulation 46 (short periods of sickness), after paragraph (5) there were inserted-

"(6) Where-
  (a) a person has been treated under regulation 55(1) of the Jobseeker's Allowance Regulations 1996 as capable of work or as not having limited capability for work for a certain period; and
  (b) these Regulations apply to that person with effect from a day ("the relevant day") within that period,
  the person is to be treated for the part of that period that begins with the relevant day as capable of work or as not having limited capability for work.

(7) Where paragraph (6) applies to a person and the conditions in paragraph (1)(a) to (c) are fulfilled in relation to that person on any day within the part of a period referred to in paragraph (6), the requirement of paragraph (1) to treat the person as capable of work or as not having limited capability for work is to be regarded as satisfied with respect to the fulfilment of those conditions on that day.

(8) For the purposes of paragraph (3), where paragraph (6) applies to a person, paragraph (3) is to apply to the person as though the preceding provisions of this regulation had applied to the person with respect to the person having been treated for a period, under regulation 55(1) of the Jobseeker's Allowance Regulations 1996 and paragraph (6), as capable of work or as not having limited capability for work.".

(4) Where this article applies, the 1995 Act is to be read as though, in section 5 of the 1995 Act, the reference to a jobseeker's allowance in subsection (1) and the first reference to a jobseeker's allowance in subsection (2) included a reference to a contribution-based jobseeker's allowance.

(5) For the purposes of this article, "joint-claim couple" has the meaning given in section 1(4) of the 1995 Act.".

DEFINITIONS

"the Act"–art.2(1).
"the 1995 Act"–*ibid.*
"appointed day"–*ibid.*
"contribution-based jobseeker's allowance"–*ibid.*
"contributory employment and support allowance"–*ibid.*
"jobseeker's allowance"–*ibid.*
"joint-claim couple"–*ibid.*
"new style JSA award"–*ibid.*
"the No. 9 Order"–*ibid.*
"old style JSA award"–*ibid.*

Transition from new style JSA to old style JSA

6.106   **11.**-(1) Paragraph (2) applies in relation to a case where-
(a)   (i)   a person makes, or is treated as making, a claim for a jobseeker's allowance (whether or not as a member of a joint-claim couple);
(ii)   the 1995 Act, as it has effect apart from the provisions of Part 1 of Schedule 14 to the Act that remove references to an income-based jobseeker's allowance, applies in relation to the claim; and
(iii)   the claim is made or treated as made on or after 1st July 2013; or
(b)   (i)   a person has a new style JSA award and article 6(2) of the No. 9 Order applies in relation to the award (which award therefore continues as an old style JSA award); and
(ii)   the first day on which the person in question is entitled to a jobseeker's allowance under the old style JSA award occurs on or after 1st July 2013.

(2) Where this paragraph applies, for article 13 of the No. 9 Order substitute-

"Transition from new style JSA

13.-(1) This article applies where a person-
(a)   makes, or is treated as making, a claim for a jobseeker's allowance (whether or not as a member of a joint-claim couple) and the 1995 Act, as it has effect apart from the provisions of Part 1 of Schedule 14 to the Act that remove references to an income-based jobseeker's allowance, applies in relation to the claim; or
(b)   has a new style JSA award and article 6(2) applies in relation to the award such that it continues as an old style JSA award,
and, in the case of sub-paragraph (a), the condition referred to in paragraph (2) is satisfied.
(2) the condition is that the person previously-
(a)   made, or was treated as having made, a claim for a jobseeker's allowance and, under article 4, the 1995 Act, as amended by the

provisions of Part 1 of Schedule 14 to the Act that remove references to an income-based jobseeker's allowance, applied in relation to the claim; or

(b) (i) had an old style JSA award immediately before the appointed day in relation to a case of a claim for universal credit referred to in article 4(2)(a) to (d) (and any award made in respect of the claim), or an award of universal credit referred to in article 4(2)(e) or (f); and

    (ii) the old style JSA award consisted of or included a contributory employment and support allowance (which allowance therefore continued as a new style JSA award).

(3) Where this article applies, the JSA Regulations 1996 are to be read as if-

(a) in regulation 14A (victims of domestic violence), for the purposes of paragraph (3)(b) of that regulation, a person had been treated as available for employment on a day (under paragraph (2) of that regulation) where regulation 15 of the JSA Regulations 2013 applied to that person on that day;

(b) in regulation 46 (waiting days)-

    (i) where a person was entitled to a new style JSA award with effect from the first day of a jobseeking period by virtue of regulation 36(1) of the JSA Regulations 2013 and, with effect from the second or third day of that period, that award continued as an old style JSA award in the circumstances referred to in paragraph (1)(b) of this article, the reference to a jobseeker's allowance in paragraph (1)(a) included a reference to the new style JSA award; and

    (ii) the second reference to a jobseeker's allowance in paragraph (1)(d) included a reference to a new style JSA award;

(c) in regulation 47 (jobseeking period)-

    (i) the jobseeking period in relation to a claimant included any period that, under regulation 37 of the JSA Regulations 2013 (jobseeking period) forms part of the jobseeking period for the purposes of the 1995 Act; and

    (ii) in paragraph (4), the reference to any day that is to be treated as a day in respect of which the claimant was entitled to a contribution-based jobseeker's allowance included a reference to a day that, under regulation 37(3) of the JSA Regulations 2013 (jobseeking period), is to be treated as a day in respect of which the claimant was entitled to a jobseeker's allowance;

(d) in regulation 50 (persons temporarily absent from Great Britain), where a person had a new style JSA award in the circumstances referred to in paragraph (1)(b) of this article, the reference in paragraph (2)(b), (3)(a) and (c), (5)(a) and (c), (6AA)(a) and (6D)(b) to entitlement to a jobseeker's allowance included a reference to the new style JSA award; and

(e) in regulation 55 (short periods of sickness), after paragraph (5) there were inserted-

"(6) Where-

(a) a person has been treated under regulation 46(1) of the Jobseeker's Allowance Regulations 2013 as capable of work or as not having limited capability for work for a certain period; and

(b) these Regulations apply to that person with effect from a day ("the relevant day") within that period,

the person is to be treated for the part of that period that begins with the relevant day as capable of work or as not having limited capability for work.

(7) Where paragraph (6) applies to a person and the conditions in paragraph (1)(a) to (c) are fulfilled in relation to that person on any day within the part of a period referred to in paragraph (6), the requirement of paragraph (1) to treat the person as capable of work or as not having limited capability for work is to be regarded as satisfied with respect to the fulfilment of those conditions on that day.

(8) For the purposes of paragraph (3), where paragraph (6) applies to a person, paragraph (3) is to apply to the person as though the preceding provisions of this regulation had applied to the person with respect to the person having been treated for a period, under regulation 46(1) of the Jobseeker's Allowance Regulations 2013 and paragraph (6), as capable of work or as not having limited capability for work.".

(4) Where this article applies, the 1995 Act is to be read as though, in section 5 of the 1995 Act, the reference to a contribution-based jobseeker's allowance in subsection (1) and the first reference to a contribution-based jobseeker's allowance in subsection (2) included a reference to a new style JSA award.

(5) For the purposes of this article, "joint-claim couple" has the meaning given in section 1(4) of the 1995 Act.".

DEFINITIONS

"the Act"–art.2(1).
"the 1995 Act"–*ibid.*
"appointed day"–*ibid.*
"contribution-based jobseeker's allowance"–*ibid.*
"contributory employment and support allowance"–*ibid.*
"jobseeker's allowance"–*ibid.*
"joint-claim couple"–*ibid.*
"new style JSA award"–*ibid.*
"the No. 9 Order"–*ibid.*
"old style JSA award"–*ibid.*

Article 2(1)

6.107

SCHEDULE

PART 1

The No.2 relevant districts

1. WN1 1 and WN1 2.
2. WN2 1 to WN2 5.

3. WN3 0.
4. WN3 4 to WN3 6.
5. WN5 0.
6. WN5 6 to WN5 9.
7. WN6 0.
8. WN6 7 to WN6 9.

PART 2

The No.3 relevant districts

6.108

1. M35 0 to M35 4.
2. M35 6 and M35 7.
3. M35 9.
4. OL1 0 to OL1 6.
5. OL1 8 and OL1 9.
6. OL2 1.
7. OL2 3 to OL2 9.
8. OL3 1.
9. OL3 5 to OL3 7.
10. OL3 9.
11. OL4 0 to OL4 5.
12. OL8 and OL9.
13. WA1 and WA2.
14. WA3 4 to WA3 7.
15. WA4 and WA5.
16. WA13 0.
17. WA13 9.

Welfare Reform Act 2012 (Commencement No. 13 and Transitional and Transitory Provisions) Order 2013

(SI 2013/2657) (C.103) (as amended)

ARRANGEMENT OF ARTICLES

6.109

The Secretary of State, in exercise of the powers conferred by section 150(3) and (4)(a), (b)(i) and (c) of the Welfare Reform Act 2012, makes the following Order:

GENERAL NOTE

This Commencement Order ("the Commencement No. 13 Order") extended the universal credit scheme to certain postcode districts in West London, Manchester and Wigan ("the No. 4 relevant districts") as from October 28, 2013. In addition, of course, the claimant had initially to fall within the Pathfinder Group, i.e. be a person who meets the requirements of regs 5 to 12 of the Transitional Provisions Regulations 2013, and now meet the gateway conditions in Sch.5 to the Commencement No. 9 Order.

Citation

6.110   1. This Order may be cited as the Welfare Reform Act 2012 (Commencement No. 13 and Transitional and Transitory Provisions) Order 2013.

Interpretation

6.111   2. (1) In this Order—

"the Act" means the Welfare Reform Act 2012;
"the amending provisions" means the provisions referred to in article 4(1)(a) to (c) of the No. 9 Order (day appointed for the abolition of income-related employment and support allowance and income-based jobseeker's allowance);
[¹ . . . [² . . . .] . . . [² . . .] . . .]
[⁴ "claimant"—
> (a) in relation to an employment and support allowance, has the same meaning as in Part 1 of the Welfare Reform Act 2007, save as mentioned in article 5(1A) of the No. 9 Order as applied by article 4(7);
> (b) in relation to a jobseeker's allowance, has the same meaning as in the Jobseekers Act 1995 (as it applies apart from the amendments made by Part 1 of Schedule 14 to the Act that remove references to an income-based jobseeker's allowance), save as mentioned in article 5(1A) of the No. 9 Order as applied by article 4(7);
> (c) in relation to universal credit, has the same meaning as in Part 1 of the Act;]

"employment and support allowance" means an employment and support allowance under Part 1 of the Welfare Reform Act 2007;
[¹ "First-tier Tribunal" has the same meaning as in the Social Security Act 1998;
[² [³ "gateway conditions" means the conditions specified in Schedule 5 to the No. 9 Order]]]
[² "jobseeker's allowance" means a jobseeker's allowance under the Jobseekers Act 1995;]
""joint claimants" in relation to universal credit, has the same meaning as in Part 1 of the Act;"
"No. 4 relevant districts" means the postcode part-districts specified in the Schedule;
"the No. 9 Order" means the Welfare Reform Act 2012 (Commencement No. 9 and Transitional and Transitory Provisions and Commencement No. 8 and Savings and Transitional Provisions (Amendment)) Order 2013.

[² "single claimant", in relation to universal credit, has the same meaning as in Part 1 of the Act;]

[¹ "Upper Tribunal" has the same meaning as in the Social Security Act 1998.]

[¹ (2) For the purposes of this Order, the Universal Credit, Personal Independence Payment, Jobseeker's Allowance and Employment and Support Allowance (Claims and Payments) Regulations 2013 apply for the purpose of deciding—

(a) whether a claim for universal credit is made; and

(b) the date on which such a claim is made.]

[² (3) [³ . . .]

(4) [³ . . .]]

AMENDMENTS

1. Welfare Reform Act 2012 (Commencement No. 9, 11, 13, 14 and 16 and Transitional and Transitory Provisions (Amendment)) Order 2014 (SI 2014/1452) art.19(2) (June 16, 2014).
2. Welfare Reform Act 2012 (Commencement No. 9, 11, 13 14, 16 and 17 and Transitional and Transitory Provisions (Amendment)) Order 2014 (SI 2014/1661) art.6(1)(a) and 6(3) (June 30, 2014).
3. Welfare Reform Act 2012 (Commencement No. 9, 11, 13, 14, 16 and 17 and Transitional and Transitory Provisions (Amendment) (No. 2)) Order 2014 (SI 2014/1923) art.7(2) (July 28, 2014).
4. Welfare Reform Act 2012 (Commencement No. 9, 11, 13 14, 16, 17 and 19 and Transitional and Transitory Provisions (Amendment)) Order 2014 (SI 2014/3067) art.6(3) (November 24, 2014).

Day appointed for commencement of the universal credit provisions in Part 1 of the Act

3. (1) The day appointed for the coming into force of the provisions of the Act listed in Schedule 2 to the No. 9 Order, in so far as they are not already in force, in relation to the case of a claim referred to in paragraph (2), and any award that is made in respect of the claim, is the day appointed in accordance with paragraph (3).   **6.112**

[¹(2) The claims referred to are—

(a) a claim for universal credit where, on the date on which the claim is made, the claimant resides in one of the No. 4 relevant districts and meets the gateway conditions; and

[²(b) a claim for universal credit where—

(i) in the case of a single claimant, the claimant gives incorrect information regarding the claimant residing in a No. 4 relevant district or meeting the gateway conditions and the claimant does not reside in such a district or does not meet the gateway conditions on the date on which the claim is made;

(ii) in the case of joint claimants, either or both of the joint claimants gives or give incorrect information regarding his or her (or their) residing in such a district or meeting the gateway conditions and one or both of them does not or do not reside in such a district or does not or do not meet those conditions on the date on which the claim is made; and

(iii) after a decision is made that the single claimant is, or the joint claimants are, entitled to universal credit and one or more payments have been made in respect of the single claimant or the joint claimants, the Secretary of State discovers that incorrect information has been given regarding residence or meeting the gateway conditions.]]

(3) The day appointed in relation to the case of a claim referred to in paragraph (2), and any award that is made in respect of the claim, is the first day of the period in respect of which the claim is made [² . . .].

(4) [¹ . . .]

(5) Article 3(6) of the No. 9 Order applies for the purposes of paragraph (3) as it applies for the purposes of article 3(4)(a) of the No. 9 Order.

[¹ [² [³ (6) Article 3A of the No. 9 Order applies in connection with a claim for universal credit where a single claimant, or, as the case may be, either or both of joint claimants, gives incorrect information regarding his or her (or their) residing in a No. 4 relevant district or meeting the gateway conditions, as it applies in connection with the giving of incorrect information regarding a claimant residing in a relevant district (as defined in the No. 9 Order) or meeting the gateway conditions.]]]

AMENDMENTS

1. Welfare Reform Act 2012 (Commencement No. 9, 11, 13, 14 and 16 and Transitional and Transitory Provisions (Amendment)) Order 2014 (SI 2014/1452) art.19(3) (June 16, 2014).
2. Welfare Reform Act 2012 (Commencement No. 9, 11, 13 14, 16 and 17 and Transitional and Transitory Provisions (Amendment)) Order 2014 (SI 2014/1661) art.6(1)(b) and 6(4) (June 30, 2014).
3. Welfare Reform Act 2012 (Commencement No. 9, 11, 13, 14, 16 and 17 and Transitional and Transitory Provisions (Amendment) (No. 2)) Order 2014 (SI 2014/1923) art.7(3) (July 28, 2014).

DEFINITIONS

"the Act"–art.2(1).
"the No. 4 relevant districts"–*ibid.*
"the No. 9 Order"–*ibid.*

GENERAL NOTE

Para. (1)

6.114   This brings into force provisions relating to universal credit in Part 1 of the WRA 2012, as set out in Sch.2 to the Commencement No. 9 Order, in so far as they are not already in force, in relation to the further categories of case set out in para.(2).

Para. (2) (a)

6.115   This covers the making of a claim for universal credit on or after October 28, 2013, in respect of a period that begins on or after that date, where a person lives in a "No. 4 relevant district" at the time that the claim is made. The "No. 4 relevant districts" are those Manchester, Wigan but principally West London postcodes (the latter mainly dealt with by Hammersmith Jobcentre) set out in the Schedule. The other conditions for making a claim for universal credit, originally known as the "Pathfinder Group conditions", are set out in regs 5-12 of the Transitional Provisions Regulations 2013, and are now called "gateway conditions" (see Sch. 5 to the Commencement No. 9 Order).

Para. (2) (b)

This relates to the making of a claim for universal credit on or after October 28, 2013 in respect of a period that begins on or after that date but provides incorrect information as to their residence in a No. 4 relevant district or meeting the gateway conditions. Such a claim remains within the universal credit regime despite the error. **6.116**

Para. (3)

The day appointed for the commencement of the universal credit provisions in the above cases is the first day of the period in respect of which the claim is made. **6.117**

Para. (5)

Article 3(6) of the Commencement No. 9 Order deals with the situation where there is an extension of time for making a claim. **6.118**

Para. (6)

Article 3A of the Commencement No. 9 Order makes consequential provision for cases where incorrect information has been given. **6.119**

Day appointed for the abolition of income-related employment and support allowance and income-based jobseeker's allowance

[¹ **4.** (1) The day appointed for the coming into force of the amending provisions, in relation to the case of a claim referred to in paragraph (2) and any award that is made in respect of the claim, is the day appointed in accordance with paragraph (3). **6.120**

(2) The claims referred to are—

(a) a claim for universal credit, an employment and support allowance or a jobseeker's allowance where, on the date on which the claim is made [³ or treated as made], the claimant—
   (i) resides in one of the No. 4 relevant districts; and
   (ii) meets the gateway conditions;
[² (b) a claim for universal credit where—
   (i) in the case of a single claimant, the claimant gives incorrect information regarding the claimant residing in a No. 4 relevant district or meeting the gateway conditions and does not reside in such a district or does not meet the gateway conditions on the date on which the claim is made;
   (ii) in the case of joint claimants, either or both of the joint claimants gives or give incorrect information regarding his or her (or their) residing in such a district or meeting those conditions and one or both of them does not or do not reside

431

in such a district or does not or do not meet those conditions on the date on which the claim is made; and

    (iii) after a decision is made that the single claimant is, or the joint claimants are, entitled to universal credit and one or more payments have been made in respect of the single claimant or the joint claimants, the Secretary of State discovers that incorrect information has been given regarding residence or meeting the gateway conditions;

[³ (c) a claim for an employment and support allowance or a job-seeker's allowance other than one referred to in sub-paragraph (a) that is made or treated as made during the relevant period by a single claimant of universal credit or by either of two joint claimants of universal credit who has or have made a claim for universal credit within sub-paragraph (a) or (b).]]

(3) The day appointed in relation to the case of a claim referred to in paragraph (2), and any award that is made in respect of the claim, is the first day of the period in respect of which the claim is made.

(4) For the purposes of paragraph (2)(c), "relevant period" means, in relation to a claim for universal credit referred to in paragraph (2)(a) or (b), any UC claim period, and any period subsequent to any UC claim period in respect of which the claimant is entitled to an award of universal credit in respect of the claim.

(5) For the purposes of paragraph (4), a "UC claim period" is a period when—

    (a) a claim for universal credit as referred to in paragraph (2)(a) [2, (b)(i) or (ii)] has been made but a decision has not yet been made on the claim; or

    (b) a decision has been made that the claimant is not entitled to universal credit and—

        (i) the Secretary of State is considering whether to revise that decision under section 9 of the Social Security Act 1998, whether on an application made for that purpose, or on the Secretary of State's own initiative; or

        (ii) the claimant has appealed against that decision to the First-tier Tribunal and that appeal or any subsequent appeal to the Upper Tribunal or to a court has not been finally determined.

(6) Paragraphs (6) and (7) of article 4 of the No. 9 Order apply in relation to the case of a claim for universal credit referred to in paragraph (2) (and any award that is made in respect of the claim) as they apply in relation to the case of a claim for universal credit referred to in sub-paragraphs (a) and (b) of article 4(2) of the No. 9 Order (and any award that is made in respect of the claim).

[² [³ . . .]] [⁴ (7) Paragraphs (1) to (1B) of article 5 of the No. 9 Order apply for the purposes of paragraph (2)(a) as they apply for the purposes of article 4(2)(a) of the No. 9 Order.]

(8) Paragraphs (5) to (7) of article 5 of the No. 9 Order apply for the purposes of sub-paragraphs (a) and (c) of paragraph (2) as they apply for the purposes of sub-paragraphs (a) and (g) of article 4(2) of the No. 9 Order.

(9) Article 5(8) of the No. 9 Order applies for the purposes of paragraph (3) as it applies for the purposes of article 4(3)(a) of the No. 9 Order.]

AMENDMENTS

1. Welfare Reform Act 2012 (Commencement No. 9, 11, 13, 14 and 16 and Transitional and Transitory Provisions (Amendment)) Order 2014 (SI 2014/1452) art.19(4) (June 16, 2014).
2. Welfare Reform Act 2012 (Commencement No. 9, 11, 13 14, 16 and 17 and Transitional and Transitory Provisions (Amendment)) Order 2014 (SI 2014/1661) art.6(5) (June 30, 2014).
3. Welfare Reform Act 2012 (Commencement No. 9, 11, 13, 14, 16 and 17 and Transitional and Transitory Provisions (Amendment) (No. 2)) Order 2014 (SI 2014/1923) art.7(4) (July 28, 2014).
4. Welfare Reform Act 2012 (Commencement No. 9, 11, 13 14, 16, 17 and 19 and Transitional and Transitory Provisions (Amendment)) Order 2014 (SI 2014/3067) art.6(4) (November 24, 2014).

DEFINITIONS

"the amending provisions"–art.2(1)
"employment and support allowance"–*ibid.*
"jobseeker's allowance"–*ibid.*
"the No. 4 relevant districts"–*ibid.*
"the No. 9 Order"–*ibid.*
"a person who . . . falls within the Pathfinder Group"–art.2(2).

GENERAL NOTE

Para. (1)

This brings into force provisions relating to the abolition of income-related   **6.121**
employment and support allowance and of income-based jobseeker's allowance where the case falls within one of the categories set out in para.(2) (see also the incorporation by reference of other provisions as made by paras (6)-(9) below).

Para. (2) (a)

This provides that the new provisions come into force in relation to a claim for   **6.122**
(and any subsequent award of) universal credit, employment and support allowance or jobseeker's allowance, where a person makes such a claim on or after October 28, 2013 for a period that begins on or after that date and, at the time that the claim is made, the claimant both lives in a No. 4 relevant district (see Schedule) and meets the Pathfinder Group conditions (now the gateway conditions).

Para. (2) (b)

This provides that the new provisions come into force in relation to a claim for   **6.123**
(and any subsequent award of) universal credit where a person claims universal credit, again on or after October 28, 2013 for a period that begins on or after that date, but provides incorrect information as to either their residence in a No. 4 relevant district (see Schedule) or as to their meeting the Pathfinder Group or gateway conditions. As with reg.3(2)(b), such a claim remains within the universal credit regime despite the error.

Para. (2) (c)

6.124   This covers universal credit claimants who make an ESA or JSA claim and are not otherwise covered by art.4(2)(a). See further art.4(4) and (5).

Para. (3)

6.125   The day appointed for the coming into force of the amending provisions in the above cases is the first day of the period in respect of which the claim is made or treated as made.

Para. (4)

6.126   Article 4(4) and (5) of the Commencement No. 9 Order extend the universal credit provisions to include certain claims and awards that follow on from the conversion process that applies to recipients of incapacity benefit and severe disablement allowance.

Para. (5)

6.127   Article 5(1) of the Commencement No. 9 Order provides that the Claims and Payments Regulations 1987 determine whether and when a claim for employment and support allowance or jobseeker's allowance is made or is treated as made. Article 5(2) simply deems any reference in regs 5-12 of the Transitional Provisions Regulations 2013 to a claim for universal credit as including a claim to employment and support allowance or jobseeker's allowance as appropriate.

Para. (7)

6.128   Article 5(1) of the Commencement No. 9 Order provides that the Claims and Payments Regulations 1987 determine whether and when a claim for employment and support allowance or jobseeker's allowance is made or is treated as made.

Amendment of the No. 9 Order

6.129   5. With effect from 29th October 2013—
   (a) in article 11(2)(f)(ii) of the No. 9 Order, for "paragraph (2)(b)(iii)" substitute "paragraph (4)(c)"; and
   (b) in article 5 of the Welfare Reform Act 2012 (Commencement No. 11 and Transitional and Transitory Provisions and Commencement No. 9 and Transitional and Transitory Provisions (Amendment)) Order 2013(1), the reference to article 11 of the No. 9 Order is a reference to article 11 as amended by paragraph (a).

GENERAL NOTE

6.130   This article makes a minor amendment to the Commencement No. 9 Order (which is noted in the statutory text above) and makes a consequential clarification of the effect of a provision in the Commencement No. 11 Order.

Application of the No. 9 Order

6.131   6. [¹ Articles] 9 to 22 of the No. 9 Order apply in connection with the coming into force of the amending provisions in relation to the case of a claim referred to in article 4(2), and any award made in respect of the claim, as they apply in connection with the coming into force of the amending provisions in relation to the case of a claim referred to in [2 sub-paragraphs (a), (b) and (g) of article 4(2)] of the No.9 Order and any award made in respect of the claim.

AMENDMENTS

1. Welfare Reform Act 2012 (Commencement No. 9, 11, 13, 14 and 16 and Transitional and Transitory Provisions (Amendment)) Order 2014 (SI 2014/1452) art.19(5) (June 16, 2014).
2. Welfare Reform Act 2012 (Commencement No. 9, 11, 13 14, 16 and 17 and Transitional and Transitory Provisions (Amendment)) Order 2014 (SI 2014/1661) art.6(6) (June 30, 2014).

DEFINITION

"the amending provisions"–art.2(1).

GENERAL NOTE

This is in the same terms as art.5 of the Commencement No. 11 Order.   **6.132**

Article 2(1)

SCHEDULE

The No. 4 relevant districts

1. M35 5.
2. W6 0.
3. W6 6 to W6 9.
4. W14 0.
5. W14 4.
6. W14 8 and W14 9.
7. WN1 3.

The Welfare Reform Act 2012 (Commencement No. 14 and Transitional and Transitory Provisions) Order 2013

SI 2013/2846 (C.114) (as amended)

ARRANGEMENT OF ARTICLES   **6.133**

The Secretary of State, in exercise of the powers conferred by section 150(3) and (4)(a), (b)(i) and (c) of the Welfare Reform Act 2012, makes the following Order:

GENERAL NOTE

6.134   This Commencement Order ("the Commencement No. 14 Order") extends the universal credit scheme to certain postcode districts in Rugby, Inverness and Perth ("the No. 5 relevant districts") as from November 25, 2013. In addition, of course, the claimant must fall within the Pathfinder Group, i.e. be a person who meets the requirements of regs 5 to 12 of the Transitional Provisions Regulations 2013, now the "gateway conditions" (see Sch.5 to the Commencement No. 9 Order).

Citation

6.135   1. This Order may be cited as the Welfare Reform Act 2012 (Commencement No. 14 and Transitional and Transitory Provisions) Order 2013.

Interpretation

6.136   2. (1) In this Order—

"the Act" means the Welfare Reform Act 2012;

"the amending provisions" means the provisions referred to in article 4(1)(a) to (c) of the No. 9 Order (day appointed for the abolition of income-related employment and support allowance and income-based jobseeker's allowance);

[¹ ... [² ....] ... [² ...] ...]

[⁴ "claimant"—

   (a) in relation to an employment and support allowance, has the same meaning as in Part 1 of the Welfare Reform Act 2007, save as mentioned in article 5(1A) of the No. 9 Order as applied by article 4(7);

   (b) in relation to a jobseeker's allowance, has the same meaning as in the Jobseekers Act 1995 (as it applies apart from the amendments made by Part 1 of Schedule 14 to the Act that remove references to an income-based jobseeker's allowance), save as mentioned in article 5(1A) of the No. 9 Order as applied by article 4(7);

   (c) in relation to universal credit, has the same meaning as in Part 1 of the Act;]

"employment and support allowance" means an employment and support allowance under Part 1 of the Welfare Reform Act 2007;

[¹ "First-tier Tribunal" has the same meaning as in the Social Security Act 1998;

[² [³ "gateway conditions" means the conditions specified in Schedule 5 to the No. 9 Order";]]

"jobseeker's allowance" means a jobseeker's allowance under the Jobseekers Act 1995;

[² "joint claimants" in relation to universal credit, has the same meaning as in Part 1 of the Act;]

"No. 5 relevant districts" means the postcode part-districts specified in the Schedule;

"the No. 9 Order" means the Welfare Reform Act 2012 (Commencement No. 9 and Transitional and Transitory Provisions and Commencement No. 8 and Savings and Transitional Provisions (Amendment)) Order 2013.

[² "single claimant", in relation to universal credit, has the same meaning as in Part 1 of the Act;]

[¹ "Upper Tribunal" has the same meaning as in the Social Security Act 1998.]

[¹ (2) For the purposes of this Order, the Universal Credit, Personal Independence Payment, Jobseeker's Allowance and Employment and Support Allowance (Claims and Payments) Regulations 2013 apply for the purpose of deciding—

(a) whether a claim for universal credit is made; and

(b) the date on which such a claim is made.]

[² (3) [³ . . .]]

AMENDMENTS

1. Welfare Reform Act 2012 (Commencement No. 9, 11, 13, 14 and 16 and Transitional and Transitory Provisions (Amendment)) Order 2014 (SI 2014/1452) art.20(2) (June 16, 2014).
2. Welfare Reform Act 2012 (Commencement No. 9, 11, 13 14, 16 and 17 and Transitional and Transitory Provisions (Amendment)) Order 2014 (SI 2014/1661) art.7(1)(a) and 7(3) (June 30, 2014).
3. Welfare Reform Act 2012 (Commencement No. 9, 11, 13, 14, 16 and 17 and Transitional and Transitory Provisions (Amendment) (No. 2)) Order 2014 (SI 2014/1923) art.8(2) (July 28, 2014).
4. Welfare Reform Act 2012 (Commencement No. 9, 11, 13 14, 16, 17 and 19 and Transitional and Transitory Provisions (Amendment)) Order 2014 (SI 2014/3067) art.6(3) (November 24, 2014).

Day appointed for commencement of the universal credit provisions in Part 1 of the Act

3. (1) The day appointed for the coming into force of the provisions of   **6.137** the Act listed in Schedule 2 to the No. 9 Order, in so far as they are not already in force, in relation to the case of a claim referred to in paragraph (2), and any award that is made in respect of the claim, is the day appointed in accordance with paragraph (3).

[¹ (2) The claims referred to are—

(a) a claim for universal credit where, on the date on which the claim is made, the claimant resides in one of the No. 5 relevant districts and meets the gateway conditions; and

[² (b) a claim for universal credit where—

(i) in the case of a single claimant, the claimant gives incorrect information regarding the claimant residing in a No. 5 relevant district or meeting the gateway conditions and the claimant does not reside in such a district or does not meet the gateway conditions on the date on which the claim is made;

(ii) in the case of joint claimants, either or both of the joint claimants gives or give incorrect information regarding his or

437

her (or their) residing in such a district or meeting the gateway conditions and one or both of them does not or do not reside in such a district or does not or do not meet those conditions on the date on which the claim is made; and

(iii) after a decision is made that the single claimant is, or the joint claimants are, entitled to universal credit and one or more payments have been made in respect of the single claimant or the joint claimants, the Secretary of State discovers that incorrect information has been given regarding residence or meeting the gateway conditions.]]

(3) The day appointed in relation to the case of a claim referred to in paragraph (2), and any award that is made in respect of the claim, is the first day of the period in respect of which the claim is made [² . . .].

(4) [¹ . . .]

(5) Article 3(6) of the No. 9 Order applies for the purposes of paragraph (3) as it applies for the purposes of article 3(4)(a) of the No. 9 Order.

[¹ [² [³ (6) Article 3A of the No. 9 Order applies in connection with a claim for universal credit where a single claimant, or, as the case may be, either or both of joint claimants, gives incorrect information regarding his or her (or their) residing in a No. 5 relevant district or meeting the gateway conditions, as it applies in connection with the giving of incorrect information regarding a claimant residing in a relevant district (as defined in the No. 9 Order) or meeting the gateway conditions.]]]

AMENDMENTS

1. Welfare Reform Act 2012 (Commencement No. 9, 11, 13, 14 and 16 and Transitional and Transitory Provisions (Amendment)) Order 2014 (SI 2014/1452) art.20(3) (June 16, 2014).
2. Welfare Reform Act 2012 (Commencement No. 9, 11, 13 14, 16 and 17 and Transitional and Transitory Provisions (Amendment)) Order 2014 (SI 2014/1661) art.7(1)(b) and 7(4) (June 30, 2014).
3. Welfare Reform Act 2012 (Commencement No. 9, 11, 13, 14, 16 and 17 and Transitional and Transitory Provisions (Amendment) (No. 2)) Order 2014 (SI 2014/1923) art.8(3) (July 28, 2014).

DEFINITIONS

"the Act"–art.2(1).
"the No. 5 relevant districts"–*ibid.*
"the No. 9 Order"–*ibid.*

GENERAL NOTE

Para. (1)

6.138   This brings into force provisions relating to universal credit in Part 1 of the WRA 2012, as set out in Sch.2 to the Commencement No. 9 Order, in so far as they are not already in force, in relation to the further categories of case set out in para.(2).

Para. (2) (a)

6.139   This covers the making of a claim for universal credit on or after November 25, 2013, in respect of a period that begins on or after that date, where a person lives in a "No. 5 relevant district" at the time that the claim is made. The "No. 5 relevant districts" are those postcodes in Rugby, Inverness and Perth set out in the Schedule. The other conditions for making a claim for universal credit, previously known as the "Pathfinder Group conditions", as set out in the Transitional Provisions Regulations 2013 are now the "gateway conditions" (see Sch.5 to the Commencement No.9 Order).

Para. (2) (b)

This relates to the making of a claim for universal credit on or after November 25, 2013 in respect of a period that also begins on or after that date but where the claimant provides incorrect information as to their residence in a No. 5 relevant district or meeting the gateway conditions. Such a claim remains within the universal credit regime despite the error.   **6.140**

Para. (3)

The day appointed for the commencement of the universal credit provisions in the above cases is the first day of the period in respect of which the claim is made.   **6.141**

Para. (5)

Article 3(6) of the Commencement No. 9 Order deals with the situation where there is an extension of time for making a claim.   **6.142**

Para. (6)

Article 3A of the Commencement No. 9 Order makes consequential provision for cases where a claimant gives incorrect information about either their area of residence or meeting the gateway conditions.   **6.143**

Day appointed for the abolition of income-related employment and support allowance and income-based jobseeker's allowance

[¹ **4.** (1) The day appointed for the coming into force of the amending provisions, in relation to the case of a claim referred to in paragraph (2) and any award that is made in respect of the claim, is the day appointed in accordance with paragraph (3).   **6.144**
(2) The claims referred to are—
(a) a claim for universal credit, an employment and support allowance or a jobseeker's allowance where, on the date on which the claim is made [³ or treated as made], the claimant—
   (i) resides in one of the No. 5 relevant districts; and
   (ii) meets the gateway conditions;
[² (b) a claim for universal credit where—
   (i) in the case of a single claimant, the claimant gives incorrect information regarding the claimant residing in a No. 5 relevant district or meeting the gateway conditions and does not reside in such a district or does not meet the gateway conditions on the date on which the claim is made;
   (ii) in the case of joint claimants, either or both of the joint claimants gives or give incorrect information regarding his or her (or their) residing in such a district or meeting those conditions and one or both of them does not or do not reside

439

in such a district or does not or do not meet those conditions on the date on which the claim is made; and

(iii) after a decision is made that the single claimant is, or the joint claimants are, entitled to universal credit and one or more payments have been made in respect of the single claimant or the joint claimants, the Secretary of State discovers that incorrect information has been given regarding residence or meeting the gateway conditions;

[³ (c) a claim for an employment and support allowance or a job-seeker's allowance other than one referred to in sub-paragraph (a) that is made or treated as made during the relevant period by a single claimant of universal credit or by either of two joint claimants of universal credit who has or have made a claim for universal credit within sub-paragraph (a) or (b).]]

(3) The day appointed in relation to the case of a claim referred to in paragraph (2), and any award that is made in respect of the claim, is the first day of the period in respect of which the claim is made.

(4) For the purposes of paragraph (2)(c), "relevant period" means, in relation to a claim for universal credit referred to in paragraph (2)(a) or (b), any UC claim period, and any period subsequent to any UC claim period in respect of which the claimant is entitled to an award of universal credit in respect of the claim.

(5) For the purposes of paragraph (4), a "UC claim period" is a period when—

(a) a claim for universal credit as referred to in paragraph (2)(a) or [² (b)(i) or (ii)] has been made but a decision has not yet been made on the claim; or

(b) a decision has been made that the claimant is not entitled to universal credit and—

(i) the Secretary of State is considering whether to revise that decision under section 9 of the Social Security Act 1998, whether on an application made for that purpose, or on the Secretary of State's own initiative; or

(ii) the claimant has appealed against that decision to the First-tier Tribunal and that appeal or any subsequent appeal to the Upper Tribunal or to a court has not been finally determined.

(6) Paragraphs (6) and (7) of article 4 of the No. 9 Order apply in relation to the case of a claim for universal credit referred to in paragraph (2) (and any award that is made in respect of the claim) as they apply in relation to the case of a claim for universal credit referred to in sub-paragraphs (a) and (b) of article 4(2) of the No. 9 Order (and any award that is made in respect of the claim).

[² [³ . . .]] [⁴ (7) Paragraphs (1) to (1B) of article 5 of the No. 9 Order apply for the purposes of paragraph (2)(a) as they apply for the purposes of article 4(2)(a) of the No. 9 Order.]

(8) Paragraphs (5) to (7) of article 5 of the No. 9 Order apply for the purposes of sub-paragraphs (a) and (c) of paragraph (2) as they apply for the purposes of sub-paragraphs (a) and (g) of article 4(2) of the No. 9 Order.

(9) Article 5(8) of the No. 9 Order applies for the purposes of paragraph (3) as it applies for the purposes of article 4(3)(a) of the No. 9 Order.]

AMENDMENTS

1. Welfare Reform Act 2012 (Commencement No. 9, 11, 13, 14 and 16 and Transitional and Transitory Provisions (Amendment)) Order 2014 (SI 2014/1452) art.20(4) (June 16, 2014).
2. Welfare Reform Act 2012 (Commencement No. 9, 11, 13 14, 16 and 17 and Transitional and Transitory Provisions (Amendment)) Order 2014 (SI 2014/1661) art.7(5) (June 30, 2014).
3. Welfare Reform Act 2012 (Commencement No. 9, 11, 13, 14, 16 and 17 and Transitional and Transitory Provisions (Amendment) (No. 2)) Order 2014 (SI 2014/1923) art.8(4) (July 28, 2014).
4. Welfare Reform Act 2012 (Commencement No. 9, 11, 13 14, 16, 17 and 19 and Transitional and Transitory Provisions (Amendment)) Order 2014 (SI 2014/3067) art.6(4) (November 24, 2014).

DEFINITIONS

"the amending provisions"–art.2(1).
"employment and support allowance"–*ibid*.
"jobseeker's allowance"–*ibid*.
"the No. 4 relevant districts"–*ibid*.
"the No. 9 Order"–*ibid*.
"a person who . . . falls within the Pathfinder Group" –art.2(2).

GENERAL NOTE

Para. (1)

This brings into force provisions relating to the abolition of income-related 6.145 employment and support allowance and of income-based jobseeker's allowance where the case falls within one of the categories set out in para.(2) (see also the incorporation by reference of other provisions as made by paras (6)-(9) below).

Para. (2) (a)

This provides that the new provisions come into force in relation to a claim for 6.146 (and any subsequent award of) universal credit, employment and support allowance or jobseeker's allowance, where a person makes such a claim on or after November 25, 2013 for a period that begins on or after that date and, at the time that the claim is made, the claimant both lives in a No. 5 relevant district (see Schedule) and meets the Pathfinder Group (now gateway) conditions.

Para. (2) (b)

This provides that the new provisions come into force in relation to a claim for 6.147 (and any subsequent award of) universal credit where a person claims universal credit, again on or after November 25, 2013 for a period that begins on or after that date, but provides incorrect information as to either their residence in a No. 5 relevant district (see Schedule) or as to their meeting the Pathfinder Group or gateway conditions. As with reg.3(2)(b), such a claim remains within the universal credit regime despite the error.

Para. (3)

6.148   The day appointed for the coming into force of the amending provisions in the above cases is the first day of the period in respect of which the claim is made.

Para. (7)

6.149   Article 5(1) of the Commencement No. 9 Order provides that the Claims and Payments Regulations 1987 determine whether and when a claim for employment and support allowance or jobseeker's allowance is made or is treated as made.

Application of the No. 9 Order

6.150   5. [¹Articles] 9 to 22 of the No. 9 Order apply in connection with the coming into force of the amending provisions in relation to the case of a claim referred to in article 4(2), and any award made in respect of the claim, as they apply in connection with the coming into force of the amending provisions in relation to the case of a claim referred to in [² sub-paragraphs (a), (b) and (g) of article 4(2)] of the No. 9 Order and any award made in respect of the claim.

AMENDMENTS

    1. Welfare Reform Act 2012 (Commencement No. 9, 11, 13, 14 and 16 and Transitory and Transitory Provisions (Amendment)) Order 2014 (SI 2014/1452) art.20(5) (June 16, 2014).
    2. Welfare Reform Act 2012 (Commencement No. 9, 11, 13 14, 16 and 17 and Transitory and Transitory Provisions (Amendment)) Order 2014 (SI 2014/1661) art.7(6) (June 30, 2014).

DEFINITION

"the amending provisions"–art.2(1).

GENERAL NOTE

6.151   This provision is in the same terms as art.5 of the Commencement No. 11 Order.

Article 2(1)

6.152   SCHEDULE
The No. 5 relevant districts

    1. CV21 1 to CV21 4.
    2. CV21 9.
    3. CV22 5 to CV22 7.
    4. IV1 1.
    5. IV1 3.
    6. IV1 9.
    7. IV2 3 to IV2 7.
    8. IV3 5.
    9. IV3 8.
    10. IV4 7.
    11. IV5 7.
    12. IV8 8.
    13. IV9 8.

14. IV10 8.
15. IV11 8.
16. IV12 4 and IV12 5.
17. IV12 9.
18. IV13 7.
19. IV21 2.
20. IV22 2.
21. IV26 2.
22. IV54 8.
23. IV63 6 and IV63 7.
24. PH19 1.
25. PH20 1.
26. PH21 1.
27. PH22 1.
28. PH23 3.
29. PH24 3.
30. PH25 3.
31. PH26 3.
32. PH26 9.
33. PH32 4.

The Welfare Reform Act 2012 (Commencement No. 16 and Transitional and Transitory Provisions) Order 2014

SI 2014/209 (C. 7) (as amended)

ARRANGEMENT OF ARTICLES
6.153

1. Citation
2. Interpretation
3. Day appointed for commencement of the universal credit provisions in Part 1 of the Act
4. Day appointed for the abolition of income-related employment and support allowance and income-based jobseeker's allowance
5. Application of the No. 9 Order
6. Day appointed for the coming into force of section 139 of the Act

Schedule: The No. 6 and No. 7 relevant districts

The Secretary of State, in exercise of the powers conferred by section 150(3) and (4)(a), (b)(i) and (c) of the Welfare Reform Act 2012, makes the following Order:

GENERAL NOTE

This Commencement Order ("the Commencement No. 16 Order") extended the universal credit scheme to certain postcode districts in Bath and Harrogate ("the No. 6 relevant districts") as from February 24, 2014 and to others in Shotton ("the No. 7 relevant districts") as from April 7, 2014. In addition, of course, the claimant had to fall within the Pathfinder Group, i.e. be a person who meets the requirements of regs 5 to 12 of the Transitional Provisions Regulations 2013, now the "gateway conditions" (see Sch.5 to the Commencement No.9 Order).

6.154

Citation

6.155   **1.** This Order may be cited as the Welfare Reform Act 2012 (Commencement No. 16 and Transitional and Transitory Provisions) Order 2014.

Interpretation

6.156   **2.** (1) In this Order—

"the Act" means the Welfare Reform Act 2012;

"the amending provisions" means the provisions referred to in article 4(1)(a) to (c) of the No. 9 Order (day appointed for the abolition of income-related employment and support allowance and income-based jobseeker's allowance);

[¹ ... [² ....] ... [² ...] ...]

[⁴ "claimant"—

(a) in relation to an employment and support allowance, has the same meaning as in Part 1 of the Welfare Reform Act 2007, save as mentioned in article 5(1A) of the No. 9 Order as applied by article 4(7);

(b) in relation to a jobseeker's allowance, has the same meaning as in the Jobseekers Act 1995 (as it applies apart from the amendments made by Part 1 of Schedule 14 to the Act that remove references to an income-based jobseeker's allowance), save as mentioned in article 5(1A) of the No. 9 Order as applied by article 4(7);

(c) in relation to universal credit, has the same meaning as in Part 1 of the Act;]

"employment and support allowance" means an employment and support allowance under Part 1 of the Welfare Reform Act 2007;

[¹ "First-tier Tribunal" has the same meaning as in the Social Security Act 1998;

[² [³ "gateway conditions" means the conditions specified in Schedule 5 to the No. 9 Order;]]]

"jobseeker's allowance" means a jobseeker's allowance under the Jobseekers Act 1995;

[² "joint claimants" in relation to universal credit, has the same meaning as in Part 1 of the Act;]

"No. 6 relevant districts" means the postcode part-districts specified in Part 1 of the Schedule;

"No. 7 relevant districts" means the postcode part-districts specified in Part 2 of the Schedule;

"the No. 9 Order" means the Welfare Reform Act 2012 (Commencement No. 9 and Transitional and Transitory Provisions and Commencement No. 8 and Savings and Transitional Provisions (Amendment)) Order 2013;

[² "single claimant", in relation to universal credit, has the same meaning as in Part 1 of the Act;]

[¹ "Upper Tribunal" has the same meaning as in the Social Security Act 1998.]

[¹ (2) For the purposes of this Order, the Universal Credit, Personal Independence Payment, Jobseeker's Allowance and Employment and Support Allowance (Claims and Payments) Regulations 2013 apply for the purpose of deciding—

(a) whether a claim for universal credit is made; and

(b) the date on which such a claim is made.]

[² (3) [³ . . .]]

AMENDMENTS

1. Welfare Reform Act 2012 (Commencement No. 9, 11, 13, 14 and 16 and Transitional and Transitory Provisions (Amendment)) Order 2014 (SI 2014/1452) art.21(2) (June 16, 2014).
2. Welfare Reform Act 2012 (Commencement No. 9, 11, 13 14, 16 and 17 and Transitional and Transitory Provisions (Amendment)) Order 2014 (SI 2014/1661) art.8(1)(a) and 8(3) (June 30, 2014).
3. Welfare Reform Act 2012 (Commencement No. 9, 11, 13, 14, 16 and 17 and Transitional and Transitory Provisions (Amendment) (No. 2)) Order 2014 (SI 2014/1923) art.9(2) (July 28, 2014).
4. Welfare Reform Act 2012 (Commencement No. 9, 11, 13 14, 16, 17 and 19 and Transitional and Transitory Provisions (Amendment)) Order 2014 (SI 2014/3067) art.6(3) (November 24, 2014).

Day appointed for the coming into force of the universal credit provisions in Part 1 of the Act

3. (1) The day appointed for the coming into force of the provisions of the Act listed in Schedule 2 to the No. 9 Order, in so far as they are not already in force, in relation to the case of a claim referred to in paragraph (2), and any award that is made in respect of the claim, is the day appointed in accordance with paragraph (3). 6.157

[¹ (2) The claims referred to are—

(a) a claim for universal credit where, on the date on which the claim is made or treated as made, the claimant resides in one of the No. 6 or No. 7 relevant districts and meets the gateway conditions; and

[² (b) a claim for universal credit where—

(i) in the case of a single claimant, the claimant gives incorrect information regarding the claimant residing in a No. 6 or a No. 7 relevant district or meeting the gateway conditions and the claimant does not reside in such a district or does not meet the gateway conditions on the date on which the claim is made;

(ii) in the case of joint claimants, either or both of the joint claimants gives or give incorrect information regarding his or her (or their) residing in such a district or meeting the gateway conditions and one or both of them does not or do not reside in such a district or does not or do not meet those conditions on the date on which the claim is made; and

(iii) after a decision is made that the single claimant is, or the joint claimants are, entitled to universal credit and one or more

445

payments have been made in respect of the single claimant or the joint claimants, the Secretary of State discovers that incorrect information has been given regarding residence or meeting the gateway conditions.]]

(3) The day appointed in relation to the case of a claim referred to in paragraph (2), and any award that is made in respect of the claim, is the first day of the period in respect of which the claim is made [² . . .].

(4) [¹ . . .]

(5) Article 3(6) of the No. 9 Order applies for the purposes of paragraph (3) as it applies for the purposes of article 3(4)(a) of the No. 9 Order.

[¹ [² [³ (6) Article 3A of the No. 9 Order applies in connection with a claim for universal credit where a single claimant, or, as the case may be, either or both of joint claimants, gives incorrect information regarding his or her (or their) residing in a No. 6 or a No. 7 relevant district or meeting the gateway conditions, as it applies in connection with the giving of incorrect information regarding a claimant residing in a relevant district (as defined in the No. 9 Order) or meeting the gateway conditions.]]]

AMENDMENTS

1. Welfare Reform Act 2012 (Commencement No. 9, 11, 13, 14 and 16 and Transitional and Transitory Provisions (Amendment)) Order 2014 (SI 2014/1452) art.21(3) (June 16, 2014).
2. Welfare Reform Act 2012 (Commencement No. 9, 11, 13 14, 16 and 17 and Transitional and Transitory Provisions (Amendment)) Order 2014 (SI 2014/1661) art.8(1)(b) and 8(4) (June 30, 2014).
3. Welfare Reform Act 2012 (Commencement No. 9, 11, 13, 14, 16 and 17 and Transitional and Transitory Provisions (Amendment) (No. 2)) Order 2014 (SI 2014/1923) art.8(3) (July 28, 2014).

Day appointed for the abolition of income-related employment and support allowance and income-based jobseeker's allowance

6.158   [¹ **4.** (1) The day appointed for the coming into force of the amending provisions, in relation to the case of a claim referred to in paragraph (2) and any award that is made in respect of the claim, is the day appointed in accordance with paragraph (3).

(2) The claims referred to are—

(a) a claim for universal credit, an employment and support allowance or a jobseeker's allowance where, on the date on which the claim is made [3 or treated as made], the claimant—

(i) resides in one of the No. 6 or No. 7 relevant districts; and

(ii) meets the gateway conditions;

[² (b) a claim for universal credit where—

(i) in the case of a single claimant, the claimant gives incorrect information regarding the claimant residing in a No. 6 or a No. 7 relevant district or meeting the gateway conditions and

446

does not reside in such a district or does not meet the gateway conditions on the date on which the claim is made;

(ii) in the case of joint claimants, either or both of the joint claimants gives or give incorrect information regarding his or her (or their) residing in such a district or meeting those conditions and one or both of them does not or do not reside in such a district or does not or do not meet those conditions on the date on which the claim is made; and

(iii) after a decision is made that the single claimant is, or the joint claimants are, entitled to universal credit and one or more payments have been made in respect of the single claimant or the joint claimants, the Secretary of State discovers that incorrect information has been given regarding residence or meeting the gateway conditions;

[³ (c) a claim for an employment and support allowance or a job-seeker's allowance other than one referred to in sub-paragraph (a) that is made or treated as made during the relevant period by a single claimant of universal credit or by either of two joint claimants of universal credit who has or have made a claim for universal credit within sub-paragraph (a) or (b).]]

(3) The day appointed in relation to the case of a claim referred to in paragraph (2), and any award that is made in respect of the claim, is the first day of the period in respect of which the claim is made.

(4) For the purposes of paragraph (2)(c), "relevant period" means, in relation to a claim for universal credit referred to in paragraph (2)(a) or (b), any UC claim period, and any period subsequent to any UC claim period in respect of which the claimant is entitled to an award of universal credit in respect of the claim.

(5) For the purposes of paragraph (4), a "UC claim period" is a period when—

(a) a claim for universal credit as referred to in paragraph (2)(a) [2, (b)(i) or (ii)] has been made but a decision has not yet been made on the claim; or

(b) a decision has been made that the claimant is not entitled to universal credit and—

(i) the Secretary of State is considering whether to revise that decision under section 9 of the Social Security Act 1998, whether on an application made for that purpose, or on the Secretary of State's own initiative; or

(ii) the claimant has appealed against that decision to the First-tier Tribunal and that appeal or any subsequent appeal to the Upper Tribunal or to a court has not been finally determined.

(6) Paragraphs (6) and (7) of article 4 of the No. 9 Order apply in relation to the case of a claim for universal credit referred to in paragraph (2) (and any award that is made in respect of the claim) as they apply in relation to the case of a claim for universal credit referred to in sub-paragraphs (a) and (b) of article 4(2) of the No. 9 Order (and any award that is made in respect of the claim).

[² [³ . . .]] [⁴ (7) Paragraphs (1) to (1B) of article 5 of the No. 9 Order apply for the purposes of paragraph (2)(a) as they apply for the purposes of article 4(2)(a) of the No. 9 Order.]

(8) Paragraphs (5) to (7) of article 5 of the No. 9 Order apply for the purposes of sub-paragraphs (a) and (c) of paragraph (2) as they apply for the purposes of paragraphs (a) and (g) of article 4(2) of the No. 9 Order.

(9) Article 5(8) of the No. 9 Order applies for the purposes of paragraph (3) as it applies for the purposes of article 4(3)(a) of the No. 9 Order.]

AMENDMENTS

1. Welfare Reform Act 2012 (Commencement No. 9, 11, 13, 14 and 16 and Transitional and Transitory Provisions (Amendment)) Order 2014 (SI 2014/1452) art.21(4) (June 16, 2014).
2. Welfare Reform Act 2012 (Commencement No. 9, 11, 13 14, 16 and 17 and Transitional and Transitory Provisions (Amendment)) Order 2014 (SI 2014/1661) art.8(5) (June 30, 2014).
3. Welfare Reform Act 2012 (Commencement No. 9, 11, 13, 14, 16 and 17 and Transitional and Transitory Provisions (Amendment) (No. 2)) Order 2014 (SI 2014/1923) art.9(4) (July 28, 2014).
4. Welfare Reform Act 2012 (Commencement No. 9, 11, 13 14, 16, 17 and 19 and Transitional and Transitory Provisions (Amendment)) Order 2014 (SI 2014/3067) art.6(4) (November 24, 2014).

Application of the No. 9 Order

6.159   **5.** [¹ Articles] 9 to 22 of the No. 9 Order apply in connection with the coming into force of the amending provisions in relation to the case of a claim referred to in article 4(2), and any award made in respect of the claim, as they apply in connection with the coming into force of the amending provisions in relation to the case of a claim referred to in [² sub-paragraphs (a), (b) and (g) of article 4(2)] of the No. 9 Order and any award made in respect of the claim.

AMENDMENTS

1. Welfare Reform Act 2012 (Commencement No. 9, 11, 13, 14 and 16 and Transitional and Transitory Provisions (Amendment)) Order 2014 (SI 2014/1452) art.21(5) (June 16, 2014).
2. Welfare Reform Act 2012 (Commencement No. 9, 11, 13 14, 16 and 17 and Transitional and Transitory Provisions (Amendment)) Order 2014 (SI 2014/1661) art.8(6) (June 30, 2014).

Day appointed for the coming into force of section 139 of the Act

6.160   **6.** The day appointed for the coming into force of section 139 of the Act (recovery of child support maintenance by deduction from benefit) is the day following the day on which this Order is made.

448

SCHEDULE 1   **6.161**

                                    Article 2(1)

PART 1

The No.6 relevant districts

1. BA1 0 to BA1 7.
2. BA2 0 to BA2 6.
3. BA2 9.
4. BA3 2 and BA3 3.
5. BA3 9.
6. BS31 1.
7. BS31 3.
8. BS31 9.
9. BS39 4 and BS39 5.
10. BS39 7.
11. HG1 1 to HG1 5.
12. HG1 9.
13. HG2 0.
14. HG2 7 to HG2 9.
15. HG3 1 to HG3 4.
16. HG4 1 to HG4 3.
17. HG4 9.
18. HG5 0.
19. HG5 5.
20. HG5 8 and HG5 9.
21. LS17 0.
22. YO51 9.

PART 2   **6.162**

The No. 7 relevant districts

1. CH5 1 to CH5 4.
2. CH5 9.

Universal Credit (Transitional Provisions) Regulations 2014

2014/1230 (as amended)
In force June 16, 2014

ARRANGEMENT OF REGULATIONS   **6.163**

PART 1

PART 2

CHAPTER 1

CHAPTER 2

CHAPTER 3

The Secretary of State for Work and Pensions makes the following Regulations in exercise of the powers conferred by section 42(2) and (3) of and paragraphs 1(1) and (2)(b), 3(1)(a) to (c), 4(1)(a), 5(1), (2)(c) and (d) and (3)(a) and 6 of Schedule 6 to the Welfare Reform Act 2012.

In accordance with section 172(1) of the Social Security Administration Act 1992 ("the 1992 Act"), the Secretary of State has referred proposals in respect of these Regulations to the Social Security Advisory Committee.

In accordance with section 176(1) of the 1992 Act and, in so far as these Regulations relate to housing benefit, the Secretary of State has consulted with organisations appearing to him to be representative of the authorities concerned in respect of proposals for these Regulations.

PART 1

Citation and commencement

1. (1) These Regulations may be cited as the Universal Credit (Transitional Provisions) Regulations 2014.   6.164

(2) These Regulations come into force on 16th June 2014.

Interpretation

2. (1) In these Regulations—   6.165

"the 2002 Act" means the Tax Credits Act 2002;
"the 2007 Act" means the Welfare Reform Act 2007;
"the Act" means the Welfare Reform Act 2012;

"assessment period" has the same meaning as in the Universal Credit Regulations;

"the Claims and Payments Regulations" means the Universal Credit, Personal Independence Payment, Jobseeker's Allowance and Employment and Support Allowance (Claims and Payments) Regulations 2013;

"contributory employment and support allowance" means a contributory allowance under Part 1 of the 2007 Act as that Part has effect apart from the amendments made by Schedule 3, and Part 1 of Schedule 14, to the Act that remove references to an income-related allowance;

[¹ . . .]

"existing benefit" means income-based jobseeker's allowance, income-related employment and support allowance, income support, housing benefit and child tax credit and working tax credit under the 2002 Act, but see also regulation 25(2);

"First-tier Tribunal" has the same meaning as in the Social Security Act 1998;

"housing benefit" means housing benefit under section 130 of the Social Security Contributions and Benefits Act 1992;

"income-based jobseeker's allowance" has the same meaning as in the Jobseekers Act 1995;

"income-related employment and support allowance" means an income-related allowance under Part 1 of the 2007 Act;

"income support" means income support under section 124 of the Social Security Contributions and Benefits Act 1992;

"joint-claim jobseeker's allowance" means old style JSA, entitlement to which arises by virtue of section 1(2B) of the Jobseekers Act 1995;

"new claimant partner" has the meaning given in regulation 7;

"new style ESA" means an allowance under Part 1 of the 2007 Act as amended by the amendments made by Schedule 3, and Part 1 of Schedule 14, to the Act that remove references to an income-related allowance;

"new style JSA" means an allowance under the Jobseekers Act 1995 as amended by the amendments made by Part 1 of Schedule 14 to the Act that remove references to an income-based allowance;

"old style ESA" means an employment and support allowance under Part 1 of the 2007 Act as that Part has effect apart from the amendments made by Schedule 3, and Part 1 of Schedule 14, to the Act that remove references to an income-related allowance;

"old style JSA" means a jobseeker's allowance under the Jobseekers Act 1995 as that Act has effect apart from the amendments made by Part 1 of Schedule 14 to the Act that remove references to an income-based allowance;

[¹ "specified accommodation" means accommodation to which one or more of sub-paragraphs (2) to (5) of paragraph 3A of Schedule 1 to the Universal Credit Regulations applies;]

"partner" in relation to a person ("A") means a person who forms part of a couple with A;

"tax credit" (including "child tax credit" and "working tax credit"), "tax credits" and

"tax year" have the same meanings as in the 2002 Act;

"the Universal Credit Regulations" means the Universal Credit Regulations 2013;

"Upper Tribunal" has the same meaning as in the Social Security Act 1998.

(2) For the purposes of these Regulations—

(a) the date on which a claim for universal credit is made is to be determined in accordance with the Claims and Payments Regulations;

(b) where a couple is treated, in accordance with regulation 9(8) of the Claims and Payments Regulations, as having made a claim for universal credit, references to the date on which the claim is treated as made are to the date of formation of the couple;

(c) where a regulation refers to entitlement to an existing benefit on the date on which a claim for universal credit is made or treated as made, such entitlement is to be taken into account notwithstanding the effect of regulations 5, 7 and 8 or termination of an award of the benefit before that date by virtue of an order made under section 150(3) of the Act.

AMENDMENTS

1. Universal Credit (Transitional Provisions) (Amendment) Regulations 2014 (SI 2014/1626) reg.3 (November 3, 2014).

Revocation and saving of the Universal Credit (Transitional Provisions) Regulations 2013

3. (1) The Universal Credit (Transitional Provisions) Regulations 2013 ("the 2013 Regulations") are revoked, subject to the savings in paragraphs (2) to (4).   **6.166**

(2) Chapters 2 and 3 of Part 2 (Pathfinder Group and treatment of invalid claims) of the 2013 Regulations continue to have effect in relation to a claim for universal credit—

(a) which was made before the date on which these Regulations come into force ("the commencement date"); and

(b) in respect of which no payment has been made to the claimant before the commencement date.

(3) Regulation 19 of the 2013 Regulations (advance payments of universal credit) continues to have effect in relation to an advance payment which was made in accordance with that regulation before the commencement date and regulation 17 of these Regulations does not apply to such a payment.

(4) Any other provision of the 2013 Regulations continues to have effect in so far as is necessary to give full effect to paragraphs (2) and (3).

PART 2

CHAPTER 1

Secretary of State discretion to determine that claims for universal credit may not be made

6.167   **4.** (1) Where the Secretary of State considers it necessary, in order to—

(a) safeguard the efficient administration of universal credit; or

(b) ensure the effective testing of systems for the administration of universal credit,

to cease to accept claims in any area, or in any category of case (either in all areas or in a specified area), the Secretary of State may determine that claims for universal credit may not be made in that area, or in that category of case.

(2) A determination under paragraph (1) has effect until it ceases to have effect in accordance with a further determination made by the Secretary of State.

(3) More than one determination under paragraph (1) may have effect at the same time.

CHAPTER 2

Exclusion of entitlement to certain benefits

6.168   **5.** (1) Except as provided in paragraph (2), a claimant is not entitled to—

(a) income support;

(b) housing benefit;

(c) a tax credit; or

(d) state pension credit under the State Pension Credit Act 2002,

in respect of any period when the claimant is entitled to universal credit.

(2) Entitlement to universal credit does not preclude the claimant from entitlement—

(a) to housing benefit in respect of [1 specified accommodation]; or

(b) during the first assessment period for universal credit, where the claimant is a new claimant partner, to—

(i) income support, where an award to which the new claimant partner is entitled terminates, in accordance with regulation 7(4), after the first date of entitlement to universal credit;

(ii) housing benefit, where regulation 7(5)(b) applies and an award of housing benefit to which the new claimant partner is entitled terminates after the first date of entitlement to universal credit; or

(iii) a tax credit, where an award to which the new claimant partner is entitled terminates, in accordance with the 2002 Act, after the first date of entitlement to universal credit.

AMENDMENTS

1. Universal Credit (Transitional Provisions) (Amendment) Regulations 2014 (SI 2014/1626) reg.3 (November 3, 2014).

Exclusion of claims for certain existing benefits

6. (1) Except as provided in paragraphs (5) to (9) a universal credit claimant may not make a claim for income support, housing benefit or a tax credit.

6.169

(2) For the purposes of this regulation, a person is a universal credit claimant if—

(a) the person is entitled to universal credit;

(b) the person has made a claim for universal credit, a decision has not yet been made on that claim and the person has not been informed (in accordance with an order made under section 150(3) of the Act) that he or she is not entitled to claim universal credit;

(c) the person was previously entitled to a joint award of universal credit which terminated because the person ceased to be a member of a couple, he or she is not exempt (by virtue of regulation 9(6) of the Claims and Payments Regulations) from the condition of entitlement to universal credit that he or she makes a claim for it and the period of one month, starting with the date on which the person notified the Secretary of State that he or she had ceased to be a member of a couple, has not expired;

(d) the person is treated, under the Claims and Payments Regulations, as having made a claim for universal credit, or may be entitled to an award of universal credit in circumstances where, by virtue of those Regulations, it is not a condition of entitlement that he or she makes a claim for it, but no decision has yet been made as to the person's entitlement;

(e) a decision has been made that the person is not entitled to universal credit and—

(i) the Secretary of State is considering whether to revise that decision under section 9 of the Social Security Act 1998, whether on an application made for that purpose, or on the Secretary of State's own initiative; or

(ii) the person has appealed against that decision to the First-tier Tribunal and that appeal or any subsequent appeal to the Upper Tribunal or to a court has not been finally determined.

(3) For the purposes of paragraph (1)—

(a) a universal credit claimant makes a claim for benefit mentioned in that paragraph if the claimant takes any action which results in a decision on a claim being required under the relevant Regulations; and

(b) except as provided in paragraphs (5) to (7), it is irrelevant that the effect of any provision of the relevant Regulations is that, for the purposes of those Regulations, the claim is made or treated as made at a time when the claimant was not a universal credit claimant.

(4) The relevant Regulations are—

(a) in relation to a claim for income support, the Social Security (Claims and Payments) Regulations 1987 ("the 1987 Regulations");

(b) in relation to a claim for housing benefit, the Housing Benefit Regulations 2006("the 2006 Regulations") or, as the case may be, the Housing Benefit (Persons who have attained the qualifying age for state pension credit) Regulations 2006 ("the 2006 (SPC) Regulations");

(c) in relation to a claim for a tax credit, the Tax Credits (Claims and Notifications) Regulations 2002.

(5) A universal credit claimant is not precluded from making a claim for income support if—

(a) first notification of the claimant's intention to make that claim was made, or deemed to be made, for the purposes of regulation 6(1A)(c) of the 1987 Regulations, before the date on which the claim for universal credit was made or treated as made; and

(b) in accordance with the 1987 Regulations, the claimant's entitlement to income support in connection with the claim will (if the claimant is entitled to income support) pre-date—

(i) the date, or anticipated date, of the claimant's entitlement to universal credit in connection with the current award or claim; or

(ii) where the claimant is a new claimant partner and regulation 7(4) would apply to the award, the date on which it would terminate in accordance with that provision.

(6) A universal credit claimant is not precluded from making a claim for housing benefit if—

(a) first notification of the claimant's intention to make that claim was given (within the meaning of regulation 83(5)(d) of the 2006 Regulations or, as the case may be, regulation 64(6)(d) of the 2006 (SPC) Regulations before the date on which the claim for universal credit was made or treated as made; and

(b) in accordance with the 2006 Regulations or, as the case may be, the 2006 (SPC) Regulations, the claimant's entitlement to housing benefit in connection with the claim will (if the claimant is entitled to housing benefit) pre-date—

(i) the date, or anticipated date, of the claimant's entitlement to universal credit in connection with the current award or claim; or

(ii) where the claimant is a new claimant partner and regulation 7(5)(b) would apply to the award, the date on which it would terminate in accordance with the 2006 Regulations or, as the case may be, the 2006 (SPC) Regulations.

(7) A universal credit claimant is not precluded from correcting or completing a claim for housing benefit which was defective within the meaning of the 2006 Regulations or the 2006 (SPC) Regulations if—

(a) the defective claim was made before the date on which the claim for universal credit was made or treated as made; and

(b) in accordance with the 2006 Regulations or, as the case may be, the 2006 (SPC) Regulations, the claimant's entitlement to housing benefit in connection with the claim will (if the claimant is entitled to housing benefit) pre-date—

(i) the date, or anticipated date, of the claimant's entitlement to universal credit in connection with the current award or claim; or

(ii) where the claimant is a new claimant partner and regulation 7(5)(b) would apply to the award, the date on which it would terminate in accordance with the 2006 Regulations or, as the case may be, the 2006 (SPC) Regulations.

(8) A universal credit claimant is not precluded from making a claim for housing benefit in respect of [¹ specified accommodation].

(9) A universal credit claimant is not precluded from making a claim for a tax credit which the claimant is treated as having made by virtue of regulation 7(7) or 8(4)(a).

AMENDMENTS

1. Universal Credit (Transitional Provisions) (Amendment) Regulations 2014 (SI 2014/1626) reg.3 (November 3, 2014).

Termination of awards of certain existing benefits: new claimant partners

7. (1) This regulation applies where—   6.170

(a) a person ("A") who was previously entitled to universal credit as a single person ceases to be so entitled on becoming a member of a couple;

(b) the other member of the couple ("the new claimant partner") was not entitled to universal credit as a single person immediately before formation of the couple;

(c) the couple is treated, in accordance with regulation 9(8) of the Claims and Payments Regulations, as having made a claim for universal credit; and

(d) the Secretary of State is satisfied that the claimants meet the basic conditions specified in section 4(1)(a) to (d) of the Act (other than any of those conditions which they are not required to meet by virtue of regulations under section 4(2) of the Act).

(2) Subject to paragraphs (4) and (5), where this regulation applies, all awards of income support or housing benefit to which the new claimant partner would (were it not for the effect of these Regulations) have been entitled during the relevant period are to terminate, by virtue of this regulation—

(a) on the day before the first date on which the joint claimants are entitled to universal credit in connection with the claim; or

457

(b) if the joint claimants are not entitled to universal credit, on the day before the first date on which they would have been so entitled, if all of the basic and financial conditions applicable to them had been met; or

(c) if the new claimant partner became entitled to an award after the date on which it would otherwise terminate under sub-paragraph (a) or (b), at the beginning of the first day of entitlement to that award.

(3) For the purposes of this regulation, "the relevant period" is the period starting with the first day of the assessment period (in relation to A's award of universal credit) during which A and the new claimant partner formed a couple and ending with the date of formation of the couple.

(4) Where the new claimant partner was entitled during the relevant period to income support, he or she was at that time a member of a couple and the award included an amount in respect of the new claimant partner and their partner at that time ("P"), the award of income support terminates, by virtue of this regulation, on the date on which the new claimant partner and P ceased to be a couple for the purposes of the Income Support (General) Regulations 1987, unless it terminates on that date in accordance with other legislative provision, or terminated on an earlier date.

(5) An award of housing benefit to which the new claimant partner is entitled does not terminate by virtue of this regulation where—

(a) the award is in respect of [1 specified accommodation]; or

(b) the new claimant partner leaves the accommodation in respect of which housing benefit was paid, in order to live with A.

(6) Where an award terminates by virtue of this regulation, any legislative provision under which the award terminates on a later date does not apply.

(7) Where the new claimant partner was, immediately before forming a couple with A, treated by regulation 11 as being entitled to a tax credit, the new claimant partner is to be treated, for the purposes of the 2002 Act, as having made a claim for the tax credit in question for the current tax year.

AMENDMENTS

1. Universal Credit (Transitional Provisions) (Amendment) Regulations 2014 (SI 2014/1626) reg.3 (November 3, 2014).

Termination of awards of certain existing benefits: other claimants

6.171   **8.**—(1) This regulation applies where—

(a) a claim for universal credit (other than a claim which is treated, in accordance with regulation 9(8) of the Claims and Payments Regulations, as having been made) is made; and

(b) the Secretary of State is satisfied that the claimant meets the basic conditions specified in section 4(1)(a) to (d) of the Act (other than any of those conditions which the claimant is not required to meet by virtue of regulations under section 4(2) of the Act).

(2) Subject to paragraph (3), where this regulation applies, all awards of income support, housing benefit or a tax credit to which the claimant (or, in the case of joint claimants, either of them) is entitled on the date on which the claim is made are to terminate, by virtue of this regulation—

   (a) on the day before the first date on which the claimant is entitled to universal credit in connection with the claim; or

   (b) if the claimant is not entitled to universal credit, on the day before the first date on which he or she would have been so entitled, if all of the basic and financial conditions applicable to the claimant had been met.

(3) An award of housing benefit to which a claimant is entitled in respect of [1 specified accommodation] does not terminate by virtue of this regulation.

(4) Where this regulation applies and the claimant (or, in the case of joint claimants, either of them) is treated by regulation 11 as being entitled to a tax credit—

   (a) the claimant (or, as the case may be, the relevant claimant) is to be treated, for the purposes of the 2002 Act and this regulation, as having made a claim for the tax credit in question for the current tax year; and

   (b) if the claimant (or the relevant claimant) is entitled on the date on which the claim for universal credit was made to an award of a tax credit which is made in respect of a claim which is treated as having been made by virtue of sub-paragraph (a), that award is to terminate, by virtue of this regulation—

      (i) on the day before the first date on which the claimant is entitled to universal credit; or

      (ii) if the claimant is not entitled to universal credit, on the day before the first date on which he or she would have been so entitled, if all of the basic and financial conditions applicable to the claimant had been met.

(5) Where an award terminates by virtue of this regulation, any legislative provision under which the award terminates on a later date does not apply.

AMENDMENTS

   1. Universal Credit (Transitional Provisions) (Amendment) Regulations 2014 (SI 2014/1626) reg.3 (November 3, 2014).

Treatment of ongoing entitlement to certain benefits: benefit cap

9. (1) This regulation applies where a claimant who is a new claimant partner, or who has (in accordance with regulation 26 of the Universal Credit Regulations) been awarded universal credit in respect of a period preceding the date on which the claim for universal credit was made or treated as made—

   6.172

(a) is entitled, in respect of the whole or part of the first assessment period for universal credit, to a welfare benefit (other than universal credit) mentioned in regulation 79(4) of the Universal Credit Regulations (circumstances where the benefit cap applies); and

(b) is entitled to housing benefit at any time during the first assessment period for universal credit, or would be so entitled were it not for the effect of these Regulations.

(2) Where this regulation applies, regulation 79 of the Universal Credit Regulations applies, in relation to the claimant, as if the benefit in question was not included in the list of welfare benefits in paragraph (4) of that regulation.

Treatment of overpayments

6.173   **10.** (1) This regulation applies where—

(a) an award of universal credit is made to a claimant who was previously entitled to an existing benefit other than a tax credit or a joint-claim jobseeker's allowance; and

(b) a payment of the existing benefit is made which includes payment ("the overpayment") in respect of a period—

   (i) during which the claimant is not entitled to that benefit (including non-entitlement which arises from termination of an award by virtue of an order made under section 150(3) of the Act or regulation 7, 8, or 14); and

   (ii) which falls within an assessment period for universal credit.

(2) Where this regulation applies, for the purposes of calculating the amount of an award of universal credit in respect of an assessment period—

(a) regulation 66 of the Universal Credit Regulations (what is included in unearned income?) applies as if the overpayment which was made in respect of that assessment period were added to the descriptions of unearned income in paragraph (1)(b) of that regulation; and

(b) regulation 73 of the Universal Credit Regulations (unearned income calculated monthly) does not apply to the overpayment.

(3) In so far as any overpayment is taken into account in calculating the amount of an award of universal credit in accordance with this regulation, that payment may not be recovered as an overpayment under—

(a) the Social Security (Payments on account, Overpayments and Recovery) Regulations 1988;

(b) the Housing Benefit Regulations 2006; or

(c) the Housing Benefit (Persons who have attained the qualifying age for state pension credit) Regulations 2006.

Ongoing awards of tax credits

6.174   **11.** (1) For the purposes of regulations 7(7) and 8(4)—

(a) a person is to be treated as being entitled to working tax credit with effect from the start of the current tax year even though a decision has not been made under section 14 of the 2002 Act in respect of a claim for that tax credit for that tax year, if the person was entitled to working tax credit for the previous tax year and any of the cases specified in paragraph (2) applies; and

(b) a person is to be treated as being entitled to child tax credit with effect from the start of the current tax year even though a decision has not been made under section 14 of the 2002 Act in respect of a claim for that tax credit for that tax year, if the person was entitled to child tax credit for the previous tax year and any of the cases specified in paragraph (2) applies.

(2) The cases are—

(a) a final notice has not been given to the person under section 17 of the 2002 Act in respect of the previous tax year;

(b) a final notice has been given, which includes provision by virtue of subsection (2) or (4) of section 17, or a combination of those subsections and subsection (6) and—

  (i) the date specified in the notice for the purposes of section 17(2) and (4) or, where different dates are specified, the later of them, has not yet passed and no claim for a tax credit for the current tax year has been made, or treated as made; or

  (ii) a claim for a tax credit has been made, or treated as made, on or before the date mentioned in paragraph (i), but no decision has been made in relation to that claim under section 14(1) of the 2002 Act;

(c) a final notice has been given, no claim for a tax credit for the current year has been made, or treated as made, and no decision has been made under section 18(1) of the 2002 Act in respect of entitlement to a tax credit for the previous tax year; or

(d) a final notice has been given and—

  (i) the person did not make a declaration in response to provision included in that notice by virtue of section 17(2)(a), (4)(a) or (6)(a), or any combination of those provisions, by the date specified in the notice;

  (ii) the person was given due notice that payments of tax credit under section 24(4) of the 2002 Act had ceased due to his or her failure to make the declaration; and

  (iii) the person's claim for universal credit is made during the period of 30 days starting with the date on the notice referred to in paragraph (ii) or, where the person is a new claimant partner, notification of formation of a couple with a person entitled to universal credit is given to the Secretary of State during that period.

Modification of tax credits legislation: overpayments and penalties

12. (1) This regulation applies where—   6.175

(a) a claim for universal credit is made, or is treated as having been made;

(b) the claimant is, or was at any time during the tax year in which the claim is made or treated as made, entitled to a tax credit; and

461

(c) the Secretary of State is satisfied that the claimant meets the basic conditions specified in section 4(1)(a) to (d) of the Act (other than any of those conditions which the claimant is not required to meet by virtue of regulations under section 4(2) of the Act).

(2) Where this regulation applies, the 2002 Act applies in relation to the claimant with the following modifications.

(3) In section 28—

(a) in subsection (1)—

(i) after "tax year" in both places where it occurs, insert "or part tax year";

(ii) at the end insert "or treated as an overpayment of universal credit";

(b) in subsections (3) and (4), after "repaid" insert "to the Board or, as the case may be, to the Secretary of State";

(c) omit subsection (5);

(d) in subsection (6) omit "(apart from subsection (5))".

(4) In section 29(4)—

(a) after "regulations" insert "or, as the case may be, regulations made by the Secretary of State under the Social Security Administration Act 1992";

(b) after "any tax credit" insert ", or universal credit,".

(5) In section 48 after the definition of "overpayment" insert—

""part tax year" means a period of less than a year beginning with 6th April and ending with the date on which the award of a tax credit terminated,".

(6) In Schedule 2, in paragraph 6(1)(a) and (c) and (2)(a), after "for the tax year" insert "or part tax year".

[¹ Modification of tax credits legislation: finalisation of tax credits

6.176   **12A.** (1) This regulation applies where—

(a) a claim for universal credit is made, or is treated as having been made;

(b) the claimant is, or was at any time during the tax year in which the claim is made or treated as made, entitled to a tax credit; and

(c) the Secretary of State is satisfied that the claimant meets the basic conditions specified in section 4(1)(a) to (d) of the Act (other than any of those conditions which the claimant is not required to meet by virtue of regulations under section 4(2) of the Act).

(2) Subject to paragraph (3), where this regulation applies, the amount of the tax credit to which the person is entitled is to be calculated in accordance with the 2002 Act and regulations made under that Act, as modified by the Schedule to these Regulations ("the modified legislation").

(3) Where, in the opinion of the Commissioners for Her Majesty's Revenue and Customs, it is not reasonably practicable to apply the modified legislation in relation to any case or category of cases, the 2002

Act and regulations made under that Act are to apply without modification in that case or category of cases.]

AMENDMENTS

    1. Universal Credit (Transitional Provisions) (Amendment) Regulations 2014 (SI 2014/1626) reg.4 (October 13, 2014).

Appeals etc relating to certain existing benefits

13. (1) This regulation applies where, after an award of universal credit has been made to a claimant—   **6.177**

  (a) an appeal against a decision relating to the entitlement of the claimant to income support, housing benefit or a tax credit (a "relevant benefit") is finally determined;

  (b) a decision relating to the claimant's entitlement to income support is revised under section 9 of the Social Security Act 1998 ("the 1998 Act") or superseded under section 10 of that Act;

  (c) a decision relating to the claimant's entitlement to housing benefit is revised or superseded under Schedule 7 to the Child Support, Pensions and Social Security Act 2000; or

  (d) a decision relating to the claimant's entitlement to a tax credit is revised under section 19 or 20 of the 2002 Act, or regulations made under section 21 of that Act, or is varied or cancelled under section 21A of that Act.

(2) Where the claimant is a new claimant partner and, as a result of determination of the appeal or, as the case may be, revision or supersession of the decision the claimant would (were it not for the effect of these Regulations) be entitled to income support or housing benefit during the relevant period mentioned in regulation 7(3), awards of those benefits are to terminate in accordance with regulation 7.

(3) Where the claimant is not a new claimant partner and, as a result of determination of the appeal or, as the case may be, revision, supersession, variation or cancellation of the decision, the claimant would (were it not for the effect of these Regulations) be entitled to a relevant benefit on the date on which the claim for universal credit was made, awards of relevant benefits are to terminate in accordance with regulation 8.

(4) The Secretary of State is to consider whether it is appropriate to revise under section 9 of the 1998 Act the decision in relation to entitlement to universal credit or, if that decision has been superseded under section 10 of that Act, the decision as so superseded (in either case, "the UC decision").

(5) Where it appears to the Secretary of State to be appropriate to revise the UC decision, it is to be revised in such manner as appears to the Secretary of State to be necessary to take account of—

  (a) the decision of the First-tier Tribunal, Upper Tribunal or court, or, as the case may be, the decision relating to entitlement to a relevant benefit, as revised, superseded, varied or cancelled; and

(b) any finding of fact by the First-tier Tribunal, Upper Tribunal or court.

Appeals etc relating to universal credit

6.178   **14.** (1) This regulation applies where—

(a) a decision is made that a claimant is not entitled to universal credit ("the UC decision");

(b) the claimant becomes entitled to income support, housing benefit or a tax credit (a "relevant benefit");

(c) an appeal against the UC decision is finally determined, or the decision is revised under section 9 of the Social Security Act 1998;

(d) an award of universal credit is made to the claimant in consequence of entitlement arising from the appeal, or from the decision as revised; and

(e) the claimant would (were it not for the effect of regulation 5 and this regulation) be entitled to both universal credit and a relevant benefit in respect of the same period.

(2) Subject to paragraph (3), where this regulation applies—

(a) all awards of a relevant benefit to which the claimant would (were it not for the effect of these Regulations) be entitled are to terminate, by virtue of this regulation, at the beginning of the first day of entitlement to that award; and

(b) any legislative provision under which an award would otherwise terminate on a later date does not apply.

(3) An award of housing benefit to which a claimant is entitled in respect of [¹ specified accommodation] does not terminate by virtue of this regulation.

AMENDMENTS

1. Universal Credit (Transitional Provisions) (Amendment) Regulations 2014 (SI 2014/1626) reg.3 (November 3, 2014).

Modification of Claims and Payments Regulations in relation to universal credit claimants

6.179   **15.** (1) Where a claim for universal credit is made by a person who was previously entitled to an existing benefit, regulation 26 of the Claims and Payments Regulations (time within which a claim for universal credit is to be made) applies in relation to that claim with the modification specified in paragraph (2).

(2) In paragraph (3) of regulation 26, after sub-paragraph (a) insert—

"(aa) the claimant was previously in receipt of an existing benefit (as defined in the Universal Credit (Transitional Provisions) Regulations 2014) and notification of expiry of entitlement to that benefit was not sent to the claimant before the date that the claimant's entitlement expired;".

Persons unable to act

16. (1) Paragraph (2) applies where—
(a) a person ("P2") has been appointed, or treated as appointed, under regulation 33(1) of the Social Security (Claims and Payments) Regulations 1987(1) ("the 1987 Regulations") (persons unable to act) to exercise rights and to receive and deal with sums payable on behalf of a person who is unable to act ("P1"); or
(b) a person ("P2") has been appointed under regulation 18(3) of the Tax Credits (Claims and Notifications) Regulations 2002 ("the 2002 Regulations") (circumstances where one person may act for another in making a claim—other appointed persons) to act for a person who is unable to act ("P1") in making a claim for a tax credit.

(2) Where this paragraph applies and P1 is, or may be, entitled to universal credit, the Secretary of State may, if P2 agrees, treat the appointment of P2 as if it were made under regulation 57(1) of the Claims and Payments Regulations (persons unable to act) and P2 may carry out the functions set out in regulation 57(4) of those Regulations in relation to P1.

(3) Paragraph (4) applies where a person ("P2") was appointed, or treated as appointed, under regulation 57(1) of the Claims and Payments Regulations to carry out functions in relation to a person who is unable to act ("P1") and who was, or might have been, entitled to universal credit, but who has ceased to be so entitled, or was not in fact so entitled.

(4) Where this paragraph applies—
(a) the Secretary of State may, if P2 agrees, treat the appointment of P2 as if it were made under regulation 33(1) of the 1987 Regulations and P2 may exercise rights and receive and deal with sums payable in respect of existing benefits on behalf of P1; and
(b) the Board (within the meaning of the 2002 Regulations) may, if P2 agrees, treat the appointment of P2 as if it were made under regulation 18(3) of the 2002 Regulations and P2 may act for P1 in making a claim for a tax credit.

Advance payments of universal credit

17. (1) This regulation applies where—
(a) the Secretary of State is deciding a claim for universal credit, other than a claim which is treated as having been made, in accordance with regulation 9(8) of the Claims and Payments Regulations;
(b) the claimant is, or was previously, entitled to an existing benefit ("the earlier award"); and
(c) if the earlier award terminated before the date on which the claim for universal credit was made, the claim for universal credit was made during the period of one month starting with the date of termination.

(2) Where this regulation applies—
(a) a single claimant may request an advance payment of universal credit;

(b) joint claimants may jointly request such a payment,

at any time during the first assessment period for universal credit.

(3) Where a request has been made in accordance with this regulation, the Secretary of State may make an advance payment to the claimant, or joint claimants, of such amount in respect of universal credit as the Secretary of State considers appropriate.

(4) After an advance payment has been made under this regulation, payments of any award of universal credit to the claimant or, in the case of joint claimants, to either or both of them, may be reduced until the amount of the advance payment is repaid.

Deductions from benefits

6.182   **18.** (1) This regulation applies where—

(a) an award of universal credit is made to a claimant who—

    (i) was entitled to income-based jobseeker's allowance, income-related employment and support allowance or income support (a "relevant award") on the date on which the claim for universal credit was made or treated as made;

    (ii) is a new claimant partner who was, immediately before forming a couple with a person entitled to universal credit, the partner of a person ("P") who was at that time entitled to a relevant award; or

    (iii) is not a new claimant partner and was, immediately before making a claim for universal credit, the partner of a person ("P") who was at that time entitled to a relevant award, where the award of universal credit is not a joint award to the claimant and P; and

(b) on the relevant date, deductions in respect of fuel costs or water charges were being made under regulation 35 of the Social Security (Claims and Payments) Regulations 1987, in accordance with Schedule 9 to those Regulations.

(2) In this regulation, the "relevant date" means—

(a) where paragraph (1)(a)(i) applies and the claimant is not a new claimant partner, the date on which the claim for universal credit was made;

(b) where paragraph (1)(a)(i) applies and the claimant is a new claimant partner, the date on which the claim for universal credit was treated as made;

(c) where paragraph (1)(a)(ii) or (iii) applies, the date on which the claimant ceased to be the partner of P.

(3) Where this regulation applies, deductions in respect of fuel costs or, as the case may be, water charges, may be made from the award of universal credit in accordance with Schedule 6 to the Claims and Payments Regulations, without the need for any consent which would otherwise be required under paragraph 3(3) of that Schedule.

(4) For the purposes of this regulation, a deduction is to be taken into account even if the relevant award subsequently terminated by virtue of an order made under section 150(3) of the Act, regulation 7 or, as the

case may be, regulation 8, before the date on which the deduction was first applied.

Transition from old style ESA

19. (1) This regulation applies where— 6.183

(a) an award of universal credit is made to a claimant who was entitled to old style ESA on the date on which the claim for universal credit was made or treated as made ("the relevant date"); and

(b) on or before the relevant date it had been determined that the claimant was entitled to the work-related activity component or to the support component.

(2) Where, on or before the relevant date, it had been determined that the claimant was entitled to the work-related activity component—

(a) regulation 27(3) of the Universal Credit Regulations (award to include LCW and LCWRA elements) does not apply; and

(b) the claimant is to be treated as having limited capability for work for the purposes of regulation 27(1)(a) of those Regulations and section 21(1)(a) of the Act.

(3) Unless the assessment phase applied and had not ended at the relevant date, in relation to a claimant who is treated as having limited capability for work under paragraph (2)—

(a) regulation 28 of the Universal Credit Regulations (period for which the LCW or LCWRA element is not to be included) does not apply; and

(b) the LCW element is (subject to the provisions of Part 4 of the Universal Credit Regulations) to be included in the award with effect from the beginning of the first assessment period.

(4) Where, on or before the relevant date, it had been determined that the claimant was entitled to the support component—

(a) regulation 27(3) of the Universal Credit Regulations does not apply; and

(b) the claimant is to be treated as having limited capability for work and work-related activity for the purposes of regulation 27(1)(b) of those Regulations and section 19(2)(a) of the Act.

(5) Unless the assessment phase applied and had not ended at the relevant date, in relation to a claimant who is treated as having limited capability for work and work-related activity under paragraph (4)(4)(b)—

(a) regulation 28 of the Universal Credit Regulations does not apply; and

(b) the LCWRA element is (subject to the provisions of Part 4 of the Universal Credit Regulations) to be included in the award of universal credit with effect from the beginning of the first assessment period.

(6) For the purposes of this regulation, a determination that the claimant was entitled to the work-related activity component or, as the case may be, the support component, is to be taken into account even if

467

the award of old style ESA subsequently terminated (in so far as it was an award of income-related employment and support allowance) before the date on which that determination was made, by virtue of an order made under section 150(3) of the Act.

(7) Where a claimant is treated, by virtue of this regulation, as having limited capability for work or, as the case may be, limited capability for work and work-related activity, the Secretary of State may at any time make a fresh determination as to these matters, in accordance with the Universal Credit Regulations.

(8) In this regulation and in regulations 20 to 27—

"assessment phase", "support component" and "work-related activity component" have the same meanings as in the 2007 Act;

"incapacity benefit" and "severe disablement allowance" have the same meanings as in Schedule 4 to that Act;

"LCW element" and "LCWRA element" have the same meanings as in the Universal Credit Regulations.

(9) For the purposes of this regulation and regulation 20, references to cases in which the assessment phase applied are references to cases in which sections 2(2)(a), 2(3)(a), 4(4)(a) and 4(5)(a) of the 2007 Act applied and references to cases in which the assessment phase did not apply are references to cases in which those sections did not apply.

Transition from old style ESA before the end of the assessment phase

6.184   **20.** (1) This regulation applies where—

(a) an award of universal credit is made to a claimant who was entitled to old style ESA on the date on which the claim for universal credit was made or treated as made ("the relevant date"); and

(b) on the relevant date, the assessment phase in relation to the claimant applied and had lasted for less than 13 weeks.

(2) Where this regulation applies—

(a) regulation 28(2) of the Universal Credit Regulations (period for which the LCW or LCWRA element is not to be included) does not apply; and

(b) for the purposes of regulation 28 of those Regulations, the relevant period is—

(i) the period of 13 weeks starting with the first day of the assessment phase; or

(ii) where regulation 5 of the Employment and Support Allowance Regulations 2008 (the assessment phase—previous claimants) applied to the claimant, the period which ends when the sum of the periods for which the claimant was previously entitled to old style ESA and the period for which the claimant is entitled to universal credit is 13 weeks.

(3) Where, on the relevant date, the assessment phase in relation to the claimant applied and had not ended and had lasted for more than 13 weeks—

(a) regulation 28 of the Universal Credit Regulations does not apply;

(b) if it is subsequently determined in accordance with Part 5 of those Regulations that the claimant has limited capability for work the LCW element is (subject to the provisions of Part 4 of those Regulations) to be included in the award of universal credit with effect from the beginning of the first assessment period;

(c) if it is subsequently determined in accordance with Part 5 of the Universal Credit Regulations that the claimant has limited capability for work and work-related activity the LCWRA element is (subject to the provisions of Part 4 of those Regulations) to be included in the award of universal credit with effect from the beginning of the first assessment period.

(4) For the purposes of this regulation, the fact that an assessment phase applied in relation to a claimant on the relevant date is to be taken into account even if the award of old style ESA subsequently terminated (in so far as it was an award of income-related employment and support allowance) before that date by virtue of an order made under section 150(3) of the Act.

Other claimants with limited capability for work: credits only cases

21. (1) This regulation applies where— 6.185

(a) an award of universal credit is made to a claimant who was entitled to be credited with earnings equal to the lower earnings limit then in force under regulation 8B(2)(iv), (iva) or (v) of the Social Security (Credits) Regulations 1975 ("the 1975 Regulations") on the date on which the claim for universal credit was made or treated as made (the "relevant date"); and

(b) neither regulation 19 nor regulation 20 applies to that claimant (whether or not, in the case of joint claimants, either of those regulations apply to the other claimant).

(2) Where, on or before the relevant date, it had been determined that the claimant would have limited capability for work (within the meaning of Part 1 of the 2007 Act) if he or she was entitled to old style ESA—

(a) regulation 27(3) of the Universal Credit Regulations does not apply; and

(b) the claimant is to be treated as having limited capability for work for the purposes of regulation 27(1)(a) of those Regulations and section 21(1)(a) of the Act.

(3) Unless the notional assessment phase applied and had lasted for less than 13 weeks at the relevant date, in relation to a claimant who is treated as having limited capability for work under paragraph (2)—

(a) regulation 28 of the Universal Credit Regulations does not apply; and

(b) the LCW element is (subject to the provisions of Part 4 of the Universal Credit Regulations) to be included in the award with effect from the beginning of the first assessment period.

(4) Where, on or before the relevant date, it had been determined that the claimant would have limited capability for work-related activity (within the meaning of Part 1 of the 2007 Act) if he or she was entitled to old style ESA—

(a) regulation 27(3) of the Universal Credit Regulations does not apply; and

(b) the claimant is to be treated as having limited capability for work and work-related activity for the purposes of regulation 27(1)(b) of those Regulations and section 19(2)(a) of the Act.

(5) Unless the notional assessment phase applied and had lasted for less than 13 weeks at the relevant date, in relation to a claimant who is treated as having limited capability for work and work-related activity under paragraph (4)—

(a) regulation 28 of the Universal Credit Regulations does not apply; and

(b) the LCWRA element is (subject to the provisions of Part 4 of the Universal Credit Regulations) to be included in the award of universal credit with effect from the beginning of the first assessment period.

(6) Where, on the relevant date, the notional assessment phase in relation to the claimant to whom the award was made applied and had lasted for less than 13 weeks—

(a) regulation 28(2) of the Universal Credit Regulations does not apply; and

(b) for the purposes of regulation 28 of those Regulations, the relevant period is the period of 13 weeks starting with the first day of the notional assessment phase.

(7) Where, on the relevant date, the notional assessment phase in relation to the claimant applied and had not ended and had lasted for more than 13 weeks—

(a) regulation 28 of the Universal Credit Regulations does not apply;

(b) if it is subsequently determined in accordance with Part 5 of those Regulations that the claimant has limited capability for work, the LCW element is (subject to the provisions of Part 4 of those Regulations) to be included in the award of universal credit with effect from the beginning of the first assessment period;

(c) if it is subsequently determined in accordance with Part 5 of those Regulations that the claimant has limited capability for work and work-related activity, the LCWRA element is (subject to the provisions of Part 4 of those Regulations) to be included in the award of universal credit with effect from the beginning of the first assessment period.

(8) Where a claimant is treated, by virtue of this regulation, as having limited capability for work or, as the case may be, limited capability for work and work-related activity, the Secretary of State may at any time

make a fresh determination as to these matters, in accordance with the Universal Credit Regulations.

(9) For the purposes of this regulation—

(a) a determination that the claimant would have limited capability for work or, as the case may be, limited capability for work-related activity, if the claimant was entitled to old style ESA is to be taken into account even if the claimant subsequently ceased to be entitled as mentioned in paragraph (1)(a) before the date on which that determination was made because he or she became entitled to universal credit;

(b) the fact that a notional assessment phase applied in relation to a claimant on the relevant date is to be taken into account even if the claimant subsequently ceased to be entitled as mentioned in paragraph (1)(a) before that date because the claimant became entitled to universal credit.

(c) references to a determination that the claimant would have limited capability for work if the claimant was entitled to old style ESA do not include a determination made under regulation 30 of the Employment and Support Allowance Regulations 2008 (conditions for treating a claimant as having limited capability for work until a determination about limited capability for work has been made);

(d) references to cases in which the notional assessment phase applied are references to cases in which sections 2(2)(a), 2(3)(a), 4(4)(a) and 4(5)(a) of the 2007 Act would have applied to the claimant if he or she had been entitled to old style ESA in addition to the entitlement mentioned in paragraph (1)(a), but do not include cases in which the claimant is entitled as mentioned in paragraph (1)(a) under regulation 8B(2)(iva) of the 1975 Regulations;

(e) subject to sub-paragraph (f), the "notional assessment phase" is the period of 13 weeks starting on the day on which the assessment phase would have started in relation to the claimant, if he or she had been entitled to old style ESA and sections 2(2)(a), 2(3)(a), 4(4)(a) and 4(5)(a) of the 2007 Act had applied;

(f) the notional assessment phase has not ended if, at the end of the 13 week period referred to in sub-paragraph (e), no determination has been made as to whether a claimant would have limited capability for work (within the meaning of Part 1 of the 2007 Act) if the claimant was entitled to old style ESA.

Transition from income support payable on the grounds of incapacity for work or disability [¹ and other incapacity benefits]

22. (1) This regulation applies where an award of universal credit is made to a claimant [1 (other than a claimant to whom regulation 23 or 24 applies)] who was entitled to income support on the grounds of incapacity for work or disability on the date on which the claim for universal credit was made or treated as made [¹ or is entitled to incapacity benefit or severe disablement allowance].   **6.186**

471

(2) Where this regulation applies—

(a) if it is determined in accordance with Part 5 of the Universal Credit Regulations that the claimant has limited capability for work—

    (i) the claimant is to be treated as having had limited capability for work for the purposes of regulation 27(1)(a) of the Universal Credit Regulations (award to include LCW and LCWRA elements) from the beginning of the first assessment period;

    (ii) regulation 28 of those Regulations (period for which the LCW or LCWRA element is not to be included) does not apply; and

    (iii) the LCW element is (subject to the provisions of Part 4 of the Universal Credit Regulations) to be included in the award with effect from the beginning of the first assessment period;

(b) if it is determined in accordance with Part 5 of the Universal Credit Regulations that the claimant has limited capability for work and work-related activity—

    (i) the claimant is to be treated as having had limited capability for work and work-related activity for the purposes of regulation 27(1)(b) of the Universal Credit Regulations from the beginning of the first assessment period;

    (ii) regulation 28 of those Regulations does not apply; and

    (iii) the LCWRA element is (subject to the provisions of Part 4 of the Universal Credit Regulations) to be included in the award of universal credit with effect from the beginning of the first assessment period.

(3) In this regulation—

"income support on the grounds of incapacity for work or disability" means an award of income support which is an "existing award" within the meaning of Schedule 4 to the 2007 Act.

AMENDMENTS

    1. Universal Credit (Transitional Provisions) (Amendment) Regulations 2014 (SI 2014/1626) reg.5(1) (October 13, 2014).

Transition from other incapacity benefits [¹: assessment under the 2010 Regulations]

6.187   **23.** (1) This regulation applies where—

(a) an award of universal credit is made to a claimant who is entitled to incapacity benefit or severe disablement allowance [¹ ("the relevant award")]; and

[¹ (b) on or before the date on which the claim for universal credit is made or treated as made, a notice has been issued to the claimant under regulation 4 of the Employment and Support Allowance (Transitional Provisions, Housing Benefit and

Council Tax Benefit) (Existing Awards) (No.2) Regulations 2010 ("the 2010 Regulations") (notice commencing the conversion phase).]

[¹ (1A) Where this regulation applies, regulations 27(3) (award to include LCW and LCWRA elements) and 38 (determination of limited capability for work and work-related activity) of the Universal Credit Regulations do not apply and the question whether a claimant has limited capability for work, or for work and work-related activity, is to be determined, for the purposes of the Act and the Universal Credit Regulations, in accordance with this regulation.]

(2) [¹ Where it is determined in accordance with the 2010 Regulations that the relevant award qualifies for conversion into an award in accordance with regulation 7 of those Regulations (qualifying for conversion) and that award includes the work-related activity component]—

(a) [¹ . . .];

(b) the claimant is to be treated as having had limited capability for work for the purposes of regulation 27(1)(a) of the Universal Credit Regulations from the beginning of the first assessment period;

(c) regulation 28(1) of those Regulations (period for which LCW or LCWRA element is not to be included) does not apply;

(d) the LCW element is (subject to the provisions of Part 4 of the Universal Credit Regulations) to be included in the award of universal credit with effect from the beginning of the first assessment period; and

(e) the claimant is to be treated as having limited capability for work for the purposes of section 21(1)(a) of the Act.

(3) [¹ Where it is determined in accordance with the 2010 Regulations that the relevant award qualifies for conversion into an award in accordance with regulation 7 of those Regulations and that award includes the support component]—

(a) [¹ . . .];

(b) the claimant is to be treated as having had limited capability for work and work-related activity for the purposes of regulation 27(1)(b) of the Universal Credit Regulations from the beginning of the first assessment period;

(c) regulation 28(1) of those Regulations does not apply;

(d) the LCWRA element is (subject to the provisions of Part 4 of the Universal Credit Regulations) to be included in the award of universal credit with effect from the beginning of the first assessment period; and

(e) the claimant is to be treated as having limited capability for work and work-related activity for the purposes of section 19(2)(a) of the Act.

AMENDMENTS

1. Universal Credit (Transitional Provisions) (Amendment) Regulations 2014 (SI 2014/1626) reg.5(2) (October 13, 2014).

Transition from other incapacity benefits: claimants approaching pensionable age

6.188   **24.** (1) This paragraph applies where—

(a) an award of universal credit is made to a claimant who is entitled to incapacity benefit or severe disablement allowance;

(b) no notice has been issued to the claimant under regulation 4 (notice commencing the conversion phase) of the Employment and Support Allowance (Transitional Provisions, Housing Benefit and Council Tax Benefit) (Existing Awards) (No.2) Regulations 2010 ("the 2010 Regulations");

(c) the claimant will reach pensionable age (within the meaning of the 2010 Regulations) within the period of one year; and

(d) the claimant is also entitled to—

(i) personal independence payment, where neither the daily living component nor the mobility component is payable at the enhanced rate;

(ii) disability living allowance under section 71 of the Social Security Contributions and Benefits Act 1992 ("the 1992 Act"), where the care component is payable at the middle rate within the meaning of section 72(4) of that Act or the mobility component is payable at the lower rate within the meaning of section 73(11) of that Act (or both components are payable at those rates);

(iii) attendance allowance under section 64 of the 1992 Act, where the allowance is payable at the lower rate in accordance with section 65 of that Act;

(iv) an increase in the weekly rate of disablement pension under section 104 of the 1992 Act (increase where constant attendance needed), where the increase is of an amount which is equal to or less than the amount specified in paragraph 2(a) of Part V of Schedule 4 to that Act; or

(v) any payment based on the need for attendance which is paid as an addition to a war disablement pension (which means any retired pay or pension or allowance payable in respect of disablement under an instrument specified in section 639(2) of the Income Tax (Earnings and Pensions) Act 2003), where the amount of that payment is equal to or less than the amount specified in paragraph 2(a) of Part V of Schedule 4 to the 1992 Act.

(2) Where paragraph (1) applies and paragraph (3) does not apply—

(a) regulation 27(3) of the Universal Credit Regulations (award to include LCW and LCWRA elements) does not apply;

(b) the claimant is to be treated as having limited capability for work for the purposes of regulation 27(1)(a) of those Regulations from the beginning of the first assessment period;

(c) regulation 28(1) of the Universal Credit Regulations (period for which LCW or LCWRA element is not to be included) does not apply;

(d) the LCW element is (subject to the provisions of Part 4 of the Universal Credit Regulations) to be included in the award of universal credit with effect from the beginning of the first assessment period; and

(e) the claimant is to be treated as having limited capability for work for the purposes of section 21(1)(a) of the Act.

(3) This paragraph applies where—

(a) an award of universal credit is made to a claimant who is entitled to incapacity benefit or severe disablement allowance;

(b) no notice has been issued to the claimant under regulation 4 of the 2010 Regulations;

(c) the claimant will reach pensionable age (within the meaning of the 2010 Regulations) within the period of one year; and

(d) the claimant is also entitled to—

   (i) personal independence payment, where either the daily living component or the mobility component is (or both components are) payable at the enhanced rate;

   (ii) disability living allowance under section 71 of the 1992 Act, where the care component is payable at the highest rate within the meaning of section 72(4) of that Act or the mobility component is payable at the higher rate within the meaning of section 73(11) of that Act (or both components are payable at those rates);

   (iii) attendance allowance under section 64 of the 1992 Act, where the allowance is payable at the higher rate in accordance with section 65 of that Act;

   (iv) armed forces independence payment under the Armed Forces and Reserve Forces (Compensation Scheme) Order 2011;

   (v) an increase in the weekly rate of disablement pension under section 104 of the 1992 Act, where the increase is of an amount which is greater than the amount specified in paragraph 2(a) of Part V of Schedule 4 to that Act; or

   (vi) any payment based on the need for attendance which is paid as an addition to a war disablement pension (which means any retired pay or pension or allowance payable in respect of disablement under an instrument specified in section 639(2) of the Income Tax (Earnings and Pensions) Act 2003), where the amount of that payment is greater than the amount specified in paragraph 2(a) of Part V of Schedule 4 to the 1992 Act.

(4) Where paragraph (3) applies (whether or not paragraph (1) also applies)—

(a) regulation 27(3) of the Universal Credit Regulations does not apply;

(b) the claimant is to be treated as having limited capability for work and work-related activity for the purposes of regulation 27(1)(b) of those Regulations from the beginning of the first assessment period;

(c) regulation 28(1) of the Universal Credit Regulations does not apply;

(d) the LCWRA element is (subject to the provisions of Part 4 of the Universal Credit Regulations) to be included in the award of universal credit with effect from the beginning of the first assessment period; and

(e) the claimant is to be treated as having limited capability for work and work-related activity for the purposes of section 19(2)(a) of the Act.

Transition from other incapacity benefits: supplementary

6.189   **25.** (1) Where an award of universal credit is made to a claimant who is entitled to incapacity benefit or severe disablement allowance, regulation 66 of the Universal Credit Regulations (what is included in unearned income?) applies to the claimant as if incapacity benefit or, as the case may be, severe disablement allowance were added to the descriptions of unearned income in paragraph (1)(b) of that regulation.

(2) For the purposes of regulations [1 22,] 23 and 24 and this regulation only, incapacity benefit and severe disablement allowance are prescribed benefits under paragraph 1(2)(b) of Schedule 6 to the Act.

AMENDMENTS

1. Universal Credit (Transitional Provisions) (Amendment) Regulations 2014 (SI 2014/1626) reg.5(3) (October 13, 2014).

Other claimants with incapacity for work: credits only cases where claimant is approaching pensionable age

6.190   **26.** (1) This regulation applies where—

(a) an award of universal credit is made to a claimant who was entitled to be credited with earnings equal to the lower earnings limit then in force under regulation 8B(2)(a)(i), (ii) or (iii) of the Social Security (Credits) Regulations 1975 on the date on which the claim for universal credit was made or treated as made;

(b) the claimant will reach pensionable age within the meaning of the Employment and Support Allowance (Transitional Provisions, Housing Benefit and Council Tax Benefit) (Existing Awards) (No.2) Regulations 2010 within the period of one year; and

(c) [1 none of regulations 22, 23 or 24 apply] to that claimant (whether or not, in the case of joint claimants, [1 any] of those regulations apply to the other claimant).

(2) Where the claimant is entitled to a payment, allowance or increased rate of pension specified in regulation 24(1)(d) and is not entitled to a payment, allowance or increased rate of pension specified in regulation 24(3)(d)—

(a) regulation 27(3) of the Universal Credit Regulations (award to include LCW and LCWRA elements) does not apply;

(b) the claimant is to be treated as having limited capability for work for the purposes of regulation 27(1)(a) of those Regulations from the beginning of the first assessment period;

(c) regulation 28(1) of the Universal Credit Regulations (period for which the LCW or LCWRA element is not to be included) does not apply;

(d) the LCW element is (subject to the provisions of Part 4 of the Universal Credit Regulations) to be included in the award of universal credit with effect from the beginning of the first assessment period; and

(e) the claimant is to be treated as having limited capability for work for the purposes of section 21(1)(a) of the Act.

(3) Where the claimant is entitled to a payment, allowance or increased rate of pension specified in regulation 24(3)(d) (whether or not the claimant is also entitled to a payment, allowance or increased rate of pension specified in regulation 24(1)(d))—

(a) regulation 27(3) of the Universal Credit Regulations does not apply;

(b) the claimant is to be treated as having limited capability for work and work-related activity for the purposes of regulation 27(1)(b) of those Regulations from the beginning of the first assessment period;

(c) regulation 28(1) of the Universal Credit Regulations does not apply;

(d) the LCWRA element is (subject to the provisions of Part 4 of the Universal Credit Regulations) to be included in the award of universal credit with effect from the beginning of the first assessment period; and

(e) the claimant is to be treated as having limited capability for work and work-related activity for the purposes of section 19(2)(a) of the Act.

[¹ (4) Where the claimant is not entitled to a payment, allowance or increased rate of pension specified in either regulation 24(1)(d) or regulation 24(3)(d)—

(a) if it is determined in accordance with Part 5 of the Universal Credit Regulations that the claimant has limited capability for work—

(i) the claimant is to be treated as having had limited capability for work for the purposes of regulation 27(1)(a) of the Universal Credit Regulations from the beginning of the first assessment period;

(ii) regulation 28 of the Universal Credit Regulations does not apply; and

(iii) the LCW element is (subject to the provisions of Part 4 of the Universal Credit Regulations) to be included in the award with effect from the beginning of the first assessment period; and

(b) if it is determined in accordance with Part 5 of the Universal Credit Regulations that the claimant has limited capability for work and work-related activity—

     (i) the claimant is to be treated as having had limited capability for work and work-related activity for the purposes of regulation 27(1)(b) of the Universal Credit Regulations from the beginning of the first assessment period;

    (ii) regulation 28 of the Universal Credit Regulations does not apply; and

    (iii) the LCWRA element is (subject to the provisions of Part 4 of the Universal Credit Regulations) to be included in the award of universal credit with effect from the beginning of the first assessment period.]

AMENDMENTS

   1. Universal Credit (Transitional Provisions) (Amendment) Regulations 2014 (SI 2014/1626) reg.5(4) (October 13, 2014).

Other claimants with incapacity for work: credits only cases

6.191   **27.** (1) This regulation applies where—

  (a) an award of universal credit is made to a claimant who was entitled to be credited with earnings equal to the lower earnings limit then in force under regulation 8B(2)(a)(i), (ii) or (iii) of the Social Security (Credits) Regulations 1975 on the date on which the claim for universal credit was made or treated as made; and

  (b) none of regulations 22, 23, 24 or 26 apply to that claimant (whether or not, in the case of joint claimants, any of those regulations apply to the other claimant).

  (2) Where this regulation applies—

  (a) if it is determined in accordance with Part 5 of the Universal Credit Regulations that the claimant has limited capability for work—

    (i) the claimant is to be treated as having had limited capability for work for the purposes of regulation 27(1)(a) of the Universal Credit Regulations (award to include LCW and LCWRA elements) from the beginning of the first assessment period;

    (ii) regulation 28 of the Universal Credit Regulations (period for which the LCW or LCWRA element is not to be included) does not apply; and

    (iii) the LCW element is (subject to the provisions of Part 4 of the Universal Credit Regulations) to be included in the award with effect from the beginning of the first assessment period;

  (b) if it is determined in accordance with Part 5 of the Universal Credit Regulations that the claimant has limited capability for work and work-related activity—

    (i) the claimant is to be treated as having had limited capability for work and work-related activity for the purposes of regulation 27(1)(b) of the Universal Credit Regulations from the beginning of the first assessment period;

    (ii) regulation 28 of the Universal Credit Regulations does not apply; and

    (iii) the LCWRA element is (subject to the provisions of Part 4 of the Universal Credit Regulations) to be included in the award of universal credit with effect from the beginning of the first assessment period.

Meaning of "qualifying young person"

28. Where a person who would (apart from the provision made by this   **6.192** regulation) be a "qualifying young person" within the meaning of regulation 5 of the Universal Credit Regulations is entitled to an existing benefit—

(a) that person is not a qualifying young person for the purposes of the Universal Credit Regulations; and

(b) regulation 5(5) of those Regulations applies as if, after "a person who is receiving" there were inserted "an existing benefit (within the meaning of the Universal Credit (Transitional Provisions) Regulations 2014),".

Support for housing costs

29. (1) Paragraph (3) applies where—   **6.193**

(a) an award of universal credit is made to a claimant who—

    (i) was entitled to income-based jobseeker's allowance, income-related employment and support allowance or income support (a "relevant award") at any time during the period of one month ending with the day on which the claim for universal credit was made or treated as made (or would have been so entitled were it not for termination of that award by virtue of an order made under section 150(3) of the Act or the effect of these Regulations); or

    (ii) was at any time during the period of one month ending with the day on which the claim for universal credit was made or treated as made, the partner of a person ("P") who was at that time entitled to a relevant award, where the award of universal credit is not a joint award to the claimant and P; and

(b) on the relevant date, the relevant award included an amount in respect of housing costs under—

    (i) paragraphs 14 to 16 of Schedule 2 to the Jobseeker's Allowance Regulations 1996 ("the 1996 Regulations");

    (ii) paragraphs 16 to 18 of Schedule 6 to the Employment and Support Allowance Regulations 2008 ("the 2008 Regulations"); or, as the case may be,

    (iii) paragraphs 15 to 17 of Schedule 3 to the Income Support (General) Regulations 1987 ("the 1987 Regulations").

(2) In this regulation, the "relevant date" means—

(a) where paragraph (1)(a)(i) applies and the claimant was not entitled to the relevant award on the date on which the claim for universal credit was made or treated as made, the date on which the relevant award terminated;

(b) where paragraph (1)(a)(i) applies, the claimant is not a new claimant partner and he or she was entitled to the relevant award on the date on which the claim for universal credit was made, that date;

(c) where paragraph (1)(a)(i) applies, the claimant is a new claimant partner and he or she was entitled to the relevant award on the date on which the claim for universal credit was treated as made, that date;

(d) where paragraph (1)(a)(ii) applies, the date on which the claimant ceased to be the partner of P or, if earlier, the date on which the relevant award terminated.

(3) Where this paragraph applies, paragraph 5 of Schedule 5 to the Universal Credit Regulations (no housing costs element under this Schedule for qualifying period) does not apply.

(4) Paragraph (5) applies where paragraph (1)(a) applies, but the relevant award did not include an amount in respect of housing costs because the claimant's entitlement (or, as the case may be, P's entitlement) was nil by virtue of—

(a) paragraph 6(1)(c) or 7(1)(b) of Schedule 2 to the 1996 Regulations;

(b) paragraph 8(1)(c) or 9(1)(b) of Schedule 6 to the 2008 Regulations; or, as the case may be,

(c) paragraph 6(1)(c) or 8(1)(b) of Schedule 3(4) to the 1987 Regulations.

(5) Where this paragraph applies—

(a) paragraph 5(2) of Schedule 5 to the Universal Credit Regulations does not apply; and

(b) the "qualifying period" referred to in paragraph 5 of that Schedule is the period of 91 days starting with the first day on which the claimant (or, as the case may be, P) was entitled to the relevant award, taking into account any period which was treated as a period of continuing entitlement under—

   (i) paragraph 13 of Schedule 2 to the 1996 Regulations;

   (ii) paragraph 15 of Schedule 6 to the 2008 Regulations; or, as the case may be,

   (iii) paragraph 14 of Schedule 3 to the 1987 Regulations,

provided that, throughout that part of the qualifying period after the award of universal credit is made, receipt of universal credit is continuous and the claimant otherwise qualifies for the inclusion of an amount calculated under Schedule 5 to the Universal Credit Regulations in their award.

(6) For the purposes of—

(a) paragraph (1)(b) of this regulation, inclusion of an amount in respect of housing costs in a relevant award is to be taken into account even if the relevant award subsequently terminated by virtue of an order made under section 150(3) of the Act, regulation 7 or, as the case may be, regulation 8, before the date on which that amount was included in the award;

(b) paragraph (5)(b) of this regulation, entitlement to a relevant award is to be treated as having continued until the relevant date even if the award subsequently terminated by virtue of an order made under section 150(3) of the Act, regulation 7 or, as the case may be, regulation 8, before that date.

Sanctions: transition from old style ESA

30. (1) This regulation applies where—   6.194

(a) an award of universal credit is made to a claimant who was previously entitled to old style ESA ("the ESA award"); and

(b) on the relevant date, payments in respect of the ESA award were reduced under regulation 63 of the Employment and Support Allowance Regulations 2008 ("the 2008 Regulations").

(2) In this regulation, the "relevant date" means—

(a) where the claimant was not entitled to old style ESA on the date on which the claim for universal credit was made or treated as made, the date on which the ESA award terminated;

(b) where the claimant is not a new claimant partner and was entitled to old style ESA on the date on which the claim for universal credit was made, that date;

(c) where the claimant is a new claimant partner and was entitled to old style ESA on the date on which the claim for universal credit was treated as made, that date.

(3) Where this regulation applies—

(a) the failure which led to reduction of the ESA award ("the ESA failure") is to be treated, for the purposes of the Universal Credit Regulations, as a failure which is sanctionable under section 27 of the Act;

(b) the award of universal credit is to be reduced in relation to the ESA failure, in accordance with the provisions of this regulation and Chapter 2 of Part 8 of the Universal Credit Regulations (sanctions), as modified by this regulation; and

(c) the reduction is to be treated, for the purposes of the Universal Credit Regulations, as a reduction under section 27 of the Act.

(4) The reduction period for the purposes of the Universal Credit Regulations(2) is a period of the number of days which is equivalent to the length of the fixed period applicable to the person under regulation 63(7) of the 2008 Regulations in relation to the ESA failure, minus—

(a) the number of days (if any) in that period in respect of which the amount of old style ESA was reduced; and

(b) if the ESA award terminated before the first date of entitlement to universal credit in connection with the current award, the number of days (if any) in the period after termination of that award, before the start of the universal credit award.

(5) Accordingly, regulation 101 of the Universal Credit Regulations (general principles for calculating reduction periods) applies in relation to the ESA failure as if, in paragraphs (1) and (3), for "in accordance with regulations 102 to 105", there were substituted "in accordance with

481

regulation 30 of the Universal Credit (Transitional Provisions) Regulations 2014".

(6) For the purposes of this regulation, a determination that payments in respect of the ESA award are to be reduced under regulation 63 of the 2008 Regulations is to be taken into account even if the ESA award subsequently terminated (in so far as it was an award of income-related employment and support allowance) on a date before the date on which that determination was made, by virtue of an order made under section 150(3) of the Act.

Escalation of sanctions: transition from old style ESA

6.195 **31.** (1) This regulation applies where an award of universal credit is made to a claimant who was at any time previously entitled to old style ESA.

(2) Where this regulation applies, for the purposes of determining the reduction period under regulation 104 of the Universal Credit Regulations (low-level sanction) in relation to a sanctionable failure by the claimant, other than a failure which is treated as sanctionable by virtue of regulation 30—

    (a) a reduction of universal credit in accordance with regulation 30; and

    (b) any reduction of old style ESA under the Employment and Support Allowance Regulations 2008 ("the 2008 Regulations") which did not result in a reduction under regulation 30,

is, subject to paragraph (3), to be treated as arising from a sanctionable failure for which the reduction period which applies is the number of days which is equivalent to the length of the fixed period which applied under regulation 63 of the 2008 Regulations.

(3) In determining a reduction period under regulation 104 of the Universal Credit Regulations in accordance with paragraph (2), no account is to be taken of—

    (a) a reduction of universal credit in accordance with regulation 30 if, at any time after that reduction, the claimant was entitled to an existing benefit;

    (b) a reduction of old style ESA under the 2008 Regulations if, at any time after that reduction, the claimant was entitled to universal credit, new style ESA or new style JSA, and was subsequently entitled to an existing benefit.

Sanctions: transition from old style JSA

6.196 **32.** (1) This regulation applies where—

    (a) an award of universal credit is made to a claimant who was previously entitled to old style JSA ("the JSA award");

    (b) on the relevant date, payments in respect of the JSA award were reduced under section 19 (as it applied either before or after substitution by the Act) or section 19A of the Jobseekers Act 1995 ("the 1995 Act"), or under regulation 69B of the Jobseeker's Allowance Regulations 1996 ("the 1996 Regulations"); and

(c) if the JSA award was made to a joint-claim couple within the meaning of the 1995 Act and the reduction related to—

    (i) in the case of a reduction under section 19 as it applied before substitution by the Act, circumstances relating to only one member of the couple; or,

    (ii) in the case of a reduction under section 19 as it applied after substitution by the Act, a sanctionable failure by only one member of the couple,

the award of universal credit was made to that person.

(2) In this regulation, the "relevant date" means—

(a) where the claimant was not entitled to old style JSA on the date on which the claim for universal credit was made or treated as made, the date on which the JSA award terminated;

(b) where the claimant is not a new claimant partner and was entitled to old style JSA on the date on which the claim for universal credit was made, that date;

(c) where the claimant is a new claimant partner and was entitled to old style JSA on the date on which the claim for universal credit was treated as made, that date.

(3) Where this regulation applies—

(a) the circumstances or failure which led to reduction of the JSA award (in either case, "the JSA failure") is to be treated, for the purposes of the Universal Credit Regulations, as—

    (i) a failure which is sanctionable under section 26 of the Act, where the reduction was under section 19 of the 1995 Act; or

    (ii) a failure which is sanctionable under section 27 of the Act, where the reduction was under section 19A of the 1995 Act or regulation 69B of the 1996 Regulations;

(b) the award of universal credit is to be reduced in relation to the JSA failure, in accordance with the provisions of this regulation and Chapter 2 of Part 8 of the Universal Credit Regulations (sanctions), as modified by this regulation; and

(c) the reduction is to be treated, for the purposes of the Universal Credit Regulations, as a reduction under section 26 or, as the case may be, section 27 of the Act.

(4) The reduction period for the purposes of the Universal Credit Regulations is a period of the number of days which is equivalent to the length of the period of reduction which is applicable to the person under regulation 69, 69A or 69B of the 1996 Regulations, minus—

(a) the number of days (if any) in that period in respect of which the amount of old style JSA was reduced; and

(b) if the award of old style JSA terminated before the first date of entitlement to universal credit in connection with the current award, the number of days (if any) in the period after termination of that award, before the start of the universal credit award.

(5) Accordingly, regulation 101 of the Universal Credit Regulations applies in relation to the JSA failure as if, in paragraphs (1) and (3), for

"in accordance with regulations 102 to 105", there were substituted "in accordance with regulation 32 of the Universal Credit (Transitional Provisions) Regulations 2014".

(6) Where the JSA award was made to a joint-claim couple within the meaning of the 1995 Act and the JSA failure related to only one member of the couple, the daily reduction rate for the purposes of the Universal Credit Regulations is the amount calculated in accordance with regulation 70(3) of the 1996 Regulations in respect of the JSA award, divided by seven and rounded down to the nearest 10 pence, unless regulation 111(2) or (3) of the Universal Credit Regulations (daily reduction rate) applies.

(7) Where the daily reduction rate is to be determined in accordance with paragraph (6), regulation 111(1) of the Universal Credit Regulations applies in relation to the JSA failure as if, for the words from "an amount equal to" to the end there were substituted the words "an amount determined in accordance with regulation 32 of the Universal Credit (Transitional Provisions) Regulations 2014".

(8) For the purposes of this regulation, a determination that payments in respect of the JSA award are to be reduced under regulation 69, 69A or 69B of the 1996 Regulations is to be taken into account even if the JSA award subsequently terminated (in so far as it was an award of income-based jobseeker's allowance) on a date before the date on which that determination was made, by virtue of an order made under section 150(3) of the Act.

Escalation of sanctions: transition from old style JSA

6.197   **33.**—(1) This regulation applies where an award of universal credit is made to a claimant who was at any time previously entitled to old style JSA.

(2) Where this regulation applies, for the purposes of determining the applicable reduction period under regulation 102 (higher-level sanction), 103 (medium-level sanction) or 104 (low-level sanction) of the Universal Credit Regulations in relation to a sanctionable failure by the person, other than a failure which is treated as sanctionable by virtue of regulation 32—

    (a) a reduction of universal credit in accordance with regulation 32; and

    (b) any reduction of old style JSA under section 19 or 19A of the Jobseekers Act 1995 ("the 1995 Act"), or under regulation 69B of the 1996 Regulations which did not result in a reduction under regulation 32,

is, subject to paragraph (3), to be treated as arising from a sanctionable failure for which the reduction period is the number of days which is equivalent to the length of the period which applied under regulation 69, 69A or 69B of the 1996 Regulations.

(3) In determining a reduction period under regulation 102, 103 or 104 of the Universal Credit Regulations in accordance with paragraph (2), no account is to be taken of—

(a) a reduction of universal credit in accordance with regulation 32 if, at any time after that reduction, the claimant was entitled to an existing benefit;

(b) a reduction of old style JSA under section 19 or 19A of the 1995 Act, or under regulation 69B of the 1996 Regulations if, at any time after that reduction, the claimant was entitled to universal credit, new style ESA or new style JSA, and was subsequently entitled to an existing benefit.

Sanctions: temporary return to certain existing benefits

34. If an award of universal credit terminates while there is an outstanding reduction period (within the meaning of regulation 107 of the Universal Credit Regulations) and the claimant becomes entitled to old style JSA, old style ESA or income support ("the relevant benefit") during that period— 6.198

(a) regulation 107 of the Universal Credit Regulations (reduction period to continue where award terminates) ceases to apply; and

(b) the reduction period is to terminate on the first date of entitlement to the relevant benefit.

Loss of benefit penalties: transition from existing benefits other than tax credits

35. (1) Subject to paragraph (6), this regulation applies in the cases set out in paragraphs (2) to (4). 6.199

(2) The first case is where—

(a) an award of universal credit is made to a claimant who is an offender;

(b) the claimant was entitled to old style JSA, old style ESA, income support or housing benefit ("the earlier award") at any time during the period of one month ending with the date on which the claim for universal credit was made or treated as made (or would have been so entitled were it not for termination of that award by virtue of an order made under section 150(3) of the Act or, as the case may be, the effect of these Regulations); and

(c) payments in respect of the earlier award were, on the relevant date, subject to a restriction under section 6B (loss of benefit in case of conviction, penalty or caution for benefit offence), 7 (repeated benefit fraud) or 8 (effect of offence on joint-claim jobseeker's allowance) of the 2001 Act.

(3) The second case is where—

(a) an award of universal credit is made to a claimant who is an offender;

(b) another person who was the offender's family member (but is no longer their family member) was entitled to old style JSA, old style ESA, income support or housing benefit ("the earlier award") at any time during the period of one month ending with the date on which the claim for universal credit was made or treated as made; and

(c) payments in respect of the earlier award were, on the relevant date, subject to a restriction under section 9 (effect of offence on benefits for members of offender's family) of the 2001 Act.

(4) The third case is where—

(a) an award of universal credit is made to a claimant who is an offender's family member;

(b) the offender, or the claimant, was entitled to old style JSA, old style ESA, income support or housing benefit ("the earlier award") at any time during the period of one month ending with the date on which the claim for universal credit was made or treated as made; and

(c) payments in respect of the earlier award were, on the relevant date, subject to a restriction under section 6B, 7, 8 or, as the case may be, 9 of the 2001 Act.

(5) Where this regulation applies—

(a) any subsequent payment of universal credit to the claimant in respect of an assessment period which falls wholly or partly within the remainder of the disqualification period applicable to the offender is to be reduced in accordance with regulation 36; and

(b) regulation 3ZB of the 2001 Regulations does not apply.

(6) This regulation does not apply if the earlier award was a joint-claim jobseeker's allowance and—

(a) payments in respect of the award were, on the relevant date, subject to a restriction under section 8(2) of the 2001 Act; or

(b) the award of universal credit is not made to joint claimants who were, on the relevant date, both entitled to the joint-claim job-seeker's allowance.

(7) In this regulation and in regulation 36—

"the 2001 Act" means the Social Security Fraud Act 2001;

"the 2001 Regulations" means the Social Security (Loss of Benefit) Regulations 2001;

"disqualification period" has the meaning given in the 2001 Act, interpreted in accordance with the 2001 Regulations;

"earlier award" is to be interpreted in accordance with paragraph (2)(b), (3)(b) or, as the case may be, (4)(b) and, for the purposes of regulation 36, where there is more than one earlier award, the term refers to the award to which the claimant became entitled most recently;

"offender" means an offender within the meaning of the 2001 Act;

"offender's family member" has the same meaning as in the 2001 Act;

"the relevant date" means—

(a) in relation to the first case—

(i) where the claimant was not entitled to the earlier award on the date on which the claim for universal credit was made or treated as made, the date on which the earlier award terminated;

(ii) where the claimant is not a new claimant partner and was entitled to the earlier award on the date on which the claim for universal credit was made, that date;

(iii) where the claimant is a new claimant partner and was entitled to the earlier award on the date on which the claim for universal credit was treated as made, that date;

(b) in relation to the second case, the date on which the person entitled to the earlier award ceased to be the offender's family member or, if the award terminated before that date, the date on which the earlier award terminated;

(c) in relation to the third case—

(i) where the claimant was entitled to the earlier award but that entitlement terminated before the date on which the claim for universal credit was made or treated as made, the date on which the earlier award terminated;

(ii) where the claimant is not a new claimant partner and was entitled to the earlier award on the date on which the claim for universal credit was made, that date;

(iii) where the claimant is a new claimant partner and was entitled to the earlier award on the date on which the claim for universal credit was treated as made, that date;

(iv) where the offender's family member was entitled to the earlier award, the date on which that person ceased to be the offender's family member or, if earlier, the date on which the earlier award terminated.

(8) For the purposes of this regulation, the fact that payments in respect of an earlier award were subject to a restriction is to be taken into account, even if the earlier award subsequently terminated before the date on which payments became subject to a restriction by virtue of an order made under section 150(3) of the Act (in so far as it was an award of income-based jobseeker's allowance or income-related employment and support allowance), regulation 7 or, as the case may be, regulation 8.

Loss of benefit penalties: reduction of universal credit

36. (1) Subject to paragraph (6) [¹ and to regulation 38], where regulation 35 applies, the amount of a reduction of universal credit in respect of an assessment period is to be calculated by multiplying the daily reduction rate by the number of days in the assessment period, unless paragraph (2) applies.   6.200

(2) Where the disqualification period ends during an assessment period, the amount of the reduction for that assessment period is (subject to paragraph (6)) to be calculated by multiplying the daily reduction rate by the number of days in the assessment period which are within the disqualification period.

(3) Subject to paragraphs (4) and (5), the daily reduction rate where regulation 35 applies is an amount which is equal to—

(a) the monetary amount by which payments in respect of the earlier award were reduced in accordance with section 6B or 7 of the

2001 Act or, as the case may be, regulation 3, 3ZA or 17 of the 2001 Regulations in respect of the last complete week before the relevant date (within the meaning of regulation 35);

(b) multiplied by 52;

(c) divided by 365; and

(d) rounded down to the nearest 10 pence.

(4) Where the monetary amount by which payments in respect of the earlier award would have been reduced would, if the claimant had remained entitled to the earlier award, have changed during the disqualification period because of an order made under section 150 of the Social Security Administration Act 1992 (annual up-rating of benefits)—

(a) the daily reduction rate is to be calculated in accordance with paragraph (3), but on the basis of the new amount by which payments would have been reduced; and

(b) any adjustment to the reduction of universal credit is to take effect from the first day of the first assessment period to start after the date of the change.

(5) Where the earlier award was a joint-claim jobseeker's allowance, the daily reduction rate is an amount which is equal to—

(a) the amount of the standard allowance applicable to the joint claimants under regulation 36 of the Universal Credit Regulations (table showing amounts of elements);

(b) multiplied by 12;

(c) divided by 365;

(d) reduced by 60%; and

(e) rounded down to the nearest 10 pence.

(6) The amount of the reduction under this regulation in respect of any assessment period is not to exceed the amount of the standard allowance which is applicable to the claimant in respect of that period.

AMENDMENTS

1. Universal Credit (Transitional Provisions) (Amendment) Regulations 2014 (SI 2014/1626) reg.6(1) (October 13, 2014).

[¹ Loss of benefit penalties: transition from working tax credit

6.201   **37.** (1) This regulation applies where an award of universal credit is made to a claimant who—

(a) was previously entitled to working tax credit; and

(b) is an offender, within the meaning of the 2002 Act.

(2) Where this regulation applies, the Social Security (Loss of Benefit) Regulations 2001 apply as if in regulation 3ZB of those Regulations—

(a) in paragraph (1) at the beginning there were inserted "Subject to regulation 38 of the Universal Credit (Transitional Provisions) Regulations 2014,";

(b) "disqualification period" includes a disqualification period within the meaning of the 2002 Act;

(c) "offender" includes an offender within the meaning of the 2002 Act; and

(d) "offender's family member" includes a person who is a member of the family (within the meaning of section 137(1) of the Social Security Contributions and Benefits Act 1992 of a person who is an offender within the meaning of the 2002 Act.]

AMENDMENTS

1. Universal Credit (Transitional Provisions) (Amendment) Regulations 2014 (SI 2014/1626) reg.6(2) (October 13, 2014).

[¹ Loss of benefit penalties: maximum total reduction

38. Where regulations 35 and 37 both apply to a claimant, the total amount of a reduction of universal credit in respect of any assessment period under— **6.202**
(a) regulation 36; and
(b) regulation 3ZB of the Social Security (Loss of Benefit) Regulations 2001,
    must not exceed the amount of the standard allowance which is applicable to the claimant in respect of that period.]

AMENDMENTS

1. Universal Credit (Transitional Provisions) (Amendment) Regulations 2014 (SI 2014/1626) reg.6(2) (October 13, 2014).

SCHEDULE

Regulation 12A

MODIFICATION OF TAX CREDITS LEGISLATION (FINALISATION OF TAX CREDITS)

Modifications to the Tax Credits Act 2002

1. Paragraphs 2 to 10 prescribe modifications to the application of the 2002 Act where **6.203**
regulation 12A of these Regulations applies.
2. In section 7 (income test)—
(a) in subsection (3), before "current year income" in each place where it occurs, insert "notional";
(b) in subsection (4)—
    (i) for "current year" substitute "current part year";
    (ii) in paragraphs (a) and (b), before "tax year" insert "part";
(c) after subsection (4), insert—

> "(4A) In this section "the notional current year income" means—
>   (a) in relation to persons by whom a joint claim for a tax credit is made, the aggregate income of the persons for the part tax year to which the claim relates, divided by the number of days in that part tax year, multiplied by the number of days in the tax year in which the part tax year is included and rounded down to the next whole number of pence; and
>   (b) in relation to a person by whom a single claim for a tax credit is made, the income of the person for that part tax year, divided by the number of days in that part tax year, multiplied by the number of days in the tax year in which the part tax year is included and rounded down to the next whole number of pence.".

3. In section 17 (final notice)—
(a) in subsection (1)—
    (i) omit "the whole or"; and
    (ii) in sub-paragraph (a), before "tax year" insert "part";

(b) in subsection (3), before "tax year" insert "part";

(c) in subsections (4)(a) and (4)(b), for "current year" in both places where it occurs, substitute "current part year";

(d) in subsection (5)(a) for "current year" in both places where it occurs, substitute "current part year";

(e) omit subsection (8).

4. In section 18 (decisions after final notice)—

(a) in subsection (1), before "tax year" insert "part";

(b) omit subsections (6) to (9);

(c) in subsection (10), for "subsection (1), (5), (6) or (9)" substitute "subsection (1) or (5)";

(d) in subsection (11)—

(i) after "subsection (5)" omit "or (9)";

(ii) omit paragraph (a);

(iii) in paragraph (b) omit "in any other case,";

(iv) before "tax year" in each place where it occurs, insert "part".

5. In section 19 (power to enquire)—

(a) in subsection (1)(a) and (b), before "tax year" insert "part";

(b) in subsection (3), before "tax year" insert "part";

(c) for subsection (5) substitute—

"(5) "The relevant section 18 decision" means the decision under subsection (1) of section 18 in relation to the person or persons and the part tax year.";

(d) for subsection (6) substitute—

"(6) "The relevant section 17 date" means the date specified for the purposes of subsection (4) of section 17 in the notice given to a person or persons under that section in relation to the part tax year.";

(e) in subsection (11), before "tax year" insert "part";

(f) in subsection (12), before "tax year" in each place where it occurs, insert "part".

6. In section 20 (decisions on discovery)—

(a) in subsection (1), before "tax year" insert "part";

(b) in subsection (4)(a), before "tax year" insert "part";

(c) in subsection (5)(b), before "tax year" insert "part";

(d) in subsection (6)—

(i) before "tax year" insert "part";

(ii) in paragraph (a), for "section 18(1), (5), (6) or (9)" substitute "section 18(1) or (5)";

(e) in subsection (7), before "tax year" in each place where it occurs, insert "part".

7. In section 21 (decisions subject to official error), for "18(1), (5), (6) or (9)" substitute "18(1) or (5)".

8. In section 23 (notice of decisions)—

(a) in subsection (1), for "18(1), (5), (6) or (9)" substitute "18(1) or (5)";

(b) in subsection (3)—

(i) after "18(1)" omit "or (6)";

(ii) for paragraph (b) substitute—

"(b) the notice of the decision under subsection (1) of section 18,".

9. In section 30(1) (underpayments), before "tax year" in each place where it occurs, insert "part".

10. In section 38 (appeals)—

(a) in subsection (1)(b), before "tax year" insert "part";

(b) for subsection (2), substitute—

"(2) "The relevant section 18 decision" means the decision under subsection (1) of section 18 in relation to the person or persons and the tax credit for the part tax year.".

Modifications to the Tax Credits (Definition and Calculation of Income) Regulations 2002

11. Paragraphs 12 to 23 prescribe modifications to the application of the Tax Credits (Definition and Calculation of Income) Regulations 2002 where regulation 12A of these Regulations applies. **6.204**

12. In regulation 2(2) (interpretation), after the definition of "the Macfarlane Trusts" insert—

""part tax year" means a period of less than a year beginning with 6th April and ending with the date on which the award of a tax credit terminated;".

13. In regulation 3 (calculation of income of claimant)—
(a) in paragraph (1)—
    (i) before "tax year" insert "part";
    (ii) in Steps 1 and 2, after "of the claimant, or, in the case of a joint claim, of the claimants" insert "received in or relating to the part tax year";
    (iii) in the second and third sentences of Step 4, before "year" insert "part";
(b) in paragraph (6A), for the words from "ending on 31st March" to the end, substitute "ending on the last day of the month in which the claimant's award of a tax credit terminated";
(c) in paragraph (8)(b), before "year" insert "part".

14. In regulation 4 (employment income)—
(a) in paragraph (1)(a), before "tax year" insert "part";
(b) in paragraph (1)(b), (c), (d), (e), (g) and (k), before "year" insert "part";
(c) in paragraph (1)(f), after "ITEPA" insert "which is treated as received in the part tax year and in respect of which the charge arises in the part tax year";
(d) in paragraph (1)(h), after "week" insert "in the part tax year";
(e) in paragraph (1)(i), for "that year" substitute "the tax year" and after "ITEPA" insert "which is treated as received in the part tax year";
(f) in paragraph (1)(j), after "applies" insert "which is received in the part tax year";
(g) in paragraph (1)(l), for "that year" substitute "the tax year" and after "ITEPA" insert "in respect of which the charge arises in the part tax year";
(h) in paragraph (1)(m), after "paid" insert "in the part tax year";
(i) in paragraph (4), in the first sentence and in the title of Table 1, after "employment income" insert "received in the part tax year";
(j) in paragraph (5), after "calculating earnings" insert "received in the part tax year".

15. In regulation 5 (pension income)—
(a) in paragraph (1), after ""pension income" means" insert "any of the following received in or relating to the part tax year";
(b) in paragraph (2), in the first sentence and in the title of Table 2, after "pension income" insert "received in or relating to the part tax year";
(c) in paragraph (3), after "income tax purposes", insert "in relation to the part tax year".

16. In regulation 6 (trading income)—
(a) re-number the existing regulation as paragraph (1);
(b) in paragraph (1) (as so re-numbered)—
    (i) in sub-paragraph (a), for "taxable profits for the tax year" substitute "actual or estimated taxable profits attributable to the part tax year";
    (ii) in sub-paragraph (b), for "taxable profit for the" substitute "actual or estimated taxable profit attributable to the part tax";
(c) after paragraph (1) insert—

"(2) Actual or estimated taxable profits attributable to the part tax year ("the relevant trading income") is to be calculated by reference to the basis period (determined by reference to the rules in Chapter 15 of Part 2 of ITTOIA) ending during the tax year in which the claimant made, or was treated as making, a claim for universal credit.
(3) The relevant trading income is to be calculated by—
(a) taking the figure for the actual or estimated taxable income earned in the basis period;

(b) dividing that figure by the number of days in the basis period to give the daily figure; and

(c) multiplying the daily figure by the number of days in the part tax year on which the trade, profession or vocation was carried on.".

17. In regulation 7 (social security income)—

(a) in paragraph (1), after "social security income" insert "received in the part tax year";

(b) in paragraph (3), in the opening words and in the title of Table 3, after "social security income" insert "received in the part tax year".

18. In regulation 8 (student income), after "in relation to a student" insert ", any of the following which is received in the part tax year".

19. In regulation 10 (investment income)—

(a) in paragraph (1), after "gross amount" insert "received in the part tax year";

(b) in paragraph (1)(e), before "year" insert "part tax";

(c) in paragraph (2), in the opening words and in the title of Table 4, after "investment income" insert "received in the part tax year".

20. In regulation 11(1) (property income)—

(a) omit "annual";

(b) after "taxable profits" insert "for the part tax year".

21. In regulation 12(1) (foreign income), before "year" insert "part tax".

22. In regulation 13 (notional income), after "means income" insert "received in the part tax year".

23. In regulation 18 (miscellaneous income), after "means income" insert "received in the part tax year".

Modifications to the Tax Credits (Income Thresholds and Determination of Rates) Regulations 2002

6.205   24. Paragraphs 25 to 27 prescribe modifications to the application of the Tax Credits (Income Thresholds and Determination of Rates) Regulations 2002 where regulation 12A of these Regulations applies.

25. In regulation 2 (interpretation)—

(a) after the definition of "the income threshold" insert—

> ""part tax year" means a period of less than a year beginning with 6th April and ending with the date on which the award of a tax credit terminated;";

(b) in the definition of "the relevant income" insert "as modified by the Universal Credit (Transitional Provisions) Regulations 2014" at the end.

26. In regulation 7(3) (determination of rate of working tax credit)—

(a) in Step 1, in the definition of "MR", after "maximum rate" insert "(determined in the manner prescribed at the date on which the award of the tax credit terminated)";

(b) in Step 3—

  (i) in the definition of "I", before "tax year" insert "part";

  (ii) in the definition of "N1", before "tax year" insert "part".

27. In regulation 8(3) (determination of rate of child tax credit)—

(a) in Step 1, in the definition of "MR", after "maximum rate" insert "(determined in the manner prescribed at the date on which the award of the tax credit terminated)";

(b) in Step 3—

  (i) in the definition of "I", before "tax year" insert "part";

  (ii) in the definition of "N1", before "tax year" insert "part".

Modifications to the Tax Credits (Claims and Notifications) Regulations 2002

6.206   28. Paragraphs 29 to 34 prescribe modifications to the application of the Tax Credits (Claims and Notifications) Regulations 2002 where regulation 12A of these Regulations applies.

29. In regulation 4 (interpretation), omit paragraph (b).

30. Omit regulation 11 (circumstances in which claims to be treated as made).

31. Omit regulation 12 (further circumstances in which claims to be treated as made).

32. In regulation 13 (circumstances in which claims made by one member of a couple to be treated as also made by the other)—

(a) in paragraph (1), after "prescribed by paragraph" omit "(2) or";

(b) omit paragraph (2).

33. In regulation 15(1)(c) (persons who die after making a claim)—

(a) omit "the whole or" and "after the end of that tax year but"; and

(b) for "section 18(1), (5), (6) or (9)" substitute "section 18(1) or (5)".

34. In regulation 33 (dates to be specified in notices)—

(a) in paragraph (a), for the words from "not later than 31st July" to "if later", substitute "not less than 30 days after the date on which the notice is given";

(b) omit paragraph (b) and the "and" which precedes it.

Modification to the Tax Credits (Payment by the Commissioners) Regulations 2002

35. Paragraph 36 prescribes a modification to the application of the Tax Credits (Payment by the Commissioners) Regulations 2002 where regulation 12A of these Regulations applies.

6.207

36. Omit regulation 7 (prescribed circumstances for certain purposes).

Modification to the Tax Credits (Residence) Regulations 2003

37. Paragraph 38 prescribes a modification to the application of the Tax Credits (Residence) Regulations 2003 where regulation 12A of these Regulations applies.

6.208

38. In regulation 3(5)(a) (circumstances in which a person is treated as not being in the United Kingdom)(26), omit "under regulation 11 or 12 of the Tax Credits (Claims and Notifications) Regulations 2002 or otherwise".

AMENDMENTS

1. Universal Credit (Transitional Provisions) (Amendment) Regulations 2014 (SI 2014/1626) reg.4 (October 13, 2014).

The Welfare Reform Act 2012 (Commencement No. 17 and Transitional and Transitory Provisions) Order 2014

SI 2014/1583 (C. 61) (as amended)

ARRANGEMENT OF ARTICLES

6.209

The Secretary of State, in exercise of the powers conferred by sections 150(3) and (4)(a), (b)(i) and (c) of the Welfare Reform Act 2012, makes the following Order:

GENERAL NOTE

This Commencement Order ("the Commencement No. 17 Order") extended the universal credit scheme to certain postcode districts and as from various dates in areas known as the No. 8, No. 9, No. 10, No. 11, No. 12 and No. 13 relevant districts (see Schedule). All the scheduled postcode districts are in the

6.210

North West. "The No. 8 relevant districts" are in Hyde, Stalybridge, Stretford and Altrincham (as from June 23, 2014). "The No. 9 relevant districts" are in Southport, Crosby, Bootle, Bolton (Great Moor Street; Blackhorse Street) and Farnworth (as from June 30, 2014). "The No. 10 relevant districts" are in the Wirral (as from July 7, 2014). "The No. 11 relevant districts" are in Bolton, Bury and Preston (as from July 14, 2014). "The No. 12 relevant districts" are in Liverpool, Greater Manchester and Warrington (as from July 21, 2014). "The No. 13 relevant districts" are in Chester, Crewe, Stockport and Warrington (as from July 28, 2014). In addition, of course, the claimant had to fall within the Pathfinder Group, i.e. be a person who meets the requirements of regs 5 to 12 of the Transitional Provisions Regulations 2013, now the "gateway conditions" (see Sch.5 to the Commencement No.9 Order).

Citation

6.211   **1.** This Order may be cited as the Welfare Reform Act 2012 (Commencement No. 17 and Transitional and Transitory Provisions) Order 2014.

Interpretation

6.212   2. (1) In this Order—

"the Act" means the Welfare Reform Act 2012;

"the amending provisions" means the provisions referred to in article 4(1)(a) to (c) of the No. 9 Order (day appointed for the abolition of income-related employment and support allowance and income-based jobseeker's allowance);

[¹ . . .] [³ "claimant"—

(a) in relation to an employment and support allowance, has the same meaning as in Part 1 of the Welfare Reform Act 2007, save as mentioned in article 5(1A) of the No. 9 Order as applied by article 4(7);

(b) in relation to a jobseeker's allowance, has the same meaning as in the Jobseekers Act 1995 (as it applies apart from the amendments made by Part 1 of Schedule 14 to the Act that remove references to an income-based jobseeker's allowance), save as mentioned in article 5(1A) of the No. 9 Order as applied by article 4(7);

(c) in relation to universal credit, has the same meaning as in Part 1 of the Act;]

"employment and support allowance" means an employment and support allowance under Part 1 of the Welfare Reform Act 2007;

"First-tier Tribunal" has the same meaning as in the Social Security Act 1998;

[³ "gateway conditions" means the conditions specified in Schedule 5 to the No. 9 Order save that where, for the purposes of article 3(2)(e), (f), (k) or (l) or 4(2)(e), (f), (k) or (l), the claimant resides in one of the No. 10 relevant districts, or in postcode part-district CH62 9, on the date on which the claim is made, it means those conditions as if the No. 9 Order were amended as referred to in paragraph (3);]

"jobseeker's allowance" means a jobseeker's allowance under the Job-seekers Act 1995;

[² "joint claimants" in relation to universal credit, has the same mean-ing as in Part 1 of the Act;]

"the No. 9 Order" means the Welfare Reform Act 2012 (Commence-ment No. 9 and Transitional and Transitory Provisions and Com-mencement No. 8 and Savings and Transitional Provisions (Amendment)) Order 2013;

"No. 8 relevant districts" means the postcode districts and part-districts specified in Part 1 of the Schedule;

"No. 9 relevant districts" means the postcode districts and part-districts specified in Part 2 of the Schedule;

"No. 10 relevant districts" means the postcode districts and part-districts specified in Part 3 of the Schedule;

"No. 11 relevant districts" means the postcode districts and part-districts specified in Part 4 of the Schedule;

"No. 12 relevant districts" means the postcode districts and part-districts specified in Part 5 of the Schedule;

"No. 13 relevant districts" means the postcode districts and part-districts specified in Part 6 of the Schedule;

[² "single claimant", in relation to universal credit, has the same meaning as in Part 1 of the Act;]

"Upper Tribunal" has the same meaning as in the Social Security Act 1998.

(2) For the purposes of this Order, the Universal Credit, Personal Independence Payment, Jobseeker's Allowance and Employment and Support Allowance (Claims and Payments) Regulations 2013 apply for the purpose of deciding—

(a) whether a claim for universal credit is made; and

(b) the date on which such a claim is made.

[³ (3) The amendments of the No. 9 Order referred to are—

(a) in article 2(1)—

(i) after the definition of "the Decisions and Appeals Regula-tions 2013" insert—

""disability living allowance" means an allowance under section 71 of the Social Security Contributions and Benefits Act 1992;"; and

(ii) after the definition of "old style JSA award" insert—

""personal independence payment" means an allowance under Part 4 of the Act;"; and

(b) in paragraph 6 of Schedule 5 (caring responsibilities)—

(i) for sub-paragraph (1) substitute—

"(1) There must not be a child or young person living with the claimant some or all of the time if the child or young person—

(a) has been certified as severely sight impaired or blind by a consultant ophthalmologist;

(b) is looked after by a local authority, within the meaning of section 22 of the Children Act 1989 or section 17(6) of the Children (Scotland) Act 1995, save where the child or young person is so looked after during any period referred to in regulation 4A(1)(a) of the Universal Credit Regulations; or

(c) is entitled to a disability living allowance or personal independence payment.";

(ii) for sub-paragraph (2)(a) substitute—

"(a) be an adopter (within the meaning of the Universal Credit Regulations) with whom a child has been placed within the period of 12 months ending immediately before the date on which the claim for universal credit is made or with whom a child is expected to be placed during the period of two months beginning with that date; or";

(iii) omit sub-paragraph (2)(c) and (d); and

(iv) in sub-paragraph (3), at the end insert—

";

(c) "young person" means a person—

(i) who is not a child but who is under the age of 20; and

(ii) for whom the claimant would be responsible for the purposes of regulation 4 of the Universal Credit Regulations, if the person were a qualifying young person within the meaning of regulation 5 of those Regulations."]

AMENDMENTS

1. Welfare Reform Act 2012 (Commencement No. 9, 11, 13 14, 16 and 17 and Transitional and Transitory Provisions (Amendment)) Order 2014 (SI 2014/1661) art.9 (June 30, 2014).

2. Welfare Reform Act 2012 (Commencement No. 9, 11, 13, 14, 16 and 17 and Transitional and Transitory Provisions (Amendment) (No. 2)) Order 2014 (SI 2014/1923) art.10(2) (July 28, 2014).

3. Welfare Reform Act 2012 (Commencement No. 9, 11, 13 14, 16, 17 and 19 and Transitional and Transitory Provisions (Amendment)) Order 2014 (SI 2014/3067) art.5(a), (b) and 6(3) (November 24, 2014).

Day appointed for the coming into force of the universal credit provisions

6.213 **3.** (1) The day appointed for the coming into force of the provisions of the Act listed in Schedule 2 to the No. 9 Order, in so far as they are not already in force, in relation to the case of a claim referred to in paragraph (2), and any award that is made in respect of the claim, is the day appointed in accordance with paragraph (3).

(2) The claims referred to are—

(a) a claim for universal credit that is made on or after 23rd June 2014 in respect of a period that begins on or after 23rd June 2014 where, on the date on which the claim is made, the claimant resides in one of the No. 8 relevant districts and meets the gateway conditions;

[¹ (b) a claim for universal credit that is made in respect of a period that begins on or after 23rd June 2014 where—

    (i) in the case of a single claimant, the claimant gives incorrect information regarding the claimant residing in a No. 8 relevant district or meeting the gateway conditions and the claimant does not reside in such a district or does not meet the gateway conditions on the date on which the claim is made;

    (ii) in the case of joint claimants, either or both of the joint claimants gives or give incorrect information regarding his or her (or their) residing in such a district or meeting the gateway conditions and one or both of them does not or do not reside in such a district or does not or do not meet those conditions on the date on which the claim is made; and

    (iii) after a decision is made that the single claimant is, or the joint claimants are, entitled to universal credit and one or more payments have been made in respect of the single claimant or the joint claimants, the Secretary of State discovers that incorrect information has been given regarding residence or meeting the gateway conditions;]

(c) a claim for universal credit that is made on or after 30th June 2014 in respect of a period that begins on or after 30th June 2014 where, on the date on which the claim is made, the claimant resides in one of the No. 9 relevant districts and meets the gateway conditions;

[¹ (d) a claim for universal credit that is made in respect of a period that begins on or after 30th June 2014 where—

    (i) in the case of a single claimant, the claimant gives incorrect information regarding the claimant residing in a No. 9 relevant district or meeting the gateway conditions and the claimant does not reside in such a district or does not meet the gateway conditions on the date on which the claim is made;

    (ii) in the case of joint claimants, either or both of the joint claimants gives or give incorrect information regarding his or her (or their) residing in such a district or meeting the gateway conditions and one or both of them does not or do not reside in such a district or does not or do not meet those conditions on the date on which the claim is made; and

    (iii) after a decision is made that the single claimant is, or the joint claimants are, entitled to universal credit and one or more payments have been made in respect of the single claimant or the joint claimants, the Secretary of State discovers that incorrect information has been given regarding residence or meeting the gateway conditions;]

(e) a claim for universal credit that is made on or after 7th July 2014 in respect of a period that begins on or after 7th July 2014 where, on the date on which the claim is made, the claimant resides in one of the No. 10 relevant districts and meets the gateway conditions;

[¹ (f) a claim for universal credit that is made in respect of a period that begins on or after 7th July 2014 where—

    (i) in the case of a single claimant, the claimant gives incorrect information regarding the claimant residing in a No. 10 relevant district or meeting the gateway conditions and the claimant does not reside in such a district or does not meet the gateway conditions on the date on which the claim is made;

    (ii) in the case of joint claimants, either or both of the joint claimants gives or give incorrect information regarding his or her (or their) residing in such a district or meeting the gateway conditions and one or both of them does not or do not reside in such a district or does not or do not meet those conditions on the date on which the claim is made; and

    (iii) after a decision is made that the single claimant is, or the joint claimants are, entitled to universal credit and one or more payments have been made in respect of the single claimant or the joint claimants, the Secretary of State discovers that incorrect information has been given regarding residence or meeting the gateway conditions;]

(g) a claim for universal credit that is made on or after 14th July 2014 in respect of a period that begins on or after 14th July 2014 where, on the date on which the claim is made, the claimant resides in one of the No. 11 relevant districts and meets the gateway conditions;

[¹ (h) a claim for universal credit that is made in respect of a period that begins on or after 14th July 2014 where—

    (i) in the case of a single claimant, the claimant gives incorrect information regarding the claimant residing in a No. 11 relevant district or meeting the gateway conditions and the claimant does not reside in such a district or does not meet the gateway conditions on the date on which the claim is made;

    (ii) in the case of joint claimants, either or both of the joint claimants gives or give incorrect information regarding his or her (or their) residing in such a district or meeting the gateway conditions and one or both of them does not or do not reside in such a district or does not or do not meet those conditions on the date on which the claim is made; and

    (iii) after a decision is made that the single claimant is, or the joint claimants are, entitled to universal credit and one or more payments have been made in respect of the single claimant or the joint claimants, the Secretary of State discovers that incorrect information has been given regarding residence or meeting the gateway conditions;]

(i) a claim for universal credit that is made on or after 21st July 2014 in respect of a period that begins on or after 21st July 2014 where, on the date on which the claim is made, the claimant resides in one of the No. 12 relevant districts and meets the gateway conditions;

[¹ (j) a claim for universal credit that is made in respect of a period that begins on or after 21st July 2014 where—

  (i) in the case of a single claimant, the claimant gives incorrect information regarding the claimant residing in a No. 12 relevant district or meeting the gateway conditions and the claimant does not reside in such a district or does not meet the gateway conditions on the date on which the claim is made;

  (ii) in the case of joint claimants, either or both of the joint claimants gives or give incorrect information regarding his or her (or their) residing in such a district or meeting the gateway conditions and one or both of them does not or do not reside in such a district or does not or do not meet those conditions on the date on which the claim is made; and

  (iii) after a decision is made that the single claimant is, or the joint claimants are, entitled to universal credit and one or more payments have been made in respect of the single claimant or the joint claimants, the Secretary of State discovers that incorrect information has been given regarding residence or meeting the gateway conditions;]

(k) a claim for universal credit that is made on or after 28th July 2014 in respect of a period that begins on or after 28th July 2014 where, on the date on which the claim is made, the claimant resides in one of the No. 13 relevant districts and meets the gateway conditions;

[¹ (l) a claim for universal credit that is made in respect of a period that begins on or after 28th July 2014 where—

  (i) in the case of a single claimant, the claimant gives incorrect information regarding the claimant residing in a No. 13 relevant district or meeting the gateway conditions and the claimant does not reside in such a district or does not meet the gateway conditions on the date on which the claim is made;

  (ii) in the case of joint claimants, either or both of the joint claimants gives or give incorrect information regarding his or her (or their) residing in such a district or meeting the gateway conditions and one or both of them does not or do not reside in such a district or does not or do not meet those conditions on the date on which the claim is made; and

  (iii) after a decision is made that the single claimant is, or the joint claimants are, entitled to universal credit and one or more payments have been made in respect of the single claimant or the joint claimants, the Secretary of State discovers that incorrect information has been given regarding residence or meeting the gateway conditions.]

(3) The day appointed in relation to the case of a claim referred to in paragraph (2), and any award that is made in respect of the claim, is the first day of the period in respect of which the claim is made.

(4) Article 3(6) of the No. 9 Order applies for the purposes of paragraph (3) as it applies for the purposes of article 3(4)(a) of the No. 9 Order.

[¹ (5) Article 3A of the No. 9 Order applies in connection with a claim for universal credit where a single claimant, or, as the case may be, either or both of joint claimants, gives incorrect information regarding his or her (or their) residing in a No. 8, No. 9, No. 10, No. 11, No. 12 or No. 13 relevant district or meeting the gateway conditions, as it applies in connection with the giving of incorrect information regarding a claimant residing in a relevant district (as defined in the No. 9 Order) or meeting the gateway conditions]

AMENDMENTS

1. Welfare Reform Act 2012 (Commencement No. 9, 11, 13, 14, 16 and 17 and Transitional and Transitory Provisions (Amendment) (No. 2)) Order 2014 (SI 2014/1923) art.10(3) (July 28, 2014).

Day appointed for the abolition of income-related employment and support allowance and income-based jobseeker's allowance

6.214   **4.** (1) The day appointed for the coming into force of the amending provisions, in relation to the case of a claim referred to in paragraph (2), and any award that is made in respect of the claim, is the day appointed in accordance with paragraph (3).

(2) The claims referred to are—

(a) a claim for universal credit, an employment and support allowance or a jobseeker's allowance that is made [¹ or treated as made] on or after 23rd June 2014 in respect of a period that begins on or after 23rd June 2014 where, on the date on which the claim is made [¹ or treated as made], the claimant resides in one of the No. 8 relevant districts and meets the gateway conditions;

[¹ (b) a claim for universal credit that is made in respect of a period that begins on or after 23rd June 2014 where—

(i) in the case of a single claimant, the claimant gives incorrect information regarding the claimant residing in a No. 8 relevant district or meeting the gateway conditions and the claimant does not reside in such a district or does not meet the gateway conditions on the date on which the claim is made;

(ii) in the case of joint claimants, either or both of the joint claimants gives or give incorrect information regarding his or her (or their) residing in such a district or meeting the gateway conditions and one or both of them does not or do not reside in such a district or does not or do not meet those conditions on the date on which the claim is made; and

(iii) after a decision is made that the single claimant is, or the joint claimants are, entitled to universal credit and one or more payments have been made in respect of the single claimant or the joint claimants, the Secretary of State discovers that incorrect information has been given regarding residence or meeting the gateway conditions;]

(c) a claim for universal credit, an employment and support allowance or a jobseeker's allowance that is made [¹ or treated as made] on or after 30th June 2014 in respect of a period that begins on or after 30th June 2014 where, on the date on which the claim is made [¹ or treated as made], the claimant resides in one of the No. 9 relevant districts and meets the gateway conditions;

[¹ (d) a claim for universal credit that is made in respect of a period that begins on or after 30th June 2014 where—

(i) in the case of a single claimant, the claimant gives incorrect information regarding the claimant residing in a No. 9 relevant district or meeting the gateway conditions and the claimant does not reside in such a district or does not meet the gateway conditions on the date on which the claim is made;

(ii) in the case of joint claimants, either or both of the joint claimants gives or give incorrect information regarding his or her (or their) residing in such a district or meeting the gateway conditions and one or both of them does not or do not reside in such a district or does not or do not meet those conditions on the date on which the claim is made; and

(iii) after a decision is made that the single claimant is, or the joint claimants are, entitled to universal credit and one or more payments have been made in respect of the single claimant or the joint claimants, the Secretary of State discovers that incorrect information has been given regarding residence or meeting the gateway conditions;]

(e) a claim for universal credit, an employment and support allowance or a jobseeker's allowance that is made [1 or treated as made] on or after 7th July 2014 in respect of a period that begins on or after 7th July 2014 where, on the date on which the claim is made [¹ or treated as made], the claimant resides in one of the No. 10 relevant districts and meets the gateway conditions;

[¹ (f) a claim for universal credit that is made in respect of a period that begins on or after 7th July 2014 where—

(i) in the case of a single claimant, the claimant gives incorrect information regarding the claimant residing in a No. 10 relevant district or meeting the gateway conditions and the claimant does not reside in such a district or does not meet the gateway conditions on the date on which the claim is made;

(ii) in the case of joint claimants, either or both of the joint claimants gives or give incorrect information regarding his or her (or their) residing in such a district or meeting the gateway conditions and one or both of them does not or do not reside in such a district or does not or do not meet those conditions on the date on which the claim is made; and

(iii) after a decision is made that the single claimant is, or the joint claimants are, entitled to universal credit and one or more payments have been made in respect of the single claimant or the joint claimants, the Secretary of State discovers that incorrect information has been given regarding residence or meeting the gateway conditions;]

(g) a claim for universal credit, an employment and support allowance or a jobseeker's allowance that is made [¹ or treated as made] on or after 14th July 2014 in respect of a period that begins on or after 14th July 2014 where, on the date on which the claim is made [¹ or treated as made], the claimant resides in one of the No. 11 relevant districts and meets the gateway conditions;

[¹ (h) a claim for universal credit that is made in respect of a period that begins on or after 14th July 2014 where—

(i) in the case of a single claimant, the claimant gives incorrect information regarding the claimant residing in a No. 11 relevant district or meeting the gateway conditions and the claimant does not reside in such a district or does not meet the gateway conditions on the date on which the claim is made;

(ii) in the case of joint claimants, either or both of the joint claimants gives or give incorrect information regarding his or her (or their) residing in such a district or meeting the gateway conditions and one or both of them does not or do not reside in such a district or does not or do not meet those conditions on the date on which the claim is made; and

(iii) after a decision is made that the single claimant is, or the joint claimants are, entitled to universal credit and one or more payments have been made in respect of the single claimant or the joint claimants, the Secretary of State discovers that incorrect information has been given regarding residence or meeting the gateway conditions;]

(i) a claim for universal credit, an employment and support allowance or a jobseeker's allowance that is made [¹ or treated as made] on or after 21st July 2014 in respect of a period that begins on or after 21st July 2014 where, on the date on which the claim is made [¹ or treated as made], the claimant resides in one of the No. 12 relevant districts and meets the gateway conditions;

[¹ (j) a claim for universal credit that is made in respect of a period that begins on or after 21st July 2014 where—

(i) in the case of a single claimant, the claimant gives incorrect information regarding the claimant residing in a No. 12 relevant district or meeting the gateway conditions and the claimant does not reside in such a district or does not meet the gateway conditions on the date on which the claim is made;

(ii) in the case of joint claimants, either or both of the joint claimants gives or give incorrect information regarding his or her (or their) residing in such a district or meeting the gateway conditions and one or both of them does not or do not reside in such a district or does not or do not meet those conditions on the date on which the claim is made; and

    (iii) after a decision is made that the single claimant is, or the joint claimants are, entitled to universal credit and one or more payments have been made in respect of the single claimant or the joint claimants, the Secretary of State discovers that incorrect information has been given regarding residence or meeting the gateway conditions;]

(k) a claim for universal credit, an employment and support allowance or a jobseeker's allowance that is made [¹ or treated as made] on or after 28th July 2014 in respect of a period that begins on or after 28th July 2014 where, on the date on which the claim is made [¹ or treated as made], the claimant resides in one of the No. 13 relevant districts and meets the gateway conditions;

[¹ (l)   a claim for universal credit that is made in respect of a period that begins on or after 28th July 2014 where—

    (i) in the case of a single claimant, the claimant gives incorrect information regarding the claimant residing in a No. 13 relevant district or meeting the gateway conditions and the claimant does not reside in such a district or does not meet the gateway conditions on the date on which the claim is made;

    (ii) in the case of joint claimants, either or both of the joint claimants gives or give incorrect information regarding his or her (or their) residing in such a district or meeting the gateway conditions and one or both of them does not or do not reside in such a district or does not or do not meet those conditions on the date on which the claim is made; and

    (iii) after a decision is made that the single claimant is, or the joint claimants are, entitled to universal credit and one or more payments have been made in respect of the single claimant or the joint claimants, the Secretary of State discovers that incorrect information has been given regarding residence or meeting the gateway conditions;]

[¹ (m) a claim for an employment and support allowance or a jobseeker's allowance other than one referred to in sub-paragraph (a), (c), (e), (g), (i) or (k) that is made or treated as made during the relevant period by a single claimant of universal credit or by either of two joint claimants of universal credit who has or have made a claim for universal credit within one of sub-paragraphs (a) to (l).]

(3) The day appointed in relation to the case of a claim referred to in paragraph (2), and any award that is made in respect of the claim, is the first day of the period in respect of which the claim is made.

(4) For the purposes of paragraph (2)(m), "relevant period" means, in relation to a claim for universal credit within paragraph (2)(a) to (l), any UC claim period, and any period subsequent to any UC claim period in respect of which the claimant is entitled to an award of universal credit in respect of the claim.

(5) For the purposes of paragraph (4), a "UC claim period" is a period when—

(a) a claim for universal credit within paragraph [1 (2)(a), (b)(i) or (ii), (c), (d)(i) or (ii), (e), (f)(i) or (ii), (g), (h)(i) or (ii), (i), (j)(i) or (ii), (k) or (l)(i) or (ii)] has been made but a decision has not yet been made on the claim; or

(b) a decision has been made that the claimant is not entitled to universal credit and—

    (i) the Secretary of State is considering whether to revise that decision under section 9 of the Social Security Act 1998, whether on an application made for that purpose, or on the Secretary of State's own initiative; or

    (ii) the claimant has appealed against that decision to the First-tier Tribunal and that appeal or any subsequent appeal to the Upper Tribunal or to a court has not been finally determined.

(6) Paragraphs (6) and (7) of article 4 of the No. 9 Order apply in relation to a claim for universal credit referred to in paragraph (2) (and any award that is made in respect of the claim) as they apply in relation to a claim for universal credit referred to in sub-paragraphs (a) and (b) of article 4(2) of the No. 9 Order (and any award that is made in respect of the claim).

[² (7) Paragraphs (1) to (1B) of article 5 of the No. 9 Order apply for the purposes of paragraph (2)(a), (c), (e), (g), (i) and (k) as they apply for the purposes of article 4(2)(a) of the No. 9 Order.]

(8) Paragraphs (5) to (7) of article 5 of the No. 9 Order apply for the purposes of sub-paragraphs (a), (c), (e), (g), (i), (k) and (m) of paragraph (2) as they apply for the purposes of sub-paragraphs (a) and (g) of article 4(2) of the No. 9 Order.

(9) Article 5(8) of the No. 9 Order applies for the purposes of paragraph (3) as it applies for the purposes of article 4(3)(a) of the No. 9 Order.

AMENDMENTS

1. Welfare Reform Act 2012 (Commencement No. 9, 11, 13, 14, 16 and 17 and Transitional and Transitory Provisions (Amendment) (No. 2)) Order 2014 (SI 2014/1923) art.10(4) (July 28, 2014).
2. Welfare Reform Act 2012 (Commencement No. 9, 11, 13 14, 16, 17 and 19 and Transitional and Transitory Provisions (Amendment)) Order 2014 (SI 2014/3067) art.6(5) (November 24, 2014).

Application of the No. 9 Order

6.215   **5.** Articles 9 to 22 of the No. 9 Order apply in connection with the coming into force of the amending provisions in relation to the case of a claim referred to in article 4(2), and any award made in respect of the claim, as they apply in connection with the coming into force of the amending provisions in relation to the case of a claim referred to in sub-paragraphs (a), (b) and (g) of article 4(2) of the No. 9 Order and any award made in respect of the claim.

SCHEDULE   **6.216**

Article 2(1)

POSTCODE DISTRICTS AND PART-DISTRICTS

PART 1

THE NO. 8 RELEVANT DISTRICTS

M31.
M32.
M33 2.
M33 4 to M33 7.
M34.
M41.
OL5.
SK14 1 and SK14 2.
SK14 4.
SK14 6.
SK14 9.
SK15.
WA14 1 and WA14 2.
WA14 5.
WA15 5 and WA15 6.
WA15 9.

PART 2   **6.217**

THE NO. 9 RELEVANT DISTRICTS

BL1.
BL2.
BL3.
BL4.
BL5 1.
BL5 3.
BL6 4.
BL6 9.
L20 0.
L20 3 to L20 6.
L21.
L22.
L23.
L29.
L30.
L31 0.
L31 2 and L31 3.
L31 5 to L31 9.
L37 1 to L37 4.
L37 6 to L37 8.
L38.
M26 3.
PR8 1 and PR8 2.
PR8 6.
PR8 9.
PR9 0.
PR9 7.
PR9 9.

505

6.218

PART 3

THE NO. 10 RELEVANT DISTRICTS

CH41.
CH42.
CH43.
CH44.
CH45.
CH46.
CH47.
CH48.
CH49.
CH60.
CH61.
CH62 0 to CH62 8.
CH63.

6.219

PART 4

THE NO. 11 RELEVANT DISTRICTS

BL0 9.
BL8 1 to BL8 3.
BL8 9.
BL9 0.
BL9 5.
BL9 8 and BL9 9.
M25 1.
M25 3.
M25 9.
M26 1 and M26 2.
M26 4.
M45.
PR0.
PR1.
PR2.
PR4 4 and PR4 5.
PR5 4 and PR5 5.
PR11.
PR25 1 to PR25 3.
PR25 9.
PR26 6.

6.220

PART 5

THE NO. 12 RELEVANT DISTRICTS

L10 0.
L10 2 and L10 3.
L10 6.
L10 8.
L28 3 to L28 7.
L32.
L33 0 to L33 2.
L33 5 to L33 9.
L34.
L35 0 to L35 5.
L35 7 to L35 9.
L36 0 to L36 4.
L36 6 to L36 9.

M17 1.
M17 8.
M27 0.
M27 5.
M27 8 and M27 9.
M28.
M30.
M38.
WA9.
WA10.
WA11 0.
WA11 8 and WA11 9.
WA12.

PART 6

THE NO. 13 RELEVANT DISTRICTS

CH1.
CH2.
CH3.
CH4 7 and CH4 8.
CH62 9.
CW1.
CW2 6 to CW2 8.
CW3 0.
CW4.
CW5.
CW10.
CW11.
CW12 1 and CW12 2.
CW12 4.
CW12 9.
SK9.
WA 6.
WA14 3 and WA14 4.
WA16.

The Welfare Reform Act 2012 (Commencement No. 9, 11, 13, 14, 16 and 17 and Transitional and Transitory Provisions (Amendment)) Order 2014

(SI 2014/1661) (C.69)

ARRANGEMENT OF ARTICLES

6.222

8. Amendment of the No. 16 Order
9. Amendment of the No. 17 Order

The Secretary of State, in exercise of the powers conferred by sections 150(3) and (4)(a), (b)(i) and (c) of the Welfare Reform Act 2012, makes the following Order:

Citation

6.223 **1.** This Order may be cited as the Welfare Reform Act 2012 (Commencement No. 9, 11, 13, 14, 16 and 17 and Transitional and Transitory Provisions (Amendment)) Order 2014.

Interpretation

6.224 **2.** (1) In this Order—

"the Act" means the Welfare Reform Act 2012;

"claimant", in relation to an employment and support allowance or a jobseeker's allowance, has the same meaning as in Part 1 of the Welfare Reform Act 2007 and the Jobseekers Act 1995 (as it applies apart from the amendments made by Part 1 of Schedule 14 to the Act that remove references to an income-based jobseeker's allowance) respectively and, in relation to universal credit, has the same meaning as in Part 1 of the Act;

"employment and support allowance" means an employment and support allowance under Part 1 of the Welfare Reform Act 2007;

"jobseeker's allowance" means a jobseeker's allowance under the Jobseekers Act 1995;

"joint claimants", in relation to universal credit, has the same meaning as in Part 1 of the Act;

"the No. 9 Order" means the Welfare Reform Act 2012 (Commencement No. 9 and Transitional and Transitory Provisions and Commencement No. 8 and Savings and Transitional Provisions (Amendment)) Order 2013;

"the No. 11 Order" means the Welfare Reform Act 2012 (Commencement No. 11 and Transitional and Transitory Provisions and Commencement No. 9 and Transitional and Transitory Provisions (Amendment)) Order 2013;

"the No. 13 Order" means the Welfare Reform Act 2012 (Commencement No. 13 and Transitional and Transitory Provisions) Order 2013;

"the No. 14 Order" means the Welfare Reform Act 2012 (Commencement No. 14 and Transitional and Transitory Provisions) Order 2013;

"the No. 16 Order" means the Welfare Reform Act 2012 (Commencement No. 16 and Transitional and Transitory Provisions) Order 2014;

"the No. 17 Order" means the Welfare Reform Act 2012 (Commencement No. 17 and Transitional and Transitory Provisions) Order 2014;

"relevant districts" has the meaning given in the No. 9 Order;

"No. 2 relevant districts" and "No. 3 relevant districts" have the meanings given in the No. 11 Order;

"No. 4 relevant districts" has the meaning given in the No. 13 Order;

"No. 5 relevant districts" has the meaning given in the No. 14 Order;

"No. 6 relevant districts" and "No. 7 relevant districts" have the meanings given in the No. 16 Order;

"No. 8 relevant districts", No. 9 relevant districts", "No. 10 relevant districts", "No. 11 relevant districts", "No. 12 relevant districts" and "No. 13 relevant districts" have the meanings given in the No. 17 Order;

"single claimant", in relation to universal credit, has the same meaning as in Part 1 of the Act;

"specified districts" means the relevant districts, No. 2 relevant districts, No. 3 relevant districts, No. 4 relevant districts, No. 5 relevant districts, No. 6 relevant districts, No. 7 relevant districts, No. 8 relevant districts, No. 9 relevant districts, No. 10 relevant districts, No. 11 relevant districts, No. 12 relevant districts and No. 13 relevant districts.

(2) For the purposes of this Order—

(a) the Universal Credit, Personal Independence Payment, Jobseeker's Allowance and Employment and Support Allowance (Claims and Payments) Regulations 2013 apply for the purpose of deciding—

    (i) whether a claim for universal credit is made; and

    (ii) the date on which such a claim is made; and

(b) the Social Security (Claims and Payments) Regulations 1987 apply for the purpose of deciding—

    (i) whether a claim for an employment and support allowance or a jobseeker's allowance is made; and

    (ii) the date on which the claim is made or is to be treated as made.

Amendment of the No. 9, 11, 13, 14, 16 and 17 Orders: cases to which the amendments apply.

3. This article applies in relation to a case where—
          6.225

(a) a claim is made for universal credit, an employment and support allowance or a jobseeker's allowance and, on the date on which the claim is made or treated as made, the claimant resides in one of the specified districts; or

(b) a claim for universal credit is made where—

    (i) in the case of a single claimant, the claimant gives incorrect information regarding the claimant residing in a specified district and does not reside in such a district on the date on which the claim is made;

    (ii) in the case of joint claimants, either or both of the joint claimants gives or give incorrect information regarding his or her (or their) residing in such a district and one or both of them does not or do not reside in such a district on the date on which the claim is made; and

(iii) after a decision is made that the single claimant is, or the joint claimants are, entitled to universal credit and one or more payments have been made in respect of the single claimant or the joint claimants, the Secretary of State discovers that incorrect information has been given regarding residence,

and where the claim is made or treated as made on or after 30th June 2014.

Amendment of the No. 9 Order

6.226   **4.** *[Amendments incorporated into No. 9 Order]*

Amendment of the No. 11 Order

6.227   **5.** *[Amendments incorporated into No.11 Order]*

Amendment of the No. 13 Order

6.228   **6.** *[Amendments incorporated into No. 13 Order]*

Amendment of the No. 14 Order

6.229   **7.** *[Amendments incorporated into No. 14 Order]*

Amendment of the No. 16 Order

6.230   **8.** *[Amendments incorporated into No. 16 Order]*

Amendment of the No. 17 Order

6.231   **9.** *[Amendments incorporated into No. 17 Order]*

The Welfare Reform Act 2012 (Commencement No. 9, 11, 13, 14, 16 and 17 and Transitional and Transitory Provisions (Amendment) (No. 2)) Order 2014

(SI 2014/1923) (C.88)

The Secretary of State, in exercise of the powers conferred by section 150(3) and (4)(a), (b)(i) and (c) of the Welfare Reform Act 2012, makes the following Order:

6.232   ARRANGEMENT OF ARTICLES

1.   Citation
2.   Interpretation
3.   Amendment of the No. 9, 11, 13, 14, 16 and 17 Orders: cases to which the amendments apply

510

The Secretary of State, in exercise of the powers conferred by section 150(3) and (4)(a), (b)(i) and (c) of the Welfare Reform Act 2012, makes the following Order:

Citation

1. This Order may be cited as the Welfare Reform Act 2012 (Commencement No. 9, 11, 13, 14, 16 and 17 and Transitional and Transitory Provisions (Amendment) (No. 2)) Order 2014. **6.233**

Interpretation

2. (1) In this Order— **6.234**

"the Act" means the Welfare Reform Act 2012;

"the 1995 Act" means the Jobseekers Act 1995;

"the 2007 Act" means the Welfare Reform Act 2007;

"claimant", in relation to an employment and support allowance or a jobseeker's allowance, has the same meaning as in Part 1 of the 2007 Act and the 1995 Act (as it applies apart from the amendments made by Part 1 of Schedule 14 to the Act that remove references to an income-based jobseeker's allowance) respectively and, in relation to universal credit, has the same meaning as in Part 1 of the Act;

"the Claims and Payments Regulations 2013" means the Universal Credit, Personal Independence Payment, Jobseeker's Allowance and Employment and Support Allowance (Claims and Payments) Regulations 2013;

"employment and support allowance" means an employment and support allowance under Part 1 of the 2007 Act;

"jobseeker's allowance" means a jobseeker's allowance under the 1995 Act;

"joint claimants", in relation to universal credit, has the same meaning as in Part 1 of the Act;

"the No. 9 Order" means the Welfare Reform Act 2012 (Commencement No. 9 and Transitional and Transitory Provisions and Commencement No. 8 and Savings and Transitional Provisions (Amendment)) Order 2013;

"the No. 11 Order" means the Welfare Reform Act 2012 (Commencement No. 11 and Transitional and Transitory Provisions and Commencement No. 9 and Transitional and Transitory Provisions (Amendment)) Order 2013;

"the No. 13 Order" means the Welfare Reform Act 2012 (Commencement No. 13 and Transitional and Transitory Provisions) Order 2013;

"the No. 14 Order" means the Welfare Reform Act 2012 (Commencement No. 14 and Transitional and Transitory Provisions) Order 2013;

"the No. 16 Order" means the Welfare Reform Act 2012 (Commencement No. 16 and Transitional and Transitory Provisions) Order 2014;

"the No. 17 Order" means the Welfare Reform Act 2012 (Commencement No. 17 and Transitional and Transitory Provisions) Order 2014;

"relevant districts" has the meaning given in the No. 9 Order;

"No. 2 relevant districts" and "No. 3 relevant districts" have the meanings given in the No. 11 Order;

"No. 4 relevant districts" has the meaning given in the No. 13 Order;

"No. 5 relevant districts" has the meaning given in the No. 14 Order;

"No. 6 relevant districts" and "No. 7 relevant districts" have the meanings given in the No. 16 Order;

"No. 8 relevant districts", "No. 9 relevant districts", "No. 10 relevant districts", "No. 11 relevant districts", "No. 12 relevant districts" and "No. 13 relevant districts" have the meanings given in the No. 17 Order;

"single claimant", in relation to universal credit, has the same meaning as in Part 1 of the Act;

"specified districts" means the relevant districts, No. 2 relevant districts, No. 3 relevant districts, No. 4 relevant districts, No. 5 relevant districts, No. 6 relevant districts, No. 7 relevant districts, No. 8 relevant districts, No. 9 relevant districts, No. 10 relevant districts, No. 11 relevant districts, No. 12 relevant districts and No. 13 relevant districts.

(2) For the purposes of this Order—

(a) the Claims and Payments Regulations 2013 apply for the purpose of deciding—

    (i) whether a claim for universal credit is made or treated as made; and

    (ii) the date on which such a claim is made;

(b) where a couple is treated, in accordance with regulation 9(8) of the Claims and Payments Regulations 2013, as making a claim for universal credit, references to the date on which the claim is treated as made are to the date of formation of the couple; and

(c) the Social Security (Claims and Payments) Regulations 1987 apply for the purpose of deciding—

    (i) whether a claim for an employment and support allowance or a jobseeker's allowance is made; and

    (ii) the date on which such a claim is made or is to be treated as made.

Amendment of the No. 9, 11, 13, 14, 16 and 17 Orders: cases to which the amendments apply

3. This article applies in relation to a case where— **6.235**

(a) a claim is made for universal credit, an employment and support allowance or a jobseeker's allowance and, on the date on which the claim is made or treated as made, the claimant resides in one of the specified districts;

(b) a claim for universal credit is made and it is subsequently discovered by the Secretary of State that—

   (i) in the case of a single claimant, the claimant gave incorrect information regarding the claimant residing in a specified district and the claimant did not reside in such a district on the date on which the claim was made; or

   (ii) in the case of joint claimants, either or both of the joint claimants gave incorrect information regarding his or her (or their) residing in such a district and one or both of them did not reside in such a district on the date on which the claim was made;

(c) a claim for universal credit is treated as made by a couple in the circumstances referred to in regulation 9(8) of the Claims and Payments Regulations 2013 (claims for universal credit by members of a couple);

(d) a claim for universal credit is made by a former member of a couple who were joint claimants of universal credit, whether or not the claim is made jointly with another person, where the former member is not exempt from the requirement to make a claim by virtue of regulation 9(6) of the Claims and Payments Regulations 2013 (claims for universal credit by members of a couple), where the claim is made during the period of one month starting with the date on which notification is given to the Secretary of State that the former joint claimants have ceased to be a couple;

(e) an award of universal credit is made without a claim in the circumstances referred to in regulation 6(1) or (2) of the Claims and Payments Regulations 2013 (claims not required for entitlement to universal credit in some cases); or

(f) an award of universal credit is made without a claim in the circumstances referred to in regulation 9(6), (7) or (10) of the Claims and Payments Regulations 2013 (claims for universal credit by members of a couple),

and the claim for universal credit, an employment and support allowance or a jobseeker's allowance is made or treated as made, or, as the case may be, the award of universal credit is made without a claim, on or after 28th July 2014.

Amendment of the No. 9 Order

4. *[Amendments incorporated into No. 9 Order]* **6.236**

Application of parts of the No. 9 Order amended by article 4

6.237   **5.** Where article 3 applies, any reference—
  (a) in the No. 11 Order and the No. 17 Order to article 5(1) of, or Schedule 5 to, the No. 9 Order is a reference to those provisions as amended by article 4(6)(a) and (7) respectively;
  (b) in the No. 11 Order, the No. 13 Order, the No. 14 Order, the No. 16 Order and the No. 17 Order to article 5(7) of the No. 9 Order is a reference to that provision as amended by article 4(6)(c).

Amendment of the No. 11 Order

6.238   **6.** *[Amendments incorporated into No.11 Order]*

Amendment of the No. 13 Order

6.239   **7.** *[Amendments incorporated into No. 13 Order]*

Amendment of the No. 14 Order

6.240   **8.** *[Amendments incorporated into No. 14 Order]*

Amendment of the No. 16 Order

6.241   **9.** *[Amendments incorporated into No. 16 Order]*

Amendment of the No. 17 Order

6.242   **10.** *[Amendments incorporated into No. 17 Order]*

The Welfare Reform Act 2012 (Commencement No. 19 and Transitional and Transitory Provisions and Commencement No. 9 and Transitional and Transitory Provisions (Amendment)) Order 2014

(SI 2014/2321) (C.99) (as amended)

6.243   ARRANGEMENT OF ARTICLES

1. Citation
2. Interpretation
3. Day appointed for the coming into force of the universal credit provisions
4. Day appointed for the abolition of income-related employment and support allowance and income-based jobseeker's allowance
5. Application of the No. 9 Order
6. Day appointed for the coming into force of section 41 of the Act.
7. Amendment of the No. 9 Order

SCHEDULE: POSTCODE DISTRICTS AND PART-DISTRICTS

The Secretary of State makes the following Order in exercise of the powers conferred by sections 150(3) and (4)(a), (b)(i) and (c) of the Welfare Reform Act 2012:

GENERAL NOTE

This Commencement Order ("the Commencement No. 19 Order") extended **6.244** the universal credit scheme to certain postcode districts in a wide range of different areas (known as the No. 14, No. 15, No. 16, No. 17, No. 18, No. 19, No. 20, No. 21, No. 22, No. 23, No. 24, No. 25, No. 26 or No. 27 relevant districts—see Schedule). In addition, of course, the claimant must meet the gateway conditions in Sch.5 to the Commencement No. 9 Order.

Citation

1. This Order may be cited as the Welfare Reform Act 2012 (Com- **6.245** mencement No. 19 and Transitional and Transitory Provisions and Commencement No. 9 and Transitional and Transitory Provisions (Amendment)) Order 2014.

Interpretation

2. (1) In this Order— **6.246**

"the Act" means the Welfare Reform Act 2012;

"the amending provisions" means the provisions referred to in article 4(1)(a) to (c) of the No. 9 Order (day appointed for the abolition of income-related employment and support allowance and income-based jobseeker's allowance);

[¹ "claimant"—

    (a) in relation to an employment and support allowance, has the same meaning as in Part 1 of the Welfare Reform Act 2007, save as mentioned in article 5(1A) of the No. 9 Order as applied by article 4(7);

    (b) in relation to a jobseeker's allowance, has the same meaning as in the Jobseekers Act 1995 (as it applies apart from the amendments made by Part 1 of Schedule 14 to the Act that remove references to an income-based jobseeker's allowance), save as mentioned in article 5(1A) of the No. 9 Order as applied by article 4(7);

    (c) in relation to universal credit, has the same meaning as in Part 1 of the Act;]

"employment and support allowance" means an employment and support allowance under Part 1 of the Welfare Reform Act 2007;

"First-tier Tribunal" has the same meaning as in the Social Security Act 1998;

"gateway conditions" means the conditions specified in Schedule 5 to the No. 9 Order;

"jobseeker's allowance" means a jobseeker's allowance under the Jobseekers Act 1995;

"joint claimants", in relation to universal credit, has the same meaning as in Part 1 of the Act;

"the No. 9 Order" means the Welfare Reform Act 2012 (Commencement No. 9 and Transitional and Transitory Provisions and Commencement No. 8 and Savings and Transitional Provisions (Amendment)) Order 2013;

"No. 14 relevant districts" means the postcode districts and part-districts specified in Part 1 of the Schedule;

"No. 15 relevant districts" means the postcode districts and part-districts specified in Part 2 of the Schedule;

"No. 16 relevant districts" means the postcode districts and part-districts specified in Part 3 of the Schedule;

"No. 17 relevant districts" means the postcode districts and part-districts specified in Part 4 of the Schedule;

"No. 18 relevant districts" means the postcode districts and part-districts specified in Part 5 of the Schedule;

"No. 19 relevant districts" means the postcode districts and part-districts specified in Part 6 of the Schedule;

"No. 20 relevant districts" means the postcode districts and part-districts specified in Part 7 of the Schedule;

"No. 21 relevant districts" means the postcode districts and part-districts specified in Part 8 of the Schedule;

"No. 22 relevant districts" means the postcode districts and part-districts specified in Part 9 of the Schedule;

"No. 23 relevant districts" means the postcode districts and part-districts specified in Part 10 of the Schedule;

"No. 24 relevant districts" means the postcode districts and part-districts specified in Part 11 of the Schedule;

"No. 25 relevant districts" means the postcode districts and part-districts specified in Part 12 of the Schedule;

"No. 26 relevant districts" means the postcode districts and part-districts specified in Part 13 of the Schedule;

"No. 27 relevant districts" means the postcode districts and part-districts specified in Part 14 of the Schedule;

"single claimant", in relation to universal credit, has the same meaning as in Part 1 of the Act;

"Upper Tribunal" has the same meaning as in the Social Security Act 1998.

(2) For the purposes of this Order, the Universal Credit, Personal Independence Payment, Jobseeker's Allowance and Employment and Support Allowance (Claims and Payments) Regulations 2013 apply for the purpose of deciding—

(a) whether a claim for universal credit is made; and

(b) the date on which such a claim is made.

AMENDMENTS

1. Welfare Reform Act 2012 (Commencement No. 9, 11, 13 14, 16, 17 and 19 and Transitional and Transitory Provisions (Amendment)) Order 2014 (SI 2014/3067) art.6(3) (November 24, 2014).

Day appointed for the coming into force of the universal credit provisions

3. (1) The day appointed for the coming into force of the provisions of 6.247 the Act listed in Schedule 2 to the No. 9 Order, in so far as they are not already in force, in relation to the case of a claim referred to in paragraph (2), and any award that is made in respect of the claim, is the day appointed in accordance with paragraph (3).

(2) The claims referred to are—

(a) a claim for universal credit that is made on or after 15th September 2014 in respect of a period that begins on or after 15th September 2014 where, on the date on which the claim is made, the claimant resides in one of the No. 14 relevant districts and meets the gateway conditions;

(b) a claim for universal credit that is made on or after 22nd September 2014 in respect of a period that begins on or after 22nd September 2014 where, on the date on which the claim is made, the claimant resides in one of the No. 15 relevant districts and meets the gateway conditions;

(c) a claim for universal credit that is made on or after 29th September 2014 in respect of a period that begins on or after 29th September 2014 where, on the date on which the claim is made, the claimant resides in one of the No. 16 relevant districts and meets the gateway conditions;

(d) a claim for universal credit that is made on or after 6th October 2014 in respect of a period that begins on or after 6th October 2014 where, on the date on which the claim is made, the claimant resides in one of the No. 17 relevant districts and meets the gateway conditions;

(e) a claim for universal credit that is made on or after 13th October 2014 in respect of a period that begins on or after 13th October 2014 where, on the date on which the claim is made, the claimant resides in one of the No. 18 relevant districts and meets the gateway conditions;

(f) a claim for universal credit that is made on or after 20th October 2014 in respect of a period that begins on or after 20th October 2014 where, on the date on which the claim is made, the claimant resides in one of the No. 19 relevant districts and meets the gateway conditions;

(g) a claim for universal credit that is made on or after 27th October 2014 in respect of a period that begins on or after 27th October 2014 where, on the date on which the claim is made, the claimant resides in one of the No. 20 relevant districts and meets the gateway conditions;

(h) a claim for universal credit that is made on or after 3rd November 2014 in respect of a period that begins on or after 3rd November 2014 where, on the date on which the claim is made, the claimant resides in one of the No. 21 relevant districts and meets the gateway conditions;

(i) a claim for universal credit that is made on or after 10th November 2014 in respect of a period that begins on or after 10th November 2014 where, on the date on which the claim is made, the claimant resides in one of the No. 22 relevant districts and meets the gateway conditions;

(j) a claim for universal credit that is made on or after 17th November 2014 in respect of a period that begins on or after 17th November 2014 where, on the date on which the claim is made, the claimant resides in one of the No. 23 relevant districts and meets the gateway conditions;

(k) a claim for universal credit that is made on or after 24th November 2014 in respect of a period that begins on or after 24th November 2014 where, on the date on which the claim is made, the claimant resides in one of the No. 24 relevant districts and meets the gateway conditions;

(l) a claim for universal credit that is made on or after 1st December 2014 in respect of a period that begins on or after 1st December 2014 where, on the date on which the claim is made, the claimant resides in one of the No. 25 relevant districts and meets the gateway conditions;

(m) a claim for universal credit that is made on or after 8th December 2014 in respect of a period that begins on or after 8th December 2014 where, on the date on which the claim is made, the claimant resides in one of the No. 26 relevant districts and meets the gateway conditions;

(n) a claim for universal credit that is made on or after 15th December 2014 in respect of a period that begins on or after 15th December 2014 where, on the date on which the claim is made, the claimant resides in one of the No. 27 relevant districts and meets the gateway conditions;

(o) a claim for universal credit that is made on or after the date referred to in any of sub-paragraphs (a) to (n), in respect of a period that begins on or after that date where—

    (i) in the case of a single claimant, the claimant gives incorrect information regarding the claimant residing in a district as referred to in the sub-paragraph in question or meeting the gateway conditions and the claimant does not reside in such a district or does not meet the gateway conditions on the date on which the claim is made;

    (ii) in the case of joint claimants, either or both of the joint claimants gives or give incorrect information regarding his or her (or their) residing in such a district or meeting the gateway conditions and one or both of them does not or do not reside in such a district or does not or do not meet those conditions on the date on which the claim is made, and after a decision is made that the single claimant is, or the joint claimants are, entitled to universal credit and one or more payments have been made in respect of the single claimant or the joint claimants, the Secretary of State discovers that incorrect information has been given regarding residence or meeting the gateway conditions.

(3) The day appointed in relation to the case of a claim referred to in paragraph (2), and any award that is made in respect of the claim, is the first day of the period in respect of which the claim is made.

(4) Article 3(6) of the No. 9 Order applies for the purposes of paragraph (3) as it applies for the purposes of article 3(4)(a) of the No. 9 Order.

(5) Article 3A of the No. 9 Order applies in connection with a claim for universal credit where a single claimant, or, as the case may be, either or both of joint claimants, gives incorrect information regarding his or her (or their) residing in a No. 14, No. 15, No. 16, No. 17, No. 18, No. 19, No. 20, No. 21, No. 22, No. 23, No. 24, No. 25, No. 26 or No. 27 relevant district or meeting the gateway conditions, as it applies in connection with the giving of incorrect information regarding a claimant residing in a relevant district (as defined in the No. 9 Order) or meeting the gateway conditions.

Day appointed for the abolition of income-related employment and support allowance and income-based jobseeker's allowance

4. (1) The day appointed for the coming into force of the amending provisions, in relation to the case of a claim referred to in paragraph (2), and any award that is made in respect of the claim, is the day appointed in accordance with paragraph (3). **6.248**

(2) The claims referred to are—

(a) a claim for universal credit, an employment and support allowance or a jobseeker's allowance that is made or treated as made on or after 15th September 2014 in respect of a period that begins on or after 15th September 2014 where, on the date on which the claim is made or treated as made, the claimant resides in one of the No. 14 relevant districts and meets the gateway conditions;

(b) a claim for universal credit, an employment and support allowance or a jobseeker's allowance that is made or treated as made on or after 22nd September 2014 in respect of a period that begins on or after 22nd September 2014 where, on the date on which the claim is made or treated as made, the claimant resides in one of the No. 15 relevant districts and meets the gateway conditions;

(c) a claim for universal credit, an employment and support allowance or a jobseeker's allowance that is made or treated as made on or after 29th September 2014 in respect of a period that begins on or after 29th September 2014 where, on the date on which the claim is made or treated as made, the claimant resides in one of the No. 16 relevant districts and meets the gateway conditions;

(d) a claim for universal credit, an employment and support allowance or a jobseeker's allowance that is made or treated as made on or after 6th October 2014 in respect of a period that begins on or after 6th October 2014 where, on the date on which the claim is made or treated as made, the claimant resides in one of the No. 17 relevant districts and meets the gateway conditions;

(e) a claim for universal credit, an employment and support allowance or a jobseeker's allowance that is made or treated as made on or after 13th October 2014 in respect of a period that begins on or after 13th October 2014 where, on the date on which the claim is made or treated as made, the claimant resides in one of the No. 18 relevant districts and meets the gateway conditions;

(f) a claim for universal credit, an employment and support allowance or a jobseeker's allowance that is made or treated as made on or after 20th October 2014 in respect of a period that begins on or after 20th October 2014 where, on the date on which the claim is made or treated as made, the claimant resides in one of the No. 19 relevant districts and meets the gateway conditions;

(g) a claim for universal credit, an employment and support allowance or a jobseeker's allowance that is made or treated as made on or after 27th October 2014 in respect of a period that begins on or after 27th October 2014 where, on the date on which the claim is made or treated as made, the claimant resides in one of the No. 20 relevant districts and meets the gateway conditions;

(h) a claim for universal credit, an employment and support allowance or a jobseeker's allowance that is made or treated as made on or after 3rd November 2014 in respect of a period that begins on or after 3rd November 2014 where, on the date on which the claim is made or treated as made, the claimant resides in one of the No. 21 relevant districts and meets the gateway conditions;

(i) a claim for universal credit, an employment and support allowance or a jobseeker's allowance that is made or treated as made on or after 10th November 2014 in respect of a period that begins on or after 10th November 2014 where, on the date on which the claim is made or treated as made, the claimant resides in one of the No. 22 relevant districts and meets the gateway conditions;

(j) a claim for universal credit, an employment and support allowance or a jobseeker's allowance that is made or treated as made on or after 17th November 2014 in respect of a period that begins on or after 17th November 2014 where, on the date on which the claim is made or treated as made, the claimant resides in one of the No. 23 relevant districts and meets the gateway conditions;

(k) a claim for universal credit, an employment and support allowance or a jobseeker's allowance that is made or treated as made on or after 24th November 2014 in respect of a period that begins on or after 24th November 2014 where, on the date on which the claim is made or treated as made, the claimant resides in one of the No. 24 relevant districts and meets the gateway conditions;

(l) a claim for universal credit, an employment and support allowance or a jobseeker's allowance that is made or treated as made on or after 1st December 2014 in respect of a period that begins on or after 1st December 2014 where, on the date on which the claim is made or treated as made, the claimant resides in one of the No. 25 relevant districts and meets the gateway conditions;

(m) a claim for universal credit, an employment and support allowance or a jobseeker's allowance that is made or treated as made on or after 8th December 2014 in respect of a period that begins on or after 8th December 2014 where, on the date on which the claim is made or treated as made, the claimant resides in one of the No. 26 relevant districts and meets the gateway conditions;

(n) a claim for universal credit, an employment and support allowance or a jobseeker's allowance that is made or treated as made on or after 15th December 2014 in respect of a period that begins on or after 15th December 2014 where, on the date on which the claim is made or treated as made, the claimant resides in one of the No. 27 relevant districts and meets the gateway conditions;

(o) a claim for universal credit that is made on or after the date referred to in any of sub-paragraphs (a) to (n), in respect of a period that begins on or after that date where—

    (i) in the case of a single claimant, the claimant gives incorrect information regarding the claimant residing in a district as referred to in the sub-paragraph in question or meeting the gateway conditions and the claimant does not reside in such a district or does not meet the gateway conditions on the date on which the claim is made;

    (ii) in the case of joint claimants, either or both of the joint claimants gives or give incorrect information regarding his or her (or their) residing in such a district or meeting the gateway conditions and one or both of them does not or do not reside in such a district or does not or do not meet those conditions on the date on which the claim is made,

and after a decision is made that the single claimant is, or the joint claimants are, entitled to universal credit and one or more payments have been made in respect of the single claimant or the joint claimants, the Secretary of State discovers that incorrect information has been given regarding residence or meeting the gateway conditions;

(p) a claim for an employment and support allowance or a jobseeker's allowance other than one referred to in sub-paragraphs (a) to (n) that is made or treated as made during the relevant period by a single claimant of universal credit or by either of two joint claimants of universal credit who has or have made a claim for universal credit within one of sub-paragraphs (a) to (o).

(3) The day appointed in relation to the case of a claim referred to in paragraph (2), and any award that is made in respect of the claim, is the first day of the period in respect of which the claim is made.

(4) For the purposes of paragraph (2)(p), "relevant period" means, in relation to a claim for universal credit within paragraph (2)(a) to (o), any UC claim period, and any period subsequent to any UC claim period in

respect of which the claimant is entitled to an award of universal credit in respect of the claim.

(5) For the purposes of paragraph (4), a "UC claim period" is a period when—

    (a) a claim for universal credit within one of sub-paragraphs (a) to (n) of paragraph (2), or within sub-paragraph (o)(i) or (ii) of that paragraph, has been made but a decision has not yet been made on the claim; or

    (b) a decision has been made that the claimant is not entitled to universal credit and—

        (i) the Secretary of State is considering whether to revise that decision under section 9 of the Social Security Act 1998, whether on an application made for that purpose, or on the Secretary of State's own initiative; or

        (ii) the claimant has appealed against that decision to the First-tier Tribunal and that appeal or any subsequent appeal to the Upper Tribunal or to a court has not been finally determined.

(6) Paragraphs (6) and (7) of article 4 of the No. 9 Order apply in relation to a claim for universal credit referred to in paragraph (2) (and any award that is made in respect of the claim) as they apply in relation to a claim for universal credit referred to in sub-paragraphs (a) and (b) of article 4(2) of the No. 9 Order (and any award that is made in respect of the claim).

[¹ (7) Paragraphs (1) to (1B) of article 5 of the No. 9 Order apply for the purposes of paragraph (2)(a) to (n) as they apply for the purposes of article 4(2)(a) of the No. 9 Order.]

(8) Paragraphs (5) to (7) of article 5 of the No. 9 Order apply for the purposes of sub-paragraphs (a) to (n) and (p) of paragraph (2) as they apply for the purposes of sub-paragraphs (a) and (g) of article 4(2) of the No. 9 Order.

(9) Article 5(8) of the No. 9 Order applies for the purposes of paragraph (3) as it applies for the purposes of article 4(3)(a) of the No. 9 Order.

AMENDMENTS

    1. Welfare Reform Act 2012 (Commencement No. 9, 11, 13 14, 16, 17 and 19 and Transitional and Transitory Provisions (Amendment)) Order 2014 (SI 2014/3067) art.6(6) (November 24, 2014).

Application of the No. 9 Order

6.249   **5.** Articles 9 to 22 of the No. 9 Order apply in connection with the coming into force of the amending provisions in relation to the case of a claim referred to in article 4(2), and any award made in respect of the claim, as they apply in connection with the coming into force of the amending provisions in relation to the case of a claim referred to in sub-paragraphs (a), (b) and (g) of article 4(2) of the No. 9 Order and any award made in respect of the claim.

Day appointed for the coming into force of section 41 of the Act.

6. 15th September 2014 is the day appointed for the coming into force of section 41 of the Act (pilot schemes) for all purposes.   **6.250**

Amendment of the No. 9 Order

7. *(Amendments incorporated into text of No. 9 Order)*   **6.251**

SCHEDULE   **6.252**

Article 2(1)

POSTCODE DISTRICTS AND PART-DISTRICTS

PART 1

THE NO. 14 RELEVANT DISTRICTS

BL9 7.
L31 1.
L31 4.
L33 3 and L33 4.
L37 0.
L37 5.
L37 9.
L39.
L40 0 and L40 1.
L40 4 to L40 9.
M24 0 to M24 2.
M24 5 and M24 6.
OL10.
OL11.
OL12 6.
OL12 9.
OL15 0.
OL15 8.
OL16.
PR8 3 to PR8 5.
PR9 8.
WA11 7.
WN8.

PART 2   **6.252**

THE NO. 15 RELEVANT DISTRICTS

L10 1.
L10 4 and L10 5.
L10 7.
L14.
L15.
L18 0 to L18 2.
L18 5.
L20 1 and L20 2.
L20 7 to L20 9.
L28 0 and L28 1.
L28 8.
L36 5.
M4.

M7 4.
M8.
M9.
M22 0 to M22 2.
M22 5.
M22 8 and M22 9.
M23.
M24 4.
M25 0.
M25 2.
M33 3.
M40.
WA15 0.
WA15 7 and WA15 8.

6.253   PART 3

THE NO. 16 RELEVANT DISTRICTS

L1.
L2.
L3.
L4 0 to L4 4.
L4 7.
L5.
L6.
L7.
L8.
L17 1 to L17 4.
L17 7 to L17 9.

6.254   PART 4

THE NO. 17 RELEVANT DISTRICTS

BB4.
BB5.
BB8.
BB9 0.
BB9 4 and BB9 5.
BB9 7 to BB9 9.
BB10.
BB11.
BB12 0.
BB12 6.
BB12 8.
BB18 5.
BB18 9.
BL0 0.
BL9 6.
OL12 0.
OL12 7 and OL12 8.
OL13.

6.255   PART 5

THE NO. 18 RELEVANT DISTRICTS

BL5 2.
M29.
M46.

WA3 1 to WA3 3.
WN4.
WN7.

PART 6   **6.256**

THE NO. 19 RELEVANT DISTRICTS

L4 6.
L4 8 and L4 9.
L11.
M15.
M16.
SK10.
SK11 6 to SK11 9.

PART 7   **6.257**

THE NO. 20 RELEVANT DISTRICTS

L4 5.
L9.
L12.
L13.
L16.
L17 0.
L17 5 and L17 6.
L18 3 and L18 4.
L18 6 to L18 9.
L19.
L24 0 to L24 3.
L24 6 to L24 9.
L25.
L26.
L27.

PART 8   **6.258**

THE NO. 21 RELEVANT DISTRICTS

FY5.
FY6.
FY7.
PR4 0.

PART 9   **6.259**

THE NO. 22 RELEVANT DISTRICTS

M12.
M13.
M14.
M19 0.
M21.

PART 10   **6.260**

THE NO. 23 RELEVANT DISTRICTS

L24 4 and L24 5.
L35 6.

M11.
M18.
M19 1 to M19 3.
M20.
M22 4.
SK1.
SK2.
SK3.
SK4.
SK5.
SK6.
SK7.
SK8.
SK12.
SK14 3.
SK14 5.
WA7.
WA8.

6.261

PART 11

THE NO. 24 RELEVANT DISTRICTS

BB1.
BB2.
BB3.
BB6 7 and BB6 8.
BB9 6.
BB12 7.
BB12 9.
BL6 5 to BL6 7.
BL7.
BL8 4.
L40 2 and L40 3.
PR4 6.
PR5 0.
PR5 6.
PR5 8.
PR6.
PR7.
PR25 4 and PR25 5.
PR26 7 to PR26 9.

6.262

PART 12

THE NO. 25 RELEVANT DISTRICTS

CH64.
CH65.
CH66.
CW6.
CW7.
CW8.
CW9.
M1.
M2.
M3.
M5.
M6.
M7 1 to M7 3.
M27 4.

M27 6.
M50.

PART 13

THE NO. 26 RELEVANT DISTRICTS

FY1.
FY2.
FY3.
FY4.
FY8.
LA1.
LA2 0.
LA2 6.
LA2 9.
LA3.
LA4.
LA5 0.
LA5 8 and LA5 9.
LA6 1 and LA6 2.
LA7.
LA8.
LA9.
LA11.
LA12.
LA13.
LA14.
LA15.
LA16.
LA17.
LA18.
LA19.
LA20.
LA21.
LA22.
LA23.
M44.
PR3.
PR4 1 to PR4 3.

PART 14

THE NO. 27 RELEVANT DISTRICTS

BB7.
CA1.
CA2.
CA3.
CA4.
CA5.
CA6.
CA7.
CA8 0 and CA8 1.
CA8 9.
CA10 1 to CA10 3.
CA11.
CA12.
CA13.
CA14.
CA15.

CA16.
CA17.
CA18.
CA19.
CA20.
CA21.
CA22.
CA23.
CA24.
CA25.
CA26.
CA27.
CA28.

The Welfare Reform Act 2012 (Commencement No. 9, 11, 13 14, 16, 17 and 19 and Transitional and Transitory Provisions (Amendment)) Order 2014

SI 2014/3067 (C.129)

6.265 ARRANGEMENT OF ARTICLES

The Secretary of State for Work and Pensions makes the following Order in exercise of the powers conferred by sections 150(3) and (4)(a), (b)(i) and (c) of the Welfare Reform Act 2012

Citation

6.266 **1.** This Order may be cited as the Welfare Reform Act 2012 (Commencement No. 9, 11, 13, 14, 16, 17 and 19 and Transitional and Transitory Provisions (Amendment)) Order 2014.

Interpretation

6.267 **2.** (1) In this Order—

"the Act" means the Welfare Reform Act 2012;
"claimant"—
(a) in relation to an employment and support allowance, has the same meaning as in Part 1 of the Welfare Reform Act 2007;

(b) in relation to a jobseeker's allowance, has the same meaning as in the Jobseekers Act 1995 (as it applies apart from the amendments made by Part 1 of Schedule 14 to the Act that remove references to an income-based jobseeker's allowance);

(c) in relation to universal credit, has the same meaning as in Part 1 of the Act;

"employment and support allowance" means an employment and support allowance under Part 1 of the Welfare Reform Act 2007;

"jobseeker's allowance" means a jobseeker's allowance under the Jobseekers Act 1995;

"joint claimants", in relation to universal credit, has the same meaning as in Part 1 of the Act;

"the No. 9 Order" means the Welfare Reform Act 2012 (Commencement No. 9 and Transitional and Transitory Provisions and Commencement No. 8 and Savings and Transitional Provisions (Amendment)) Order 2013;

"the No. 11 Order" means the Welfare Reform Act 2012 (Commencement No. 11 and Transitional and Transitory Provisions and Commencement No. 9 and Transitional and Transitory Provisions (Amendment)) Order 2013;

"the No. 13 Order" means the Welfare Reform Act 2012 (Commencement No. 13 and Transitional and Transitory Provisions) Order 2013;

"the No. 14 Order" means the Welfare Reform Act 2012 (Commencement No. 14 and Transitional and Transitory Provisions) Order 2013;

"the No. 16 Order" means the Welfare Reform Act 2012 (Commencement No. 16 and Transitional and Transitory Provisions) Order 2014;

"the No. 17 Order" means the Welfare Reform Act 2012 (Commencement No. 17 and Transitional and Transitory Provisions) Order 2014;

"the No. 19 Order" means the Welfare Reform Act 2012 (Commencement No. 19 and Transitional and Transitory Provisions and Commencement No. 9 and Transitional and Transitory Provisions (Amendment)) Order 2014;

"prescribed districts" means the relevant districts and the areas each of which is described by a number preceding the expression "relevant districts" as specified in article 2(1) of the No. 11 Order, the No. 13 Order, the No. 14 Order, the No. 16 Order, the No. 17 Order and the No. 19 Order;

"relevant districts" has the same meaning as in the No. 9 Order;

"single claimant", in relation to universal credit, has the same meaning as in Part 1 of the Act.

(2) For the purposes of this Order—

(a) the Universal Credit, Personal Independence Payment, Jobseeker's Allowance and Employment and Support Allowance (Claims and Payments) Regulations 2013 apply for the purpose of deciding—

      (i) whether a claim for universal credit is made; and

      (ii) the date on which such a claim is made; and

(b) the Social Security (Claims and Payments) Regulations 1987 apply for the purpose of deciding—

      (i) whether a claim for an employment and support allowance or a jobseeker's allowance is made; and

      (ii) the date on which such a claim is made or is to be treated as made.

Amendment of the No. 9, No. 11, No. 13, No. 14, No. 16, No. 17 and No. 19 Orders: cases to which the amendments apply

6.268

3. Articles 4 to 6 apply where—

(a) a claim is made for universal credit, an employment and support allowance or a jobseeker's allowance and, on the date on which the claim is made or treated as made, the claimant resides in one of the prescribed districts; or

(b) a claim for universal credit is made where—

      (i) in the case of a single claimant, the claimant gives incorrect information regarding the claimant residing in a prescribed district and does not reside in such a district on the date on which the claim is made; or

      (ii) in the case of joint claimants, either or both of the joint claimants gives or give incorrect information regarding his or her (or their) residing in such a district and one or both of them does not or do not reside in such a district on the date on which the claim is made,

and where the claim is made or treated as made on or after 24th November 2014.

Amendment of the No. 11 Order: the gateway conditions

6.269

4. *(Amendments incorporated into text of No. 11 Order)*

Amendment of the No. 17 Order: the gateway conditions

6.270

5. *(Amendments incorporated into text of No. 17 Order)*

Meaning of "claimant": amendment of the No. 9, No. 11, No. 13, No. 14, No. 16, No. 17 and No. 19 Orders

6.271

6. *(Amendments incorporated into text of No. 9, No. 11, No. 13, No. 14, No. 16, No. 17 and No. 19 Orders)*

Amendment of the No. 9 Order: transitional provisions on waiting periods

6.272

7. With effect from 24th November 2014—

(a) in articles 10(2)(gb), 11(2)(gb), 12(3)(b) and 13(3)(b)(i) of the No. 9 Order (transition from old style ESA to new style ESA and vice versa; transition from old style JSA to new style JSA and vice versa)(1), for "the second or third day of that period" substitute "a day between the second and the seventh day of that period (including the second and the seventh day)"; and

(b) any reference in the No. 11 Order, the No. 13 Order, the No. 14 Order, the No. 16 Order, the No. 17 Order or the No. 19 Order to article 10, 11, 12 or 13 of the No. 9 Order is a reference to that article as amended by paragraph (a).

The Welfare Reform Act 2012 (Commencement No. 20 and Transitional and Transitory Provisions and Commencement No. 9 and Transitional and Transitory Provisions (Amendment)) Order 2014

(SI 2014/3094) (C.133)

ARRANGEMENT OF ARTICLES

6.273

The Secretary of State for Work and Pensions makes the following Order in exercise of the powers conferred by sections 150(3) and (4)(a), (b)(i) and (c) of the Welfare Reform Act 2012:

GENERAL NOTE

This Commencement Order ("the Commencement No. 20 Order") extended the universal credit scheme to the part postcode district in Sutton (SM5 2) known as "the No. 28 relevant district". This applied for a limited period only, namely November 26, 2014 until December 20, 2014. In this instance there was no further requirement that the claimant had to meet the gateway conditions (in Sch.5 to the Commencement No. 9 Order). This is because this extension involved the testing of the enhanced digital service for universal credit for the full scope of universal credit households in a limited area (i.e. the part postcode SM5 2). See also the Universal Credit (Digital Service) Amendment Regulations 2014 (SI 2014/2887), introduced with effect from 26 November 2014, which were limited to any claimant who lived in the digital trial area and who was referred to as a 'Digital service claimant'. There is no Schedule to this Commencement Order as the relevant part postcode area is simply defined by reference to the definition of "the No. 28 relevant district" in art.2(1).

6.274

Citation

6.275   **1.** This Order may be cited as the Welfare Reform Act 2012 (Commencement No. 20 and Transitional and Transitory Provisions and Commencement No. 9 and Transitional and Transitory Provisions (Amendment)) Order 2014.

Interpretation

6.276   **2.** (1) In this Order—

"the Act" means the Welfare Reform Act 2012;

"the 1998 Act" means the Social Security Act 1998;

"the amending provisions" means the provisions referred to in article 4(1)(a) to (c) of the No. 9 Order (day appointed for the abolition of income-related employment and support allowance and income-based jobseeker's allowance);

"claimant"—

(a) in relation to an employment and support allowance, has the same meaning as in Part 1 of the Welfare Reform Act 2007, save as mentioned in article 5(1A) of the No. 9 Order as applied by article 4(7);

(b) in relation to a jobseeker's allowance, has the same meaning as in the Jobseekers Act 1995 (as it applies apart from the amendments made by Part 1 of Schedule 14 to the Act that remove references to an income-based jobseeker's allowance), save as mentioned in article 5(1A) of the No. 9 Order as applied by article 4(7);

(c) in relation to universal credit, has the same meaning as in Part 1 of the Act;

"the Claims and Payments Regulations 2013" means the Universal Credit, Personal Independence Payment, Jobseeker's Allowance and Employment and Support Allowance (Claims and Payments) Regulations 2013;

"the Digital Service Regulations 2014" means the Universal Credit (Digital Service) Amendment Regulations 2014;

"employment and support allowance" means an employment and support allowance under Part 1 of the Welfare Reform Act 2007;

"First-tier Tribunal" has the same meaning as in the 1998 Act;

"housing benefit" means housing benefit under section 130 of the Social Security Contributions and Benefits Act 1992;

"income support" means income support under section 124 of the Social Security Contributions and Benefits Act 1992;

"jobseeker's allowance" means a jobseeker's allowance under the Jobseekers Act 1995;

"joint claimants", in relation to universal credit, has the same meaning as in Part 1 of the Act;

"the No. 9 Order" means the Welfare Reform Act 2012 (Commencement No. 9 and Transitional and Transitory Provisions and Commencement No. 8 and Savings and Transitional Provisions (Amendment)) Order 2013;

532

"the No. 28 relevant district" means the postcode part-district SM5
  2;

"single claimant", in relation to universal credit, has the same meaning
  as in Part 1 of the Act;

"specified condition" means the condition that a claimant is a British
  citizen who—

(d) has resided in the United Kingdom throughout the period of two
  years ending with the date on which the claim for universal credit
  is made; and

(e) has not, during that period, left the United Kingdom for a continuous period of four weeks or more;

"state pension credit" means state pension credit under the State
  Pension Credit Act 2002;

"tax credit" (including "child tax credit" and "working tax credit")
  and "tax year" have the same meanings as in the Tax Credits Act
  2002;

"Upper Tribunal" has the same meaning as in the 1998 Act.

(2) For the purposes of this Order—

(a) the Claims and Payments Regulations 2013 apply for the purpose
  of deciding—

  (i) whether a claim for universal credit is made or treated as
    made; and

  (ii) the date on which such a claim is made; and

(b) where a couple is treated, in accordance with regulation 9(8) of
  the Claims and Payments Regulations 2013, as making a claim for
  universal credit, references to the date on which the claim is
  treated as made are to the date of formation of the couple.

Day appointed for the coming into force of the universal credit provisions

3. (1) The day appointed for the coming into force of the provisions of
the Act listed in Schedule 2 to the No. 9 Order, in so far as they are not
already in force, in relation to the case of a claim referred to in paragraph
(2), and any award that is made in respect of the claim, is the day
appointed in accordance with paragraph (3).

6.277

(2) The claims referred to are—

(a) a claim for universal credit that is made on or after 26th November 2014 and before 20th December 2014 in respect of a period
  that begins on or after 26th November 2014 where, on the date on
  which the claim is made, the claimant resides in the No. 28
  relevant district and meets the specified condition;

(b) a claim for universal credit that is made on or after 26th November 2014 and before 20th December 2014, in respect of a period
  that begins on or after 26th November 2014 where—

  (i) in the case of a single claimant, the claimant gives incorrect
    information regarding the claimant residing in the No. 28
    relevant district or meeting the specified condition and the
    claimant does not reside in that district or does not meet the

specified condition on the date on which the claim is made;

(ii) in the case of joint claimants, either or both of the joint claimants gives or give incorrect information regarding his or her (or their) residing in that district or meeting the specified condition and one or both of them does not or do not reside in such a district or does not or do not meet the specified condition on the date on which the claim is made,

and after a decision is made that the single claimant is, or the joint claimants are, entitled to universal credit and one or more payments have been made in respect of the single claimant or the joint claimants, the Secretary of State discovers that incorrect information has been given regarding such residence or meeting the specified condition as the case may be.

(3) The day appointed in relation to the case of a claim referred to in paragraph (2), and any award that is made in respect of the claim, is the first day of the period in respect of which the claim is made.

(4) Article 3(6) of the No. 9 Order applies for the purposes of paragraph (3) as it applies for the purposes of article 3(4)(a) of the No. 9 Order.

(5) Article 3A of the No. 9 Order applies in connection with a claim for universal credit where a single claimant, or, as the case may be, either or both of joint claimants, gives or give incorrect information regarding his or her (or their) residing in a No. 28 relevant district or meeting the specified condition, as it applies in connection with the giving of incorrect information regarding a claimant residing in a relevant district (as defined in the No. 9 Order) or meeting the gateway conditions (as defined in the No. 9 Order).

Day appointed for the abolition of income-related employment and support allowance and income-based jobseeker's allowance

6.278   **4.** (1) The day appointed for the coming into force of the amending provisions, in relation to the case of a claim referred to in paragraph (2), and any award that is made in respect of the claim, is the day appointed in accordance with paragraph (3).

(2) The claims referred to are—

(a) a claim for universal credit that is made on or after 26th November 2014 and before 20th December 2014 in respect of a period that begins on or after 26th November 2014 where, on the date on which the claim is made, the claimant resides in the No. 28 relevant district and meets the specified condition;

(b) a claim for universal credit that is made on or after 26th November 2014 and before 20th December 2014, in respect of a period that begins on or after 26th November 2014 where—

(i) in the case of a single claimant, the claimant gives incorrect information regarding the claimant residing in the No. 28 relevant district or meeting the specified condition and the claimant does not reside in that district or does not meet the specified condition on the date on which the claim is made;

(ii) in the case of joint claimants, either or both of the joint claimants gives or give incorrect information regarding his or her (or their) residing in that district or meeting the specified condition and one or both of them does not or do not reside in such a district or does not or do not meet the specified condition on the date on which the claim is made,

and after a decision is made that the single claimant is, or the joint claimants are, entitled to universal credit and one or more payments have been made in respect of the single claimant or the joint claimants, the Secretary of State discovers that incorrect information has been given regarding such residence or meeting the specified condition as the case may be;

(c) a claim for an employment and support allowance or a jobseeker's allowance that is made or treated as made on or after 26th November 2014 and before 20th December 2014 where, on the date on which the claim is made or treated as made, the claimant resides in the No. 28 relevant district and meets the specified condition;

(d) a claim for an employment and support allowance or a jobseeker's allowance other than one referred to in sub-paragraph (c) that is made or treated as made during the relevant period by a single claimant of universal credit or by either of two joint claimants of universal credit who has or have made a claim for universal credit within sub-paragraph (a) or (b).

(3) The day appointed in relation to the case of a claim referred to in paragraph (2), and any award that is made in respect of the claim, is the first day of the period in respect of which the claim is made.

(4) For the purposes of paragraph (2)(d), "relevant period" means, in relation to a claim for universal credit within paragraph (2)(a) or (b), any UC claim period, and any period subsequent to any UC claim period in respect of which the claimant is entitled to an award of universal credit in respect of the claim.

(5) For the purposes of paragraph (4), a "UC claim period" is a period when—

(a) a claim for universal credit within sub-paragraph (a) of paragraph (2), or within sub-paragraph (b)(i) or (ii) of that paragraph, has been made but a decision has not yet been made on the claim; or

(b) a decision has been made that the claimant is not entitled to universal credit and—

(i) the Secretary of State is considering whether to revise that decision under section 9 of the 1998 Act, whether on an application made for that purpose, or on the Secretary of State's own initiative; or

(ii) the claimant has appealed against that decision to the First-tier Tribunal and that appeal or any subsequent appeal to the Upper Tribunal or to a court has not been finally determined.

(6) Paragraphs (6) and (7) of article 4 of the No. 9 Order apply in relation to a claim for universal credit referred to in paragraph (2) (and any award that is made in respect of the claim) as they apply in relation to a claim for universal credit referred to in sub-paragraphs (a) and (b) of article 4(2) of the No. 9 Order (and any award that is made in respect of the claim).

(7) Paragraphs (1A) and (1B) of article 5 of the No. 9 Order apply for the purposes of paragraph (2)(c) as they apply for the purposes of article 4(2)(a) of the No. 9 Order (but as if the reference in paragraph (1A) to Schedule 5 of the No. 9 Order were omitted).

(8) Paragraphs (5) to (7) of article 5 of the No. 9 Order apply for the purposes of sub-paragraphs (c) and (d) of paragraph (2) as they apply for the purposes of sub-paragraphs (a) and (g) of article 4(2) of the No. 9 Order.

(9) Article 5(8) of the No. 9 Order applies for the purposes of paragraph (3) as it applies for the purposes of article 4(3)(a) of the No. 9 Order.

Application of the No. 9 Order

6.279   **5.** Articles 9 to 22 of the No. 9 Order apply in connection with the coming into force of the amending provisions in relation to the case of a claim referred to in article 4(2), and any award made in respect of the claim, as they apply in connection with the coming into force of the amending provisions in relation to the case of a claim referred to in sub-paragraphs (a), (b) and (g) of article 4(2) of the No. 9 Order and any award made in respect of the claim.

Transitional provision: claims for housing benefit, income support or a tax credit

6.280   **6.** (1) Except as provided by paragraphs (2) to (5) and (8), a person may not make a claim for housing benefit, income support or a tax credit (in the latter case, whether or not as part of a Tax Credits Act couple) on any date where, if that person made a claim for universal credit on that date (whether or not as part of a couple), the provisions of the Act listed in Schedule 2 to the No. 9 Order would come into force under article 3(1) and (2)(a) of this Order in relation to that claim for universal credit.

(2) Paragraph (1) does not apply to a claim for housing benefit in respect of specified accommodation.

(3) Paragraph (1) does not apply to a claim for housing benefit or a tax credit where—

(a) in the case of a claim for housing benefit, the claim is made by a person who has reached the qualifying age for state pension credit, or by a person who is a member of a State Pension Credit Act couple the other member of which has reached that age;

(b) in the case of a claim for a tax credit, the claim is made by—

(i) a person who has reached the qualifying age for state pension credit;

(ii) a Tax Credits Act couple both members of which have reached, or either member of which has reached, that age; or

(iii) in a case not covered by paragraph (i), a person who is a member of a State Pension Credit Act couple where the other member of the couple has reached that age.

(4) Paragraph (1) does not apply to a claim for a tax credit where a person or persons makes or make a claim for child tax credit or working tax credit and on the date on which he or she (or they) makes or make the claim he or she (or they) is or are entitled to working tax credit or child tax credit respectively.

(5) Paragraph (1) does not apply to a claim for a tax credit where a person is or was, or persons are or were, entitled to child tax credit or working tax credit in respect of a tax year and that person or those persons makes or make (or is or are treated as making) a claim for that tax credit for the next tax year.

(6) In paragraph (4), the reference to a person being entitled to a tax credit includes where a person is treated as being entitled to a tax credit in the circumstances referred to in regulation 11 of the Universal Credit (Transitional Provisions) Regulations 2014 but as if regulation 11 were amended as follows—

(a) in paragraph (1), for "For the purposes of regulations 7(7) and 8(4)" substitute "For the purposes of article 6(4) of the Welfare Reform Act 2012 (Commencement No. 20 and Transitional and Transitory Provisions and Commencement No. 9 and Transitional and Transitory Provisions (Amendment)) Order 2014"; and

(b) for paragraph (2)(d)(iii), substitute—
"(iii) the person's claim for child tax credit or working tax credit is made during the period of 30 days starting with the date on the notice referred to in paragraph (ii).".

(7) For the purposes of this article—

(a) a person makes a claim for income support, housing benefit or a tax credit if the person takes any action which results in a decision on a claim being required under the relevant Regulations; and

(b) except as provided in paragraph (8), it is irrelevant that the effect of any provision of the relevant Regulations is that, for the purpose of those Regulations, the claim is made or treated as made on a date that is earlier than the date on which that action was taken.

(8) Paragraph (1) does not apply to a claim for housing benefit or income support where—

(a) in the case of a claim for housing benefit—
(i) first notification of the person's intention to make the claim is given (within the meaning of regulation 83(5)(d) of the Housing Benefit Regulations 2006 ("the 2006 Regulations") or, as the case may be, regulation 64(6)(d) of the Housing Benefit (Persons who have attained the qualifying age for state pension credit) Regulations 2006 ("the 2006 (SPC) Regulations")) before 26th November 2014; or

(ii) a defective claim for housing benefit (within the meaning of the 2006 Regulations or the 2006 (SPC) Regulations) is made before 26th November 2014 and it is corrected or completed on or after that date;

(b) in the case of a claim for income support, first notification of the person's intention to make the claim is made, or deemed to be made, for the purposes of regulation 6(1A)(c) of the Social Security (Claims and Payments) Regulations 1987, before 26th November 2014.

(9) Paragraph (10) applies where a person makes a claim for universal credit and the provisions of the Act listed in Schedule 2 to the No. 9 Order come into force under article 3(1) and (2)(a) or (b) of this Order in relation to that claim (and any award made in respect of the claim).

(10) Where this paragraph applies, regulation 6 of the Universal Credit (Transitional Provisions) Regulations 2014 applies in relation to the person who makes the claim as referred to in paragraph (9), in relation to any time when they are a "universal credit claimant" as referred to in paragraph (2) of that regulation, as if, in paragraphs (5) to (7) of that regulation, the reference to the date on which the claim for universal credit was made were a reference to 26th November 2014.

(11) For the purposes of this article—

(a) "couple" (apart from in the expressions "State Pension Credit Act couple" and "Tax Credit Act couple"), has the meaning given in section 39 of the Act;

(b) "qualifying age for state pension credit" means the qualifying age referred to in section 1(6) of the State Pension Credit Act 2002;

(c) the "relevant Regulations" means—

(i) in the case of a claim for income support, the Social Security (Claims and Payments) Regulations 1987;

(ii) in the case of a claim for housing benefit, the 2006 Regulations or, as the case may be, the 2006 (SPC) Regulations;

(iii) in the case of a claim for a tax credit, the Tax Credits (Claims and Notifications) Regulations 2002;

(d) "specified accommodation" means accommodation to which one or more of sub-paragraphs (2) to (5) of paragraph 3A of Schedule 1 to the Universal Credit Regulations 2013 applies;

(e) "State Pension Credit Act couple" means a couple as defined in section 17 of the State Pension Credit Act 2002;

(f) "Tax Credits Act couple" means a couple as defined in section 3(5A) of the Tax Credits Act 2002.

Amendment of the No. 9 Order: claim for universal credit treated as made and awards of universal credit without a claim

6.281   7. (1) Paragraph (2) applies in relation to a case where—

(a) an award of universal credit is made without a claim as a consequence of a couple forming or separating at a time when both members of the couple in question were entitled to an award of universal credit;

(b) a claim for universal credit is treated as made as a consequence of a couple forming at a time when one member of the couple was entitled to an award of universal credit;

(c) a claim for universal credit is made by a former member of a couple who were joint claimants of universal credit, whether or not the claim is made jointly with another person, where the former member is not exempt from the requirement to make a claim by virtue of regulation 9(6) of the Claims and Payments Regulations 2013 (claims for universal credit by members of a couple), as that provision has effect apart from the amendments made by the Digital Service Regulations 2014, where the claim is made during the period of one month starting with the date on which notification is given to the Secretary of State that the former joint claimants have ceased to be a couple; or

(d) an award of universal credit is made without a claim in the circumstances referred to in regulation 6(1) or (2) of the Claims and Payments Regulations 2013 (claims not required for entitlement to universal credit in some cases),

and the claim for universal credit is made or treated as made, or, as the case may be, the award of universal credit is made without a claim, on or after 26th November 2014.

(2) *[Amendments are incorporated in No. 9 Commencement Order]*

(3) For the purposes of paragraph (1), "couple" has the meaning given in section 39 of the Act.

SECTION B

UPDATER TO VOLUME V

p.42, *annotation to the Welfare Reform Act 2012 s.1(2) (Universal credit)*

6.282   The reference to reg.40 in the second sentence of the annotation to s.1(2) should be to s.40, not reg.40.

p.61, *annotation to the Welfare Reform Act 2012 s.20 (Claimants subject to work-focused interview requirement only)*

6.283   Note that, by virtue of the amendment of reg.91(1) of the Universal Credit Regulations 2013 with effect from April 28, 2014 by reg.16(2) of the Income Support (Work-Related Activity) Miscellaneous Amendments Regulations 2014 (SI 2014/1097) (entry for p.205 below), a responsible carer now comes within subs.(1)(a), and is so exempted from the imposition of any work-related requirements other than the work-focused interview requirement, only if the child in question is under the age of three (previously five). But see the effect of the new reg.91A and s.21 (entries for pp.62 and 207).

p.62, *annotation to the Welfare Reform Act 2012 s.21 (Claimants subject to work preparation requirement)*

6.284   Note that, by virtue of the insertion of reg.91A of the Universal Credit Regulations 2013 with effect from April 28, 2014 by reg.16(3) of the Income Support (Work-Related Activity) Miscellaneous Amendments Regulations 2014 (SI 2014/1097) (see the entry for p.207 below), a category of claimant has now been prescribed under subs.(1)(b). This was made necessary by the amendment to reg.91(1) taking responsible carers of children aged three or four out of the exemption under s.20 from having any work-related imposed other than a work-focused interview requirement.

p.69, *annotation to the Welfare Reform Act 2012 s.26(2)(a) (Higher-level sanctions—failure to comply with requirement under a work preparation requirement to attend a work placement of a prescribed description)*

6.285   The annotation in the main volume discussing the validity or otherwise of reg.114 (Mandatory Work Activity Scheme) of the Universal

Credit Regulations 2013 under s.26(2)(a) was written on the erroneous basis that the regulation was still in its original form and had not been replaced with effect from April 29, 2013 as set out in the entry in this Supplement for p.233 of Vol.V. Regulation 114(2) as in operation from the outset of universal credit appears to give a sufficient description to meet the necessary test.

pp.79-80, *amendment to the Welfare Reform Act 2012 s.39 (Couples)*

With effect from March 13, 2014, art.2 of and para.36 of Schedule 2 to the Marriage (Same Sex Couples) Act 2013 (Consequential and Contrary Provisions and Scotland) Order 2014 (SI 2014/560) amended s.39 to read as follows in England and Wales: 6.286

"**39.**—[(1) In this Part "couple" means—
(a) two people who are married to, or civil partners of, each other and are members of the same household; or
(b) two people who are not married to, or civil partners of, each other but are living together as a married couple.]
(2) [. . .]
(3) For the purposes of this section regulations may prescribe—
(a) circumstances in which the fact that two persons are [married] or are civil partners is to be disregarded;
(b) circumstances in which [two people are to be treated as living together as a married couple];
(c) circumstances in which people are to be treated as being or not being members of the same household."

With effect from December 16, 2014, art.29 and Sch.5, para.20 of the Marriage and Civil Partnership (Scotland) Act 2014 and Civil Partnership Act 2004 (Consequential Provisions and Modifications) Order 2014 (SI 2014/3229) amended s.39 to read as above in Scotland—SI 2014/3229 art.3(4). The result is that the definition is now the same throughout Great Britain.

p.81, *annotation to the Welfare Reform Act 2012 s. 41 (pilot schemes)*

Section 41 was brought into force on September 15, 2014 by art.6 of the Welfare Reform Act 2012 (Commencement No. 19 and Transitional and Transitory Provisions and Commencement No. 9 and Transitional and Transitory Provisions (Amendment)) Order 2014 (SI 2014/2321).   6.287

p.104, *Universal Credit Regulations 2013 (SI 2013/376) (Arrangement of regulations)*

Add after entry for 90:   6.288

"91A. Claimants subject to work preparation requirement"

p.104, *amendment to the Universal Credit Regulations 2013 (SI 2013/376) reg.2 (Interpretation—definition of "maternity allowance)*

With effect from May 18, 2014, reg.6(1) of the Social Security (Maternity Allowance) (Miscellaneous Amendments) Regulations 2014   6.289

(SI 2014/884) amended the definition of "maternity allowance" in reg.2(1) to read as follows:

""maternity allowance" means a maternity allowance under section 35 [or 35B] of the Contributions and Benefits Act;".

p.107, *amendment to the Universal Credit Regulations 2013 (SI 2013/376) reg.2 (Interpretation—definition of "blind")*

6.290   With effect from November 26, 2014 reg.3(1)(a)(ii) of the Universal Credit and Miscellaneous Amendments (No.2) Regulations 2014 (SI 2014/2888) amended reg.2 by adding the following after the definition of "bereavement allowance":

""blind" means certified as severely sight impaired or blind by a consultant ophthalmologist;".

For claimants with an existing award of universal credit on November 26, 2014, the amendment has effect from the first day of the assessment period beginning on or after that day: see reg.1(2) of SI 2014/2888.

p.107, *amendment to the Universal Credit Regulations 2013 (SI 2013/376) reg.2 (Interpretation—definition of "enactment")*

6.291   With effect from April 28, 2014, reg.2(1) and (2) of the Universal Credit and Miscellaneous Amendments Regulations 2014 (SI 2014/597) amended reg.2 by adding the following definition after the definition of "employment and support allowance":

""enactment" includes an enactment comprised in, or an instrument made under, an Act of the Scottish Parliament or the National Assembly of Wales;".

p.108, *amendment to the Universal Credit Regulations 2013 (SI 2013/376) reg.2 (Interpretation—definition of "registered as blind")*

6.292   With effect from November 26, 2014 reg.3(1)(a)(i) of the Universal Credit and Miscellaneous Amendments (No.2) Regulations 2014 (SI 2014/2888) amended reg.2 by revoking the definition of "registered as blind". For claimants with an existing award of universal credit on November 26, 2014, the amendment has effect from the first day of the assessment period beginning on or after that day: see reg.1(2) of SI 2014/2888.

p.108, *amendment to the Universal Credit Regulations 2013 (SI 2013/376) reg.2 (Interpretation—definition of "statutory shared parental pay")*

6.293   With effect from December 31, 2014, reg.28(2)(c) of the Shared Parental Leave and Statutory Shared Parental Pay (Consequential Amendments to Subordinate Legislation) Order 2014 (SI 2014/3255) amended reg.2 by adding the following definition after the definition of "statutory maternity pay":

""statutory shared parental pay" means statutory shared parental pay payable in accordance with Part 12ZC of the Contributions and Benefits Act;".

p.116, *modification of the Universal Credit Regulations 2013 (SI
2013/376) reg.5 (Meaning of "qualifying young person")*

6.294

With effect from June 16, 2014, reg.26 of the Universal Credit (Transitional Provisions) Regulations 2014 (SI 2014/1230) modified reg.5 in cases where a person who would (apart from the modification) be a "qualifying young person" within the meaning of reg.5 is entitled to an "existing benefit" (i.e., as defined in reg.2(1) of SI 2014/1230). The modification is that reg.5(5) applies in such cases as if, after "a person who is receiving" there were inserted "an existing benefit (within the meaning of the Universal Credit (Transitional Provisions) Regulations 2014),".

p.128, *amendment to the Universal Credit Regulations 2013 (SI
2013/376) reg.15(2) (Claimant commitment—date and method of
acceptance)*

6.294.1

With effect from November 26, 2014, reg.3(1)(a) of the Universal Credit (Digital Service) Amendment Regulations 2014 (SI 2014/2887) amended reg.15(2) by inserting "or 3(a)" after "21(3)". Note the highly restricted area of operation of the amending Regulations by virtue of reg.5 (see Part I of this Supplement).

p.134, *amendment to the Universal Credit Regulations 2013 (SI
2013/376) reg.21 (Assessment periods)*

6.295

With effect from November 26, 2014, reg.3(1)(b) and (c) of the Universal Credit (Digital Service) Amendment Regulations 2014 (SI 2014/2887) amended reg.21 by revoking paras (5) and (6) and by substituting the following for paras (3) and (4):

"(3) Where a new award is made to a single person without a claim by virtue of regulation 9(6)(a) or (10) of the Claims and Payments Regulations (old award has ended when the claimant ceased to be a member of a couple) each assessment period for the new award begins on the same day of each month as the assessment period for the old award.

(3A) Where a new award is made to members of a couple jointly without claim by virtue of regulation 9(6)(b) or (7) of the Claims and Payments Regulations (two previous awards have ended when the claimants formed a couple) each assessment period for the new award begins on the same day of each month as the assessment period for whichever of the old awards ended earlier.

(3B) Where a claim is treated as made by virtue of regulation 9(8) of the Claims and Payments Regulations (old award ended when a claimant formed a couple with a person not entitled to universal credit), each assessment period in relation to the new award begins on the same day of each month as the assessment period for the old award.

(3C) Where a claim is made by a single person or members of a couple jointly and the claimant (or either joint claimant) meets the following conditions—

(a) the claimant was previously entitled to an award of universal credit the last day of which fell within the 6 months preceding the date on which the claim is made; and

(b) during that 6 months—

    (i) the claimant has continued to meet the basic conditions in section 4 of the Act (disregarding the requirement to have accepted a claimant commitment and any temporary period of absence from Great Britain that would be disregarded during a period of entitlement to universal credit); and

    (ii) the claimant was not excluded from entitlement by regulation 19 (restrictions on entitlement—prisoners etc.),

    each assessment period for the new award begins on the same day of each month as the assessment period for the old award or, if there was an old award in respect of each joint claimant, the assessment period that ends earlier in relation to the date on which the claim is made.

(3D) For the purposes of this regulation it does not matter if, at the beginning of the first assessment period of the new award, the following persons do not meet the basic conditions in section 4(1)(a) and (c) of the Act (at least 18 years old and in Great Britain) or if they are excluded from entitlement under regulation 19 (restrictions on entitlement—prisoners etc.) provided they meet those conditions (and are not so excluded) at the end of that assessment period—

(a) in a case to which paragraph (3B) applies, the member of the couple who was not entitled to universal credit; or

(b) in a case to which paragraph (3C) applies, the member of the couple who does not meet the conditions mentioned in that paragraph.

(3E) In this regulation "the Claims and Payments Regulations" means the Universal Credit, Personal Independence Payment, Jobseeker's Allowance and Employment and Support Allowance (Claims and Payments) Regulations 2013."

The amendment is subject to the saving provision in reg.5 of SI 2014/2887: see Part I of this Supplement.

p.138, *amendment to the Universal Credit Regulations 2013 (SI 2013/376) reg.22A (Apportionment where re-claim delayed after loss of employment)*

6.296   With effect from November 26, 2014, reg.3(1)(d) of the Universal Credit (Digital Service) Amendment Regulations 2014 (SI 2014/2887) added a new reg.22A after reg.22 as follows:

"Apportionment where re-claim delayed after loss of employment

22A.—(1) This regulation applies where—

(a) a new award is made in a case to which regulation 21(3C) (new claim within 6 months of a previous award) applies; and

(b) the claimant (or either joint claimant) is not in paid work and has ceased being in paid work since the previous award ended, other than in the 7 days ending with the date on which the claim is made.

(2) In calculating the amount of the award for the first assessment period in accordance with section 8 of the Act—

(a) the amount of each element that is to be included in the maximum amount; and

(b) the amount of earned and unearned income that is to be deducted from the maximum amount,

are each to be reduced to an amount produced by the following formula—

$$N \times \left(\frac{A \times 12}{365} \right)$$

Where—

N is the number of days in the period beginning with the date on which the claim is made and ending with the last day of the assessment period; and

A is the amount of the element that would otherwise be payable for that assessment period or, as the case may be, the amount of earned and unearned income that would otherwise be deducted for that assessment period.

(3) The period of 7 days in paragraph (1)(b) may be extended if the Secretary of State considers there is good reason for the delay in making the claim.".

The amendment is subject to the saving provision in reg.5 of SI 2014/2887: see Part I of this Supplement.

p.139, *amendment to the Universal Credit Regulations 2013 (SI 2013/376) reg.24 (The child element)*

With effect from November 26, 2014 reg.3(1)(b) of the Universal Credit and Miscellaneous Amendments (No.2) Regulations 2014 (SI 2014/2888) amended reg.26 by revoking the words "registered as" in sub-para.(2)(b)(ii). For claimants with an existing award of universal credit on November 26, 2014, the amendment has effect from the first day of the assessment period beginning on or after that day: see reg.1(2) of SI 2014/2888.   6.297

p.148, *amendment to the Universal Credit Regulations 2013 (SI 2013/376) reg.32 (The work condition)*

With effect from December 31, 2014, reg.28(3)(c) of the Shared Parental Leave and Statutory Shared Parental Pay (Consequential Amendments to Subordinate Legislation) Order 2014 (SI 2014/3255) amended reg.32(2)(b) by adding ", statutory shared parental pay" after "statutory adoption pay".   6.298

p.149, *amendment to the Universal Credit Regulations 2013 (SI 2013/376) reg.33 (The childcare costs condition)*

6.299   With effect from November 26, 2014, reg.2(1) and (3) of the Universal Credit (Digital Service) Amendment Regulations 2014 (SI 2014/2887) amended reg.33 to read as follows:

"The childcare costs condition

33.—(1) The childcare costs condition is met in respect of an assessment period if—

(za) the claimant has paid charges for relevant childcare that are attributable to that assessment period (see regulation 34A) and those charges have been reported to the Secretary of State before the end of that assessment period;"

(a) [the charges are in respect of]—

    (i) a child, or

    (ii) a qualifying young person who has not reached the 1st September following their 16th birthday,

for whom the claimant is responsible; and

(b) the charges are for childcare arrangements—

    (i) that are to enable the claimant to take up paid work or to continue in paid work, or

    (ii) where the claimant is treated as being in paid work by virtue of regulation 32(2), that are to enable the claimant to maintain childcare arrangements that were in place when the claimant ceased paid work or began to receive those benefits.

[(2) The late reporting of charges for relevant childcare may be accepted in the same circumstances as late notification of a change of circumstances may be accepted under regulation 36 of the Universal Credit, Personal Independence Payment, Jobseeker's Allowance and Employment and Support Allowance (Decisions and Appeals) Regulations 2013(4) and, in such cases, subject to regulation 34A below, all or part of any such charges may be taken into account in any assessment period to which they relate.]".

The amendment is subject to the saving provision in reg.5 of SI 2014/2887: see Part I of this Supplement.

p.150, *amendment to the Universal Credit Regulations 2013 (SI 2013/376) reg.34 (Amount of childcare costs element)*

6.300   With effect from November 26, 2014, reg.2(1) and (3) of the Universal Credit (Digital Service) Amendment Regulations 2014 (SI 2014/2887) amended reg.34 by substituting the following for sub-para.(1)(a):

"(a) 70% of the charges paid for relevant childcare that are attributable to that assessment period; or".

The amendment is subject to the saving provision in reg.5 of SI 2014/2887: see Part 1 of this Supplement.

p.150, *amendment to the Universal Credit Regulations 2013 (SI 2013/376) reg.34A (Charges attributable to an assessment period)*

With effect from November 26, 2014, reg.2(1) and (4) of the Universal Credit (Digital Service) Amendment Regulations 2014 (SI 2014/2887) added a new reg.34A after reg.34 as follows: **6.301**

"Charges attributable to an assessment period
34A.—(1) Charges paid for relevant childcare are attributable to an assessment period where—
(a) those charges are paid in that assessment period for relevant childcare in respect of that assessment period; or
(b) those charges are paid in that assessment period for relevant childcare in respect of a previous assessment period; or
(c) those charges were paid in either of the two previous assessment periods for relevant childcare in respect of that assessment period.
(2) For the purposes of paragraph (1)(c), where a claimant pays charges for relevant childcare in advance, the amount which they have paid in respect of any assessment period is to be calculated as follows:
Step 1
Take the total amount of the advance payment (leaving out of account any amount referred to in regulation 34(2)).
Step 2
Apply the formula—

$$\left(\frac{PA}{D} \right) x\, AP$$

Where—
PA is the amount resulting from step 1;
D is the total number of days covered by the payment referred to in step 1, and
AP is the number of days covered by the payment which also fall within the assessment period in question.
(3) In this regulation, a reference to an assessment period in which charges are paid, or in respect of which charges are paid, includes any month preceding the commencement of the award that begins on the same day as each assessment period in relation to a claimant's current award.".

The amendment is subject to the saving provision in reg.5 of SI 2014/2887: see Part 1 of this Supplement.

p.153, *amendment to the Universal Credit Regulations 2013 (SI 2013/376) reg.36 (Table showing amounts of the elements)*

With effect from April 7, 2014, art.13 of and Sch.5 to the Welfare Benefits Up-rating Order 2014 (SI 2014/147) and art.24(2) of and   **6.302**

Sch.16 to the Social Security Benefits Up-rating Order 2014 (SI 2014/516) amended the table in reg.36 to read as follows:

Element	Amount for each assessment period
Standard allowance—	
single claimant aged under 25	£249.28
single claimant aged 25 or over	£314.67
joint claimants both aged under 25	£391.29
joint claimants where either is aged 25 or over	£493.95
Child element—	
first child or qualifying young person	£274.58
second and each subsequent child or qualifying young person	£229.17
Additional amount for disabled child or qualifying young person—	
lower rate	£124.86
higher rate	£362.92
LCW and LCWRA elements—	
limited capability for work	£124.86
limited capability for work and work-related activity	£311.86
Carer element	£148.61
Childcare costs element—	
maximum amount for one child	£532.29
maximum amount for two or more children	£912.50

In so far as they relate to a particular beneficiary, the amended amounts in the table take effect in the assessment period which commences in the week beginning with April 7, 2014 or, if no assessment period commences in that week, the assessment period in which the whole of that week falls.

p.154, *amendment to the Universal Credit Regulations 2013 (SI 2013/376) reg.37 (Run-on after a death)*

With effect from April 28, 2014, reg.2(1) and (3) of the Universal Credit and Miscellaneous Amendments Regulations 2014 (SI 2014/597) amended reg.37 by revoking the word "or" at the end of sub-para.(b) and adding the following after sub-para.(c): 6.303

"; or
(d) a person who was a non-dependant within the meaning of paragraph 9(2) of Schedule 4,".

p.155, *amendment to the Universal Credit Regulations 2013 (SI 2013/376) reg.39 (Limited capability for work)*

With effect from April 28, 2014, reg.2(4)(a) of the Universal Credit and Miscellaneous Amendments Regulations 2014 (SI 2014/597) amended reg.39(6) by inserting at the beginning the words "Subject to paragraph (7),". 6.304

With effect from the same date, reg.2(4)(b) of the same Regulations inserted after para.(6) in reg.39 a new paragraph (7) as follows:

"(7) Where the circumstances set out in paragraph 4 or 5 of Schedule 8 apply, a claimant may only be treated as having limited capability for work if the claimant does not have limited capability for work as determined in accordance with an assessment under this Part.".

p.156, *annotation to the Universal Credit Regulations 2013 (SI 2013/376) reg.39 (Limited capability for work)*

The effect of the amendment to reg.39 is that a claimant can only be treated as having LCW under para.4 of Sch.8 (substantial risk to his/her health, or that of someone else) or para.5 of Sch.8 (life threatening disease) once a work capability assessment has been carried out and s/he has been assessed as not having LCW. This is the same as for ESA. 6.305

p.157, *amendment to the Universal Credit Regulations 2013 (SI 2013/376) reg.40 (Limited capability for work and work-related activity)*

With effect from April 28, 2014, reg.2(5)(a) of the Universal Credit and Miscellaneous Amendments Regulations 2014 (SI 2014/597) amended reg.40(5) by inserting at the beginning the words "Subject to paragraph (6),". 6.306

With effect from the same date, reg.2(5)(b) of the same Regulations inserted after para.(5) in reg.40 a new paragraph(6) as follows:

"(6) Where the circumstances set out in paragraph 4 of Schedule 9 apply, a claimant may only be treated as having limited capability for work and work-related activity if the claimant does not have limited capability for work and work-related activity as determined in accordance with an assessment under this Part.".

p.158, *annotation to the Universal Credit Regulations 2013 (SI 2013/376) reg.40 (Limited capability for work)*

6.307   The effect of the amendment to reg.40 is that a claimant can only be treated as having LCW and LCWRA under para.4 of Sch.9 (substantial risk to his/her health, or that of someone else) once a work capability assessment has been carried out and s/he has been assessed as not having LCW and LCWRA.

p.167, *amendment to the Universal Credit Regulations 2013 (SI 2013/376) reg.55 (Employed earnings)*

6.308   With effect from December 31, 2014, art.28(4)(c) of the Shared Parental Leave and Statutory Shared Parental Pay (Consequential Amendments to Subordinate Legislation) Order 2014 (SI 2014/3255) amended reg.55(4)(e) by substituting "; and" for the full stop at the end of that sub-paragraph.

With effect from the same date, the same Order amended reg.55(4) by inserting after sub-para.(e) a new sub-paragraph (f) as follows:

"(f) statutory shared parental pay."

p.167, *amendment to the Universal Credit Regulations 2013 (SI 2013/376) reg.55 (Employed earnings)*

6.309   With effect from November 26, 2014, reg.4(2) of the Universal Credit and Miscellaneous Amendments (No.2) Regulations 2014 (SI 2014/2888) amended reg.55 by inserting after para.(4) a new paragraph (4A) as follows:

"(4A) A repayment of income tax or national insurance contributions received by a person from HMRC in respect of a tax year in which the person was in paid work is to be treated as employed earnings unless it is taken into account as self-employed earnings under regulation 57(4).".

p.168, *annotation to the Universal Credit Regulations 2013 (SI 2013/376) reg.55 (Employed earnings)*

6.310   The new para.(4A) inserted into reg.55 with effect from November 26, 2014 treats a repayment of tax or NI contributions in respect of a tax year in which the person was in paid work as employed earnings, unless it is taken into account as self-employed earnings. According to the DWP (see Memo ADM 24/14), this will include repayments of income tax that relate to other sources such as unearned income, as long as the claimant was in paid work in the tax year to which the repayment relates.

p.169, *amendment to the Universal Credit Regulations 2013 (SI 2013/376) reg.57 (Self-employed earnings)*

6.311   With effect from November 26, 2014, reg.4(3) of the Universal Credit and Miscellaneous Amendments (No.2) Regulations 2014 (SI

2014/2888) amended reg.57 by inserting after para.(4) a new paragraph (5) as follows:

"(5) Where the purchase of an asset has been deducted as an expense in any assessment period and, in a subsequent assessment period, the asset is sold or ceases to be used for the purposes of a trade, profession or vocation carried on by the person, the proceeds of sale (or, as the case may be, the amount that would be received for the asset if it were sold at its current market value) are to be treated as a receipt in that subsequent assessment period.".

p.170, *annotation to the Universal Credit Regulations 2013 (SI 2013/376) reg.57 (Self-employed earnings)*

According to DWP guidance (Memo ADM 24/14), the full amount of the proceeds of sale (or deemed proceeds of sale) will be taken into account under the new reg.57(5), even if only a proportion of the purchase price had been deducted as an expense in the assessment period in which the asset was purchased because the claimant's self-employed earnings in that assessment period were less than the price of the asset.   6.312

p.174, *amendment to the Universal Credit Regulations 2013 (SI 2013/376) reg.61 (Information for calculating earned income)*

With effect from November 26, 2014, reg.4(4) of the Universal Credit and Miscellaneous Amendments (No.2) Regulations 2014 (SI 2014/2888) amended reg.61 by substituting for the existing reg.61 a new form of reg.61 as follows: 6.313

"Information for calculating earned income - real time information etc

61.—(1) Unless paragraph (2) applies, a person must provide such information for the purposes of calculating their earned income at such times as the Secretary of State may require.

(2) Where a person is, or has been, engaged in an employment in respect of which their employer is a Real Time Information employer—

(a) the amount of the person's employed earnings from that employment for each assessment period is to be based on the information which is reported to HMRC under the PAYE Regulations and is received by the Secretary of State from HMRC in that assessment period; and

(b) for an assessment period in which no information is received from HMRC, the amount of employed earnings in relation to that employment is to be taken to be nil.

(3) The Secretary of State may determine that paragraph (2) does not apply—

(a) in respect of a particular employment, where the Secretary of State considers that the information from the employer is unlikely to be sufficiently accurate or timely; or

   (b) in respect of a particular assessment period where—
      (i) no information is received from HMRC and the Secretary of State considers that this is likely to be because of a failure to report information (which includes the failure of a computer system operated by HMRC, the employer or any other person); or
      (ii) the Secretary of State considers that the information received from HMRC is incorrect, or fails to reflect the definition of employed earnings in regulation 55, in some material respect.

(4) Where the Secretary of State determines that paragraph (2) does not apply, the Secretary of State must make a decision as to the amount of the person's employed earnings for the assessment period in accordance with regulation 55 (employed earnings) using such information or evidence as the Secretary of State thinks fit.

(5) When the Secretary of State makes a decision in accordance with paragraph (4) the Secretary of State may—
   (a) treat a payment of employed earnings received by the person in one assessment period as received in a later assessment period (for example where the Secretary of State has received the information in that later period or would, if paragraph (2) applied, have expected to receive information about that payment from HMRC in that later period); or
   (b) where a payment of employed earnings has been taken into account in that decision, disregard information about the same payment which is received from HMRC.

(6) Paragraph (5) also applies where the Secretary of State makes a decision under regulation 41(3) of the Universal Credit, Personal Independence Payment, Jobseeker's Allowance and Employment and Support Allowance (Decisions and Appeals) Regulations 2013 in a case where the person disputes the information provided by HMRC.

(7) In this regulation "Real Time Information Employer" has the meaning in regulation 2A(1) of the PAYE Regulations.".

p.175, *annotation to the Universal Credit Regulations 2013 (SI 2013/376) reg.61 (Information for calculating earned income)*

6.314   According to the Explanatory Memorandum that accompanies this SI, the new form of reg.61 has been introduced because "[t]he Department's on-going process of monitoring and evaluation identified some circumstances where it is not appropriate for Universal Credit purposes simply to take the RTI [real time information] at face value or where the Secretary of State should clarify contingency arrangements".

p.176, *amendment to the Universal Credit Regulations 2013 (SI 2013/376) reg.62 (Minimum income floor)*

6.315   With effect from November 26, 2014, reg.4(5) of the Universal Credit and Miscellaneous Amendments (No.2) Regulations 2014 (SI

2014/2888) amended reg.62 by substituting for the existing reg.62 a new form of reg.62 as follows:

"Minimum income floor

62.—(1) This regulation applies to a claimant who—

(a) is in gainful self-employment (see regulation 64); and

(b) would, apart from this regulation, fall within section 22 of the Act (claimants subject to all work-related requirements).

(2) Where this regulation applies to a single claimant, for any assessment period in respect of which the claimant's earned income is less than their individual threshold, the claimant is to be treated as having earned income equal to that threshold.

(3) Where this regulation applies to a claimant who is a member of a couple, for any assessment period in respect of which—

(a) the claimant's earned income is less than their individual threshold; and

(b) the couple's combined earned income is less than the couple threshold,

the claimant is to be treated as having earned income equal to their individual threshold minus any amount by which that amount of earned income combined with their partner's earned income would exceed the couple threshold.

(4) In this regulation, references to the claimant's individual threshold and to the couple threshold are to the amounts set out in regulation 90(2) and 90(3) respectively, converted to net monthly amounts by—

(a) multiplying by 52 and dividing by 12; and

(b) deducting such amount for income tax and national insurance contributions as the Secretary of State considers appropriate.

(5) An assessment period referred to in this regulation does not include an assessment period which falls wholly within a start-up period or begins or ends in a start-up period.".

pp.177-178, *annotation to the Universal Credit Regulations 2013 (SI 2013/376) reg.62 (Minimum income floor)*

According to the Explanatory Memorandum that accompanies this SI, **6.316** the new form of reg.62 has been introduced in order to make clearer the calculation of the minimum income floor when a self-employed person is a member of a couple (or when both members of a couple are self-employed).

p.188, *amendment to the Universal Credit Regulations 2013 (SI 2013/376) reg.73 (Unearned income calculated monthly)*

With effect from November 26, 2014, reg.4 of the Universal Credit **6.317** (Digital Service) Amendment Regulations 2014 (SI 2014/2887) amended reg.73 by inserting after para.(2) a new paragraph (2A) as follows:

"(2A) Where the period in respect of which unearned income is paid begins or ends during an assessment period the amount of unearned income for that assessment period is to be calculated as follows—

$$N \times \left(\frac{M \times 12}{365} \right)$$

where N is the number of days in respect of which unearned income is paid that fall within the assessment period and M is the monthly amount referred to in paragraph (1) or, as the case may be, the monthly equivalent referred to in paragraph (2).".

Note that this amendment is subject to the saving provision in reg.5 of SI 2014/2887: see Part 1 of this Supplement.

p.189, *annotation to the Universal Credit Regulations 2013 (SI 2013/376) reg.73 (Unearned income calculated monthly)*

6.318   The effect of the saving provision in reg.5 of the Universal Credit (Digital Service) Amendment Regulations 2014 (SI 2014/2887) (see Part 1 of this Supplement) is that the amendments made by those Regulations only apply in areas where the DWP intends to test its enhanced on line service for claiming universal credit (referred to by the DWP as "the Digital Service"). As at December 31, 2014 this is only postcode part-district SM5 2 (the "No. 28 relevant district", which is part of Sutton) (see Welfare Reform Act 2012 (Commencement No. 20 and Transitional and Transitory Provisions and Commencement No. 9 and Transitional and Transitory Provisions (Amendment)) Order 2014 (SI 2014/3094)). The amendments do not apply to awards of universal credit made in postcode areas where universal credit is already in force (referred to by the DWP as "the Live Service"), except those made to:

- joint claimants, where a previous universal credit award ended when the couple formed, *or*
- a single claimant, where a previous universal credit award ended when a couple separated,

and either member of the couple is a "digital service claimant". Note the extended definition of "digital service claimant" in reg.5(3).

Note that the "gateway conditions" do not apply to digital service claimants; instead the claimant has to satisfy the "specified condition". This condition is that the claimant is a British citizen who has resided in the UK throughout the period of two years ending with the date on which the claim for universal credit is made, and who has not, during that period, left the UK for a continuous period of four weeks or more.

In the case of digital service claimants, reg.73 of the Universal Credit Regulations is amended so as to provide an exception to the general rule that unearned income is calculated as a monthly amount. For assessment periods during which unearned income starts and/or finishes, only an amount based on the actual days for which the income is paid will be taken into account. This is likely to mainly affect benefit payments.

p.192, *amendment to the Universal Credit Regulations 2013 (SI 2013/376) reg.77 (Company analogous to a partnership or one person business)*

With effect from November 26, 2014, reg.4(6) of the Universal Credit and Miscellaneous Amendments (No.2) Regulations 2014 (SI 2014/2888) amended reg.77(3)(c) by omitting the words "in relation to" to the end.

6.319

p.194, *general note to the Universal Credit Regulations 2013 (SI 2013/376) Part 7 (The benefit cap)*

At the end of the General Note, add the following:

6.320

"*Legal challenge*
On February 21, 2014, the Court of Appeal rejected a legal challenge to the benefit cap on the grounds that it (i) unlawfully discriminated against (a) women generally or (b) women who are victims of domestic violence, in breach of art.14 of, read with art.1 of the First Protocol to, ECHR; (ii) infringed art.3(1) of the United Nations Convention on the Rights of the Child; (iii) unlawfully discriminated against families in breach of art.14 read with art.8 ECHR; (iv) infringed art.8 ECHR as a free standing claim; and (v) was unlawful at common law on the grounds of irrationality: see *R (SG & Ors) v Secretary of State for Work and Pensions* [2014] EWCA Civ 156. The claimants in that case have appealed to the Supreme Court. The case was heard on April 29 and 30, 2014. However, at the time of going to press, no date has been appointed for the delivery of the Supreme Court's judgment."

p.205, *amendment to the Universal Credit Regulations 2013 (SI 2013/376) reg.91(1) (Claimants subject to work-focused interview requirement only)*

With effect from April 28, 2014, reg.16(2) of the Income Support (Work-Related Activity) Miscellaneous Amendments Regulations 2014 (SI 2014/1097) amended reg.91(1) by substituting "3" for "5". This change narrows the circumstances in which a claimant who is a "responsible carer" is exempted under s.20(1)(a) of the Welfare Reform Act 2012 from the imposition of any work-related requirement other than a work-focused interview requirement. But see the effect of the new reg.91A (below) restricting the additional requirements that can be imposed on responsible carers of children aged three or four to a work preparation requirement.

6.321

p.207, *insertion into the Universal Credit Regulations 2013 (SI 2013/376) of reg.91A (Claimants subject to work preparation requirement)*

With effect from April 28, 2014, reg.16(3) of the Income Support (Work-Related Activity) Miscellaneous Amendments Regulations 2014 (SI 2014/1097) inserted the following:

6.322

"Claimants subject to work preparation requirement
91A. For the purposes of section 21(1)(b) of the Act (claimants subject to work preparation requirement), the claimant is of a prescribed description if the claimant is the responsible carer for a child aged 3 or 4."

Before April 28, 2014, a responsible carer of a child aged three or four fell within s.20 of the Welfare Reform Act 2012, by virtue of reg.91(1) before its amendment from that date, so that no prescription was required to be made under s.21(1)(b). When the amendment to reg.91(1) took such carers out of the s.20 exemption, this new prescription under s,21(1)(b) became necessary. Its effect under s.21 is to limit the work-related requirements that can be imposed, in addition to the work-focused interview requirement, to a work preparation requirement.

p.213, *amendment to the Universal Credit Regulations 2013 (SI 2013/376) reg.98 (Victims of domestic violence)*

6.323   With effect from November 26, 2014, reg.8(2) of the Universal Credit and Miscellaneous Amendments (No.2) Regulations 2014 (SI 2014/2888) amended reg.98 by inserting a new para.(1A):

"(1A) Where a claimant referred to in paragraph (1) is a person who falls within section 22 of the Act (claimants subject to all work-related requirements) and is the responsible carer of a child, the Secretary of State must not impose a work search requirement or a work availability requirement on that claimant for a further period of 13 consecutive weeks beginning on the day after the period in paragraph (1)(a) expires."

This amendment requires the extension of the normal 13-week suspension of the imposition of any work-related requirement for recent victims of domestic violence for a further 13 weeks where the claimant is the responsible carer (see ss.19(6) and 40 of the WRA 2012 and reg.4) of a child.

p.214, *amendments to the Universal Credit Regulations 2013 (SI 2013/376) reg.98(4) (Victims of domestic violence)*

6.324   With effect from October 29, 2013, reg.3(1) of the Social Security (Miscellaneous Amendments) (No. 2) Regulations 2013 (SI 2013/1508) amended the definition of "domestic violence" by substituting new definitions of "coercive behaviour", "controlling behaviour" and "domestic violence":

"coercive behaviour" means an act of assault, humiliation or intimidation or other abuse that is used to harm, punish or frighten the victim;

"controlling behaviour" means an act designed to make a person subordinate or dependent by isolating them from sources of support, exploiting their resources and capacities for personal gain, depriving them of the means needed for independence, resistance or escape or regulating their everyday behaviour;

"domestic violence" means any incident, or pattern of incidents, of controlling behaviour, coercive behaviour, violence or abuse, including but not limited to—

(a) psychological abuse;

(b) physical abuse;

(c) sexual abuse;

(d) emotional abuse;

(e) financial abuse,

regardless of the gender or sexuality of the victim;"

This amendment renders some of the discussion in the general note obsolete. See the notes to reg.15 of the JSA Regulations 2013 in Vol.II.

With effect from April 28, 2014, reg.2(6) of the Universal Credit and Miscellaneous Amendments Regulations 2014 (SI 2014/597) amended the definition of "social worker" in reg.98(4) by substituting the following for sub-paragraph (a) formerly referring to the General Social Care Council:

"(a) The Health and Care Professions Council;"

pp.216-217, *amendments to the Universal Credit Regulations 2013 (SI 2013/376) reg.99 (Circumstances in which work-related and connected requirements must not be imposed)*

With effect from April 28, 2014, reg.2(7) of the Universal Credit and Miscellaneous Amendments Regulations 2014 (SI 2014/597) amended paras (1) and (2) of reg.99 by omitting ", (5)" in the three places it occurred and inserting new paras (2A) to (2C): **6.325**

"(2A) Where paragraph (5) applies—

(a) the Secretary of State must not impose a work search requirement on a claimant; and

(b) a work search requirement previously applying to the claimant ceases to have effect from the date on which the circumstances set out in paragraph (5) begin to apply.

(2B) Where paragraph (5A) applies "able and willing to take up work" under a work availability requirement means able and willing to take up paid work, or to attend an interview, immediately once the circumstances set out in paragraph (5A) no longer apply.

(2C) Where paragraph (5B) applies, "able and willing to take up work" under a work availability requirement means—

(a) able and willing to take up paid work immediately once the circumstances set out in paragraph (5B) no longer apply; and

(b) able and willing to attend an interview before those circumstances no longer apply."

The provision also omitted "or a work availability requirement" and "or 18(3)" in para.(5) and inserted new paras (5A) and (5B):

"(5A) This paragraph applies where the Secretary of State is satisfied that it would be unreasonable to require the claimant to comply with a work availability requirement to be able and willing to—

(a) take up paid work; and

(b) attend an interview,

(including if such a requirement were limited in accordance with section 18(3) of the Act) because the claimant falls within sub-paragraph (a), (b) or (c) of paragraph (5).

(5B) This paragraph applies where the Secretary of State is satisfied that it would be—

(a) unreasonable to require the claimant to comply with a work availability requirement to be able and willing to take up paid work because the claimant falls within sub-paragraph (a), (b) or (c) of paragraph (5); and

(b) reasonable to require the claimant to comply with a work availability requirement to attend an interview,

including if such a requirement were limited in accordance with section 18(3) of the Act."

6.326   These amendments mainly clarify the conditions of operation of the two effects previously produced under reg.99(5) (of preventing the application of a work search requirement and of altering the normal terms of a work availability requirement) in cases depending on a judgment that it would be unreasonable to apply the normal requirements (in contrast to the defined categories in paras (3), (4) and (6)). The effect on the work search requirement is now produced by paras (2A) and (5). The effect on the work availability requirement is now produced by paras (2B), (2C), (5A) and (5B), which now cater specifically for cases in which it would still be reasonable to require a claimant to be able and willing to attend an interview despite the existence of circumstances making it unreasonable to impose the requirement of being able and willing immediately to take up paid work.

With effect from November 26, 2014, reg.8(3) of the Universal Credit and Miscellaneous Amendments) (No. 2) Regulations 2014 (SI 2014/2888) amended paras (1) and (2) of reg.99 by inserting ", (4A)" after "(4)" in the three places where that occurs and inserting new paras (4A) to (4C):

"(4A) This paragraph applies for one or more periods of one month, as provided for in paragraphs (4B) and (4C), where the claimant is the responsible carer of a child and an event referred to in sub-paragraph (a) or (b) has taken place in the last 24 months and has resulted in significant disruption to the claimant's normal childcare responsibilities—

(a) any of the following persons has died—

(i) a person who was previously the responsible carer of that child;

(ii) a parent of that child;

    (iii) a brother or sister of that child; or

    (iv) any other person who, at the time of their death, normally lived in the same accommodation as that child and was not a person who was liable to make payments on a commercial basis in respect that accommodation; or

(b) the child has been the victim of, or witness to, an incident of violence or abuse and the claimant is not the perpetrator of that violence or abuse.

(4B) Paragraph (4A) is not to apply for more than one period of one month in each of the 4 consecutive periods of 6 months following the event (and, if regulation 98 or paragraph (3)(d) of this regulation applies in respect of the same event, that month is to run concurrently with any period for which that regulation or paragraph applies).

(4C) Each period of one month begins on the date specified by the Secretary of State after the claimant has notified the Secretary of State of the circumstances in paragraph (4A) provided that the Secretary of State is satisfied that the circumstances apply."

p.219, *amendment to the Universal Credit Regulations 2013 (SI 2013/376) reg.101(4) (General principles for calculating reduction periods)*

With effect from April 28, 2014, reg.2(8) of the Universal Credit and Miscellaneous Amendments Regulations 2014 (SI 2014/597) amended para.(4) of reg.99 by substituting "13" for "14".   6.327

p.220, *amendment to the Universal Credit Regulations 2013 (SI 2013/376) reg.102(2)(a)(ii) and (iii) and (b)(ii) (Higher-level sanction)*

With effect from April 28, 2014, reg.2(9) of the Universal Credit and Miscellaneous Amendments Regulations 2014 (SI 2014/597) amended para.(2)(a)(ii) and (iii) and (b)(ii) of reg.102 by substituting "364" for "365".   6.328

p.222, *amendment to the Universal Credit Regulations 2013 (SI 2013/376) reg.103(2)(a)(ii) and (b)(ii) (Medium-level sanction)*

With effect from April 28, 2014, reg.2(10) of the Universal Credit and Miscellaneous Amendments Regulations 2014 (SI 2014/597) amended para.(2)(a)(ii) and (b)(ii) of reg.103 by substituting "364" for "365".   6.329

p.223, *amendment to the Universal Credit Regulations 2013 (SI 2013/376) reg.104(2)(b)(ii) and (iii) and (3)(b) (Low-level sanction)*

With effect from April 28, 2014, reg.2(11) of the Universal Credit and Miscellaneous Amendments Regulations 2014 (SI 2014/597) amended paras (2)(b)(ii) and (iii) and (3)(b) of reg.104 by substituting "364" for "365".   6.330

p.233, *amendment to the Universal Credit Regulations 2013 (SI 2013/376) reg.114 (Sanctionable failures under section 26—work placements)*

6.331   With effect from April 29, 2013, reg.38(8) of the Universal Credit (Consequential, Supplementary, Incidental and Miscellaneous Provisions) Regulations 2013 (SI 2013/630) substituted the following form of reg.114. The change was omitted in error from the main volume:

"**114.**—(1) A placement on the Mandatory Work Activity Scheme is a prescribed placement for the purpose of section 26(2)(a) of the Act (sanctionable failure not to comply with a work placement).

(2) In paragraph (1) "the Mandatory Work Activity Scheme" means a scheme provided pursuant to arrangements made by the Secretary of State and known by that name that is designed to provide work or work-related activity for up to 30 hours per week over a period of 4 consecutive weeks with a view to assisting claimants to improve their prospects of obtaining employment."

See the entry in this Supplement for p.69 of Vol.V for the validity of this provision.

p.234, *amendments to the Universal Credit Regulations 2013 (SI 2013/376) reg.116(1) and (2) (Conditions for hardship payments)*

6.332   With effect from April 28, 2014, reg.2(12) of the Universal Credit and Miscellaneous Amendments Regulations 2014 (SI 2014/597) amended para.(1) of reg.116 by omitting "and" at the end of sub-para.(f) and inserting "; and" at the end of sub-para.(g) and a new sub-para.(h):

"(h) the daily reduction rate in regulation 111(1) applies for the purposes of the reduction in respect of the claimant under section 26 or 27 of the Act."

The same provision amended para.(2) by substituting "regulation 111(1)" for "regulation 111".

The effect of these amendments is to prevent any entitlement to a hardship payment arising for a claimant whose reduction in benefit under the sanction is only by 40% under reg.111(2), rather than by 100% under reg.111(1).

p.236, *amendment to the Universal Credit Regulations 2013 (SI 2013/376) reg.117 (The period of hardship payments)*

6.333   With effect from April 29, 2013, reg.38(9) of the Universal Credit (Consequential, Supplementary, Incidental and Miscellaneous Provisions) Regulations 2013 (SI 2013/630) substituted the following form of reg.117. The change was omitted in error from the main volume:

"**117.**—(1) A hardship payment is to be made in respect of a period which—

(a) begins with the date on which all the conditions in regulation 116(1) are met; and

(b) unless paragraph (2) applies, ends with the day before the normal payment date for the assessment period in which those conditions are met.

(2) If the period calculated in accordance with paragraph (1) would be 7 days or less, it does not end on the date referred to in paragraph (1)(b) but instead ends on the normal payment date for the following assessment period or, if earlier, the last day on which the award is to be reduced under section 26 or 27 of the Act or under section 6B(5A), 7(2A) or 9(3A) of the Social Security Fraud Act 2001.

(3) In this regulation "the normal payment date" for an assessment period is the date on which the Secretary of State would normally expect to make a regular payment of universal credit in respect of an assessment period in a case where payments of universal credit are made monthly in arrears."

This is a simplification and clarification of the original form of reg.117, but the general note in the main volume is not entirely accurate. The date of the issue of an application for a hardship does not figure as such as an alternative start date for the period of a payment, but for all the conditions in reg.116(1) to be met, so as to satisfy para.(1)(a), the claimant must have completed and submitted an application either on the approved form or in some other manner accepted by the Secretary of State.

p.239, *amendment to the Universal Credit Regulations 2013 (SI 2013/376) Sch.1 (Meaning of payments in respect of accommodation) para.1 (Interpretation)*

With effect from November 3, 2014, reg.2(2)(a)(i) of the Housing Benefit and Universal Credit (Supported Accommodation) (Amendment) Regulations 2014 (SI 2014/771) amended para.1 of Sch.1 by substituting a new definition of "exempt accommodation" for the existing definition as follows: **6.334**

""exempt accommodation" has the meaning given in paragraph 4(10) of Schedule 3 to the Housing Benefit and Council Tax Benefit (Consequential Provisions) Regulations 2006;".

With effect from the same date, reg.2(2)(a)(ii) of the same Regulations amended para.1 of Sch.1 by omitting the definition of "upper-tier county council".

p.240, *amendment to the Universal Credit Regulations 2013 (SI 2013/376) Sch.1 (Meaning of payments in respect of accommodation) para.3 (Payments excluded from being rent payments)*

With effect from November 3, 2014, reg.2(2)(b)(i) of the Housing Benefit and Universal Credit (Supported Accommodation) (Amendment) Regulations 2014 (SI 2014/771) amended para.3 of Sch.1 by omitting sub-para.(e).   **6.335**

With effect from the same date, reg.2(2)(b)(ii) of the same Regulations amended paragraph 3 of Sch.1 by adding after sub-paragraph (g) a new sub-paragraph (h) as follows:

"(h) payments in respect of accommodation specified in paragraph 3A.".

With effect from the same date, reg.2(2)(c) of the same Regulations inserted after para.3 a new paragraph 3A as follows:

"Specified accommodation

3A.—(1) The accommodation referred to in paragraph 3(h) is accommodation to which one or more of the following sub-paragraphs applies.

(2) This sub-paragraph applies to accommodation which is exempt accommodation.

(3) This sub-paragraph applies to accommodation—

(a) which is provided by a relevant body;

(b) into which the claimant has been admitted in order to meet a need for care, support or supervision; and

(c) where the claimant receives care, support or supervision.

(4) This sub-paragraph applies to accommodation which—

(a) is provided by a local authority or a relevant body to the claimant because the claimant has left the home as a result of domestic violence; and

(b) consists of a building, or part of a building, which is used wholly or mainly for the non-permanent accommodation of persons who have left their homes as a result of domestic violence.

(5) This sub-paragraph applies to accommodation—

(a) which would be a hostel within the meaning of paragraph 29(10) (renters excepted from shared accommodation) of Schedule 4 (housing costs element for renters) but
for it being owned or managed by a local authority; and

(b) where the claimant receives care, support or supervision.

(6) In this paragraph—

"domestic violence" has the meaning given in regulation 98 (victims of domestic violence);

"relevant body" means a—

(a) council for a county in England for each part of which there is a district council;

(b) housing association;

(c) registered charity; or

(d) voluntary organisation.".

p.242, *annotation to the Universal Credit Regulations 2013 (SI 2013/376) Sch.1 (Meaning of payments in respect of accommodation) para.3 (Payments excluded from being rent payments)*

6.336   The effect of the amendments made to para.3 of Sch.1 and the insertion of the new para.3A, together with the substituted definition of "exempt accommodation" in para.1 of Sch. 1, is that from November 3,

2014 there are four categories of "specified accommodation" for which universal credit is not payable (but housing benefit will be—housing benefit paid in respect of "specified accommodation" is not included when calculating benefit for the purposes of the benefit cap). The four categories are:

- "exempt accommodation", as defined in para.4(10) of Sch. 3 to the Housing Benefit and Council Tax Benefit (Consequential Provisions) Regulations 2006 (SI 2006/217);
- accommodation provided by a "relevant body" (defined as a county council, housing association, registered charity or voluntary organisation) into which the claimant has been admitted because of a need for care, support or supervision, which s/he receives;
- domestic violence refuges provided by a local authority or relevant body;
- local authority hostels where the claimant receives care, support or supervision.

p.254, *amendment to the Universal Credit Regulations 2013 (SI 2013/376) Sch.4 (Housing costs element for renters) para.2 (Interpretation)*

With effect from November 3, 2014, reg.2(3) of the Housing Benefit   6.337
and Universal Credit (Supported Accommodation) (Amendment) Regulations 2014 (SI 2014/771) amended paragraph 2 of Sch.4 by substituting for the existing definition a new definition of "exempt accommodation" as follows:

""exempt accommodation" has the meaning given in paragraph 4(10) of Schedule 3 to the Housing Benefit and Council Tax Benefit (Consequential Provisions) Regulations 2006;".

p.255, *amendment to the Universal Credit Regulations 2013 (SI 2013/376) Sch.4 (Housing costs element for renters) para.7 (Relevant payments calculated monthly)*

With effect from April 28, 2014, reg.2(13)(a) of the Universal Credit   6.338
and Miscellaneous Amendments Regulations 2014 (SI 2014/597) amended para.7 of Sch.4 by inserting after sub-para.(2)(a) of para.7 a new sub-paragraph (2)(aa) as follows:

"(aa) two-weekly payments are multiplied by 26 and divided by 12;".

With effect from the same date, reg.2(13)(b) of the same Regulations amended sub-para.(3) of para.7 by inserting after the words "rent free periods," the words "subject to sub-paragraph (3A),".

With effect from the same date, reg.2(13)(c) of the same Regulations inserted a new sub-paragraph (3A) as follows:

"(3A) Where sub-paragraph (3) applies and the relevant payments in question are—

(a) weekly payments, the total number of weekly payments which the renter is liable to make in any 12 month period shall be calculated by reference to the formula—

$$52 - RFP;$$

(b) two-weekly payments, the total number of two-weekly payments which the renter is liable to make in any 12 month period shall be calculated by reference to the formula—

$$26 - RFP;$$

(c) four-weekly payments, the total number of four-weekly payments which the renter is liable to make in any 12 month period shall be calculated by reference to the formula—

$$13 - RFP;$$

where "RFP" is the number of rent free periods in the 12 month period in question.".

p.258, *amendment to the Universal Credit Regulations 2013 (SI 2013/376) Sch.4 (Housing costs element for renters) para.14 (Amount of housing cost contributions)*

6.339   With effect from April 7, 2014, art.24(3)(a) of the Social Security Benefits Up-rating Order 2014 (SI 2014/516) amended para.14(1) of Sch.4 by substituting £68.68 for £68.00. Note that in so far as it relates to a particular claimant, the amendment takes effect in the assessment period which commences in the week beginning with April 7, 2014 or, if no assessment period commences in that week, the assessment period in which the whole of that week falls.

p.258, *amendment to the Universal Credit Regulations 2013 (SI 2013/376) Sch.4 (Housing costs element for renters) para.15 (Exempt renters)*

6.340   With effect from November 26, 2014, reg.3(1)(c) of the Universal Credit and Miscellaneous Amendments (No.2) Regulations 2014 (SI 2014/2888) amended para.15(2)(a) of Sch.4 by omitting the words "registered as".

p.267, *annotation to the Universal Credit Regulations 2013 (SI 2013/376) Sch.4 (Housing costs element for renters) para.7 (Relevant payments calculated monthly)*

6.341   The new sub-para.(2)(aa) inserted into para.7 with effect from April 28, 2014 provides a formula for the conversion of a two-weekly rent or service charge liability into a monthly figure. The amendment to sub-para.(3) and the new sub-para.(3A) clarify that, in any case where a renter has the benefit of rent or service charge free weeks, the conversion to a monthly figure must be carried out based on a standard 52 week year.

p.271, *amendment to the Universal Credit Regulations 2013 (SI 2013/376) Sch.5 (Housing costs element for owner-occupiers) para.2 (Interpretation)*

With effect from April 28, 2014, reg.2(14)(a) of the Universal Credit   **6.342**
and Miscellaneous Amendments Regulations 2014 (SI 2014/597)
amended paragraph 2 by inserting
- before the definition of "alternative finance payments", a new definition of "alternative finance arrangements" as follows:

    ""alternative finance arrangements" has the meaning given in paragraph 6(2) of Schedule 1;"; and

- after the definition of "qualifying period", a new definition of "relevant date" as follows:

    ""relevant date" means, in relation to an owner-occupier, the date on which an amount of housing costs element calculated under this Schedule is first included in the owner-occupier's award;".

p.273, *amendment to the Universal Credit Regulations 2013 (SI 2013/376) Sch.5 (Housing costs element for owner-occupiers) para.10 (Amount in respect of interest on loans)*

Note that the formula in step 4 of para.10(2) of Sch.5 should read: **6.343**

$$\frac{(A \times SR)}{12}$$

With effect from April 28, 2014, reg.2(14)(b) of the Universal Credit
and Miscellaneous Amendments Regulations 2014 (SI 2014/597)
amended paragraph 10 of Sch.5 by omitting sub-para.(5).

p.274, *amendment to the Universal Credit Regulations 2013 (SI 2013/376) Sch.5 (Housing costs element for owner-occupiers) para.11 (Amount in respect of alternative finance arrangements)*

Note that the formula in step 3 of Para.11(2) of Sch.5 should read: **6.344**

$$\frac{(A \times SR)}{12}$$

With effect from April 28, 2014, reg.2(14)(c) of the Universal Credit
and Miscellaneous Amendments Regulations 2014 (SI 2014/597)
amended para.11 of Sch. 5 by substituting for the existing sub-para.(3)
new sub-paragraphs (3) and (4) as follows:

"(3) "Purchase price" means the price paid by a party to the alternative finance arrangements other than the owner-occupier in order to acquire the interest in the accommodation to which those arrangements relate less—
(a) the amount of any initial payment made by the owner-occupier in connection with the acquisition of that interest; and

(b) the amount of any subsequent payments made by the owner-occupier before the relevant date to another party to the alternative finance arrangements which reduce the amount owed by the owner-occupier under the alternative finance arrangements.

(4) Any variation in the amount for the time being owing in connection with alternative finance arrangements is not to be taken into account after the relevant date until such time as the Secretary of State recalculates the amount under this Schedule by reference to the amount that is owing in connection with the alternative finance arrangements—

(a) on the first anniversary of the relevant date; or
(b) in respect of any variation after the first anniversary, on the next anniversary which follows the date of the variation.".

p.274, *amendment to the Universal Credit Regulations 2013 (SI 2013/376) Sch.5 (Housing costs element for owner-occupiers) para.12 (Standard rate to be applied under paragraphs 10 and 11)*

6.345   With effect from April 28, 2014, reg.2(14)(d) of the Universal Credit and Miscellaneous Amendments Regulations 2014 (SI 2014/597) amended paragraph 12(3) of Sch. 5 by substituting "0.5 percentage points" for "0.5%".

p.275, *amendment to the Universal Credit Regulations 2013 (SI 2013/376) Sch.5 (Housing costs element for owner-occupiers) para.13 (Amount in respect of service charge payments)*

6.346   With effect from April 28, 2014, reg.2(14)(e)(i) of the Universal Credit and Miscellaneous Amendments Regulations 2014 (SI 2014/597) amended paragraph 13 of Sch.5 by inserting after sub-paragraph (3)(a) of para.13 a new sub-paragraph (3)(aa) as follows:

"(aa) two-weekly payments are multiplied by 26 and divided by 12;".

With effect from the same date, reg.2(14)(e)(ii) of the same Regulations amended sub-para.(4) of para.13 by inserting after the words "service charge free periods," the words "subject to sub-paragraph (4A),".

With effect from the same date, reg.2(14)(e)(iii) of the same Regulations inserted a new sub-paragraph (4A) as follows:

"(4A) Where sub-paragraph (4) applies and the service charge payments in question are—

(a) weekly payments, the total number of weekly service charge payments which the owner-occupier is liable to make in any 12 month period shall be calculated by reference to the formula—

52 - SCFP;

(b) two-weekly payments, the total number of two-weekly service charge payments which the owner-occupier is liable to make in any 12 month period shall be calculated by reference to the formula—

$$26 - SCFP;$$

(c) four weekly payments, the total number of four-weekly service charge payments which the owner-occupier is liable to make in any 12 month period shall be calculated by reference to the formula—

$$13 - SCFP;$$

where "SCFP" is the number of service charge free periods in the 12 month period in question.".

p.277, *annotation to the Universal Credit Regulations 2013 (SI 2013/376) Sch.5 (Housing costs element for owner-occupiers) Part 3 (No housing costs element for qualifying period)*

The Universal Credit (Transitional Provisions) Regulations 2013 (SI 2013/386) were revoked on June 16, 2014 (subject to certain savings) and replaced by the Universal Credit (Transitional Provisions) Regulations 2014 (SI 2014/1230). Regulation 29 of the 2014 Regulations makes similar provision in relation to the housing costs element for owner-occupiers as that made by reg.29 of the 2013 Regulations. 6.347

p.277, *annotation to the Universal Credit Regulations 2013 (SI 2013/376) Sch.5 (Housing costs element for owner-occupiers) Part 4 (Calculation of amount of housing costs element for owner-occupiers)*

The substituted para.11(3) of Sch.5 amends the definition of "purchase price" where the claimant has entered into alternative finance arrangements in order to buy his/her home. Deductions will be made not only for any initial payment made by the claimant in connection with acquiring an interest in the accommodation but also for any subsequent payments made by the claimant before the "relevant date" which reduced the amount owed by the claimant under the alternative finance arrangements. The "relevant date" is the date on which a housing costs element calculated under Sch.5 is first included in the claimant's universal credit award (see the definition of "relevant date" in para.2 of Sch.5). 6.348

The new para.11(4) provides for changes in the outstanding amount owing under such alternative finance arrangements to be taken into account on an annual basis, in the same way as for standard mortgages.

The effect of the amendment to para.12(3) is that the current standard interest rate, which is 3.63%, will only be adjusted when the average mortgage rate increases to at least 4.13% or reduces to at least 3.13%.

The amendments to para.13 of Sch.5 (amount in respect of service charges paid by owner-occupiers) are parallel to those made to para.7 of Sch.4 (see above).

p.432-433, *revocation of the Universal Credit, Personal Independence Payment, Jobseeker's Allowance and Employment and Support Allowance (Claims and Payments) Regulations 2013 (SI 2013/380) reg.6 (Claim not required for entitlement to universal credit in certain cases)*

6.349   With effect from November 26, 2014, reg.3(2)(a) of the Universal Credit (Digital Service) Amendment Regulations 2014 (SI 2014/2887) revoked reg.6. The revocation is subject to the saving provision in reg.5 of SI 2014/2887: see Part 1 of this Supplement.

p.435, *amendment to the Universal Credit, Personal Independence Payment, Jobseeker's Allowance and Employment and Support Allowance (Claims and Payments) Regulations 2013 (SI 2013/380) reg.9 (Claims for universal credit by members of a couple)*

6.350   With effect from November 26, 2014, reg.3(2)(b) of the Universal Credit (Digital Service) Amendment Regulations 2014 (SI 2014/2887) amended reg.9 by substituting the following for para.(6):

"(6) Where an award of universal credit to joint claimants is terminated because they cease to be a couple an award may be made, without a claim, to either or each one of them—

(a) as a single person; or

(b) if either of them has formed a new couple with a person who is already entitled to universal credit, jointly with that person."

and the following for sub-para.(8)(a):

"(a) one of them ceased to be entitled to an award of universal credit (whether as a single person or as a member of a different couple) on the formation of that couple;".

The amendments are subject to the saving provision in reg.5 of SI 2014/2887: see Part 1 of this Supplement.

p.445, *modification of the Universal Credit, Personal Independence Payment, Jobseeker's Allowance and Employment and Support Allowance (Claims and Payments) Regulations 2013 (SI 2013/380) reg.26 (Time within which a claim for universal credit is to be made)*

6.351   With effect from June 16, 2014, reg.15 of the Universal Credit (Transitional Provisions) Regulations 2014 (SI 2014/1230) modified reg.26 in cases where a claim for universal credit is made by a person who was previously entitled to an existing benefit (*i.e.,* as defined in reg.2(1) of SI 2014/1230). The modification is that that reg.26(3) applies in such cases as if the following sub-paragraph were added after sub-para.(a):

"(aa) the claimant was previously in receipt of an existing benefit (as defined in the Universal Credit (Transitional Provisions) Regulations 2014) and notification of expiry of entitlement to that benefit was not sent to the claimant before the date that the claimant's entitlement expired;".

p.445, *amendment to the Universal Credit, Personal Independence Payment, Jobseeker's Allowance and Employment and Support Allowance (Claims and Payments) Regulations 2013 (SI 2013/380) reg.26 (Time within which a claim for universal credit is to be made)*

With effect from November 26, 2014, reg.3(2)(c) of the Universal Credit (Digital Service) Amendment Regulations 2014 (SI 2014/2887) amended reg.26 by revoking sub-para.(3)(e), and adding the following after para.(4):   **6.352**

"(5) In the case of a claim for universal credit referred to in regulation 21(3C) of the Universal Credit Regulations (assessment period applied from a previous award within the last 6 months) the claim for universal credit must be made before the end of the assessment period in respect of which it is made".

The amendments are subject to the saving provision in reg.5 of SI 2014/2887: see Part 1 of this Supplement.

pp.478–480, *amendment to the Universal Credit, Personal Independence Payment, Jobseeker's Allowance and Employment and Support Allowance (Claims and Payments) Regulations 2013 (SI 2013/380) Sch. 6 (Deductions from benefit and direct payment to third parties)*

With effect from November 26, 2014, reg.6 of the Universal Credit and Miscellaneous Amendments (No.2) Regulations 2014 (SI 2014/2888):   **6.353**

- amended para.4(4) (Maximum amount) by revoking the words "paragraph 7 (rent and service charges included in rent) or" and adding the words ", or the minimum amount which may be deducted under paragraph 7 (rent and service charges included in rent)" after the words "(fuel costs)";
- amended para.5(2) (priority as between certain debts) by adding the words "where the amount of the deduction equals 10% of the standard allowance" after the word "Schedule" in head (b) and adding a new head after head (p) as follows:

    "(pa) paragraph 7 (rent and service charges included in rent) where the amount of deduction exceeds the minimum amount that may be deducted under that paragraph;"

- amended para.7(5) (Rent and service charges included in rent) by substituting the words "which is no less than 10% and no more than 20%" for the words "equal to 5%".

For claimants with an existing award of universal credit on November 26, 2014, the amendment has effect from the first day of the assessment period beginning on or after that day: see reg.1(2) of SI 2014/2888.

pp.480–481, *amendment to the Universal Credit, Personal Independence Payment, Jobseeker's Allowance and Employment and Support Allowance (Claims and Payments) Regulations 2013 (SI 2013/380) Sch. 6 (Deductions from benefit and direct payment to third parties)*

6.354   With effect from April 28, 2014, reg.5(a) of the Universal Credit and Miscellaneous Amendments Regulations 2014 (SI 2014/597) amended para.11 (Eligible loans) of Sch. 6 by amending sub-para.(1) to read as follows:

"(1) This paragraph applies where [in any assessment period the claimant is in arrears in respect of a loan entered into (whether solely or jointly) with an eligible lender in respect of an eligible loan]"

and revoking sub-paras (2) and (3).

pp.481–482, *amendment to the Universal Credit, Personal Independence Payment, Jobseeker's Allowance and Employment and Support Allowance (Claims and Payments) Regulations 2013 (SI 2013/380) Sch. 6 (Deductions from benefit and direct payment to third parties)*

6.355   With effect from April 28, 2014, reg.reg.5(b) of the Universal Credit and Miscellaneous Amendments Regulations 2014 (SI 2014/597) amended para.12 (Integration loans) of Sch.6 by amending sub-para.(1) to read as follows:

"(1) This paragraph applies where [the claimant has an integration loan which is recoverable by deductions]"

and revoking sub-paras (2) and (3).

p.482, *amendment to the Universal Credit, Personal Independence Payment, Jobseeker's Allowance and Employment and Support Allowance (Claims and Payments) Regulations 2013 (SI 2013/380) Sch. 6 (Deductions from benefit and direct payment to third parties)*

6.356   With effect from April 1, 2014, reg.28 of and para.45 of the Schedule to the Financial Services and Markets Act 2000 (Regulated Activities) (Amendment) (No.2) Order 2013 (SI 2013/1881) amended para.11 (Eligible loans) of Sch. 6 by substituting the words "has permission under the Financial Services and Markets Act 2000 to enter into a contract of the kind mentioned in paragraph 23 or paragraph 23B of Schedule 2 to that Act (credit agreements and contracts for hire of goods);" for the words "is licensed under the Consumer Credit Act 1974" in the definition of "eligible lender" in sub-para.(8) and by adding the following immediately after that sub-paragraph:

"(9) The definition of "eligible lender" must be read with—
(a) section 22 of the Financial Services and Markets Act 2000,
(b) any relevant order under that section, and
(c) Schedule 2 to that Act.".

p.501, *amendment to the Universal Credit, Personal Independence Payment, Jobseeker's Allowance and Employment and Support Allowance (Decisions and Appeals) Regulations 2013 (SI 2013/381) reg.26 (Medical evidence and limited capability for work etc.)*

With effect from April 28, 2014, reg.6 of the Universal Credit and   **6.357** Miscellaneous Amendments Regulations 2014 (SI 2014/597) amended reg.26 by substituting the following for sub-para.(1)(b):

"(b) made a determination that the claimant is to be treated as having—

    (i) limited capability for work in accordance with regulation 16, 21, 22 or 29 of the Employment and Support Allowance Regulations 2013; or

    (ii) limited capability for work or for work and work-related activity in accordance with Part 5 (capability for work or work-related activity) of the Universal Credit Regulations.".

PART VII

FORTHCOMING CHANGES AND UP-RATINGS OF BENEFITS

FORTHCOMING CHANGES

7.001 This section aims to give users of Social Security Legislation 2014/15 some information on significant changes coming into force between January 1, 2015—the date up to which this Supplement is up to date—and mid-April 2015, the date to which the 2015/16 edition in turn will be up to date (as well as some advance notice of other changes further in the future). The information here reflects our understanding of sources available to us as at January 15, 2015 and users should be aware that there will no doubt be further legislative amendment between then and mid-April 2015. This Part of the Supplement will at least enable users to access the relevant legislation (and usually accompanying Explanatory Notes prepared by the Department) on the Government Legislation website (*http://www.legislation.gov.uk*) operated by the National Archives.

STATUTES

Pensions Act 2014

7.002 The Pensions Act 2014 received Royal Assent on May 14, 2014. It provides for major changes both to public pensions and private pensions. Part 1 (State Pensions) resets the regime currently established by SSCBA 1992 ss.43 to 55C and s.62. It is being brought into effect in stages, with the most important changes currently scheduled for April 6, 2016. As it does so the relevant provisions of SSCBA 1992 and amending legislation, including prospective amendments in the Pensions Act 2008, are repealed. Part 2 (option to boost old retirement pensions) is partially in effect. This enables government to introduce regulations to create a new Class 3A National Insurance contribution to allow contributors to make voluntary contributions to increase their entitlements to a state pension under the "old" provisions. This is not yet fully in effect and is largely beyond the scope of these volumes. Part 4 (State pension credit) contains measures relating to the assessed income period (AIP) in state pension credit claims. The assessed income period in effect removes the requirement for certain individuals to notify the DWP of changes to their retirement provision (broadly defined as capital, annuities and non-state pensions) for a defined period, for the purposes of assessing their entitlement to state pension credit. Section 28 of the Act provides for the phasing out of the AIP in state pension credit cases from April 2016.

For a full statement of the policy behind all these changes, including a useful executive summary, see the Government White Paper *The single-tier pension: a simple foundation for saving*, CM 8528.

REGULATIONS

The Rent Officers (Housing Benefit and Universal Credit Functions) (Local Housing Allowance Amendments) Order 2014

7.003   The Rent Officers (Housing Benefit and Universal Credit Functions) (Local Housing Allowance Amendments) Order 2014 (SI 2014/3126) comes into force on January 8, 2015. Amongst other changes it amends the Rent Officers (Universal Credit Functions) Order 2013 (SI 2013/382) to make changes to how and when the local housing allowance is determined.

The Universal Credit (Work-Related Requirements) In Work Pilot Scheme and Amendment Regulations 2015

7.003.1   The Universal Credit (Work-Related Requirements) In Work Pilot Scheme and Amendment Regulations 2015 (SI 2015/89) come into force on 19 February 2015. They first substitute a new reg.99(6) and (6A) for the existing reg.99(6) of the Universal Credit Regulations 2013 (SI 2013/376), requiring the lifting of the work search requirement and the adjustments of the work availability requirement on the ground of having earnings from employment only where they exceed a fixed level, instead of on a discretionary basis. Somewhat oddly, the fixed level is defined by reference to the personal allowance for a single person or 25 or over or a couple (plus £5 and £10 respectively) for income based JSA in the JSA Regulations 1996, which by definition have been revoked if a claimant is within the universal credit system. Then the pilot scheme allows the Secretary of State to select at random certain qualifying claimants with at lease that level of earnings to have the effect of reg.99(6) disapplied. The aim is to test what sorts of intervention involving help and support to this group, backed up by sanctions, will help them increase their earnings.

The Tax Credits (Exercise of Functions) Order 2014

7.004   Tax Credits (Exercise of Functions) Order 2014 comes into force on April 1, 2015. Article 3 allows the Secretary of State to recover, concurrently with the Commissioners for Her Majesty's Revenue and Customs, amounts specified in notices given under s.29 of the Tax Credits

Act 2002 (which specify amounts of overpayments of tax credits), the amounts of penalties imposed under ss.31 or 32 of that Act (which are imposed respectively in connection with the making of incorrect statements and failing to comply with requirements in connection with claims for, and awards of, tax credits) and interest carried on those amounts. Articles 4 and 5 provide that those amounts are to be treated as if they were amounts recoverable by the Secretary of State under certain provisions of the Social Security Administration Act 1992 and the Social Security (Overpayments and Recovery) Regulations 2013 (SI 2013/384).

The Social Fund Winter Fuel Payment (Amendment) Regulations 2014

These Social Fund Winter Fuel Payment (Amendment) Regulations 2014 (SI 2014/3270) come into force on September 21, 2015. They will amend the Social Fund Winter Fuel Payment Regulations 2000 (SI 2000/729). They restrict entitlement to winter fuel payment for some of those living abroad. These payments are presently payable to certain eligible older people ordinarily resident in the United Kingdom or habitually resident in Switzerland or an EEA state other than the United Kingdom. The payments to those living abroad will now be restricted to eligible people habitually resident in the countries in Europe listed in the Schedule inserted by these Regulations (e.g. Italy is included but France and Spain are excluded). **7.005**

NEW BENEFIT RATES FROM APRIL 2015

NEW BENEFIT RATES FROM APRIL 2014

(Benefits covered in Volume I)

	April 2014 £ pw	April 2015 £ pw
Disability benefits		
Attendance allowance		
higher rate	81.30	82.30
lower rate	54.45	55.10
Disability living allowance		
care component		
highest rate	81.30	82.30
middle rate	54.45	55.10
lowest rate	21.55	21.80
mobility component		
higher rate	56.75	57.45
lower rate	21.55	21.80
Personal independence payment		
daily living component		
enhanced rate	81.30	82.30
standard rate	54.45	55.10
mobility component		
enhanced rate	56.75	57.45
standard rate	21.55	21.80
Carer's allowance	61.35	62.10
Severe disablement allowance		
basic rate	73.75	74.65
age related addition—higher rate	11.00	11.15
age related addition—middle rate	6.15	6.20
age related addition—lower rate	6.15	6.20

New Benefit Rates from April 2015

	April 2014 £ pw	April 2015 £ pw
Maternity benefits		
Maternity allowance		
standard rate	138.18	139.58
Bereavement benefits and retirement pensions		
Widowed parent's allowance or widowed mother's allowance	110.20	112.55
Bereavement allowance or widow's pension		
standard rate	110.20	112.55
Retirement pension		
Category A	113.10	115.95
Category B (higher)	113.10	115.95
Category B (lower)	67.80	69.50
Category C	67.80	69.50
Category D	67.80	69.50
Incapacity benefit		
Long-term incapacity benefit		
basic rate	104.10	105.35
increase for age—higher rate	11.00	11.15
increase for age—lower rate	6.15	6.20
invalidity allowance—higher rate	11.00	11.15
invalidity allowance—middle rate	6.15	6.20
invalidity allowance—lower rate	6.15	6.20
Short-term incapacity benefit		
under pension age—higher rate	92.95	94.05
under pension age—lower rate	78.50	79.45
over pension age—higher rate	104.10	105.35
over pension age—lower rate	99.90	101.10
Dependency increases		
Adult		
carer's allowance	36.10	36.75
severe disablement allowance	36.30	36.55
retirement pension	64.90	65.70
long-term incapacity benefit	60.45	61.20
short-term incapacity benefit under pension age	47.10	47.65
short-term incapacity benefit over pension age	58.20	58.90
Child	11.35[1]	11.35[1]

	April 2014 £ pw	April 2015 £ pw
Industrial injuries benefits		
Disablement benefit		
100%	166.00	168.00
90%	149.40	151.20
80%	132.80	134.40
70%	116.20	117.60
60%	99.60	100.80
50%	83.00	84.00
40%	66.40	67.20
30%	49.80	50.40
20%	33.20	33.60
unemployability supplement		
basic rate	102.60	103.85
increase for adult dependant	60.45	61.20
increase for child dependant	11.35[1]	11.35[1]
increase for early incapacity—higher rate	21.25	21.50
increase for early incapacity—middle rate	13.70	13.90
increase for early incapacity—lower rate	6.85	6.95
constant attendance allowance		
exceptional rate	132.40	134.40
intermediate rate	99.60	100.80
normal maximum rate	66.40	67.20
part-time rate	33.20	33.60
exceptionally severe disablement allowance	66.40	67.20
Reduced earnings allowance		
maximum rate	66.40	67.20
Death benefit		
widow's pension		
higher rate	113.10	115.95
lower rate	33.93	34.79
widower's pension	113.10	115.95

Notes
1. These sums payable in respect of children are reduced if payable in respect of the only, elder or eldest child for whom child benefit is being paid (see reg.8 of the Social Security (Overlapping Benefits) Regulations 1979 on p.579 of Vol. 1 of the main work).

New Benefit Rates from April 2015

	April 2014 £ pw	April 2015 £ pw
Employment and support allowance		
Contribution-based personal rates		
assessment phase—*aged under 25*	57.35	57.90
aged 25 or over	72.40	73.10
main phase	72.40	73.10
Components		
work-related activity	28.75	29.05
support	35.75	36.20
Income-based personal allowances		
single person—*aged under 25*	57.35	57.90
aged 25 or over	72.40	73.10
lone parent—*aged under 18*	57.35	57.90
aged 18 or over	72.40	73.10
couple—*both aged under 18*	57.35	57.90
both aged under 18, with a child	86.65	87.50
both aged under 18, (main phase)	72.40	73.10
both aged under 18, with a child (main phase)	113.70	114.85
one aged under 18, one aged 18 or over	113.70	114.85
both aged 18 or over	113.70	114.85
Premiums		
pensioner—*single person with no component*	75.95	78.10
couple with no component	112.80	116.00
enhanced disability—*single person*	15.55	15.75
couple	22.30	22.60
severe disability—*single person*	61.10	61.85
couple (one qualifies)	61.10	61.85
couple (both qualify)	122.20	123.70
carer	34.20	34.60

7.007

NEW BENEFIT RATES FROM APRIL 2015

(Benefits covered in Volume II)

	April 2014 £ pw	April 2015 £ pw
Contribution-based jobseeker's allowance		
personal rates—*aged under 25*	57.35	57.90
aged 25 or over	72.40	73.10
Income support and income-based jobseeker's allowance		
personal allowances		
single person—*aged under 25*	57.35	57.90
aged 25 or over	72.40	73.10
lone parent—*aged under 18*	57.35	57.90
aged 18 or over	72.40	73.10
couple—*both aged under 18*	57.35	57.90
both aged under 18, with a child	86.65	87.50
one aged under 18, one aged under 25	57.35	57.90
one aged under 18, one aged 25 or over	72.40	73.10
both aged 18 or over	113.70	114.85
child	66.33	66.90
premiums		
family—*ordinary*	17.45	17.45
lone parent	17.45	17.45
pensioner—*single person (JSA only)*	75.95	78.10
couple	112.80	116.00
disability—*single person*	31.85	32.25
couple	45.40	45.95
enhanced disability—*single person*	15.55	15.75
couple	22.35	22.60
disabled child	24.08	24.43
severe disability—*single person*	61.10	61.85
couple (one qualifies)	61.10	61.85
couple (both qualify)	122.20	123.70
disabled child	59.50	60.06
carer	34.20	34.60
Pension credit		
Standard minimum guarantee		
single person	148.35	151.20
couple	226.50	230.85

	April 2014	April 2015
	£ pw	£ pw
Additional amount for severe disability		
single person	61.10	61.85
couple (one qualifies)	61.10	61.85
couple (both qualify)	122.20	123.70
Additional amount for carers	34.20	34.60
Savings credit threshold		
single person	120.35	126.50
couple	192.00	201.80
Maximum savings credit		
single person	16.80	14.82
couple	20.70	17.43

NEW TAX CREDIT AND BENEFIT RATES 2015–2016

7.009   **(Benefits covered in Volume IV)**

	2014–15	2015–16
	£ pw	£ pw
Benefits in respect of children		
Child benefit		
only, elder or eldest child (couple)	20.50	20.70
each subsequent child	13.55	13.70
Guardian's allowance	16.35	16.55
Employer-paid benefits		
Standard rates		
Statutory sick pay	87.55	88.45
Statutory maternity pay	138.18	139.58
Statutory paternity pay	138.18	139.58
Statutory adoption pay	138.18	139.58
Income threshold	110.00	112.00

	2014–15	2015–16
	£ pa	£ pa
Working tax credit		
Basic element	1,940	1,960
Couple and lone parent element	1,990	2,010
30 hour element	800	810
Disabled worker element	2,935	2,970
Severe disability element	1,255	1,275
Child care element		
maximum eligible cost for one child	*175 pw*	*175 pw*
maximum eligible cost for two or more		
children	*300 pw*	*300 pw*
per cent of eligible costs covered	*70%*	*70%*
Child tax credit		
Family element	545	545
Child element	2,750	2,780
Disabled child element	3,100	3,140
Severely disabled child element	1,255	1,275
Tax credit income thresholds		
Income rise disregard	5,000	5,000
Income fall disregard	2,500	2,500
Income threshold	6,420	6,420
Income threshold for those entitled to child tax		
credit only	16,010	16,105
Withdrawal rate	*41%*	*41%*

NEW UNIVERSAL CREDIT RATES FROM APRIL 2014

NEW UNIVERSAL CREDIT RATES FROM APRIL 2014

(Benefits covered in Volume V)   7.010

	April 2014	April 2015
	£ pw	£ pw
Standard allowances		
Single claimant—*aged under 25*	249.28	251.77
aged 25 or over	314.67	317.82
Joint claimant—*both aged under 25*	391.29	395.20
one or both aged 25 or over	493.95	498.89
Child element—*first child*	274.58	277.08
second/ subsequent child	229.17	231.67
Disabled child addition—*lower rate*	124.86	126.11
higher rate	362.92	367.92
Limited Capability for Work element	124.86	126.11
Limited Capability for Work and Work-Related Activity element	311.86	315.60
Carer element	148.61	150.39
Childcare element—*maximum for one child*	532.29	532.29
maximum for two or more children	912.50	912.50
Non-dependants' housing cost contributions	68.68	69.37
Work allowances		
Higher work allowance (no housing element)		
Single claimant—*no dependent children*	111.00	111.00
one or more children	734.00	734.00
limited capability for work	647.00	647.00
Joint claimant—*no dependent children*	111.00	111.00
one or more children	536.00	536.00
limited capability for work	647.00	647.00

New Universal Credit Rates from April 2014

	April 2013 £ pw	April 2014 £ pw
Lower work allowance		
Single claimant—*no dependent children*	111.00	111.00
one or more children	263.00	263.00
limited capability for work	192.00	192.00
Joint claimant—*no dependent children*	111.00	111.00
one or more children	222.00	222.00
limited capability for work	192.00	192.00